CHILDREN'S LITERATURE

Critical Concepts in Literary and Cultural Studies

Edited by
Peter Hunt

Volume I
Definitions and Distinctions

Routledge
Taylor & Francis Group

LONDON AND NEW YORK

First published 2006
by Routledge
2 Park Square, Milton Park, Abingdon, Oxon OX14 4RN

Simultaneously published in the USA and Canada
by Routledge
270 Madison Avenue, New York, NY 10016-0602

Routledge is an imprint of the Taylor & Francis Group, an informa business

Typeset in 10/12pt Times by Graphicraft Limited, Hong Kong
Printed and bound in Great Britain by
MPG Books Ltd, Bodmin, Cornwall

British Library Cataloguing in Publication Data
A catalogue record for this book is available from the British Library

Library of Congress Cataloging in Publication Data
A catalog record for this book has been requested

ISBN10: 0–415–37228–3 (Set)
ISBN10: 0–415–37277–1 (Volume I)

ISBN13: 978–0–415–37228–2 (Set)
ISBN13: 978–0–415–37277–0 (Volume I)

Publisher's note

References within each chapter are as they appear in the original complete work

CONTENTS

Acknowledgements   xvii
Chronological table of reprinted articles and chapters   xxi

General Introduction   1

Introduction to Volume I   9

VOLUME I   DEFINITIONS AND DISTINCTIONS

PART 1
Writing for children   15

  1 **On three ways of writing for children**   17
     C. S. LEWIS

  2 **A free gift**   27
     JOAN AIKEN

PART 2
Preliminary definitions and distinctions   43

  3 **Out on a limb with the critics**   45
     PAUL HEINS

  4 **Fiction for children and adults: some essential differences**   53
     MYLES McDOWELL

  5 **Children's literature: theory and practice**   68
     FELICITY A. HUGHES

  6 **Standards of criticism for children's literature**   86
     JOHN ROWE TOWNSEND

CONTENTS

7 Interpretation and the apparent sameness of children's novels   98
   PERRY NODELMAN

8 An important system of its own: defining children's literature   114
   RUTH B. BOTTIGHEIMER

PART 3
The subject matter   131

9 Medieval children's literature: its possibility and actuality   133
   GILLIAN ADAMS

10 Sentiment and significance: the impossibility of recovery in the
   children's literature canon or, the drowning of *The Water Babies*   155
   DEBORAH STEVENSON

11 Extracts from the 'Introduction' to *The New Oxford Book
   of Children's Verse*   172
   NEIL PHILIP

12 Children's fantasy literature: toward an anatomy   182
   DAVID GOODERHAM

13 Who 'owns' children's fantasy?   195
   ANDY SAWYER

14 The changing status of children and children's literature   211
   EVA-MARIA METCALF

15 Playing in the phase space: contemporary forms of
   fictional pleasure   220
   MARGARET MACKEY

16 Futures for children's literature: evolution or radical break?   237
   PETER HUNT

PART 4
Picture books   247

17 Introduction to picturebook codes   249
   WILLIAM MOEBIUS

18 The implied viewer: some speculations about what children's
   picture books invite readers to do and to be   264
   PERRY NODELMAN

CONTENTS

19 The dynamics of picturebook communication   282
    MARIA NIKOLAJEVA AND CAROLE SCOTT

20 The interaction of word and image in picturebooks:
    a critical survey   294
    DAVID LEWIS

21 The nature of picturebooks: theories about visual texts
    and readers   310
    EVELYN ARIZPE AND MORAG STYLES

PART 5
Criticism and texts   331

22 Beginnings   333
    RODERICK McGILLIS

23 The reader in the book   354
    AIDAN CHAMBERS

24 Problems of audience   375
    BARBARA WALL

25 Necessary misreadings: directions in narrative theory for
    children's literature   390
    PETER HUNT

26 From the editors: "cross-writing" and the reconceptualizing
    of children's literary studies   405
    MITZI MYERS AND U. C. KNOEPFLMACHER

VOLUME II   EDUCATION AND THEORY

    Acknowledgements   ix

    Introduction to Volume II   1

PART 6
Perception and response   9

27 The roots of response   11
    HUGH CRAGO

CONTENTS

28 On the success of children's books and fairy tales:
a comparative view of impact theory and reception research   21
REINBERT TABBERT AND KRISTIN WARDETZKY

29 *How Texts Teach What Readers Learn*   38
MARGARET MEEK

30 Children's literature: using text to construct reality   60
GEOFF BULL

31 Where does Cinderella live?   71
ARTHUR N. APPLEBEE

32 A defence of rubbish   78
PETER DICKINSON

PART 7
Aspects of reading and writing   **81**

33 Lessons learnt at bed-time   83
HENRIETTA DOMBEY

34 Children's literature, literacy, and literary understanding   92
LAWRENCE R. SIPE

35 "It's not all black and white": postmodern picture books
and new literacies   110
MICHÈLE ANSTEY

36 What happens when we read stories?   125
MICHAEL BENTON AND GEOFF FOX

37 Taking children's literature seriously: reading for pleasure
and social change   147
VIVIAN YENIKA-AGBAW

PART 8
Higher education   **163**

38 Extracts from *Symbolic outlining: the academic study of
children's literature*   165
MARGARET MEEK

39 Keepin' it plural: children's studies in the academy   181
KAREN S. COATS

CONTENTS

40 Into the heart of darkness? Teaching children's literature
   as a problem in theory   200
   STEPHEN SLEMON AND JO-ANN WALLACE

41 Disdain or ignorance? Literary theory and the absence of
   children's literature   218
   DEBORAH THACKER

42 Children's literature, text and theory: what are we interested
   in now?   233
   JOHN STEPHENS

43 How to get your Ph.D. in children's literature   246
   BRIAN ALDERSON

44 Thirteen ways of thumbing your nose at children's literature   251
   BEVERLY LYON CLARK

45 The future of the profession   255
   JERRY GRISWOLD

PART 9
The theory debate   261

46 Childist criticism: the subculture of the child, the book
   and the critic   263
   PETER HUNT

47 The limits of literary criticism of children's and young
   adult literature   280
   HANS-HEINO EWERS

48 The case of Peter Rabbit (and others): some reflections
   on 'the impossibility of children's fiction'   296
   BRIAN ALDERSON

49 The psychopathology of everyday children's literature
   criticism   305
   KARÍN LESNIK-OBERSTEIN

50 The delights of impossibility: no children, no books,
   only theory   323
   RODERICK McGILLIS

51 "Irony? – But children don't get it, do they?" The idea of
   appropriate language in narratives for children   336
   SUE WALSH

CONTENTS

52 Theorising and theories: the conditions of possibility of
    children's literature   356
    DAVID RUDD

53 A theory without a centre: developing childist criticism   375
    SEBASTIEN CHAPLEAU

54 Pleasure and genre: speculations on the characteristics of
    children's fiction   384
    PERRY NODELMAN

55 The pleasure of the process: same place but different   396
    RODERICK McGILLIS

56 Of dialectic and divided consciousness: intersections between
    children's literature and childhood studies   402
    THOMAS TRAVISANO

VOLUME III   CULTURAL CONTEXTS

    Acknowledgements   ix

    Introduction to Volume III   1

    PART 10
    Childhood studies   9

57 Children's culture, children's studies, and the ethnographic
    imaginary   11
    KENNETH KIDD

58 Childhood revisited: on the relationship between childhood
    studies and children's literature   29
    NINA CHRISTENSEN

59 Childhood: a narrative chronotope   46
    ROSEMARY ROSS JOHNSTON

60 Imaginary childhoods: memory and children's literature   69
    VALERIE KRIPS

CONTENTS

61 Substitute communities, authentic voices: the organic writing
    of the child   77
    STEPHEN THOMSON

PART 11
Ideology, race and politics   99

62 Ideology and the children's book   101
    PETER HOLLINDALE

63 Censorship and children's literature   120
    ANNE SCOTT MacLEOD

64 The Uncle Remus travesty, part I   132
    OPAL MOORE AND DONNARAE MacCANN

65 The Uncle Remus travesty, part II: Julius Lester and
    Virginia Hamilton   140
    OPAL MOORE AND DONNARAE MacCANN

66 Breaking the Disney spell   151
    JACK ZIPES

67 The republic of heaven   172
    PHILIP PULLMAN

PART 12
Gender   185

68 "As the Twig Is Bent . . .": gender and childhood reading   187
    ELIZABETH SEGEL

69 Enigma variations: what feminist theory knows about
    children's literature   208
    LISSA PAUL

70 *Earthsea Revisioned*   224
    URSULA K. LE GUIN

71 Fairy godmothers or wicked stepmothers? The uneasy
    relationship of feminist theory and children's criticism   236
    BEVERLY LYON CLARK

CONTENTS

72 Feminine language and the politics of children's literature   248
DEBORAH THACKER

73 "Cinderella was a Wuss": a young girl's responses to
feminist and patriarchal folktales   261
ANN M. TROUSDALE AND SALLY McMILLAN

PART 13
Publishing and television   289

74 Extracts from 'Notes on the children's book trade:
all is not well in tinsel town'   291
JOHN GOLDTHWAITE

75 Raising the issues   301
MICHAEL ROSEN

76 In the worst possible taste: children, television and
cultural value   317
HANNAH DAVIES, DAVID BUCKINGHAM AND
PETER KELLEY

PART 14
Psychology   337

77 Good friends, or just acquaintances? The relationship
between child psychology and children's literature   339
NICHOLAS TUCKER

78 Psychoanalysis and children's literature: the case for
complementarity   354
KENNETH KIDD

PART 15
Special topics   373

79 Metafictional play in children's fiction   375
ANN GRIEVE

80 The changing aesthetics of character in children's fiction   391
MARIA NIKOLAJEVA

81 The value of singularity in first- and restricted third-person
    engaging narration   416
    ANDREA SCHWENKE WYILE

VOLUME IV INTERNATIONAL AND COMPARATIVE

    Acknowledgements   ix

    Introduction to Volume IV   1

PART 16
Internationalism   9

82 **Story in orature and literature: why and how we make it
    available to children in different cultures**   11
    ANNE PELLOWSKI

83 **The right of the child to information and its practical impact
    on children's libraries**   25
    MARIAN KOREN

84 **Do children's rhymes reveal universal metrical patterns?**   39
    ANDY ARLEO

85 **Homelands: landscape and identity in children's literature** 57
    TONY WATKINS

PART 17
Translation   83

86 **The verbal and the visual: on the carnivalism and dialogics of
    translating for children**   85
    RIITTA OITTINEN

87 **Approaches to the translation of children's literature:
    a review of critical studies since 1960**   100
    REINBERT TABBERT

88 **Narratology meets translation studies, or, the voice of the
    translator in children's literature**   145
    EMER O'SULLIVAN

CONTENTS

PART 18

Colonialism/postcolonialism   159

89 Extract from the 'Introduction' to *Voices of the Other:
    Children's Literature and the Postcolonial Context*   161
    RODERICK McGILLIS

90 Hunting for history: children's literature outside, over there,
    and down under   171
    HEATHER SCUTTER

91 The end of empire? Colonial and postcolonial journeys
    in children's books   184
    CLARE BRADFORD

PART 19

Myths, folk tales and fairy tales   203

92 Myths, legends and fairy tales in the lives of children   205
    ELIZABETH COOK

93 Spells of enchantment   213
    JACK ZIPES

94 Rewritten by adults: the inscription of children's
    literature   232
    MARIA TATAR

95 Pre-texts, metanarratives, and the western metaethic   250
    JOHN STEPHENS AND ROBYN McCALLUM

96 Did they live happily ever after? Rewriting fairy tales for a
    contemporary audience   271
    LAURA TOSI

97 Folk materials, re-visions, and narrative images:
    the intertextual games they play   291
    CLAIRE MALARTE-FELDMAN

PART 20

Theatre   307

98 Political children's theater in the age of globalization   309
    JACK ZIPES

CONTENTS

99 **Carnivals, the carnivalesque, *The Magic Puddin'*, and David Almond's *Wild Girl, Wild Boy*: towards a theorizing of children's plays**   **327**
ROSEMARY ROSS JOHNSTON

Index   342

ACKNOWLEDGEMENTS

Special thanks are due to Sue Mansfield and Julie Mills and the staff of the Learning Resources Centre of Roehampton University for allowing me access to, and guiding me through, their admirable Children's Literature collections.

Thanks are also due to the many people who have helped in suggesting articles and in helping me to trace them (and their copyright holders); they include Jenny Akester, Anne Alston, Michèle Anstey, Sue Bottigheimer, Clare Bradford, Geoff Bull, Nancy Chambers, Valerie Coghlan, Geoff Fox, Matthew Grenby, Victoria de Rijke, Rosemary Johnston, Karín Lesnik-Oberstein, Gillian Lathey, Margaret Mackey, Rod McGillis, Farah Mendlesohn, Maria Nikolajeva, Perry Nodelman, Emer O'Sullivan, C. W. Sullivan III, Lissa Paul, Kim Reynolds, David Rudd, John Stephens, Morag Styles, Judy Taylor, Deborah Thacker, Lynne Vallone, Jill Paton Walsh, Jean Webb, Christine Wilkie-Stibbs, Jessica Yates and Jack Zipes.

The Publishers would like to thank the following for permission to reprint their material:

Harcourt Inc., and the C. S. Lewis Company, Ltd., for permission to reprint C. S. Lewis 'On Three Ways of Writing for Children', in *Of Other Worlds: Essays and Stories*, London: Geoffrey Bles, 1966, pp. 22–34. Copyright © 1966 by the Executors of the Estate of C. S. Lewis and renewed by 1994 by C. S. Lewis Pte., reprinted with permission of Harcourt, Inc.

The Horn Book, Inc. for permission to reprint Paul Heins, 'Out on a Limb with the Critics', *Horn Book Magazine* 46 (June 1970): 264–273.

Springer Science and Business Media for permission to reprint Myles McDowell, 'Fiction for Children and Adults: Some Essential Differences', *Children's Literature in Education* 10 (1973): 50–63. With permission from Springer Science and Business Media.

Hughes, Felicity. Children's Literature: Theory and Practice. *ELH* 45(3) (1978): 542–561. © The Johns Hopkins University Press. Reprinted with permission of The Johns Hopkins University Press.

John Rowe Townsend for permission to reprint John Rowe Townsend, 'Standards of Criticism for Children's Literature', in Nancy Chambers (ed.), *The Signal Approach to Children's Literature*, Harmondsworth: Kestrel (Penguin), 1980, pp. 193–207.

Studies in the Literary Imagination for permission to reprint Perry Nodelman, 'Interpretation and the Apparent Sameness of Children's Novels', originally published in *Studies in the Literary Imagination* 18(2) (1985): 5–20. © Copyright 1980, Department of English, Georgia State University. Reprinted with permission.

Ruth B. Bottigheimer for permission to reprint Ruth B. Bottigheimer, 'An Important System of Its Own: Defining Children's Literature', *Princeton University Library Chronicle* 59(2) (1998): 191–210.

Yale University Press for permission to reprint Gillian Adams, 'Medieval Children's Literature: Its Possibility and Actuality', *Children's Literature* 26 (1998): 1–24. Copyright © 1998 Hollins College.

Stevenson, Deborah. Sentiment and Significance: The Impossibility of Recovery in the Children's Literature Canon or, the Drowning of *The Water Babies*. *The Lion and the Unicorn* 21(1) (1997): 112–130. © The Johns Hopkins University Press. Reprinted with permission of The Johns Hopkins University Press.

Oxford University Press for permission to reprint extracts from Neil Philip, 'Introduction', *The New Oxford Book of Children's Verse*, Oxford: Oxford University Press, 1996, pp. xxv–xxxvii.

Springer Science and Business Media for permission to reprint David Gooderham, 'Children's Fantasy Literature: Toward an Anatomy', *Children's Literature in Education* 26(3) (1995): 171–183. With permission from Springer Science and Business Media.

Foundation and Andy Sawyer, Librarian of the Science Fiction Foundation Collection, University of Liverpool, for permission to reprint Andy Sawyer, 'Who "Owns" Children's Fantasy?', *Foundation* 88 (Summer 2003): 5–19.

Eva-Maria Metcalf, 'The Changing Status of Children and Children's Literature', in Sandra Beckett (ed.), *Reflections of Change: Children's Literature Since 1945*, Westport, CN: Greenwood Press, 1997, pp. 49–56. Reproduced with permission of Greenwood Publishing Group, Inc., Westport, CT.

Thimble Press for permission to reprint Margaret Mackey, 'Playing in the Phase Space: Contemporary Forms of Fictional Pleasure', *Signal* 88 (1999): 16–33.

Taylor & Francis for permission to reprint Peter Hunt, 'Futures for Children's Literature: Evolution or Radical Break?', *Cambridge Journal of Education* 30(1) (2000): 111–119.

Taylor & Francis for permission to reprint William Moebius, 'Introduction to Picturebook Codes', *Word & Image* 2(2) (April–June 1986): 141–151, 158.

CREArTA for permission to reprint Perry Nodelman, 'The Implied Viewer: Some Speculations about What Children's Picture Books Invite Readers to Do and to Be', *CREArTA* 1(1) (June 2000): 23–43.

Springer Science and Business Media and Maria Nikolajeva and Carole Scott for permission to reprint Maria Nikolajeva and Carole Scott, 'The Dynamics of Picturebook Communication', *Children's Literature in Education* 31(4) (2000): 225–239. With permission from Springer Science and Business Media.

Taylor & Francis for permission to reprint David Lewis, 'The Interaction of Word and Image in Picturebooks: A Critical Survey', in *Reading Contemporary Picture Books: Picturing Text*, London: RoutledgeFalmer, 2001, pp. 32–45.

Taylor & Francis and Evelyn Arizpe and Morag Styles for permission to reprint Evelyn Arizpe and Morag Styles, 'The Nature of Picturebooks: Theories about Visual Texts and Readers', in *Children Reading Pictures*, London: RoutledgeFalmer, 2003, pp. 19–38.

Roderick McGillis 'Beginnings', in *The Nimble Reader, Literary Theory and Children's Literature*, New York: Twayne, 1996, pp. 1–26. © Copyright 1996, Twayne Publishers. Reprinted by permission of the Gale Group.

Thimble Press for permission to reprint Aidan Chambers 'The Reader in the Book', in *Booktalk: Occasional Writing on Literature and Children*, London: Bodley Head, 1985, pp. 34–58.

Barbara Wall, 'Problems of Audience', in *The Narrator's Voice: The Dilemma of Children's Fiction*, London: Macmillan, 1991, pp. 20–36. Reproduced with permission of Palgrave Macmillan.

Studies in the Literary Imagination for permission to reprint Peter Hunt, 'Necessary Misreadings: Directions in Narrative Theory for Children's Literature', *Studies in the Literary Imagination* 18(2) (1985): 107–121. © Copyright 1985, Department of English, Georgia State University. Reprinted with permission.

Yale University Press for permission to reprint Mitzi Myers and U. C. Knoepflmacher, 'From the Editors: "Cross-Writing" and the Reconceptualizing of Children's Literary Studies', *Children's Literature* 25 (1997): vii–xvii.

Disclaimer

The publishers have made every effort to contact authors/copyright holders of works reprinted in *Children's Literature: Critical Concepts in Literary and Cultural Studies*. This has not been possible in every case, however, and we would welcome correspondence from those individuals/companies whom we have been unable to trace.

Chronological table of reprinted articles and chapters

Date	Author	Article/Chapter	References	Vol.	Chap.
1952	C. S. Lewis	On three ways of writing for children	Originally published in *Proceedings . . . of the Bournemouth Conference . . . 1952*, The Library Association. This version taken from *Of Other Worlds: Essays and Stories*, London: Geoffrey Bles, pp. 22–34.	I	1
1970	Joan Aiken	A free gift	Originally published as 'Purely for Love', Books: Journal of the National Book League (Winter): 9–21. This version taken from Edward Blishen (ed.), *The Thorny Paradise: Writers on Writing for Children*, Harmondsworth: Kestrel (Penguin), 1975, pp. 36–52.	I	2
1970	Paul Heins	Out on a limb with the critics	*Horn Book Magazine* 46 (June): 264–273.	I	3
1970	Peter Dickinson	A defence of rubbish	*Children's Literature in Education* 3: 7–10.	II	32
1971	John Rowe Townsend	Standards of criticism for children's literature	Originally published in *Top of the News*, American Library Association. This version taken from Nancy Chambers (ed.), *The Signal Approach to Children's Literature*, Harmondsworth: Kestrel (Penguin), 1980, pp. 193–207.	I	6
1973	Myles McDowell	Fiction for children and adults: some essential differences	*Children's Literature in Education* 10: 50–63.	I	4
1973	Arthur N. Applebee	Where does Cinderella live?	*The Use of English* 25(2): 136–141, 146.	II	31
1976	Elizabeth Cook	Myths, legends and fairy tales in the lives of children	*The Ordinary and the Fabulous*, Cambridge: Cambridge University Press, pp. 1–9.	IV	92

Chronological table continued

Date	Author	Article/Chapter	References	Vol.	Chap.
1977	John Goldthwaite	Extracts from 'Notes on the children's book trade: all is not well in tinsel town'	*Harper's Magazine*: 389–402.	III	74
1978	Felicity A. Hughes	Children's literature: theory and practice	*ELH* 45(3): 542–561.	I	5
1983	Anne Scott MacLeod	Censorship and children's literature	*Library Quarterly* 53(1): 26–38.	III	63
1984	Peter Hunt	Childist criticism: the subculture of the child, the book and the critic	*Signal* 43: 42–59.	II	46
1985	Perry Nodelman	Interpretation and the apparent sameness of children's novels	*Studies in the Literary Imagination* 18(2): 5–20.	I	7
1985	Aidan Chambers	The reader in the book	*Booktalk: Occasional Writing on Literature and Children*, London: Bodley Head, pp. 34–58.	I	23
1985	Peter Hunt	Necessary misreadings: directions in narrative theory for children's literature	*Studies in the Literary Imagination* 18(2): 107–121.	I	25
1985	Hugh Crago	The roots of response	*Children's Literature Association Quarterly* 10(3): 100–104.	II	27
1985	Michael Benton and Geoff Fox	What happens when we read stories?	*Teaching Literature Nine to Fourteen*, Oxford: Oxford University Press, pp. 1–18.	II	36
1986	William Moebius	Introduction to picturebook codes	*Word & Image* 2(2) (April–June): 141–151, 158.	I	17
1986	Margaret Meek	Extracts from *Symbolic outlining: the academic study of children's literature*	The 9th Annual Woodfield Lecture, Huddersfield: Woodfield and Stanley, pp. 1–17.	II	38
1986	Opal Moore and Donnarae MacCann	The Uncle Remus travesty, part I	*Children's Literature Association Quarterly* 11(2): 96–99.	III	64

Year	Author	Title	Publication		
1986	Elizabeth Segel	"As the Twig Is Bent . . .": gender and childhood reading	Elizabeth A. Flynn and Patrocinio P. Schweickart (eds), *Gender and Reading: Essays on Readers, Texts and Contexts*, Baltimore: Johns Hopkins University Press, pp. 165–186.	III	68
1986–1987	Opal Moore and Donnarae MacCann	The Uncle Remus travesty, part II: Julius Lester and Virginia Hamilton	*Children's Literature Association Quarterly* 11(4): 205–209.	III	65
1987	Lissa Paul	Enigma Variations: what feminist theory knows about children's literature	*Signal* 54: 186–202.	III	69
1988	Peter Hollindale	Ideology and the children's book	*Signal* 55 (January): 3–22.	III	62
1988	Margaret Meek	*How Texts Teach What Readers Learn*	South Woodchester: Thimble Press, pp. 3–40.	II	29
1990	Hans-Heino Ewers	The limits of literary criticism of children's and young adult literature	*The Lion and the Unicorn* 19(1) (1995): 77–94. Trans. by J. D. Stahl from the original 'Die grenzen literarischer Kinder- und Jugendbuchkritik', in Barbara Scharioth and Joachim Schmidt (eds), *Zwischen allen Stülen: zur Situation der Kinder- und Jugendbuchkritik*, Tutzing: Evangelische Akademie.	II	47
1991	Barbara Wall	Problems of audience	*The Narrator's Voice: The Dilemma of Children's Fiction*, London: Macmillan, pp. 20–36.	I	24
1991	Stephen Slemon and Jo-Ann Wallace	Into the heart of darkness? Teaching children's literature as a problem in theory	*Canadian Children's Literature* 63: 6–23.	II	40
1991	Jack Zipes	Spells of enchantment	Jack Zipes (ed.), *Spells of Enchantment*, New York: Viking Penguin, pp. 370–392.	IV	93

Chronological table continued

Date	Author	Article/Chapter	References	Vol.	Chap.
1992	Henrietta Dombey	Lessons learnt at bed-time	Keith Kimberley, Margaret Meek and Jane Miller (eds), *New Readings: Contributions to an Understanding of Literacy*, London: A. & C. Black, pp. 29–36.	II	33
1992	Beverly Lyon Clark	Thirteen ways of thumbing your nose at children's literature	*The Lion and the Unicorn* 16: 240–244.	II	44
1992	Nicholas Tucker	Good friends, or just acquaintances? The relationship between child psychology and children's literature	Peter Hunt (ed.), *Literature for Children: Contemporary Criticism*, London: Routledge, pp. 156–173.	III	77
1992	Maria Tatar	Rewritten by adults: the inscription of children's literature	*Off With Their Heads! Fairy Tales and the Culture of Childhood*, Princeton: Princeton University Press, pp. 3–21, 241–244.	IV	94
1993	Brian Alderson	The case of Peter Rabbit (and others): some reflections on 'the impossibility of children's fiction'	Enid Bassom, Rowena Knox and Irene Whalley (eds), *Beatrix Potter's Little Books: Beatrix Potter Studies V*, Ambleside: The Beatrix Potter Society, pp. 9–18.	II	48
1993	Ursula K. Le Guin	*Earthsea Revisioned*	Cambridge: Children's Literature New England in association with Green Bay Publications, pp. 5–26.	III	70
1993–1994	Beverly Lyon Clark	Fairy godmothers or wicked stepmothers? The uneasy relationship of feminist theory and children's criticism	*Children's Literature Association Quarterly* 18(4): 171–176.	III	71
1994	Tony Watkins	Homelands: landscape and identity in children's literature	Wendy Parsons and Robert Goodwin (eds), *Landscape and Identity: Perspectives from Australia*, Adelaide: Auslib Press, pp. 3–20.	IV	85
1995	Geoff Bull	Children's literature: using text to construct reality	*Australian Journal of Language and Literacy* 18(4) (November): 259–269.	II	30

Year	Author	Title	Source	Vol.	Page
1995	David Gooderham	Children's fantasy literature: toward an anatomy	*Children's Literature in Education* 26(3): 171–183.	I	12
1995	Reinbert Tabbert and Kristin Wardetzky	On the success of children's books and fairy tales: a comparative view of impact theory and reception research	*The Lion and the Unicorn* 19(1): 1–19.	II	28
1995	Jack Zipes	Breaking the Disney spell	Elizabeth Bell, Lynda Haas and Laura Sells (eds), *From Mouse to Mermaid: The Politics of Film, Gender, and Culture*, Bloomington, Indiana University Press, pp. 21–42.	III	66
1995	Michael Rosen	Raising the issues	*Signal* 76: 26–44.	III	75
1995	Riitta Oittinen	The verbal and the visual: on the carnivalism and dialogics of translating for children	*Compar(a)ison: An International Journal of Comparative Literature* 2: 49–65.	IV	86
1996	Neil Philip	Extracts from the 'Introduction' to *The New Oxford Book of Children's Verse*	*The New Oxford Book of Children's Verse*, Oxford: Oxford University Press, pp. xxv–xxxvii.	I	11
1996	Roderick McGillis	Beginnings	*The Nimble Reader, Literary Theory and Children's Literature*, New York: Twayne, pp. 1–26.	I	22
1997	Brian Alderson	How to get your Ph.D. in children's literature	*Horn Book Magazine* 52(4) (July/August): 437–441.	II	43
1997	Lawrence R. Sipe	Children's literature, literacy, and literary understanding	*Journal of Children's Literature* 23(2) (Fall): 6–19.	II	34
1997	Vivian Yenika-Agbaw	Taking children's literature seriously: reading for pleasure and social change	*Language Arts* 74(6) (October): 446–453.	II	37
1997	Deborah Stevenson	Sentiment and significance: the impossibility of recovery in the children's literature canon or, the drowning of *The Water Babies*	*The Lion and the Unicorn* 21: 112–130.	I	10

Chronological table continued

Date	Author	Article/Chapter	References	Vol.	Chap.
1997	Eva-Maria Metcalf	The changing status of children and children's literature	Sandra Beckett (ed.), *Reflections of Change: Children's Literature Since 1945*, Westport, CN: Greenwood Press, pp. 49–56.	I	14
1997	Mitzi Myers and U. C. Knoepflmacher	From the editors: "cross-writing" and the reconceptualizing of children's literary studies	*Children's Literature* 25: vii–xvii.	I	26
1997	Valerie Krips	Imaginary childhoods: memory and children's literature	*Critical Quarterly* 39(3): 42–50.	III	60
1997	Anne Pellowski	Story in orature and literature: why and how we make it available to children in different cultures	International Board on Books for Young People, *Proceedings, 25th Congress, 12–16 August 1996, Telling the Tale*, Amsterdam: Dutch Section of IBBY, pp. 81–86.	IV	82
1997	Heather Scutter	Hunting for history: children's literature outside, over there, and down under	*ARIEL: A Review of International English Literature* 28(1) (January): 21–36.	IV	90
1998	Ruth B. Bottigheimer	An important system of its own: defining children's literature	*Princeton University Library Chronicle* 59(2): 191–210.	I	8
1998	Gillian Adams	Medieval children's literature: its possibility and actuality	*Children's Literature* 26: 1–24.	I	9
1998	Stephen Thomson	Substitute communities, authentic voices: the organic writing of the child	Karin Lesnik-Oberstein (ed.), *Children in Culture: Approaches to Childhood*, Basingstoke: Macmillan, pp. 248–273.	III	61
1998	Ann Grieve	Metafictional play in children's fiction	*Papers: Explorations into Children's Literature* 8(3): 5–15.	III	79
1998	Marian Koren	The right of the child to information and its practical impact on children's libraries	*The New Review of Children's Literature and Librarianship* 4: 1–16.	IV	83

Year	Author	Title	Source	Vol.	Page
1998	John Stephens and Robyn McCallum	Pre-texts, metanarratives, and the western metaethic	Retelling Stories, Framing Culture: Traditional Story and Metanarratives in Children's Literature, New York: Garland, pp. 3–23.	IV	95
1999	Margaret Mackey	Playing in the phase space: contemporary forms of fictional pleasure	Signal 88: 16–33.	I	15
1999	Roderick McGillis	The delights of impossibility: no children, no books, only theory	Children's Literature Association Quarterly 23(4): 202–208.	II	50
2000	Karin Lesnik-Oberstein	The psychopathology of everyday children's literature criticism	Cultural Critique 45 (Spring): 222–242.	II	49
2000	Perry Nodelman	The implied viewer: some speculations about what children's picture books invite readers to do and to be	CREArTA 1(1) (June): 23–43.	I	18
2000	Peter Hunt	Futures for children's literature: evolution or radical break?	Cambridge Journal of Education 30(1): 111–119.	I	16
2000	Maria Nikolajeva and Carole Scott	The dynamics of picturebook communication	Children's Literature in Education 31(4): 225–239.	I	19
2000	David Lewis	The interaction of word and image in picturebooks: a critical survey	Reading Contemporary Picture Books: Picturing Text, London: RoutledgeFalmer, pp. 31–45.	I	20
2000	Deborah Thacker	Disdain or ignorance? Literary theory and the absence of children's literature	The Lion and the Unicorn 24(1): 1–17.	II	41
2000	John Stephens	Children's literature, text and theory: what are we interested in now?	Papers: Explorations into Children's Literature 10(2): 12–20.	II	42
2000	Perry Nodelman	Pleasure and genre: speculations on the characteristics of children's fiction	Children's Literature 28: 1–14.	II	54

Chronological table continued

Date	Author	Article/Chapter	References	Vol.	Chap.
2000	Roderick McGillis	The pleasure of the process: same place but different	*Children's Literature* 28: 15–21.	II	55
2000	Thomas Travisano	Of dialectic and divided consciousness: intersections between children's literature and childhood studies	*Children's Literature* 28: 22–29.	II	56
2000	Hannah Davies, David Buckingham and Peter Kelley	In the worst possible taste: children, television and cultural value	*European Journal of Cultural Studies* 3(1): 5–24.	III	76
2000	Roderick McGillis	Extract from the 'Introduction' to *Voices of the Other: Children's Literature and the Postcolonial Context*	*Voices of the Other: Children's Literature and the Postcolonial Context*, New York: Garland, pp. xix–xxviii.	IV	89
2001	Maria Nikolajeva	The changing aesthetics of character in children's fiction	*Style* 35(3) (Fall): 430–454.	III	80
2001	Philip Pullman	The republic of heaven	*Horn Book Magazine* 57(7) (November/December): 655–667.	III	67
2001	Karen S. Coats	Keepin' it plural: children's studies in the academy	*Children's Literature Association Quarterly* 26(3): 140–150.	II	39
2001	Deborah Thacker	Feminine language and the politics of children's literature	*The Lion and the Unicorn* 25(1): 3–16.	III	72
2001	Andy Arleo	Do children's rhymes reveal universal metrical patterns?	*Bulletin de la Société de Stylistique Anglaise* 22: 125–145.	IV	84
2001	Clare Bradford	The end of empire? Colonial and postcolonial journeys in children's books	*Children's Literature* 29: 196–218.	IV	91

Year	Author	Title	Source	Part	Page
2001	Laura Tosi	Did they live happily ever after? Rewriting fairy tales for a contemporary audience	*Hearts of Lightness: The Magic of Children's Literature*, Venice: Cafoscarina, pp. 101–124.	IV	96
2002	Michèle Anstey	"It's not all black and white": postmodern picture books and new literacies	*Journal of Adolescent and Adult Literacy* 45(6) (March): 444–457.	II	35
2002	Jerry Griswold	The future of the profession	*The Lion and the Unicorn* 26(2): 236–242.	II	45
2002	Kenneth Kidd	Children's culture, children's studies, and the ethnographic imaginary	*Children's Literature Association Quarterly* 27(3): 146–155.	III	57
2002	Rosemary Ross Johnston	Childhood: a narrative chronotope	Roger D. Sell (ed.), *Children's Literature as Communication*, Amsterdam/Philadelphia: John Benjamins, pp. 137–157.	III	59
2002	Reinbert Tabbert	Approaches to the translation of children's literature: a review of critical studies since 1960	*Target: International Journal of Translation Studies* 14(2): 303–351.	IV	87
2003	Ann M. Trousdale and Sally McMillan	'Cinderella was a Wuss': a young girl's responses to feminist and patriarchal folktales	*Children's Literature in Education* 34(1) (March): 1–28.	III	73
2003	Rosemary Ross Johnston	Carnivals, the carnivalesque, *The Magic Puddin'*, and David Almond's *Wild Girl, Wild Boy*: towards a theorizing of children's plays	*Children's Literature in Education* 34(2) (June): 131–146.	IV	99
2003	Andy Sawyer	Who 'owns' children's fantasy?	*Foundation* 88 (Summer): 5–19.	I	13
2003	Evelyn Arizpe and Morag Styles	The nature of picturebooks: theories about visual texts and readers	*Children Reading Pictures*, London: RoutledgeFalmer, pp. 19–38.	I	21
2003	Sue Walsh	"Irony? — But children don't get it, do they?" The idea of appropriate language in narratives for children	*Children's Literature Association Quarterly* 28(1): 26–36.	II	51
2003	Andrea Schwenke Wyile	The value of singularity in first- and restricted third-person engaging narration	*Children's Literature* 31: 116–141.	III	81

Chronological table continued

Date	Author	Article/Chapter	References	Vol.	Chap.
2003	Emer O'Sullivan	Narratology meets translation studies, or, the voice of the translator in children's literature	*Meta* 48(1–2): 197–207.	IV	88
2003	Jack Zipes	Political children's theater in the age of globalization	*Theater* 33(2): 3–25.	IV	98
2003–2004	Nina Christensen	Childhood revisited: on the relationship between childhood studies and children's literature	*Children's Literature Association Quarterly* 28(4): 230–239.	III	58
2003–2004	Claire Malarte-Feldman	Folk materials, re-visions, and narrative images: the intertextual games they play	*Children's Literature Association Quarterly* 28(4): 210–219.	IV	97
2004	David Rudd	Theorising and theories: the conditions of possibility of children's literature	Peter Hunt (ed.), *International Companion Encyclopedia of Children's Literature,* Volume I, London and New York: Routledge, pp. 29–43.	II	52
2004	Sebastien Chapleau	A theory without a centre: developing childist criticism	Celia Keenan and Mary Shine Thompson (eds), *Studies in Children's Literature 1500–2000,* Dublin: Four Courts Press, pp. 130–137.	II	53
2004	Kenneth Kidd	Psychoanalysis and children's literature: the case for complementarity	*The Lion and the Unicorn* 28(1): 109–130.	III	78

GENERAL INTRODUCTION

Reading children's literature and 'Children's Literature'

Children's literature – as a body of texts in various media – is immensely influential across much of the world. It is fundamental to functional and socio-cultural literacy; it is important commercially and creatively; it is inevitably complex and ideologically and politically potent and it is the source of possibly the most formative and satisfying literary experiences in the lives of vast numbers of people.

This collection makes available the key articles and chapters written about children's literature theory and criticism over the past fifty years or so, the period during which an academic discipline has become established – 'Children's Literature'. It rehearses the major debates about why and how texts for children can be approached, and how to deal with the unique literary and cultural matrix of texts, adult readers and child readers involved.

One of the most striking features of 'Children's Literature' as a study is that it is, perhaps uniquely, inter-disciplinary, impinging on, or emanating from psychology, language studies, history, bibliography, librarianship, education, childhood studies and many other disciplines. Partly as a result, it has been marginalised by mainstream academia and this marginalisation has been compounded by its association with the child, the female, the practical and the popular. The advantage has been that its theorists and critics have tended to be, necessarily, eclectic and radical; as Aidan Chambers noted in 1985:

> ... the best demonstration of almost all [that literary theorists] say when they talk about phenomenology or structuralism or deconstruction or any other critical approach can be most clearly and easily demonstrated in children's literature.
>
> (1985, p. 133)

In addition, children's literature has often been seen as an international, inter-cultural phenomenon, on the assumption that aspects of childhood and storying are common across the world – with clear cultural and political implications.

Because texts for children touch on so many readers for such a variety of purposes, Children's Literature has become a singularly democratic area

1

of cultural and literary study. The texts are accessible to everyone; they are 'owned' by everyone. Adult readers are looking back to, or down on, childhood; they are in the position of mediating texts to children (as teachers, parents, carers), or they are visiting (or revisiting) childhood and childhood reading. In every case, they are entering into a power relationship in which *they* are empowered. Consequently, these adult readers feel that they can make judgements and contribute to debates more robustly than they might in other literary or cultural areas where 'professional readers' – critics, academics – appear to have 'superior' knowledge. Thus, clearly audible in these volumes is a remarkable range of voices and what those voices consider to be worth talking about varies considerably. This is a field not confined to academics, and the academics themselves are variously preoccupied with theory, affect, history, culture and many diverse and often conflicting issues. As a result, the debates tend to be self-aware, uninhibited, lively and to a large extent consciously free of arcane and exclusive (in the sense of excluding) language.

Children's Literature is now a fully-fledged academic area; as Susan Gannon has described it:

> Children's literature studies [is] a network of related scholarly, pedagogical and practical inquiries, all equal in status, their immediate importance depending on their usefulness in answering whatever question needs to be addressed at a particular point.
>
> (2000, p. 38)

However, these developments have not been seen universally as admirable. In her novel, *Foreign Affairs*, Alison Lurie, a Professor of English who teaches Children's Literature at Columbia University, New York, has her protagonist – also a Professor of Children's Literature – reflect:

> The very idea of making children's literature into a scholarly discipline, of forcing all that's most imaginative and free . . . into a grid of solemn pedantry, pompous platitude, and dubious textual analysis – psychological, sociological, moral, linguistic, structural – such a process invites divine retribution. . . .
>
> Vinnie has a bad conscience about her profession. The success of children's literature as a field of study – her own success – has an unpleasant side to it. At times she feels as if she were employed in enclosing what was once open heath or common. First she helped to build a barbed-wire fence about the field; then she helped to pull apart the wildflowers that grow there in order to examine them scientifically.
>
> (1986, pp. 235–236)

2

She is not alone. Russell Hoban, the American novelist who has written extensively and successfully for children, writes:

> The fact is that now there are not only books for children, there are books about books about books for children, there are courses where one learns about the books about the books for children; there's this tremendous tottering edifice, piled upon the sagging and beaten down back of the child at the end of the chain, and I must say that I question it.
>
> (Fox 1995, p. 119)

(And see also Alderson (Chapters 43 and 48).)

There is also the related difficulty that the huge range of interests and applications involved may seem to pull in destructive directions. As Roderick McGillis points out in 'The Delights of Impossibility: No Children, No Books, Only Theory' (Chapter 50):

> The rarefied theorising of the literary academic strikes the practising teacher as arid beyond tolerance, whereas the practical aims of the educationalist seem too limited and limiting to the theorist and historian of children's literature. The interest in bibliotherapy, sometimes expressed by the psychologically oriented critic . . . is often dismissed as lacking the formalist rigor of serious literary analysis. And the interest in accumulating data, the purview of the librarian/media specialist, some [regard as] interesting but hardly intellectually stimulating or socially engaged.
>
> (p. 325)

Nevertheless, these tensions are generally highly productive. As this collection shows, those who work with children's books may be concerned with the most abstruse theory and philosophy, the widest social and political philosophy, or the most intimate interpretation of an individual text to an individual child – but they are all *aware* of the fact that they subsist within a highly complex network.

Principles of selection and arrangement

These complexities have necessarily influenced the selection and arrangement of the articles in these volumes. Almost all of them have been selected to assist the reader in understanding how children's literature (or some facet of it) might be approached, rather than (as the vast majority of contemporary articles do) *demonstrating* various approaches. This accounts in part for the balance of journals represented: for example, *Signal* has been more inclined to discuss the fundamental issues involved in writing about children's literature than *Papers*.

As the same basic arguments recur in discussions of children's literature, I have included articles such as those by Hughes (Chapter 5) and Crago (Chapter 27) that were starting points for the discipline and which remain useful starting points for students. Myles McDowell's views in his famous 1973 article, 'Fiction for Children and Adults: Some Essential Differences' (Chapter 4), would probably find very few supporters thirty years later, but it is important that the article is available so that students can work through the arguments.

Other articles, which might perhaps seem a little dated now (to experts), have had huge formative influence – such as Aidan Chambers' 'The Reader in the Book' (Chapter 23), which introduced reception theory to non-specialists, Arthur N. Applebee's 'Where Does Cinderella Live?' (Chapter 31), Peter Dickinson's squib, 'A Defence of Rubbish' (Chapter 32) and Lissa Paul's 'Enigma Variations: What Feminist Theory Knows About Children's Literature' (Chapter 69). These remain classics – essential (and very readable) reading; the introductions to each volume provide some contextualisation.

The division of the material into four themed volumes, and broad sections within them, is designed to cater for very broad audiences and areas of interest. However, the material could have been arranged in many other ways, primarily because the vast majority of chapters address several themes. Thus, Stephen Thomson's 'Substitute Communities, Authentic Voices: The Organic Writing of the Child' (Chapter 61) which appears in the 'Childhood studies' section, could have found a home in 'The theory debate'; Michèle Anstey's 'It's Not All Black and White' (Chapter 35), which appears in 'Aspects of reading and writing' could have appeared in 'The subject matter' or 'Picture books' – and so on, more or less indefinitely. To help readers in finding their way through this luxuriant forest, I have suggested links to other articles on related themes.

Essential distinctions

Not far beneath the surface of even the most 'advanced' of the essays collected here is an awareness of the plurality of the subject matter and the discipline. As Emer O'Sullivan has put it:

> The two defining characteristics which distinguish children's literature ... are first that it is a body of literature which belongs simultaneously to two systems, the literary and the pedagogical ... and second ... that the communication in children's literature is asymmetrical. At every stage ... we find adults acting for children.
> (2004, pp. 194–195)

Defining the limits of the subject matter (explored especially in Chapters 5 and 6) is thus as important as defining the limits of the discipline (as in Chapters 38, 39, 42 and 50). It might be useful, therefore, to summarise the terminology attached to the body of creative texts being addressed. Definitions in general are either pragmatic and organisational, designed to exclude materials that would make the subject unmanageable (Townsend, Chapter 6), or are based on features attributed to texts or to readers. Thus, distinctions based on content (as in Chapters 63 and 66), form (Chapters 4 and 54), or 'quality' (Chapters 3 and 6) often lead out into discussions of affect and cultural agreements (or disagreements). Others, based on analyses of language, look to the implied reader (Chapters 23 and 46), the mode of address (Chapters 24 and 26) or a tone-content combination, such as Peter Hollindale's concept of 'Childness':

> [Childness is] the quality of being a child which is shared ground, although differently experienced and understood, between child and adult. . . . Childness is the distinguishing property of a text in children's literature . . . and it is also the property that a child brings to the reading of a text. The childness of the text can change the childness of the child, and vice versa.
>
> (1997, p. 47)

The value-term 'literature' has caused – and continues to cause – problems, as can be seen in Heins (Chapter 3), Rowe Townsend (Chapter 4), Bottigheimer (Chapter 8) and several others. The very term 'children's literature' seems to many to be an oxymoron. After all, as Henry James remarked,

> [With] the Literature, as it may be called for convenience, of children . . . the sort of taste that used to be called 'good' has nothing to do with the matter: we are so demonstrably in the presence of millions for whom taste is but an obscure, confused, immediate instinct.
>
> (Hunt, 1990, p. 75)

It may be more convenient for the reader of this book to re-configure the term 'children's literature' – except where the context specifies otherwise – as *texts for children*, allowing that the meanings of all three words have to be highly flexible.

> – *Texts* can be taken to mean virtually any form of communication. One of the distinguishing features of children's literature has been its lack of generic 'purity' . . . and in the twenty-first [century], it seems safe to say, the idea of the book as a 'closed' form will be

replaced by the multi-dimensional experience. The book, the film, the video, the re-tellings, the prequels and sequels, the merchandising, the diaries, the TV series with 'new' episodes, the 'making of the TV series', the 'back stories', the biographies of the stars who appear in the TV series . . . all of these are part of the 'experience' of what, reductively, we call the 'text'. And – because it passes constantly across the borders of high and popular culture – children's literature is now taken to include virtually *anything* produced for the entertainment, exploitation, or enculturation of children. In academic terms (that is, in terms of arbitrary, organisational convenience) our texts reside in literature, media studies, graphic art, history, folklore, theatre, dance . . . and so on.

– *for* can be declared by the author, assumed by the publisher, or – less manageably for those trying to create a coherent discipline – assumed by either those who give books to children, or (even more confusingly) by the children themselves. None of these categories is reliable. . . . The *'forness'* is [perceived and] judged differently by different generations and by those with different interests. . . .

– *children* The relationship between children and childhood, and adults and adulthood is extremely complex, and is continuously reflected in the [texts]. . . . Thus although it is possible to make some generalisations about how a culture or a society constructs the child – and publishers have made, and make (probably self-fulfilling) assumptions – 'the child' is an infinitely varied concept, from house to house, and from day to day. In talking about children's books, some generalisations have to be made, or the language becomes unmanageable, but the fact that the concept of the child is an ever-present problem for children's literature criticism cannot be forgotten.

(Hunt 2001, pp. 3–6)

In short, the question of whether a child is addressed, and the nature of the child addressee resides in the interpretation of the text by *any* reader – and here lies a shift in power between text and reader that characterises Children's Literature. As Perry Nodelman has put it, describing his move from mainstream to Children's Literature:

[Guides to children's literature] all made judgements of excellence in terms of the effects of books on their audience – and that astonished me, for in the ivory tower of literary study I had hitherto inhabited, one certainly did not judge books by how they affected audiences; in fact, one often judged audiences by the extent to which they were affected by books, so that, for instance, anyone who wasn't overwhelmed by Shakespeare was simply assumed to be an intransigent dummy.

(Nodelman 1985, p. 4)

Children's Literature (the study) and children's literature (the texts) are, as this collection demonstrates, complex and challenging. Even now, *pace* optimistic writers such as Jerry Griswold (Chapter 45), studying children's literature is assumed to be simple and it is worth bearing in mind Elizabeth Rigby's riposte (in 1844) to those who have denigrated books for children in the past, for it applies to everything in these volumes:

The whole mistake hinges upon the slight but important distinction between *childish* books and *children*'s books. The first are very easy – the second as much the reverse – the first require no mind at all – the second mind of no common class.

(1844, p. 26)

References

Chambers, A. (1985) *Booktalk: Occasional Writing on Literature and Children*, London: The Bodley Head.

Fox, G. (ed.) (1995) *Celebrating Children's Literature in Education*, London: Hodder and Stoughton.

Gannon, S. (2000) 'Children's Literature Studies in a New Century', *Signal* 91: 25–40.

Hollindale, P. (1997) *Signs of Childness in Children's Books*, South Woodchester: Thimble Press.

Hunt, P. (ed.) (1990) *Children's Literature: The Development of Criticism*, London and New York: Routledge.

—— (2001) *Children's Literature*, Blackwell Guides to Literature, Oxford: Blackwell.

Lurie, A. (1986) *Foreign Affairs*, London: Abacus.

Nodelman, P. (ed.) (1985) *Touchstones: Reflections on the Best in Children's Literature*, Vol. 1, West Lafayette, IN: Children's Literature Association.

O'Sullivan, E. (2004) 'Comparative Children's Literature', in P. Hunt (ed.) *International Companion Encyclopedia of Children's Literature*, 2nd edn, London and New York: Routledge.

Rigby, E. (1844) 'Children's Books', *The Quarterly Review* 74(1–3): 16–26.

INTRODUCTION TO VOLUME I

Writing for children

Sure it's simple, writing for kids. Just as simple as bringing them up.
(Le Guin 1989, p. 49)

Away from the pressures of marketing, and the need to provide striking quotations, children's authors have provided many thoughtful contributions to the debate about writing for non-peer audiences and the cultural rôle of children's literature. For example, the Australian novelist, Ivan Southall, has questioned the (common) suggestion that writing for children is a 'lesser' activity:

> The viewpoint mystifies me – that works for children must necessarily be minor works by minor writers, that deliberately they are generated and projected at reduced voltage, that they evade truth, that they avert passion and sensuality and the subtleties of life and are unworthy of the attention of the serious artist or craftsman. . . . Adult scaling-down of the intensity of the child state is a crashing injustice, an outrageous distortion of what childhood is about.
> (1980, p. 85)

The two quotations reprinted here (and see also Chapters 23, 32, 67 and 75) raise many of the questions – of suitability, reception, quality, style, social responsibility, and so on – that are explored throughout this collection. One of the fundamental issues is approached by C. S. Lewis, when he notes in Chapter 1 that 'a children's story which is enjoyed only by children is a bad children's story' (p. 19). This, like W. H. Auden's dictum that 'there are good books which are only for adults . . . there are no good books that are only for children' (1972, p. 11) needs to be, and has been, challenged. The first of these views privileges the adult; the second privileges the adult concept of literature. More recent critics have taken the opposite view, notably David Rudd in *Enid Blyton and the Mystery of Children's Literature*; he maintains, in effect, that the *purest* children's literature is that which *excludes* adults. And, he adds, 'this recognition, that there are some texts that might be good only for children, has been slow in coming' (p. 204).

9

Preliminary definitions and distinctions

The initial problem for writers wanting to write about children's literature was to forge a mode of criticism distinct from the adult-value-dominated critical modes of the past. The chapters by Heins, McDowell, Hughes and Rowe Townsend (Chapters 3–6) have been among the most influential in negotiating this difficult area.

However, the result of the lingering attachment to a value-based concept of literature, and the new-found preoccupation with audience, has been twofold. One, which has produced a continuing debate about the purpose and methodology of criticism, is that, as Karín Lesnik-Oberstein put it: 'How to find the *good* book for the child is children's literature criticism's purpose, whichever way it is dressed up' – rather than the more abstract purposes of 'adult' criticism (1994, p. 3). (See especially Lesnik-Oberstein (Chapter 49) and also Chapters 50 and 52.)

Equally, the idea of bringing the child-readers into the equation was strongly resisted, notably by Brian Alderson:

> Ultimately, of course, the referral of critical issues to young readers themselves raises the question of the validity in critical terms of majority opinions. . . . The adage that 'we needs must love the highest when we see it' has always seemed to me of doubtful application and it is at its most doubtful applied to children when they are left to themselves among books. But for the critic to collapse under popular clamour for the lowest is not only undignified, it is also evidence of his failure to analyse where his position lies in the no-man's-land between young readers and literacy.
>
> It may be objected that to assess children's books without reference to children is to direct some absolute critical standard relating neither to the author's purpose nor the reader's enjoyment. To do much less, however, is to follow a road that leads to a morass of contradictions and subjective responses, the most serious result of which will be the confusion of what we are trying to do in encouraging children to read. From the tone of reviews in the popular press, our aim would appear to be not much more than that of keeping the children quiet for half an hour or fitting them out to be competent participants in a bureaucratic society. But once one assigns to reading the vital role, which I believe that it has, of making children more perceptive and more aware of the possibilities of language, then it becomes necessary to hold fast to qualitative judgements formed upon the basis of adult experience. Naturally a knowledge of and sympathy with children (beyond mere remembrance of things past) must play a vital part in this

judgement, but just as vital is a personal response based upon knowledge of the resources of contemporary children's literature.

(1969, pp. 10–11)

This may be an 'adultist' view, but Alderson is far from being in what John Rowe Townsend (Chapter 6) called the 'book people' camp (whose interest lies in either the text-as-phenomenon, or the book-as-object); his concern here is with books and readers – 'creating intelligently literate young people'.

Paul Heins, in the article 'Coming to Terms with Criticism', which followed up the arguments in 'Out on a Limb with the Critics', reprinted here as Chapter 3, argued rather uneasily that, 'if children's literature is part of all literature, then the criticism of children's literature becomes a part of the criticism of all literature', admitting that the fact of the child as reader 'is a subject only occasionally related to literary criticism'. He concluded prophetically:

Perhaps one should distinguish, in the long run, between the two different ways of approaching children's books: (1) the criticism of these books as they concern the different kinds of people who use and work with these books and (2) the literary criticism of children's literature. But I still feel that a conscious and enlightened literary criticism should direct and govern our whole approach to children's literature.

(1970, p. 375)

It is this kind of fundamental debate that infuses Chapters 4–6, and further discussion can be found in McGillis (22), Crago (27), Dickinson (32) and, in the context of higher education, in Chapters 46–56.

The subject matter

This section ranges from an argument for early children's literature to an exploration of the effect of new media and new modes of storytelling. Children's literature draws on a huge range of genres (even, recently, pornography) and a great deal of time has been spent in trying to chart its boundaries. It has been argued that one essential condition for the existence of children's literature is a recognisable, or distinct, childhood that can be addressed. Gillian Adams' argument for Sumerian texts (2400 BC), 'The First Children's Literature? The Case for Sumer' (1986), acknowledged that, although the Mesopotamians had books that were 'routinely associated with childhood' (p. 1) and had a literature which they considered 'particularly suited for children' (p. 25), their ideas may well not fit with contemporary ideas of childhood or the function of children's books –

but that does not mean that such books should be excluded from the field.

Something of the difficulty of establishing the boundaries of children's literature can be seen in discussions of poetry and fantasy. In the first case, poetry for children has long been seen as an oxymoron – poetry is profound and reflective; children are not. As Anna Laetitia Barbauld wrote in 1781:

> It may well be doubted whether poetry ought to be lowered to the capacities of children . . . for the very essence of poetry is an elevation in thought and style above the common standard.
>
> (Hunt 2001, p. 293)

Until very recently, fantasy and science fiction have been regarded (at least by the academic 'establishment') as in some ways inferior to realism. As Jill Paton Walsh has observed, however:

> If a book has a dragon in it, then maybe one dismisses it as rubbish. . . . There are no dragons in the world, but there are ferocious, greedy and destructive keepers of goldhoards. And there is greed in one's own soul. A work of fantasy compels a reader into a metaphorical state of mind. A work of realism, on the other hand, permits very literal-minded readings, even downright stupid ones. . . . Even worse, it is possible to read a realistic book as though it were not fiction at all. . . .
>
> (Hearne and Kaye 1981, p. 38)

(See also another area of literature that has become associated with children more or less by default, myths, folk, and fairy tales (Chapters 92–97).)

One of the attractions of children's literature as a body of texts is that there are relatively few 'canonical' texts – this is not a discipline of relativity. Deborah Stevenson (Chapter 10) suggests that the viability of titles and the survival of canonical (and other) texts is linked very much to their status; for further discussion of the publishing imperatives impinging on children's literature, see Chapters 74 and 75.

Picture books

A separate section has been devoted to picture books (or picture-books or picturebooks) because they are, as Perry Nodelman asserted in his pioneering *Words about Pictures*, 'unlike any other form of verbal or visual art' in their combination of pictures and words (1988, p. vii). They are not merely (complex) narratives, but (complex) art; as Jane Doonan has suggested, the view that honours the picture-book most fully, holds that pictures, through their expressive powers, enable the book to function as an art object.... The value lies ... in the aesthetic experience and the contribution the picture book can make to our aesthetic development. In an aesthetic experience we are engaged in play of the most enjoyable and demanding kind.... And in that play we have ... to deal with abstract concepts logically, intuitively and imaginatively.

(1993, p. 7)

It can be cogently argued that picture books are the single most original contribution that children's books have made to general literature, requiring a good deal of new theorising to understand the process of perception (see also Chapters 35, 58 and 97).

Criticism and texts

How most effectively and appropriately to write about children's literature can be explored in terms of (among others) reception and response (see especially Chapter 29), literacy (Chapter 34), literary and cultural theory (Chapters 42, 46–53 and 61) and 'metanarratives' (Chapters 59 and 95).

However, it may be useful for the reader to look at ways in which critical theory (as summarised by McGillis in Chapter 22) has responded to the specific characteristics of the texts, such as the implied reader (Chapter 23), single, double, and dual address (Chapter 24) and narrative patterns and the reader (Chapter 25 and see also Chapters 27 and 31). Myers and Knoepflmacher also distinguish between multiple voices within a single narrator, in their idea of 'cross-writing' (Chapter 26). These ideas can also be usefully linked to the ideological debates about who 'owns' children's literature (Chapters 13, 49, 51 and 94).

References

Adams, G. (1986) 'The First Children's Literature? The Case for Sumer', *Children's Literature* 14: 1–30.

Alderson, B. (1969) 'The Irrelevance of Children to the Children's Book Reviewer', *Children's Book News* (January/February): 10–11.

Auden, W. H. (1972) 'Today's "wonder-world" needs Alice', in R. Philips (ed.) *Aspects of Alice*, London: Gollancz.

Doonan, J. (1993) *Looking at Pictures in Picture-Books*, South Woodchester: Thimble Press.

Hearne, B. and Kaye, M. (1981) *Celebrating Children's Books*, New York: Lothrop, Lee and Shepard.

Heins, P. (1970) 'Coming to Terms With Criticism', *Horn Book Magazine* 46: 370–375.

Hunt, P. (2001) *Children's Literature*, Blackwell Guides to Literature, Oxford: Blackwell.

Le Guin, U. K. (1989) *The Language of the Night*, New York: HarperCollins.

Lesnik-Oberstein, K. (1994) *Children's Literature: Criticism and the Fictional Child*, Oxford: Clarendon Press.

Nodelman, P. (1988) *Words about Pictures*, Athens, GA: The University of Georgia Press.

Rudd, D. (2000) *Enid Blyton and the Mystery of Children's Literature*, London: Macmillan.

Southall, I. (1980) 'Sources and Responses', in V. Haviland (ed.) *The Openhearted Audience: Ten Authors Talk About Writing for Children*, Washington DC: Library of Congress.

Part 1

WRITING FOR CHILDREN

1

ON THREE WAYS OF
WRITING FOR CHILDREN

C. S. Lewis

Source: *Of Other Worlds: Essays and Stories*, London: Geoffrey Bles, 1966, pp. 22–34. Originally published in *Proceedings . . . of the Bournemouth Conference . . . 1952*, The Library Association.

I think there are three ways in which those who write for children may approach their work; two good ways and one that is generally a bad way.

I came to know of the bad way quite recently and from two unconscious witnesses. One was a lady who sent me the MS of a story she had written in which a fairy placed at a child's disposal a wonderful gadget. I say 'gadget' because it was not a magic ring or hat or cloak or any such traditional matter. It was a machine, a thing of taps and handles and buttons you could press. You could press one and get an ice cream, another and get a live puppy, and so forth. I had to tell the author honestly that I didn't much care for that sort of thing. She replied, 'No more do I, it bores me to distraction. But it is what the modern child wants.' My other bit of evidence was this. In my own first story I had described at length what I thought a rather fine high tea given by a hospitable faun to the little girl who was my heroine. A man, who has children of his own, said, 'Ah, I see how you got to that. If you want to please grown-up readers you give them sex, so you thought to yourself, "That won't do for children, what shall I give them instead? I know! The little blighters like plenty of good eating."' In reality, however, I myself like eating and drinking. I put in what I would have liked to read when I was a child and what I still like reading now that I am in my fifties.

The lady in my first example, and the married man in my second, both conceived writing for children as a special department of 'giving the public what it wants'. Children are, of course, a special public and you find out what they want and give them that, however little you like it yourself.

The next way may seem at first to be very much the same, but I think the resemblance is superficial. This is the way of Lewis Carroll, Kenneth

Grahame, and Tolkien. The printed story grows out of a story told to a particular child with the living voice and perhaps *ex tempore*. It resembles the first way because you are certainly trying to give that child what it wants. But then you are dealing with a concrete person, this child who, of course, differs from all other children. There is no question of 'children' conceived as a strange species whose habits you have 'made up' like an anthropologist or a commercial traveller. Nor, I suspect, would it be possible, thus face to face, to regale the child with things calculated to please it but regarded by yourself with indifference or contempt. The child, I am certain, would see through that. In any personal relation the two participants modify each other. You would become slightly different because you were talking to a child and the child would become slightly different because it was being talked to by an adult. A community, a composite personality, is created and out of that the story grows.

The third way, which is the only one I could ever use myself, consists in writing a children's story because a children's story is the best art-form for something you have to say: just as a composer might write a Dead March not because there was a public funeral in view but because certain musical ideas that had occurred to him went best into that form. This method could apply to other kinds of children's literature besides stories. I have been told that Arthur Mee never met a child and never wished to: it was, from his point of view, a bit of luck that boys liked reading what he liked writing. This anecdote may be untrue in fact but it illustrates my meaning.

Within the species 'children's story' the sub-species which happened to suit me is the fantasy or (in a loose sense of that word) the fairy tale. There are, of course, other sub-species. E. Nesbit's trilogy about the Bastable family is a very good specimen of another kind. It is a 'children's story' in the sense that children can and do read it: but it is also the only form in which E. Nesbit could have given us so much of the humours of childhood. It is true that the Bastable children appear, successfully treated from the adult point of view, in one of her grown-up novels, but they appear only for a moment. I do not think she would have kept it up. Sentimentality is so apt to creep in if we write at length about children as seen by their elders. And the reality of childhood, as we all experienced it, creeps out. For we all remember that our childhood, as lived, was immeasurably different from what our elders saw. Hence Sir Michael Sadler, when I asked his opinion about a certain new experimental school, replied, 'I never give an opinion on any of those experiments till the children have grown up and can tell us *what really happened.*' Thus the Bastable trilogy, however improbable many of its episodes may be, provides even adults, in one sense, with more realistic reading about children than they could find in most books addressed to adults. But also, conversely, it enables the children who read it to do something much more mature than they realize. For the whole book is a character study of Oswald, an unconsciously satiric self-portrait, which every intelligent child can fully appreciate: but no child would sit down to read a character study in any other form. There is another way in which children's stories mediate this psychological interest, but I will reserve that for later treatment.

In this short glance at the Bastable trilogy I think we have stumbled on a principle. Where the children's story is simply the right form for what the author has to say, then of course readers who want to hear that, will read the story or re-read it, at any age. I never met *The Wind in the Willows* or the Bastable books till I was in my late twenties, and I do not think I have enjoyed them any the less on that account. I am almost inclined to set it up as a canon that a children's story which is enjoyed only by children is a bad children's story. The good ones last. A waltz which you can like only when you are waltzing is a bad waltz.

This canon seems to me most obviously true of that particular type of children's story which is dearest to my own taste, the fantasy or fairy tale. Now the modern critical world uses 'adult' as a term of approval. It is hostile to what it calls 'nostalgia' and contemptuous of what it calls 'Peter Pantheism'. Hence a man who admits that dwarfs and giants and talking beasts and witches are still dear to him in his fifty-third year is now less likely to be praised for his perennial youth than scorned and pitied for arrested development. If I spend some little time defending myself against these charges, this is not so much because it matters greatly whether I am scorned and pitied as because the defence is germane to my whole view of the fairy tale and even of literature in general. My defence consists of three propositions.

1. I reply with a *tu quoque*. Critics who treat *adult* as a term of approval, instead of as a merely descriptive term, cannot be adult themselves. To be concerned about being grown up, to admire the grown up because it is grown up, to blush at the suspicion of being childish; these things are the marks of childhood and adolescence. And in childhood and adolescence they are, in moderation, healthy symptoms. Young things ought to want to grow. But to carry on into middle life or even into early manhood this concern about being adult is a mark of really arrested development. When I was ten, I read fairy tales in secret and would have been ashamed if I had been found doing so. Now that I am fifty I read them openly. When I became a man I put away childish things, including the fear of childishness and the desire to be very grown up.

2. The modern view seems to me to involve a false conception of growth. They accuse us of arrested development because we have not lost a taste we had in childhood. But surely arrested development consists not in refusing to lose old things but in failing to add new things? I now like hock, which I am sure I should not have liked as a child. But I still like lemon-squash. I call this growth or development because I have been enriched: where I formerly had only one pleasure, I now have two. But if I had to lose the

taste for lemon-squash before I acquired the taste for hock, that would not be growth but simple change. I now enjoy Tolstoy and Jane Austen and Trollope as well as fairy tales and I call that growth: if I had had to lose the fairy tales in order to acquire the novelists, I would not say that I had grown but only that I had changed. A tree grows because it adds rings: a train doesn't grow by leaving one station behind and puffing on to the next. In reality, the case is stronger and more complicated than this. I think my growth is just as apparent when I now read the fairy tales as when I read the novelists, for I now enjoy the fairy tales better than I did in child-hood: being now able to put more in, of course I get more out. But I do not here stress that point. Even if it were merely a taste for grown-up literature added to an unchanged taste for children's literature, addition would still be entitled to the name 'growth', and the process of merely dropping one parcel when you pick up another would not. It is, of course, true that the process of growing does, incidentally and unfortunately, involve some more losses. But that is not the essence of growth, certainly not what makes growth admirable or desirable. If it were, if to drop parcels and to leave stations behind were the essence and virtue of growth, why should we stop at the adult? Why should not *senile* be equally a term of approval? Why are we not to be congratulated on losing our teeth and hair? Some critics seem to confuse growth with the cost of growth and also to wish to make that cost far higher than, in nature, it need be.

3. The whole association of fairy tale and fantasy with childhood is local and accidental. I hope everyone has read Tolkien's essay on Fairy Tales, which is perhaps the most important contribution to the subject that anyone has yet made. If so, you will know already that, in most places and times, the fairy tale has not been specially made for, nor exclusively enjoyed by, children. It has gravitated to the nursery when it became unfashionable in literary circles, just as unfashionable furniture gravitated to the nursery in Victorian houses. In fact, many children do not like this kind of book, just as many children do not like horsehair sofas: and many adults do like it, just as many adults like rocking chairs. And those who do like it, whether young or old, probably like it for the same reason. And none of us can say with any certainty what that reason is. The two theories which are most often in my mind are those of Tolkien and of Jung.

According to Tolkien[1] the appeal of the fairy story lies in the fact that man there most fully exercises his function as a 'subcreator'; not, as they love to say now, making a 'comment upon life' but making, so far as poss-ible, a subordinate world of his own. Since, in Tolkien's view, this is one of man's proper functions, delight naturally arises whenever it is successfully performed. For Jung, fairy tale liberates Archetypes which dwell in the collective unconscious, and when we read a good fairy tale we are obeying the old precept 'Know thyself'. I would venture to add to this my own theory, not indeed of the Kind as a whole, but of one feature in it: I mean, the presence of beings other than human which yet behave, in varying degrees, humanly: the giants and dwarfs and talking beasts. I believe these to be at least (for they may have many other sources of power and beauty) an admirable hieroglyphic which conveys psychology, types of character, more briefly than novelistic presentation and to readers whom novelistic presentation could not yet reach. Consider Mr Badger in *The Wind in the Willows*—that extraordinary amalgam of high rank, coarse manners, gruffness, shyness, and goodness. The child who has once met Mr Badger has ever afterwards, in its bones, a knowledge of humanity and of English social history which it could not get in any other way.

Of course as all children's literature is not fantastic, so all fantastic books need not be children's books. It is still possible, even in an age so ferociously anti-romantic as our own, to write fantastic stories for adults: though you will usually need to have made a name in some more fashionable kind of literature before anyone will publish them. But there may be an author who at a particular moment finds not only fantasy but fantasy-for-children the exactly right form for what he wants to say. The distinction is a fine one. His fantasies for children and his fantasies for adults will have very much more in common with one another than either has with the ordinary novel or with what is sometimes called 'the novel of child life'. Indeed the same readers will probably read both his fantastic 'juveniles' and his fantastic stories for adults. For I need not remind such an audience as this that the neat sorting-out of books into age-groups, so dear to publishers, has only a very sketchy relation with the habits of any real readers. Those of us who are blamed when old for reading childish books were blamed when children for reading books too old for us. No reader worth his salt trots along in obedience to a time-table. The distinction, then, is a fine one: and I am not quite sure what made me, in a particular year of my life, feel that not only a fairy tale, but a fairy tale addressed to children, was exactly what I must write—or burst. Partly, I think, that this form permits, or compels you to leave out things I wanted to leave out. It compels you to throw all the force of the book into what was done and said. It checks what a kind, but discerning critic called 'the expository demon' in me. It also imposes certain very fruitful necessities about length.

If I have allowed the fantastic type of children's story to run away with this discussion, that is because it is the kind I know and love best, not because I wish to condemn any other. But the patrons of the other kinds very frequently want to condemn it. About once every hundred years some wiseacre gets up and tries to banish the fairy tale. Perhaps I had better say a few words in its defence, as reading for children.

It is accused of giving children a false impression of the world they live in. But I think no literature that children could read gives them less of a false impression. I think what profess to be realistic stories for children are far more likely to deceive them. I never expected the real world to be like the fairy tales. I think that I did expect school to be like the school stories. The fantasies did not deceive me: the school stories did. All stories in which children have adventures and successes which are possible, in the sense that they do not break the laws of nature, but almost infinitely improbable, are in more danger than the fairy tales of raising false expectations.

Almost the same answer serves for the popular charge of escapism, though here the question is not so simple. Do fairy tales teach children to retreat into a world of wish-fulfilment—'fantasy' in the technical psychological sense of the word—instead of facing the problems of the real world? Now it is here that the problem becomes subtle. Let us again lay the fairy tale side by side with the school story or any other story which is labelled a 'Boy's Book' or a 'Girl's Book', as distinct from a 'Children's Book'. There is no doubt that both arouse, and imaginatively satisfy, wishes. We long to go through the looking glass, to reach fairy land. We also long to be the immensely popular and successful schoolboy or schoolgirl, or the lucky boy or girl who discovers the spy's plot or rides the horse that none of the cowboys can manage. But the two longings are very different. The second, especially when directed on something so close as school life, is ravenous and deadly serious. Its fulfilment on the level of imagination is in very truth compensatory: we run to it from the disappointments and humiliations of the real world: it sends us back to the real world undivinely discontented. For it is all flattery to the ego. The pleasure consists in picturing oneself the object of admiration. The other longing, that for fairy land, is very different. In a sense a child does not long for fairy land as a boy longs to be the hero of the first eleven. Does anyone suppose that he really and prosaically longs for all the dangers and discomforts of a fairy tale?— really wants dragons in contemporary England? It is not so. It would be much truer to say that fairy land arouses a longing for he knows not what. It stirs and troubles him (to his life-long enrichment) with the dim sense of something beyond his reach and, far from dulling or emptying the actual world, gives it a new dimension of depth. He does not despise real woods because he has read of enchanted woods: the reading makes all real woods a little enchanted. This is a special kind of longing. The boy reading the school story of the type I have in mind desires success and is unhappy (once the book is over) because he can't get it: the boy reading the fairy tale desires and is happy in the very fact of desiring. For his mind has not been concentrated on himself, as it often is in the more realistic story.

I do not mean that school stories for boys and girls ought not to be written. I am only saying that they are far more liable to become 'fantasies' in the clinical sense than fantastic stories are. And this distinction holds for adult reading too. The dangerous fantasy is always superficially realistic. The real victim of wishful reverie does not batten on the *Odyssey*, *The Tempest*, or *The Worm Ouroboros*: he (or she) prefers stories about millionaires, irresistible beauties, posh hotels, palm beaches and bedroom scenes—things that really might happen, that ought to happen, that would have happened if the reader had had a fair chance. For, as I say, there are two kinds of longing. The one is an *askesis*, a spiritual exercise, and the other is a disease.

A far more serious attack on the fairy tale as children's literature comes from those who do not wish children to be frightened. I suffered too much from night-fears myself in childhood to undervalue this objection. I would not wish to heat the fires of that private hell for any child. On the other hand, none of my fears came from fairy tales. Giant insects were my specialty, with ghosts a bad second. I suppose the ghosts came directly or indirectly from stories, though certainly not from fairy stories, but I don't think the insects did. I don't know anything my parents could have done or left undone which would have saved me from the pincers, mandibles, and eyes of those many-legged abominations. And that, as so many people have pointed out, is the difficulty. We do not know what will or will not frighten a child in this particular way. I say 'in this particular way' for we must here make a distinction. Those who say that children must not be frightened may mean two things. They may mean (1) that we must not do anything likely to give the child those haunting, disabling, pathological fears against which ordinary courage is helpless: in fact, *phobias*. His mind must, if possible, be kept clear of things he can't bear to think of. Or they may mean (2) that we must try to keep out of his mind the knowledge that he is born into a world of death, violence, wounds, adventure, heroism and cowardice, good and evil. If they mean the first I agree with them: but not if they mean the second. The second would indeed be to give children a false impression and feed them on escapism in the bad sense. There is something ludicrous in the idea of so educating a generation which is born to the Ogpu and the atomic bomb. Since it is so likely that they will meet cruel enemies, let them at least have heard of brave knights and heroic courage. Otherwise you are making their destiny not brighter but darker. Nor do most of us find that violence and bloodshed, in a story, produce any haunting dread in the minds of children. As far as that goes, I side impenitently with the human race against the modern reformer. Let there be wicked kings and beheadings, battles and dungeons, giants and dragons, and let villains be soundly killed at the end of the book. Nothing will persuade me that this causes an ordinary child any kind or degree of fear beyond what it wants, and needs, to feel. For, of course, it wants to be a little frightened.

The other fears—the phobias—are a different matter. I do not believe one can control them by literary means. We seem to bring them into the world with us ready made. No doubt the particular image on which the child's terror is fixed can sometimes be traced to a book. But is that the source, or only the occasion, of the fear? If he had been spared that image, would not some other, quite unpredictable by you, have had the same effect? Chesterton has told us of a boy who was more afraid of the Albert Memorial than anything else in the world. I know a man whose great childhood terror was the India paper edition of the *Encyclopaedia Britannica*—for a reason I defy you to guess. And I think it possible that by confining your child to blameless stories of child life in which nothing at all alarming ever happens, you would fail to banish the terrors, and would succeed in banishing all that can ennoble them or make them endurable. For in the fairy tales, side by side with the terrible figures, we find the immemorial comforters and protectors, the radiant ones; and the terrible figures are not merely terrible, but sublime. It would be nice if no little boy in bed, hearing, or thinking he hears, a sound, were ever at all frightened. But if he is going to be frightened, I think it better that he should think of giants and dragons than merely of burglars. And I think St George, or any bright champion in armour, is a better comfort than the idea of the police.

I will even go further. If I could have escaped all my own night-fears at the price of never having known 'faerie', would I now be the gainer by that bargain? I am not speaking carelessly. The fears were very bad. But I think the price would have been too high.

But I have strayed far from my theme. This has been inevitable for, of the three methods, I know by experience only the third. I hope my title did not lead anyone to think that I was conceited enough to give you advice on how to write a story for children. There were two very good reasons for not doing that. One is that many people have written very much better stories than I, and I would rather learn about the art than set up to teach it. The other is that, in a certain sense, I have never exactly 'made' a story. With me the process is much more like bird-watching than like either talking or building. I see pictures. Some of these pictures have a common flavour, almost a common smell, which groups them together. Keep quiet and watch and they will begin joining themselves up. If you were very lucky (I have never been as lucky as all that) a whole set might join themselves so consistently that there you had a complete story: without doing anything yourself. But more often (in my experience always) there are gaps. Then at last you have to do some deliberate inventing, have to contrive reasons why these characters should be in these various places doing these various things. I have no idea whether this is the usual way of writing stories, still less whether it is the best. It is the only one I know: images always come first.

Before closing, I would like to return to what I said at the beginning. I rejected any approach which begins with the question 'What do modern children like?' I might be asked, 'Do you equally reject the approach which begins with the question "What do modern children need?"—in other words, with the moral or didactic approach?' I think the answer is Yes. Not because I don't like stories to have a moral: certainly not because I think children dislike a moral. Rather because I feel sure that the question 'What do modern children need?' will not lead you to a good moral. If we ask that question we are assuming too superior an attitude. It would be better to ask 'What moral do I need?' for I think we can be sure that what does not concern us deeply will not deeply interest our readers, whatever their age. But it is better not to ask the question at all. Let the pictures tell you their own moral. For the moral inherent in them will rise from whatever spiritual roots you have succeeded in striking during the whole course of your life. But if they don't show you any moral, don't put one in. For the moral you put in is likely to be a platitude, or even a falsehood, skimmed from the surface of your consciousness. It is impertinent to offer the children that. For we have been told on high authority that in the moral sphere they are probably at least as wise as we. Anyone who *can* write a children's story without a moral, had better do so: that is, if he is going to write children's stories at all. The only moral that is of any value is that which arises inevitably from the whole cast of the author's mind.

Indeed everything in the story should arise from the whole cast of the author's mind. We must write for children out of those elements in our own imagination which we share with children: differing from our child readers not by any less, or less serious, interest in the things we handle, but by the fact that we have other interests which children would not share with us. The matter of our story should be a part of the habitual furniture of our minds. This, I fancy, has been so with all great writers for children, but it is not generally understood. A critic not long ago said in praise of a very serious fairy tale that the author's tongue 'never once got into his cheek'. But why on earth should it?—unless he had been eating a seed-cake. Nothing seems to me more fatal, for this art, than an idea that whatever we share with children is, in the privative sense, 'childish' and that whatever is childish is somehow comic. We must meet children as equals in that area of our nature where we are their equals. Our superiority consists partly in commanding other areas, and partly (which is more relevant) in the fact that we are better at telling stories than they are. The child as reader is neither to be patronized nor idolized: we talk to him as man to man. But the worst attitude of all would be the professional attitude which regards children in the lump as a sort of raw material which we have to handle. We must of course try to do them no harm: we may, under the Omnipotence, sometimes dare to hope that we may do them good. But only such good as involves treating them with respect. We must not imagine that we are Providence or Destiny. I will not say that a good story for children could never be written by someone in the Ministry of Education, for all things are possible. But I should lay very long odds against it.

Once in a hotel dining-room I said, rather too loudly, 'I loathe prunes.' 'So do I,' came an unexpected six-year-old voice from another table. Sympathy was instantaneous. Neither of us thought it funny. We both

25

knew that prunes are far too nasty to be funny. That is the proper meeting between man and child as independent personalities. Of the far higher and more difficult relations between child and parent or child and teacher, I say nothing. An author, as a mere author, is outside all that. He is not even an uncle. He is a freeman and an equal, like the postman, the butcher, and the dog next door.

Note

1 J. R. R. Tolkien, 'On Fairy–Stories', *Essays Presented to Charles Williams* (1947), p. 66 ff.

2

A FREE GIFT

Joan Aiken

Source: Edward Blishen (ed.), *The Thorny Paradise: Writers on Writing for Children*, Harmondsworth: Kestrel (Penguin), 1975, pp. 36–52. Originally published as 'Purely for Love', Books: Journal of the National Book League (Winter 1970): 9–21.

This is not so much an essay as a rambling series of disjointed meditations, and some questions without any answers, and some impracticable suggestions.

To start with, a couple of quotations: their relevance will probably be guessed. The first:

> 'Do you know where the wicked go after death?'
>
> 'They go to hell,' was my ready and orthodox answer.
>
> 'And should you like to fall into that pit and be burning there for ever?'
>
> 'No, Sir.'
>
> 'What must you do to avoid it?'
>
> I deliberated for a moment; my answer, when it did come, was objectionable. 'I must keep in good health and not die.'
>
> 'How can you keep in good health? Children younger than you die daily . . . Here is a book entitled *The Child's Guide*; read it with prayer, especially that part containing an account of the awfully sudden death of Martha G—, a naughty child addicted to falsehood and deceit'. . .
>
> 'I am not deceitful; if I were I should say I loved *you*; but I declare I do not love you . . . I dislike you the worst of anybody in the world, and this book about the liar, you may give it to your girl Georgiana, for it is she who tells lies . . .'

That, of course, is from *Jane Eyre*. And the other, quite different, is shorter:

> 'Me and my brother were then the victims of his feury since which we have suffered very much which leads us to the arrowing belief

that we have received some injury in our insides, especially as
no marks of violence are visible externally. I am screaming out
loud all the time I write and so is my brother which takes off
my attention and I hope will excuse mistakes . . .'

I'll leave those for the moment in the air . . .

I keep my gramophone records in old wooden coalboxes. Quite by
chance I discovered a long time ago that old wooden coalboxes are exactly
the right shape and size for keeping gramophone records in. Don't worry –
there is a connection here: for someone who has been writing children's
stories on and off for the last thirty years, the sudden rise to importance of
children's literature has affected me rather as if I woke one day and found
that university courses and seminars were being held on the necessity of
keeping one's discs in old wooden coalboxes, and journals being printed
called *Wooden Coalbox News*, and even an industry had sprung up for
making imitation plastic wooden coalboxes . . . I don't wish to sound snide
or ungrateful. In a way it's wonderful suddenly to find one's occupation
so respectable, at least in certain company – for it isn't yet so with the
general public. In most circles, the confession that one writes children's
books always produces the same response, and very daunting it is. I was
taken once to a party by friends. It was a very mixed party – all incomes,
classes and professions, young and old: some guests were in television, some
in films or advertising, some wrote. The only common factor was that they
were all very intelligent, because the host was very intelligent. My friends
started off by introducing me as their friend Joan who wrote children's
books. But they soon stopped that. Because at the phrase *children's books*
an expression of blank horror would close down on every face. People
would be unable to think of a single conversational topic; they obviously
expected me to start reciting poetry about fairies in a high, piping voice, and
they couldn't wait to get away from that part of the room to somewhere
safer and more interesting. Having observed this Phenomenon, my friends
changed their tactics – they began introducing me as somebody who wrote
thrillers. Instantly all was well, and faces lit up – people love thriller-writers
because everybody reads a thriller at one time or another. So they felt
able to talk to me, and I had a good time and came away from the party
with a curious feeling of the relativity of identity. And wondering, too, who
is a real adult – if anybody is: all the time, that is to say.

Obviously, writing for children is regarded by society as a fairly childish
occupation. But then it occurred to me that most people's occupations
are pursued at a number of different levels – at varying mental ages. A
man runs his business affairs with a fifty-year-old intelligence, conducts his
marriage on a pattern formed when he was twenty, has hobbies suitable
to a ten-year-old, and a reading age that stuck at Leslie Charteris. Is he an
adult or not? And if he is not, how would you classify his reading-

matter? There's a lot of what I'd classify as non-adult reading: thrillers, funny books, Regency romances, horror stories, westerns, for instance. Of course, some of these, because of outstanding qualities, may fall into the adult sphere: but many don't. And yet it is considered perfectly all right for a forty-five-year-old company director to read, say, Ian Fleming, whereas he would be thought odd if he read, say, Alan Garner – a much better writer. And there is the same ambivalence in the social attitude to the writers. If you say you write books for children because you enjoy doing so, people instantly assume that you are retarded. Whereas, sad but true, if you say: 'Of course, I'd *rather* write adult fiction, but writing for children is more paying' (which, incidentally, is not so), people accept that as a perfectly logical, virtuous viewpoint. But to write children's books for pleasure – that, nine times out of ten, is considered almost as embarrassing as making one's money from the manufacture of contraceptives or nappy liners. And yet writing thrillers is all right. It's odd – because the really interesting point here is the strong similarity that in fact exists between thrillers and children's fiction; the moral outlook is the same: the pattern of mystery, danger, capture, escape, revenge, triumph of good over evil, is very similar indeed.

So society regards people who write for children as odd. And – if one does write for children – one can't help stopping from time to time and saying to oneself: 'Maybe society is right about this? Why do people write for children anyway? Is it a good thing that they should? Up to the nineteenth century, children managed all right without having books specially written for them; they were not regarded as a different species, but were clothed, fed, and treated in most ways as adults of a smaller size. Are they, in fact, better off for being treated as a separate minority? And, turning to the people who write for children, ought they to indulge themselves in this way? And what started them doing so, in the middle of the nineteenth century? Was it the need of the children, or the need of the writers to write in that particular way? And, if people are to be allowed to write for children, what ought they to write?'

I've started a lot of hares there, some of which I don't intend to pursue. The last question is particularly silly – almost as silly as saying: What ought people to write for adults? But I'd like to return to the first of my questions. Why do people write for children?

I'm afraid there are some – quite a number – who do it because it seems like easy money, especially in the recent boom in children's literature. Their idea is that in children's fiction you can get away with a minimum of factual background, a skimpy story, and a poverty-stricken vocabulary. But let's set such people on one side. If they found an easier racket, they'd switch to it. Let's consider the ones who *like* to write for children. Let's consider why, in spite of its being an embarrassing, ill-paid, guilt-producing and socially unacceptable thing to do, quite a number of people in fact *do* it – instead of writing adult novels or plays or TV scripts or biographies, or as well as doing these things. What sort of people are they?

The answers to some of these questions may exist, and be available, in detail. For some years ago the Department of Motivational Studies in an American university set out to conduct a massive research project into the motivations of children's writers. They sent out a great questionnaire, which took a solid six hours to fill in, going at top speed: the results to be tabulated by computers. Though of course those results were bound to be an average only of the writers they selected – and who did the selecting, one wonders? I guess they'll have come up with such conclusions as that most children's writers are from broken families, and may have been ill when young, or handicapped, or misfits, or at least unsociably inclined. And I'm not sure where such a result would get us. We have left behind the era when boys were castrated so they'd always be sure of a part in opera; and you could hardly break up your home in the hope that your child might become a second Lewis Carroll. (It really is too bad that this project started too late for the questionnaire to be sent to *him!*)

However, let's – rather sketchily – survey a few peaks sticking up out of the general landscape of children's literature. We can agree that, yes, Dickens had a very unhappy childhood. (I include Dickens because, though not a children's writer, he has so many of the essential qualities of one: mystery, slapstick, simple emotion, intricate plots, marvellous language – and anyway, children enjoy him, and you could say that he wrote for a mental age of fifteen.) Kipling and Masefield were also unhappy as children. Beatrix Potter had tyrannical, dominating parents, and so did Charlotte Yonge. Ruskin and Lewis Carroll never entirely grew up. Hans Andersen's father died when he was small and his mother drank. Blake suffered from visions – and his being so gifted must in itself have made his childhood a troubled one. De la Mare was delicate, and so was Robert Louis Stevenson – who, moreover, had to endure a hellfire upbringing which caused him to have frightful nightmares and guilt fantasies. The theme certainly seems clear enough. Writers who had unhappy childhoods tend to address themselves to children: not necessarily all the time, not necessarily through their whole output – but, obviously, as a sort of compensation, to replace part of the childhood they lost, or to return to the happier periods which may have seemed particularly radiant in retrospect compared with the black times. They address themselves to children because they need to; they are writing for the unfulfilled part of themselves. It would be invidious to talk about living writers in this context; but I can think of a couple among the top rank who were ill when young or suffered from broken homes. It's interesting, though, that this seems to apply to male writers more than to females. Plenty of well-known female children's writers had stable, happy childhoods and led normal lives. Maybe women just take naturally to producing children's tales: it's an occupational occupation. They don't get such a complete break from childhood as men do, because they are more likely to be in continuous touch with children, one way or another, between youth and middle age. (This certainly happened in my own case.)

So we can guess that, as part of that American university's profile of the children's writer, there's a troubled childhood in the background. A probability that leads me to put yet another question, with the intention of causing argument: Is it a good thing that these disturbed, unhappy characters should be doing this particular job? Are the people who write for children the ones who *ought* to be doing so?

There are quite a few professions – for instance, politics, the police, the prison service, maybe the civil service – which, one suspects, attract the very last people who ought to be in them. The mere desire to be a prison warder or a prime minister should disbar one from eligibility. I dare say by the next century anybody expressing a wish to go into politics will be psychoanalysed and put through all kinds of vocational tests, as they ought to be before matrimony or being allowed to drive a car on the public roads. I know this is a shocking suggestion, verging on fascism: but we are moving into a more and more controlled way of living. Our environment has to be controlled: we are subject to restraints in many areas already – fluoridation, smokeless zones, no-parking areas, contraception, industrial regulations, the decision whether to die of nicotine cancer. Control isn't enjoyable – it's just necessary because there are so many of us. Some industries already have their own personnel selection tests; before taking an advertising job in which I wrote copy for Campbells' soup tin labels, I had to undergo a whole series of ability tests, and finally a psychologist spent two hours trying to make me lose my temper. If one needs such stringent tests in order to write advertising copy, the end-purposes of which may reasonably be regarded as frivolous, if not downright nefarious, then how much more necessary might it not be thought to subject to some kind of psychological screening those people who are directing their energies into such a frighteningly influential area as children's books? After all, they produce material that can affect the outlook of whole generations to an incalculable degree.

I know this is an outrageous suggestion. Who would give the tests? What would they consist of? Who would assess the results? The whole idea bristles with impossibilities, and certainly runs counter to the growing permissiveness in the adult field as to what can be written and published. I'm not making the suggestion quite seriously. But it's worth thinking around. Bear in mind that you need a licence to keep a dog: you need all kinds of official authority before you can adopt or foster a child or start a school or even run a playgroup. Yet any paranoid can write a children's book – the only direct control is the need to find a publisher, and that's not too difficult.

Wouldn't some control over the production of children's books be a good thing? I'll stick my neck out even further. The average child, I've heard, is estimated in the course of childhood to have time to read six hundred books. Judging from myself and my friends and children, the figure probably ought to be less, because children read books over and over again – which is a good thing: better to read *Tom Sawyer* four times than four second-rate stories. So, six hundred books or less. But the book industry is unlike nearly all other industries in one marked particular: its products never perish. So those six hundred books have already been written. Without a shadow of doubt, any children's librarian could produce a list of six hundred titles, including all the classics and plenty of good modern books: enough to last any child right through. So where is the need to write any more? Particularly since writing for children is such a suspect, self-indulgent, narcissistic activity.

I'll leave that question in the air, with the others, and continue to think about writers. Of course, a troubled childhood in the background isn't the only contributory factor, or the world would be stuffed with children's writers. Many people who suffer from childhood handicaps go on to become politicians or psychoanalysts or bank robbers. To be a writer you must have the potential; to be a children's writer, you need imagination, iconoclasm, a deep instinctive morality, a large vocabulary, a sense of humour, a powerful sense of pity and justice . . . In addition, the ideal writer for children – I for one feel this very strongly – should do something else most of the time. Writing for children ought not to be a full-time job. I want to underline that – it's perhaps the most important thing I have to say in this essay: *writing for children should not be a full-time job.* Another thing Dickens, Masefield, de la Mare, Lewis Carroll, Ruskin, Kipling, Hans Andersen, William Blake had in common – children's writing was a sideline with them. (If indeed they were really writing for children at any time?) They had plenty of other professional interests. And that meant, first, that their writing was enriched by their other activities, other knowledge and background. It had great depth. It meant, second, that they wrote, when they did write for children, purely for love. And that is the way children's writing should be done; it should not be done for any other reason. Think of those six hundred books again – what a tiny total it is! It's frightful to think that a single one of them should have been written primarily to earn an advance of £250 on a 5 per cent royalty rising to 12$\frac{1}{2}$ per cent – or to propagate some such idea as that it's a very enjoyable thing to be a student nurse. And while I'm at this point I might as well add that I don't think any kind of fringe activity connected with children's literature should be a full-time occupation – editing, reviewing, publishing, anything. Everyone connected with these professions ought to leave the children's field from time to time in order to get a different perspective. After all, children live in the world with the rest of us, they aren't a separate race.

I'm uneasy about this cult of treating children as creatures utterly divorced from adult life. In a television series, *Family of Man*, which compared the social habits of different races, what struck me forcibly about the New Guinea tribesmen, the Himalayans, the Kalahari bushmen, the Chinese, was how very serene and well-adjusted their children seemed to be, because they had their established place in the adult world. And yet I'm ready to bet that not a single one of them had a children's book.

There's no need to point a moral here – and anyway, we can't reverse the course of civilization. So I'll go on to mention a danger that every children's writer is likely to encounter.

Most writers – most people – have at some point the idea for a good children's book. And maybe something fetches it out: an unresolved trauma from childhood to dispose of, or simply the circumstance of having children and telling them stories which seem worth writing down. In one way or another, this person, owing to some environmental factor, writes a good book – maybe two or three. And then, although the formative circumstances no longer exist, he or she is too caught up in the business to quit. Financial pressure, pressure of success, pressure of habit – it's easy to succumb. I can think of several people who wrote one or two good children's books; and then their interests developed elsewhere in a natural progression and they stopped. I can think of several more who wrote one or two good children's books; and should have stopped there, but didn't. And I need hardly say, since my previous remarks will have made this opinion clear – but I will say it again because I feel so strongly about it: Writing anything for children unless one has a strong, genuine impulse not only to write but to write that one, particular thing – writing anything without such an impulse is every bit as wicked as selling plastic machine-gun toys, or candies containing addictive drugs, or watered-down penicillin.

Another reason why children's writers should have some other, predominant occupation is simply that children have a greater respect for them if they do. Children, bless their good sound sense, are naturally suspicious of adults who devote themselves to nothing but children. For one thing, such adults are too boringly familiar – there aren't any mysteries about them. How, at school, we respected the teachers who disappeared to their own pursuits when school was over! How we despised those who were always at hand, doing things with the children as if they had nothing else to do – no better way of occupying themselves! Elizabeth Jenkins, in her book *Young Enthusiasts*, says: 'It is, of course, admirable to want to teach children, but the question all too seldom asked is: What have you got to teach them?' Parents, after all, are not exclusively occupied with their children – or heaven help both parties! Surveys of distraught young mothers in housing estates who never have a chance to get away show what a very unnatural state of affairs this is, and how undesirable.

When I was a child, one of my greatest pleasures was listening to my elder brother playing the piano. He was a lot older, and he played pretty well. But the point was that he was playing for his benefit, and not for mine. Part of my pleasure was the feeling that it was a free gift, that my brother and I were independent of one another. Another part was the understanding that some of the music was beyond my scope, which intensified my enjoyment of the easier bits. If my brother had said, 'I'll play for you now. Choose what you'd like,' I would have been not only embarrassed and nonplussed, but also horribly constricted by such a gesture: it would have completely changed the whole experience. I think the essence of the very best children's literature is this understanding that it is a free gift – no, not a gift, but a treasure trove – tossed out casually from the richness of a much larger store. Of course, there are exceptions to such a generalization: I can think of several fine children's writers now at work who *at present* address themselves only to children. But my feeling is that they have the capacity to do something else – and will do so, in due course.

I listened once to a fascinating broadcast by Arthur Koestler. Its subject was literature and the law of diminishing returns, and Mr Koestler was discussing whether or not there is progress in art comparable with progress in science, where discoveries and the growth of knowledge can be continually recorded and tabulated. He came to the conclusion that there *is* progress in art, but of a different kind. It proceeds by leaps and bounds instead of in a measurable upward graph, and it skips from one form to another: each art-form proceeding through four stages. There's a stage of revolution, a stage of expansion, a stage of saturation – when the audience has had enough of it, and the only way their attention can be held is by exaggeration or involution – and then a final collapse, as something else comes to the fore. I suppose, judged in those terms, one could say that writing for children is just leaving its revolutionary stage, having been going for less than a hundred years, and is still expanding. Just now, because it is expanding, it attracts people who fifty years ago would have been writing novels. I wonder what will have happened in, say, another twenty years? Maybe involution will have set in, and there will be a kind of Kafka vogue in children's literature. I wouldn't be surprised at that – I believe one can see traces of it already. Anyway, I was thinking, after Koestler's talk, about this question of progress – that you can't have progress without loss. You acquire nylon, you lose the spinning-wheel. You acquire colour photography, you lose Breughel. You acquire logic, you lose fairy-tales. Our brains now have to contain such a frightening amount of *stuff*, just in order to carry on normal life: electronics, the decimal system, knowledge of what is happening all over the world, psychology, ecology, how to deal with parking meters and supermarkets and yellow tube tickets. When you think of all this information that has to be rammed in and stored at the front of our minds – compared, say, with the necessary equipment for comfortable and rational living at the beginning of the nineteenth century – you can see why some people worry about what in the meantime may be trickling away at the back and being irretrievably lost. Sherlock Holmes had an idea that the brain's capacity was strictly limited; when Dr Watson, rather scandalized, discovered that Holmes knew nothing about the solar system, and began explaining it to him, Holmes brushed his proffered instruction aside, saying: 'I managed very well before, without this information, and what you have told me I shall now do my best to forget.' I'm sure that, whether or not this idea of the mind's limited capacity is correct, many people entertain it; consciously or unconsciously it forms part of their fear of progress – the feeling that if you acquire enough basic data about space flight to be able to understand what is going on in the lunar module, you will probably forget your wife's birthday or the theme of the first movement of the third Brandenburg Concerto. I sometimes cheer myself up by remembering that in Peru they didn't learn about the wheel until bicycles were invented. I'm convinced that most children's writers are natural opponents of progress, unable to adapt to the world entirely, fighting a rearguard action, like people salvaging treasures in a bombardment. For growing up, of course, involves the severest loss of all, the one that is hardest to accept. Children's writers are natural conservatives in the sense that they want to *conserve*.

*

Let me go back to that question I asked, not very seriously: If people are to be allowed to write for children at all, what should they be allowed to write?

I hope it's a question that makes the reader's blood run cold. I'm glad to think that the notion of any restraints or controls over writers is a horrifying one. And yet on the other side of the Iron Curtain – for instance – such controls are in force. And in the field of children's literature, both in this country and America, I've come across educators who made fairly plain their feeling that some children's writers are a bunch of tiresome anarchists who could perfectly well be a bit more helpful if they chose, in the way of incorporating educational material and acceptable ethics into their writing. As if they were a kind of hot-drink vending machine, and you had only to press the right knob to produce an appropriately flavoured bit of nourishment! I need hardly say that I don't agree with this point of view. I don't think it's possible to exercise any control over what a creative artist produces, without the risk of wrecking the product. The only possible control is to shoot the artist.

This view may seem inconsistent with what I said before about who should be allowed to write for children. So it is. I don't pretend to have consistent views.

I wouldn't dream of making suggestions to other writers as to what they should write. But I do have strong opinions about the kind of intentions one should *not* have when setting out to write for children. Childhood is so desperately short, and becoming shorter all the time; children are reading adult novels at fourteen, which leaves only about nine years in which to get through those six hundred books – nearly two books a week. Furthermore, children have so little reading-time, compared with adults, and it's growing less. There's school, there's bedtime, and there are all the extracurricular activities they now have. I'm not decrying adventure playgrounds and drama groups and classes in clay-modelling and organized camp holidays . . . I think they are splendid: and even television has its points. But it all means a loss of reading time, and *that* means that when children do read, it really is a wicked shame if they waste any time at all on what I'll group together under the heading of Filboid Studge. That, you may recall, was the title of a short story by Saki, about a breakfast food so dull and tasteless that it sold extremely well because everybody believed it *must* be good for them. (Really it's a pity we don't have an excretory system for mental as well as physical waste matter. Children, at an age when their minds are as soft and impressionable as a newly tarred road, pick up such a mass of unnourishing stuff – and what happens to it? It soaks down into the subconscious and does no good there, or it lies around taking up room that could be used to better purpose.)

It's lucky that at least children have a strong natural resistance to phoney morality. They can see through the adult with some moral axe to grind almost before he opens his mouth. The smaller the child, the sharper the instinct. I suppose it's the same kind of ESP that one finds in animals – the telepathy that transmits to one's cat exactly which page of the Sunday paper one wishes to read, so that he can go and sit on it. Small children have this to a marked degree. You have only to say, 'Eat your nice spinach', for a negative reaction to be triggered off. You don't even have to add: 'Because it's good for you.' They pick that up out of the atmosphere. They sense at once when we want them to do something because it suits *us*. Sad to think how much at our mercy children are! Ninety per cent of their time we are organizing and guiding them and making them do things for utilitarian reasons – and then, for the remaining ten per cent, as likely as not, we are concocting pretexts for getting rid of them. I can remember the exact tone of my mother's voice as she invented some errand that would get me out from under the grown-ups' feet for half an hour. And I now remember too, with frightful guilt, how pleased I was when my children learned to read; apart from my real happiness at the thought of the pleasure that lay ahead of them, I looked forward to hours of peace and quiet.

On account of this tough natural resistance, I'm not bothered about hypocritical moral messages. That, as the reader will have guessed, is where the quotation from *Jane Eyre* comes in – the one I began this essay with. It's a beautiful example of the calm and ruthless logic with which children bypass any piece of moral teaching they are not going to concern themselves with.

> 'What must you do to avoid it [going to hell?]' . . .
> 'I must keep in good health and not die.'

It's an example of lateral thinking, anticipating Edward de Bono by 120 years.

Unfortunately, as children grow older, this faculty becomes blunted because of education. So much of education consists in having inexplicable things done at one for obscure reasons, that it's no wonder the victims presently almost cease to resist. I can see that some education is necessary – just as the wheel is necessary. We have to learn to get into gear with the rest of the world. But it's remarkable how little education one *can* get along with.

It's a dangerous thing to decry education. But I feel there is something wrong with our whole attitude to it. The trouble is that we have taken away the role of children in the adult world. Instead of being with their parents, learning how: helping on the farm, blowing the forge fire, making flint arrowheads with the grown-ups, as would be natural, they are all shoved off together into a corner. And what happens then? We have to find them something to do to keep them out of mischief. I think too much – far, far too much – of education is still fundamentally just this: something cooked up to keep children out of their parents' hair till they are grown. I don't see how you can learn to have a spontaneous, creative, intelligent, sensitive reaction to the world when for your first six or twelve or eighteen years there is so much of this element of hypocrisy in how you are treated. And the worst of it is that this element is present not only in education, but in reading matter too.

There's a whole range of it – from *The Awfully Sudden Death of Martha G—*, through *A Hundred and One Things to Do on a Wet Saturday and not Plague Daddy* – and *Sue Jones has a Super Time as Student Nurse* – to the novels (some of them quite good) intended to show teen-agers how to adjust to the colour problem and keep calm through parents' divorce and the death of poor Fido. My goodness, I even saw in a publisher's catalogue a series of situation books for *under-sixes*. I suppose they serve some purpose. But just the same I count them as Filboid Studge. And how insulting they are! Adults are not expected to buy books called *Mrs Sue Jones – Alcoholic's Wife*, or *A Hundred and One Ways to Lose Your Job and Keep Calm*. Maybe some adults would be better adjusted if they did. It's true people will swallow things wrapped in this form of fictional jam. They will swallow it because they have been conditioned to do so all their lives: because from the first primer their reading has become more impure.

(I'm not using impure in the sense of obscene, but in the sense of being written with a concealed purpose.) In that same publisher's catalogue, advertising a series of basic vocabulary classics aimed at backward readers, the blurb said that in secondary schools a surprising number of children read nothing for pleasure except comics. Can you wonder at that, if the poor things have had nothing but situation books handed out to them? If you are bombarded with Filboid Studge, either you go on strike, or you become dulled and cease to recognize propaganda when you see or hear it. I'm sure if children's reading were kept unadulterated, they would be quicker and clearer-minded as adults, more confident in making judgements for themselves.

I can see an objection coming up here: some of the greatest and best-known children's books have a moral message. C. S. Lewis and George MacDonald: the Christian religion. Kipling: How to Maintain the British Empire. Arthur Ransome: How to get along without parents just the same as if they were there. They had a moral message mostly because they were rooted in the nineteenth century, when moral messages came naturally; everybody wore them like bustles. As we get farther and farther away from the nineteenth century, the moral message has become more cautious and oblique, though it is still often there. Don't mistake me – I'm not opposed to a moral if it is truly felt. You can't have life without opinions, you can't have behaviour without character. I just don't like tongue-in-cheek stuff. Konrad Lorenz said somewhere that our intuitive judgements of people are partly based on their linguistic habits. An interesting idea – I'm sure it's true. I certainly find it true in myself, and not only on an intuitive level: from someone who uses sloppy, second-hand phrases I'd expect sloppy, inconsiderate behaviour, whereas a person who uses vigorous, thoughtful, individual language will apply the same care to their behaviour – and this applies with double force to the written word. What I find myself meaning is that the author of a really well-written book needn't worry about inserting some synthetic moral message – the message will *be* there, embodied in the whole structure of the book.

Back to that other quotation with which I began – the quotation from Dickens: '"I am screaming out loud all the time I write and so is my brother which takes off my attention rather and I hope will excuse mistakes."'

The reason why I love that so much is because it's plain that it was written with extreme pleasure. You can feel his smile as the idea came to him and he wrote it down. You can feel this smile in plenty of children's masterpieces – in Jemima Puddleduck, and in James Reeves's poem *Cows* and in Jane Austen's youthful history of the kings and queens of England – to pick a few random examples. And there's a serious counterpart of the smile – a kind of intensity – you feel the author's awareness that he is putting down *exactly* what he intended – oh, for instance, in *The King of the Golden River*, and *A Cricket in Times Square*, and *Huckleberry Finn*, to pick some more at random. Really good writing should come out with the force of Niagara, it ought to be concentrated; it needs to have everything that's in adult writing squeezed into a smaller compass. I mean that both literally and metaphorically: in a form adapted to children's capacities, and at shorter length, because of this shortage of reading-time. But the emotional range ought to be the same, if not greater; children's emotions are just as powerful as those of adults, and more compressed, since children have less means of expressing themselves, and less capacity for self-analysis. The Victorians really had a point with all those deathbed scenes.

Some time ago I had a home-made picturebook sent me from a primary school in Cornwall: it was about Miss Slighcarp, the villainness in one of my books. Each of the children had drawn a picture of her and written on the back why they hated her. And then, under that, their teacher had evidently suggested that each should write down his own personal fear: 'In the kitchen, where the boiler is, the ventilator rattles and frightens me.' 'I hate Mrs Rance next door. Every time the ball goes in her garden she keeps it and I am frightened of her.' 'I am frightened of the teacher and my mum and dad when they are angry.' At first it was rather a worrying thought that my book had triggered off all this hate and fear, but then I thought – well, at least they are expressing their fears, and plainly they had an interesting time comparing their bogies and nightmares. Maybe it was really a good thing for them.

This is another thing a children's story ought to do, I suppose – put things in perspective; if you think about it, a story is the first step towards abstract thought. It is placing yourself on one side and looking at events from a distance: in psychological terms, mixing primary mental process – dream-imagery, wish-fulfilling fantasy – with secondary process – verbalization, adaptation to reality, logic. A story is like a roux – in cookery by the chemical process of rubbing fat into dry flour you can persuade it to mix with a liquid. So by means of a story you can combine dream with reality and make something nourishing. I think this mixing dream with reality, far from confusing children, helps them to define areas of both.

There's something I've said elsewhere that I'd like to repeat here: it's about the texture of children's books. Children read in a totally different way from adults. It's a newer activity for them – to begin with, they have to be wooed and kept involved. And then, when they are involved, reading for them isn't just a relaxation, something to be done after work. It's a real activity. (Children, after all, don't differentiate between work and non-work.) You see a child reading: he is standing on one leg, or squatting, or lying on his stomach – holding his breath, absolutely generating force. Children's reading-matter is going to be subjected to all sorts of strains and tensions, and it needs to be able to stand up to this at every point. Children read the same book over and over, or just make for the bits they like best, or read the book backwards. There's a psychological explanation for all this re-reading; apparently it fulfils a need for security, a need to make sure the story is still there. (Or you could just call it love, of course.) And children may read very slowly or very fast; they gulp down books or chew them, they believe passionately in the characters and identify with them, they really participate. In order to stand up to all this wear and tear, a book needs almost to be tested in a wind-tunnel before being launched. Furthermore, if it is going to be read and re-read, by the same child, over a span of perhaps ten years – my children certainly did this – then it needs to have something new to offer at each re-reading. It's impossible to predict what a child's mind will seize on at any stage. Their minds are like houses in a staggered process of building – some rooms complete with furniture, others just bare bricks and girders. Many children will miss humour in a story at first reading while they concentrate on the plot. Richness of language, symbolism, character – all these emerge at later readings. Conversely, anything poor or meretricious or cheap may be missed while attention is held by the excitement of the story, but sticks out like a sore thumb on a later reading. Reading aloud, of course, is the ultimate test – an absolutely basic one for a children's book. And I must add here that any adult who isn't willing to read aloud to its child for an hour a day doesn't deserve to *have* a child. I know this is probably an impossible ideal – both parents may be working, and there are so many counter-attractions and distractions – but just the same, there is nothing like reading aloud for enjoyment, and for building up a happy relationship between the participants.

Another factor which I think is of tremendous importance in this enrichment of texture is a sense of mystery and things left unexplained – references that are not followed up, incidents and behaviour that have to be puzzled over, language that is going to stretch the reader's mind and vocabulary. (Words, in themselves, are such a pleasure to children – and even the most deprived childhood can be well supplied with *them*.) Talking about mystery, I once came across a fascinating analysis of Wilkie Collins's *Moonstone*, in psychological terms, by Dr Charles Rycroft. He begins his essay by saying that people who have a compulsion to read detective novels do so as a kind of fantasy defence against incomprehensible infantile memories connected with their parents; they, as it were, keep on solving the problem over and over to their own satisfaction and pinning the guilt firmly on to somebody else. It's a very ingenious theory. I'm not sure that I agree with it altogether – I can think of plenty of reasons for reading thrillers – but I daresay that is one of the reasons why we all love a mystery.

As I've said, there's a very close connection between writing thrillers and writing for children – I know two or three people who, like myself, do both. And since, presumably, a wish to keep solving the unresolved problems of childhood, over and over again, characterizes the writer as well as the reader of detective fiction, then this ties in neatly with our image of the children's writer as someone with a troubled past.

As for children themselves – it's not surprising they are fascinated by mysteries. An immense proportion of the world they live in, after all, must be mysterious to them, since they are expected to take most adult behaviour on trust, without explanations. And not only adult behaviour, but anything else that adults themselves can't explain or haven't time to account for. And there's no doubt that children do love mysteries; they are poets, too; they have a natural affinity for the crazy logic of magic. And they like open endings that they can keep in mind and ponder.

Since children's reading needs richness and mystery, and a sense of intense pleasure, and dedication, and powerful emotion, and an intricate story, and fine language, and humour, it's plain that only one group of people are competent to write for children. They, of course, are poets – or at least people with the mental make-up of poets: writers who can condense experience and make it meaningful by the use of symbols. Not surprisingly, the best children's writers *are* poets – I wonder if the American university found that out!

I've said that I don't think children should be filled with Filboid Studge. And that the best children's writers should be mostly otherwise occupied, and should be poets. And I've ruminated a little about what should be written or not be written. But – except in so far as what I have said may have been a conscious summing-up of unconscious processes – I can't claim to practise what I preach. There is a relevant fairy-tale, which crops up in many folklores and so must carry a pretty basic message: the one about the helpful pixies. Mysterious little helpers do the farmwife's work for her every night – spin the flax, collect the eggs, make the butter, and so forth; but when she watches and discovers who is helping her and, to reward them, makes them all tiny suits of clothes, they put on the clothes, and they are pleased, to be sure, and dance all about: but that's the end of them. They disappear and never return. That tale is a powerful warning against too much tinkering with one's subterranean creative processes. I can't claim to write according to any of the lofty ideals I have put forward. But I said nobody should write for children unless they do it with their whole heart. And I can claim to do that.

Part 2

PRELIMINARY DEFINITIONS AND DISTINCTIONS

3

OUT ON A LIMB WITH THE CRITICS

Paul Heins

Source: *Horn Book Magazine* 46 (June 1970): 264–273.

To be a critic—a literary critic—is almost, by definition, to be out on a limb. In addition to being in a precarious position, one never knows whether one will be top-heavy and crack the limb because of his weight or whether somebody will come along with a saw. Either way, the position is fraught with danger. Yet, since critics rush in where angels fear to tread, there must be some justification or explanation for their existence.

I do not think we have to be concerned about the criticism of what might be called adult literature. Aristotle started the business long ago, and it is enough to mention Coleridge and Goethe, Dr. Johnson and Matthew Arnold, I. A. Richards and Allen Tate, to show that whenever literature is produced, critics are sure to follow. What does concern us, however, is the criticism of children's literature—a formidable task, and much more difficult than the criticism of adult literature.

Children's literature—for good or for bad—is not the concern of children alone. Parents, teachers, and librarians as well as authors, illustrators, and publishers are potential judges of books for children. Questions of suitability and vocabulary jostle with personal likes and dislikes, and there is always the question of whether a particular book written for children will appeal to children. We have also been made painfully aware of the fact that we are dealing with a generation conditioned by television; and we are being told that children's literature should be realistic and should absorb, in some form or other, the social and psychological problems of the day.

Even a philosopher can say something—at times—that has a bearing on children's literature. In 1957, Suzanne K. Langer, in *Problems of Art: Ten Philosophical Lectures*, made a number of statements worth considering:

> Every generation has its styles of feeling. One age shudders and blushes and faints, another swaggers, still another is godlike in a universal indifference. These styles in actual emotion are not insincere. They are largely unconscious—determined by many social causes, but *shaped* by artists, usually popular artists of the screen, the jukebox, the shop window, and the picture magazine. (That, rather than incitement to crime, is my objection to the comics.)

Furthermore, she comes to a rather stringent conclusion about what she calls "art education"; and if we think about children's literature at all, it does not seem too farfetched to consider it in the category of the arts.

According to Mrs. Langer, "Art education is the education of the feeling, and a society that neglects it gives itself up to a formless emotion. Bad art is corruption of feeling." How many of us are willing to say that the moving-picture versions of *Mary Poppins* and *Dr. Dolittle* were bad art? Some of us will, because we believe that each picture version failed to capture the spirit of the book on which it was based. How many of us would go so far as to say these cinematic productions were not only bad art, but—because they were bad art—were corrupt in feeling? I, for one, am willing to say so.

Incidentally, critics of children's literature have frequently spoken up against shoddy methods and shoddy productions. Perhaps three of the most famous *Horn Book* articles represented this kind of frontal attack on mediocrity: "Walt Disney Accused" (Frances Clarke Sayers, *Horn Book*, December 1965), "Not Recommended" (Ruth Hill Viguers, *Horn Book*, February 1963), and "An Imaginary Correspondence" (Rumer Godden, *Horn Book*, August 1963), which delightfully accomplished its aim indirectly—by satire, humor, and irony. The chief value of this kind of criticism—of debased classics, of vocabularized texts—consists of clearing the decks for a more positive kind of criticism.

It has been said that people who insist that they have no philosophy or no religion will ultimately, in the course of conversation or discussion, reveal their explanation of the universe or of the beliefs which guide their lives. We are all critics whether we know it or not; and every time we pass judgment on a book or express enthusiasm for it, we are engaging in a critical act.

In her recent amusing book *The Girl on the Floor Will Help You*, Lavinia Russ speaks of "that crashing bore of a question which inevitably totters into any discussion of children's books, 'Are they written for children or for adults?'" Now, Mrs. Russ is naturally entitled to her opinion, not to say to her emotions; but she immediately follows up her condemnation by adding two statements: "She [E. Nesbit] didn't write for adults; she didn't write for children; she wrote for herself. Not her adult self, but to please and delight the child in herself—the child she remembered with fondness." In spite of her boredom, in spite of her initial outburst, Mrs. Russ was drawn

46

into an act of criticism; and although she did not develop a point of view at length—as did Eleanor Cameron in her article "Why *Not* for Children?" (*Horn Book*, February 1966)—Mrs. Russ was actually delivering herself of an opinion on a topic which—as she herself states—unavoidably crops up in many discussions concerning children's literature. Mrs. Russ is a critic in spite of herself.

Children's books and authors, naturally, are not exempt from the random impressions and evaluations of readers. Perhaps the time has come for the criticism of children's literature to be more conscious than ever before of its existence—and better still of its function. It should learn to speak with precision and to qualify its enthusiasms. There is certainly available a large body of worthwhile children's books that invites critical consideration. As a matter of fact, because of the proliferation of good books for children during the last fifty years, the era has been termed a "golden age."

Incidentally, the term "golden age" is not without its difficulties. It can be a confusing term, for it seems that there are two golden ages. Both of them are mentioned in John Rowe Townsend's brief but excellent literary history *Written for Children: An outline of English children's literature*. In it we find an interesting summary of the last years of the first golden age:

> In children's literature at least, the opening years of the century were the last of a golden age. . . . the shortest of short lists . . . must include nearly all of E. Nesbit's work and much of Kipling; the play of *Peter Pan*; *The Wind in the Willows*; *The Secret Garden*; and—Beatrix Potter's splendid little books for small children.
>
> The Victorian–Edwardian era ended gloriously.

Elsewhere in Townsend's book, the two golden ages are brought into focus:

> The half century before 1914 was the first golden age of children's literature. The second golden age is now.

In *A Critical History of Children's Literature*, Part Four is entitled The Golden Age 1920–1950. In this book, the term is applied to children's literature in both the United States and England, and Ruth Hill Viguers naturally discusses both American and English books. In "The Book and the Person" (*Horn Book*, December 1968), Mrs. Viguers names more than two dozen men and women who during the twentieth century have written outstanding books that "give pleasure to children"; and in her list of ". . . Twentieth-century Children's Books Every Adult Should Know" she supplies titles by thirty authors. Although voices are occasionally raised deploring what the uninitiated call the inadequacy of children's literature, students of children's literature and people working with books and children know that there is almost an embarrassment of riches.

Along with the growth in the number of outstanding books for children, there has crystallized a feeling—to use Eleanor Cameron's words—that "children's literature does not exist in a narrow world of its own, but is enmeshed in a larger world of literature. . . ." Moreover, this perception of the locus of children's literature carries with it a further consequence. To quote again from Mrs. Cameron: "the highest standards of the one hold good for the other." And more than twenty years ago Bertha Mahony Miller wrote in a *Horn Book* editorial (May–June 1946):

> Arts flourish where there is sound critical judgment to examine and appraise. The critic must, first of all, have a real point of view about his subject. The essential point of view grows out of acquaintance with the best children's books past and present, and also with the world's best literature for everyone.

This high standard for the criticism of children's literature may be seen exemplified in such works as *Books, Children and Men* and *The Unreluctant Years*. It continues with unabated significance in Mrs. Cameron's recent volume *The Green and Burning Tree*.

About the relationship between children's literature and literature in general, John Rowe Townsend also has made some clear and definite statements:

> I believe that children's books must be judged by much the same standards as adult literature. A good children's book must not only be pleasing to children: it must be a good book in its own right.
>
> Where the works of the past are concerned, I have much faith in the sifting process of time—"time" being the shorthand for the collective wisdom of a great many people over a long period of time. . . . Survival is a good test of a book. . . . With present-day books, the sifting process is incomplete and judgments [Townsend is modestly referring to his own] are provisional.

But what of reviewing? Is reviewing criticism, or should it be criticism? Actually, criticism cannot be kept out of reviewing. Even the short capsulelike review cannot avoid making some critical comment, and a long review tends to become a critical essay.

What is the function of reviewing? I know of no better discussion of the subject than is found in a pamphlet published by the Hogarth Press in England in 1939. Entitled *Reviewing*, it was written by Virginia Woolf, some of whose previously unsigned reviews have recently been identified and republished in the London *Times Literary Supplement*. She states her observations in a definitive manner. When reviewing rose in importance at the beginning of the nineteenth century, "Its complex task was partly to inform the public, partly to criticize the book and partly to advertise its existence." During the present century, "The critic is separate from the reviewer; the function of the reviewer is partly to sort current literature; partly to advertise the author; partly to inform the public." Present-day authors will doubtless acquiesce in her opinion that "it is a matter of very great interest to a writer to know what an honest and intelligent reader thinks about his work." And when Virginia Woolf states that "It is impossible for the living to judge the works of the living," one recognizes the confession of an honest reviewer, who was also a critic in her own right.

Although a review serves the practical purpose of giving information and of advertising—using the word in its Woolfian sense—it cannot avoid making certain critical gestures. To consider only children's books: Of the thousands published yearly, how many of them is it physically possible to review? If a journal, like *The Horn Book Magazine*, reviews only books considered worthy of mention, the very task of selection is, by its very nature, a task of criticism—of judgment. Any form of literary classification, comparison, or evaluation must also be considered a form of criticism. Actual—one should even dare to say serious—criticism will occur only when judgments are being made in a context of literary knowledge and literary standards. If a reviewer perceives clearly the intention of the author and states it, the author will surely appreciate the intelligence—that is, the critical acumen of the reviewer. If the reviewer tries to indicate how well the author has succeeded in accomplishing his intention, the reviewer—once again—assumes the role of the critic.

Reviewing, however, is only concerned with what is imminent in publishing, with what is being produced at the present time; and does its job well by selecting, classifying, and evaluating—evaluating for the time being. Criticism deals with literature in perspective and places a book in a larger context—be it historical, aesthetic, psychological, or what you will. I deliberately say "what you will" for there are—as we all well know— Marxian critics, Thomistic critics, and psychoanalytical critics, who concern themselves with evaluations which are not always purely literary.

As I have suggested before, the reviewing and criticism of children's literature is more complex and more fraught with misconceptions than any other kind of reviewing and criticism. If children's literature—at its best —is worthy of consideration with the rest of literature, if the understanding and appreciation of children's literature is to lead to the development of relevant and reliable criticism, one must never forget that the term *children's* remains a specifying term and, willy-nilly, must be respected.

It is certainly important and necessary at times to consider children's literature purely as literature. Questions of style, structure, and technical subtlety are as applicable to children's literature as to any of the other branches of literature. Julia Cunningham's *Dorp Dead* (Pantheon) may be considered as an exemplar of the Gothic novel; and one could learn much by comparing the structure of her story with that of *Jane Eyre*. Incidentally, a good reviewer's critical apparatus should obviously include a wide knowledge of universal literature. The reviewer of Scott O'Dell's *The Dark Canoe* (Houghton) who confessed to an ignorance of—that is, of having never read—*Moby Dick* could scarcely begin to do justice to Mr. O'Dell's book, whatever its ultimate literary significance or value may be.

However, even if children's literature should be considered as literature, it does not cease to be children's literature. But, unfortunately, there is no simple, or clear and easy way by which to determine the proper relationship between the term *children's* and the term *literature*. The most one can do is to consider a few varying points of view.

To ask a child invites defeat. Often his response is primitive or rudimentary; a child's enthusiasm for a book is a much better indication of what the book means to him and does for him than any direct answer to a question posed at him. Jean Karl, editor of children's books, Atheneum, has stated the child's case with great common sense:

> No book is for every child and no book should be made to appeal to every child. A book is made to be loved and cherished by the child it is right for and rejected by those who prefer others.

Or one may consider the point of view of the literary purist, as in Brian Alderson's article "The Irrelevance of Children to the Children's Book Reviewer" (*Children's Book News*, London, January–February 1969). One may agree with Alderson that such remarks as "My Euphemia loved the tasteful blue and yellows" does not get one very far; but when he states that

> It may be objected that to assess children's books without reference to children is to erect some absolute critical standard relating neither to the author's purpose or the reader's enjoyment. To do much less, however, is to follow a road that leads to a morass of contradictions and subjective responses, the most serious result of which will be the confusion of what we are trying to do in encouraging children to read.

I wonder whether Mr. Alderson has not sidetracked one of the chief problems in the consideration of children's literature—literary merit—by speaking of "encouraging children to read," which is a pedagogical point of view and therefore should also be irrelevant to the children's book reviewer.

Interestingly enough, John Rowe Townsend looks upon "acceptability to a child as a preliminary hurdle rather than a final test." Personally, I question whether Mr. Townsend has not put the cart before the horse. In discussions of recently published children's books, generally after a discussion of a book of rare value, one often hears the voice of the devil's advocate: "But, will children like it?" or more pessimistically, "What child will read it?" Surely the question of acceptability to a child is a question concerning book selection and not a fundamental critical question—not a question of literary criticism.

A conciliatory point of view is found in the editorial by Bertha Mahony Miller previously referred to. In it, she modified her statement about the criticism of children's literature by adding an important qualification. "This point of view—this measuring stick—" (by which she meant literary standards) "must also bear some relation to children themselves and their reaction to books today." The word "some" is significant. Mrs. Miller's chief accomplishment was to have considered the child and the book together, not in an intellectually critical way, but appreciatively—one may say, intuitively. Some of her intuitions still bear repeating:

> Who can say what is the right book for the right child? That, thank God, is the child's own adventure (*Horn Book* editorial, November 1933).

> . . . it is foolish to say "we ought only to give the child conceptions it can understand." His soul grows by wonder over things it cannot understand (*Horn Book* editorial, January 1934).

These statements may seem both inspirational and idealistic in form and utterance, but in essence they show a deep respect for the child as a person.

Except by taking polls and by compiling statistics, one could not determine the frequency of appeal of William Mayne's *Earthfasts* (Dutton) or Alan Garner's *The Owl Service* (Walck) among children. But popularity is only a descriptive, not a critical term. Among mature readers, how many are there who read *Paradise Lost* or *Finnegan's Wake* for the sheer pleasure of it? There are some, of course, who do; and if children's literature has so developed in richness and scope as to have produced a number of recondite masterpieces, these works should first be respected and treated as works of literature before one goes through the agony of deciding: To how many, to what kinds of children will these works appeal?

Finally, reviewers and critics are but readers; and if they function properly, should simply be better readers than most. Perhaps they should try to be humble rather than clever. Lewis Carroll once managed to be both in a letter that was disarmingly simple and devastatingly logical:

> As to the meaning of the Snark (he wrote to a friend in America), I'm very much afraid that I didn't mean anything but nonsense. Still, you know, words mean more than we mean to express when we use them; so a whole book ought to mean a great deal more than the writer means. So whatever good meanings are in the book,

I'm glad to accept as the meaning of the book. The best that I've seen is by a lady (she published it in a letter to a newspaper), that the book is an allegory on the search after happiness. I think this fits in beautifully in many ways—particularly about the bathing machines: when people get weary of life, and can't find happiness in towns or in books, then they rush off to the seaside to see what bathing machines will do for them.

One of Carroll's statements—"whatever good meanings are in the book, I am glad to accept as the meaning of the book"—invites speculation. He does not consider a possible logical loophole—the possible bad meanings. I am sure that Freudian critics have already taken care of the loophole. As for the lady's idea that "the book is an allegory on the search after happiness," Carroll delightfully and logically destroys her interpretation by pursuing it to its absurd extreme. And yet, Maurice Sendak was to give creative vitality to a very similar bizarre situation in *Higglety-Pigglety Pop!* by transforming nonsense into allegory. During the past year, the editor of *The Horn Book Magazine* received a letter from a student of children's literature who was planning to investigate symbolism in Beatrix Potter. She was—unfortunately—unacquainted with Lewis Carroll's letter.

In *Notes Towards the Definition of Culture*, T. S. Eliot stated what he considered to be "the three permanent reasons for reading: the acquisition of wisdom, the enjoyment of art, and the pleasure of entertainment." It is certainly the third of these reasons which is the most nearly universal. Most children become aware of words at an early age and advance naturally to the more complicated pleasure of listening to stories. If conditions are favorable, children will discover that the world of books can still further augment their verbal pleasures. The prime function, then, of the reviewer and even of the critic of children's books is to signalize those books which appealing at present to children will seem even better when they are reread by those same children in their adulthood.

4

FICTION FOR CHILDREN AND ADULTS
Some essential differences

Myles McDowell

Source: *Children's Literature in Education* 10 (1973): 50–63.

Is there such a thing as a children's book? Is the children's book an art form, distinct from other fiction, having its own particular excellence? Or is it just the novel made easy, in which everything is the same as in an adult book, only less so? (Jill Paton Walsh 'The Rainbow Surface' *Times Literary Supplement* 3 December 1971)

The only definition of a children's book, John Rowe Townsend avers, in *A Sense of Story*, is that its name appears on a publisher's list of children's books. The distinction between adult and children's fiction is an artificial one maintained for administrative convenience. Now there is enough of truth in this to make us stop and ask, is there really no difference at all? But it seems to me to be the sort of special pleading to expect from one who is known as a writer for children, and is hardly the assertion one would expect from a purely 'adult' novelist. Townsend's statement is more important for the questions it raises than for the truth it contains, for while clearly the line between children's and adult fiction is blurred and broad, equally clearly there are vast numbers of books that fall very definitely on one side or the other. For the sake of examples one might pick, almost at random, Joyce's *Ulysses* and Clive King's *Stig of the Dump*. Now this is not to say that there is nothing in *Stig* that an adult might read with pleasure and profit, nor indeed that there are not bits of *Ulysses* that a child might confidently approach. C. S. Lewis was undoubtedly right to claim that a book that could only be read by a child was a poor child's book, but he might have added that an exclusive diet of children's fiction can hardly be satisfying to an adult, any more than an exclusive diet of the 'available bits' from adult books is a satisfactory diet for a child. An adult reading *Stig* does not read it as a child, full of wonder and delight and discovery, but as one perhaps blandly aware (because it is a rather 'thin' book), of an evocation of childhood, and aware too of some rather naively oblique comments on the Consumer Society. Neither does the adult read *Stig* as he reads an adult book. His mental approach and his expectations would be markedly different.

Is then the distinction we think we discern between *Tom's Midnight Garden* (Philippa Pearce) and *The Shrimp and the Anemone* (L. P. Hartley), between *The Piemakers* (Helen Cresswell) and *Mill on the Floss* (George Eliot), merely one conditioned in us by publishers anxious to serve their own conveniences? Or are there real differences; are there two distinct general categories, even if the two merge and run together freely at the point of contact? A pot of green and a pot of orange paint might be spilled on the floor. The two pools have a yellow base in common, and where they run together a murky brown is formed that doesn't happily belong to either pot, but he is a fool who cannot distinguish the green from the orange. Unless he's colour-blind. But then the difference is a fact, only he is inadequately equipped to see it.

As between the green and the orange, there are observable differences: children's books are generally shorter; they tend to favour an active rather than a passive treatment, with dialogue and incident rather than description and introspection; child protagonists are the rule; conventions are much used; the story develops within a clear-cut moral schematism which much adult fiction ignores; children's books tend to be optimistic rather than depressive; language is child-oriented; plots are of a distinctive order, probability is often disregarded; and one could go on endlessly talking of magic, and fantasy, and simplicity, and adventure. The point here is not to legislate for essential differences but simply to note observable general orders of differences between the large body of children's fiction and that of adult fiction. The question immediately to be raised is how far these observable differences are inherent rather than accidental or conventional. Must a child's book necessarily be different from an adult book, or are the reasons for the differences merely conventions introduced by publishers, or by teachers, librarians, parents or others who direct choice and influence the supply?

Wherein lies the difference between the two following extracts? The first is from Philippa Pearce's *Tom's Midnight Garden* and the second is from Angus Wilson's *Night Call.*

> Only one thing went badly amiss that Thursday. Just as he was getting into bed, he remembered: 'I never wrote to Peter yesterday!'
>
> 'Never mind,' said his aunt, tucking him up.
>
> 'But I promised to.'

'It's bad to break a promise, but I'm sure you didn't mean to. Luckily, it won't matter very much to Peter. Why, he'll be seeing you the day after tomorrow.'

Tom knew that it did matter. The broken promise was bad enough; but he knew, as well, that Peter would be feeling desperate without his letter. Peter needed all that Tom could write to him, to feed his imaginings – to feed his dreams. 'Write to me more about the garden and Hatty,' he had begged Tom. 'Tell me what you did. . . . Be sure to tell me what you're going to do.' 'Sorry, Pete,' Tom murmured into his pillow, and felt wretched. He hoped that Peter had by now got over the bitterness of this betrayal. Peter went to bed earlier than Tom, so that probably he had already ended his day of disappointment with sleep.

* * *

Mrs Longmore put on her white silk nightgown, unloosened her long black hair and sat brushing it before the little stained dressing-table mirror. Then suddenly she thought of something. She opened one of the trunks she had so painfully packed in the afternoon, and rummaging at the side, pulled out a long lemon-coloured piece of tulle. She had worn it one evening round her head, to the little Tuffield girl's great wonder. Now, tiptoeing across the corridor, she entered the Tuffield children's bedroom. She had not somehow expected to find them all sleeping in one large bed, with the eldest girl lying on her stomach in the middle. She was moaning still, but it seemed, in her sleep. Mrs Longmore bent down and placed the chiffon scarf on the hump which she guessed to be the little girl's feet. She was glad to get out of the stuffy, ill-smelling room. It was little enough she had done, God knew, but it was something.

In both the character involved is facing regret. Tom regrets his failure to write to his brother, and the reasons why a letter would have been import-ant are complex; so is the sense of responsibility, of accountability, that it raises. A child reading this passage may well grow in an important dimension of awareness. But though complex and potent, the experience is made available to quite a young child reader by the carefully unobtru-sive way Philippa Pearce leads him through it by the hand. Angus Wilson offers very little help. The confusion of regret, culpable blindness, guilt and insensitivity, rationalization, despairing ineffectuality in the face of brutal atavistic emotions (she has been the cause of the little girl being whipped 'till the blood run') is created by Wilson in all its complexity. He has evoked the emotional condition; it is not his function to analyse it and to present the elements separately to the reader. And I think this comes close to the heart of the difference between a children's and an adult novel: a good children's book makes complex experience available to its readers; a good adult book draws attention to the inescapable complexity of experience.

These differences are essential, I think, simply because children think quantitatively differently from adults. The peculiar variety of emotional response in Mrs Longmore simply isn't conceptually accessible to children (and perhaps, in fact, to many adults), and the reason is that the average child has not reached, until the mid-teens at the earliest, a sufficiently advanced stage of conceptual maturity to understand, to grasp, let alone appreciate, such a condition.

Piaget's work on the stages of mental growth is well known. P. H. Hirst and R. S. Peters speak of the work of Kohlberg:

> Children, Kohlberg claims, start by seeing rules as dependent upon power and external compulsion; they then see them as instrumental to rewards and to the satisfaction of their needs; then as ways of obtaining social approval and esteem; then as upholding some ideal order and finally as articulations of social principles necessary for living together with others. Varying contents given to rules are fitted into invariant forms of conceiving rules. Of course, in many cultures there is no progression through to the final stages, the rate of development will be different in different cultures, and in the same culture there are great individual differences. All this can be granted and explained. But his main point is that this sequence in levels of conceiving of rules is constitutive if moral development and that it is a cultural invariant. Also, because of the conceptual relations involved, which are connected with stages of role-taking, it could not occur in any other order (*The Logic of Education*).

There are, it seems, whole areas of moral, emotional, psychological, understanding which are beyond the child's cognitive range, exactly as there are physical skills like walking which are dependent on maturational factors. St Paul put it more simply: 'When I was a child, I spoke as a child, I understood as a child . . .'. Tom, in pushing at the frontiers of understanding, is exemplary in that he is as aware as one could hope any child might be; Mrs Longmore has regressed into an emotional and rational infantility in order to escape the pain of accountability, and is therefore blameworthy.

If therefore some peculiarly adult emotions and experiences are not accessible to children this does not necessarily mean that a writer will find himself excessively restricted in his range nor compelled to simplify experience. Restrictions there are, of course, but then every writer is restricted to some degree by the cultural expectations against which he writes. It has been argued, indeed, that present day 'adult' writers are peculiarly restricted to themes of personal relationships, or to man in society, and that to be free to write of adventure, of fantasy, of initiation and personal growth, to write of a period other than our own, to explore some of the great archetypal experiences such as the quest or the great dichotomous morality patterns, a writer must turn to children's fiction, or to the adult 'pulp' market. 'Keep off sex', it seems, is, rather like 'Keep off the grass'. Not so much a restriction as a license to walk anywhere else you choose. And it has been said that Dickens, were he writing today, would not be expected to command a large adult audience.

But what of simplicity? Is to write in terms of a child's experience to write up experience simplistically? I don't think this need necessarily be so, though of course some writers do just that – some notoriously so, such as Enid Blyton, some because their concern is not principally with individually felt experience but with, say, wider historical themes. Cynthia Harnett is a case in point here. One also thinks of Rosemary Sutcliff, whose concern is with typical, even archetypal experience in distanced, powerfully evoked, historical settings, rather than with the psychological study of one child's experience. Those children who follow Drem's adventures in *Warrior Scarlet* (Rosemary Sutcliff) easily sense that this is the story of the runt of every litter that ever was, and that Drem exemplifies a recurring, universal experience. In a sense Drem's story reiterates the experience of every reader, offering comfort and encouragement rather than new knowledge. This is at a far remove from the intensely personal discovery of the complex notion of another's individual worth and sanctity, of the necessary distinction between wishful dreaming and reality, and the responsibilities of reality, the tempering of values in the fire of experience: the discoveries, as I see them, which can be made by a sensitive child reading *A Dog so Small* (Philippa Pearce). There is new knowledge discoverable here; a child might grow in reading it rather than, as it were, consolidate what he already has (and this latter, of course, were no inconsequential thing).

What is one to say, moreover, of the view of life expressed in, for example, *Smith*, by Leon Garfield: is that simplistic? The word hardly seems an apt description for a kaleidoscopic view of fortune and deservings such as Garfield presents. Schematic, I suggest, is the more appropriate word. And in this word, I think, is contained one of the essential differences between an adult's and a child's view of life. By and large adults have effected a bifurcation between the moral and the physical imperatives. But this understanding is itself of fairly recent growth, having its springs in the development of scientific rationality during the last three centuries; and in popular terms perhaps is restricted to presently living generations of 'advanced' countries. A common nineteenth-century European view, in all strata of society, would have been that a moral power could, and frequently did, overrule the physical laws. A personal accident that befell one was not explicable in terms of a chain of physical cause and effect, but as a 'judgement' for some earlier moral failing. This schematic moral view of life is essentially childlike; and what is more, it is inconceivable that one should reach the more sophisticated state of discriminatory thinking about the varieties of cause and effect without going through the more primitive stage of belief that an omnipotent, omnipresent, omniactive power controlled all manifestations. From a child's point of view not only is such a view safe and reassuring, it is also optimistic. Good *will* triumph, and not because it has public support and sympathy (that being almost one of the characteristics of what we call good), but because it *must*. Evil *will* be punished, again a benign power reigns.

Part of Leon Garfield's, William Mayne's and others' optimism rests in their acceptance of this schematic view, not, I suggest, as an article of personal belief, but as an appropriate matrix against which to present details of experience for children. In *A Parcel of Trees* (William Mayne) Susan wins from the Railways the right of possession of the orchard because on the whole she deserves to. She has proved herself worthy of the heritage. It isn't merely a conventionally happy ending; no other ending for the child reader would have made sense.

A schematic view of life is then not merely an observable difference between adult and children's literature – it is an essential difference. What of the other observable differences, are they essential too?

Children's books are shorter than adult books. It depends on the age of the child, but it is common sense that the younger the child the less he will be able to grasp and retain, the shorter will be his period of concentration. Indeed, we wouldn't want a child to concentrate on reading all day, believing that varied experience and activity is beneficial. Not much need be made of this. It is obvious that a four or five hundred page novel is something of an acquired taste, something one graduates towards.

More important is the bias towards an active rather than a passive presentation of the material. By active I mean that the text concentrates on dialogue and incident rather than on the more passive mood which characterises description and reflection. Again it is more obvious: good children's books do follow the rule; those which ignore it risk rejection by the child reader. Children, in their reading as in their lives, are more active than ruminant: it is just happily so. And a skilful writer such as Leon Garfield accepts this, as the following extract from *Smith* shows.

> His favourite spot was Ludgate Hill, where the world's coaches, chairs and curricles were met and locked, from morning to night, in a horrible, blasphemous confusion. And here, in one or other of the ancient doorways, he leaned and grinned while the shouting and cursing and scraping and raging went endlessly, hopelessly

on – till, sooner or later, something prosperous would come his way. At about half past ten of a cold December morning an old gentleman got furiously out of his carriage. . . .

This is description, but *active* description, loud and colourful: 'met . . . locked . . . confusion . . . leaned and grinned . . . shouting . . . cursing . . . scraping . . . raging . . .'. It is achieved in short bold strokes and quickly moves on again to action: 'an old gentleman got furiously out of his carriage . . .'. Furiously? Not surprisingly, and in gleeful anticipation the fun begins. The reader wishes to move in for a closer view, and, being with Garfield, gets more than he bargained for.

In *A Parcel of Trees* Mayne evokes a languid, summery world of long and lazy days and slow quest. He unfolds his story unhurriedly, drowsing and droning, so it seems. But the impression is deceptive – a retrospective impression. In fact, the story seldom stands still, and then only for the shortest passages.

> Susan felt melancholy rise in her like joy. Here she was alone, but there was a way back. Here she was not in the year that surrounded the rest of the world, but in the first year and the last year of time. This vision was perfect. It began in the mist, like a dream, and then the sky began to be blue overhead, and the mist sank, until the treetops were out of it and the sun shone on the apples. Then it was warm on her face and warm on the wall, and then was slanting across the grass and mottling it with the indistinct profiles of the branches above. The sunshine showed in the still heavy air, and the shadows were hollow, so that the air was veined. The day began to be hot. Susan thought she must have been out all morning, and went back in again, hoping not to be late for dinner.

Back to action again! Though the sun has been active and changing throughout this relatively still passage, Mayne's art is to give the impression of languidness without lulling the reader to sleep. He does this, among other means, by the obliquity of his dialogue.

> Mr Ferriman looked into the shop on his way home at midday.
>
> 'Burwen rock,' he said, and went at once.
>
> 'Caerphilly Castle,' said Rosemary.
>
> 'Don't stock it,' said Mum, shaking her head. 'I don't believe it's made. Weston-Super-Mare is what he's thinking of.'
>
> 'Tom Royal,' said Susan. 'That's the name of something. He doesn't mean seaside rock.'

'Are you sure?' said Mum. 'We'll go and look at Burwen Hill and be certain.'

She went outside. Susan went with her. Burwen Hill, with its rocky top, stood out clear against the paler edge of the sky. 'That's it,' said Mum. 'It looks no different, so he must mean what you think.'

'He does,' said Susan.

There is with Mayne a sense of a slow, deep, steady current of understanding underlying the lighter surface show. The surface carries the reader buoyantly; the undercurrent it is which is remembered. And this, of course, is Mayne's strength, this hiding of the introspective, reflective quality in dialogue and incident.

> 'It must be water,' said David. 'It's water rocking a stone about, or a boulder or something, and then it's going to break out here and be another spring. At least, it won't be another spring, because there isn't one in this field, even though it's called High Keld. This must be the High Keld itself, and it dried up and went. Now it's coming back.'
>
> 'Oh well,' said Keith. 'I'd rather have badgers.'
>
> 'Of course,' said David. 'Of course.'

What a wealth of private understanding, of a history of reflection, of a scale of values, of a way of life shared is conveyed in those short strokes, 'Of course . . . Of course.'

Another major difference between the children's and the adult novel is the almost invariable use in children's fiction of the child central character, which rarely appears in adult fiction, and then most frequently from the adult point of view as a recollection of childhood (L. P. Hartley is the great exception here, and perhaps Joyce Cary). Wallace Hildick says that:

> Assuming . . . that identification is the key to one's enjoyment of a story and to the refreshment and sustenance to be had from it, it is possible to see why so many children's books deal with child characters. A child *can* identify with adult characters – but only if they are sympathetically drawn and simple enough. By this I am not suggesting that the only adult characters a child can get under the skin of are simple-*minded* ones. Quite complex adults – adults who can be presumed to have complex personalities by virtue of their positions in life, like kings, prime ministers, witches, wizards and wise old nurses – abound in fairy tales of high quality. But in such a context only single aspects of their personalities are

60

presented at a time: the predominantly greedy become greed itself, the generally envious become envy, the honest honesty, the brave bravery – and so on. (*Children and Fiction*)

The central character of the novel must be created in the illusion of fullness, roundness – must be made to 'live', and that almost necessarily means must be shown as a complex being. There are complexities of adult being that are beyond the comprehension of a child, and an author is left with little choice; either he writes of simple, child-like, adult characters (for example George and Lennie in Steinbeck's *Of Mice and Men* – one of those awkward books that defies the classifications I am dealing with here), or if he wants to draw a complex character he must draw a child. This, I think, accounts for the recurring similarities between many of William Mayne's adult characters. They have their individual traits, of course, but they are, many of them, remarkably similar too. And for children adults *are* alike. They have the common quality of being adult, which perhaps looms larger than all their differences in a child's eye.

Adults are, however, often conveniently absent from the world of the children's story. Either they are ill, or they are too busy to notice, or they are misty background figures lost in their own tea and conversation. George Layton dismisses the mother in *The Balaclava Story* with the economical line, 'Well, it's my bingo night, so make yourself some cocoa before you go to bed.'

Whatever the design, the convention is that they don't intrude for a large part of the story, and *conventions*, of one sort or another, are an essential ingredient of children's fiction. There is, I think, a certain assurance to be found, and also a certain necessary aesthetically pleasing sense of the predictability (as in music) in meeting a story that runs on predictable lines.

The old conventions, therefore, are much used. The quest is a favourite. But this is really, in the hands of a clever writer, the general form of the story rather than its substance. Within the 'form' of the quest the experience can be unique. Compare *Ravensgill* (William Mayne), where the object of the quest is unknown until it is found, with *A Parcel of Trees* (William Mayne), where the ostensible object is always in sight, and what is really discovered is a sense of place, and continuing time and change and adjustment, a sense of community.

Travel in time is another recurring convention. This varies from the use of the idea of time travel to produce simply another exotic locale, to the use of time to explore a philosophical concept (*Earthfasts*, William Mayne) or an emotional one (*Tom's Midnight Garden*, Philippa Pearce). In many respects, the use of the time travel convention is similar to the convention of historical setting. Again it can be a mere exotic locale (C. S. Forester's *Hornblower* stories), or the deliberate distancing of a story to a relatively simpler and less cluttered time, where the issues can be presumed to be clearer and bolder. Again, one thinks of Rosemary Sutcliff and Cynthia Harnett. A geographical distancing, as in *Walkabout* (James Vance Marshall) or *Lord of the Flies* (William Golding), can be used for a similar purpose.

Initiation into manhood, or womanhood, is another much-used convention or theme, but this can vary from the relatively simple task and achievement outline of *Warrior Scarlet* (Rosemary Sutcliff), to the complexities of self-discovery forced upon the protagonists of *Walkabout* (James Vance Marshall) or *To the Wild Sky* (Ivan Southall). The initiation can be into reality based self-confidence, as in the case of the plain girl, Maggie, in Zindel's *My Darling, My Hamburger* (Paul Zindel), or into the responsibilities and self-abnegating role playing of young womanhood as in *Marianne Dreams* (Catherine Storr), or into self-knowledge, as in *A Dog so Small* (Philippa Pearce).

The rise and fall of fortune is another favourite theme (*Black Hearts in Battersea*, Joan Aiken) which on occasions can be neatly inverted as in *Devil-in-the-Fog* (Leon Garfield), with its happy 'riches to rags' theme. But, of course, children's fiction has no monopoly of conventions, though it might be thought richer in available conventions than much adult fiction which retreads the 'boy meets girl' theme, or the 'eternal triangle' theme, endlessly.

There are other aspects of plot which characterize children's stories. Not many threads run through the story. There will be twists and turns and reversals as much and as often as you like, but the main thread, or threads if it is a two-in-hand, must be kept going and not be held up by subplots rising and dying across the path of the action. *Devil-in-the-Fog* is, I think, a good example of a plot running smoothly two-in-hand. The story of George Tweet-Dexter and the story of Captain Richard trot along comfortably together to a final resolution which draws them together satisfactorily.

There are possibilities of growth in the plot. If the hero emerges substantially the same as he began the book, then the story has very little but romance to offer. Nicholas Tucker refers to the value of building something of the unknown into the known areas of the plot: stretching the child's knowledge, especially his self-knowledge, or extending the story beyond the reader's expectations ('How Children respond to fiction' *Children's literature in education* 9, November 1972). He instances *The Intruder* of John Rowe Townsend which, he says, starts off very black and white, but the colours merge and dimensions of uncertainty enter and force Arnold Haithwaite to adjust and grow. *Smith* (Leon Garfield) would be another fine example of colours continually changing and merging and forcing independent reappraisal onto the young hero. Tucker is right, I think, and Joan Robinson hopelessly confused when she says,

> Before . . . making judgments we must start with some basic assumptions. And we can't arrive at those by just thinking about them. They are emotionally based, which is why I am only interested

in books which, apart from helping myself, may help children in their growing up. ('Writing for children: a social engagement?' *Children's literature in education* 6, November 1971.)

Judgments that are emotionally based, far from helping growth, will just precisely retard it. The system is closed. Emotions and judgments both must be based, if they are to be capable of development, on increasing knowledge, on growing understanding, on confrontations with the details and truth of experience, and not just emotional reaction to it. That would be to have Tom emerge from his midnight garden with no more than a feeling of regret for a passing dream, instead of a growth in understanding of the meaning of time and change and loss.

Such growth is usually linked with the optimism of children's literature, upon which I have already touched. I think however that it is as well to recognize that this optimism is perhaps as much a part of the cultural traditions of Christendom as it is an essential ingredient of children's fiction. Adult literature today tends often to be depressive simply because ours is an optimistic culture, and optimism is so often betrayed. In other cultures which are perhaps more melancholy, or fatalistic, other sorts of children's literature might be written, but optimism is ingrained in our habits and traditions of thought. This is why I think that the newer sub-Salinger writers, such as Zindel, despite their virtues of freshness and an authentic teenage voice are on the whole unsuitable for children. There is such an overall cynical depressive quality about Zindel's books, which seems to me to be destructive of values before values have properly had time to form. It is the depression I would want to protect emergent minds from, rather than the promiscuity. For even the sexual adventures of his young heroes and heroines are presented in a depressive light, and this presentation of sexuality arguably is as potentially harmful as direct licentiousness. So though Zindel obviously understands the confusion and amorality of teenagers and their frequent failure to associate consequences with actions, rather better than does K. M. Peyton, I feel the work of the latter is preferable because of its underlying optimism, even if it is sometimes clumsily handled (the professor, deus ex machina, of *Pennington's Seventeenth Summer*, for example), although Peyton's language does not have the same adolescent ring as Zindel's.

For at its best, Zindel's language does provide an illustration of the peculiar qualities of writing that distinguish good children's fiction. In this passage from *I Never Loved Your Mind*, he manages that awkward mixture of irony, strained posing, uncertainty of touch, throw-away affectation and hollow pretentiousness and ingenuous charm, that gaucherie that *is* adolescence:

I remember regaining consciousness (I only passed out once before in my life, and that was last summer when I was bombed at Lake

George and went water-skiing at midnight with a lantern in my teeth) and still thinking I was unconscious because when I opened my eyes, I couldn't see anything. It took me a minute of blinking before I realized I was staring at a white ceiling. Anybody else would have been relieved they hadn't croaked, but I let out a scream. It was a little, manly scream, like the kind an actor lets out when he's playing the movie role of an archaeologist who pooh-poohs the mummy's curse but the mummy gets him anyway. I knew I was looking at a white ceiling, but I was scared because the thought crossed my mind that maybe that's what death was – one big white glossy ceiling.

Eleanor Cameron, in *The Green and Burning Tree*, talks about 'an elusive quality (of language) . . . it may be its flavour, tone, atmosphere, or its force of association, all of which have deeply to do with meaning.' One can see immediately how 'right' is the text of Sendak's *Where the Wild Things Are*, for example. Again, consider this extract from *Black Hearts in Battersea*, by Joan Aiken:

'Mr Cobb,' said Simon that evening as he mended the springs of a lady's perch-phaeton. 'What would you do if you thought you had discovered a Hanoverian plot?'

Mr Cobb lowered the wash leather with which he was polishing the panels and regarded Simon with a very shrewd expression. 'Me boy,' he said, 'it's all Lombard Street to a China orange that I'd turn a blind eye and do nothing about it. Yes, yes, I know –' raising a quelling hand – 'I know the Hanoverians are a crew of fire-breaching traitors who want to turn good King James, bless him, off the throne and bring in some flighty German boy. But, I ask you, what do they actually do? Nothing. It's all a lot of talk and moonshine, harmless as a kettle on a guinea-pig's tail. Why trouble about them when they trouble nobody?'

Simon wondered whether Mr Cobb would think them so harmless if he were to see the contents of the Twites' cellar. But just as he was opening his mouth to speak the Chelsea church clock boomed out the hour of nine and he had to hurry off to Battersea Castle.

and the appropriateness is obvious. In this example there is raciness, there is fun, there is inventiveness and a mad kind of logic – 'harmless as a kettle on a guinea-pig's tail' – and the plot is effortlessly forwarded, time moves on. It is as easy to pick good as bad examples. But why are some uses not appropriate? Vocabulary might be too remote (though a few long words will often add to the fun of language), the concepts it handles too abstract.

A child's most telling condemnation often is, 'It's boring!', and perhaps there it is. The language must have an attractive or interesting personality of its own. It might be a benign adult voice (*Tom's Midnight Garden*, Philippa Pearce), or the authentic voice of childhood (*There is a Happy Land*, Keith Waterhouse). There will perhaps be musical qualities, rhythms, unexpected moments of delight, variations in texture. Eleanor Cameron quotes Kipling's

> It was indeed a Superior Comestible (that's magic) and he put it on the stove because *he* was allowed to cook on that stove, and he baked it and he baked it till it was all done brown and smelt most sentimental.

Impossible to lay down rules. Perhaps it springs from a writer's caring for his tale and caring to set it down well. What one misses in the following extract from a story in the magazine *Fab 208* is precisely this sense of caring; one regrets also the missed opportunities:

> It was a hot sunny afternoon and the end of another failure day. I didn't think much about the failure, I was used to all that. It was one of the conditions of my life and I had to live with it. But it was a long climb up the hill to the common. The brown paper carrier bag was heavy and the string was biting into my fingers, so I changed hands and took a look inside it. It wasn't groceries I was carrying. Nothing so sensible. Being me and my daffy sort of universe it had to be a cat inside the carrier bag.

I want finally to say something about probability, the last of the 'observable differences' mentioned at the outset of this article. To say that probability is not terribly important for a child is really only another way of saying that it looms large for an adult. The adult's habit of rational enquiry and explanation gets in the way of enjoyment of the book with improbabilities written into it. But it seldom occurs to children to seek rational explanation of some parts of the plot, probable or improbable. The world of the story is there, it is given, and is accepted as a schematically coherent whole. To listen to a group of adults frantically searching for a rational explanation of time in *Tom's Midnight Garden* (Philippa Pearce) – 'Is it happening *now* in Mrs Bartholomew's dream?' 'Then how can Abel see Tom?' 'Are they real skates or imaginary ones – which are the imaginary pair?' – is to realize that they, like Uncle Allen, have quite simply failed to understand. The explanation is conveyed in a metaphor, not a logical system of relationships:

> He had longed for someone to play with and for somewhere to play; and that great longing, beating about unhappily in the

65

big house, must have made its entry into Mrs Bartholomew's dreaming mind and had brought back to her the little Hatty of long ago.

The child reader who accepts the 'thirteenth hour' as being as unnecessary of explanation as any of the everyday phenomena described in the book is operating more totally in the world of the novel than the unfortunate adult hindered from full response to the experience by his shackling habit of rational enquiry. Adults, indeed, may make intrusive interpreters for the child reader, for it would seem that a child's book (and I hope I have established that there is such a thing) is one a child can enter and need no other guide than the author.

References

Aiken, Joan (1965) *Black Hearts in Battersea* London: Cape, Penguin; New York: Doubleday

Cameron, Eleanor (1969) *The Green and Burning Tree* Boston: Little, Brown

Cresswell, Helen (1967) *The Piemakers* London: Faber; Philadelphia: Lippincott

Eliot, George (1860) *The Mill on the Floss* various editions London: Collins, Chatto, Dent; New York: Collins, Dutton, New American Library

Forester, C. S. (1953) *Captain Hornblower* and other titles London: Michael Joseph, Penguin; Boston: Little, Brown

Garfield, Leon (1967) *Devil-in-the-Fog* London: Longman, Penguin; New York: Pantheon

Garfield, Leon (1967) *Smith* London: Longman, Penguin; New York: Pantheon

Golding, William (1954) *Lord of the Flies* London: Faber, Penguin; New York: Coward, Putnam

Hartley, L. P. (1963) *The Shrimp and the Anemone* London: Faber

Hildick, E. W. (1970) *Children and Fiction* London: Evans

Hirst, Paul H. and Peters, Richard (1970) *The Logic of Education* London: Routledge

Joyce, James (1922) *Ulysses* London: Bodley Head, Penguin; New York: Random House

King, Clive (1965) *Stig of the Dump* London: Hamish Hamilton, Penguin

Marshall, James Vance (1971) *Walkabout* London: Hamish Hamilton, Penguin; New York: Morrow (reissue)

Mayne, William (1966) *Earthfasts* London: Hamish Hamilton, Penguin; New York: Dutton

Mayne, William (1963) *A Parcel of Trees* London: Hamish Hamilton, Penguin; Baltimore: Penguin

Mayne, William (1970) *Ravensgill* London: Hamish Hamilton; New York: Dutton

Pearce, Philippa (1962) *A Dog So Small* London: Longman, Penguin; Philadelphia: Lippincott

Pearce, Philippa (1958) *Tom's Midnight Garden* London: Oxford University Press; Philadelphia: Lippincott

Peyton, K. M. (1970) *Pennington's Seventeenth Summer* London: Oxford University Press; New York: Crowell

Sendak, Maurice (1962) *Where the Wild Things Are* London: Bodley Head, Penguin; New York: Harper and Row

Southall, Ivan (1967) *To the Wild Sky* London: Angus and Robertson, Penguin; New York: St Martin's

Steinbeck, John (1937) *Of Mice and Men* London: Heinemann, Penguin; New York: Viking, Bantam

Storr, Catherine (1959) *Marianne Dreams* London: Faber, Penguin; New York: Transatlantic, Baltimore: Penguin

Sutcliff, Rosemary (1958) *Warrior Scarlet* London: Oxford University Press; New York: Walck

Townsend, John Rowe (1969) *The Intruder* London: Oxford University Press; Philadelphia: Lippincott

Townsend, John Rowe (1971) *A Sense of Story* London: Longman

Waterhouse, Keith (1957) *There is a Happy Land* London: Longman, Penguin

Wilson, Angus (1964) *Night Call* London: Secker and Warburg, Penguin; New York: Viking

Zindel, Paul (1971) *I Never Loved Your Mind* London: Bodley Head; New York: Harper and Row

Zindel, Paul (1970) *My Darling, My Hamburger* London: Bodley Head; New York: Harper and Row.

5

CHILDREN'S LITERATURE

Theory and practice

Felicity A. Hughes

Source: *ELH* 45(3) (1978): 542–561.

The theory of Children's Literature has been for some time in a state of confusion. That so many good and important works of literature have been produced in that time is a cheering reminder that art can survive even the worst efforts of critical theorists. There are no grounds for complacency in this state of affairs, however, because although theoretical confusion may not stifle good art, it can impose significant constraints and directions upon it.

I suggest that the origin of some confused beliefs, including the belief that there is, in some significant literary sense, such a thing as children's literature at all, is to be found in the theory of the novel. The history of children's literature coincides, more or less, with that of the novel. What historians of children's literature often call the first real children's book, Newbery's *A Little Pretty Pocket-Book* was published within a decade of Richardson's *Pamela*. It is probable that more than mere coincidence is involved since similar social conditions are conducive to both. In fact, the development of a separate body of literature addressed to children has been crucially associated with that of the novel, and the critical fortunes of the one have been strongly affected by those of the other. In this paper I shall discuss that dependence with respect to twentieth-century novels for children, and argue that it accounts for some of the many confusions which hamper attempts to construct theories of children's literature.

The crisis in the novel which occurred in the eighteen eighties is generally agreed to have determined the development of the twentieth-century novel. In that decade a new view of the novel is held to have triumphed over an older one. David Stone writes of the eighties, 'with the deaths of the established Victorian novelists, not only a younger group of novelists, but an entirely new set of attitudes towards fiction appeared'.[1] John Goode suggests that the change involved 'a reappraisal of the possibilities and responsibilities of the novel which is important because it represents the beginning of the dividing line between the Victorian novel and the twentieth century novel'.[2] The emergent view is characterised by Walter Allen as 'a heightened, more serious conception of the novel as art'.[3] Further, it is agreed by these and other writers that this change came about at least partly in response to changing social conditions and in particular what were seen as profound changes in the readership of the novel. I propose to consider the implications of this crisis for the development of a separate literature for children.

From its inception in the eighteenth century the novel had been seen in England as at least potentially *family* reading. A glance through the material collected in Ioan Williams' *Novel and Romance 1700–1800* will amply bear this out.[4] The words 'young people' or 'our youth' appear in virtually every review or essay. The debate on the relative merits of Richardson and Fielding seems to have revolved around the question of which novel was more appropriate for the moral, social and literary education of British youth. In spite of occasional deprecatory murmurs, Victorian novelists also accepted the constraints that a family readership was held to impose on them. In light of this it is clear that Moore, when he protested in 1885 that 'never in any age or country have writers been asked to write under such restricted conditions' was either taking a very large view of his 'age' or wrong.[5] Judgement of novels had always involved a hypothetical young reader.

Moreover, throughout the same history, the status of the novel as a genre was comparable to that of the bourgeoisie it largely predicted. In spite of its rapid rise to dominance as preferred reading, it failed to gain the accolade of critical and learned opinion. Lacking the long and distinguished classical ancestry of poetry and drama, the novel was engaged in a struggle to live down the stigma of being a 'low' form, not art but entertainment. Critics turned their attention to novels cursorily and with distaste, real or feigned, recommending the best novels only in the context of a general caveat against the genre.

The crisis of the eighties effected changes in both these circumstances. By the turn of the century it was clear that at least some English novelists would no longer allow themselves to be held responsible for the moral welfare of the nation's youth. By about 1910, moreover, the novel seemed to have risen above its old inferior status. It received more critical recognition; it was old enough to have something of a history; it had, as Allen Tate later put it, 'caught up with poetry'.[6] There was acknowledged to be an 'art of fiction' and there were some novels that could be referred to as 'art novels' or 'serious novels'.

It was also true that by the turn of the century something was emerging that might be called 'children's literature'. Just as D. H. Lawrence's titles seem to proclaim themselves as 'M', for mature readers only, so Edith Nesbit's books equally clearly announce themselves as 'C', for child readers only. Stevenson's *Treasure Island*, which had been read with pleasure by Henry James, was reclassified as a 'children's classic' and the days when novels could confidently be dedicated to 'boys of all ages' were over.

I doubt whether this particular development, initiating as it did a trend in fiction writing which has continued to the present, was a mere accident of literary history. I suggest that a plausible explanation of it can be found in the acceptance by writers and critics of a theory about fiction which directly attributed the low status of the novel *to* its family readership. The theory in question is that developed by Henry James in his essays. Setting aside, for the moment, the question of whether the theory is true or false, I shall argue that one major consequence of its acceptance was that novelists, in a bid for critical respectability, tried to dissociate the novel from its family readership and redirect it towards what was seen as art's traditional elite audience of educated adult males outside the home, at court, the coffee house, or the club. The 'serious novel' would have to earn its laurels, or win its spurs, at the cost of being unsuitable for women and children – beyond their reach not only because it dealt with facts of life from which such people had to be 'protected', but because it was too difficult, requiring not only maturity but discrimination beyond the reach of all but the highly educated. Since no-one can start off life highly educated, children are *ipso facto* disqualified.

The implications of this particular aspect of the crisis in the novel can best be studied by a consideration of the controversy between James and R. L. Stevenson. It is generally agreed that James was making a bid to establish the novel as serious art in his manifesto, 'The Art of Fiction'.[7] In that essay, it will be remembered, he claimed that the novelist's function was 'to attempt to represent life' and that the novel should not be presented by its author as 'just a story' or as 'make believe', but as something akin to history. Novel-writing being an art which 'undertakes immediately to reproduce life', it must take itself seriously if it wishes to be taken seriously and, in particular, 'it must demand that it be perfectly free'. 'It goes without saying', he says, 'that you will not write a good novel unless you possess the sense of reality'. He gave *Treasure Island* only qualified praise, saying that it is delightful 'because it appears to me to have succeeded wonderfully in what it attempts', and compared it to its disadvantage with a story by a French writer which attempted to 'trace the moral consciousness of a child'. Although he acknowledged that the French story failed in what it attempted, he nevertheless preferred it to *Treasure Island* because he could measure it against his own sense of reality; 'I can at successive steps . . . say Yes or No, as it may be, to what the artist puts before me.' In *Treasure Island* he could not make that decision, because

'I have been a child in fact, but I have been on a quest for buried treasure only in supposition'. James here suggests a criterion for critical approval which would exclude all stories except those the reader can measure against his own sense of reality. It may be inferred from this that a 'sense of reality' is required of the reader as well as of the writer, so that he is actually as well as theoretically able to say 'Yes or No' to what the writer offers. Writer and reader, then, are to enter into a sophisticated contract by which, although illusion is held to be the object of the exercise, no one is actually taken in, the reading having constantly to judge the merit of the novel *as illusion* by measuring it against something else.

Since James' principal criterion for the seriousness of a novel was the degree to which it gave the illusion of portraying real life, when Stevenson came to answer the essay he found himself in the position of defending the notion of the novel as 'make believe'. He called it 'a peculiarity of our attitude to any art' that 'No art produces illusion'.[8] Yet his requirement of the reader seems to require the involuntary assent appropriate to illusion. In '*A Gossip on Romance*', he wrote,

> In anything fit to be called by the name of reading, the process itself should be absorbing and voluptuous; we should gloat over a book, be rapt clean out of ourselves, and rise from the perusal, our mind filled with the busiest kaleidoscopic dance of images, incapable of sleep or of continuous thought... It was for this pleasure that we read so closely and loved our books so dearly, in the bright, troubled period of boyhood.[9]

Stevenson admired novels which made intense demands of sympathy and identification, whereas James required that characters in novels be presented 'objectively' in a way that prevents the reader from entering into any extraordinary sympathy with them. Their disagreement over *Crime and Punishment* was reported by Stevenson in a letter thus:

> it was easily the greatest book I have read in ten years: Many find it dull. Henry James could not finish it: all I can say is that it nearly finished me. It was like having an illness. James did not care for it because the character of Raskolnikov was not objective: and at that I divined a great gulf between us and... a certain impotence in many minds of today which prevents them from living *in* a book or character, and keeps them standing afar off, spectators of a puppet show.[10]

While it is difficult to see the consistency of either writer's position, it is clear enough that they were opposed on the two points under discussion. James claimed that novels are serious in so far as they attempt to provide 'the intense illusion of real life'. Stevenson denied this claim. Secondly, James required characters to be 'objective' and the reader to be detached, impartial and sceptical, whereas Stevenson saw reader involvement and the submersion of self to be the triumph of art.

In reviewing this controversy we should also bear in mind that other great item of discussion in the eighties and nineties – the early years of State Education in England – the spread of literacy, which was assumed to be proceeding rapidly through the agency of universal compulsory education. By the turn of the century these two issues had come together in James' thinking in a way that was to be widespread not long after his death. The attitude I wish to discuss is that expressed in an essay called 'The Future of the Novel' which he published in 1899.[11] What that essay expresses is an undisguised dismay at the galloping popularity of the novel, the great increase in novel readers, which he attributed to the fact that

> The diffusion of the rudiments, the multiplication of the common schools, has more and more had the effect of making readers of women and of the very young. Nothing is so striking in a survey of this field . . .

and he observes the growth of writing for children in these terms:

> The literature, as it may be called for convenience, of children is an industry that occupies by itself a very considerable quarter of the scene. Great fortunes, if not great reputations, are made we learn, by writing for schoolboys . . . The published statistics are extraordinary and of a sort to engender many kinds of uneasiness. The sort of taste that used to be called 'good' has nothing to do with the matter: we are so demonstrably in the presence of millions for whom taste is but an obscure, confused, immediate instinct.

The distaste and even fear of the mass of women and children readers which James manifests here springs, I suggest, from his suspicion that the popularity of the novel will diminish its chances of finding the elite audience the existence of which will justify its status as art. He thinks that being exclusive is a necessary condition for novels being serious. Popular novels cannot be good, they must be vulgar. Commercial success therefore is a sign of declining standards:

> The high prosperity of our fiction has marched very directly, with another 'sign of the times', the demoralisation, the vulgarisation of literature in general, the increasing familiarity of all such methods

CHILDREN'S LITERATURE: THEORY AND PRACTICE

of communication, the making itself supremely felt, as it were, of the presence of the ladies and children – by whom I mean, in other words, the reader irreflective and uncritical.

So serious a menace did James take this to be that he prophesied on the brink of this century:

By what it decides to do in respect to 'the young', the great prose fable will, from any serious point of view, practically see itself stand or fall.

He refrains from making any specific suggestions as to what should be done with respect to the young but his general drift is clear when he goes on to demand again 'freedom' for the serious novelist. If the novelist's business is to present 'life' he must be able to select his material from the whole of life: nothing must be prohibited. And he refers to the 'immense omission in our fiction'. It was, he claimed, 'because of the presence of ladies and children' that in novels 'there came into being a mistrust of all but the most guarded treatment of the great relation between men and women, the constant world-renewal'. In fact James' solution seems to be the same as that suggested by Moore in 1885:

We must write as our poems, our histories, our biographies are written, and give up at once and forever asking that most silly of all silly questions 'Can my daughter of eighteen read this book?' Let us renounce the effort to reconcile these two irreconcilable things – art and young girls. That these young people should be provided with a literature suited to their age and taste, no artist will deny; all I ask is that some means may be devised by which the novelist will be allowed to describe the moral and religious feeling of his day as he perceives it to exist, and to be forced no longer to write with a view of helping parents and guardians to bring up their charges in all the traditional beliefs.[12]

In the course of their respective essays, Moore and James both imply that keeping children in heavily guarded ignorance is not only bad for the novel but bad for the children. Neither chooses to pursue that point, however, since, unlike their eighteenth-century predecessors, they are exclusively concerned about the rights of novelists. Hence the proposed solution is not that adults should allow formerly prohibited topics to be discussed in front of the children, but that [the] child should be excluded so that adults can discuss such matters among themselves. The children are to be sent away to play, with their mothers presumably, so that the serious novelist can be free to pursue his art and write about sex.

Within twenty years of the publication of 'The Future of the Novel', the views expressed in it were widespread; in particular the view that the serious novel is one that children cannot read was generally accepted among writers and critics. The impact that this exclusion has had not only on the development of children's literature, but on attitudes towards it is still overwhelming. The segregation of adult's and children's literature is rationalised, even celebrated on all sides. It has assumed the status of a fact, a piece of knowledge about the world, that children read books in a different way and have to have special books written for them.

The consequence of this *de facto* segregation of children's literature from the rest can be seen in general aesthetic theory, in literary theory, in the theory and criticism of children's literature and in the literature itself. I shall deal briefly with the first two and more fully with the last two.

In aesthetic theory it is a not uncommon assumption that children cannot have aesthetic satisfactions. Professor F. J. Coleman, for instance, introduces aesthetics in *Contemporary Essays in Aesthetics* (1968) by suggesting that we can rank pleasures in a sequence which 'depends on the degree of intelligence and discrimination needed to experience the feelings those terms designate':

> The lowest pleasures would be those that any sentient human being can feel – children, idiots, the senile; they are such pleasures that do not require any power of discrimination. To call a pleasure an 'aesthetic' pleasure is to imply that it would fall on the highest end of the continuum; therefore aesthetic pleasures are those that require discrimination, intelligence and imagination to be experienced. For surely we do not speak of children or the mentally deficient as *experiencing* art, though of course they may *hear* a symphony or see a painting . . .[13]

Professor Coleman's argument is circular and proves nothing, but it at least affords a clear view of the prejudice under discussion.

Children have also continued to figure as scapegoats in the controversy over 'aesthetic distance' raised in the debate between James and Stevenson. In literary theory, the question is 'what constitutes a proper attitude on the part of the reader: detachment (which James felt to be characteristic of the good reader) or involvement (which Stevenson preferred and was universally believed to characterise the child reader)?' Over the last few decades the requirement that the mature reader, qualified to be discriminating, keep his proper distance has been increasingly questioned. It is acknowledged that even the most judicious readers do become involved in the books they read. But, even so, the children have not been rescued from the scapegoat role in this debate. It seems that the prejudice against child readers is so strong that it will be the last element in the theory to be relinquished. For instance, the celebrated attack on the theory in Wayne Booth's *The Rhetoric of Fiction* turned on an analysis of Jane Austen's *Emma* in which he showed that during the course of the novel 'our emotional reaction to every event concerning Emma tends to become like her own'.[14] It seems then that Booth is acknowledging that even critics do identify with characters in books – that it doesn't make one an inferior reader to do so. *But*, that is only the last half of the sentence, the first half of which goes, 'While only immature readers ever really identify with any character, losing all sense of distance and hence all chance of an artistic experience . . .' Even Booth feels he has to make a concession to the prejudice he is trying to overcome, and the concession he chooses to make is once again to deny 'immature readers' any chance of 'an artistic experience'.

If the assumptions outlined here were held universally, then we would not be able to talk of children's literature but only, as James would have it, of the children's book industry. Critics and theorists who want to talk about 'children's literature' have had to find a way round this pervasive prejudice. Few have been bold enough to take issue with authorities such as Professor Coleman. Many have taken a way out by arguing that children *do* have aesthetic satisfactions but that these are different in kind from those of adults. Cornelia Meigs, for example, introducing a critical history of children's literature, says:

> Just as children, in spite of having long been treated as no more than smaller and more helpless editions of their elders, have always been *something apart* in vigour of personality, of vision, and enterprise of mind, so has the reading of their choice, even though unrecognised as something separate, had its own characteristics, its own individuality, and its own greatness.[15]

This is to make the best of a bad thing and it leads to a great deal of effort on the part of such writers to give an account of the mysteriously different way of experiencing books that children are supposed to have. Criticism, it may be noted, becomes virtually impossible in the face of this supposed fundamental difference between adults' and children's responses to the same book. Some, despairing of bridging the gap, have suggested that only children should review children's books. Such reviews are invariably disappointing to their advocates because they give no evidence whatsoever of a fundamentally different way of responding to books. Rather than explain this away on the grounds of teacher interference, we should regard the original hypothesis that children's responses are different in kind from those of adults as not proven.

The exclusion of children's literature from the class of serious literature has of course resulted in its being classed as a branch of popular literature. Just as the unsubstantiated claim that the aesthetic experiences of adults are not available to children created a need for theories of what children do experience, so the equally arbitrary categorisation of children's literature as 'popular' has fostered the belief that the popularity of a children's book is a proper index of its worth which has in turn attracted the curious explanation that children, unlike adults, are possessed of natural good taste in reading, hence if they generally approve of a book it must be good. Further confusions arise from the fact that at times 'popularity' is understood as a set of critical criteria rather than a function of sales and readers. Kipling, for instance, had considerable respect for Rider Haggard and tried to base a theory on Haggard's writing. In a letter, Kipling exclaimed:

> How the dickens do you do it? How do you keep and outpour the vitality and the conviction and *how* do you contrive to nail down and clinch the *interest* that keeps a man lying along one elbow till the whole arm is tone-cramped? I don't pretend to judge the book in the least. I only know in my own person, that it held me as a drug might – but it was a good drug – . . . You have the incommunicable gift of catching and holding . . .[16]

Although at the time of writing Kipling was himself a top best-seller whilst Haggard's popularity was declining, Kipling still regarded Haggard as the master popular writer, indicating that for him the popularity of a novel could be determined by criteria other than its sales. What these were may be deduced from Haggard's *Autobiography* in which he tries to communicate the incommunicable gift:

> the story is the thing and every word in the book should be a brick to build its edifice . . . Let the character be definite, even at the cost of a little crudeness. Tricks of style and dark allusions may please the superior critic; they do not please the average reader, and . . . a book is written to be read. The first duty of a story is to keep him who peruses it awake . . . 'grip' is about everything.[17]

This passage is interesting in that, if you replace 'the superior critic' by 'the adult reader' and 'the average reader' by 'the child reader' it could be interpolated without being noticed into any textbook on children's literature. Nor is that because the audience for such textbooks are assumed to be interested in writing for children as a commercial venture. A recent critical book dealing with a handful of the best authors of books for children was called *A Sense of Story*.[18] It is thought to be the prerequisite for the good children's writer in the way that James required the 'sense of reality' in the serious novelist. The source of the requirement lies in the perception of children's literature as a branch of popular literature.

This perception originated, I suggest, in the vagueness with which the group of unwelcome new readers was perceived in the eighties by those who felt threatened by them. Class, sex, and age were conflated as causes of a supposed inability to appreciate the best in art and literature, those 'millions to whom taste is but an obscure, confused, immediate instinct', Walter Allen, writing in 1954 saw the class division as most important:

It was probably not accidental that this heightened, more serious conception of the novel as art should have triumphed in the eighties, for the split between the old novel and the new coincided with a cultural revolution. Forster's education Acts of 1870 provided compulsory primary education for all, and the result, over the years, was an enormous increase in the reading public. But the gap between the best education and the worst was so great that the highbrow–lowbrow dichotomy with which we are now wearisomely familiar was inevitable. Before 1870, the poor man who strove to learn to read and, having done so, went on to read beyond the newspapers, did so because he was to some degree a superior man. To be able to read was a key to enfranchisement; it opened the door to a better position as a tradesman or to succeed in business; it was essential to the politically minded working man who dreamed of power for his class; and for a few more disinterested spirits it offered the freedom of a culture traditionally an upper-class preserve. But whatever the motive for learning to read, the Victorian working man, by and large, accepted the cultural standards of classes higher in the social scale. After 1870 this was no longer necessarily so. The provision of reading matter for a semi-literate public became the concern of a vast industry which set its own standards, standards which had nothing to do with the literary and artistic standards as normally understood. Indeed the notion of a single standard ceased practically to exist, and perhaps this was inevitable, for when you give a semi-literate person the vote and persuade him that thereby he is an arbiter of his countries [sic] destiny, it is not easy at the same time to convince him that he is not also the arbiter of what is excellent in art: there is a natural tendency for every man to believe that what he prefers must be the best.[19]

In the closing sentences of this passage, Allen echoes James, who wrote of 'an industry that occupies a very considerable quarter of the scene' with which 'the sort of taste that used to be called "good" has nothing to do'. Allen similarly writes of 'a vast industry' setting 'standards which had nothing to do with literary and artistic standards as normally understood'. James had in mind the child reader, Allen the enfranchised adult male working-class reader, but from the point of view of literary theory they are treated as interchangeable.

It was claimed at the beginning of this paper that theoretical confusion can impose significant constraints on art. One of the most striking features of English children's literature is the amount and quality of fantasy offered to children especially in the last quarter century. The prominence and excellence of fantasy in children's literature has often been remarked on, yet the criticism of those works has been confused and superficial. I believe that both of these phenomena can be explained in terms of the theory I have offered in this paper.

I have shown that the exclusion of children from the readership of the serious novel was associated with the acceptance of a version of realism. One consequence of the acceptance of realism was that fantasy was immediately déclassé. Since fantasy can be seen as the antithesis of realism, it seemed to follow, to those who espoused the realist cause, that fantasy was also the opposite of serious, i.e., trivial or frivolous. That is precisely how Forster used the term in *Aspects of the Novel*.[20] In that book, he devoted two chapters to non-realistic aspects of the novel, one called 'Fantasy' and one called 'Prophecy', characterising both by what they require of the reader. Fantasy, he says, 'asks us to pay something extra'. It is, he suggests, 'like a side-show in an exhibition where you pay sixpence as well as the original entrance fee'. The analogy is damaging, raising the question as to whether the show is worth even sixpence. He divides the potential audience into two groups. Of the first group, those who 'pay with delight' (i.e. enjoy fantasy), Forster claims, 'it is only for the side shows that they entered the exhibition', i.e., a taste for fantasy precludes a taste for other literature; to the second group who 'refuse with indigna-tion' (i.e., detest fantasy), he offers 'our sincere regards, for to dislike the fantastic in literature as not to dislike literature. It does not even imply poverty of imagination, only a disinclination to meet certain demands that are made on it'. So, while a taste for fantasy is said to be incompatible with a taste for any other literature, a distaste for fantasy is said to be quite compatible and, not surprisingly, wins Forster's regard. Although he finds the demands made by fantasy unfulfillable, he admits that he cannot show that they are unreasonable:

> No doubt this approach is not critically sound. We all know that a work of art is an entity, etc. etc.; it has its own laws which are not those of daily life, anything that suits it is true, so why should any question arise about the angel etc., except whether it is suitable to its book? Why place an angel on a different basis from a stockbroker – once in the realm of the fictitious what difference is there between an apparition and a mortgage? I see the soundness

of this argument, but my heart refuses to assent. The general tone of novels is so literal that when the fantastic is introduced it produces a special effect.

In comparison with fantasy, Prophecy is, according to Forster, a much more serious affair and demands to be taken seriously. Fantasy and prophecy are said to be 'alike in having gods, and unlike in the gods they have'. In comparison with the gods of prophecy, those of fantasy are 'small'. 'I would call them fairies if the word were not consecrated to imbecility.' He suggests that fantasies should be saved from 'the claws of critical apparatus', that 'their appeal is specially personal – they are side-shows inside the main show'. The implication here is that the appeal of fantasy is so ephemeral that critical inspection would destroy it – show it to be a trick, an illusion, a device. In fact, he suggests that fantasy can be identified by its 'devices' and 'the fact that their number is strictly limited is of interest'. Prophecy, on the other hand, demands of the reader, 'humility and a suspension of the sense of humour'. It is interesting to note that in this case Forster feels that *refusal* to submit is childish:

> Humility is a quality for which I have only a limited admiration. In many phases of life it is a great mistake and degenerates into defensiveness and hypocrisy. But humility is in place just now. Without its help we shall not hear the voice of the prophet, and our eyes will behold a figure of fun instead of his glory. And the sense of humour – that is out of place: that estimable adjunct of the educated man must be laid aside. Like the school-children in the Bible, one cannot help laughing at the prophet – his bald head is so absurd – but one can discount the laughter and realise that it has no critical value and is merely food for bears.

In *Aspects of the Novel*, 'Fantasy' and 'Prophecy' together represent a by-way in Forster's train of thought on the novel – he calls them interludes 'gay and grave'. Neither can be dealt with properly by his critical equipment, which was designed for novels that arc 'literal in tone', though prophetic novels induce him to consider the possibility that this critical equipment is not the best, or that there may be no such thing as critical equipment at all. Such doubts are momentary, however, and characteristically, brushed off with a sigh. 'It is a pity that Man cannot be at the same time impressive and truthful.'

In those 1927 lectures Forster reflected and helped disseminate a widespread prejudice against fantasy. A consequence of the prejudice that fantasy is childish has been that the writer of fantasy has been directed into writing for children no matter how good he or she might be. The realistic writer has had a choice and indeed been encouraged to regard writing for adults as more satisfying. In writing for children the realistic writer has been conscious of taking second best since realism was defined in terms which excluded children as readers hence 'real' realism was impossible in a children's book. The fantasist has written under no such shadow – has had no such option – all fantasy goes on the children's list. Some excellent writers have found themselves writing for children for this reason, which partially explains the high amount and quality of fantasy in children's literature this century.

Moreover, writers of children's literature have been able to turn to advantage the fact that a work which announces itself as fantasy is deemed frivolous, childish and not worth critical attention. Edith Nesbit referred to this situation at the beginning of *Five Children and It*:

> I could go on and make this into a most interesting story about all the ordinary things that the children did – just the kind of things you do yourself you know – and you would believe every word of it, and when I told you about the children being tiresome, as you are sometimes, your aunts would perhaps write in the margin of the story with a pencil 'How true!' or 'how like life!' And you would see it and very likely be annoyed. So I will only tell you about the really astonishing things that happened, and you may leave the book about quite safely, for no aunts and uncles either are likely to write 'How true!' on the edge of the story.[21]

Using fantasy thus as a protective cover to save the work from prying adult eyes, writers have managed to extend considerably the range of subjects dealt with in children's literature.

An inevitable consequence of the way that children's literature came into being was that a certain restraint has been imposed on children's writers in the realist tradition when it comes to topics such as terror, politics and sex. That such censorship has been found too restrictive by some writers is clear from books like William Mayne's *A Game of Dark* (1971) and Philippa Pearce's *A Dog so Small* (1962). The protagonist of the former is schizoid, of the latter, obsessive, which enables the writers to present intense fears and resentments. But such shifts are of limited use: one can't write about deranged people all the time, nor is it true that only the mad get frightened. What is clear is that these devices will never accommodate what are, after all, incompatible demands made on the writer in this tradition, that he be true to life and also that he avoid certain topics. Moore's solution was to exclude the children: the children's writer's solution is to turn to fantasy. Even Mayne, who is inventive enough to write a highly schematic book like *Sand* (1970) or a mythopoeic book like *The Jersey Shore* (1973) and remain, technically, within the conventions of realism-for-children, found it necessary, in order to deal with the more terrifying aspects of his earlier preoccupation, the alien time-scheme of the earth, to resort to fantasy, in *Earthfasts* (1966).

The so-called 'new realism' in children's books proves on inspection, to be an attempt to introduce adolescent sex into children's books. In fact the acclaimed writers of the 'new realism' have a long way to go before they can deal with the range of sexual feelings including jealousy, possessiveness, despair and the desire for liberation that Alan Garner dealt with in *The Owl Service* (1967) by using fantasy.

Political topics such as class and race have recently been self-consciously injected into children's realistic fiction, but again the fantasists have set the standard to be met. Those writers who are attempting accurate description of working class life in realistic terms are only attempting what Mary Norton did so brilliantly in the Borrowers series (1953 *et seq.*) in which, by one fantastic stroke, she invented a way of presenting the experience of being small and propertyless in a society in which that entails constant vulnerability. Accounts of dispossession and exploitation given in fantasy by Mary Norton and by Russell Hoban in *The Mouse and His Child* (1969) are much more penetrating that those given in books like Serrailler's *Silver Sword* (1956) and Rugters Van der Loeff's *Children On the Oregon Trail, (Oregon at Last)* (New York, 1961) though the latter make the strongest claim to verisimilitude – that of being based on the real experiences of real children. Similarly, in *A Stranger at Green Knowe* (1961) Lucy Boston depicts the relationship between a Chinese boy and an escaped gorilla in a way that makes the self-consciously anti-racist realistic literature look crass.

A preoccupation with the role of the imagination in relation to time would appear unduly sophisticated in a realistic children's book as is suggested by the reaction of reviewers to Mayne's *The Jersey Shore*. So Philippa Pearce was able to contribute to that immemorial topic only by writing fantasy in *Tom's Midnight Garden* (1958). Finally and by a just revenge, fantasy gives cover to parody, the children's own traditional weapon, to mount attacks on the pretensions of adult art and artists in Randolph Stow's *Midnite* (Melbourne, 1967) and Hoban's *The Mouse and His Child*.[22]

These admirable novels have not received the critical appreciation they deserve. I suggest this also stems from the fact that the rejection of the child reader by influential critics and writers was accompanied by the rejection of fantasy and the associated claim that fantasy does not appeal to the mature mind. Scholes and Kellogg's *The Nature of Narrative* is often cited as a work which challenges the domination of realism in the novel. In so far as they champion Romance, however, it is with a reservation similar to that made by Booth concerning reader-involvement and identification:

Romance, the only narrative form which is ineluctably artistic since it is the product of the story telling impulse at its purest, diminishes in interest as its perfection carries it too far from the world of ideas or from the actual world. A pure story, without ideas or imitation of actuality to tie it to human concerns and experiences would be, if such a possibility were realized, totally uninteresting to adult readers. In some children's stories this infinitude of inanity is approached. But in general, narrative artists have sensed the dangers of purity in their art and shied away from it consciously or not.[23]

The use of the term 'inanity' here is reminiscent of Forster's identification of fairies with 'imbecility' and Coleman's association of 'children, idiots, the senile'. A tendency to class children with the mentally defective seems to have supplanted the older prejudices which classed children with women or with working class men. From the point of view of thinking clearly about children as readers this can hardly be counted progress.

The first and major impediment to useful criticism, then, lies in the acceptance by critics of the idea that fantasy is peculiarly suitable for children, not for adults. In order to interpret this supposed fact in a way that attributes no inferiority to children (a considerable feat) many critics rely on some version of the 'culture epoch' theory which states that individual human development recapitulates the development of the race. According to this view children are primitives and are most appropriately served by primitive literature – myths, fables, folk tales and fairy tales. It should be remembered that until recently, fantasies were called 'invented fairy tales' or 'modern fairy tales'. Thus Lillian Smith writes, in *The Unreluctant Years*:

> A child of today asks 'why' and 'how' as he wonders about the natural world which he does not understand. So, in the childhood of the race, without knowledge of the discoveries with which science has enlarged our understanding, primitive peoples made their own explanations of the physical world in terms of themselves.[24]

And Elizabeth Cook documents the 'natural afinity [*sic, passim*] between the childhood of the race and the childhood of the individual human being' in matters of taste:

> They expect a story to be a good yarn, in which the action is swift and the characters are clearly and simply defined. And legends and fairy tales are just like that. Playground games show that children like catastrophes and exhibitions of speed and power, and a clear differentiation between cowboys, cops and spacemen who are good, and Indians, robbers and spacemonsters who are bad.[25]

This 'natural afinity' is brought forward to explain why fantasy appeals to children, but it is not taken as a sufficient explanation as to why fantasy is *good* for children. The Romantic version of the recapitulation theory was inclined to rate the child's and primitive's view of the world highly and to regard growing up as a process of losing touch with essentials. Since that time other theories of development have prevailed, the one most in point here being that which views growing up as a progress towards maturity and that people, as part of that process, gradually acquire a grip of reality in the course of their childhood; that to do so is a vital advance in child development, and that anything which interferes with a child's acquisition of a sense of reality is harmful to his development. Fantasy might according to this theory, constitute just such a hazard to a child's healthy acquisition of a sense of reality. Indeed, the eighteenth century Rousseauists who held an analogous theory about the acquisition of reason, acted consistently with it in banning all fairy tales (thus annoying Lamb and Coleridge). Mrs Barbauld, for instance, supported a programme almost the reverse of the modern, namely that children should be offered informative, factual material about the actual world and that only the most highly educated and developed tastes would reach the 'pure poetry' of, say, Collins, the literature least concerned with actuality.

The inconsistencies in our position lead to an anxiety about children reading 'too much' fantasy and the advocacy of a 'balanced diet'. The range of critical opinion on the issue includes those who, like W. J. Scott, are inclined to place severe limits on the reading of fantasy:

> An acceptance with such enthusiasm of a representation of human beings in action that is so patently false must tend to create some misunderstanding in the mind of the young reader of the nature and motives of human behaviour. Further it compels him to lead a dual existence, using part of his energy in an excessive emotional participation in a life of fantasy at a time when he needs so much to grapple with the real world. Granted that it is still necessary for him to withdraw sometimes from the real world into one of fantasy, it is of great importance that the experience given in fantasy should be of good quality, indirectly extending his understanding of reality.[26]

and those who, like Lillian Smith, are prepared to adopt the Romantic position:

> A child's acceptance of fantasy is based on imagination and wonder. An adult lacking these universal attributes of childhood is often at a loss when he is asked to consider seriously a work of purely imaginative content, far removed from the reality of his

experience of life. Before the adult can feel at ease in this different world of fantasy he must discover a means of approach. There is an interesting discussion of fantasy by E. M. Forster in his *Aspects of the Novel*, in which he says 'What does fantasy ask us? It asks us to pay something extra'. That is to say that over and above what we ordinarily bring to the reading of a story, fantasy demands something extra, perhaps a kind of sixth sense. All children have it, but most adults leave it behind with their cast off childhood.[27]

Lillian Smith's misinterpretations of Forster's remarks is a clear example of the way that such apologists for fantasy have had to close their eyes to the manifest change in the critical climate, in order to feel justified in what they are doing.

Obviously, the whole issue is distorted by the almost universal assumption that fantasy appeals to children because they believe it is true or at least don't know that it is false, and that adults reject it because they know it is not true. The question as to whether any art produces belief in any reader of any age is too big to go into here. I merely point out that confusions and disagreements on that question add to the confusions on this one. The issue of belief is introduced in an attempt to answer an irrelevant question on to which critics have allowed themselves to be diverted, namely, 'why does fantasy appeal to children and not to adults?' They have discussed that question because they were unwilling to face the fact that fantasy had been merely abandoned to the child reader. Even where critics have avoided the distracting question, they have found themselves ill-equipped to deal with fantasy properly, perhaps because they have only secondhand equipment of the Forster design.

The theory of children's literature has been for some time in a state of confusion. The achievements of the writers, in particular the fantasists, in spite of the lack of critical and theoretical support has been remarkable and provided a challenge to the critic which should be taken up.

Notes

1 Donald David Stone, *Novelists in a Changing World* (Cambridge, Mass., 1972), p. 1.
2 John Goode, 'The Art of Fiction: Walter Besant and Henry James' in David Howard, John Lucas, John Goode (eds), *Tradition and Tolerance in Nineteenth-Century Fiction: Critical Essays on some English and American Novels* (London, 1966), p. 245.
3 Walter Allen, *The English Novel: A Short Critical History* (London, 1954), p. 249.
4 (London, 1970).
5 George Moore, *Literature at Nurse or Circulating Morals* (London, 1885), p. 18.
6 Allen Tate, 'Techniques of Fiction', *Sewanee Review*, 53 (1944), p. 225.
7 First published 1884. From Henry James, *Selected Literary Criticism*, ed. Morris Shapiro (London, 1963), p. 49.

8 'A Humble Remonstrance', first published 1884. In *Works*, ed. Swanson (London, 1911–12), IX, p. 148.
9 First published 1882. In *Works*, IX, p. 134.
10 S. Colvin (ed.), *Letters of Robert Louis Stevenson* (London, 1901), II, p. 20.
11 This essay was discovered 'long buried' by Leon Edel and given pride of place in *Henry James: The Future of the Novel. Essays on the Art of Fiction* (New York, 1956). It was not completely unknown before that time, however, and seems to have influenced Walter Allen. See below n. 19.
12 George Moore, p. 21.
13 Introduction, p. 17.
14 Wayne Booth, *The Rhetoric of Fiction* (Chicago, 1961), p. 284.
15 Cornelia Meigs (and others), *A Critical History of Children's Literature* (New York, 1969), p. 3 (my emphasis).
16 Dated 5 May 1925. Quoted in Morton Cohen, *Rider Haggard, His Life and Work*, 2nd edn (London, 1968), p. 281.
17 H. Rider Haggard, *The Days of My Life*, ed. C. J. Longman, II, 92. Quoted in Cohen, pp. 284–5.
18 John Rowe Townsend, *A Sense of Story: Essays on Contemporary Writers for Children* (London, 1971). The book however advocates and offers proper, serious criticism.
19 Walter Allen, p. 249.
20 E. M. Forster, *Aspects of the Novel* (London, 1927), chapters 6 and 7.
21 E. Nesbit, *Five Children and It* (London, 1902), p. 18.
22 The place of publication of novels mentioned in the preceding paragraphs is London except where otherwise stated.
23 Robert Scholes and Robert Kellogg, *The Nature of Narrative* (New York, 1966), p. 232.
24 Lillian Smith, *The Unreluctant Years* (Chicago, 1953), p. 65.
25 Elizabeth Cook, *The Ordinary and the Fabulous* (Cambridge, 1969), p. 7.
26 W. J. Scott, quoted, without reference, in Geoffrey Trease, *Tales Out of School*, 2nd edn (London, 1964), p. 73.
27 Lillian Smith, p. 152.

6

STANDARDS OF CRITICISM FOR CHILDREN'S LITERATURE

John Rowe Townsend

Source: Nancy Chambers (ed.), *The* Signal *Approach to Children's Literature*, Harmondsworth: Kestrel (Penguin), 1980, pp. 193–207. Originally published in *Top of the News*, American Library Association, 1971.

To give the May Hill Arbuthnot Honour Lecture is the greatest privilege that can fall to a commentator on books for children. It is with some idea of matching my response to the size of the honour that I have decided at last to attempt the largest and most difficult subject I know in this field: namely, the question of standards by which children's literature is to be judged. This is not only the most difficult, it is the most important question; indeed, it is so basic that none of us who are professionally concerned with children and books ought really to be functioning at all unless we have thought it out to our own satisfaction and are prepared to rethink it from time to time. But, as in many other areas of life, we tend to be so busy doing what we have to do that we never have time to stop and consider why and how we do it. True, Mrs. Arbuthnot herself had a good deal to say on the subject of critical standards, but she would not have claimed to say the last word.

It seems to me that the assessment of children's books takes place in an atmosphere of unparalleled intellectual confusion. There are two reasons for this. One is a very familiar one which I need not elaborate on. It was neatly expressed by Brian Alderson in an article in *Children's Book News* of London for January/February 1969, when he said that "everyone in the children's book business subsists in a slightly unreal world, where time, brains and energy are expended on behalf of a vast and largely nonparticipating audience". It has been pointed out time and time again that children's books are written by adults, published by adults, reviewed by adults, and, in the main, bought by adults. The whole process is carried out at one, two, three, or more removes from the ultimate consumer.

This situation is inescapable, but it is an uneasy one. Most of us think we know what is good for ourselves, but the more sensitive we are, the more seriously we take our obligations, the less we feel sure we know what is good for others.

The second cause of confusion is that children's literature is a part of the field, or adjoins the field, of many different specialists; yet it is the *major* concern of relatively few, and those not the most highly placed in the professional or academic pecking-order. Furthermore, the few to whom children's literature is central cannot expect, within one working lifetime, to master sufficient knowledge of the related fields to meet the experts on their own ground and at their own level. And yet, while the children's literature person obviously cannot operate at a professional level in all these various fields, the people operating in the various fields can and quite properly do take an interest in children's reading as it affects their own specialities, and quite frequently pronounce upon it. But, understandably, such people are often unaware of or have not thought deeply about the aspects of children's literature that do *not* impinge upon their own field. The subject is one on which people are notoriously willing to pronounce with great confidence but rather little knowledge. Consequently, we have a flow of apparently authoritative comment by people who are undoubtedly experts but who are not actually experts on *this*.

I am not here to quarrel with those who see children's literature in terms of social or psychological adjustment, advancement of deprived or minority groups, development of reading skills, or anything else. I have said in the foreword to my book, *A Sense of Story*, that "most disputes over standards are fruitless because the antagonists suppose their criteria to be mutually exclusive; if one is right the other must be wrong. This is not necessarily so. Different kinds of assessment are valid for different purposes." I would only remark that the viewpoints of psychologists, sociologists, and educationists of various descriptions have rather little in common with each other or with those whose approach is mainly literary.

We face, in fact, a jungle of preoccupations, ideas, and attitudes. I should like to begin my discussion by clearing, if I can, some small piece of common ground which will accommodate most of us who care about children and books.

Let me borrow a phrase used by Edgar Z. Friedenberg in a book entitled *Coming of Age in America*, published in 1965. I do not agree with all that is said in the book, but I think the phrase I have my eye on is admirable. Friedenberg used it to describe the true function of the schools; I would use it to describe the duty of all of us, either as parents or, in a broad sense, as guardians. This aim, he said, was "the respectful and affectionate nurture of the young, and the cultivation in them of a disciplined and informed mind and heart".

Extending this formulation to cover the special interest which has brought us here today, I should like to add that in furtherance of these ends we would wish every child to experience to his or her full capacity the enjoyment, and the broadening of horizons, which can be derived from literature. Diffidently I invite my hearers, and my readers, if any, to subscribe to this modest and unprovocative creed. What it asks is the acceptance of literary experience as having value in itself for the general enrichment of life, over and above any virtue that may be claimed for it as a means to a non-literary end. Anyone who cannot accept the proposition is of course fully entitled to stand aloof; but I cannot think of anything to say to such a person, because if literature is *solely* a means to an end, then the best literature is the literature which best serves that end, and the only matters worth arguing about are whether the end is a good one and how effectively it is served. Furthermore, those points cannot be argued in general terms, but only in relation to a particular cause and a particular book.

I wonder if from the tiny clearing we have made we can begin to find a way through the tangle that surrounds us. Let us try to consider what literature is, what it offers and what is children's literature. I do not want to spend a lot of time on questions which, although they may present theoretical difficulties, are not really perplexing in practice. I am going to define literature, without appeal to authority, as consisting of all works of imagination which are transmitted primarily by means of the written word or spoken narrative – that is, in the main, novels, stories, and poetry – with the addition of those works of non-fiction which by their qualities of style or insight may be said to offer experience of a literary nature. This is a rather loose definition, but in practical terms I think it will do.

What does literature offer? Summarizing ruthlessly, I will say that it is, above all, enjoyment: enjoyment not only in the shallow sense of easy pleasure, but enjoyment of a profounder kind; enjoyment of the shaping by art of the raw material of life, and enjoyment, too, of the skill with which that shaping is performed; enjoyment in the stretching of one's imagination, the deepening of one's experience, and the heightening of one's awareness; an enjoyment which may be intense even if the material of the literary work is sad or painful. I should add that obviously not all literature can offer such a range of enjoyments; that no work of literature outside such short forms as the lyric poem can offer these enjoyments throughout; and that the deliberate restriction of aim is often necessary in children's literature as in much else.

What in particular is children's literature? That is quite a hard question. There is a sense in which we don't need to define it because we know what it is. Children's literature is *Robinson Crusoe* and *Alice* and *Little Women* and *Tom Sawyer* and *Treasure Island* and *The Wind in the Willows* and *Winnie-the-Pooh* and *The Hobbit* and *Charlotte's Web*. That's simple: but it won't quite do. Surely *Robinson Crusoe* was not written for children, and do not the *Alice* books appeal at least as much to grownups?; if *Tom Sawyer* is children's literature, what about *Huckleberry Finn*?; if the *Jungle Books* are children's literature, what about *Kim* or *Stalky*?; and if *The Wind in the Willows* is children's literature, what about *The Golden Age*?; and so on.

Since any line-drawing must be arbitrary, one is tempted to abandon the attempt and say that there is no such thing as children's literature, there is just literature. And in an important sense that is true. Children are not a separate form of life from people; no more than children's books are a separate form of literature from just books. Children are part of mankind; children's literature is part of literature. Yet the fact that children are part of mankind doesn't save you from having to separate them from adults for certain essential purposes: nor does the fact that children's literature is part of literature save you from having to separate it for practical purposes (in the libraries and bookshops, for instance). I pondered this question for some time while working on *A Sense of Story*, and came to the conclusion that in the long run children's literature could only be regarded as consisting of those books which by a consensus of adults and children were assigned to the children's shelves – a wholly pragmatic definition. In the short run it appears that, for better or worse, the publisher decides. If he puts a book on the children's list, it will be reviewed as a children's book and will be read by children (or young people), if it is read at all. If he puts it on the adult list, it will not – or at least not immediately.

Let us assume that we have found, in broad terms, a common aim; that we know roughly what literature is and the nature of the experience it offers: that we have a working definition of children's literature, even if it is more pragmatic than we would wish. Can we now make some sense out of the question of differing standards? So far I have tried to examine what exists rather than to project a theoretical system out of my own head. We all know how often the application of a new mind to an old problem will fail because the new thinking is insufficiently grounded in what has been thought and done before; indeed, it often overestimates its own originality.

When we look for individual assessments of actual books (as distinct from general articles on children's literature and reading) we find that most of what is written comes under the headings of (a) overwhelmingly, reviews, (b) aids to book selection, and (c) general surveys. There is little writing that I think could be dignified with the name of criticism, a point to which I will return later. While examining reviews, selection aids, and surveys, in both the United States and Britain and in relation to imaginative literature, I asked myself not whether they were sound and perceptive or whether I agreed with them, but what they were actually doing and what their standards appeared to be. I was aware that similar enquiries had been carried out by others, and more thoroughly; but I was aware, too, that my findings would be matters of judgement which were not of simple fact, and the scheme of my over-all study required that the judgements should be my own. I will spare you the raw material of my investigation and will keep my conclusions brief. I found, naturally, some differences between reviews in general and specialist publications, but from my point of view they were not crucial.

What the reviewers and selectors were largely concerned with, more often than not, it seemed to me, was telling you what the story was about: a necessary activity, but not an evaluative one. I came to the conclusion that where they offered judgements the writers always concerned themselves with one or more of four attributes, which I do not place in order of importance or frequency. These were (1) suitability, (2) popularity, or potential popularity, (3) relevance, and (4) merit. "Suitability" is rather a blanket term, under which I include appropriateness to the supposed readership or reading age or purpose, and also attempts by the reviewer or selector to assign books to particular age groups or types of child. "Popularity" needs no explanation. By "relevance" I mean the power, or possible power, of theme or subject matter to make the child more aware of current social or personal problems, or to suggest solutions to him; where a story appears to convey a message I include under "relevance" the assessment of the message. Finally, by "merit" I mean on the whole, literary merit, although often one finds that what might be called undifferentiated merit is discerned in a book.

Of the four attributes I have mentioned (please remember that my classifications are arbitrary and that there is some overlap) it may well have occurred to you that the first three are child-centred: suitability to the child, popularity with the child, relevance to the child. The fourth is book-centred: merit of the book. This is an important distinction: failure to perceive it has given us a great deal of trouble in the past, preventing us from understanding each other and understanding what we are about. In an article in *Wilson Library Bulletin* for December 1968 I rashly coined a phrase about "book people" and "child people". "Book people," I said, were those primarily concerned with books: authors, publishers, a great many reviewers, and public librarians. "Child people," I said, were those primarily concerned with children: parents, teachers, and (in England at any rate) most school librarians. This division was useful in a way, because it helped to account for two diametrically opposed views of the state of English children's literature: that it was in a very healthy state, with so many good books being published; and that it was in a very unhealthy state, because so many children didn't find pleasure in reading. "Book people," I thought, tended to take the former view; "child people" to take the latter. Incidentally, it was reflection on the fact that such totally opposite views could be held that led me to feel we needed an examination of standards and, in part, led me to offer my present hesitant contribution to that formidable task.

However, I did not and do not intend to set any group against any other group, and I must say at once that all children's "book people" I know are also "child people" in that they care about children; and all the "child people" I know who are interested in books are on that account "book people". And I will repeat here what I said earlier in another context: that different kinds of assessment are valid for different purposes. Not only that, but different standards can co-exist within the mind of the same person at the same time. This is why we get mixed up. Our judgements are rarely made with a single, simple purpose in mind, and we do not stop to separate our purposes any more than we normally stop to analyse our own processes of thought. Because we are both "book people" and "child people" and because we care about both books and children, book-centred and child-centred views are all jumbled together in our heads. Is it a good book, will children like it, will it have a beneficial effect on them? We ask ourselves all these questions at once, and expect to come up with a single answer.

It is easy for mental sideslips to occur, even when we are writing for publication. A simple instance (one of many that could be cited) is in the London *Times Literary Supplement* of 16 April 1970, where the anonymous reviewer of a book of verse by Alan Brownjohn discusses the book with much intelligence in the language of literary criticism, and finishes by saying that "this is a book all children will most definitely enjoy". The statement is unrelated to the rest of what is said and, unfortunately, cannot be true. Nobody has yet found a book that "all" children enjoy, and if there were such a book I do not think it would be a book of poems. The reviewer cannot have *thought* before writing that; he or she has made the remark either as a general expression of approval or as an unrealistic inference: "It is good, so they will all enjoy it."

There are people – Brian Alderson in an article provocatively entitled "The Irrelevance of Children to the Children's Book Reviewer"; Paul Heins, if I understand him correctly, in two articles in the *Horn Book* called "Out on a Limb with the Critics" and "Coming to Terms with Criticism", in June and August 1970, respectively – who maintain that reviewing should be strictly critical. Alderson says: "It may be objected that to assess children's books without reference to children is to erect some absolute critical standard relating neither to the author's purpose nor to the reader's enjoyment. To do much less, however, is to follow a road that leads to a morass of contradictions and subjective responses."

I do not wish to prolong my discussion of a subject already so much discussed as reviewing. On the whole I agree with Heins and Alderson, whose positions, I think, can fairly be described as purist. I would prefer the reviewer to address himself sensitively to the book which is there in front of him, rather than to use his space for inevitably crude assessments of suitability for some broad notional category of child or speculations that the book will or will not sit long on the shelf, or that it will or will not help its readers to adjust to reality or understand how the other half of the world lives. Readers can use their intelligence and make these assessments or pursue these speculations for themselves. I suspect that library systems can manage the practical task of book selection without undue dependence on the individual reviewer. What they need to know from him, if they need to know anything from him (and if it isn't too late anyway by the time the review appears), is: does the book have literary merit?

Suitability, popularity, relevance – are these not questions for the buyer, and perhaps above all for those who are closest to the ultimate consumer? "Will this be suitable for *my* child, will this be popular with *my* class, will this be relevant for children in the area served by *my* library?" Surely only the parent, teacher, or librarian there on the spot can find the answer. He will find it in his own judgement and experience. And he will soon learn whether he was right.

I hope I have cleared the ground sufficiently to allow myself to move on to a discussion of critical principles in relation to children's literature. I am not sure whether I have sufficiently indicated the *usefulness* of the critical approach. If I have not, then I ought to do so; for although some of us would no doubt practise it quite happily for its own sake, if it is not useful we cannot reasonably expect others to give their time and attention, their paper and print, to the result of our endeavours. So I will suggest first that a standard of literary merit is required, and indeed in practice is accepted, as the *leading edge*, so to speak, of book assessment since non-literary standards relate so largely to specific aims and situations, times, places, and audiences. Literary standards are not fixed forever, but they are comparatively stable; that is part of their essence. Without this leading edge, this backbone if you prefer it, there can only be a jumble of criteria, a haphazard mixture of personal responses. And I have found in my own numerous discussions with people concerned with various aspects of books for children, that even those who most strongly condemn what they consider to be an excessively literary approach do in fact take it for granted that there is some independent standard of quality other than what children like or what is good for them or what brings them face to face with contemporary issues. "Wonderful stuff, but not for *my* kids" is a frequent comment.

I would suggest, too, and have suggested in the introduction to *A Sense of Story*, that a critical approach is desirable not only for its own sake but also as a stimulus and discipline for author and publisher, and, in the long run, for the improvement of the breed. Donnarae MacCann, introducing a series of articles in the *Wilson Library Bulletin* for December 1969, made this point and quoted from Henry S. Canby's *Definitions* (second series, 1967):

> Unless there is somewhere an intelligent critical attitude against which the writer can measure himself . . . one of the chief requirements for good literature is wanting. . . . The author degenerates.

Donnarae MacCann goes on to say that "there is no body of critical writing to turn to, even for those books which have been awarded the highest literary prizes in children's literature in Britain and America". That seems to me to indicate a serious lack, and to suggest a further use for the literary criticism of children's books: to help them to achieve their proper status. There is a parallel between the standing of children's literature now and that of the novel a hundred years or so ago. Listen to Henry James in *The Art of Fiction* (1884):

> Only a short time ago it might have been supposed that the English novel was not what the French call "discutable" . . . there was a comfortable, good-humoured feeling abroad that a novel is a novel as a pudding is a pudding, and that our only business with it could be to swallow it. . . . Art lives upon discussion, upon experiment, upon curiosity, upon variety of attempt, upon the exchange of views and the comparison of standpoints. . . . [The novel] must take itself seriously for the public to take it so.

We can apply Henry James's statements to children's literature today. As yet, it is barely discussible at a respectable intellectual level. But if we are to move onward from kiddy lit and all that the use of that squirmy term implies, then children's books must be taken seriously *as literature*, and this means they must be considered with critical strictness. Vague approval, praise for the work of established writers because they are established and, above all, sentimental gush will get us nowhere.

I have suggested, diffidently, what I consider to be literature and what I believe in broad terms to be the nature of literary experience. From the latter it would be possible to derive, in equally broad terms, an elementary criterion for the assessment of literary merit. But we need something more detailed and sophisticated, which could hardly be drawn by legitimate processes of deduction from my simple premises; and I feel even more diffident when I think of the amount of distinguished American and British literary criticism in print. Is this even a case where the construction and application of abstract rules are proper? Perhaps we ought to see what some of the critics say.

We find in fact that the literary critics, both modern and not-so-modern, are rather reluctant to pin themselves down to theoretical statements. In the introduction to *Determinations* (1934), F. R. Leavis expresses the belief that "the way to forward true appreciation of literature and art is to examine and discuss it"; and again, "out of agreement or disagreement with particular judgements of value a sense of relative value in the concrete will define itself, and, without this, no amount of talk about values in the abstract is worth anything". The late T. S. Eliot was elusive about critical standards, but when he did make a firm statement it could be startlingly down-to-earth. He said, in *The Use of Poetry and the Use of Criticism* (1933):

> The rudiment of criticism is the ability to select a good poem and reject a bad poem: and its most severe test is of its ability to select a good *new* poem, to respond properly to a new situation.

I should mention that Eliot, like many other critics, sometimes used the word "poem" as shorthand for any work of imaginative literature. Whether he was doing so here I am not sure, but his statement is a statement about criticism, not about poetry, and if for "poem" you substituted "novel", "painting", or "piece of music" it would be equally true.

In the same book, Eliot remarked that "if you had no faith in the critic's ability to tell a good poem from a bad one, you would put little reliance on the value of his theories". I do not recall that Eliot ever explained by what standard you were to judge whether the critic could tell a good poem, but obviously it was some standard other than the person's own theory and, in fact, I am fairly sure that it was the consensus of informed opinion over a period of time. And that comes originally from Dr. Johnson, who said in the *Preface to Shakespeare* that the only test that could be applied to works of literature was "length of duration and continuance of esteem"; and also, in the *Life of Gray*, that "it is by the common sense of readers uncorrupted by literary prejudice that all claim to literary honours is finally decided".

Matthew Arnold in *The Study of Poetry* (1880) proposed, as aids to distinguishing work of the highest class, not rules but touchstones, examples from the great masters. Arnold says:

> Critics give themselves great labour to draw out what in the abstract constitutes the character of a high quality of poetry. It is much better simply to have recourse to concrete examples; – to take specimens of poetry of high, the very highest quality, and to say: The characters of a high quality of poetry are what is expressed *there*. They are far better recognised by being felt in the verse of the master than by being perused in the prose of the critic. . . . If we are asked to define this mark and accent (of "high beauty, worth and power") in the abstract, our answer must be: No, for we should thereby be darkening the question, not clearing it.

Here Arnold was undoubtedly talking about poetry and not using the word as shorthand. His touchstone principle could be extended to prose, although it strikes me as not entirely satisfactory anyway since it would not help you to judge really original work. The main point is, however, that Johnson, Arnold, Eliot, Leavis – and Henry James, too, if I correctly interpret his critical writings – are reluctant to prescribe an abstract framework against which a work of literature can be measured. They see the danger. "People are always ready," T. S. Eliot said, "to grasp at any guide which will help them to recognize the best poetry without having to depend upon their own sensibility and taste." Once establish a formula (this is myself speaking, not Eliot) and you open the door to bad and pedantic criticism by people who rely on rules instead of perceptions. Not only that but you risk creating a structure within which writers can be imprisoned. Writers should never be given the idea that there is one approved way of doing things. Far better to keep an open critical mind and encourage them with the words of Kipling:

> There are nine and sixty ways of constructing tribal lays,
> And – every – single – one – of – them – is – right!

Am, I, you may ask, suggesting that there should be no formal standards at all? Well, not quite that. It depends on the critic. Some find formal principles helpful in organizing their thought. Mrs. Arbuthnot did; and I am sure the "criteria for stories" which she sets out on pages 17–19 of *Children and Books* have been valuable to a great many people, especially those who are feeling their way into the subject. Mrs. Arbuthnot suggests looking at stories with an eye to theme, plot, characters, and style, and that is excellent; it gives you somewhere to start; it gets you moving. The guidelines for the award in England of the Carnegie Medal are almost identical and are laid down with staccato brevity; they are not expanded and explained, as Mrs. Arbuthnot expanded and explained hers. But I believe that Mrs. Arbuthnot's standards are less valuable than her example, as seen in the perceptive, practical literary criticism and, I might add, art criticism all through her book. It may well be that the British Library Association realized that what mattered for the Carnegie were not a few bald words about plot, style, and characterization, but the knowledge and judgement of the people who were appointed to apply them. The terms of the *Guardian* award for children's fiction, with which I am associated, say only that it is to go to an outstanding work; everything else is left to the judges, and I see nothing wrong with that. A good critic will indeed be aware of theme, plot, style, characterization, and many other considerations, some of them not previously spelled out but arising directly from the work; he will be sensitive; he will have a sense of balance and rightness; he will respond. Being only human he cannot possibly know all that it would be desirable for him to know; but he will have a wide knowledge of literature in general as well as of children and their literature, and probably a respectable acquaintance with cinema, theatre, television, and current affairs. That is asking a lot of him, but not too much. The critic (this is the heart of the matter) counts more than the criteria.

He will have his standards, but they will have become part of himself; he will hardly be conscious of them. Certainly he will not cart them around with him like a set of tools ready for any job. He will, I think, if I may now quote myself again from *A Sense of Story*, approach a book with an open mind and respond to it as freshly and honestly as he is able; then he will go away, let his thoughts and feelings about it mature, turn them over from time to time, consider the book in relation to others by the same author and by the author's predecessors and contemporaries. If the book is for children, he should not let his mind be dominated by the fact, but neither, I believe, should he attempt to ignore it. Just as I feel the author must write for himself yet with awareness of an audience of children, so I feel the critic must write for himself with an awareness that the books he discusses are children's books.

This last point gives me my cue to return very briefly to an issue which I touched on but put aside at its logical place in my discussion, because I wanted to keep some edges clear and I feared it might blur them. I think I can now safely go back to it. When I indicated that a critical approach was book-centred rather than child-centred, when I said I agreed on the whole with the purists, I did not, emphatically not, mean to imply that the book exists in some kind of splendid isolation, and that whether it actually speaks to the child does not matter. Rather, I think that purists can go too far in their apparent disregard for popularity. There is a sense in which the importance, the value even, of a work, is linked with its capacity to appeal to the multitude. To take some exalted examples: does not common sense tell us that part of the greatness of a Beethoven, a Shakespeare, a Michelangelo lies in the breadth of their appeal, the fact that their works are rewarding not only to a few cognoscenti but to *anyone* in possession of the appropriate faculties? A book is a communication; if it doesn't communicate, does it not fail? True, it may speak to posterity, if it gets the chance; it may be ahead of its time. But if a children's book is not popular with children here and now, its lack of appeal may tell us something. It is at least a limitation, and it *may* be a sign of some vital deficiency which is very much the critic's concern.

Those of us with purist tendencies are also perhaps too much inclined to turn up our noses at the "book with a message". For the message may be of the essence of the work, as in the novels of D. H. Lawrence or George Orwell. The revelation of the possibilities of human nature for good or ill is a major concern of literary art, probably *the* major concern of literary art. If the writer engages himself with a contemporary problem, he may be engaging himself most valuably with the mind and feelings of the reader; and to demand that he be neutral on the issues raised is to demand his emasculation. Nevertheless, it needs to be said from time to time that a book can be good without being immensely popular and without solving anybody's problems.

You will have noticed that in this talk, now drawing to a close, I have refrained from discussing specific contemporary books for children. This has been a self-denying ordinance. We would all rather talk about books than principles. But to illustrate adequately – not just casually – the various general points I have made would require reference to many books and to many pieces of writing about them; it would be the task of a course of lectures, not a single one. And so, having reluctantly maintained a some-what abstract level throughout, I want to finish, as it were, on the theoretical summit of children's literature. T. S. Eliot, in the book already cited, remarks that:

> In a play of Shakespeare you get several levels of significance. For the simplest auditors there is the plot, for the more thoughtful the character and conflict of character, for the more musically sensi-tive the rhythm, and for the auditors of greater sensitiveness and understanding a meaning which reveals itself gradually.

Now authors cannot all be Shakespeares, nor for that matter can critics all be Eliots. And even within our own limitations we cannot aim at the peaks of achievement all the time. But no one compels us to be modest in our ambitions; no one has compelled me to be modest in making claims on behalf of children's literature, nor have I any intention of being so. Let's all remember with pride and pleasure that children's books of the highest merit will work on several levels; they will work indeed on the same person at successive stages of development. The best children's books are infinitely rereadable; the child can come back to them at increasing ages and, even as a grownup, still find new sources of enjoyment. Some books, a few books, need never be grown away from; they can always be shared with children and with the child within. The writer for children need feel no lack of scope for high endeavour, for attempting the almost but not quite impossible. For of books that succeed in this comprehensive way, that bind the generations together, parents with children, past with present with future, we are never likely to have too many.

7

INTERPRETATION AND
THE APPARENT SAMENESS
OF CHILDREN'S NOVELS

Perry Nodelman

Source: *Studies in the Literary Imagination* 18(2) (1985): 5–20.

The critical theory of the past few decades has focused on the similarities of different works of literature—on archetypes, on considerations of genre, on intertextuality; yet for most of us, the reason for criticism remains what it has always been. Like Samuel Johnson, like Matthew Arnold, like T. S. Eliot, we want to determine what makes the poems and novels we consider good different from the ones we consider mediocre; and we want to explore what makes the works we consider masterpieces special. In other words, we still want to know how works of literature are different from each other.

For that reason, we assume that good books are those that transcend genre or archetype, and that demand our close attention to their distinguishing qualities—those qualities that we can, as we say, "interpret." Above all, we assume that the act of interpretation will reveal the sources of uniqueness, somewhere below the surface, in a central core of distinct meanings and patterns; and we assume that in being distinct, such a central core is the exact opposite of the archetypal or the generic. In other words, distinctive details on the surface are evidence of uniqueness at the core.

That causes a serious problem for critics of children's literature. Most children's books are "simple," undetailed, and consequently, so similar to each other that their generic similarities and their evocations of archetypes are breathtakingly obvious. Such books have few qualities distinct enough to need interpreting, and attempts to interpret them as we interpret important adult books reveal surprisingly similar central cores of meanings and patterns—cores not much different from the generic or the archetypal.

Of course, most adult novels are more alike each other than different. But when we suspect that there's little difference between an adult novel's central core and its generic qualities or its archetypes, we happily identify it as formula fiction, and happily acknowledge that it requires no individual interpretation. Children's fiction thwarts would-be interpreters simply because so *few* children's novels move much beyond the formulaic or the stereotypical. Lois Kuznets has shown how respected children's novels by both Lois Lenski and Noel Streatfeild contain the underlying formulas of popular literature for adults that John G. Cawelti has outlined: "both seem to have produced only a layer of realism imposed upon a stereotypical structure, which in turn rested upon an archetypal base."[1] Kuznets suggests that these books and many other "good" children's novels are "individualized formulaic narratives," as distinguished not only from crude formula novels, but also from more complex children's novels, which she sees as open to interpretation.

Yet even those more complex children's novels seem to have more in common with works of popular fiction and with each other than do interpretable books for adults. A quick glance through any journal devoted to the criticism of children's literature reveals how frequently interpretations of quite different sorts of excellent children's books uncover the same or quite similar patterns and themes: not only is E. B. White's *Charlotte's Web* as much about acceptance of one's lot as are R. L. Stevenson's *Treasure Island* and Virginia Hamilton's *Arilla Sun Down*, but it brings its characters to that acceptance by similar means.

This apparent sameness of even important children's books demands one of two conclusions. We can accept the implications of the critical endeavour throughout history, and say that "good" children's novels are not in fact good novels, because interpretation cannot show us how they are different from each other. Or we can accept what our instinct tells us— that some children's novels stand out, and are, indeed, especially worthy of critical attention, even though interpretation tells us that they are much like other children's novels. If we are wise enough to make the second choice, then we face another choice. We may conclude that the similarity of good children's books to each other makes children's fiction different from adult fiction—different enough that it requires its own interpretive approach. Or we may reach a quite different, and, to my mind, more sensible conclusion—that in fact, children's fiction is less significantly a special sort of fiction than a serious challenge to conventional ideas about interpretation and distinctness, that traditional means of interpretation are *always* misleading, and that the central cores critics uncover in complex adult novels do not actually explain what is special about those novels either. Perhaps Susan Sontag was right when she suggested that interpretation as conventionally practised "violates" art.[2]

I began thinking of these matters as I listened to a talk by Eleanor Cameron about time fantasies, children's novels in which children of the present come into contact with people from the past. Cameron is the author of two such books, and also of an earlier discussion of time fantasies in *The Green and Burning Tree*;[3] her talk called "The Eternal Moment" was about books that have been published since that earlier discussion appeared in 1969. Near the end of the talk, Cameron said, "You may have noted the number of instances when I have said of one or another of these fantasies that in some respect it is like another."[4] I had, in fact, noted exactly that, and been intrigued by it.

All the books Cameron described have a reputation for excellence; and the ones I had read seemed to me to live up to that reputation. In fact, few of these books are widely popular with children, simply because they are good enough, that is, complex enough, to demand some literary sophistication of their readers. They are the sort of children's books that adult readers who like to interpret literature find most attractive. Yet they are indeed very much like each other, in a way that the novels for adults that we consider excellent rarely are; and an exploration of their similarities clearly reveals how children's fiction challenges conventional ideas about interpretation.

Good novels for adults often have clear relationships with earlier novels that may have impressed or otherwise influenced their authors; but, perhaps because of what Harold Bloom calls "the anxiety of influence,"[5] these relationships tend to be ironic ones. Distinguished novelists pay homage to their sources by subverting or re-inventing them; they become distinguished by making themselves distinct from their forebears. It seems likely, then, that the unquestionably distinguished children's time fantasies of recent years similarly pay homage to earlier books about contact across time—especially since this kind of fantasy is relatively new. Or perhaps more exactly, the possibility that this kind of fantasy might be considered a kind, a genre, is relatively new; for many years, Alison Uttley's *A Traveller in Time* was merely a unique novel based on an unusual idea, and it's only in the light of later novels that we can look back and see it as the first of a series of similar books.[6]

In fact, a look at earlier time fantasies revels how very much recent writers do pay homage to them. It also shows how these earlier writers paid homage to each other, how Lucy M. Boston was influenced by Alison Uttley and how Phillipa Pearce was influenced by both. But surprisingly, the relationships of books by these writers are hardly a matter of re-invention, and certainly not subversive; there is influence, but little anxiety about it. Considered as a series in the chronological order of their writing, these early time fantasies are like the same picture seen in increasingly sharper focus. Each repeats the situation of the one before it in a way that makes that situation more obviously meaningful, so that one can look backwards and interpret the older books in terms of the meanings of the newer ones.

In *A Traveller in Time*, first published in 1939, a child comes alone to an old house and has contact with people who once lived there; and the solitary child and the place that survives time's passage come to be common features of most later time fantasies. So does Uttley's focus on the continuity of the house as the heart of the novel's meaning. The passage of time means that everything must change, so that everything must die; but the continuance of the house and of old ways of doing things within it means that time's passage does not matter, for despite it, things do continue in the same way.

In Lucy M. Boston's *The Children of Green Knowe* (1954),[7] similarly, the word "always" appears again and again in relation to a house and its inhabitants. The family faces "always come back" (p. 18). "There's always a boat called Linnet on the river" (p. 32). "Tolly felt as if he had lived here always instead of just one day" (p. 37). "There is always a St. Christopher by an old ford" (p. 49). "Everybody who works here is a son or nephew of someone who has always been here" (pp. 80–81). Yet throughout *The Children of Green Knowe*, there are signs of disruption: the youngest Boggis retains the family name only because his parents weren't married, Tolly's mother is dead, his father has remarried, his stepmother distorts his own old family name into "Toto." Greene Knowe represents custom and continuity just as Thackers did, but now those qualities stand more explicitly for the past as opposed to the present; they are receding into it, and the house stands less for the fact that things do continue than for the wish that they might.

While that seems to reverse what Uttley suggested, in fact it merely makes obvious an implication of time fantasy that Uttley did suggest: that if the past can still be entered by people in the present, then it is not yet over. That represents a triumph over death, over the destructiveness of transience, over the separation of people from each other, even over scientific knowledge based on what our senses tell us of reality. Almost all later time fantasists consider contact with the past a sort of wish-fulfillment, a transcendence of what actually is.

Because Tolly's contact with the past represents his getting what he wants and needs, but cannot find in the contemporary world outside Green Knowe, *The Children of Green Knowe* has a psychological dimension not explicitly explored in *A Traveller in Time*. Penelope came to Thackers to be cured of physical illness; Tolly's malady is loneliness and lack of love, caused by the disruptiveness of the passage of time, which has killed his mother, destroyed his home, and brought war and disruption. Both children are cured by their stay in an old house and their contact with the past; but the psychological cure is more explicitly symbolic than the physical one. It's not just fresh country air that makes Tolly better; it's his contact with enduring values directly antithetical to those aspects of the world outside Green Knowe that threaten to damage him.

Yet Penelope did gain psychological strength, even if Uttley never directly says so; in fact, *The Children of Green Knowe* reads like an interpretation of *A Traveller in Time*, different only in its more explicit statement of themes. There is a similar relationship between *Children of Green Knowe* and Phillipa Pearce's *Tom's Midnight Garden.*[8]

Both books are mostly about children playing. But Pearce makes the Victorian Hatty an equal partner in the modern Tom's play, quite unlike the mysterious presences of Jacobean children that flit around the edges of Tolly's consciousness; and she describes Tom and Hatty's play from some distance, so that it seems to have more thematic relevance to the novel as a whole than did the more mysteriously evoked playing of Tolly and the Jacobean children. The games Tom and Hatty play all involve freedom from the constrictions imposed on them by circumstances, by adults, by the very fact that they are children. Again and again, they use play to escape —Hatty to escape her hateful relatives in the past, Tom to escape his "cooped up" life in the present. They have secret places to escape to; they climb walls to see over the constricting boundaries of the garden; they free birds from the gooseberry nets; and Hatty wants to skate because "I feel as free as a bird—as I've never felt before" (p. 116).

Not surprisingly, the very fact that Tom and Hatty can play with each other means they have escaped the confines of reality that isolate them in different times. The young Hatty can have a *real* imaginary friend, the old Hatty who lives upstairs can dream of Tom in her past, and Tom can enter that older Hatty's dream and actually play with the younger Hatty, because they need to escape confines and because they get what they need. Looking back, we can see that both Penelope and Tolly also got what they needed, in contacts across time afforded them by activities that usually offer only imaginary experience; Penelope dreams her way into the past and Tolly plays his way there, even though neither Uttley nor Boston insists that that is the meaning of her book.

Pearce also balances the benefits of wish-fulfillment with a consideration of its dangers; she explores the negative as well as the positive implications of escape, of freedom, and of nostalgia for the past. While both Hatty and Tom view the garden as a place where they can escape from the constrictions of their actual circumstances, it contains danger for both— and paradoxically, not because it is free, but because it is confining. When Tom walks on the garden wall, he realizes that he "had known only the garden, and a very little beyond its limits; now, from his walltop, he saw what seemed to be the whole world" (p. 83). At first the garden "tempted" Tom (p. 15), and it tempts him into a solitary existence, a self-enclosure that ignores family responsibilities until almost the end. The presence of a man called Abel in this tempting place has biblical overtones. Abel thinks Tom is the snake in Hatty's paradise, and in a sense, he is; by escaping into her play with Tom, Hatty can ignore real life. Hatty says that if she's caught talking to him, "Aunt Grace will say it shows how unfit I am to go anywhere with other children, outside, in the village" (p. 54). Later, her cousin says, "Hatty is young for her age. . . . Perhaps it comes from her being by herself so much—playing alone—always in the garden. . . . She should see more of the world" (p. 95). As well as representing the way a child's world of play and fantasy is a necessary escape from the constrictions of reality, Pearce's garden also stands for the dangers of that escape—its distancing from other people, its preference for the security of the limited known, its refusal to face what must be faced "outside." As Hatty's aunt says, "she doesn't want to grow up; she wants only her garden" (p. 96).

But one must grow up; and both Hatty and Tom learn to move beyond the garden, and in doing so, to accept the inevitability of time's passage. The last part of this novel is not about the joy of being in the garden, but the necessity of getting out of it. Pearce makes the passage of time *within* the garden a key issue, so that Hatty grows beyond Tom and the garden is therefore no longer an attractive place for him. She balances nostalgia with a commitment to the present and the future; and in doing so she makes brilliant use of the main quality of time fantasy: that it is both fantasy and history, and for that reason can balance the desire for escape with the inevitability of what is.

In this way, too, she clarifies a theme only implied in both *A Traveller in Time* and *Children of Green Knowe*; for while neither Uttley nor Boston draw much attention to it, ugly things happened in the past as well as pleasant ones, in both those books: Mary Queen of Scots did not escape despite Penelope's wish that she could forewarn her, Penelope falls in love with a man who died hundreds of years before she was born, the topiary of Noah has been cursed, the children Tolly plays with died long ago in a plague.

Interpretations of the traditional sort I've just attempted—explorations of central patterns and meanings—would almost inevitably reveal important differences in three apparently similar, complex adult books. My explorations of these three undeniably complex children's books which share a basic story idea reveals that they have quite different plots and quite different tones but that their central cores are astonishingly alike. In other words, my attempt at interpretation reveals the opposite of what it should have—it shows how the theoretically superficial details that make these novels seem quite different are actually underpinned by the same themes and attitudes. And while we might expect similar themes in books with such clear generic connections with each other, we could hardly expect similar attitudes toward these themes; but interpretation of these books does in fact reveal influence without anxiety.

Upon interpretation, more recent time fantasies seem even more alike. Once Philippa Pearce made explicit the themes and attitudes only implied in earlier time fantasies, writers seem surprisingly content to restate those themes and retain those attitudes. I chose four fairly recent books to explore because, while their similarities were obvious, they did seem to have important differences from each other: Eleanor Cameron's *The Court of the Stone Children* replaces the old house of the tradition with a museum, and in Nancy Bond's *A String in the Harp*,[9] an entire district of Wales represents the past; and because Janet Lunn's *The Root Cellar*[10] is set in North America and Ruth Park's *Playing Beatie Bow* in Australia,[11] the circumstances of life in these books in both the past and present are quite different from those found in the English country houses of earlier books. These should be significant differences, ones that provide these books with the uniqueness we expect of good literature. But the more I explored these books, the more I found they had in common with each other—while, paradoxically, the more I confirmed my original impression that each is an excellent novel, and excellent exactly because its surface details *do* sustain a subtle central core of meaning, just as we expect good novels to. The curious thing, again, is that such different surface details seem to sustain such similar central cores. Before I consider the implications of that similarity, I'd like to show just how similar they are.

All four novels involve a child with family difficulties. Just as Tom's brother is sick in *Tom's Midnight Garden*, Nina's father is sick in *Court of the Stone Children*. In *The Root Cellar*, Rose's grandmother has just died, in *A String in the Harp*, the children's mother has died, and Abigail's parents in *Playing Beatie Bow* compound a painful separation by thinking of ending it and thus changing the status quo again. In all cases, the passage of time has meant that something has changed; and as a result, a child is conscious that things are not now as good as they once were. Almost all the children express the wish that things had not changed; all want back the security and the comfort they have lost. They want their own personal pasts back.

But as the novels begin, these children are all lonely. There are two reasons for the loneliness, one physical, the other psychological; both involve separations. The child feels that he or she does not belong in the physical place he now resides in; Nina prefers her old home in Silver Springs to San Francisco, where she must live in a place that is "not home, but where temporarily she had to come" (p. 25). Jen says that Wales "sure isn't like home" (p. 50), and her brother Peter resents the move from his old home in Amherst to Wales; forced to move to Canada, Rose longs for her old life in Paris and New York, and Abigail resents her current home because it was a gift from the father who broke up an earlier one in a "two-car garden suburb" (p. 6).

While Abigail can't help feeling proud that her father designed the building she now lives in, the others find their new home horrifying. For Nina, modern San Francisco is "ugly" and Rose "had never dreamed of any place uglier than this one" (p. 16). In the first pages of *String in the Harp*, words like "strange," "foreign," and "unfamiliar" occur again and again; the kitchen is "completely strange, totally unfamiliar" (p. 10), and "Jen couldn't help feeling foreign" (p. 53). In fact, and like Tom at the beginning of Pearce's novel, the children all feel exiled—deprived of the security and comforts of home, they hate where they now must live.

The exile is not just a physical fact. It symbolizes a movement away from the secure innocence of childhood, the development of greater consciousness of the world and its nasty habit of not always giving one what one wants. But since these novels have been written for children who are themselves likely to resent the world's refusal to be what we wish it to be, rather than for adults who have supposedly learned how to accept it, they all provide good reasons for their young protagonists' resentment. They all demand more sympathy for their main characters than they do impatience with their refusal to accept—and they all do so by making them feel psychological as well as physical exile.

Rose, deprived of parents in early childhood, has been orphaned again by the loss of her grandmother. While the other children still have at least one parent, the parents are involved in problems of their own. The father in *A String in the Harp* is too submerged in his own grief over his wife's death to cope with the children's grief, the parents in *Playing Beatie Bow* must sort out their own confusing relationship, Nina's parents must cope with his illness and their new poverty.

Consequently, these children all are right to feel isolated—exiled from affection. Rose "came to the conclusion when she was about eight that she didn't belong in the world" (p. 3). Nina's friend in the past, Domi, says, "I'm a little odd. Are you?" (p. 40). She is, for her love of old things isolates her from other children. Abigail is an "outsider" who feels "a hundred years older and wiser than the love-mad rabble in her class" (p. 4). In *A String in the Harp*, the children's loneliness is less an aspect of character than it has been imposed on them by their move to a strange land; but there, Peter, who used to be surrounded by friends, has become a lonely solitary.

Isolation is so central to these books that it involves characters beyond the main one. Beatie Bow is as feisty and difficult as Abigail. Nina meets both the "odd" Domi in the past and the "insufferable oddity" Gil in the present (p. 94). Rose first hates and then learns to admire the "frightening strangeness" (p. 22) of her aunt's family. In *A String in the Harp*, the children befriend the "shy" Gwilym, a solitary birdwatcher whose mother "wants him to spend time with kids his own age" (p. 34).

Furthermore, these novels contain many actual exiles in addition to psychological ones. In *A String in the Harp*, Gwilym's mother comes from elsewhere: "He doesn't quite belong, and she doesn't belong at all. Oh, she fits in, but she doesn't belong" (p. 49); and Mrs Rhys says, "I shall be a foreigner here no matter how many years I have!" (p. 137). In the past meanwhile, Peter relives episodes in the life of the harpist Taliesen in which he is exiled first from his own home, then from various other countries he adopts as home. In *Court of the Stone Children*, Auguste and Mamzelle have come to San Francisco from France; in *Playing Beatie Bow*, Abigail's father came from Norway, and in the past, the Bows and Talliskers have come to New South Wales from Great Britain. The family Rose encounters at Hawthorn Bay is almost as new to the island as she is; in the past, Will's family came to Canada from the United States, just as Rose does: "I guess what matters is where you belong. Me, I ain't always sure. I was born here but Ma comes from across the lake in the States" (p. 57).

In all these books, in fact, the central issue the main characters face is the one implied by their real or imagined exile: where do I belong? The words "belong" and "belonging" occur often in *The Root Cellar*, less often in the others; but in all the books, all the children finally learn that they belong where they are—Nina in San Francisco, Rose at Hawthorn Bay, Abigail with her mother and father, for as she says, "I have to go home, I don't belong here" (p. 107). Home is where you are now, not a place in the past that you feel nostalgia for. Even the children in *A String in the Harp* decide to extend their stay in Wales. What Becky says in that book is true for all of the exiles in all of these novels: "We've started to belong" (p. 356).

They can say that for two reasons. First, the events of the novel have brought an end to their isolation. They have found others who share their eccentricity and alienation from the norm, and in doing so, have learned their need for psychological belonging; Peter thinks how he has "learned that he was part of other people and they part of him and he was glad" (p. 365). All the children who have felt alienated from their parents learn to love them again; Rose, who never had parents, has found some good substitutes.

But in addition, the children have had some version of what they thought they wanted—a return to the past—and it has first intensified and then brought an end to their isolation. As it does for Tom in Pearce's novel, the intensification occurs because their fascination with the odd experiences they are having separates them from others; his sister notices that "Peter just seemed to be getting further away from them" (p. 180), and we are told of Rose that "She had been so engrossed in the strange events of her own life that she had missed everything going on in the Henry household" (p. 84). But, just as Tom's friendship helps Hatty, all do something in the past that helps the people who live there; and like Tom, all are helped in some significant way by those people. In the midst of exile comes the end of isolation.

Nina finds the clue that restores the reputation of Domi's's father— and while doing so, learns a socially acceptable way of dealing with her "museum feeling," gains the respect of new friends, and gets a summer job; she even finds a new apartment for her family, so that she no longer feels as imprisoned as she once did. Peter restores Taliesen's harp key, and his possession of the key brings an end to his grief and forces him to make contact with the other members of his family. Rose helps Susan find Will in an army hospital in Georgetown, and learns from that experience to value her new family in the present. As the Stranger of the Prophecy, Abigail saves young Gibbie from a fire in the past; and both her exile from home and the Talliskers' closeness that she observes while exiled teach her to value her own family in the present again.

In all these books, then, a physical impossibility—the meeting of different people across the barrier of time—represents an emotional possibility—the meeting of different people across the barrier of self. In fact, that point is made by all the books in some specific way. In a variation of Tom's meeting with the now aged Hatty at the end of *Tom's Midnight Garden*, Abigail in *Beatie Bow* meets and loves a man who looks like the boy she loved in the past, and who is actually the great grandson of the child whose life she saved in the past. In *A String in the Harp*, the children's father explicitly says, "I suppose the thing to remember is that if we're together then none of us has to be alone. Pretty heavy stuff!" (p. 154) A little less obviously, Cameron and Lunn both have large groups of once-isolated people sit down to a meal together.

These children come into contact with the past by means of a place that exists similarly in both past and present: the rooms of Domi's house, the Welsh landscape, the root cellar, the streets of Sydney. But whereas earlier books focused on the continuing sameness of houses like Thackers and Green Knowe, the settings of these more recent books have more in common with the once magnificent house Phillippa Pearce describes that is now divided into small flats. The place is quite different in the present than it was in the past—and that difference is as essential to the meaning of these books as it is in *Tom's Midnight Garden*.

While *Beatie Bow* takes place in both past and present in Sydney, there is no continuity of anything but the land under the buildings. In fact, Abigail quickly confirms her conviction that the past as it was is totally unlike the present as it is; but it is not what she thought it would be. The present distorts the past, as seen both in the absorption of Beatie's name into a game, and in the uncomprehending nostalgia represented by Abigail's wearing of an Edwardian dress and by her mother's shop, Magpies, which is filled with Victorian objects that distort the real circumstances of Victorian life. That uncomprehending nostalgia is like Abigail's treatment of her own past; she sees her early life when her parents were together incorrectly, through rose-colored glasses, and must learn to view them more accurately.

In *A String in the Harp*, a similar point is made by the counterpointing of Wales as it once was and Wales as it is now. As Abigail first felt nostalgia for the past, Peter first sees Taliesen's world as a green paradise; later visions give him a more balanced picture, in which Taliesen's feelings of pain and exile compare rather than contrast with his own. Meanwhile, modern Wales turns out to be less bleak and sterile than the children had first imagined it, so that the present takes on the qualities of the past as well as the past taking on the qualities of the present. At the beginning of the book, the strangeness of Wales contrasts with the familiarity of home; later, strangeness and familiarity balance each other, as Jen hears Christmas carols, "many of them unfamiliar but telling a familiar story" (p. 103), and as Peter thinks, "He and his father and Gwilym would always be foreigners . . . it didn't matter as much as he had once thought" (p. 246); for every human being is a foreigner to every other human being, and all must meet across a gulf.

In *Root Cellar*, Rose first feels she belongs in the past because the Edenic freshness of the past as she first sees it so contrasts with the disruption of her present life; "it all seemed brighter and more interesting than any place she had ever seen" (p. 47). But just as Peter must live through the desolation of Taliesen's life, Rose must live through the desolation of the American civil war; and a symbol of that desolation is the contrast of a tree-less Washington in the past with the "tree-lined streets" Rose remembers experiencing in modern Washington (p. 179). Like Peter and like Abigail, Rose's realization that the past was not just paradise causes her to realize that the present is not just hell, and allows her to conclude that she belongs in the place she first wished to escape from.

Nina too discovers that the idyllic beauty of Domi's house in the past did not prevent violence and pain, and that she can find a way of belonging in contemporary San Francisco despite its ugliness. But in *Court of the Stone Children*, a paradox common to all these novels becomes clear. These children all first yearn for the past because they think it better than the present, and then turn back to the present as they discover that life is equally pleasurable and painful in both; yet in turning back to the present, all acknowledge that the past *is* significantly different—that in fact, to remain there would be to be truly exiled. Cameron succinctly expresses that paradox by replacing the house found in older time fantasies with a museum.

A museum does not represent the past triumphing over time by continuing into the present, but rather, what the present makes of the past; the French Museum contains the rooms of Domi's house, but as she says herself, "this is a kind of strange, twisted dream of my home, the same and yet weirdly not the same" (p. 43). A house that remains the same in a changing world represents a potentially stultifying regard for something no longer alive—a turning away from the flux of time. But it is our consciousness of the flux of time that causes us to create museums, in which the past remains alive through contact with the present, so that both may affect each other. Thus Domi contacts Nina, not because she wants the present itself, but because she needs something the present has to offer the past—the distance of historical perspective. And for Nina, the museum does not represent the past itself so much as something that allows her to cope with the present; when she speaks of her "museum feeling" as "being freed of the moment" (p. 17), she does not mean nostalgic immersion in a different moment, but rather, a special sort of health-giving consciousness that signals a temporary escape from all moments—a sense that time is not real which signals the transcending of ordinary reality.

In fact, these novelists all insist that the past's value for us is in its being over—in its being different from the present—because they all want to focus on how past and present, foreign and familiar, may meet despite their differences; they are not permanently exiled from each other. So all the books begin with the horror of change and separation, and all find a way of seeing change and separation positively. The word "pattern" occurs throughout *A String in the Harp*; it signifies the order and unity created by the coming together of disparate things that are themselves disorderly and isolated—including past and present. A similar idea is expressed by the chaos and anarchy Abigail first perceives in both past and present; as the two come together, she discovers the order in both that she is first blind to. And in all these books, it is not the past that heals the present, but rather, contact between the different values of past and present that heals in both the past and present. Peter and Nina and Rose and Abigail help Taliesen and Domi and Will and the Bow family as much as they are helped into greater knowledge and self-acceptance by them. For Rose and for Abigail, moreover, it is modern assertiveness that allows them to act, while those who belong in the past express what is for them a socially acceptable passivity; similarly, Domi needs modern techniques of detecting forgeries in painting, and the existence of Gwilym's contemporary motor-bike is essential in Peter's task of restoring Taliesen's key.

In all these novels, as in *Tom's Midnight Garden*, the doorway between past and present closes after the two-sided healing, the balancing of present and past values, occurs; Nina loses contact with Domi, Abigail's piece of lace disintegrates, the root cellar washes away, and Peter returns the key to its rightful place. That healing has indeed occurred is signalled in all cases by the main characters conceding that they no longer require the contact.

But before that happens, all of these novels deal with the question most obviously raised by the magical coming together of past and present: it isn't logical or rational, so how could it have happened? In these books, characters who distrust the inexplicable are condemned as dangerously narrow—imprisoned in what is familiar and secure; as Dr. Rhys says in *A String in the Harp*, "People do not like not understanding, do you see, because as long as we understand, we feel we have control" (p. 196).

And the idea of control is central in these books. They all grow from their main characters' feeling that they lack control—that circumstances have control over them; and they all allow these characters to regain control by means of an inexplicable entry into another time, an event beyond reason—an event that ought to signify the opposite of control because it lets in the irrational. All are frightened by that. As Tom and Hatty are both distraught about each other's assumption that the other is a ghost, Nina is frightened "right to the gut of your being" when Domi's hand goes through hers; she feels "fear, or more nearly terror, and yet just as deeply a very powerful attraction" (p. 69). Peter feels the same way about his experiences with the key: "He was drawn to the key even as it frightened him" (p. 66); Jen, his sister, feels constantly frightened by it. Abigail's first response to entering the past is "both terror and desperation" (p. 32), and Rose's first response to seeing a room in the house as it once was is to make it tidy as it now is: "she felt that by making her own order there the room would be less likely to change itself into some other room" (p. 29). While all these children feel disorder in their lives in the present, they fear the massive disorder implied by their contact with the past; yet their eventual acceptance of the possibility that one can have contact with others over apparently insurmountable barriers is what heals them, for it tells them that it is possible to live happily without that control, by accepting what must be accepted and dealing with it. Paradoxically, acceptance of what is—the world one is stuck with and cannot control—comes from acceptance of what ought not to be possible: escape through movement across time. Once again, the greatest similarity of these books is their use of cross-temporal experience to signify the transcendence of psychological barriers and acceptance of the inevitable passage of time.

After commenting on the similarities of time fantasies in "The Eternal Moment," Cameron goes on to say, "But it is never alone the core of plot that is of foremost importance, but always tone, characterization, theme, style, evocation of place, and private vision that determine the difference in quality between one fantasy and another. . . . In this way there is no end to originality, to the ability of private vision to give us something new and treasurable" (p. 164). And that ought to be true; when I first contemplated this essay, I planned to show how these novels are different despite their apparent similarities, and I fully expected that interpretation would show me "something new and treasurable" in each of them.

I discovered just the opposite. As I analysed them, these novels began to seem more and more alike, not more and more different from each other. They all balance the same sets of opposites: home and exile, escape and security, the familiar and the foreign, the strange and the comfortable, fear and acceptance, isolation and togetherness, the disorderly and the patterned. All reach similar conclusions about these things, and do so by similar means; and while their settings are different, these different places come to mean much the same thing to the characters. My acts of interpretation seemed only to deprive these novels of their personality, and make the "personal" visions at their core seem astonishingly alike.

But the word "vision" can have two different meanings: not only what one thinks life is all about, but also, how one sees it. Any two people will see the same thing differently enough to make their description of it different; as I showed earlier, different degrees of explicitness make the atmospheres of earlier time fantasies seem different from each other. And of course, there are differences of tone and style in these more recent books also, so that Eleanor Cameron's presentation by similar means of a similar vision is quite different from Philippa Pearce's or Nancy Bond's or Janet Lunn's or Ruth Park's.

In fact, the Victorian Sydney that Park evokes in *Playing Beatie Bow* is distinctly crude and horrifying, and Cameron's focus on clear bright colors, particularly gold and green, and on damp, ferny places, gives *Court of the Stone Children* a feel quite unlike Bond's travelogue-like descriptions of Wales or Lunn's stark, understated descriptions of the horrors of war. *A String in the Harp* and *The Root Cellar* are more problematic, for they both have that clear, straightforward, undetailed prose that we find in *Tom's Midnight Garden*, indeed in much children's fiction; yet there is still something distinct in the atmosphere each of these writers create. In fact, there is something distinct about the atmosphere of each of these books.

I could, I suppose, be content with simply realizing that; but I would like to *understand* it. Unfortunately, I know no means of understanding it but exploring it by means of conventional interpretation—by trying to relate the details that create atmosphere to a central core of meanings; and doing that makes these differences of tone and atmosphere seem less striking than they first seem to be—just as the differences in earlier fantasies come to seem less striking than their shared attitudes. Indeed, the mere fact that they do share those patterns and attitudes implies an impeccably logical conclusion: the distinctness in the tone and style of these books really doesn't matter at all, as it would in a consideration of adult novels. It doesn't matter simply because exploration of the apparently unique surface details that create tone and atmosphere only reveals how they actually point, not to private visions, but to central cores so similar to each other that they transcend the personal. These books are, in fact, more noticably similar to each other than they are different; they lack any significant uniqueness.

That is impeccably logical. But it cannot possibly be right. Any perceptive reader must acknowledge that differences in tone and style do in fact make these books significantly unlike each other, even if the differences are not ones that traditional interpretation can uncover. As I suggested of earlier time fantasies, these novels challenge our most basic conviction about both style and interpretation—that distinctive details are worth interpreting because they do point to a distinct personal vision.

Furthermore, it may well be their shared central core that makes these quite complex time fantasies quite recognizable as children's books, even though we usually expect children's books to be simple. And if that's true, then the problems interpretation of them creates may well apply to the interpretation of children's fiction as a whole.

As I worked my way through interpretations of these books, I began to realize how very much of what I was discovering can be found in numerous other children's books also. Children's literature frequently combines fantasy with history, escape with necessity, wish-fulfillment with acceptance of what is—perhaps because our desires to entertain children conflict with our desires to educate them. Our attempts to entertain make much children's literature wish-fulfillment, escape from what is into what one imagines one wants; but our attempts to teach children truth turn that around and make much children's literature an escape from what one imagines one wants into what actually is. Consequently, time fantasy as Pearce left it and current writers practice it, a combination of what one wants and what is, sums up some central concerns of children's fiction in a particularly concentrated form.

Those concerns are thematic matters, ideas about and attitudes toward what matters in life. If children's fiction is indeed significantly different from other kinds of fiction (and it obviously is), then the main distinguishing factor may turn out to be, not necessarily the simplicity of style that children's fiction shares with all popular writing, not even the shared set of archetypal plots and characters that children's fiction shares with most fantasy; it may be a fascination with the same basic sets of opposite ideas, and a propensity for bringing them into balance, so that both can be included in a vision of what life is. Even books as complex as *A String in the Harp* or *Beatie Bow* may be identified as children's fiction because of their concentration on the same themes in much the same way; and so may many complex children's books that are not time fantasies: to name just a few, *Charlotte's Web*, *Treasure Island*, and *Arilla Sun Down*, all in some way combine what one wishes for with what one must accept, all deal with freedom and constriction, home and exile, escape and acceptance, and all create balances between these extremes.

Perhaps that's not surprising; those themes are central issues in our conceptions of childhood and of the process of maturing, and children's fiction is more than anything else fiction for children and about childhood. Furthermore, the lack of anxiety in the way children's writers accept influence and pay homage to their forebears may imply a conservatism that nicely explains their constant dwelling upon themes of acceptance. Nevertheless, the possibility that children's fiction may be defined by a specific group of thematic concerns and a specific way of treating them would certainly explain why interpretation of children's books so often seems pointless. Since interpretation as we usually practice it is designed to reveal a book's uniqueness by uncovering its central core of ideas and attitudes, it can do nothing but reveal an apparent lack of uniqueness in the many children's novels that share a central core. Because it can only show that a children's novel is indeed a children's novel, it cannot tell us what we still want to know, and what it does often seem to tell us of adult books: how unique books are unique.

Consequently, my discovery that traditional interpretation could not explain how these books are different from each other does not so much deny their value as literature as it challenges our usual assumptions about interpretation. If interpretation of these books does not give us any insight into what makes them unique, then perhaps the information that interpretation of more "complex" novels provides is equally misleading. Perhaps the apparently unique themes and patterns we find in those more complex novels do not adequately explain their uniqueness either; perhaps we must search for other means of interpretation.

We must certainly do so if we wish to understand excellence in children's fiction, for traditional interpretation of children's novels can do little more than uncover the expected and the obvious. Until we develop a new approach, we will not understand how a children's novel can in fact be unique even though its characters, its story, its "simple" language, and even its central core of patterns and ideas are not.

Notes

1 Lois R. Kuznets, "Family as Formula: Cawelti's Formulaic Theory and Streatfeild's 'Shoe' Books," *ChLA Quarterly*, 9 (Winter 1984–85), 148. Kuznets refers to *Adventure, Mystery, and Romance* by John Cawelti (Chicago: University of Chicago Press, 1976).
2 Susan Sontag, *Against Interpretation* (Delta) (New York: Dell, 1966), p. 10.
3 The two time fantasies by Cameron are *The Court of the Stone Children* (New York: Dutton, 1973) and *Beyond Silence* (New York: Dutton, 1980). All further references to these novels are to these Dutton editions. *The Green and Burning Tree: On the Writing and Enjoyment of Children's Books* was published by Little Brown (Boston, 1969).
4 Eleanor Cameron, "The Eternal Moment," *ChLA Quarterly*, 9 (Winter 1984–85), 164.
5 The phrase is from the title of Bloom's book *The Anxiety of Influence* (New York: Oxford University Press, 1973).
6 Alison Uttley, *A Traveller in Time* (London: Faber and Faber, 1939). All further references to this novel are to this edition.
7 L. M. Boston, *The Children of Green Knowe* (New York: Harcourt Brace, 1954). All further references to this novel are to this edition.
8 Phillipa Pearce, *Tom's Midnight Garden* (London: Oxford University Press, 1958; 1970). All further references to this novel are to this edition.
9 Nancy Bond, *A String in the Harp* (New York: Atheneum, 1976). All further references to this novel are to this edition.
10 Janet Lunn, *The Root Cellar* (Toronto: Lester & Orpen Denys, 1981). All further references to this novel are to this edition.
11 Ruth Park, *Playing Beatie Bow* (Harmondsworth, England: Kestrel, 1980). All further references to this novel are to this edition.

8

AN IMPORTANT SYSTEM
OF ITS OWN

Defining children's literature

Ruth B. Bottigheimer

Source: *Princeton University Library Chronicle* 59(2) (1998): 191–210.

Children's literature is "an important system of its own," in the words of a distinguished contemporary scholar. And yet its historians and critics are still in the process of defining the field as well as the methods proper to its study. They wonder, for example, about "childist" or "adultist" perspectives.[1] There is no consensus about which discipline's (or disciplines') analytic approaches to use, because those of literary criticism, child psychology, education, ethics, and social history are each appropriate at various times. In this respect children's literature resembles other disciplines in the humanities whose boundaries and critical tools have changed dramatically within the last fifteen years.

Children's literature has also been marked by an underlying but rarely articulated uncertainty about what actually constitutes the subject. Is it belletristic *literature* for children or *books* for children? Does it, and should it, treat *intended* child readers or *actual* child readers? Is the study of children's literature about the problematics of *writing for* children or about the mechanics, aesthetics, or psychology of *reading by* children? Each of these approaches overlaps neighboring ones, each is independently legitimate, and each generates assumptions and conclusions that potentially undermine or actually contradict basic premises within others.

In my view the distinguishing element of children's literature is its normative nature. Within this framework it is possible to reconcile external historical and social differences as well as internal aesthetic and structural contradictions. To justify this position, I would like to explore past and present children's literature and to outline the many ways in which scholars and collectors have viewed and continue to view children's books.

Discrete areas of study within "children's literature"—literature, books, children, reading, and writing—require different theoretical and historical approaches, but at the same time they also require and produce fundamentally separate inquiries peculiar to themselves. The approaches to children's literature listed above ultimately express the disparate concerns of the disciplines of history, sociology, psychology, and pedagogy. Only rarely, however, do these individual approaches come to grips with children's literature in and of itself, that is, as an independent system. As the study of children's literature matures, however, the nature and structure of its inherent system is becoming increasingly apparent. In this article I will sketch out where the study of children's literature is today and how it got there.[2]

* * *

A cluster of entertaining secular writings specifically for children appeared suddenly in England in the 1740s: Thomas Boreman's *History of Cajanus, the Swedish Giant* (1742), Mary Cooper's *The Child's New Play-Thing* (1743), and John Newbery's *A Little Pretty Pocket-Book* (1744). Newbery, philosophically an apostle of John Locke and personally a man of remarkable energy, broad perspective, and wide acquaintance, is generally credited with inaugurating English children's literature, because his press initiated a sustained production of clearly identifiable children's books. His were light and amusing fictions that meant to delight as they instructed. Newbery probably wrote his first children's book, *A Little Pretty Pocket-Book*, himself, although for many of his later books he hired outside authors. His son-in-law, the poet Christopher Smart, composed children's lyrics for him; Oliver Goldsmith is widely believed to have written *Giles Gingerbread*; and there is evidence that even Samuel Johnson contributed anonymously to Newbery's broader oeuvre.[3]

A large bibliography has grown up around Newbery and his press, the most recent of which is John Rowe Townsend's *John Newbery and His Books: Trade and Plumb-Cake For Ever, Huzza!* (1994). But early collectors of Newbery's and other publishers' eighteenth-century children's books have faced a hard task. Children, archetypal intensive readers, often quite literally read their books to pieces, with the not surprising result that first editions became exceedingly rare and even more rarely survived in good condition. Title pages were frequently lost, and, as I have learned through my work with children's Bibles, it was, and is, often impossible to ascertain basic bibliographic information about many books, despite the existence of that marvelous research tool, the *English Short Title Catalogue*. Even England's depository libraries—the British Library, the Bodleian, and the Cambridge University Library—have occasionally been casual about keeping records of their children's books, some of which have been unaccounted for for more than a century.[4] To date, no compilation of

English and American books for children is as broad-ranging and detailed as those in the chef-d'oeuvre of German children's literature, *Handbuch zur Kinder und Jugendliteratur*.[5]

Difficulties, however, only intensify collectors' avid pursuit and devoted chronicling, and it was from possessors and collectors of children's literature such as Harvey Darton, A. S. W. Rosenbach, and D'Alté Welch that the earliest appreciations and histories of children's books came.[6] Prizing small size and celebrating rarity and beauty, their loving descriptions have laid, and continue to lay, a foundation for the still incomplete project of a comprehensive bibliography of children's books in English.

Books published before the 1740s pose additional problems, because classifying them as children's or adults' is often difficult. After all, not all publishers addressed their books unambiguously to readers like "Little Master Tommy and Pretty Miss Polly," as did Newbery. In questionable cases, book design can sometimes be analyzed to identify children's books. For instance, eighteenth-century children's books use white space to emphasize text to a far greater extent than do books for adults, as is evident from two children's Bibles in Princeton's Cotsen Children's Library, *The History of Genesis* and *A Compendious History of the Old and New Testament*.[7] This aspect of book design also confirms the fact that the first buyers of early children's books were either wealthy or distinctly well off: wasting paper by using it as white space to set off text signaled luxury, for paper was one of a printer's principal expenses in the eighteenth century.

* * *

In publishing *Some Thoughts Concerning Education* in 1693, John Locke was expressing plainly many ideas already in circulation among his English and European contemporaries. Yet he was so effective in discussing educating the young in terms of religion, food, travel, speech, and learning to read that his name entered children's book prefaces, and his ideas permeated their contents. Locke advised against "promiscuous reading" of the Holy Bible, while others among England's educators condemned the bawdy bloody chapbooks that were available to children in their day.[8] Early children's authors castigated the same writings: "Let not your Children read these vain Books, prophane Ballads, and filthy Songs. . . . Throw away all fond and amorous Romances, and fabulous Histories of Giants, the bombast Atchievements of Knight Errantry, for these fill them with wanton Thoughts, and nasty and obscene Discourse," and offered their own works—refined, uplifting, and educational—as remedial replacements for those books' "false Notions and irregular Conceits."[9] The mere appearance of a new literature for children, in England and all over Europe, did not, however, mean that all children switched their reading allegiance. On the contrary, there is much evidence that despite Locke's and others' advice, chapbooks'

sensational stories continued to be published and read alongside, and sometimes instead of, improved (and improving) children's literature.

In the late 1800s, historians who believed that great men steered the
course of history provided a new cue for European and American educators. Many of them concluded positivistically that literary masterpieces
proceed from the sum total of an author's own literary experience. What
better model for children's reading, then, than the reported childhood reading of literary worthies themselves? And so, in Germany, for example, the
youthful reading material of writers like Johann Wolfgang von Goethe
(1749–1832) was prescribed for children growing up more than a century
after Goethe's own childhood, in an effort to elevate children's reading by
urging it towards "high" cultural values.[10]

A low-versus-high distinction in children's literature has until recently
been fundamental to its history. On one side stand crude chapbooks, blood-
and-thunder novels, and slick formula fiction, books eagerly devoured by
many children. On the other rises a Golden-Age literature for children,
together with its progenitors and its progeny. "Low" and "high" have also
informed criticism, particularly in the nineteenth century, when critics and
educators alike defined children's literature as a body of writing that
manifested fine style and praiseworthy ethics found in contemporaneous
"high" literature for adults. And when mainstream literary scholars began
to take children's literature seriously in the late twentieth century, they
too examined it with the same critical tools that they had developed for
adult reading.[11]

In the 1960s and 1970s, new definitions of and critical tools for analyzing children's literature emerged from the German schools of children's
literature in Cologne and Frankfurt, radically redefining children's literature as a set of writings that its authors had *intended* for children, vastly
expanding the kinds and numbers of books the field included. Unlike their
predecessors, who had viewed historical children's literature narrowly as
a fictional form that took shape in the mid-eighteenth century, these
schools understood it as a corpus of writing intended for children that
extended hundreds—and, if we accept the evidence of what appears to be a
Sumerian schoolbook, even thousands—of years into the past.[12] To the
traditional fictions, German scholars' reformulated corpus of "children's
literature" added medieval and early modern instructional books (both
secular and religious), miscellanies and periodicals (beginning in the eighteenth century), comic books (in the twentieth century), and modern
media-related spinoffs.

Equating intentional production with children's literature, however,
entailed further problems of definition, because intention can fall far short
of realization. For instance, in the history of children's (and other) literature, many books have been published at their authors' own expense in
small print runs that reached a similarly small number of children. If such

books failed, that is, were *not* read, then the very fact that they had *not* been used and had remained in good condition meant that they were likely to be added to library collections. The paradoxical result? Precisely these *un*-read books would be preserved, their presence on library shelves misleadingly suggesting a currency that, in fact, they had not enjoyed during their circulating lifetime. Such books tell us about the concerns of the adults who wrote them, but little about the children who did or did not read them.

Literary style itself can be analyzed to identify the reader an author addresses. From the time that literary theorist Wolfgang Iser's *Implied Reader* (1974) appeared in English, anglophone children's literature critics have used his concept to "establish the author's relationship with the (child) reader implied in the story to see how he creates that relationship."[13] If a text was intended for children rather than for adults, or for a mixed audience of literate children and simple adults, then both content and style should betray the presence, and identity, of those readers, as implied by the author.

Insights from modern developmental psychology have also contributed to efforts to define readerships, as studies of children's literature suggest that a book's psychological and aesthetic success requires matching its text to the psychological and intellectual level(s) of the intended child readers. That, in turn, implies that the kinds of plots typical of children's books —for example, youthful difficulties followed by adolescent or adult resolution—are reused one century after another, because they parallel regularly occurring steps in children's social, psychological, and intellectual maturation processes.[14]

Vocabulary, too, can be utilized to determine whether an author intended a book for adult or child readers. In "The Reader in the Book," Aidan Chambers noted that English children's literature was characterized by a high incidence of Anglo-Saxon rather than Latin-based vocabulary, tellings from a child's point of view, identifiable referential gaps that imply immediate childhood experience, and authorial alliances forged with child readers for the express purpose of guiding those readers "towards the meanings [the authors] wish to negotiate."[15] Chambers's indicators work well for confirming contemporary authors' intents, but less well for identifying historical children's books, for whose intended readers authors often provided sexually sophisticated plots (like Potiphar's wife attempting to seduce Joseph), explicit vocabulary (blood and gore in eighteenth-century histories of "Tom Thumb"), and mature thematic concerns (early death and the torments of Hell) that are fundamentally alien to contemporary views of child-oriented reading material.[16]

The books described in the preceding paragraphs are all characterized by ambiguity, as far as their intended readers are concerned. This is particularly true of religious books by earnest educators for whom heavenly and earthly agenda were equally insistent in the seventeenth and eighteenth centuries.[17] Their titles often included the word "children," but it frequently had a dual referent: those who were young in age as well as those who were young in God, i.e., newly awakened to religion. Secular instructional books, in contrast, are nearly always free of ambiguity as far as their readers are concerned, and they include the most familiar kinds of early books published for children: universal histories (in Latin or in the vernacular), geographies, books of manners (separate ones for girls and for boys), Comenius's bi- or multilingual depictions of the world's treasury of objects, and Aesopic fables with their worldly observations (mainly for boys) all appeared in print form between the fifteenth and eighteenth centuries.

It was only when amusement began to temper instruction that children's literature, as we moderns understand it, emerged. New literary forms, such as the serial miscellany, soon joined it. Newbery's *Lilliputian Magazine* (1752, with subsequent reprints) was the first, and produced a modest three issues. Madame Leprince de Beaumont's *Magasin*, begun in 1756, was enormously successful and ran to scores of reprintings in French and in translations and had nearly as many imitators.[18]

* * *

Redefining children's literature as writings intended for a child readership dramatically extended the bounds of children's literature. At the same time the category of intentional production for child readers established parameters that led critics to search out, and to examine, readers themselves.[19]

One important limit on readership in eighteenth-century children's books was social class. For eighteenth-century authors like Newbery, virtue led to literacy (as in *The History of Little Goody Two-Shoes*), and then to prosperity, and he, like his contemporaries, recognized that money conferred advantage. Class per se was rarely acknowledged overtly; more often than not it remained an implicit category. Nonetheless, plots in most books for children were visibly class-related: childish disobedience and youthful insubordination, it was alleged in book after book, led to a fall from moral grace (lying, gambling, or stealing) and thence to a fall from social grace (class-specific poverty), which ultimately delivered young miscreants to an early death (either from illness or the hangman's rope).[20]

As literacy expanded in the nineteenth century among both old and young, authors and publishers defined readerships more closely. Age parameters, supposedly natural indicators of the ability to read and to comprehend, were defined in the eighteenth century, refined (e.g., for ages 2–4, 5–7, 8–10, and 12 and up) and set in place by educators in the nineteenth, and have survived through the twentieth.[21] Title pages often name the explicitly intended readers: some were deaf, some were "thinking youths," some were "country children." But more often than not, readers' natures —rational before 1850, Romantic afterward, at least in America—formed an integral part of the implied reader's identity.[22]

Increasingly, studies of the books children read have focused on where and how they were read.[23] In so doing, they have attempted characterizations of contemporaneous child readers, whom they have begun to incorporate into the titles of their studies: *English Children and Their Magazines* (1988), *Children and Their Books* (1989), and *Behold the Child* (1994), a trend that developed first in Germany, continued in America, and is now beginning to emerge in France.[24]

One of the earliest forms of narrative writing for literate and preliterate children grew from the Bible and appeared as Bible "histories." Religious in origin and social in intent, children's Bibles did not adhere strictly to their canonical source. Instead, their stories changed so greatly over time that the changes themselves make it possible to chart evolving attitudes towards and about Bible history readers as dramatically as secular children's fictions do. Although the historical readers of Bible story texts were Catholic, Jewish, and Protestant, their Catholicism was nationally inflected, their Jewishness temporally defined, and their Protestantism denominationally distinct, with Puritan-tinged, Anglican, Lutheran, Reformed, and Mormon texts easily distinguishable from one another.

The language and methods appropriate to investigating class, confession, and change over time in children's literature would at first glance appear to be solely those of literary criticism, and to center on and to grow out of an exploration of the editorial practices and rhetorical devices used to craft texts for the young. Yet each literary exploration is affiliated with neighboring disciplines, such as the history of children and childhood, or the history of education and general social history, or even a historical-linguistic study of age and class-related language development. Considered in this light, the study of children's literature as intentional production lends itself easily to studies of child readers that cross disciplinary boundaries and embed literary readings in neighboring disciplines. Historical, pedagogical, philosophical, and even sociopolitical documents are properly introduced into discussions of historical children's literature. For example, Martin Luther's pedagogical writings illuminate the content of his "children's Bible," the *Passionalbüchlein* of 1529, as surely as Isaac Watts's "Discourse on the Education of Children and Youth" supplies some of the foundation of his eighteenth-century moral literature. Similarly, eighteenth- and nineteenth-century child-labor statistics illuminate Mary Martha Sherwood's morally couched threats of expulsion from cozy bourgeois comfort in *The Fairchild Family* (1818), an expulsion that would precipitate little miscreants into starveling street life or worse.

* * *

Reception-oriented critics focus on children's responses to their reading.[25] This simple statement cloaks a different attitude to reception from that employed by critics of canonical adult literature. In the case of children's literature, evidence of reception often depends on visible child use, that is, rips and tears, picture and text defacements, marginal ABC practice, adolescent comments, and ownership notations and markings. Together and separately these identify the presence of one or more child readers who left traces of their readings on the pages of individual books.

Reception-oriented critics' skepticism about whether a significant number of children actually read many of the (often improving) books *intended* for their use has led some of them to subtract titles from the theoretical *oeuvre* of children's literature. But their insistence on *use* as the principal determinant for including titles among listings of historical children's literature has also led them to add titles from the adult canon if it can be shown that a particular book was once read by someone known to have been a child at the time, and that proof has been relatively simple to find, since intellectually curious children routinely scavenge their parents' libraries to feed their appetite as soon as they are able to read fluently. But the books children found on their parents' shelves were often held to be damaging. Referring probably to Boccaccio's stories, which were then being published in England, Roger Ascham (1515–1568), tutor to the young Princess Elizabeth, warned against "your mery books of Italie of late translated out of Italian into English, sold in every shop in London, commended by honest titles the soner to corrupt honest maners."[26] There is copious evidence that boys in particular continued to devour story collections and chapbooks for the next three hundred years, and as a result Ascham's sentiments were repeated by every teacher who expressed thoughts on the subject of children's reading from then until the nineteenth century.

Chapbooks included tales of King Arthur's court; histories of Guy of Warwick, Fortunatus, Valentine and Orson, the destruction of Troy, and Parismus, Prince of Bohemia; and accounts of Jack the Giant Killer's bloody adventures and Tom Thumb's romps. Such stories smack of Camelot and fairy tales and sound innocent enough, and yet they were as coarse and violent and as likely to "corrupt honest maners" as anything against which Ascham had inveighed.

Followed to its logical conclusion, reception-oriented critics' definition of children's literature as based on use (children's reading) rather than intention (adults' writing for them) aligns children's literature neatly (and solely) with child literacy. This, however, represents an extreme position that no reception-oriented critic has yet adopted. However, it is true that the chapbooks that were available to literate and semiliterate adults of the sixteenth, seventeenth, and eighteenth centuries, were what literate boys —and probably some girls—were also reading. But, since the later 1700s, palpable differences in plot, style, and design have distinguished books written for children from those for adults.

If use is to define the corpus of children's literature, then continuing to document actual reading and response beyond signs of use in books themselves remains important. Biographical evidence is spotty, but fascinating. By his own account William Godwin was ready to die a child martyr after reading James Janeway's *Token for Children*.[27] Statistical studies, such as story element preferences among girls and boys or library borrowing patterns organized by age, cast a broader net and identify the specific books or kinds of books that many children actually read.[28]

Book ownership is a good, though not foolproof index of child reading, while memories of childhood reading, such as Joseph Buckingham's of his *Robinson Crusoe, Goody Two-Shoes, Tom Thumb*, and "six or seven other similar books," offer a close approximation of historical reading experience.[29] Numerous memoirs affirm the importance of Robinsonades and Christoph von Schmid's sentimental books all over Europe as well as confirming the fact that children have always sneaked books from their parents' shelves.[30]

* * *

The theory of responsive reception assumes that children's literature produces a response among its readers, which in turn leads to a more general inquiry about the kinds of response individual books have been designed to elicit. Writers have historically hoped to persuade their readers to reproduce their books' pious thoughts, polite acts, and in the case of instructional manuals for apprentices, craftsmanlike handiwork; the promised rewards included an improvement in readers' chances of rising spiritually, socially, or financially. Now I would like to shift my focus from historical children's literature to issues central to contemporary writing for children.

Authors still mean to influence their readers, and critics still assume that they will, but in recent decades the mode has become intensely personal. Against a background of Freudian psychoanalysis that posits the preeminence of childhood experience in forming identity, children's literature has been seen as a source of psychological succour in dealing with the vicissitudes of youth; however, authors no longer promise a happy result, and many stories end badly.[31] And yet a doubt remains: does children's literature actually produce a response, and if so, what kind? Answers to these questions hinge on the extent to which children identify with characters in the books they read, and on researchers' sensitivity to cultural issues like race, class, and gender.

Herbert Kohl's title question, *Should We Burn Babar?* was not altogether rhetorical, because his essays on the power of stories persuasively document the existence of racism, classism, and sexism in children's literature. His sustained analysis of numerous versions of "The Story of Rosa Parks," for example, jarringly details racially blindered reformulations of Parks's act of resistance.[32] Kohl's concerns, like all reception-oriented approaches to the criticism and analysis of children's literature, are rooted in the act of reading. Reading in the modern world is preponderantly a solitary act, but reading in the past, as historians of that subject have shown, was often a social act. Consider the contexts in which group reading has historically taken place: in school (where teachers read aloud, with changing intonations, dramatic pauses, or dull drones, each of which conferred additional layers of meaning on a set text); in church (where Bible stories or moral tales came alive or stopped dead according to a pastor's, priest's, or lay teacher's interpretive skill); at home (where in the eighteenth century an English family's Bible included prepared remarks to be inserted as the father read aloud to his assembled family); among apprentices (whose lewd reception of bawdy stories intensified their appreciation of sexual content); among workers' reading groups (whose earnest desire for knowledge led them to pool their resources to subscribe jointly to newspapers or to rent or buy useful books); and in social groups (like Biedermeier coffee klatsches where fairy tales and other stories were read aloud among tenderly reared young women and men).

Each of these reading occasions provided a venue, a company of fellow readers, a set of implicitly or explicitly expressed interpretations, and a consequent sense of story as an implied commentary on, a guide to coping with, or a critique of working conditions, practical religion, literary tropes, family life, or, in the shorthand of contemporary criticism, race, class, and gender. Only some of these reading occasions included child readers, but those that did—school, church, and family—amply demonstrate the extent to which individual presentation and group dynamics had the potential to reconfigure story content and to condition its meaning well before individual reception came into play.

Kohl's outrage at racism (in the Rosa Parks stories) and colonialist attitudes (in the Babar tales) suggests that the contemporary prevalence of unmediated reading, even within the wide range of psychological states and social conditions in which any given child reader might approach a text, ought to urge authors to exert greater care in their writing. Another word for this "care" is self-censorship, an act that has long characterized the writing of children's books. With a few modern exceptions, children's literature authors have generally presented, and continue to present, the world as—in their view—it should be, if not in the acts of individual characters, then in the underlying social framework that sustains those characters. That unquestioning presentation of social and family structure is of great historical and critical importance. It embeds contemporary children's literature—with its fantasy, its chocolate wars, and its sexual explorations—in a centuries-long tradition of moralizing ardor on the one hand and magic escapism on the other, which ultimately rests on an acceptance of prevailing social orders shared by authors and readers.

* * *

Successful writers of children's literature evoke the world of childhood in memorable prose that captures moments of enchantment or pathos and avoids stereotyped images. And above all, good children's book writing shouldn't try to explain the attitudes and problems of childhood. These are the introductory thoughts of a meditation on children's literature published in 1974.[33] The latter statement hints at an incipient theory of an unbridgeable chasm, an irreconcilable difference, a perpetual mismatch between adult authors of children's literature and their child readers. Children are children, and adults are adults, and ne'er the twain shall meet. Some variant of this statement underlies the recently expressed conviction that "children's literature" is an impossible oxymoron, precisely because its socially independent and psychologically formed adult authors cannot possibly, so the theory goes, communicate with socially dependent and psychologically unformed child readers. To Jacqueline Rose, for instance, "[C]hildren's fiction is impossible . . . [because] it hangs on . . . the impossible relation between adult and child. Children's fiction is clearly about that relation, but it has the remarkable characteristic of being about something which it hardly ever talks of." For Karin Lesnik-Oberstein, "the child" whose responses critics discuss remains a construction, as do critics' notions of any single child or group of children for whom works of children's literature are written.[34] Her legitimate objection is one that could be raised in many areas of the humanities, because scholars, of necessity, construct and propound entities and identities as a matter of course in their efforts to understand what is essentially unknowable.

The ever-present gaps in human knowing that both Rose and Lesnik-Oberstein explore have led Rose to posit an irremediable separation between adult author and child reader and to suggest a two-world literary system. From a broader perspective, Rose's and Lesnik-Oberstein's studies form part of a deepening awareness of the social and psychological peculiarities of adult authors of children's literature like John Ruskin and Lewis Carroll, as well as a more refined understanding of contemporary and historical child readers.[35]

Rose's sweeping dismissal of the possible existence of children's literature has not only theoretical but also practical implications. Her conclusions —disquieting but hard to disregard—suggest that successful communication can only take place between an author and reader when the author is similar to the reader. Taken to its absurd but logical conclusion, that means boy (not man) authors for boys, girls for girls, black authors for black readers, and Plains Indian authors for Plains Indian readers. Such a conclusion prompts reactions ranging from alarmed consternation to mocking rejection, but the problem will not go away simply because it can be dismissed on logical grounds.

Insensitivity and ignorance on issues of religion, race, gender, and class have long existed, and no doubt will continue to do so. Racism distorted numerous portrayals of Rosa Parks and her community, obscuring or erasing her own commitment and that of her community to resisting racist practices. Classism evident in children's Bibles between 1750 and 1850 reveals the extent to which class interests superseded religious ones in those years. Gender inequities are equally demonstrable when men and women write about the same subjects. Rare was the male author of children's Bibles who portrayed Jael's courage in the Old Testament story of her murder of Sisera. Nor would it have been very likely for a man to have come up with the plot of Frances Hodgson Burnett's novel *A Lady of Quality* (1899), with its heroine growing into an independent and responsible womanhood from an unfettered and positively portrayed quasiboyhood. Reading, too, is gendered, because girls and boys perceive texts and contexts increasingly differently as they grow older.[36]

Rose's thesis about the impossibility of children's literature resurrects central questions about its nature and purpose. Its purpose, unchanged since Locke's *Thoughts Concerning Education*, is still preparatory, an intention that distinguishes it fundamentally from literature for adults. Rose's objection regarding authors' inadequacy in writing for children, however, grows out of modern sensibilities about individual and group identity and is directly relevant to contemporary concerns that literature reaffirm its young readers socially and psychologically. Her stance aligns itself with requirements that writers parallel and reproduce readers' identities, and seems to understand the writing and reading of children's literature as processes for confirming personal and group identity.

Identity confirmation in literature for children is not peculiar to 1990s political correctness. Newbery's books confirmed his middle- and upper-class readers' identities in class terms. Conduct books did the same for gender. Devotional and instructional books did so for religion. Race, physical condition, and sexual orientation are simply a few new categories added in the modern world. In the past, religion (usually Protestant, occasionally Catholic), race (white), gender (primarily male), and class (middle, upper-middle, and upper) were so broadly accepted as defining parameters in children's literature that it was easy for readers as well as critics to overlook their presence, at the same time that, paradoxically, children's literature was believed to encourage expanding its readers' imaginative horizons.

There has always existed a tension between aesthetic autonomy and the need to provide workable models for a child's future life. This tension is, in my view, the defining point that separates children's literature from the adult literary enterprise. It is a dynamic and never fully resolvable literary

125

problem, for as one generation defines the nature of children's identity, childhood's proper occupations, and children's reading, its children have already entered a society altered by those decisions. Childhood, its expectations, and its literature are as historically rooted and expressed as individual children themselves.

Just as all children exist in history, so do all authors of children's literature. It makes a difference that children's literature is for historical children. That difference offers the principal reason why the child, the child's world, and the adult world for which children are being prepared are as central to the system of children's literature as its aesthetics, its authors, and their intentions.[37]

Notes

1 Peter Hunt, *An Introduction to Children's Literature* (Oxford: Oxford University Press, 1994), p. 7. On defining methods, see my review essays, "Recent Scholarship in Children's Literature, 1980 to the Present [i.e., 1990]," *Eighteenth-Century Life* 17, n.s. 3 (November 1993): 89–103, which also includes discussion of German children's literary studies, and "Zur englischsprachigen Kinder- und Jugendliteraturforschung der 90er Jahre—ein aktueller Überblick" (forthcoming). In this essay I will discuss the texts of American and English children's literature and its criticism, but not its illustrations. For a discussion of the terms "childist" and "adultist," see Hunt's "Childist Criticism: The Subculture of the Child, the Book, and the Critic," *Signal* 43 (1984): 42–59.

2 *Compar(a)ison*, an international journal of comparative literature, devoted its II/1995 issue to scholarship in children's literature from the United States, several European countries, Nigeria, and Israel. See Bettina Kümmerling-Meibauer, ed., *Current Trends in Comparative Literature Research* (Bern: Peter Lang, 1995).

3 Harvey Darton wrote in 1924 that Goldsmith "very likely did write 'Goody Two-Shoes,'" an assessment that subsequent scholars have generally accepted. See F. J. Harvey Darton, "A Note on Old Children's Books," typescript (Teachers College Library, Columbia University), p. 6; John D. C. Buck, "John Newbery and Literary Merchandising, 1744–1767" (Ph.D. diss., University of California, 1972), pp. 289–291; M. F. Thwaite, "Introduction," *John Newbery, A Little Pretty Pocket-Book* (London: Oxford University Press, 1966).

4 The British Library's move to new premises [1988] raises hope for the reappearance of books that have been missing for a century or more.

5 For example, Sydney Roscoe, *John Newbery and His Successors 1740–1814* (Wormley, England: Five Owls Press, 1973; F. J. Harvey Darton, *Children's Books in England*, 3rd ed. (Cambridge: Cambridge University Press, 1982); Marjorie Moon, *John Harris's Books for Youth 1801–1843* (1976; repr. Folkstone, England: Dawsons, 1992); William Sloane, *Children's Books in England & America in the Seventeenth Century. A History and a Checklist, Together with The Young Christian's Library, the First Printed Catalogue of Books for Children* (New York: Columbia University Press, 1955). Theodor Brüggemann and Otto Brunken, eds., *Handbuch zur Kinder und Jugendliteratur*, 3 vols. (Stuttgart: Metzler, 1987–1992), vol. 3, *Von 1750 bis 1800*, ed. Theodor Brüggemann and Hans-Heino Ewers (1992).

6 F. J. Harvey Darton, *Children's Books in England* (Cambridge: Cambridge University Press, 1958); see also note 5; A. S. W. Rosenbach, *Early American*

Children's Books (New York: Kraus, 1966); D'Alté Welch, *A Bibliography of American Children's Books Printed Prior to 1821* (Worcester, Mass.: American Antiquarian Society, 1971).

7 The full title of *The History of Genesis* contains the words "Fitted for the Use of Schools"; this printing appeared in London, printed by "J. D." for W. Fisher and R. Mount in 1691. The foreword of *A Compendious History* (London: J. Hazard, 1726) notes that it is "proper for schools" and cheap enough to be "no greater a Burthen to the Parents Pockets than . . . to the Learners Memory" (A3ᴿ).

8 John Locke, *Some Thoughts Concerning Education* (London: A. and J. Churchill, 1693), p. 188. See also Samuel F. Pickering, Jr., *John Locke and Children's Books in Eighteenth-Century England* (Knoxville: University of Tennessee Press, 1981), pp. 116–122.

9 *History of Genesis*, pp. vi–vii.

10 Heinrich Wolgast, *Das Elend unserer Jugendliteratur: Ein Beitrag zur künstlerischen Erziehung der Jugend*, 3rd ed. (Leipzig: B. G. Teubner, 1905), p. 25.

11 François Caradec, *Histoire de la littérature enfantine en France*, 2 vols. (Paris: Albin Michel, 1977), 1:35. An early plea for a poetic awareness of children's literature appeared in Klaus Doderer, ed., *Ästhetik der Kinderliteratur. Plädoyer für ein poetisches Bewußtsein* (Weinheim: Beltz, 1981).

12 See Gillian Adams, "The First Children's Literature? The Case for Sumer," *Children's Literature* 14 (1986): 1–30.

13 Aidan Chambers, "The Reader in the Book," in *The Signal Approach to Children's Books*, ed. Nancy Chambers (Metuchen, N. J.: Scarecrow Press, 1981), p. 253.

14 Nicholas Tucker, *The Child and the Book: A Psychological and Literary Exploration* (Cambridge: Cambridge University Press, 1981), pp. 4, 5–15.

15 Chambers, "The Reader," pp. 254–269.

16 Donald Milton Smith, "English Religious and Moral Verse for Children, 1686–1770" (Ph.D. diss., New York University, 1989).

17 See Patricia Demers, *Heaven upon Earth: The Form of Moral and Religious Children's Literature, to 1850* (Knoxville: University of Tennessee Press, 1993); Ruth B. Bottigheimer, *The Bible for Children from the Age of Gutenberg to the Present* (New Haven: Yale University Press, 1996).

18 For an excellent detailed study of the chronology and mechanics of producing *The Lilliputian Magazine*, see Jill E. Grey, "*The Lilliputian Magazine*: A Pioneering Periodical," *Journal of Librarianship* 2.2 (1970): 107–115. Isabelle Havelange and Ségolène Le Men, *Le Magasin des Enfants. La littérature pour la jeunesse (1750–1830)* (Montreuil: Bibliothèque Robert-Desnos, Association Bicentenaire, 1988).

19 Warren W. Wooden, *Children's Literature of the English Renaissance* (Lexington: University of Kentucky Press, 1986); Percy Muir, *English Children's Books 1600–1900* (1954; repr. London: Batsford, 1979); and F. J. Harvey Darton, *Children's Books in England. Five Centuries of Social Life* (1932; repr. Cambridge: Cambridge University Press, 1982), which remains a standard work, revised by Brian Alderson and now in its third edition; Brüggemann and Brunken, *Handbuch zur Kinder- und Jugendliteratur*.

20 For other investigations of social class, see Hugo Cerda, *Literatura Infantil y Clases Sociales* (Madrid: Akal Bolsillo, 1982); Isaac Kramnick, "Children's Literature and Bourgeois Ideology: Observation on Culture and Industrial Capitalism in the Later Eighteenth Century," in *Culture and Politics from Puritanism to the Enlightenment*, ed. Perez Zagorin (Berkeley: University of California Press, 1981), pp. 203–240; Claire-Lise Malarte-Feldman, "La Comtesse de Ségur, a Witness of Her Time," *Children's Literature Association Quarterly* 20.3 (1995): 135–139.

21 In early- to mid-twentieth-century Germany, pedagogical principles amalgamated age with genre and produced the concept of "Märchenalter," the age during which a child was susceptible to fairy tales. The concept allowed pedagogues to align specific fairy tales and their morals with specified age groups.

22 Wilhelm Arnold, *Biblische Geschichten: ein Lesebuch für Unmündige, zunächst für Taubstumme* (Basel: Bahnmeier, 1848); Johann Caspar Lavater, *Christliche Religionsunterricht für denkende Jünglinge* (Zürich: n.p., 1788); Georg Gessner, *Biblische Geschichten zum Gebrauche der Landschulen* (Zürich: Johann Kaspar Ziegler, 1774); Anne Scott MacLeod, "From Rational to Romantic: The Children of Children's Literature in the Nineteenth Century," *Poetics Today* (Spring 1992): 141–153.

23 See, for example, Dennis Butts, ed., *Stories and Society: Children's Literature in Its Social Context* (London: Macmillan, 1992).

24 Kirsten Drotner, *English Children and Their Magazines 1751–1945* (New Haven: Yale University Press, 1988); Gillian Avery and Julia Briggs, eds., *Children and Their Books: A Celebration of the Work of Iona and Peter Opie* (Oxford: Clarendon Press, 1989); and Gillian Avery, *Behold the Child. American Children and Their Books 1621–1922* (London: Bodley Head, 1994). For a recent overview, see Hugh Cunningham, *Children and Childhood in Western Society since 1500* (London: Longman, 1995). See also Georg Jäger, *Schule und literarische Kultur. Sozialgeschichte des deutschen Unterrichts an höheren Schulen von der Spätaufklärung bis zum Vormärz* (Stuttgart: Metzler, 1981); Reinbert Tabbert, *Kinderbuchanalysen* (Frankfurt: Dipa, 1991); Jean Perrot, *Art Baroque, Art d'Enfance* (Nancy: Presses Universitaires de Nancy, 1991); and Mary V. Jackson, *Engines of Instruction, Mischief and Magic: Children's Literature in England from Its Beginnings to 1839* (Lincoln: University of Nebraska Press, 1989).

25 See, for example, the essays in Bettina Hurrelmann, ed., *Kinderliteratur und Rezeption. Beiträge der Kinderliteraturforschung zur literaturwissenschaftlichen Pragmatik* (Baltmannsweiler: Burgbücherei Wilhelm Schneider, 1980).

26 Roger Ascham, *The Scholemaster of plaine and perfite way of teachyng children, to understand, write, and speake the Latin tong, but specially purposed for the private bryngyng up of youth in Ientlemen and Noble mens houses* (London: Iohn Daye, 1570), leaf 26ᵛ.

27 Ruth K. MacDonald, *Literature for Children in England and America from 1646 to 1774* (Troy, N. Y.: Whitston Publishing Co., 1982), p. 24.

28 Clara Vostrovsky, *Studies in Education*, cited in the introduction to George Hamilton Archibald, *Bible Lessons for Little Beginners* (London: Sunday School Union, 1903), p. vii. See also Tabbert, *Kinderbuchanalysen II*; Roger Sale, "The Audience in Children's Literature," in *Bridges to Fantasy*, ed. George E. Slusser, Eric S. Rabbin, and Robert Scholes (Carbondale: Southern Illinois University Press, 1982), pp. 78–89.

29 Margery Fisher, "Stories from a Victorian Nursery," *Signal* 69 (September 1992): 176–189. Describing the book collection of a Manchester girl in the 1880s, Fisher infers her likes and dislikes from the books' condition, i.e., revealing heavy or light use. Buckingham is quoted in Avery, *Behold the Child*, p. 38.

30 Ingeborg Weber-Kellermann, "Was die Großen lasen als sie noch klein waren," in *Erzählen-Sammeln-Deuten: Hessische Blätter für Volks- und Kulturforschung* Bd. 18, neue Folge (1985), ed. Charlotte Oberfeld and Peter Assion; see also the essays in Dietmar Larcher and Christine Spieß, eds., *Lesebilder. Geschichten und Gedanken zur literarischen Sozialisation* (Reinbek: Rowohlt, 1980).

31 Francelia Butler and Richard Rotert, eds., *Triumphs of the Spirit in Children's Literature* (Hamden, Conn.: Shoe String Press, 1986); Isobel Jan, *On Children's Literature* (New York: Schocken, 1974), p. 118; Margaret Rustin and Michael Rustin, *Narratives of Love and Loss: Studies in Modern Children's Fiction* (London: Verso, 1987).

32 Herbert Kohl, *Should We Burn Babar?: Essays on Children's Literature and the Power of Stories* (New York: New Press, 1995), pp. 305–306. Kohl found that although Parks had been active in the NAACP for years, and previously ejected from public buses, white authors had regularly portrayed her only as a poor, tired, simple but stubborn working woman whose refusal to relinquish her seat was completely unpremeditated, as was the black community's ensuing support. See also Rudine Sims, *Shadow and Substance. Afro-American Experience in Contemporary Children's Fiction* (Urbana, Ill.: National Council of Teachers of English, 1982) for an early description and analysis of books about and for African-American children by African-American and non-African-American writers.

33 Reformulated from Anna Pellouski, in her preface to Jan's *On Children's Literature*, p. 8.

34 Jacqueline Rose, *The Case of Peter Pan: The Impossibility of Children's Fiction* (1984; repr. Philadelphia: University of Pennsylvania Press, 1992), p. 1; Lesnik-Oberstein, *Children's Literature*, pp. 9, 163.

35 See, for example, U. C. Knoepflmacher, "Resisting Growth through Fairy Tale in Ruskin's *The King of the Golden River*," *Children's Literature* 13 (1985): 3–30.

36 Frances Hodgson Burnett, *A Lady of Quality* (New York: International Book and Publishing Co., 1899). For discussions of class, gender, race, and religion in children's literature, see my "God and the Bourgeoisie: Class, the Two-Tier Tradition, Work, and Proletarianization in Children's Bibles," in *Lion and the Unicorn* 17.2 (1993): 124–134; "Philogyny, Misogyny, and Erasure," in *The Bible for Children*, pp. 142–151; and "Fairy Tale Illustrations: Children's Drawings and the Male Imagination," in *Papers of the 4th Congress of the Société Internationale d'Ethnologie et de Folklore*, ed. Bente Gullveig Alver and Torunn Selberg (1991), 2:55–62.

37 For an overview of a comparative approach to children's literature, see Emer O'Sullivan, "Ansätze zu einer komparatistischen Kinder- und Jugendliteraturforschung," in *Theorien der Jugendlektüre: Beiträge zur Kinder- und Jugendliteraturkritik seit Heinrich Wolgast*, ed. Bernd Dolle-Weinkauff and Hans-Heino Ewers (Weinheim: Juventa Verlag, 1996), pp. 285–315.

Part 3

THE SUBJECT MATTER

9

MEDIEVAL CHILDREN'S LITERATURE

Its possibility and actuality

Gillian Adams

Source: *Children's Literature* 26 (1998): 1–24.

Years ago, while taking a graduate course in medieval Latin, I was struck by the wide disparity in the difficulty of the works that were assigned, a disparity that often did not coincide with other variables such as the historical period or the author's social class, profession, or region. In that course it was assumed that all the texts we addressed, whatever their degree of difficulty, were written for adults. I concluded at the time that there must have been a substantial number of adult readers with literacy skills below the third-grade level. I have since become convinced that some of the works we were looking at were written not only or even initially for semiliterate adults, a group often equated with children in the earlier periods, but for children.[1] In order to support my claim that such works should be considered children's literature I draw on evidence provided by cultural and literary historians to dispute two widely held convictions that have hampered previous critical and theoretical studies. The first is the nonspecialist belief that there can be no medieval children's literature because a conception of childhood as we know it did not exist in the Middle Ages. The second is the specialist assertion, typified by the medievalist Bennett Brockman, that "the Middle Ages made no provision for a separate literature for children, apart from pedagogical texts designed to teach them to read, to write, to cipher, and to behave civilly" ("Juvenile" 18). Finally, I discuss the ways in which some medieval works and their contexts indicate a child audience and why such works warrant further exploration as children's literature.

I

First it is necessary to dispose of the myths about medieval children that have prevented scholars from seriously considering that a literature for them might exist. There are three initial barriers, primarily hypothetical, to recognizing medieval children's literature. To begin with, there is the still-widespread belief in the "Ariès thesis," in brief that childhood was "discovered" in the seventeenth century (according to Philippe Ariès) or the eighteenth century (according to some other researchers). Ariès, as he admits in his introduction to *Centuries of Childhood*, was not a specialist in the periods for which he claims that "the idea of [*sentiment*, a separate feeling about] childhood did not exist" (128), and in fact, if his book is deconstructed, it is evident that there was a cognizance of childhood throughout those earlier periods. What his thesis amounts to is that previous centuries thought quite differently about children than did seventeenth-century France. A statement of this nature is true for any time and for any region even today: for example, the conception of childhood is different for the first half of the twentieth century and the second; for the rich, the urban poor, and the comfortable, usually suburban, middle class; and most notably for Americans and those who live in countries where poor children go to work in factories at six or seven and parents sell children into prostitution and even slavery.[2] Nevertheless, Ariès's insistence on the social construction of childhood and on not naively reading the past in terms of the present is an essential contribution to the study of past children's literatures. His work has informed many subsequent critical and historical studies and has given rise to the examination of specific works within a wide-ranging sociohistorical context that includes nonliterary texts.

It was not long after the Ariès book appeared (in 1960 in France and in 1962 in English translation) that specialists in the medieval and early modern periods began to point out what was wrong with its ideas and with the data used to support them. As early as 1975 Meradith McMunn wrote in *Children's Literature*, on the basis of her examination of the description of children in French medieval literature, that Ariès's claims are "not supported by a close look at medieval literature" ("Children" 54). She was followed by C. H. Talbot, who asserted in *Children's Literature* in 1977 that "anyone who is at all conversant with the biographies of the saints; with the lives of abbots, monks, and nuns; or with the chronicles of monasteries and cathedral churches written between the eighth and the twelfth century will realize that such a theory [as Ariès's] is untenable" (17). Books criticizing Ariès soon followed: recent works accessible to nonspecialists and available in paperback are John Boswell's *The Kindness of Strangers* (1988, see particularly 36–38), Shulamith Shahar's *Childhood in the Middle Ages* (1990), and Barbara A. Hanawalt's *Growing up in Medieval London* (1993).[3] By 1995, Hugh Cunningham can comment in *Children and Childhood in*

Western Society Since 1500 that disproving Ariès is "an easy goal" and that what is needed is greater attention to "the contradictions and changes over time and place in medieval thought and practice" (40). In short, medieval and early modern scholars are unanimous in discarding the Ariès thesis, in spite of the interest of many of his observations; it is time for children's literature scholars to do the same.

Ariès's claim that childhood as we now think of it did not exist before the seventeenth or the eighteenth century as well as his chapters on the ages of life, the discovery of childhood (in art), and children's dress have resulted in two additional barriers to locating medieval children's literature. The first is the idea that parents did not love (or were afraid to love) their children because infant and child mortality was so high. One finds this claim made, in spite of ample evidence to the contrary, for periods ranging from antiquity through the eighteenth century. Such a claim is logically absurd; for the greater part of human existence, life for most has been nasty, brutish, and short. Death rates have often been almost as high for adults as for children, particularly in the case of childbearing women and warriors, yet there is no lack of early literature about love. In fact, a high value was placed on children and on parental love (see Boswell, Hanawalt, Shahar, and Talbot passim), although often on a sliding scale: some children—for example, male heirs of the wealthy and powerful—were more valuable than others, and a separate literature for them was more likely to develop and to survive.

The second and more damaging idea, as far as children's literature studies is concerned, is based primarily on Ariès's discussion of medieval dress and art and his claim that children were viewed as "miniature adults." Ariès was not an art historian, and his interpretation of the evidence he presents is flawed, given that for the period he discusses artists were not interested in realism as we conceive of it. There is other medieval art, notably sculpture and manuscript illustration, that better represents the child as distinct from the adult. In Ariès's day, in contrast to the present, European children and sometimes adolescents were strongly differentiated by their clothing (for example, short pants and school smocks), so it would be natural for him to be struck by the similarity of adults' and children's clothing in medieval art. Moreover, Ariès's claim that childhood was not viewed as a separate stage of life is not supported by the ample evidence of the interest shown during the Middle Ages in discussing and defining the ages and characteristics of *infantia* (birth to six or seven years), *pueritia* (seven to twelve for girls, to fourteen for boys), *adolescentia* (the period between biological and social puberty and legal and social majority), and *juventus* (see, for example, Shahar 22 and notes; Hanawalt, passim).

Nevertheless, these myths about medieval children persist. For example, in the most recent edition of *The Pleasures of Children's Literature* (1996), although Perry Nodelman cites Pollock's and Shahar's studies, he continues to assert that in the earlier periods "a *different* conception of child-hood operated, [and] that conception required no special literature for children" (70, emphasis in original).[4] If we contend that a society whose conception of childhood is alien to our own is incapable of developing children's literature, we should also argue that there could have been no children's literature in the eighteenth and nineteenth centuries in England and the United States either, since the ideas operative then about the "innocent" child and about family structure, clothing, age- and gender-appropriate activities, and social status are not identical to today's. In fact, there is no logical reason why societies with constructions of childhood that differ widely from our own (for example, China) should not develop literature for children, whether or not they actually do. To assert that only *our* conception of childhood can result in children's literature, a literature that only we are able to judge as literature in terms of its literary value (which for some reason must include "entertainment"), is the kind of cultural imperialism and ideological colonialism that modern critics, Nodelman among them, often seek to avoid (see Nodelman's often-cited essay "The Other: Orientalism, Colonialism, and Children's Literature").

II

Even if we admit, then, that the period roughly from the sack of Rome (410) to the invention of printing had different conceptions of childhood from those current in most of Europe and America today, such conceptions do not logically preclude the possibility of a literature for children. More problematic is the narrowness of vision of those who do recognize and write about medieval and early modern texts for children and youth as exemplified by the quotation from Brockman with which I began this chapter. Brockman makes two claims: first, that there is literature but that it is "pedagogical," and second, that apart from this literature there is no separate literature for children (i.e., that it was a part of adult literature that children shared with adults). Brockman is not alone; on the basis of the scholarship that I have seen to date, the only medieval texts recognized as exclusively for children are considered nonfiction: instruction manuals and courtesy books. The idea that this sort of work is all that exists is fostered by bibliographies, collections of excerpts such as that edited by Patricia Demers and Gordon Moyles, and the early chapters of F. J. Harvey Darton's *Children's Books in England*.[5]

Like Brockman, most children's literature specialists who are also medievalists address themselves to a shared literature whose content or circumstances may indicate a child audience, or they tell us how good or poor a job modern children's literature does in portraying the medieval period. I find particularly distressing the essays on medieval children's literature in volume 1 of *Children's Literature*.[6] Although Hugh Keenan's piece on Old

English children's literature is suggestive, mentioning not only Aelfric's *Colloquy* (ca. 1000) but also the Exeter and Cotton gnomes, the McMunns' essay, in spite of some excellent citations, writes off the fourteenth-century French *Book of the Knight of La Tour-Landry* (translated into English in the fifteenth century) as "an encyclopedic catalogue of anecdotes, each with a very explicit moral" (23); Brockman terms its stories "crudely manipulative" ("Medieval" 40). Anyone who has read this work knows that it contains fascinating narratives of some length, some readily accessible to students today. Nothing has changed in volume 4 of *Children's Literature*, where William McMunn asserts in his introduction to the four papers from the MLA panel "Children and the Middle Ages" that "all of us on the panel agree that 'children's literature' did not exist in the Middle Ages" ("Literacy" 36).

Why will these scholars not consider as children's literature "the pedagogical texts designed to teach [children] to read, to write, to cipher, and to behave civilly" (Brockman, "Juvenile" 18) or the "entertaining stories [that] were used in programs of instruction" (McMunn and McMunn, "Children's" 22)? I believe that there are two reasons, and the case of the McMunns' and Brockman's condemnation of *The Book of the Knight of La Tour-Landry* provides a clue to the first. It seems to be the belief in the romantic notion, based on Darton's 1932 definition of children's literature, that didactic works do not count, are not truly "literature": "By 'children's books' I mean printed works produced ostensibly to give children spontaneous pleasure, and not primarily to teach them, nor solely to make them good, nor to keep them *profitably* quiet" (1, emphasis in original). Such a narrow definition of literature has been repudiated by a number of scholars, ably led for some years now by the new historicist Mitzi Myers, whose groundbreaking review of Geoffrey Summerfield castigates his book for its "presentism" and espousal of "Romantic values" (108). Brockman's essay on medieval poetry, in spite of valuable observations on lullabies and on different types of medieval didacticism, is a sad example of such "presentism." Recently Patricia Demers in *Heaven upon Earth: The Form of Moral and Religious Children's Literature, to 1850*, which begins its study of children's literature with Erasmus's 1540 *Sermon of the Chylde Jesus*, has provided a telling critique of Darton's antididactic position.

In fact, in certain countries and periods, among them medieval Europe, didacticism has been highly valued (as it is by many education students today); typical is the classical poet Horace's proclamation in his *Ars Poetica* (often part of the medieval curriculum) that *Scribendi recte sapere est et principium et fons* [The source and first principle of good writing is wisdom] (l. 310). In a dictum often referred to by medieval theorists, Horace adds, *omne tulit punctum qui miscuit utile dulci / lectorem delectando pariterque monendo* [he has won the day who has mixed the useful with the pleasurable / equally delighting the reader and instructing him] (ll. 343–44).

In Horace's own work the needle was closer to *dulci* on the continuum between *utile* and *dulci*; in most medieval literature, it tended to be closer to *utile*. Thus the works of the great literary figures of the High Middle Ages, for example, Dante and Chaucer, are explicit about the lessons to be drawn from their fictions. Yet their situation as stars of the literary canon—along with that supremely didactic work, the Bible—has never been denied. Of course, as Marxist and other ideological critics often remind us, all literature has an agenda, however carefully disguised.

I suspect that the second reason for refusing to believe that anything connected with pedagogy could be literature has to do with the need perceived by many American academic children's literature specialists to divorce themselves from the fields of education and library science. Nevertheless, from its beginnings in the ancient world, children's literature has been intimately related to pedagogics and remains so today (see Adams). European scholars appear much more comfortable with the connection than we do, on the evidence of Maria Nikolajeva's introduction to the essays in *Aspects and Issues in the History of Children's Literature* and many of the essays themselves. There is no logical reason why texts used for educational purposes should not also qualify as literature, whether they appeal to us or not. The history of education demonstrates that poetry, drama, and narrative have been used to supplement nonfiction in the schools from their beginning, whether adult material used and sometimes adapted for children or material created especially for them and whether used in ways that seem familiar to us or alien. To investigate fully the possibilities of medieval children's literature, then, we must begin with medieval education and the texts used within or as supplements to the curriculum.

III

Once we have disposed of the mythologies and prejudices that have prevented specialists and nonspecialists alike from admitting that medieval children's literature may exist, two important barriers to an accurate, scholarly assessment of that literature remain, and they have to do with the nature of medieval education. The first concerns what was once thought to be the low percentage of the population for whom literacy was deemed necessary or even desirable, the second the admittedly high price of codices. Of late, scholars have been revising literacy figures upward, led by Rosamond McKitterick for the earlier periods; for the later periods see the historical studies mentioned at the beginning of this essay. The Middle Ages are not monolithic, and certain groups of people placed a high value on literacy: the Jews (the people of the book), whose males were required by religious law to be literate enough to read the Scriptures;[7] the church (monks, nuns, and the secular clergy); royalty and the high nobility (and the clerks and legal experts who served them); and, beginning with the twelfth century, those engaged in commerce. Of course, the situation in urban areas was different from that in the countryside, and some regions were more learned and literate than others. For example, many parts of Italy, particularly the regions under Arab and Byzantine influence, never lost a respect for learning. Once most of Spain came under Muslim domination, high culture flourished. Southern France was ahead of northern France until the Renaissance of the twelfth century; there were pockets of culture in Germany; and England tended to lag behind, even with respect to Ireland. But because of the high value placed on books—both as objects sometimes worth enough to hold for ransom and as containers of text that was also highly esteemed—they, and the ability to read them, were indicators of power and status. Literacy was not only useful but necessary for upward mobility.[8]

But it is exactly the high value of a book before the invention of printing, and even for a time afterwards, that most scholars assume makes it unlikely that any but a child from a wealthy family would actually have possessed a book of his or (even more rarely) her own; if there were books for children in a household or school, they would be shared and as likely to be heard as read. There obviously could be no children's book trade in the modern sense, although there is plenty of evidence of the buying and selling of codices: as early as the eighth century certain ecclesiastical establishments depended on the money they gained from copying (see McKitterick, "Nuns' Scriptoria"; *Carolingians* ch. 4), and books for children must have been part of this trade.

Nevertheless, some children did learn how to read, whether taught in schools run by monks and nuns or by the secular clergy, at home by parents, or at court by tutors. Exactly how this teaching was done is detailed by Suzanne Reynolds in *Medieval Reading: Grammar, Rhetoric, and the Classical Text*. Although her account is based on a description in a twelfth-century English text by Alexander Neckham, *Sacerdos ad altare accessurus*, scholars agree that the general shape of the curriculum as Neckham describes it is characteristic of the whole medieval period. The student began with the alphabet, perhaps inscribed on an object in daily use such as a bowl or a belt (8), and went on to the proper pronunciation of Latin syllables by memorizing the Paternoster, the Creed, and perhaps parts of the Psalter. Much of this learning would be done by rote at a level of "uncomprehending reiteration" (10).[9] Texts were also written on parchment attached to wooden paddles or in large letters glued to a wooden board (Shahar 189). Many institutions had extremely large service books that could be seen at a distance by a number of readers, and books were often chained to bookstands so that they could be read seriatim.

Reynolds emphasizes the orality of education, arguing that students "do not read (in our sense of the term) the text at all, for it remains at all moments and in all senses in the teacher's hands. . . . This is a communal reading, communicated orally. . . . Reasons of economy and availability make it very unlikely that individual students, even if they could write, would have had access to copies of the text. If they did write, it was probably on wax tablets. . . . [And] the wax tablet of *memoria* is fundamental in medieval literacy" (29). On the other hand, in her studies of the Carolingian period, McKitterick emphasizes the dominance of the written text and of writing from the earliest periods. Talbot (22) and R. H. and M. A. Rouse describe the slates framed in wood and the wax-covered wooden *tabellae* on which students did their first writing exercises (4–5), usually, according to Reynolds, short or long paraphrases (21). It seems probable that the balance between memorized and written text varied according to time, place, the institution and its resources, and the status of its pupils.

The next text in the learning sequence was a grammar book, usually the Donatus *Ars Minor* or part of the *Ars Maior*, with local variants, which was used from the fourth until at least the fifteenth century;[10] its question-and-answer format is characteristic of other medieval master-pupil dialogues specifically designed for children. At least one child owned his own copy of Donatus, a ninth-century schoolboy named Sado, "who wrote in a mixture of rather straggling capitals and minuscule . . . with a notably shaky command of grammar" across the top of the page: "*Sadoniis iste liber est sua mater dedit illi Magnum onor illa sit qui dedit hunc librum*" [this book is Sados his mother gave it to him may she be greatly honored who gave him this book] (McKitterick, "Ninth" 228). In her study of this manuscript, which is "rather inferior quality vellum" and gives other indications of an attempt at economy (for example, leaves erased and reused), McKitterick details the ways in which it has been prepared for "a learner's eye": it has clearly punctuated sentences, section headings in "rustic capitals," and "extravagantly wide margins" (227), some of which have been ruled with narrow lines for the "annotations of the struggling student" who has written (incorrectly) on one of them, *stultissimo grammatica* [extremely stupid grammar] (228). McKitterick concludes, "Phillips 16308 in fact contradicts a frequent assumption that books in the early Middle Ages were too costly and scarce to be owned by the ordinary schoolboy" (228). The multiple copies of Donatus in the library lists of monasteries known to have flourishing schools, and the many copies that still survive, are further confirmation of McKitterick's claim.

A second work found in multiple copies, falsely attributed to the Roman philosopher Cato and universally coupled with Donatus in the elementary curriculum, is the *Catonis Disticha* [Cato's distichs]. It is a third-century collection of 152 moral couplets in four books, prefaced by a short introductory epistle and about fifty-four very short sentences, some as little as two words. The introduction addresses a child, "Cato"'s son: *Nunc te, fili karissime, docebo quo pacto morem animi tui componas* [Now I will teach you, dearest son, how you can put your mind in order] (T. Hunt 9). The work ends with *Hic finit Cato dans castigamina nato / ostendens quare mundum non debet amare* [Here Cato finishes admonishing his son / showing how he ought not to love this world].[11] From the tenth century onward "Cato" was the first item in an elementary reading book, the *Liber Catonianus*. Tony Hunt gives a full account of how the selections in this reading book varied according to location and period, but three items in addition to "Cato" were constant. First there were fables, usually Avianus's expansion of those by Babrius; then something about the Trojan war—in the earlier period the *Ilias Latina*, a shortened version of the *Iliad* from A.D. 65, which was later replaced by the medieval version of Statius's *Achilleis*, valued for its account of how Achilles obeyed his mother Thetis, her concern for him, and his upbringing by Chiron (Hunt 69). The third item was usually the *Eclogues* of the tenth-century author Theodolus, a debate between Truth and Falsehood about Christianity and paganism that owes much to Virgil's third and seventh eclogues and that was viewed as preparatory to his study. None of the works Hunt mentions, aside from "Cato" and Avianus, was originally composed for children; rather, all were appropriated (and glossed, often heavily) for and by them. Donatus, "Cato," the fables, and some of the other texts exist in multiple versions and variants with interpolations and excisions; I cannot emphasize their fluidity too strongly.

It was at this point, before the serious student went on to Virgil's *Eclogues* and the fixed texts of the classical and late Latin *auctores* (Cicero, Horace, Ovid, Lucan, Terence, and others), that according to Alexander Neckham, he was to read "*quibusdam libellis informationi rudium necessariis*" [certain shorter works necessary for the instruction of the unlearned] (Reynolds 7).[12] And, I would argue, it is at this point that we should find, between the elementary texts and the medieval equivalent of Shakespeare and other works in today's high-school canon, the optional material in a curriculum otherwise dominated by classical and late Latin texts: the poems, fables, and stories adapted or specially written for children, the "separate literature" that, according to Brockman and others, does not exist in the Middle Ages.

IV

Now that I have established that there is no reason why medieval children's literature—even material with an agenda covert enough for critics such as Brockman to accept as literature—should not exist, and that there is a place in the curriculum for such works, I would like to name a few candidates and the genres in which they occur. Most of the examples that I describe below happen to be in Latin; I am convinced that further material is available not only in Latin but in the vernaculars. Because there are medievalists who have no interest in children as an audience, indeed to whom the idea of children as a potential audience might seem utterly foreign, it is important to find as many indications as possible that a text has a connection with child readers or auditors. To discover features that indicate a child audience, absent the kind of smoking gun that McKitterick finds in Sado's grammar book, I ask the following questions: in terms of the text itself (internal evidence), is there a dedication to a named child or introductory material indicating that the work is intended for children or younger students? What is the language like—is it very simple or simpler and more direct than that in other works by the same author clearly directed at adults, and is the language in the prefatory material more complex than the language in the body of the text? Is a child directly addressed or portrayed as a major character? How is he or she presented? What is the appearance of the manuscript or manuscripts of the text? Are there explanatory glosses directed at inexpert readers, as in the case of Sado's grammar and the *Liber Catonianus*? Does the calligraphy of some versions indicate inexpert copyists? If there are illustrations, what do they reveal about an implied audience, keeping in mind that the primary audience for illustrated material was an adult one? Are the manuscripts inexpensively produced, or are they so lavish that they imply a princely owner?

In terms of external evidence, what is the nature of the scriptoria from which the earliest examples come? What establishments owned the manuscripts? Are they also the sites of schools? What do we know about the author, whether actual or ascribed (for example, "Cato" or "Aesop")? How popular is the text and how fluid? Does it exist in multiple versions, or in Latin and the vernaculars? With what other works is it bound? (For example, works bound with "Cato" or the popular grammars are more likely to be directed at children.) What is the historical and cultural context of the work, its period and location? Do selections from it appear in *florilegia*, collections of excerpts for use in the schools? Is it referred to in other texts as somehow connected with children or with education?

I have already mentioned that fables, usually about animals, were a curriculum standard for young readers. They were often grouped with *aenigmata* (riddles) by Symphosius, Aldhelm, and others, also used in the schools from an early period (see Ziolkowski 40–46). The best-known fables are found in collections such as "Aesop" and those by Babrius and Phaedrus in versions known as Avianus and Romulus (see Ben Edwin Perry for an extended discussion of various versions and their use). On the basis of what has survived, apart from classical fable material, narratives containing speaking animals begin with ninth-century animal poems by Alcuin of York and others who were members of Charlemagne's palace school; Alcuin's poem "The Cock and the Wolf" is the earliest known analogue of Chaucer's "Nun's Priest's Tale."[13]

These and other short poems are followed by *The Ecbasis Captivi*, an eleventh-century Latin frame tale intended on one level to serve as a warning to young novices against attempting escape from the monastery (a major problem, according to Boswell). The inner story is about a calf (*vitulus*), a common term for a novice, who is imprisoned by a wolf, rescued by a fox, and taken to the court of the lion king. The work is a cento; that is, it is made up of multiple short quotations, which may be intended as embellishment, parody, or a kind of contextual gloss, from the set texts that children would have encountered in their studies. It is bound with school texts in the two surviving manuscripts. The *Ecbasis* is followed in turn by animal epics such as the twelfth-century *Ysengrimus* (attributed to "Nivardus"), which is the first fully worked-out version of the Reynard the Fox material. On the basis of its complex structure, difficult language, learned jokes, and inclusion of a smutty passage, it was probably intended for an audience of ecclesiastics. The questionable passage, however, was early removed for a presumably younger audience in a version of the manuscript that comes from a teaching establishment, and selections from the *Ysengrimus* found their way into *chrestomathies* and *florilegia* bound together with grammatical and other teaching texts.[14]

Although nonspecialists will be familiar with the medieval Reynard cycle and its offshoots only from modern versions, the association of medieval children with drama, both as actors and as part of the audience, should be common knowledge (see, for example, Brockman, "Children"; Hanks; and M. and W. McMunn). In the second half of the tenth century Froumund of Tegernsee refers to using props and animal masks to get the attention of his pupils; Ziolkowski suggests that some animal poems "were perhaps scripts for schoolroom performances in which pupils donned animal masks" (5, see also 147–52). But I know only one dramatic corpus specifically written for children: the plays of Hrotswitha of Gandersheim, a late-tenth-century nun who taught in an establishment limited to female children of the German royal family and important nobility. Her series of playlets, written in simple Latin with short, snappy, often amusing dialogue and some slapstick, celebrates the victories of prepubescent girls—the major characters—over threats to their chastity and integrity. The language of the plays is totally unlike the grandiose rhetoric of works by Hrotswitha dedicated to the king and to other important adults, and there are additional internal and external features that indicate a youthful audience. The plays are still performed today, primarily in academic situations.[15]

In the later periods there appear didactic works intended for the young containing fictional narratives among their moral precepts; a prime example is the *Fecunda ratis* of Egbert of Liège. An early-eleventh-century collection of Latin verse texts of varying lengths and degrees of difficulty written and compiled for Egbert's young pupils, it is a "gallimaufry of proverbs, fables, fairytales, and anecdotes" (Ziolkowski 42–43). Among its treasures is the first known version of "Little Red Riding Hood," complete with moral (see Berlioz; Lontzen).

Whereas Egbert, to my knowledge, has not been translated into English, a medieval best-seller, the *Disciplina Clericalis*, has two fine translations. It is by Petrus Alfonsi, a Spanish Jew who converted to Christianity in 1106. Written in very simple Latin at a time when the language often reflected Ciceronian splendors, this collection of stories primarily from Semitic and Arab sources, is, on the evidence of Alfonsi's ornate preface and an addressee in the text ("a little boy like you"), especially intended for young students. Termed "the oldest story book of the Middle Ages" (Beeson 84), its tales are usually short, as are its easy sentences; there is much dialogue, and the anecdotes are far less didactic than one would expect given both the agenda the author promotes in the preface and the genre: wisdom literature.[16] From slightly later in the same period comes a frame tale enclosing similar stories, Johannes de Alta Silva's *Dolopathos*, or *The King and the Seven Wise Men*.[17] Versions of Alfonsi's stories appear in the *Gesta Romanorum*, Marguerite of Navarre's *Heptameron*, Boccacio's *Decameron*, and other later collections; both his and Alta Silva's tales are quite familiar to folklorists.

Jonathan Nicholls sees the *Dolopathos* and *Disciplina Clericalis* as forerunners of the somewhat later courtesy books, observing that the teaching of courtesy as a part of the grammar course began in the twelfth century, when these works were written and when the nobility became more universally literate (58). Courtesy books are the one medieval genre that has been recognized as primarily directed at children or adolescents by children's literature scholars. But readers of the McMunns' "Children's Literature in the Middle Ages" or Ann Hildebrand's helpful study of the relation between courtesy books and the *Babar* stories would be ignorant of the fact that courtesy manuals contain more than just short, basic precepts of table etiquette. The narrative material they include may be part of the reason for their wide popularity; it certainly bears further investigation.[18] Allied to the courtesy books are the "mirrors for princes," handbooks for those expected to be in positions of power, for example, the manual that Dhuoda wrote for her sixteen-year-old son, arguably an adult by Carolingian standards, when he set out for Charlemagne's court (see McKitterick, *Carolingians* 223–25).

Religious texts are another popular medieval genre that scholars who write about children's literature seem reluctant to include as true children's literature, probably because they are didactic and thus presumably not entertaining. But when Chaucer's Prioress begins her sad tale of Little Hugh of Lincoln she is embarking on a topic, if not an actual story, no doubt well known to and enjoyed by most of her audience from their childhoods. Stories about exemplary children abound throughout the history of children's literature, and stories about child saints in simple language, especially when bound with school texts, would repay close examination. In a letter of 25 February 1997, Ruth Bottigheimer suggests for consideration as children's texts the narratives taken from the Vulgate by Peter

Comestor, the author of the best-selling twelfth-century *Historia Scholastica* (see Bottigheimer, *Bible* 14–23). The stories in John the Monk's fourteenth-century *Liber de Miraculis* are another possibility. And Milla B. Riggio notes that in the fifth century Claudius Marius Victor's paraphrase of Genesis, *Alethia*, was "expressly written to train the young" (48).

Neither space nor the limits of my investigations to date permit addressing the possibility of medieval children's literature in the vernaculars. Geoffrey Chaucer's *Treatise on the Astrolabe*, written for his ten-year-old son Lewis, is an obvious example of nonfiction (see T. and K. Jambeck). On the basis of manuscript evidence, Mary Shaner has discussed the ways in which a medieval romance was revised for a child reader, and Brockman argues that *Sir Orfeo* is an example of shared, or family, literature because of its internal accessibility for children and the content of the codices in which the three surviving manuscripts of it are contained ("Juvenile"). Brockman has also examined how the Robin Hood narratives were transformed from an entertainment shared by adults and children into one exclusively for children, and Harriet Spiegel has looked at the way Marie of France's *Fables* work as shared literature since "[they] not only seem well suited to children but directly address them or their well-being," and "some present a child actually being taught by a parent" (29). More work needs to be done along these lines, and perhaps in the course of scholarly explorations, more compelling evidence on the order of Shaner's discoveries will be found to connect vernacular fiction directly with children. It seems likely that examples of cross-written or threshold literature—for example, the *Morall Fabillis* of Master Robert Henryson or *Aucassin and Nicolette*—will be more frequent in the vernaculars because of their less intimate connection with education.

Thus the works that I have argued are clearly children's literature are in Latin, although there came to be vernacular versions of some of them (for example, the stories in Petrus Alfonsi, the Reynard the Fox stories, and most of the fables). This is because most education was conducted in Latin throughout the European Middle Ages, and if a text is associated with a church or a secular school, there is a strong likelihood that it was used for its pupils. The fact that the extant translations are often in extremely stilted, even pretentious, English has helped to disguise the true nature of these works. Moreover, the little excerpts of medieval Latin published for Latin students in textbooks such as *Fons Perennis* tend to lead to the conclusion that medieval Latin is a simple language—thus a simple text is just as likely to be for adults as for children. But in actuality medieval Latin comes in a wide variety of styles and complexities. It has its Dr. Seusses, Virginia Woolfs, and James Joyces, just as other languages do. If a text is short and in very simple Latin, it is proper to ask why this so. What evidence exists that it is written for semiliterate adults as opposed to children learning how to read? Is there, for example, a more difficult, perhaps more "adult" version extant?

If we wish to certify such texts as children's literature, however, we must examine their use of language, the local meaning of terms such as *infans* (infant or child), *puer* (boy), and *puella* (girl), the literary and legal evidence for what constituted a child at that time, location, and situation, other possible audiences, and the textual criteria that I mentioned at the beginning of this section. All of these matters, one might object, are just old-fashioned philology and not a legitimate literary pursuit. But philology is no longer old-fashioned; the "new philology," according to Leah Marcus, constitutes the new frontier of modern literary studies (*Renaissance* 22–30, passim).[19] What the new philological approaches add to the old philology is a greater interest in and ease with textual instability in its material context, just as new historicism has brought a special appreciation of literary works within their cultural context. Such methodologies should help us strip away as much as possible our preconceptions, in this case of what a child and children's literature *ought* to be, and take a look at what fiction was actually written for children and what they actually read. It is a good bet that the works that I have cited above were both valued and enjoyed, because if such had not been the case, the costly material on which they were written would have been erased and used again.

I hope that younger scholars who do not suffer from misconceptions about children as unloved and as miniature adults or participate in the presentism of earlier critics will join me in the exciting search for medieval children's literature. We need fresh eyes, better scholarship, more lively translations, and new children's books reworking the old texts. In addition, I hope to begin a process whereby the many books and articles about children's literature that are operating on incorrect assumptions or that are simply wrong will be changed in subsequent editions. We also need to avoid in the future theoretical constructs built on inaccurate information such as Zohar Shavit's attempt at a historical model for the development of children's literature.

And finally, I hope to counter the current wave of ahistoricism among some children's literature scholars. They seem blind to the fact that, like readers at the end of the Middle Ages, we face a radical transformation in both the way that words are transmitted and, according to some observers, the way that children are constructed (see Cunningham 179–90). At the children's literature conference in Charlotte in 1996, a critic with a distinguished publication record asked me why the existence or nonexistence of medieval children's literature should matter. "It is so long ago," he said. Peter Hunt has written several pieces recently along similar lines; for example, in his column "Passing on the Past: The Problem of Books That Are for Children and That Were for Children," he distinguishes between "live" books and "dead" books, which he claims concern no one except historians. He challenges the view that all books for children are connected and that "we in the present can learn from the past about books and children" (200). Although Hunt claims that "different skills" are required to read books from earlier periods (202), no different skills are needed for the imaginative works that I have mentioned when they are well translated.

Moreover, such works are not "dead." I would argue, on the contrary, that, with the exception of Hrotswitha and apart from the nonfiction, most of the material in the texts that I cite in the last part of this essay is an integral part of "the sea of stories" and continues to be found in the modern period in works now generally agreed to be children's literature. The *Ecbasis Captivi* and the *Ysengrimus* were discovered and copied by Jacob Grimm in the Bibliothèque Nationale during his researches there in the 1830s; material from them is alive today in various versions of Reynard the Fox and in some of Joel Chandler Harris's Uncle Remus stories. At the same time, Grimm copied shorter medieval texts that he included in his *Kinder- und Hausmärchen* and that are now classed as fairy tales (for example, in the Jack Zipes translation, nos. 73 and 146). Grimm could recognize a fine story when he saw one, and some of the originals he transcribed continue to be a good read. We need to recognize similar medieval narratives, plays, and poems for what they originally were: fictions provided to children, most probably initially for educational purposes. But they are a far cry from *Fun with Dick and Jane*. They are children's literature.

Notes

1 For the semiliterate adult–child equation see, among others, Ruth Bottigheimer's "The Child-Reader of Children's Bibles" (45). Children's literature is not a tidy genre: the boundary between it and adult literature is indeterminate, as the Perry Nodelman–Michael Steig exchange in the *Children's Literature Association Quarterly* (spring 1993) makes clear. All children's literature is shared with adults (if only parents and teachers) to a greater or lesser degree; some works read by children remain popular with adults; some adult literature has become children's literature (often in special versions for them); some literature is marketed simultaneously to adults and to children with the same text presented in different formats (see Sandra Beckett) or with a different target audience in another country (*Watership Down*); a work marketed as childred's literature may be claimed by adults (*The Adventures of Huckleberry Finn*); some children's literature is "cross-written" (see the 1997 special volume of *Children's Literature*); some authors claim that they let their editors decide whether their work is for children or for adults; and even picture books, once thought to be for children only, are now enjoyed by and used for teaching young adults and adults. For the purposes of this essay, I am defining children's literature as texts that, on the basis of internal or external evidence, are written with a child audience in mind or for which a child audience actually existed.

2 Readers of the international journal *Bookbird: World of Children's Books* and its reports on the state of children's literature in non-Western countries are familiar with the often striking differences between Western and non-Western constructions of children and the impact of these differences on the literature to which those who are literate are exposed. Rosamond McKitterick notes the similarities between the situation of the medieval Carolingians and that of contemporary

multilingual countries seeking to develop a literature apart from that of their former English or French colonizers (*Carolingians* passim).

3 Also important are the first chapter of new historicist Leah Marcus's *Childhood and Cultural Despair* (1978), Linda Pollock's *Forgotten Children* (1983), and most recently, the first two chapters of James A. Schultz's *The Knowledge of Childhood in the German Middle Ages* (1995). The bibliographies and footnotes of these works cite numerous studies in learned journals critiquing Ariès's theories, however much their interests and conclusions may differ. Talbot offers tantalizing leads to potential children's literature, but his references are so sketchy that it is impossible to follow them up. Shahar concentrates on the central and late Middle Ages (roughly from the twelfth century on) and devotes the second half of her book to education in "the second stage" (*pueritia*), roughly ages seven to fourteen. Although Hanawalt occasionally draws in material from other countries and periods, she divides her book according to the stages of childhood and provides a picture of each stage on the basis of evidence found in court records, wills, and other archival, as well as literary, sources from fourteenth- and fifteenth-century London. Schultz bases his study on the way aristocratic children are portrayed in Middle High German texts by poets who sought to please the German aristocracy and would thus be conservative in their views; he is closer to Ariès, concluding that these children are viewed as separate from adults but "deficient" and that their attempts to play adult roles are deemed inadequate. There is a split between scholars who emphasize the biological (nature) and those who emphasize the cultural (nurture); for example, Schultz criticizes Shahar's book for its "confident sentimentality" and the too-easy identification of medieval with modern children (6). Nevertheless, Schultz agrees that medieval society saw childhood as a separate stage and that medieval children were loved.

4 I mention Nodelman's book in particular, although there are many similar examples, because it is arguably the best of the general books likely to be used by students and graduate students in children's literature studies. Roderick McGillis in *The Nimble Reader* (1996) is more judicious: "As nearly all the handbooks and histories of children's literature state, literature for children as we know it—a distinct body of works written and published for the edification and enjoyment of children—only came into being in an organized way in the eighteenth century" (52). But McGillis, like many others, is by implication defining children's literature in terms of its commodification; the idea that its very existence as a separate entity is tied to commercial interests was pointed out by Francelia Butler long ago in her introduction to *Children's Literature 1*. Nevertheless, the researches of scholars such as Gillian Avery and Margaret Kinnell into the children's literature of the early modern period in England have already established the existence of "a distinct body of works" prior to the eighteenth century. German scholars have pushed even further back, as Theodor Brüggemann and Otto Brunken's bibliography of 484 books and broadsides intended for children with accompanying essays and commentary demonstrates; it begins with Ulrich Boner's 1461 *Der Edelstein*.

5 Jane Bingham and Grayce Scholt's annotated bibliography, limited to England, includes works for adults by Boethius, Bede, Geoffrey of Monmouth, and others, appropriated in whole or in part, they argue, for children. Among such works they list *Beowulf*, which, according to David Howlett, was originally children's literature: "I see *Beowulf* as Boethius for babies, teaching the young king [Aethelstan] how to behave in a time of extreme danger.... But the establishment will resist the idea that the national epic was written for a little boy" (qtd. Dugdale 51).

6 For example, in his essay on *Aesopica*, Robert G. Miner Jr. claims that "none of these editions [of Aesop] were for children (children, of course, were not invented until the seventeenth century)" (10). That fables and fable collections were associated with children throughout the classical and medieval periods is well known. For a recent discussion of the use of fable texts in the education of children during that time span see Jan M. Ziolkowski's *Talking Animals* (21–24). For Caxton's *Aesop* and later fable versions see the special issue of the *Children's Literature Association Quarterly* 9, no. 2 (Summer 1994).

7 For an introduction to the topic of Jewish literacy see Stefan Reif, particularly 149–55. For those with the linguistic skills, the topic of medieval Jewish children and any material that may have been written for them would be a rich, and apparently uninvestigated, field.

8 McKitterick claims that an esteem for books and their contents—and a literacy level much higher than originally thought for the laity as well as the church—are as characteristic of the so-called Dark Ages as the High Middle Ages; see particularly her *Carolingians and the Written Word*. William McMunn also argues for a higher literacy rate than was once thought ("Literacy"). In her fourth chapter, "The Production and Possession of Books," McKitterick details the high cost of the many skins, the binding, and the pigments used for an illuminated book (*Carolingians*).

9 Reynolds emphasizes that even at this early stage, learning to read is learning to read in a foreign language, Latin, and it is the Latin pronunciation of the alphabet that is learned. McKitterick argues, however, that in the Frankish regions, through the Carolingian period and even extending beyond it, students were learning the learned version of their own language (perhaps on the order of standard English and "ebonics"); this practice was even more widespread in Spain and Italy (*Carolingians* passim).

10 McKitterick notes the shortcomings for elementary educational purposes of the original "Donatus" (by a fourth-century Roman grammarian), which dealt only with the parts of speech. She discusses some of the additions, variants, and substitutes made for it, even as early as the Carolingian period, in order to meet local needs (*Carolingians* 13–20).

11 The short phrases at the beginning commence with *Itaque deo supplica* [And so pray to God], *Parentes ama* [Love your parents], and *cognatos cole* [honor your relatives] (i, nos. 1–3). The longer couplets in the second section are along the lines of *Plus vigila semper nec somno deditus esto / nam diuturna quies vitiis alimenta ministrat* [Always devote yourself more to waking than sleeping / since long repose gives nourishment to the vices] (ii, no. 2). Jonathan Nicholls comments that "such was the popularity of the original idea that, in translation and paraphrase, [Cato] reached an enormous public in every country in Europe" (64). The distichs were still popular enough in the early modern period for Benedict Burgh's fifteenth-century English paraphrase to be one of Caxton's earlier productions, *Cato*, in 1477; it went into a second edition within a year and a third in 1481 (Childs 176). For the most accessible original and translation see [Cato]. After the second half of the twelfth century the anonymous *Facetus*, "a disorganized collection of precepts that dealt with moral welfare, points of etiquette, and semi-proverbial wisdom," is often found together with the distichs (Nicholls 182).

12 For the many shifts in the upper-division classical curriculum in the medieval period, see Ernst Robert Curtius's chapter "Curriculum Authors" (48–54). He notes that "medieval reverence for the *auctores* was so great that every source [of their texts] was held to be good. The historical and the critical sense were both lacking" (52).

13 Ziolkowski provides a detailed analysis of this poem (48–53). Alcuin spent the first half of his adult life in York and was head of the cathedral school there. At the International Research Society for Children's Literature conference at York in August 1997 I presented a paper on Alcuin and his writing for children in which I argued that his poem was an example of a work "cross-written" for a dual audience of children and adults.

14 It is a shame that Zeydel's English translation of the *Ecbasis Captivi* is so unreadable; for an analysis that emphasizes the work's religious symbolism and connection to Easter, see Ziolkwoski 153–197. Mann's prose translation of the *Ysengrimus*, on the other hand, is clear and direct and has excellent notes. For the most recent work on medieval animal literature in general see Ziolkowski's authoritative book, which is sensitive throughout to the possibility of a child audience and mentions when the works he addresses are bound with school texts.

15 Hrotswitha has not been well served by the English translations, which obscure the vividness and immediacy of her text. The two most recent ones I have seen, by Larissa Bonfante (1979) and Katharina Wilson (1989), are no exception; Bonfante's is slightly preferable.

16 I presented a paper on this text, "A Medieval Storybook: The Urban Tales of Petrus Alfonsi," at the Children's Literature Association Conference in Omaha, Nebraska, in June 1997.

17 The original audience for *Dolopathos* is not easily specified because there is only one manuscript from a time (about 1200) and location close to the author; the other five that the editor Alfons Hilka cites are from the fifteenth century (vii–x). There are also later vernacular variants. Although it is dedicated to Bertrand, the bishop of Metz, I believe that this work had a youthful audience. The framing story is a rousing account of how a fourteen-year-old pagan, Lucinius, is saved from the lust of his wicked stepmother and from being burned to death by a series of tales told by seven wise men; the secular frame concludes with a tedious account of Lucinius's conversion to Christianity later in life, added no doubt to get the bishop's approval. *Dolopathos* has been well translated by Brady B. Gilleland and is an excellent read.

18 For a detailed description of each of these medieval courtesy books in Latin, Anglo-Norman, and English with all known texts and preferred editions, see Nicholls, Appendix B (179–97).

19 The introductory chapter to Marcus's study of problematic early modern texts, *Unediting the Renaissance*, applies to critical approaches to literary works of all periods and should be required reading for graduate students who plan to deal with the material text as a network or force field linked to a wider historical and cultural matrix.

Works cited

Adams, Gillian. "The First Children's Literature? The Case for Sumer." *Children's Literature* 14 (1986): 1–30.

Alfonsi, Petrus. *Die Disciplina Clericalis des Petrus Alfonsi (das älteste Novellenbuch des Mittelalters)*. Ed. Alfons Hilka and Werner Söderhjelm. Shorter edition. Heidelberg: Carl Winter, 1911. Trans. Joseph Ramon Jones and John Esten Keller as *The Scholar's Guide: A Translation of the Twelfth-Century Disciplina Clericalis of Pedro Alfonso*. Toronto: Pontifical Institute, 1969, and P. R. Quarrie as *The Disciplina Clericalis of Petrus Alfonsi*. Berkeley: University of California Press, 1977.

Alta Silva, Johannes de. *Dolopathos sive De rege et septem sapientibus.* Ed. Alfons Hilka. Heidelberg: Carl Winter, 1913. Trans. Brady B. Gilleland. *Johannes de Alta Silva: Dolopathos, or The King and the Seven Wise Men.* Binghamton, N.Y.: Center for Medieval and Early Renaissance Studies, 1981.

Ariès, Philippe. *Centuries of Childhood: A Social History of Family Life.* 1960. Trans. Robert Baldick. New York: Vintage, 1962.

Beckett, Sandra. "Crosswriting Child and Adult: Henri Bosco's *L'Enfant et la rivière.*" *Children's Literature Association Quarterly* 21, no. 4 (winter 1996–97): 189–99.

Beeson, Charles H. *A Primer of Medieval Latin: An Anthology of Prose and Poetry.* Chicago: Scott, Foresman, 1925.

Berlioz, Jacques. "Un Petit chaperon rouge médiéval? 'La petite fille épargnée par les loups' dans la *Fecunda ratis* d'Egbert de Liège (début du XIe siècle)." *Merveilles & Contes* 55 no. 2 (December 1991): 246–63.

Bingham, Jane, and Grayce Scholt. *Fifteen Centuries of Children's Literature: An Annotated Chronology of British and American Works in Historical Context.* Westport, Conn.: Greenwood, 1980.

Boswell, John. *The Kindness of Strangers.* 1988. New York: Vintage, 1990.

Bottigheimer, Ruth B. *The Bible for Children: From the Age of Gutenberg to the Present.* New Haven: Yale University Press, 1996.

——. "The Child-Reader of Children's Bibles, 1656–1753." In *Infant Tongues: The Voice of the Child in Children's Literature.* Ed. Elizabeth Goodenough et al. Detroit: Wayne State University Press, 1994. Pp. 44–56.

——. Letter to the author. 25 February 1997.

Brockman, Bennett A. "Children and Literature in Late Medieval England." *Children's Literature* 4 (1975): 58–63.

——. "The Juvenile Audiences of Sir Orfeo." *Children's Literature Association Quarterly* 10, no. 1 (Spring 1985): 18–20.

——. "Medieval Songs of Innocence and Experience." *Children's Literature* 2 (1973): 40–49.

——. "Robin Hood and the Invention of Children's Literature." *Children's Literature* 10 (1982): 1–17.

Brüggemann, Theodor, with Otto Brunken. *Handbuch zur Kinder- und Jugendliteratur vom Beginn des Buchdrucks bis 1570.* Stuttgart: Metzler, 1987.

Butler, Francelia. "From the Editor's High Chair." *Children's Literature* 1 (1972): 7–8.

[Cato]. "'Dicta Catonis': Introduction to *Disticha.* Text." In *Minor Latin Poets* vol. 2. Ed. and trans. J. Wight Duff and Arnold M. Duff. 1934. Loeb Classical Library. 1982. Pp. 585–621.

Childs, Edmund. *William Caxton: A Portrait in a Background.* London: Northwood, 1976.

Comestor, Petrus. *Historia Scholastica Excellens Opus. Editio altera post Beneventam anni MDCIC. Accessit Index locupletissimus.* Venice: Antonius Bortolus, 1729.

Cunningham, Hugh. *Children and Childhood in Western Society Since 1500.* London and New York: Longman, 1995.

Curtius, Ernst Robert. *European Literature and the Latin Middle Ages.* 1948. Trans. Willard Trask. Bollingen Series no. 36. New York: Pantheon, 1953.

Darton, Harvey F. J. *Children's Books in England.* 1932. 3d rev. ed. Ed. Brian Alderson. Cambridge: Cambridge University Press, 1982.

Demers, Patricia. *Heaven upon Earth: The Form of Moral and Religious Children's Literature, to 1850.* Knoxville: University of Tennessee Press, 1993.

Demers, Patricia, and Gordon Moyles. *From Instruction to Delight: An Anthology of Children's Literature to 1850.* Toronto: Oxford University Press, 1982.

Dhuoda. *A Handbook for William: A Carolingian Woman's Counsel for Her Son.* Trans. Carol Neel. Regents Studies in Medieval Culture. Lincoln: University of Nebraska Press, 1991.

Dugdale, John. "Who's Afraid of *Beowulf?*" *The New Yorker*, 23 and 30 December 1996, 50–51.

Ecbasis Cuiusdam Captivi per Tropologiam (Escape of a Certain Captive Told in a Figurative Manner: An Eleventh-Century Beast Epic). Ed. and trans. Edwin H. Zeydel. University of North Carolina Studies in the Germanic Languages and Literatures 46. Chapel Hill: University of North Carolina Press, 1964.

Egbert of Liège. *Fecunda ratis Egberts von Lüttich.* Ed. Ernst Voigt. Halle: Max Niemeyer, 1889.

Gordon, E. V., ed. *Pearl.* 1953. Oxford: Clarendon, 1974.

Grimm, Jacob, and Wilhelm Grimm. *The Complete Fairy Tales of the Brothers Grimm.* 1812–1857. Trans. and with an introduction by Jack Zipes. New York: Bantam, 1987.

Hanawalt, Barbara A. *Growing up in Medieval London: The Experience of Childhood in History.* New York: Oxford University Press, 1993.

Hanks, D. Thomas, Jr. "Not for Adults Only: The English Corpus Christi Plays." *Children's Literature Association Quarterly* 10, no. 1 (Spring 1985): 21–22.

Hildebrand, Ann M. "Jean de Brunhoff's Advice to Youth: The *Babar* Books as Books of Courtesy." *Children's Literature* 11 (1983): 76–95.

Horace. *Satires, Epistles, and Ars Poetica*, with English trans. by H. Rushton Fairclough. Loeb Classical Library. 1926. Revised 1929.

Hrotswitha of Gandersheim. *The Plays of Hrotsvit of Gandersheim.* Trans. Katharina Wilson. Garland Library of Medieval Literature 62, Series B. New York: Garland, 1989.

———. *The Plays of Hrotswitha of Gandersheim.* Trans. Larissa Bonfante. New York: New York University Press, 1979.

Hunt, Peter. "Passing on the Past: The Problem of Books That Are for Children and That Were for Children." *Children's Literature Association Quarterly* 21, no. 4 (Winter 1996–97): 200–202.

Hunt, Tony. *Teaching and Learning Latin in 13th-Century England.* Vol. 1, *Texts.* Cambridge, U.K.: Brewer, 1991.

Jambeck, Thomas J., and Karen K. Jambeck. "Chaucer's *Treatise on the Astrolabe*: A Handbook for the Medieval Child." *Children's Literature* 3 (1974): 117–22.

Lontzen, Günter. "Das Gedicht 'De Puella A Lupellis Servata' von Egbert von Lüttich—eine Parabel zum Thema der Taufe." *Merveilles & Contes* 6, no. 1 (May 1992): 20–44.

Marcus, Leah Sinanoglou. *Childhood and Cultural Despair: A Theme and Variation in Seventeenth-Century Literature.* Pittsburgh: University of Pittsburgh Press, 1978.

———. *Unediting the Renaissance: Shakespeare, Marlowe, Milton.* London and New York: Routledge, 1996.

McGillis, Roderick. *The Nimble Reader: Literary Theory and Children's Literature.* New York: Twayne, 1996.

McKitterick, Rosamond. *The Carolingians and the Written Word*. Cambridge: Cambridge University Press, 1989.

——. "A Ninth-Century Schoolbook from the Loire Valley: Phillipps MS 16308." In *Books, Scribes, and Learning in the Frankish Kingdoms, 6th–9th Centuries*. Aldershot: Variorum, 1994. Essay 9 (225–31).

——. "Nuns' Scriptoria in England and Francia in the Eighth Century." In *Books, Scribes, and Learning in the Frankish Kingdoms, 6th–9th Centuries*. Aldershot: Variorum, 1994. Essay 7 (1–35).

——, ed. *The Uses of Literacy in Early Medieval Europe*. Cambridge: Cambridge University Press, 1990.

McMunn, Meradith Tilbury. "Children and Literature in Medieval France." *Children's Literature* 4 (1975): 51–58.

McMunn, Meradith Tilbury, and William Robert McMunn. "Children's Literature in the Middle Ages." *Children's Literature* 1 (1972): 21–29.

McMunn, William Robert. "The Literacy of Medieval Children." *Children's Literature* 4 (1975): 36–41.

Miner, Robert G., Jr. "Aesop as Litmus: The Acid Test of Children's Literature." *Children's Literature* 1 (1972): 9–15.

Morris, Sidney. *Fons Perennis: An Anthology of Medieval Latin for Schools*. London: Harrap, 1962.

Myers, Mitzi. "Wise Child, Wise Peasant, Wise Guy: Geoffrey Summerfield's Case Against the Eighteenth Century." *Children's Literature Association Quarterly* 12, no. 2 (Summer 1987): 107–10.

Nicholls, Jonathan. *The Matter of Courtesy: Medieval Courtesy Books and the Gawain-Poet*. Woodbridge, Suffolk: D. S. Brewer, 1985.

Nikolajeva, Maria, ed. *Aspects and Issues in the History of Children's Literature*. Contributions to the Study of World Literature 60. Westport, Conn. and London: Greenwood, 1995.

[Nivardus]. *Ysengrimus*. Ed. and trans. Jill Mann. Mittellateinische Studien und Texte 12. Leiden: Brill, 1987.

Nodelman, Perry. "The Other: Orientalism, Colonialism, and Children's Literature." *Children's Literature Association Quarterly* 17.1 (Spring 1992): 29–35.

——. *The Pleasures of Children's Literature*. 1992. Rev. ed. White Plains, N.Y.: Longman, 1996.

——, ed. "Literary Theory and Children's Literature." *Children's Literature Association Quarterly* 18.1 (Spring 1993): 36–46.

Perry, Ben Edwin. *Babrius and Phaedrus*. Newly Edited and Translated into English, Together with an Historical Introduction and a Comprehensive Survey of Greek and Latin Fables in the Aesopic Tradition. Loeb Classical Library. 1965.

Pollock, Linda A. *Forgotten Children: Parent-Child Relations from 1500 to 1900*. Cambridge: Cambridge University Press, 1983.

Reif, Stefan C. "Aspects of Medieval Jewish Literacy." In *The Uses of Literacy in the Early Medieval Period*. Cambridge: Cambridge University Press, 1990. Pp. 134–55.

Reynolds, Suzanne. *Medieval Reading: Grammar, Rhetoric and the Classical Text*. Cambridge: Cambridge University Press, 1996.

Riggio, Milla B. "The Schooling of the Poet: Christian Influences and Latin Rhetoric in the Early Middle Ages." *Children's Literature* 4 (1975): 44–51.

Rouse, R. H., and M. A. Rouse. "The Vocabulary of Wax Tablets." *Harvard Library Bulletin* n.s., 1.3 (Fall 1990): 2–19.

Schultz, James A. *The Knowledge of Childhood in the German Middle Ages, 1100–1350.* Philadelphia: University of Pennsylvania Press, 1995.

Shahar, Shulamith. *Childhood in the Middle Ages.* 1990. London and New York: Routledge, 1992.

Shaner, Mary. "Instruction and Delight: Medieval Romances as Children's Literature." *Poetics Today* 31 (1992): 5–15.

Shavit, Zohar. "The Historical Model of the Development of Children's Literature." In *Aspects and Issues in the History of Children's Literature.* Contributions to the Study of World Literature 60. Westport, Conn. and London: Greenwood, 1995. Pp. 27–38.

Smith, Elva Sophronia. *The History of Children's Literature: A Syllabus with Selected Bibliographies.* 1937. Rev. ed. Ed. Margaret Hodges and Susan Stein. Chicago: American Library Association, 1980.

Spiegel, Harriet. "Instructing the Children: Advice from the Twelfth-Century *Fables* of Marie of France." *Children's Literature* 17 (1989): 25–46.

Talbot, C. H. "Children in the Middle Ages." *Children's Literature* 6 (1977): 17–33.

Victor, Claudius Marius. *Alethia.* Ed. C. Schenkl. *Corpus Scriptorum Ecclesiasticorum Latinorum* 16. Vienna, 1888.

Wright, Thomas, ed. *The Book of the Knight of La Tour-Landry: Compiled for the Instruction of His Daughters.* Early English Text Society orig. ser. 33, 1906. London: Kegan Paul, 1968.

Ziolkowski, Jan M. *Talking Animals: Medieval Latin Beast Poetry, 750–1150.* Philadelphia: University of Pennsylvania Press, 1993.

10

SENTIMENT AND SIGNIFICANCE

The impossibility of recovery in the
children's literature canon or,
the drowning of *The Water Babies*

Deborah Stevenson

Source: *The Lion and the Unicorn* 21 (1997): 112–130.

Recovery of a forgotten author always sounds like a wonderful idea; one takes a writer whose work, like a dropped stitch, fell out of its place, and knits it back into its row in the canonical garment. I use "recovery" here to mean not just a return to print but a return to broad awareness of a book as indispensable, as, in short, a children's literature classic to be passed on to ensuing generations. A hypothetical version of recovery works something like this: a critic writes a brilliant new book on Charles Kingsley's *The Water-Babies* (1863), causing people to reassess its importance. The book is favorably reviewed not only in academic journals, but in "gatekeeper" periodicals such as the *New York Times Book Review* and the *New York Review of Books*. Other scholars find this work relevant to their own, and *Water-Babies* articles begin to appear in PMLA, contesting, restructuring, and expanding on the original pivotal volume. At the same time, non-academics who have read the monograph's reviews and seen the author on the *Today* show exhibit heightened interest in *The Water-Babies* itself, buying it in greater numbers for their children. Soon, Spielberg's plans for a new live-action movie are announced, the book is repackaged with a flashy film tie-in (while the Norton edition steadily infiltrates universities), and the children and scholars of the 1990s rediscover the magic and/or import of Mrs. Doasyouwouldbedoneby and Mrs. Bedonebyasyoudid and then pass them onto the next generations as treasures of their own childhood.

It is an appealing picture, but it is not going to happen. Children's literature depends upon a canon of sentiment, and such canons are proof

155

against attempts at academic recovery; the academic curriculum, which is based on a canon of significance, may rediscover the historical significance of a children's author but can never truly recover it to the literature's dominant popular canon.

Canons are an increasingly problematized notion in our time; children's literature, with its conflicting and often polarized formative currents, offers a particularly complex response to the issue. In common academic discourse, we employ "canon" to refer to that list of works we consider requisite for understanding a part of literature; that, in short, is what we must teach if we wish students to comprehend a subject. While there is heated debate about how such texts should be chosen and perpetuated, or even what they mean, there have been some excellent analyses, both from those who approve of the process and those who do not, of how canon formation operates. Yet the academic canon formation described by Richard Ohmann as taking place "in the interaction between large audiences and gatekeeper intellectuals," is not the process that creates lasting classics in children's literature ("Shaping" 383).

Canon formation is largely a concern of literary scholarship, which has, as opposed to the disciplines of library science and education, lately turned its attention to the genre of children's literature; only recently have academic rankings of significance for the books within the genre begun to appear. While children's literature does not yet offer academic anthologies of the same weight and importance as the Heath or the Norton collections, which operate as arbiters or thermostats of canonical status, other works such as Charles Frey and John Griffith's *Classics of Children's Literature* (which offers a similar compendium flavor and paperback textbook format and which just appeared in its fourth edition) seem to want to emulate them. If academic criticism of children's literature continues to burgeon, doubtless such books will gain in popularity and number.

As Brian McCrea discusses in *Addison and Steele Are Dead* (1990), academic canons exist to fill a variety of needs, both artistic and professional; scholars are likelier to discuss books about which they have something to say. The long academic silence on children's literature seems likely to stem from the absence of its critical cachet as well as a lack of critical tools for its analysis. Now that criticism of the genre is increasing, this tendency to lionize what is useful to the critic exists in the study of and response to children's literature. Some authorities of children's literature note the existence of "critics' books," or "reviewers' books," texts that appeal strongly to the adults who, after encountering scores of formula novels, appreciate the originality of a technical innovation without being distanced, as its child audience might be, by its sophistication (Gerhardt 122). Similarly, scholarly interest in text recovery is a well-established phenomenon in all walks of literature; scholars of children's literature, too, are interested in the merit of works whose reputation may have dimmed over the decades.

As a teaching canon, children's literature feels a need to document its history; the canon is not, however, closed to change, particularly as many contemporary books provide yet more interesting theoretical challenges. Despite the genre's conservatism, it is not closed to the new: Maurice Sendak's *Where the Wild Things Are* (1963) is canonical; Jon Scieszka's *The Stinky Cheese Man and Other Fairly Stupid Tales* (1992) has made an impressive attempt on the academic canon in four short years. The community of the genre's scholars, too, is expanding as children's literature gets taught as literature in college, high school, and lower schools.

These academic readers, however, are not the significant audience of children's literature. A canonical work such as *Hamlet* is read almost exclusively by members of the community of scholars, which includes high-school students as well as professors of literature. Purely popular incarnations or readings of the play, without awareness of its academic role, do not exist. *Where the Wild Things Are*'s popular role exists alongside its academic role; in fact, its popular significance overshadows its academic impact. Children's literature scholarship is by no means invalid; it sheds much light on literature as a whole as well as the genre it discusses. But its power to affect the literature it studies is slight compared to the effect of criticism on other contemporary genres, and its judgment over the literature is not supreme. Ultimately, popular judgments of sentimental regard, not academic lists of significance, create and control the canon of children's literature.

Literary critics are not the only professionals with authority over children's literature: educators and librarians have studied and distributed the genre for years. Yet while curricular use of titles enhances their sales figures, a reader's association with such a text is controlled by its mandatory nature, so that scholastic use of a title rarely affects its uncoerced status. The impact of librarians has been much more significant; in addition to being for decades the genre's most noted scholars, they influence distribution, marketing, and readership. But they too have professional considerations that influence their choices, and it is the non-professional canon, the judgments of amateurs—in both that word's original meaning of "one who does it only for love" and in its contemporary sense—which figures most prominently in popular conception of the literature. There is, however, one common characteristic between those non-academic adult categories: none of the adults who deal directly with children's reading—parents, teachers, librarians, "practitioners" (Peter Hunt's term)—has much occasion for recovering the truly forgotten (6). They, not literary critics (although they may take that role at times), determine which books are passed on to children, and they hand down the familiar and beloved, not the merely historically significant or the forgotten.

"Popular canon" may initially seem an oxymoronic concept, but children's books have never depended on the academy for the creation of classic status. Ohmann notes that "lay" readers generally valued literature "where they discovered the values in which they believed or where they found needed moral guidance when shaken in their own beliefs" (*Politics* 70), and the popular canon seems to reflect such values. While no canon, springing as it does from a variety of social and economic forces, can truly be termed "natural," the canon of sentiment is less self-conscious than academic rankings or anthologies. As an accidental canon, it takes one book at a time with little thought to overall effect. Unlike the canon of significance, it makes no attempt at breadth, considers no issues of representation (in fact, is wildly non-representative in many ways), and suffers from few exigencies of time and space. It ultimately defines children's literature in the popular understanding of the term. Whereas the academic canon of significance exists to justify, document, chronicle, or explain, the canon of sentiment exists to preserve—to preserve the childhood of those adults who create that canon and to preserve the affection those adults feel for the books within it. Instead of Norton anthologies, it has the manifold treasuries, both mass-market and elegantly produced keepsakes, of children's literature.

Like the academic canon, the popular canon is problematically conceived and misleadingly weighted; it too selects its entries based on shifting and arguable notions of what fills a need and what is valuable. It reflects the taste and intentions of those adults empowered to affect the purchase of books, which has in the past excluded and continues to exclude large groups of people who have lacked the opportunity and economic capability to enforce any textual choices they might make. Though there are signs that the patterns of influence may be changing (although the greater interest in multicultural literature does not always relate directly to the interests of people from a given culture, as Thelma Seto points out [169–74]), the disproportion seems merely to shift rather than to disappear. The combination of unevenly concentrated power and the retroactive nature of the genre means that the standards employed in judging these canon entries are rooted in the Great Books tradition (which, of course, is shaped by the books already in the canon). The fact of a book's moving millions does matter to the popular canon. Moving which millions, however, and moving them in what way, is an important consideration. The kitschy chic of an old Nancy Drew title cannot popularly compete with *Alice in Wonderland* (1865). The sentimental canon has its own belletristic standards, despite its different criteria for what makes a text "belle."

The sentimental canon, then, is formed largely on custom: it favors books that comfort over books that challenge, books that reinforce the status quo over books that attempt to change it; it renders all books safe by their very inclusion therein. Therefore the canon of sentiment, even more than the academic canon, is following Frederick Crews' description of the conservative idea of academia as "a pantheon for the preservation of great works and great ideas," which follows a "'transfusion' model of education, whereby the stored-up wisdom of the classics is considered a kind of plasma that will drip beneficially into our veins if we only stay sufficiently passive in its presence" (xiv). We talk about viewing classics afresh with each new generation, but we do not wish to evade the viewpoint of those older generations entirely; the point is to add layers of contemplation, not to replace the previous layers.

Other popular literatures, too, have their rankings. While few canons are as dependent on the popular viewpoint as that of children's literature, it is instructive to consider those that have a similar duality of audience and purpose. The discernment shown by the dedicated romance readers featured in Janice Radway's *Reading the Romance* (1984) differs from the scholarly differentiation a critic might make; Janice Radway is not her subject readers.[1] The Victorianist writing on M. E. Braddon or E.D.E.N. Southworth does not consider his or her subject in the same light as a pleasure reader would, and that scholar cannot consider those authors as their contemporaries might have.

Both of those Victorians have been subject to modest academic recovery efforts, but the recovery of *Lady Audley's Secret* (1862) into a graduate English classroom is not a return to its original status. A melodrama that pounds no pulses is not recovered but taxidermized: Braddon academically recovered is not resurrected; there is still no life in the corpse. *Lady Audley's Secret*, to be truly recovered in the modern world, needs to be sold in airport bookstalls and converted to made-for-TV dramas. There has been no such occurrence; the text has not been recovered to its initial place or read in its initial sense. Braddon does not rub shoulders with Mary Higgins Clark in the popular canon.

Reading as the original readers is always a problem. The challenge of returning into the past is one that scholars face, and fail, constantly. Even if one does accept the idea that the Victorian self was in some ways a child of the contemporary self, that merely peeling off layers permits one to understand the Victorian point of view, one cannot un-know what one knows. There is a similarity between one adulthood and another, however, that there is not between adulthood and childhood. *Lady Audley's Secret* is not favored contemporary reading, but some of those adults who do peruse Braddon's work today have found the reading pleasurable for, apparently, many of the same reasons their Victorian counterparts did: the spirit of the popular audience remains. Scholarship not being proof against suspense, there is a possibility of similarity between Braddon's nineteenth-century readers and twentieth-century Braddon scholars that does not exist for a children's book such as *The Water-Babies*.

The canon cannot, then, dispense entirely with children, but neither is there any independent, adult-free canon of children's literature. Children's literature must, at least nominally, speak to a state in which the readers of power no longer participate. Librarians have a professional awareness of what books are popular among children, but their own standards and financial restraints affect their selections. Educators choose books to suit their pedagogic purposes. Parents too choose books for their children based not only on their knowledge of their children's preferences but their desire for their children's growth. Yet this separation from the putative audience may well be the point of the canon and indeed the literature, as readers find an excuse for what Virgil Nemoianu, discussing the popular regard for Evelyn Waugh, terms "contrasting imaginative relief . . . from prevailing social discourses" (231).

It is instructive to examine some pragmatic considerations in connection with the issue of canonical status. Other popular literatures, for instance, are largely purchased by their actual audience; most children's books are not. They are purchased by librarians, by parents—in short, by adults. Librarians purchase books for libraries that will allow many non-purchasers to read the book; library purchases were, in the 1960s and 1970s, ninety percent of children's book sales. Private purchasing having grown and public funding having shrunk, that share has dwindled to approximately fifty percent—but the non-library purchases are hardly dominated by children's direct purchasing. While occasionally adults will buy children's books for their own enjoyment or their own research, generally someone other than the buyer is the intended reader. Purchasers of adult books are much likelier to be their readers as well as their buyers.

Children do purchase books, of course; the Goosebumps phenomenon, like the Stratemeyer syndicate before it, is almost entirely driven by a direct child market, and Stine's series is even more successful than its mass-market forerunners. Yet adults do not offer the same respect to totally child-driven successes—the awareness of the lower status of a book keeps it from entering the sentimental canon no matter how much it makes it into sentimental recollection. There are standards of perceived quality even in this popular canon and even within this popular literature. The sentimental canon contains books that one must be able to pass on with approval, not just cherish for oneself; the child an adult once was has some power, but the adult that is wields more.

Hardback editions of a text, for instance, are proof of an adult market. A profitable survival of a hardback edition indicates a sufficiency of adult audience. Reillustrated hardback classics appear on the shelves of every children's section in a bookstore; adults who purchase such books are not likely to be librarians or educators, who have access to versions more likely to be appealing to children, but non-professional adults giving literary symbols of childhood to children; they are books so redolent of treasure that adults will spend twenty dollars on them in order to give a keepsake rather than seven or eight merely to give a title.

Comparatively few children's backlist books remain in hardback printing. Those that do, however, are in print as hardback because they are in somebody's canon. "If you are a dead author and not in the canon," Marilyn Butler observes about adult literature, "you are probably not in print," and a similar relationship exists in children's literature (70). Many canonical works have passed into the public domain and made reprinting even easier and more profitable. Often these hardback editions coexist with a lower-priced paperback edition, or even several: *Little Women* (1868) has its academic versions, its hardback children's versions, and its paperback children's versions (some abridged, some not, and some with stills from the recent movie on the cover), and even *The Wind in the Willows* (1908) has several different illustrated versions in hardback in addition to plainer and less expensive paperbacks. Such production does not seem to encourage the recovery of the lost but the perpetuation of the already successful.

Children, practically speaking, have two effects on their literature: they buy books and they cause books to be bought, whether by importuning relatives or by wearing out library copies. The first of these effects, however, is slight compared to adult market influence; it is the second, and often the illusion of the second, that molds the genre. Though this literature nominally belongs to children, their role in the formation of these various canons is a vexed one. Children's literature cannot exist without adults, but neither the genre nor its canon can exist without children. As Jacqueline Rose has pointed out, children's literature's apparent embrace of the child is deceptive, but the genre does demand a continual awareness of children (2). The constraints upon child readers, however, limit their ability to shape the canon directly.

While practitioners note that different children have different tastes, we tend to treat child readers more egalitarianly—and more homogeneously—than adult readers: in the absence of a recognized, linked child intelligentsia, the gatekeepers of which Richard Ohmann speaks, the opinion of one child bears no more weight than that of any other. There is no limited child coterie whose known approval, even should it fail to extend beyond the bounds of the group, can make a book's reputation. As a result, audience numbers in child readership become more important to status than they do for adult literature, where only a few of the "right" readers count as much as hundreds or thousands of the wrong. Smart or precocious child readers merely move to a different reading level; they often slot themselves or are slotted according to that level, rather than their age, which means that they have comparatively lost *status*, in this mythical peer audience, because they are younger than the others reading that level of book. Sometimes they simply move up to adult literature, which removes them from the children's literature reading pool entirely. The best child readers rise longitudinally rather than exerting power latitudinally, which means that there are no child gatekeepers of the canon.

Children are culturally and financially powerless; more specifically, child readers are judged and categorized in a way that precludes their contribution to an academic canon. Children's literature practitioners are fairly conscious of the tendency of children's literature to please adults rather than children; as a result, however, a book ostensibly aimed at, say, sixth graders that contains a complexity that most sixth graders will not have dealt with is viewed with suspicion. Yet even if most sixth-graders cannot or will not take in this hypothetical title, it seems likely that there will be some—perhaps only a few hundred more or less—who will read and profit from this text. This number is too few to carry the book forward to the next generation, or perhaps even to the next printing, without adult support, and adult support will be in spite of, not because of, the child readership; too small a child readership suggests to adults that the book is either a bad children's book or an adult book. While highly specialized subject matter receives a tolerant acknowledgment of a narrow but deserving audience, a similarly specialized level of sophistication arouses wariness.

The sentimental canon may appear to connect more closely to the child audience than the academy, but it too essentially excludes them from its formation. Childish affection for a text exerts some influence on a text's status, but a far more important influence is the affection of the children today's adults once were, the affection demonstrated when that fond child grows up and arrives at a position of transmission—s/he becomes a librarian, or a parent, or an editor, or a teacher. The sentimental canon of children's literature depends upon a text's ability to call up a connection with childhood even more than a connection with children.

It is ultimately unclear just how long a text can persist in the canon without the readership of actual children, or how large a readership that must be. The sentimental canon demands popularity at some level with children, but it does not require that popularity to remain for canonicity. The difficulty of obtaining reader statistics and audience information makes it nearly impossible to state just how many contemporary children have read *The Water-Babies*, or, for that matter, *The Wind in the Willows* or *Alice in Wonderland*. The latter two texts have had their positions bolstered by other media versions, many of which children encounter in lieu of the books but which contribute to the awareness of the original texts (and hence the retention in, though not a recovery to, the sentimental canon). *Alice* is part of the culture, and it is part of the culture as a children's book. It will never change categories; adults who read it today still read it as a children's book, because that is what it is. It depends on that identity.[2]

A text's usefulness to children is relevant; more important is its connection to childhood. There are both old and new children's books that are more significant to adult readers than children; *Alice*, with its Martin Gardner annotations and its adult culthood, is a good example of that phenomenon. These books still depend on their linkage with childhood for success, for significance, and for their place in the world. Adults enjoy hip children's books not merely because the books are so adult, but because they are children's books; the sense of slipping into an entitlement of the past provides their appeal.[3] The undercutting and usage of the children's genre is the basis of adult affection for such books; were they to be understood as entirely adult works they would have no place or power.

A text need not be popular with a multitude of contemporary children in order to be a classic. It must, however, speak of childhood, not just of literature, to adults. The halo of affection around classic children's literature texts is more important than the texts themselves. Despite periodic argument, for instance, that *Alice in Wonderland* is really an adult book (and probably more adults than children read the text these days), *Alice* is read as a cherished children's book in a way that *The Water-Babies* is ceasing to be. And *The Wind in the Willows* has diminished in actual readership but has yet to disappear from the canon of sentiment. At a recent conference panel devoted to Grahame's book, surprisingly few academics present had read this book in their childhood (and we had been bookish children). All of us had been aware of it in our childhoods, however, and had perhaps coexisted with a copy that we simply had refused to open. Even unread, *The Wind in the Willows* was associated with our childhoods in a way that *The Water-Babies* was not. Even if we never read it as children, we knew it belonged to us, and that it was a beloved classic.

The most successful books in the canon of sentiment are those such as C. S. Lewis' Narnia books (1950–56), which call forth affection both from the adult recalling a childhood reading (and sometimes a more recent reading) and from the child reading these books for the first time. The affection of the contemporary child enriches the adult's experience of transmission, and the affection of the adult enhances the child's experience by branding the books as classic and previously beloved. This process is the sort of self-reinvigorating chain lionized by books extolling the virtues of sharing literature with children.

That word "beloved" is crucial to the canon of sentiment. Several adult books over the last century, ranging from classics such as Lillian Smith's *The Unreluctant Years* (1953) to recent additions such as Regina Higgins' *Magic Kingdoms: Discovering the Joys of Childhood Classics with Your Child* (1992), emphasize the joy of sharing loved books with children; Higgins says, "When parents ask me which books they should read to their children for enjoyment . . . I begin by asking them about the books they enjoyed when they were growing up" (14). Love, as much as literature, is being canonized. In *The History in Literature*, Herbert Lindenberger suggests that the discourse of literary criticism approximates not the discourse of science or history, but that of love; we persuade ourselves and others that this one person, this particular book, matters more than others and for all time, when both lovers and literary critics know that such persuasions are prone to alteration (157). In regard to a genre of popular literature such as children's literature, the allusion to love ceases to be an analogy and becomes an analysis.

Herbert Lindenberger links canonization with love; Lillian R. Furst looks at the converse, pointing out that "to dislike the canon is therefore taken automatically as a sign of boorishness, without much inquiry into what is subsumed into the idea of an adequate explanation or a proper grasp, let alone a discerning reading" and that "the orthodox belief has been, as illustrated in those exam questions, that a failure to like the accepted canon could only be attributed to a deficiency in education" (39). In the canon of sentiment, a disliked classic is an oxymoron; if books are largely disliked they do not belong in the canon and do not stay there. More important than the text itself is the idea of the text; people who have never read *Alice* have an affectionate regard for the book that they do not extend to *The Water-Babies*.[4]

Although, as Lindenberger suggests, academic canon formation too is about love, adult literary criticism rarely discusses the issue while criticism of children's literature embraces it. The goal of teaching the love of literature has been a commonly stated aim of libraries and library associations for years; children's literature criticism, which for years came almost entirely from library science, speaks with similar enthusiasm of the love of individual books and of literature. The assumption of the necessity of such love is so great that the reasons for it are never explained; it is never clear why a love of literature or reading is necessary in order to profit from the activity. No other crucial activity or cornerstone of society is couched in terms of affection: we do not attempt to instill a love of law, a love of eating right, a love of exercise, a love of regular dental checkups. We do not even try to instill, or publicly exhort trying to instill, a love of thinking. This insistence on love suggests the possibility that the other rewards of reading are not sufficiently clear to make the practice regular. One need not love the law in order to observe it; the rewards of doing so and consequences of failing are assumed (often incorrectly) to speak for themselves. The emphasis on love, when it comes to reading, suggests that the non-emotional benefits may not suffice. True, if one develops a love of something readily available then a certain amount of pleasure is guaranteed through life, but if a reliable source of pleasure were the only goal then something even simpler and easier, such as breathing, might well have been a better choice on which to center a lifelong affection. The practice of reading is a commonly lauded goal in American society. But why do we demand not only competence in reading but also love? Are those who read capably without loving the activity really less successful or less worthy?

Children are the main targets of this intention to instill love. One does not instill a love of reading in an adult; it is tacitly admitted to be too late. Either adults are readers or they are not (we seem to balance our tabula rasa view of youth with a view of immutable adulthood). Reading is not only worthy of affection, it is praiseworthy; a child's developed affection for reading will presumably keep him or her in the habit of reading throughout life, so affection has become a reward for desirable behavior. The fact that this literature belongs to children further increases the relevance of the subject of love; it is difficult to discuss children without talking about love. How and in what ways we must love our children is a topic fraught with controversy, but *that* we must love them seems to be generally agreed upon. Perhaps in a world where the fear of loving children wrongly seems to be increasing, the safety of loving literature and loving children through literature is increasingly appealing.

The canon of sentiment approves of this emphasis on love. Carey Kaplan and Ellen Rose refer to Gertrude Himmelfarb's dichotomy of culture into "academic" and "society" (44); the sentimental canon knows it is not an academic-based canon, and is proud of that fact. The differences between academic and sentimental criteria are obvious, and the transmission of children's literature in the popular sphere depends on the latter. Just as the cry goes out to "let children be children," to refrain from frightening them with the more unpleasant truths of the world, so many people seek to protect children's literature from what is in their eyes the adultification—or adulteration—of analysis. Affection for individual books and indeed the entire genre is considered desirable and laudable; most scholars of children's literature can relate the eagerness with which people respond to the announcement of their profession, which contrasts considerably with the response engendered by an announcement of any other kind of literary scholarship. The idea of this literature and of the books within it prompt affection.

Sometimes, however, affection takes a different turn. Some of the closest approximations of revival involve affection for a different version of a text. Filmed or televised literary adaptations can enhance the audience numbers of a lesser-known text or shore up a book's place in the canon, and reillustrations and readaptations can allow for new recognition of folktales. It is worth considering both the scope and limitations of such reinvigorations.

Film and television adaptations are the one form of literary reinvigoration to which children do have access. The last few years have seen several critically acclaimed films with connections to children's books: *The Secret Garden* (1994), *The Little Princess* (1995), *Jumanji* (1995), *Babe* (1995); this summer brings us *James and the Giant Peach*, *Harriet the Spy*, and *Matilda*, and the fall promises a live-action *101 Dalmatians*. Animated tales based on books have, over the years, included *101 Dalmatians* (1961), *The Rescuers* (1977), and *The Secret of NIMH* (1982); I would also argue that films based upon folk and fairytales such as *Snow White* (1937), *Sleeping Beauty* (1959), *The Little Mermaid* (1989), and *Beauty and the Beast* (1991) should be considered in this category, because their source material is now considered nearly exclusively the domain of child readers and was chosen as an animated subject for that very reason.

The existence of other versions can work to the advantage of a book's popularity; Dodie Smith's *101 Dalmatians* (1956) is not, at least in the U.S., canonical, and its place in American culture stems from its film version, not its print version. The movie may well be what keeps the book in print when other excellent books of its era have long since fallen off backlists. The watchers of a re-released *101 Dalmatians* movie seem uninclined to consider the film a stepping-stone to the text; indeed, they seem no likelier to find or to purchase copies of Dodie Smith's original book than they do mass-market movie-spinoff coloring books and retellings, which receive a stronger marketing push. Nor is there any indication that the original book receives more sustained attention than theme drinking glasses or nightshirts.

Katherine Paterson's *Bridge to Terabithia* (1977) made an affecting *Wonderworks* television movie; so did Lois Lowry's *Taking Care of Terrific* (1985). *Bridge to Terabithia* was already well on its way to sentimental canonicity, whereas *Terrific* was not; the video versions do not seem to have changed these directions. People who saw *Babe* and loved it, then read the book, will probably be likelier to take the next generation to the re-release of the movie, or to watch it on tape, than they will to pass on the book. The possibility of film "ownership" in the form of video means that the audience need not resort to the book in order to enjoy the possibility of endless repetitions of the story. The primacy effect is extremely important—the version one encounters first, be it parodic or filmic, is the real version, and the real version is the one to be transmitted. Attention-catchers such as films may temporarily increase a response to the print text, but increased availability does not necessarily imply canonicity. Nor does a resurgence of popularity, even of a canonical book, necessarily extend to an author's work in toto; teen fans of the recent *Little Women* film may have been inspired to read the book and its continuations, but it is doubtful any of them went on to read Alcott's *Moods* (1865). Canonicity does not translate between film and literary versions. While a watchable version of a text can affect a book's standing and popularity, it has yet to demonstrate an ability to restore a forgotten text to the sentimental canon.

The movie transmits its own experience, not the experience of the book. A film version may enhance book sales, but the resultant text passed on from generation to generation is filmic rather than literary. A text not already canonical benefits slightly from a movie version but will not thereby be propelled into the pantheon; a text already canonical may find such film versions helpful in maintaining its state, because the idea of the story will remain in popular consciousness.

Movies may function as parody does, wherein the derivation often eclipses the original in fame. A good example is Isaac Watts' fate compared to his parodies in *Alice in Wonderland*: Watts was an unquestionably significant figure in the sentimental canon for some time, but Carroll's memorable Watts parodies, appearing, as Watts grew less remembered, in a book itself poised for sentimental canonization, have supplanted Watts. If the book has no strong audience recognition at the time its derivation appears, the derivation may well replace it rather than reinstate it.

For books that receive no boost from other media, the opportunities for recovery are few. The possibility that seems least implausible is the recovery not of a book but of a tale or a character; the picturebook tradition of creating completely new books from readaptations and reillustrations of older works means that a story that has been in existence for decades or centuries may appear anew. Folktales seem a particularly attractive candidate for this sort of revitalization; it will be interesting to see, for instance, whether the picturebook popularity of Coyote, the American Indian trickster figure, continues not only to remain strong but to rise into something more enduring in the next twenty years, in which case one might consider Coyote as a figure recovered to the canon.[5] As yet, however, there are no instances of this kind of revival. It is too early to say whether the plethora of newly treated folktales will leave a lasting impression on another generation; nor is this form of recovery quite what academics have in mind by the term, since these readaptations involve the lionizing of a figure or tale not previously sovereign in this particular genre. Currently they cannot challenge the place of the Perrault tales in enduring popular affection.

While some texts that initially receive such affection fade away, several have not: not every book is doomed to slide downwards in and disappear from the sentimental canon over time. Old books such as *Little Women* and *Alice* are still firmly entrenched. The genre is young, but it loves to preserve, depending on retrospection in a way that other genres do not. There will undoubtedly be a paring down of older books, as some sink like *The Water-Babies* while newer books rise. This tendency towards weeding down does not mean that all books, over time, are doomed to slide downwards in the sentimental canon, simply because fewer and fewer people remember them. The Perrault tales are still strongly canonical and show no sign of flagging; *Little Women* is still going strong. For a popular genre, children's literature has in fact been unusually gifted with lasting potential; adults do not hand down E.D.E.N. Southworth, or even Dickens, in the same way as they do Alcott.

Eventually, a children's literature classic masters being beloved without actually being read, with a sufficiently protective affection to keep the book enshrined in the sentimental canon despite its not being read. Eventually, just as Shakespeare becomes "Shakespeare," *Alice* becomes "Alice." Kaplan and Rose note that "you do not have to believe in *Hamlet*; you will simply be deemed culturally illiterate if you have not read it" (85). Similarly, you do not have to have read *Alice*, but you will be deemed culturally illiterate should you not acknowledge it as a children's literature classic.

Even beloved books, however, can eventually fall out of favor and memory. It is difficult to imagine indifference to a book one loves, and people tend to think if a text has made it past one generation it will be beloved forever. Statements such as Richard Ohmann's that "*The Catcher in the Rye* arrived to stay; it is older than most of its audience were when they read it for the first time" (*Politics* 45) suggest a rather limited judgment of staying power and fails to acknowledge the shifts in that book's audience. There have already been books whose star has risen, hovered, and then fallen again, despite the tacit assumption that a book whose popularity has survived to the adulthood of its audience will survive forever. *The Water-Babies* achieved that goal, but it is slipping from memory nonetheless. An adult seeking a book to give to a child picks up Kingsley's fantasy thinking not with nostalgia of a childhood memory worthy of sharing, but rather, "I think I've heard of this"—if s/he picks it up at all, or can find a copy to pick up. Academics note the text's historical significance, but Kingsley's book no longer has a place in the sentimental canon; the chain of affection has been broken. At some point, for reasons of taste, or marketing, or competition, or fashion, "Mother loved this" failed to become "I loved this" and "I want my children to love this."

That failure is the loss of canonicity. Children's literature needs the generational chain of evidence, the handing down, to be canonical. Candidates for recovery, fallen as they are from this chain, can never be reinstated to it. Regina Higgins dedicates her book "to your child and to the child in you" (7); it is that curious nexus of contemporary children and the children contemporary adults used to be that forms the popular canon. Children have no significant independent access to forgotten authors and the adults have nothing to gain from recovering them. The new and exciting can be discovered together and the old and familiar will be handed down with affection, but the old and unfamiliar offers no such extraliterary benefits to adult or child. Adults who complain about the loss of old books in libraries invariably bemoan the loss of old books they knew—they are not concerned with old books they never read. They offer their children *Winnie-the-Pooh* (1926) or *The Wind in the Willows* because these books carry the captured childhood of those adults within them in a way that *The Water-Babies*, for all its historical significance, no longer does; the critic who seeks to popularize the latter, thinking it a perfect book for contemporary children, will find little audience enthusiasm and few mechanisms for doing so. The imprimatur of popular canonization on a children's book comes from the hand of a previous generation handing it down; academic attempts to reestablish a text's significance cannot confer this mark and are thereby doomed to failure.

In the popular canon, and in its abettor, the library, the status of "forgotten" is not reversible. That status does not mean anything inherent about a book, necessarily, a fact utilized by small determined bands of

SENTIMENT AND SIGNIFICANCE

adults attempting to keep beloved books from permanent obscurity, accurately remarking that there is no particular reason for other books to survive while their favorites disappear from memory as well as print. In fact, fans of an author often over-dramatize the obscurity of their darling's fate. Some fans of Maud Hart Lovelace's Betsy-Tacy series consider these books forgotten, yet the on-line library consortium lists a plethora of copies of all aspects of the series, with printings in every decade from the forties. Perhaps these books do not achieve the sine qua non status of canonical literature; they are not accorded the respect that, say, *Little Women* is, but their prevalence in libraries—if not in the academic canon—suggests that they are secure in their popular status. The efforts of adult Lovelace followers to enhance their favorites' status suggests that it is not, in fact, popular regard but academic standing they seek to enhance. The desire of many adults similarly may not just be to pass literature on but to make adults acknowledge the merits of their childhood favorites.

A recovery only in academics denies the genre's raison d'être, its popular audience. Librarians see no need to recover. The example of the Betsy-Tacy books, where adults who have been obsessed with them manage to keep a small popular interest, remains the closest thing to popular recovery. Yet a small group's forceful refusal to permit a book's consignment to obscurity does not constitute recovery and will not result in it. A publishing source (herself a Lovelace fan) discussing paperback backlist books suggests that attempts by the list-buyer to inflict personal preferences in the face of general taste are doomed to failure—in other words, mere market availability will not succeed in restoring forgotten authors without audience desire as well (Sharyn November, interview); the attempts of small coteries of adults are similarly unlikely to succeed outside of their circle.

Belletristic adult literature can effect a recovery through academia alone; it can also rediscover readers beyond the university through print reviews or on-air publicity, following paths similar to those Richard Ohmann outlines for initial entry into the canon. The children's literature audience is beyond the reach of most traditional means of recovery: children do not attend college classes, follow public-television talk shows, or peruse *The New York Times Book Review*. Children have neither access to nor interest in literary forms of reinvigoration, and most adults find the old and unfamiliar irrelevant to their desires for children's literature (nor are most other popular literatures swayed by academic rediscovery of old texts). If academic interest in children's literature continues to increase, its interest in canon formation will probably increase as well, in ways with which we are all familiar. It seems likely that over the years the academic canon of significance will become more firmly established, and the divide between it and the canon of sentiment will widen as their intentions and desires continue to diverge. While such a canon of significance can contain books of great merit and worth that might otherwise be overlooked, a text's recovery to that canon will never translate to the canon of sentiment, which insists a book meet more amorphous and often stricter standards of love and evocation of childhood. Within *The Water-Babies*, Tom found redemption and new life, but he must content himself with that internal promise; no matter what efforts scholars may make to rescue it, the book itself is sliding irrevocably below the waves.

Notes

1 The writers of romances having often sprung from—and retaining a place in —the ranks of the readers, there is a further cohesion of reader and writer that children's literature can never achieve.
2 While an excessively sophisticated children's book may please adults, I know of no instance where a book originally considered children's literature has completely shed that appellation—texts may move chronologically down to the children's category, but they seem unable to move up from it.
3 I am indebted to my colleague Roger Sutton for his insight in this and other matters concerning this topic.
4 Christa Kamenetsky, in *Children's Literature*, describes the victory of affection over ideology in the Nazis' incongruous defense of the politically undesirable adventure stories of Karl May, which Goebbels and Goering had greatly enjoyed.
5 I note the recent appearance of two high-powered but politically tamed revisions of Helen Bannerman's problematic *Little Black Sambo* (*The Story of Little Babaji* and Julius Lester's *Sam and the Tigers*); it will be interesting to see if these can repair the status of the tale, if not the book.

Works cited

Butler, Marilyn. "Repossessing the Past: The Case of an Open Literary History." *Rethinking Historicism: Critical Readings in Romantic History*. Ed. Marjorie Levinson *et al.* Oxford: Basil Blackwell, 1989. 64–84.

Crews, Frederick. *The Critics Bear It Away: American Fiction and the Academy*. New York: Random House, 1992.

Furst, Lillian R. "Reading 'Nasty' Great Books." *The Hospitable Canon: Essays on Literary Play, Scholarly Choice, and Popular Pressures*. Ed. Virgil Nemoianu and Robert Royal. Philadelphia: John Benjamins Publishing, 1991. 39–51.

Gerhardt, Lillian. "Principles in Print." Interview. *School Library Journal* 41.9 (September 1995): 118–22.

Higgins, Regina. *Magic Kingdoms: Discovering the Joys of Childhood Classics with Your Child*. New York: Simon & Schuster, 1992.

Hunt, Peter. *Children's Literature: The Development of Criticism*. London: Routledge, 1990.

Kamenetsky, Christa. *Children's literature in Hitler's Germany: The Cultural Policy of National Socialism*. Athens, OH: Ohio UP, 1984.

Kaplan, Carey and Ellen Cronan Rose. *The Canon and the Common Reader*. Knoxville: U of Tennessee P, 1990.

Lindenberger, Herbert. *The History in Literature: On Value, Genre, Institutions*. New York: Columbia UP, 1990.

McCrea, Brian, *Addison and Steele Are Dead: The English Department, Its Canon, and the Professionalization of Literary Criticism*. Newark: U of Delaware P, 1990.

Nemoianu, Virgil. "Literary Canons and Social Value Options." *The Hospitable Canon: Essays on Literary Play, Scholarly Choice, and Popular Pressures*. Ed. Virgil Nemoianu and Robert Royal. Philadelphia: John Benjamins Publishing Co., 1991. 215–47.

November, Sharyn. Personal conversation. June 25, 1995.

Ohmann, Richard. *Politics of Letters*. Middletown, CT: Wesleyan UP, 1987.

——. "The Shaping of a Canon: U.S. Fiction, 1960–1975." *Canons*. Ed. Robert von Hallberg. Chicago: U of Chicago P, 1984. 377–401.

Rose, Jacqueline. *The Case of Peter Pan, or the Impossibility of Children's Fiction*. London: Macmillan, 1984.

Seto, Thelma. "Multiculturalism Is Not Halloween." *The Horn Book Magazine* 71:2 (March/April 1995): 169–74.

11

Extracts from the
'INTRODUCTION' TO
THE NEW OXFORD BOOK
OF CHILDREN'S VERSE

Neil Philip

Source: *The New Oxford Book of Children's Verse*, Oxford: Oxford University Press, 1996, pp. xxv–xxxvii .

This anthology is, as its title proclaims, a collection of 'children's verse.' This is a term that covers a multitude of sins. In practical terms, I have taken it to mean verse written for children, or with them prominently in mind, or published for them with the explicit or implicit endorsement of the author. Even then there remains a handful of poems that are, I think, legitimately chosen—such as Poe's 'Eldorado'—which fall into none of these categories, but nevertheless seem anchored to the children's verse tradition by a kind of gravitational pull.

The problem is essentially one of definition. What is children's poetry, and how does it differ from poetry in general? This anthology is itself a full answer to this difficult question, but it is not an answer that is easy to summarize.

Some would argue that the very notion of poetry for children is a nonsense. The poetry that has been written and published for children is by no means the only poetry to which they respond; indeed some of the best anthologies for the young scarcely contain any poems expressly written for them. There is only poetry, good or bad.

Yet there is a recognizable tradition of children's verse, which this book traces. It is a tradition that is at once separate from and intermingled with the larger poetic tradition, but it has its own landmarks and its own rhetoric.

It is, most crucially, a tradition of immediate apprehension. There is in the best children's poetry a sense of the world being seen as for the first time, and of language being plucked from the air to describe it. Everything is freshly created, and the poet's senses are quiveringly alert to each new sound, scent and sight of what William Brighty Rands calls this 'great, wide, beautiful, wonderful world.'

Of course this description also fits much adult poetry, but it is important to note that the immediate sense perceptions have an overriding importance in children's poetry, quite beyond the workings of memory and reflection, or the filters of spiritual, philosophical, or political ideas. This does not necessarily mean that children's poems are 'simple' in any reductive sense. I would argue that no poem can be called a poem that does not have at its heart some unknowable mystery; as Emily Dickinson scrawled on the back of one of her poems, 'Bliss is the Plaything of the Child': 'Dont think you could understand if you tried—.' But a children's poem will in general take the direct route from one thought to another.

A true children's poem is distinguished by a clarity of thought, language and rhythm that stems from this directness. The guiding principle is that expressed by Bertolt Brecht in his poem 'And I always thought', translated here by Michael Hamburger:

> And I always thought: the very simplest words
> Must be enough.

The case of Emily Dickinson (mirrored to some extent by that of Stevie Smith) tests any makeshift boundary lines between poetry for children and poetry for adults to their limits. Shortly after her death, her poems began to appear in children's journals such as *St Nicholas* and *Youth's Companion*. Some of her poems such as 'A Narrow Fellow in the Grass' or 'Dear March—Come in—', speak strongly and directly to children. But can they, in the absence of any guidance from the author, be regarded as children's poems? A very strong case could be made for such a decision, but it would have to ignore the congruence of these poems with the remainder of her work, in which the ideas and feelings are quite definitely outside a child's grasp. So I have reluctantly confined myself in this book to three poems that Emily Dickinson herself sent to children.

If Emily Dickinson is not essentially a children's poet, it has something to do with the sense that she is not so much a participant in life as a witness to it, sworn on oath in some metaphysical court. Yet the overriding qualities of her work are also those of children's poetry: clarity, directness, mystery. She writes, for instance:

> When I have seen the Sun emerge
> From His amazing House—
> And leave a Day at every Door
> A Deed, in every place—

This is, in its clear-eyed economy, perfect children's verse.

The secret as to why a poet whose themes are profoundly unchildish should nevertheless skirt so close to being a children's poet lies in the sense of wonder. Everyone has seen the sun rise; only someone doing so as if for the first time has seen it 'leave a Day at every Door.' Emily Dickinson also wrote,

> I dwell in Possibility—
> A fairer House than Prose

and this is perhaps as good a definition as any of poetry for children. It is the poetry of Possibility. Or, as John Clare put it, 'There is nothing but poetry about the existance of childhood real simple soul moving poetry the laughter and joy of poetry and not its philosophy.'

Today, people tend to two different views about poetry for children. The first is that it is something that was defined and perfected in a lost golden age, spanning from Robert Louis Stevenson and Eugene Field to A. A. Milne and Eleanor Farjeon. Here, a succession of poets, attuned to the child's viewpoint, captured in traditional forms the essence of childhood.

The opposing view is that these are poets for the nursery, irrelevant to the modern world: comforting, sentimental, and drenched in nostalgia. Children today, it is argued, require something shorter and snappier: what Spike Milligan has proudly termed, 'silly verse for kids'.

Both views are too simplistic, and it is one of the aims of this anthology to reconcile them. Silliness has been essential to children's poetry from the beginning, and was brought to its apogee by Edward Lear; even Isaac Watts, whom I regard as the first true children's poet, urged that verse for children should be 'flowing with cheerfulness'. Word-play, parody, nonsense, and all kinds of mickey-taking and topsy-turviness are part of the central tradition of children's verse.

So, too, is the serious treatment of serious themes. A lot of early children's verse is about death; as Kenneth Grahame noted in the preface to his *Cambridge Book of Poetry for Children* in 1916, 'a compiler of Obituary Verse for the delight of children could make a fine fat volume with little difficulty'. It is in this context that the fresh unforced celebration of the child's world that we find in writers such as Stevenson and Milne should be viewed. They are such poets as Blake aspired to be, writing

> happy songs
> Every child may joy to hear.

But Blake paired his merry *Songs of Innocence* with darker *Songs of Experience*, even, as with 'Holy Thursday', writing parallel poems with the same title. Children's lives are full of wonder and delight, but they are also fraught with worries, disappointments, and sadnesses; the best children's poets come to terms with grief as well as joy.

Edward Lear, for instance, may offer a prototype for today's 'silly verse', but his nonsense is shadowed by a sense of loss and loneliness:

> Calico Pie,
> The little Birds fly
> Down to the calico tree,
> Their wings were blue,
> And they sang 'Tilly-loo!'
> Till away they flew,—
> And they never came back to me!
> They never came back!
> They never came back!
> They never came back to me!

This plangent quality in Lear, an inextricable tangle of happy and sad feelings, has resurfaced strongly in the work of one of today's finest children's poets, Charles Causley, but it can be felt in that of many others, from Walter de la Mare and Eleanor Farjeon to Roger McGough and John Mole.

Spike Milligan has it too, but the 'silly verse' of some others can seem not so much silly as empty, offering instant gratification but no sustenance. The absence of Lear's discords and minor keys turns tunes into jingles. It is easy for children's poets to fall into this trap. The resultant verse may be fun, but it offers nothing to digest, and will soon be forgotten. The basis of much of it is the pun, which is no bad thing, for at least it gives children the idea that poetry is what happens when words collide.

The problem is one of form as much as of content. Today's children's poets have deconstructed the rhetoric of children's poetry in much the same way as postmodernist writers in other modes. This has left them with a formal freedom that the skilful—Valerie Worth, or Michael Rosen, say—can exploit to powerful effect. Poets such as Sonia Sanchez and e. e. cummings make no stylistic allowances for the child reader, and as a consequence offer their readers an exhilarating experience.

But not all children's poets have the technical confidence to negotiate free verse, and the result is that some offer prose limply arranged in lines and hope for the best, while others revert to doggerel metrics. The glee with which children's poets adopted the haiku shows how far adrift many have come from the adroit mastery of traditional verse technique that we find in A. A. Milne or David McCord—you can almost hear the collective sigh of relief, 'All you've got to do is count to seventeen!'

That quintessentially English poet James Reeves published in 1971 a book entitled *How to Write Poems for Children*. It was really a study of his own practice, rather than a prescriptive 'fit one—fit all' pattern for aspiring children's poets, and it is full of insights gained from his experience. Reeves claims that 'Three things are necessary for a writer of children's poems: imagination, technique and taste.' Although Reeves himself was by nature a conservative, he does not rule out free verse, 'provided it makes its own music and fulfils its own pattern.' This, it seems to me, is the key: poetry must make its own music.

Sometimes that music can be made by the look of the poem on the page. Lewis Carroll's 'The Mouse's Tale' from *Alice in Wonderland* can probably claim to be the first concrete poem for children, the forerunner of such modern delights as Wes Magee's 'Giant Rocket' or 'Coyotes' by the Canadian, Jon Whyte. These are poems that only work on the page: you couldn't read them aloud.

Conversely, there is now a thriving tradition of performance poetry for children. Again, this has deep historical roots; for instance I would class Browning's 'The Pied Piper of Hamelin' as a performance poem. But, as with song lyrics, the virtues of performance poetry are hard to capture in print. The poets in this collection who might loosely be termed performance poets, such as Roger McGough, Michael Rosen, Adrian Mitchell, Michael Smith, and Benjamin Zephaniah, are the very best of their kind. The printed words are not so much a blueprint for performance as the performance is an expression of the text. The critic Margaret Meek writes of Michael Rosen, 'I would argue that when Michael recites his own poetry, as he often does in schools, he has to do it so that the graphematic features of its shape, what it would look like on the page, become audible rather than visible, and *not the other way round*.' In Zephaniah's case, the whole point of the poem I have chosen, 'According to My Mood', is the impossibility of confining the free voice in the strait-jacket of type.

Children's poetry is by its nature especially apt to be read aloud, and the performance qualities of many modern writers extend rather than disrupt the tradition. A lot of the poems in this book, from Blake to Prelutsky, positively beg to be read aloud. In the case of David McCord's 'Five Chants', for instance, the poem almost says the words for you:

> The goose has a hiss
> And it goes like this

'Fireflies' by Paul Fleischman (son of the children's writer Sid Fleischman man) is a virtuoso performance in two ways. Fleischman's poems are intended to be read aloud by two voices. In this particular poem, the flickering effect of the double column grid on the printed page gives a thrilling typographical equivalent of such a performance. Whether reading or listening, the form captures the pulsing quality of the subject.

Children first encounter poetry through listening to nursery rhymes. The old rhymes just go on and on, satisfying precisely because they have been shaped by so many mouths, and battered by so many accidents of life. It is one of the highest accolades of a children's poet for a verse to be silently appropriated by the world and reshaped by Anon., as happened for instance to Hughes Mearns with 'A Little Man'. Samuel Griswold Goodrich wrote his contribution to the nursery classics, 'Higglety, Pigglety, Pop!', precisely to show what facile nonsense such rhymes are, yet it has outlived all his other achievements. We can fairly assume that the best nursery rhymes of Eleanor Farjeon, Rose Fyleman, and Clyde Watson will in time join the canon, together with Christopher Isherwood's 'The Common Cormorant'—though Isherwood stole a march on the others by crediting the poem to Anon. on its first appearance, in Auden and Garrett's *The Poet's Tongue*.

Poetry for children ranges from the brevity of the new-fashioned nursery rhyme to the formidable length of a narrative poem such as 'The Pied Piper of Hamelin', or Mick Gowar's modern rewrite, 'Rat Trap'. It can accommodate every mood from lullaby to elegy, and speak both to the child and to the adult the child will become. [. . .] From early days, children's poets have attended to their predecessors and anticipated their successors. Lewis Carroll, for instance, paid homage to Isaac Watts and Jane Taylor in his parodies, and in poems such as 'Brother and Sister' ('*Moral*: Never stew your sister') laid the ground rules for the *Cautionary Verses* of Hilaire Belloc, the *Ruthless Rhymes* of Harry Graham, and their contemporary equivalents.

[. . .]

In his 1967 essay 'Poetry for Children', David McCord quotes Emerson: 'Every word was once a poem.' This is the rock bottom truth about poetry, [. . .] not every poem can be a masterpiece, but they can all aspire, in Browning's words about Christopher Smart, to adjust 'Real vision to right language.'

An example might be McCord's 'Father and I in the Woods'. This might seem on first encounter a slight poem, but in my opinion it is the best thing McCord ever wrote, over a long career that produced an œuvre to rival that of James Reeves. The reason is the perfect harmony of form, style, and subject. The elegant restraint of the language, and the delicate stepping quality of the rhythm, are inseparable from the meaning of the words.

Another test is that 'Father and I in the Woods' could not have been written by anyone else. It is original in the true sense. By originality I do not mean a straining after novelty, but a refusal to deal in second-hand words and images. Ebenezer Elliott, 'the Corn-Law Rhymer', writes in his autobiography (written 1841, published in *The Athenaeum*, 1850), 'There is not in my writings one good idea that has not been suggested to me by some real occurrence, or by some object actually before my eyes, or by some remembered object or occurrence, or by the thoughts of other men, heard or read.' Yet Elliott, though a pedestrian and unskilful writer, was 'original' in the sense I mean. What he wrote could not have been produced by any other man, and he wrote it from the centre of himself.

[. . .]

Such is the nostalgic fondness that adults brought up on Milne and Stevenson, or their American equivalent, Eugene Field, feel for the classic children's poems, it is sometimes hard for them to register the vitality and quality of more recent work. The middle years of this century saw some excellent children's poets emerge—for instance James Reeves in Britain, David McCord and Elizabeth Madox Roberts in the USA—but the last quarter of a century has seen a positive explosion of children's poetry on both sides of the Atlantic.

In Britain, there has been a seismic shift in children's poetry. The line running from Stevenson and Rossetti, through de la Mare, Farjeon, and Reeves, to Charles Causley has been disrupted by a more boisterous, less reflective street-smart poetry, characterized by the critic John Rowe Townsend as 'urchin verse'. The focus is on shared not unique experience, on the rhythms of speech not the patterns of prosody, on school not home.

Some of this new poetry is facile and superficial, but the best of it is doing something new and exciting. Each of the three leading poets in this mode— Allan Ahlberg, Roger McGough, and Michael Rosen—speaks very much in his own voice; it is not their fault if their imitators can manage the mannerisms but not the manner. Michael Rosen published a striking defence of such work in *The Times Educational Supplement* in 1984, 'Memorable Speech?', in which he argues for the availability of a variety of poetic registers in which to speak to children, one of which is 'to use a child's speech mode'. In his frequent visits to schools he sees 'children fastening on to their own speech patterns as an ideal mode for expressing themselves. I see them using my writing like a catalyst, tuning in to its small hurts, jokes and fantasies of everyday life as a means to explore their own.'

Rosen's success in the classroom is supported by Brian Morse, a teacher who is also himself a notable poet ('A Day on the Planet'), writing in the journal *Signal: Approaches to Children's Books* in 1986. 'Perhaps it's dangerous to quote children's reactions, but my class of six- and seven-year-olds are still demanding rereadings of "Eddie and the Birthday", "Eddie and the Nappy" (in fact all the baby-Eddie poems) and "Chocolate Cake" six months after they first heard them, and greeting me "Nappy nappy nappy" in the morning.' Rosen's skill, writes Morse, is 'to put children in touch with themselves'.

These poems for the classroom and the playground, rather than the solitary reading child, have injected a new energy into poetry for children, that can be felt in the work of poets such as John Mole and Jackie

Kay, who combine the subtler layered quality of the older tradition with the fresh demotic appeal of the newer. The Caribbean inflections of poets such as James Berry and John Agard have also added a new note to children's poetry in Britain.

Nevertheless the two most impressive British children's poets of this period have worked utterly outside this movement. Charles Causley and Ted Hughes are two highly regarded poets for adults who have also devoted considerable energies to children's poetry. Causley's 1970 collection *Figgie Hobbin* remains his best work, but it has been followed by a series of books nearly as good. His *Collected Poems for Children* will stand as one of the peak achievements of children's poetry, alongside Blake, Lear, and Stevenson.

'All poetry is magic,' writes Causley in the introduction to his *Puffin Book of Magic Verse*. A poem is a spell. And what is the essential of a spell? Constantine the poet, in Rebecca West's masterpiece *Black Lamb and Grey Falcon*, tells us: '*That if one word is left out it is no longer a spell.*'

Causley is essentially a poet of loss, striving to see the world anew; to see it, in a key Causley phrase, 'Eden-fresh'. Part of this task is to recapture a child's sense of wonder. He achieves this by means of subtle verbal dislocations, effecting the sort of shift of sensibility that makes one believe, sitting in a moving train, that it is the world that is moving and the train alone that is still. Thus in the ballad 'Young Edgcumbe' from his children's collection *Figure of 8*, he writes:

> Down by the Tamar river
>   As young Edgcumbe walked by
> He heard from sleep the woodcock leap
>   Into the sudden sky.

The sudden sky. There is a magic phrase. Replace it with description rather than action—'into the cloudy sky', 'into the bright blue sky'—and the whole stanza crumbles into nothing. Rephrase it—'Suddenly to the sky'— and the feeling is completely lost. It is the sky moving not the birds.

If one word is left out, it is no longer a spell.

If Causley is a poet of loss, then Ted Hughes is a poet of repossession. The intense vitality of his vision offers his readers the whole world as a gift. Like the bear in 'I See a Bear' from *Moon-Bells*,

> You have got it everything for nothing

Hughes has published several landmark collections for the young, winning the prestigious Signal Poetry Award for both *Moon-Bells*, and *What is the Truth?* Each shows a major poet working at his full power.

[. . .]

179

Children's poetry in the USA has, like American poetry in general, developed on a separate track. Much of the best American children's verse is scarcely known in Britain, and the poets themselves represented only by a few hackneyed anthology pieces. Yet since Eugene Field and James Whitcomb Riley, America has consistently produced children's poets of great energy and invention.

Donald Hall's *Oxford Book of Children's Verse in America* deftly traces the origins of American children's verse in the pages of nineteenth-century children's magazines such as *St Nicholas*. From this rich soil came poets such as Lucy Larcom, Celia Thaxter, Laura E. Richards, and Katharine Pyle (sister of the children's writer Howard Pyle).

By the middle years of this century, America's children's poets such as David McCord, Elizabeth Coatsworth, Elizabeth Madox Roberts, Rachel Field, and Aileen Fisher were producing a body of work that, in its quiet observation, delicately controlled rhythms, and child's-eye viewpoint, offers a distinctly American counterpoint to the work of English writers such as de la Mare, Farjeon, and Reeves. In the meantime, major adult poets such as Carl Sandburg, Vachel Lindsay, Theodore Roethke, e. e. cummings, and Langston Hughes were turning their attention to children's verse, producing poems, as Sandburg said of his children's stories, 'in the American lingo'.

Langston Hughes is of particular importance, as the first major African American writer to address America's children. Hughes's magnificent 1932 collection *The Dream Keeper* (reissued in 1994) contains his addendum to Whitman's 'I Hear America Singing':

> I, too, sing America.

The memory of childhood racial abuse in Hughes's colleague Countee Cullen's poem 'Incident' strikes a kind of rueful sadder-but-wiser note that also echoes in Hughes's own work. The spark of anger in a poem such as 'Children's Rhymes' was to leap into flame in the 1960s, and the work of poets such as Nikki Giovanni and Sonia Sanchez.

Sanchez's 'definition for blk/children' is about as far from the comforting nursery world of A. A. Milne as it is possible to get:

> a policeman
>   is a pig
> and he shd be in
>   a zoo
> with all the other piggy
>   animals,   and
> until he stops
>   killing blk/people

cracking open their heads
remember.
　　　　the policeman
　　is a pig.
　　　　　(oink/
　　　　　　oink.)

A less aggressive but equally uncompromising message could be found in June Jordan's verse picture book of 1969, *Who Look at Me?*, with at its heart the line,

　　　　I am black alive and looking back at you.

This process of 'looking back' at America, coming, in Langston Hughes's words, 'to sit at the table', has brought forth in recent years some marvellous children's poetry not just from African American writers but from every part of America's cultural 'melting pot'.

Today, children's poetry is thriving in America, with a multiplicity of voices and modes of expression. Writers such as Jack Prelutsky and X. J. Kennedy fill the McGough/Rosen role, while more traditional poets such as Myra Cohn Livingston continue to extend the core tradition that extends from Field to McCord to writers such as Eve Merriam, John Ciardi, and Lucille Clifton.

What connects all these poets—and their colleagues in the rest of the English-speaking world—is a commitment to the primacy of the word as the means to shape and understand our interior life. All are engaged in the task defined by Browning in the poem on Smart I quoted earlier: to pierce

　　　　the screen
'Twixt thing and word.

It is sometimes assumed that children cannot cope with undiluted poetry; that it is too difficult, too esoteric. But this is a measure of the adult's nervousness, not the child's. Children's own use of language—as shown in anthologies of their writing, such as Timothy Roger's wonderful *Those First Affections* (1979) or Jill Pirrie's inspiring collection of work from Halesworth Middle School, *Apple Fire* (1993)—shares a dimension with poetry. Indeed, the adult struggle to merge thing and word is to some extent an attempt to redeem the child's magical assumption of the identity of thought and action.

[. . .]

12

CHILDREN'S FANTASY LITERATURE

Toward an anatomy

David Gooderham

Source: *Children's Literature in Education* 26(3) (1995): 171–183.

Finding a critical language in which to speak about children's fantasy texts is not as straightforward as might first appear. Children's literature, as a younger and poorer relation of English literature, has inevitably been the recipient of critical and theoretical hand-me-downs, many of which are entirely appropriate to their tasks, but some less so. Among discussions of the genre, the theories of Todorov[1] and, in the Anglo-Saxon world, of Tolkien[2] may be taken to represent characteristic approaches, and neither seems entirely appropriate to the discussion of *children's* texts.

Todorov's location of fantasy midway between the two literary modes of "the pure uncanny" and "the pure marvellous" enables him to characterize it in terms of the radical uncertainty which opens up at that midpoint. Just what *are* we to make, for example, of the ghosts—and a good deal more—in Henry James's *Turn of the Screw?* This kind of question however is unproductive and inappropriate for children's fantasy texts.[3] Young readers are hardly ever left long in the disturbing uncertainty which Todorov regards as criterial for the genre; the vast majority of their texts belong to what he designates as "the marvellous."

An essay "On Fairy Tales," by a renowned storyteller, might be expected to offer a more amenable approach. While Tolkien's "three faces" of fantasy—"the Mystical," "the Magical," and "the Mirror of scorn and pity towards Man"—are certainly not antithetical to the character of children's texts, when tested against children's responses their relevance begins to look less unproblematic. Children can and do read texts with a "Mystical" dimension and texts which hold up "the Mirror of scorn and pity towards Man," but "The Piper at the Gates of Dawn" is just the chapter in *The Wind in the Willows* (Kenneth Grahame) which young readers are inclined to skip, and the diminutive size of the Lilliputians, rather than their satiric function, is what interests and delights children who read *Gulliver's Travels* (Jonathan Swift). The "Magical" face is a different matter but equally problematic, since, while in content it may be said to represent just what interests and delights children, it can hardly be conceived as, for children, "the refreshment and renewal of perception." Upon them "shades of the prison house" have, one hopes, not yet quite closed!

If major discussions like these fail to provide us with a critical language appropriate to children's fantasy texts, perhaps all that can be attempted is a categorization of those texts which, on the basis of some contrast with realism, seem to make up the genre (animal tales, fairy tales, nonsense, "high fantasy," etc.).[4] Categorizing of this kind, however, provides no more than lists of typical ingredients and conventions for each of the subgenres—when, for academic and professional purposes, what we are looking for is a disclosure of fundamental structures in texts and related reading responses.

Further, categorizing of this kind may well involve a covert privileging of what is often, and not insignificantly, referred to as "high fantasy." There are interesting discussions of this subgenre[5]—which doubtless came immediately to the reader's mind when, in the first sentences, I talked about the lack of a critical language. High fantasy does not, however, constitute the whole of children's fantasy literature, and the conceptual framework for its discussion cannot comprehend that range and diversity. When Cohen, for example, deploys a "high fantasy" model, he has to concede, "There are some tales which because of the mixture of fantastic elements used are extremely difficult to label. Some Victorian fantasy, such as *The Water Babies* (Charles Kingsley), falls outside the more usual sub-genres."[6] This is an admission of defeat. Kingsley's text certainly comprehends a rum assortment of materials and varieties of discourse, but this should not obscure its fecund authenticity and centrality as a children's fantasy text. It works not merely on account of its marvelous underwater world, but because it is also a bran tub of jokes, games, stories, and quaint inventions. Any model or conceptualization must be complete and discriminating enough to comprehend texts as diverse as those of, say, Kingsley and Kipling, Masefield, Ted Hughes, and Roald Dahl.

To this end, I propose an anatomy. This is, of course, a naming of parts, but it is more: It aims to describe their functional relationship. Further, in its reference to the body, it is, as I shall suggest, particularly apposite to the human experiences fundamental to children's fantasy literature. I shall proceed, first, by considering some existing approaches in formal literary discussion and in Jungian perspective; then, on the basis of these approaches, but with a different psychoanalytic perspective, I shall attempt the anatomy.

Fantasy as a metaphorical mode

Fantasy is a metaphorical mode. It works by a substitution of the purely imaginary for realistic description, in the sense not that common human experience, feeling, and ideas are removed from the text, but that metaphorical images become the vehicle by which these are rendered. It must be acknowledged that some aspects of fantasy writing rely on other devices, particularly exaggeration and incongruous conjunction and reversal, but metaphorical substitution may be claimed to constitute fantasy's figurative center of gravity. The conceptualization *fantasy* is thus seen to describe not so much a collection of marvels which divert readers from ordinary human concerns, but a distinctive and fruitful way of speaking about just these concerns. Ursula Le Guin effects this shift in focus evaluatively and combatively, opposing the literary to the sociological imagination:

> The scientist who creates a monster in his laboratory; a librarian in the library of Babel; a wizard unable to cast a spell . . . all these may be precise and profound metaphors of the human condition. The fantasist . . . may be talking as seriously as any sociologist— and a great deal more directly—about human life as it is lived, as it might be lived, and as it ought to be lived.[7]

More recently, John Stephens asserted the same conceptualization analytically, opposing two literary modes:

> The central observations I have made about the modes of fantasy and realism may be summed up as follows. The two discourses encode their concerns with the theme of language and power in quite different ways, in that fantasy is a metaphoric mode, whereas realism is a metonymic mode.[8]

Realistic children's texts speak about the child's world and to the child's condition by deploying "slices of life" which their readers have not met, but which might well form a part of the everyday world they increasingly recognize as their own social context. Fantasy texts equally speak about the child's world and to the child's condition, but metaphorically, through images of divergent and unexpected kinds which substitute either simply for the expected language of the text, or for matters that are for some reason difficult to articulate. Sexual awakening, for example, has not for the first time found a place in children's texts in the late twentieth century. It now receives ever more explicitly realistic treatment, but it has long been metaphorically expressed, from the needle pricks, glass slippers, and frog princes of fairy tale, right up to Mary's bringing her secret garden to fruition and fulfillment (F. H. Burnett, *The Secret Garden*).

184

How, then, does this mode of discourse function? It could be regarded as merely ornamental, meant to intrigue and charm readers who might become bored with the "penny plain." Motivation as bald and unapologetic as this has certainly been used to justify the production and use of fantasy texts for children but is too limited to describe adequately their diverse and powerful effects. The use, for example, of "our friends in fur," in fable and later stories,[9] has proved an eminently popular way of speaking to children about everyday human experience and pointing appropriate morals. Peter Rabbit's trespass (Beatrix Potter, *Peter Rabbit*), Pooh's overeating (A. A. Milne, *The House at Pooh Corner*) and Toad's self-willed indulgence form (Kenneth Grahame, *The Wind in the Willows*) both immediately seductive attractions to children and occasions for their instruction in morals and manners. The three stories might be translated into literal representations of transgression and indulgence, but they would then lose the wild terror of a creature stripped of his civilized clothing, the gently incorrect amusement at a fatty's indulgence and retribution, and the heady moments of incorrigible naughtiness of an unrestrained libido. These metaphorical representations are able to evoke within child readers powerful resonances, quite beyond what equivalent realistic narratives are conventionally allowed or likely to do. How, then, does this mode function?

Existential readings

Suggestive explanations of these resonances are to be found in psychoanalytic or, perhaps better, existential interpretations of children's fantasy texts.[9] One of the most interesting is that of Ravenna Helson,[10] who approaches fantasy literature as a Jungian. She sees children's texts as encoding three types of psychic drama. In the first, the ego charms the unconscious; in the second, the ego grapples with it; and in the third, the ego is reconciled with it. This theoretical conception yields three types of fantasy text: the comic, the heroic and the tender. The first type Helson sees as having "to do with wish-fulfulment, with wonderful discoveries or strokes of luck which bring riches, success . . . the heart's desire"; the second type, "whilst [dealing much in] aggression, achievement, and order, at the same time emphasise[s] humility and a sense of wonder and awe"; the last type "emphasise[s] tender feeling more than plot; they help us 'realise' how to give love or beauty or faith, how to accept and appreciate the patterns and mysteries of life and death." (Helson also identifies a different modality for each of the three types in the case of women writers.)

The approach is interesting because it provides not only an illuminating way of reading specific texts, but also a fundamental account of how the fantasy mode serves as a metaphorical vehicle for the ground of existential experience and concern. There are, however, two main problems with the theoretical framework she proposes. In the first place, it fails to comprehend an important range of children's fantasy, from Kingsley's clumsy word games and Edward Lear's absurd characters to Dahl's and Dr. Seuss's crazy constructions. Nonsense, however, as a frequent and important ingredient in texts for children, must be comprehended in any adequate account of the fantasy genre. In the second place, Helson's framework has as its basis a progressive development from charming, to grappling, and finally to reconciliation. While such a progression may be logical and desirable in developmental or therapeutic terms, when it is used as a basis for the differentiation of texts it has the less convincing effect of suggesting an ascending evaluative order: the "tenderness" of *Charlotte's Web* (E. B. White), by implication, being regarded as more mature than Bilbo's heroic venture (J. R. R. Tolkien, *The Hobbit*), and both of these as more mature than the wish fulfillment of *Charlie and the Chocolate Factory* (Roald Dahl).

Therefore, while we may follow Helson's lead in reading fantasy as a vehicle for the articulation of fundamental human feeling, we need to search out theorizing which will yield a more comprehensive and less evaluative approach.

Erik Erikson[11] offers a promising alternative. He is a Freudian who, however, lays a strong emphasis on the cultural context of human development. He conceives of Freud's psychosexual stages as a series of "growth crises," through which the emotional configuration and identity of the child, both as individual and as social being, are shaped. The first five of these crises may be described in broad terms, as, first, focused in experience at the mother's breast, where the child learns feelings of "trust and mistrust"; second, focusing in the control of, particularly, anal bodily functions, where the child learns to feel "autonomy and shame/doubt"; third, as moving out (via desire for the parent of the opposite sex) into the public world, where the child learns to feel "initiative and guilt"; fourth, in the public (school) world of know-how and technical achievement, where the child learns to feel "competence and inferiority"; and, finally, in the world of public values and ideals, where the young person develops—or fails to develop—a sense of personal identity.

Erikson does not conceive of these growth crises as progressive, in the sense that each outdates earlier ones and makes them redundant; rather, he sees emotional experience as continually recapitulating and aggregating to shape the flow of experience and its future sedimentation, so that young persons possess a widening repertoire of feeling and dispositions, learned in however many of the growth crises they have negotiated by any particular point in their lives. Youngest readers will have accrued a range of feeling developed in the first two growth crises and will be coming to terms with the third; they can therefore be touched across that narrow, but consequently intense, range of feeling. Older preadolescents and adolescents, passing through further growth crises, are likely to be affected as readers, proportionately, across a broader, more fully differentiated range of feeling.

Erikson also identifies (significantly for our discussion), in relation to each nuclear growth crisis, imaginal themes which continue to appear in later life in dream, myth, and imaginative literature. Articulating experience stemming from that of the child at the mother's breast, he distinguishes themes of "incorporation, total embracement or absorption, 'oceanic' proportions" which may be explicated as "themes of incorporation, of swallowing and being swallowed—the lollipop moon, Jonah and the whale"; for attempts at control, he lists "disappearance, reappearance, power, magic, control, impotence . . . —hidden treasures, Aladdin and his genie, Jack and the Beanstalk, etc."; for the venture out into the social world, "the classic themes of exploration, discovery, metamorphosis and origination, are expressed, for example, in the myths of Odysseus, Oedipus, Prometheus"; and so forth. In these descriptions, he provides us with an account of the metaphorical vehicles through which the fundamental configurations of human feeling are encoded in the images, themes, and stories of our culture.

Erikson's theory is thus pertinent in two ways to the construction of an anatomy of children's fantasy literature. He provides, first, what is in effect an etiology of human feeling, which offers an explanation of the *ground* of fantasy metaphor, and, then, related imaginal themes, which offer interpretations of the *vehicles* of fantasy metaphor. The task which remains in this discussion, then, is an examination of each theme and its manifestation in fantasy elements in children's texts. I shall distinguish four of these:

— The fantasy of wish fulfillment
— The fantasy of control
— The fantasy of venture
— The fantasy of competence

I shall also consider a feature deriving from the fifth growth crisis and, on this basis, identify, further:

— The fantasy of devotion:

This last fantasy element may be found in texts which count as children's literature, but because its grounding in a later growth crisis puts it beyond the feeling range of preadolescent readers, it can hardly be expected to touch them forcibly. Thus, until adolescence, the element can be expected to function differently from the earlier four in children's reading of fantasy texts.

The anatomy: the first elements

The first fantasy element which comes to light in the perspective of Erikson's theory is an uncontentious one: It derives from the close intimacy of the child with the mother, in dandling, nursing, and feeding—and, most fundamentally, in the womb—and is manifest principally in imaginal themes of being incorporated and of incorporation. These experiences and related imaginal themes of enclosure and satisfaction form a common ground in the theorizing of Freudians like Erikson and Jungians like Helson. In children's texts, the holes, burrows, and corners in which the little creatures of fantasy hide securely away and live their comfortable, protected lives are the most obvious instance of being incorporated, while the attention to food in all its forms exemplifies incorporation. A further marked characteristic of this type of fantasy, particularly in the "golden age" of children's literature, is the use of the pastoral mode. From the time of Mrs. Doasyouwouldbedoneby (Charles Kingsley, *The Water Babies*), who "took Tom in her arms, and laid him in the softest place of all," Mother Nature has been widely conceived of as one on whose bosom small creatures can take their rest, comfort, and sustenance.[12]

Whereas Helson assumes that this kind of fantasy takes a narrative form, I would argue that it more characteristically appears in single or, at best, loosely linked episodes. The pleasure of a riverbank existence in *The Wind in the Willows* (Kenneth Grahame) derives simply from clubbish days on, about, and in the river: "Where nothing seems really to matter. That's the charm of it." It functions as the central and determinative episode of George MacDonald's *At the Back of the North Wind*, where the child Diamond enters the country at the back of the North Wind—and would preferably remain there in an eternity of wondering absorption. The desire for unbroken intimacy with the mother/carer may thus manifest itself in imagery as elementary as food and eating or as complex as the mystical experience;[13] its grounding and character is nevertheless a common one: the fantasy of wish fulfillment.

The second fantasy element, following Erikson, is characterized by the imaginal themes of "disappearance, reappearance, power, magic." Powers other than those belonging to the primary world constitute a virtual defining characteristic of "high fantasy"; spells and magical control, however, wreak all kinds of havoc and spring all kinds of relief and delight on both characters and readers in a much broader range of children's texts: the Psammead grants wishes with an ironic largesse (E. E. Nesbit, *Five Children and It*), gigantic peaches grow to nurture the good child and crush wicked aunts (Roald Dahl, *James and the Giant Peach*), bronzed Australian Laura makes a witch of herself (Margaret Mahy, *The Changeover*). Further, disruptions of all kinds—whether elementary violences of language in bangs and the Iron man's "CRRRAAAASSSSSH," (Ted Hughes, *The*

Iron Man) or Alice's final triumphant gesture of defiance: "Who cares for you? You are nothing but a pack of cards!" (Lewis Carroll, *Alice's Adventures in Wonderland*)—derive their gleeful, anxious, or heady power from the ground feeling of grasp or loss of control.

One of the most important forms which this type of fantasy takes is nonsense, a genre which makes a particular appeal to children in later childhood as they are gaining cognitive control of their world. While, from early childhood, magic and general rumbustious disruption function as the metaphorical vehicles for the affective experience of grasping and exercising control, in later childhood more powerful cognition allows the risks and delighted achievements of word games and nonsense to complement these early vehicles of the fantasy of control.[14]

The third fantasy element, like the first, is a comparatively uncontentious one, which Helson describes as "the Heroic," and I have described as the fantasy of venture. The notion that children's oedipal experience can be coded in stories of heroic quest is amply confirmed by both general and reader-development literature. J. A. Appleyard designates the later years of childhood as "the Reader as Hero and Heroine" stage,[15] while Kieron Egan calls it "the Romantic stage."[16] The imaginal themes relating to this growth crisis may deploy an immense range of materials, from a young rabbit finding its way into a well-kept vegetable plot (Beatrix Potter, *Peter Rabbit*) to the grand adventures and achievements of an Odysseus or a Beowulf; all are grist to the thematic mill of "exploration, discovery, metamorphosis."

What is most striking about this type of fantasy is what may be described as its forward orientation. The imaginal themes of the fantasy of wish fulfillment take the form of static assurance or satisfaction: you idle all day on the river (Kenneth Grahame, *The Wind in the Willows*) or are lost in the beautiful dream or come to rest in a happy ending (George MacDonald, *At the Back of the North Wind*). The imaginal themes of the fantasy of control take the form of unsettling, unpredictable, risky, and perhaps haphazard disruption: Toad rushes from one disastrous excess to the next (Kenneth Grahame, *The Wind in the Willows*), Alice finds herself implicated in one nonsensical affront upon another (Lewis Carroll, *Alice's Adventures in Wonderland*), and all cacophonously—or, like the Snark, "softly and suddenly" (Lewis Carroll, *The Hunting of the Snark*)—vanish away. In the fantasy of venture, however, the hero or heroine, beginning in one state, goes out into an alien and difficult, but discoverable and even controllable, world and moves forward, through time and experience, to a new state. This forward movement is congruous with the way in which contemporary linguistic Freudians[17] associate the oedipal crisis with induction into language as a shaping and dominating structure. Seen in this perspective, the fantasy of venture may in fact be conceived of as deriving its character from the syntactical structure of language—from the sentence as model for forward-oriented narrative structure. The primordial story of heroic quest thus functions as a metaphor both for the venture out into the social world and for the venture of syntactic and narrative construction itself.

The anatomy: further elements

The three types of fantasy extrapolated thus far on the basis of Erikson's theory may be expected to form fundamentally important elements of children's fantasy texts, as well as the staple of nursery books. After infancy, however, Erikson sees children, in the psychosexual "latency" or, perhaps more significantly, social "schooling" stage, as confronting a fourth crisis, that of "Industry and inferiority." He identifies its related imaginal themes as those of "invention, construction, achievement"; we may expect these, then, also to be manifested in a further fantasy element. We have already noted the enthusiasm for language games and nonsense texts in the preadolescent years functioning (as the great expansion in children's cognitive grasp affects how they *feel* about themselves) as new manifestations of the fantasy of control. The fourth stage of emotional development, which directly parallels this cognitive development and its reminting of earlier imaginal themes, is, however, itself marked by a new set of such themes. In contrast to the sudden, disruptive, and surprising themes springing from the earlier crisis and amplified in the richer experience of this new stage, those manifesting the new crisis of "industry and inferiority" are distinguished by sustained thoroughness and painstaking rationality. Indeed, their functional propensity is to shift the texts in which they play a major part toward realism. The instances which spring immediately to mind are the meticulously detailed documentary feature of romances like R. M. Ballantyne's *Coral Island*, replete with every kind of useful knowledge and practical know-how, or those of Arthur Ransome, such as *Swallows and Amazons*, where the technicalities of sailing and its competent performance form the text's thematic and ideological center of gravity.[18]

The themes of invention, construction, and achievement manifest themselves in a similar way in fantasy texts, when the ventures of protagonists take the form not merely of brave adventure, but of clever and resourceful contrivance: the artful Charlotte weaving her cleverly conceived and competently executed webs (E. B. White, *Charlotte's Web*), or the Borrowers furnishing and providing for their way of life by a myriad such resourceful stratagems (Mary Norton, *The Borrowers*). The large, undifferentiated gesture of venture is here "cashed out" through the development and use of a broad range of precisely differentiated and thoroughgoing competences.

The fantasy text, as a whole, can itself become an image of competent construction. In Charles Kingsley's *Water Babies*, for example, the imaginal theme of achievement is realized not merely in the last literal accolade of Tom as "a great man of science, [who] can plan railroads, and steam engines, and electric telegraphs," but in the industrious, not to say obsessive, packing of the whole text with the careful and accurate natural histories of river and ocean life. This has the effect of convincing readers that the protagonist is going through a cumulative series of educational experiences; it also serves to achieve for the text as a whole a convincing solidity of specification. This technique of the painstaking—indeed, loving —piecing together of significant detail as a way of assuring readers of the "reality" of a fictive world constitutes perhaps the most important form which the imaginal themes of invention, construction, and achievement take, particularly in "high fantasy." In J. R. R. Tolkien's *The Hobbit*, for instance, besides the many holes and good meals, besides appearances, disappearances, and magic, besides the quest, there is above all the meticulous depiction of the groups that make up the world of the text, their habitats, customs, languages, and relationships. Half the success of this book derives from erudite knowledge of the folklore of the North and half from felicitous invention; the whole, however, constitutes an imaginative *tour de force*, sustained through three further volumes—and a still-aggregating corpus: *indeed* a fantasy of competence!

The final, and problematic, element of children's fantasy texts to be considered derives ultimately from the experience which Erikson describes in his *Youth, Identity and Crisis*,[19] and with which he associates the imaginal themes of "justice, revolution, reformation, utopias." He describes the quality of awareness developed in the crisis of this fifth stage in development by the term *devotion*, which I shall use to characterize this element of children's fantasy texts. It may be best understood in relation to the immediately preceding crises of "initiative and guilt" and "industry and inferiority." Seen thus, the venture out into language and the social world is confirmed and substantiated, in the fourth stage of emotional life, by the development of a broad range of linguistic, intellectual, and practical competences and then, in this fifth stage, is shaped into a sense of personal identity through fidelity or devotion to an ideal.

The imaginal themes associated with this fifth crisis also manifest themselves most obviously in relation to the fantasy of venture. In Tolkien's *The Hobbit*, not only is Bilbo's venture confirmed and substantiated by its contextualization in a skillfully contrived secondary world, but the protagonist himself becomes more than a stereotypical hero when, in the context of divided loyalties, as an act both of judicious strategy and devotion to the values he is learning, he yields up his justifiable (though surreptitiously acquired) "reward," the Arkenstone. This event would doubtless be read by Ravenna Helson as a metaphor for the relationship between the ego and the unconscious going, beyond struggle, to reconciliation: a "tender feeling" fantasy. I prefer to describe this as the fantasy of devotion in order to make clear that all such tender feeling arises out of a further differentiation of the fantasy of venture. There the protagonists's adventuring out into the world characteristically involves the binary oppositions of self and other, of the good and the evil, and of achievement for the good self through the negation of the bad other. In the more complex situation where the self and the good are conceived of in terms of personal devotion to the pursuit of some ideal or cause in a more realistic and problematic world, the final negation of the bad may be conceived of as involving the more complex act of self-abnegation: yielding the Arkenstone to overcome evil and to achieve justice. A more recent instance may be found in Margaret Mahy's *The Changeover*, where overcoming evil involves no less than the protagonist's "being born again." Helson's most illuminating instance of "tender feeling" is *Charlotte's Web* (E. B. White), where devotion is coded in a death—although transposed from Wilbur, as subject, to Charlotte, as helper.[20]

Adolescent and adult readers find no difficulty in responding to these metaphors of self-realization. They have been inducted into religious and literary traditions where, paradoxically, the losing of one's life is the way to gaining it. For preadolescent readers, however, while they may have begun to understand how others feel and to make moral judgments on a basis of more than prudence, the idealism characteristic of adolescence does not yet, for them, constitute a passion. This theoretical assertion is empirically endorsed when, for example,[21] preadolescent readers are found to enjoy *The Hobbit*, and to recall with enthusiasm the hole house, the trolls, goblins, and wargs, and the dangerous venture down into Smaug's lair, but *not* to mention the Arkenstone—or to see the episode simply as another brave and clever venture (reading it in terms simply of the third and fourth types of fantasy). An equally limited response occurs when young readers, who love *Charlotte's Web*, are delighted by her clever contrivances and pleased that Wilbur continues to enjoy his trough but are inconsolably shocked, in the movement which should provide the consolation of a happy ending, at the disappearance of Charlotte from the text. This final denial, rather than wish fulfillment, is to some degree mitigated by the reappearance of new Charlottes, in the form of the babies from the egg sack, but the dying-rising imagery which touches mature sensibilities is quite lost on the child, desolated at the loss of the mother.

In conclusion

When we consider children's fantasy literature from the perspective of Erikson's etiology we find, not several types of fantasy, which can be exemplified (as they are by Helson) in whole narratives, but a number of fantasy elements which occur in many and varied relationships in these texts. In only one case does a fantasy element consistently take a whole-narrative form: that of the fantasy of venture. This fantasy is therefore, as the argument has implied, perhaps best conceived of as an Ur narrative, in relation to which all other kinds of fantasy may be conceived of as elements in various ways impinging on and modifying the forward movement of the venture. The dreaming absorption of the fantasy of wish fulfillment and the wild power of the fantasy of control form the contrapuntal delights and excitements of the venture: at times, the fantasy of wish fulfillment may *decelerate* the narrative to a wondering stillness, while, on the other hand, the wild antics of linguistic and conceptual tomfoolery break in energetically to *disrupt* the narrative progression of the text. Similarly, the painstaking technical detail of the fantasy of competence may be seen to engage the venture in a world of ever greater *social* complexity, while the ideals of the fantasy of devotion lift it into a moral world of ever greater *ideological* complexity.

Children's fantasy literature may thus appropriately be described in terms of an anatomy: It comprises a body of texts, characterized by a number of distinctive and significantly articulated metaphors, through which first desires take their powerful course, and through which linguistic, conceptual, and social venture is celebrated and advanced.

Notes

1 See discussion in R. Jackson, *Fantasy: The Literature of Subversion*, London, Methuen, 1981.
2 J. R. R. Tolkien, *Tree and Leaf*, London, George Allen & Unwin, 1964.
3 M. Morpurgo, *The War of Jenkins Ear*, London, Heinemann, 1993. Michael Morpurgo's story about a Christ revenant in a 1950s prep-school boy gets perhaps as close as any children's text to creating unresolved uncertainty. It depends for much of its effect on a friend's (and thus the reader's) uncertainty about the ontological status of the protagonist, Christopher: Are the happy outcomes of each new situation the miracles of Chrestopher or just fortuitous matters of chance? But the ambivalences keep breaking down in the face of unambiguous evidence which the writer provides for his young readers.
4 A. Warlow, "Kinds of Fiction: A Hierarchy of Veracity" in M. Meek (Ed.), *The Cool Web*, Oxford, Bodley Head, 1977.
5 J. Curry "On the Elvish Craft," in N. Chambers (Ed.), *The Signal Approach to Children's Books*, London, Kestrel, 1980. Ann Swinfen, *In Defence of Fantasy*, London, Routledge, Kegan & Paul, 1984.
6 J. Cohen, *An Examination of Four Key Motivs found in High Fantasy for Children*, Ohio State University, Columbus 1975 (mimeograph).
7 U. Le Guin, "In Defence of Fantasy" in *Horn Book*, June 1973.
8 J. Stephens, *Language and Ideology in Children's Fiction*, London, Longmans, 1993.
9 See particularly B. Bettelheim, *The Use of Enchantment*, London, Thames & Hudson, 1976.
10 R. Helson, "Fantasy and Self-Discovery," "The Heroic, the Comic, the Tender: Patterns of Literary Fantasy and Their Authors," *Journal of Personality*, 1973, *41*(2).
11 E. Erikson, *Childhood and Society*, New York, Norton, 1950. His work has been drawn on in reader development studies: N. Tucker, *The Child and the Book*, Cambridge, 1981, and J. A. Appleyard, *Becoming a Reader*, Cambridge,

University Press, 1991. It is also drawn on most fruitfully in R. M. Jones, *Fantasy and Feeling in Education*, London, Penguin, 1968, which I use in this account.

12, 13, 14. See my "Deep Calling unto Deep: Pre-oedipal Structures in Children's Texts" in *Children's Literature in Education*, 1994, *25*(2), which provides a fuller account of the oral and anal stages of development and their manifestation in textual imagery and other linguistic devices.

15 J. A. Appleyard, op. cit.

16 K. Egan, *Individual Development and the Curriculum*, London, Hutchinson, 1986.

17 See Jacques Lacan and Julie Kristeva, introductory references in T. Eagleton, *Literary Theory: An Introduction*, Oxford, Basil Blackwell, 1983. The fantasies of wish-fulfillment and control function, in relation to the fantasy of venture, much as Kristeva sees "semiotic" functioning in relation to "symbolic" language. The competent handling of boats in Arthur Ransome's texts or the function of the Arkenstone may both be read in terms of Lacan's "phallus." Seen in these ways, the fantasy of venture is confirmed as a metaphorical statement of the momentous entry into language.

18 These fictive accounts make immediate sense to children, for whom, at this stage, linguistic play goes hand in hand with the industrious collation of information, artifacts, and every other collectible and classifiable entity; see the first paragraphs of Kenneth Grahame's, "The Twenty-first of October" in *The Golden Age*.

19 E. Erikson, *Youth, Identity and Crisis*, New York, Norton, 1968.

20 For Greimas's concept of these folktale roles, see R. Rimmon-Keenan, *Narrative Fictions: Contemporary Poetics*, London, Methuen, 1983.

21 I make reference to these responses on the basis of anecdotal evidence from teachers who have read and talked about these books with children, and of commentary from students engaged in reading-project case studies. The latter are described in "A New Practice: English and the World of Work" (forthcoming, in *Applied Aesthetics*, University of Wolverhampton).

13

WHO "OWNS" CHILDREN'S FANTASY?

Andy Sawyer

Source: *Foundation* 88 (Summer 2003): 5–19.

Or rather, what do historians and critics of children's literature *make* of fantasy? This seems a rather odd question, especially bearing in mind that fantasy is supposedly the glory of children's literature. Certain specific fantasy authors for the young – Ursula Le Guin and Alan Garner come to mind – are critiqued as *major* writers. The current "phenomena" of J. K. Rowling and Philip Pullman, gives us writers whose positioning with respect to a fantasy "mainstream" may be ambiguous (Pullman, for instance says "I have long felt that realism is a higher mode than fantasy.")[1] but who have achieved high sales and literary awards and, significantly, a large adult following. However, critics of both children's literature and fantasy acknowledge problems of what can only be "ownership". Diana Wynne Jones's latest novel, *The Merlin Conspiracy* (2003) is published as a children's book, although a related novel, *Deep Secret* (1997) was published for adults. A high proportion of the readership of Terry Pratchett's "children's" Discworld novel, *The Amazing Maurice and His Educated Rodents* (2001) will be adults who have followed the series, who see him, and the other writers mentioned, as authors they came to as part of their "adult" fantasy reading.

We do not, of course, have to give up children's fiction when we become adults, but our reading of it will come from different viewpoints. As fantasy readers, particularly, we are interested in the richness of fantasy for children, but we are also aware that this is, or ought to be, seen as part of a deep current of imaginative literature which includes works written for adults – often, as we've seen, by the same authors. From within the circle of children's literature critics, this awareness has to be tempered with a consideration that the focus is not "fantasy" but "that fantasy found on the shelves in the children's library". What the critic is seeing, or appears to be seeing, is a particular, sometimes arbitrary sub-set of fantasy, albeit one which contains many of its most interesting and creative examples. Peter Hunt in his *Criticism, Theory and Children's Literature* (1991), spends a chapter on defining the term "children's literature", considering whether it differs from "adult literature" in degree or in kind, whether we need to take the same, or different, critical approaches to a text written "for children", and what, exactly, *written for children* might mean given that many classics of the field were either not written for children at all, are read by children in abridged or adapted forms, or are aimed at a dual, adult/child, audience. (And almost all are mediated through adults – parents, teachers, librarians – as well as, naturally, written, published, and sold by adults.)[2] Like science fiction and fantasy, children's literature tends to be what we point to when we say it.[3]

Aidan Chambers, in "The Reader in the Book", one of the most important essays published on children's literature in the 1970s, discovers a gap in Maurice Sendak's picture-book *Where The Wild things Are* (1963) "so vital that, unless the reader fills it, the profound meaning of the book cannot be discovered": the fact that Max has dreamt his experiences.[4] Chambers, one of the key critics of children's literature, seems here to be here privileging that favourite standby of the baffled imagination: "And then he woke up, and it was all a dream." In the book, we have watched Max, exiled to his bedroom after a tantrum, sail "in and out of weeks and almost over a year" to the land of the Wild Things, where he tames them, joins in their wild rumpus, and, feeling lonely, returns home to his mother's love (and hot supper). As Chambers points out, there are clues in the illustrations (dolls, pictures drawn by Max) that the Wild Things of his journey are part of Max's imagination: we even see, on the page where the forest grows in his bedroom, Max standing with his eyes closed, suggesting sleep. But to read this text as *simply* a dream ignores its function as fantasy, as a text which asks its reader to believe in its unreality. It has to be real, yet imaginary. Impossible, yet take place. The "profound meaning" surely must be that this is an *ambiguous* text. The point is not that the story is Max's dream (or daydream: a third location for the imaginative "events") but that Sendak does not explicitly say so, allowing us to build up our meanings through the interplay of text and illustration, imagination and reality.

In trying to resolve the problem with this interpretation we're forced to confront how children's-literature critics consider fantasy, and the nature of children's literature (and fantasy) itself.

Reader-response criticism and the sociology of childhood have drawn attention to how socially-constructed concepts of childhood affect the stances of both writers and critics of fiction designated as "children's literature". A major debate at all levels has been how far one accepts "popularity with children" or a text's conformity with traditional "literary" values as a virtue, and how far these questions underlie questions about the didactic qualities of a children's book. Current debates over whether the Harry

Potter books are "good" because they are apparently read by masses of children or "bad" because they are narratologically and ideologically conservative, are merely the latest instalment of this argument. Karin Lesnik-Oberstein, a critic sceptical about the "place of the child" in children's books, sums up that "children's literature criticism views itself as split between critics who are quite sure that they have a knowledge of the child sufficient for their purposes and critics who claim they cannot predict the way children read."[5] One book she cites is even subtitled "The Impossibility of Children's Fiction". Its author, Jacqueline Rose, in words eerily reminiscent of what could be said about criticism of fantasy and science fiction, describes the project of children's-literature critics such as Peter Hunt and others as "the ultimate fantasy, perhaps, of children's book criticism that it should come of age and do what the adults (that is adult critics) have been doing all along."[6]

Other critics, such as John Stephens (*Language and Ideology in Children's Fiction*, 1992) consider how ideology operates in fictional discourse in a more complex manner than earlier polemicists like Bob Dixon (*Catching Them Young*, 1977). Stephens has interesting things to say about fantasy and science fiction, which he considers are areas in which "top-down" reading (drawing on higher order knowledge such as facts about the world, and narrative codes) and "bottom-up" reading (focusing upon decoding of words, semantics, and syntax) combine in significant ways. In these modes, the differences and inconsistencies between these strategies can, for instance, lead to the way the children in Nicholas Fisk's *Grinny* deduce that "Grinny" is not from this Earth.[7] Characters and objects have their meanings displaced in Diana Wynne Jones's *Castle in the Air*, meaning different things to other characters, and these "displaced signifiers", operating through a fantastic text, create a web of signification.[8]

In other words, fantasy does interesting and ambiguous things with meaning, playing with differences between what you *think* you know and what the text *says*. This fantastic inter- or meta-textuality is deliberate, but fantasy also, says Stephens, is "more prone to a kind of ideological slippage whereby implicit ideology becomes interpolated between the desired and eschewed values constructed more overtly in the text."[9] Other writers on ideology, such as Margery Hourihan (*Deconstructing the Hero*, 1997) have examined children's and adult fantasy to consider how fantasy engages with meaning in its more political or sociological senses. Hourihan's book is particularly interesting in its slippage between children's fiction and popular adventure fiction for adults. She is primarily concerned with the masculine bias of the "hero myth" in Western adventure literature, and despite the pomposity of the back-cover blurb ("Margery Hourihan shows how teaching children to read books critically can help to prevent the establishment of negative attitudes, discourage aggression and promote more positive values")[10] throws up some interesting and relevant points, even if she occasionally overlooks the very significant fault-lines which Stephens suggests fantasy can give us.[11] Nevertheless, these books are *instances* of how fantasy works, rather than, in the end, *examinations* of it.

Who writes fantasy?

In an essay originally published in 1978, Felicity Hughes wrote that "[t]he prominence and excellence of fantasy in children's literature has often been remarked on, yet the criticism of those works has been confused and superficial."[12] The reason, she suggests, is that children have been excluded from the readership of the "realistic" novel, which strove for an inclusive version of reality in which material "unsuitable" for tender sensibilities ought to be freely available for the "serious" novelist. "Not in front of the children, dear" becomes literary custom: "the children are to be sent away to play, with their mothers, presumably, so that the serious novelist can be free to pursue his art and write about sex."[13] This positioning of realism makes fantasy "déclassé". If fantasy is the opposite of realism, it means that it is the opposite of "serious" – frivolous stuff to amuse the children while Real Writers get on with charting Life As We Know It. The "demotion" of fantasy, underpinned, Hughes says, by E. M. Forster in his chapters on "Fantasy" and "Prophecy" in *Aspects of the Novel* (1927), had a further effect: "the writer of fantasy has been directed into writing for children no matter how good he or she might be."[14] While "realistic" writers *may* write for children, it could well be with a sense of being "second best": "real" realism being impossible in a book for an audience which is excluded from serious literature. "The fantasist has written under no such shadow – has had no such option – all fantasy goes on the children's list."[15]

This is a sentence which any critic of fantasy reads with incredulity. It certainly was not true in 1978, by which time Tolkien and Moorcock were major authors and the Ballantine Adult Fantasy imprint had come and gone. The availability during the late 1960s and early 1970s of paperback editions of fantasy fiction by David Lindsay, E. R. Eddison, Lord Dunsany, James Branch Cabell, William Morris, Peter Beagle, Evangeline Walton, Fritz Leiber, George MacDonald, Katherine Kurtz, Hope Mirrlees, William Hope Hodgson, William Beckford and George Meredith (as disparate a group of texts as could ever be met with) suggests that there was an audience, however specialised, for fantastic fiction written specifically for an adult audience.[16] Ironically, Hughes seems to be falling for her own "major impediment to useful criticism", the supposition that fantasy is for children, not adults.

Yet, while Hughes's writing in the present tense seem oddly myopic, it's hardly untrue. Many of the readers of the Ballantine series were young, fresh from discovering Tolkien in their teens. Diana Wynne Jones says that "there were simply no other openings for fantasy except with a children's publisher, when I started writing in earnest."[17] Ruth Nadelman Lynn, ironically, suggests that Lin Carter, responsible for the Ballantine series, was unaware of the rich tradition of children's fantasies represented by the work of Mayne, Garner or Cooper,[18] though while Carter does not name any of the "truly fine writers of children's fantasies in this century" he alludes to in his discussion of C. S. Lewis's "Narnia" books, he does so (he says) because he is making a counter-claim to the assumption that fantasy is for children. But despite Carter's attempt to justify an "adult" response to fantasy (based largely on love of the strange, imaginative and unusual) there's still, it seems, a general "lay" view that it is for children, unless it is "Magic Realism". Ironically Terry Pratchett's Carnegie Medal in 2002 for *The Amazing Maurice and his Educated Rodents* confirmed this in many eyes. Virtually all journalistic references to this award located his audience as "teenagers", even though, as his agent Colin Smythe pointed out in a letter to the *Guardian* (July 20, 2002) if that *had* once been true, those who stuck with him since *The Colour of Magic* (1983) may now have teenage children of their own. The overlapping of the first *Harry Potter* and *Lord of the Rings* movies in the Christmas blockbuster schedules seemed to have created a sense that these films shared a (juvenile) market. Each film, of course was heavily publicised in places likely to be seen by children, and each featured a computer-generated troll.

We do not, of course, need to rely on journalists working from copy supplied by movie publicists. Brian Attebery tells us that "In 1968, when Neil Isaacs and Rose Zimbardo assembled the first collection of essays on J. R. R. Tolkien, virtually nothing in the way of theory had been pro-posed for the examination of fantasy."[19] Since then, of course, a remarkable amount of discussion has taken place, with Tzvetan Todorov, Rosemary Jackson, and Christina Brooke-Rose, for example bringing the critical revo-lution of the past three decades to bear on the phenomenon and significant overview examinations of both the mode of "the fantastic" and the genre of "fantasy" presented by Kathryn Hume and, of course, Attebery himself.[20] The publication of John Clute and John Grant's *The Encyclopedia of Fantasy* in 1997 has given us, at last, much of the critical and theoretical apparatus we need to examine fantasy in detail. Yet, while there has certainly been a renaissance in the overall criticism of fantasy, John Stephens can still write in 1992 "There is a large secondary literature bearing on the concepts of fantasy and realism as they apply to children's literature, but we still lack a fully articulated theory of either."[21] When we consider how fantasy is viewed in children's literature criticism we come across a mixture of tones which is largely unsatisfactory, arising partly from the fault-lines in the theoretical constructs of each. These fault-lines (some of which I am going to describe below), are, ironically enough, partly (I believe) due to the status of both children's literature and fantasy criticism as "subordinate" criticisms.

199

First, fantasy itself is bedevilled by what Attebery calls the difference between "mode" and 'genre'. In other words, we use the same word for very different things. Following Hume, Attebery says that "There are no purely mimetic or fantastic works of fiction."[22] Hume calls fantasy an "impulse". We might regroup, therefore, and consider Tom Shippey's borrowing of the term "fabril" (for literature which is "overwhelmingly urban, disruptive, future-oriented, eager for novelty; its central image is the 'faber', the smith or blacksmith [or] . . . the creator of artefacts in general)",[23] which he contrasts with "pastoral", and add a third impulse to which we could give a relevant name but which would basically be the "fantastic". These are the three primary colours of literature from which all specific works are constructed in varying proportions. While for the purpose of this essay I am over-simplifying, this is a corrective for the common suggestion, based upon theories of child development, that fancy and imagination are child-like and serious realism is what we *grow up* to achieve.

Second, "children's literature" is haunted by its own ambiguity. Peter Hunt's use of reader-response theory and "implied readers" and the freedom given by critical theory to consider differences rather than canonical ratings, as well as the realisation that "childhood" is not a stable concept and that "[t]he literature defined by it, therefore, cannot be expected to be a stable entity" are useful.[24] But Jacqueline Rose uses very similar arguments to argue "the impossibility of children's fiction". She states that "There is no child behind the category 'children's fiction', other than the one which the category itself sets in place, which it needs to believe is there for its own purposes,"[25] and proceeds to consider J. M. Barrie's remarkably elusive *Peter Pan* as a fantasy *of* childhood rather than a fantasy *for* children. This argument is built upon by Karin Lesnik-Oberstein in *Children's Literature: Criticism and the Fictional Child* (1994). She considers the disassociation between "book-centred" critics and "child-centred" critics, the thorny questions of whether we can *know* the "child reader" and what may be "good" for them, and the socially-constructed nature of "childhood" and goes further, to dismiss the concept of specialist children's-literature criticism at all: "In making judgements and criticisms on behalf of a 'real child' who does not exist, its writings are useless to the fulfilment of its own professed aims."[26]

Well, as Douglas Adams might remark, that just about wraps it up for children's literature and its criticism. Except, of course, that a vast quantity of books presented "for children" still exist, and are read, for whatever motives, by the young of the human species. It is unclear whether Lesnik-Oberstein is arguing that "Childhood" is more socially constructed than any other identity, such as "Old Age", in terms of the social and literary assumptions that are made.

Third: as we have seen for many writers of fantasy for children this work is part of a spectrum which includes work for adults, or they have a large adult following, or the position of the book as a "juvenile" is ambiguous, due to marketing or reputation. Deborah Thacker cites adult reading of the "Harry Potter" books as evidence of the blurring of child and adult audience.[27] Alan Garner's *Red Shift*, Diana Wynne Jones's *Fire and Hemlock* or Patricia McKillip's *Winter Rose* have young protagonists, but are complex and demanding. Le Guin's fourth Earthsea novel, *Tehanu* contained references to physical and sexual abuse which made it, for many of children's literature's "gatekeepers", a book which could be only recommended for readers considerably older than those of its predecessors. There is a strong case for arguing that the target audience for this novel was those adults who had read the "Earthsea Trilogy" as young people and, like the author, had come to find its treatment of gender wanting in various respects, but Le Guin's position as one of the very few writers who are equally acclaimed in the separate spheres of adult's and children's writings make her something of a special case.

Despite the Child/Book-centred argument, most children's literature criticism seems to consider the book's effect on the child as literary artefact (Hunt) or as part of the construction of childhood either psycho-sociologically (Rose; Lesnik-Oberstein) or ideologically (Hourihan; Stephens). The child-centred nature of criticism is constantly present, either as a given, or to be reacted against. Teasing out specific references to fantasy is not always easy. When Nicholas Tucker mentions "the undemanding fantasies provided for [children] by literature which frequently has very little merit as such",[28] he seems to mean daydream or wish-fulfilment stories rather than fantasy as mode or genre, and although he uses the term a lot, for him it is a catch-all to include stories for the very young about humanised animals, Enid Blyton's "Noddy" stories, animal stories and "an imaginary land existing parallel with the real one".[29] The value of such latter fictions seems to lie in how they might comfort and enrich children with similar "daydream worlds". Tucker's model of children's fiction follows Piaget's model of child development, and interestingly, although he spends time on discussing "Who reads children's books?",[30] it is from the standpoint of children who *don't* rather than adults who *do*. Peter Hunt's *Criticism, Theory and Children's Literature* is positioned to take up that topic, and even suggests that (presumably because the "implicit child-reader" is constantly scurrying about the text, getting in the way) "reading children's literature is, for the adult, a more complex process than reading an adult book."[31] In fact, Hunt offers four ways for an adult to read children's books: first, *"as if they were peer-texts"*[32] (emphasis in the original), tending to read *against* the "implied readership" which may be a more profound but less "appropriate" reading. Second, *"on behalf of a child"*:[33] to assess the book against the perceived "appropriateness" for an implied (or sometimes actual, in the sense that this may be a parent or teacher surveying books for children they are in care of) child. Third, the adult could be reading *"with an eye to discussing [the text] with other adults*":[34] presumably, *these* adults are teachers, students or critics of children's books. The most rewarding reading, says Hunt, is "*surrender to the book on its own terms*".[35] This is acceptance of the "implied role" – but Hunt himself admits the complications. It is not "reading as a child" because the reader is *not* a child: all she can do is recall her childhood reading, get in touch with her "inner self" or in some other way fake it.

All these strategies involve the reader consciously playing a part; psyching himself up into a role before tackling the book. This, of course, assumes the separation of the children's book as something "other", to be read differently from an adult book. Even as he is trying to separate the text from the cultural contexts and networks which force our readings of it, Hunt still speaks of children's fiction as a subordinate genre which must be justified. "Children's literature," he writes, "has unique genres within it: the school story, texts designed for single sexes . . . fantasy, the folk and fairy-tale, interpretations of myth and legend . . . The re-telling of myths and legends is little found elsewhere."[36]

This *reads* like Hughes's apparent unawareness of the fact that fantasy is not confined to children's literature but in fact has a rich and thriving adult readership. Many myths and legends *do* find their way explicitly retold in the form of adult fiction.[37] In fact, Hunt is knowledgeable on fantasy and in *Alternative Worlds in Fantasy Fiction* (2001) is far more explicit about fantasy being not necessarily "for" children and indeed in some of its modes – nostalgia, regression, romantic yearnings for innocence – symptomatic of adult traits.[38] What's happening here, I think, is a defence of the concept of "children's literature" which is confining his language into the very justification which he elsewhere is trying to escape from. Fantasy may be a subordinate mode, but it's *our* subordinate mode.

This sense of "subordination", though, is rather a sense of incompleteness. In his discussion of the American fantasy tradition, Brian Attebery calls fantasy "a genre . . . with an audience of all ages" and emphasises that distinguishing between the children's writings of an author like Ray Bradbury, and the rest of his work is "arbitrary".[39] In *The Fantasy Tradition in American Literature*, and his succeeding *Strategies of Fantasy* (1992), Attebery sees fantasy as a braid-like tradition weaving in and out of an audience of children, adults, and both together, a tradition going from Hawthorne, Baum, Bradbury, Twain and Thurber to Le Guin. Looking more closely at two specific examinations of fantasy for children, the special issue of *Children's Literature Quarterly* (*CLQ*) of Spring 1987 and the above-mentioned, more recent (2001) book by Hunt and Lenz, we see a more uneasy sense of this "arbitrary". Of course, and it is a very real point, we may arrive at Lesnik-Oberstein's deconstruction of the concept of "children's literature" by a different route. If fantasy's audience is all ages, we must drop the "search for the child" within the texts of the "children's books" we, as adult readers, read: or at least relegate it to a contextually-specific paratextual coding like the audience-attracting cover which changes over time depending on the fashions of the book-buying public and the whims of the publisher's marketing division. But, pragmatically, we as adult readers do know that there is an industry which is devoted to making books appeal to children or to their adult stand-ins. C. W. Sullivan III, introducing the special section on fantasy in *CLQ* Spring 1987, distinguishes between "children's and adults' fantasy fiction" and, after briefly summarising how elements of (genre) fantasy such as magic rings, dragons, elves and talking animals have appeared in Western literature since Homeric Greece and Celtic legends, goes on to say "Children's fantasy is no less diverse".[40] Citing Hume, though, Sullivan uses her definition of fantasy as one which might obviate the "often artificially-imposed distinctions" between fantasy written for children and that written for adults.[41] In considering the *form* of fantasy, Caroline Hunt begins with the increasing popularity among adolescents for genre fantasy (that form of fiction *marketed* as fantasy), particularly that involving the quest or the search for identity. She also considers, however, the detective story, the romance and the choose-your-own adventure story to conclude that "the shift towards 'fantasy' (in its broad sense) affects nearly everything being written" and that "the common denominator is the imposition of a clear [formulaic] pattern onto the confusion of daily existence."[42]

In terms of what was going on in American popular fiction for teenagers in the late 1970s, this is interesting and locates fantasy within a wider context, but it is of lesser value in considering fantasy as mode *or* genre. Of the journal's other essays, Peter Hunt's "Landscape and Journeys, Metaphors and Maps: The Distinctive Feature of English Fantasy" allows us to extrapolate from a specific characteristic of fantasy for children – the journey, which, as readers grow, becomes *Bildungsroman* – to the importance of "place" in English fantasy which finds its "objective correlative" in the use of maps to "symbolise the tension that exists for the writer between the real landscape and the fantasy which inhabits it."[43] We may wonder though, whether the map of Le Guin's Earthsea, for example, has a similar mythopoeic function, and indeed about the wider function of those fantasies which tend to have maps almost as much as they have the word "dragon" in the title. Deiter Petzold ("Fantasy out of Myth and Fable: Animal Stories in Rudyard Kipling and Richard Adams") notes the "profound impact" these stories have on adults as well as children. Gary D. Schmidt, considering the "Doctor Dolittle" series, is taking on a character far closer to traditional conceptions of "a children's book" than most works in this section, yet his use of language in his closing paragraph is interesting "*We*" (my emphasis), will "find that Stubbins' perspective is close to that of *ours*. Dolittle, who never changes, will always remain a bit distant from *us*."[44] The implied child-reader has, apparently, dropped our, or at the very least is subsumed in Schmidt's primary audience, the adult educationalists and critics who are the journal's readership. Whether it is because of the conventional, impersonal collectivity imposed by the form of the academic essay, or a more "readerly" collectivity including "anyone who reads *Doctor Dolittle*", those influenced by the text Schmidt describes are "we" rather than "they". Cordelia Sherman, in contrast, considering the fantasy worlds of Ursula Le Guin and George MacDonald, "places" the texts she examines directly in the didactic tradition of children's literature, with a common purpose; "to teach children by dramatic example what it means to be a good adult",[45] which transcends their ideological differences. This is certainly a perfectly fair conclusion, but it may be illuminated by acknowledging that both writers, in other books, are attempting just as much "to teach *adults* by dramatic example what it means to be a good adult". Finally, Sara J. Stohler ("The Mythic World of Childhood") attempts to understand children's attachment to fictions based on myth, fairy tale and fantasy as essential to their emotional growth and development, by considering, like Tucker, Jean Piaget's model of child development which links the "egocentricism" of young children to the animistic, magic-accepting forms of thinking "found among 'primitive' or myth-oriented people".[46] Stohler's argument is persuasive if one accepts its premises, but they are premises which are uneasily rooted in images of superstitious, child-like savages and overlook both the flowering of fantasy literature among *adults* and the return of magic-like discourses (such as alien-abduction claims) among allegedly *non*-primitive people brought up outside animistic myth-systems. It may be possible to argue that children and adults will appreciate the same fantasies for different reasons, and Stohler does discuss the difference between the stages of belief and "understanding as metaphor" as children grow up, but as most children are not actually given the option that, for example "Father Christmas" is a symbolic fiction, such an argument will have to remain unresolved.[47]

The potential for a general examination of fantasy from within the children's-literature field is offered by the above-mentioned *Alternative Worlds in Fantasy Fiction*, which considers three major figures of such fantasy, Ursula Le Guin, Terry Pratchett, and Philip Pullman. As noted, Hunt's introduction takes on board the point that "it is adult writers who are interested in, or have a need for such alternatives"[48] and goes on to give us *adult* readings of classic "children's" texts such as *Peter Pan*, *The Wind in the Willows*, and *The House at Pooh Corner* in which we can recognise the role of fantasy for the *writers* and read these books – and others, such as *The Lord of the Rings* – as not too thickly disguised spiritual autobiography.[49] For the most part, though, the rest of the book does not build on this (nor does it take on what may be one riposte to this particular adult "construction" and develop how another focus might be the *aesthetic* response to the creative imagination involved in fantasy world-building). Lenz's account of Le Guin's Earthsea books is essentially a description of them for an audience relatively or completely unfamiliar with them. Like Sherman earlier, she shows us what Earthsea "teaches". Le Guin's books for adults, some at least of which readers of Earthsea might immediately move on to, are not mentioned; unlike in Hunt's survey of Pratchett which refers more widely to those of his books aimed at an adult audience. Indeed, Hunt's analysis of Pratchett contains interesting things about Pratchett's tone when he is writing for children and adults. His children's books are "not exactly what children's books are expected to be" while his adult books "do not *exclude* the child reader",[50] and he takes both modes to their limits, parodying children's literature of an earlier period (such as the way *Tom Brown's Schooldays* is parodied in *Pyramids*) in books for adults. The questions of growth, exploration and empowerment in *The Bromeliad* are equally relevant to adults, while the "Johnny" books are addressed to self-aware readers and interrogate the tropes of fantasy as much as those of the "problem" teenage novel. While a number of Hunt's contentions require further discussion, he does suggest that Pratchett is circling audiences and mediating between them in a particularly creative way. Unfortunately, Lenz on Pullman, a writer explicitly quoted as aiming for the "largest audience possible", does not take the hint and while she raises some interesting questions regarding the character of Lyra and in particularly (in view of his desire for a wide readership) Pullman's treatment of sexuality in The *Amber Spyglass* through the "double-coding" of language does not have the space to develop her argument. While fuller than her treatment of Le Guin, Lenz's section on Pullman still lists characters with gushing reviews of "breath-taking action scenes" and "an unforgettable love story".[51]

Who reads children's fantasy?

The increasing concern among adult readers of fantasy with children's books read for their *own* pleasure fits uneasily with neither main model of children's literature criticism. Much of the current wave of critical attention to Pullman and Rowling is because, whatever their status as children's writers, they have a significant adult following which is not necessarily linked to their readers' contact or work with children. Rowling, for instance, is the winner of the 2002 Hugo award for best science fiction novel of the year: an award linked to adult readers. It is not always clear that this readership is acknowledged. As a commodity, the "Harry Potter" sequence may be aimed towards children, but we know that there are editions with more sober covers (and higher prices) which reclassify the books outside this market. If children's literature criticism is focused upon the "child", the adult reader remains in limbo.

And despite the increasing awareness from publishers that certain books can he packaged for both markets, and that boundaries can also be pushed, we see the avoidance of controversial texts. It is easier to argue why a twelve-year-old *should* read William Mayne than consider why they read Guy N. Smith or Sean Hutson. Or to take a less extreme example, also taken from my experience as a children's librarian in the 1980s, Piers Anthony.

Although Anthony is listed in Ruth Nadelman Lynn's *Fantasy Literature for Children and Young Adults* along with, for example, Stephen Donaldson, Raymond Feist, J. R. R. Tolkien and Gene Wolfe as a "crossover" author in "the fast-growing genre of 'adult' fantasy", discovered by younger readers, he is rarely seen directly as a children's writer. The "Xanth" series largely charts the "Adult Conspiracy" – the child's discovery of the mechanics of sex against the wishes of their adults. Pun-based and avoiding any sense of the carnal, the Xanth series treats sexuality with a mixture of knowingness and innocence which is congenial to readers who have only recently discovered the "mystery" themselves and are unsure what to do with this knowledge. Although published as an "adult" writer, and generally reviewed as such, it makes sense to consider Anthony as a writer for young teenagers – and his own epilogues stress the response from young, especially female, teens. His "Incarnations of Immortality" series considers questions of morality in a symbolic form. His characters are often troubled young people. His plots and language have frequently been criticised for their juvenile nature – and they *are* juvenile but not necessarily, as the saying goes, in a bad way. If one accepts that his readers are children, then their coyness makes perfect sense.

The "adult" audience of children's books, on the other hand, is not – or at least is distinct from – an audience which creates fandoms out of nostalgia, although these elements should not necessarily be disparaged. Nor is it "double-voicing" of otherwise inarticulable anxieties in the sense of the way Kenneth Grahame's *Wind in the Willows* is so clearly a text "masquerading" as a children's book, although that certainly is some reason for the popularity of certain texts among adults. It *is* an audience which has developed out of the wave of fantasy reading in the past few decades – an audience which has partly responded to calls from librarian-critics that children's writers like Diana Wynne Jones have produced better and more challenging fantasy than the latest "adult" Tolkien clone or RPG novelisation, and partly an audience which has discovered this for themselves.

But children's literature critics have not (I think) really engaged with the fact that criticism of "their" writers must include an acknowledgement not that the audience is not always children (that certainly has been part of the discourse) but that readers are not at all reading "with children in mind". Quite often, there's a tip of the hat to the author who says, as Aidan Chambers quotes Arthur Ransome doing "You write not FOR children but for yourself",[52] but despite much discussion of the question whether children's literature should "forget the child" and play with the grown-ups (very like sf criticism!) and talk about *real* things such as ideology, postmodernism, or intertextuality, the focus is still on the work of fantasy for children as *part of the children's-literature spectrum* rather than *part of the fantasy spectrum*. The idea of the appeal of the children's book to the adult is subordinate to the subordinate, it seems. There is a spectrum here: the adult jokes or references inserted to appeal to an adult reading a bedtime story, the knowing asides which Piers Anthony sums up as the "Adult Conspiracy", the double-voicing of cute sentimentality and sophisticated (and rather cruel) humour at the expense of the child-figures in A. A. Milne, the psychological constructions of childhood in *Peter Pan*, are all examples of what adults may find in children's literature. But there is also the adult reading children's books for pleasure, because in these books is essentially the same factor which gives him/her pleasure in books *not* specifically denoted "for children". If "the implied reader" means anything, where, in these texts, can we find *this* person?

Only by moving away from the theory which sees fantasy as part of children's literature, rooted in folk-tale or fairy tale. More accurately, it was myth and legend. There's certainly a generation of fantasy readers brought up on retellings of *The Iliad* and Greek myths such as Charles Kingsley's *The Heros.* Later generations are as liable to come to the literature via the post-Tolkien examples, from Eddings, Feist, and other popular adult writers to (for younger readers) undemanding but effective series such as K. A. Applegate's "Ever World" or Tamora Pierce's "Alanna" sequences. *Critics* see children's literature as a temporal sequence, with a tradition, and so they should. *Children* do not.

Perhaps we need to consider the "idea of fantasy" in the same way as Westfahl does the "idea of science fiction". This is an even more complex task as what we call "fantasy" as a popular genre seems to have developed at least twice: once as "sword and sorcery" or "heroic fantasy" with Robert E. Howard's Conan stories as a touchstone and again indebted to *The Lord of the Rings*, with both weaving in and out of "Dungeons and Dragons" and other gaming scenarios. A third scenario – the fiction which slides uneasily between realities, moving on to the timeslip story – has itself a number of antecedents (George MacDonald, Lewis Carroll) more easily traced to children's literature, but is less easy to see as one genre. How, then, has children's fantasy developed? This is a question which the critics of children's literature seem to have not focused on perhaps because the answer seems obvious. But the "obvious" is not necessarily the real. The post-1945 wave of British children's fantasy owes much to cultural factors within the collective British psyche. But it also owes much to the simple presence of J. R. R. Tolkien and C. S. Lewis as lecturers at Oxford, informing a generation of students about the narratives of English literature.[53] Children's fantasy also now owes much to the tradition of adult fantasy.

This can be anaemic retelling or parody, but the post-Tolkien "big" adult fantasy is beginning to have its analogues in children's fiction.

Secondly, and more important, how does fantasy operate in children's literature? In answering this, we need to return to the theoretical quibbles about what fantasy *is*, and not even confine ourselves to what we think it is. Tucker uses the word "fantasy" a lot, and despite the confusion this sometimes arises he is not wholly wrong to do so. Can arch-realist Arthur Ransome be called a fantasy writer? I certainly think so, and have argued elsewhere that he is playing with numerous aspects of the fantastic imagination in the various viewpoints presented in the "Swallows and Amazons" sequence.[54] But it is important to realise that the "wish-fulfilment" aspect of "kids messing about in boats" is only where this process *starts*.

Third, what can critics of "adult" fantasy take from their children's literature counterparts? We have argued frequently that the field of children's fantasy is remarkably rich, but have we thoroughly *explored* these riches? Several writers have explored Maurice Sendak's picture book *Where The Wild Things Are* as a fantastic text to perceptive effect. Margery Hourihan reads it as "exactly the same as the story of Odysseus", but also as a hero-story in which the hero by the age of four or thereabouts has "learnt the trick of domination" and is ready for his place in the Patriarchy.[55] We may learn most, not from the Garners and Maynes, who write novels we can recognise as complex but from the very different techniques of the Sendaks who write epics in miniature.

Notes

1 Pullman, Philip, "Voluntary Service" in the *Guardian* Review Section, 28 December 2002, pp. 4–6.
2 Although Anselm Audley was 18 at the publication of his novel *Heresy* (Earthlight, 2001) and Catherine Webb was 14 at the time of writing *Mirror Dream* (Atom, 2002). The young age of both authors was stressed by their publishers, although Audley's novel was published in an "adult" imprint
3 A definition which is only satisfactory when we consider the word "we". All three forms are slippery: if "science fiction" is, according to Gary Westfahl (*The Mechanics of Wonder*, Liverpool: Liverpool University Press, 1998), that form of technologically-based fiction created and defined by the Gernsback magazines from the late 1920s, are we wrong in presenting *Frankenstein, Utopia*, or *The Time Machine* as science fiction? Do present-day browsers of those sections in bookshops labelled "fantasy" feel short-changed if they do not come across Borges, Barth or Calvino?
4 Chambers in Peter Hunt, ed., *Children's Literature: the Development of Criticism.* London: Routledge, 1990), pp. 103–4. First published in *Signal* 23 (May 1977), pp. 64–87.
5 Karin Lesnik-Oberstein, *Children's Literature: Criticism and the Fictional Child* (London: Clarendon Press, 1994), p. 100.
6 Jacqueline Rose, *The Case of Peter Pan, or: The Impossibility of Children's Fiction* (London: Macmillan, 1984), p. 154.

7 John Stephens, *Language and Ideology in Children's Fiction* (London; Longman, 1992), p. 30.

8 Stephens, *Language and Ideology*, pp. 272–88.

9 Stephens, *Language and Ideology*, pp. 288–89.

10 Margery Hourihan, *Deconstructing the Hero: Literary Theory and Children's Literature* (London and New York: Routledge, 1997), back cover.

11 For instance, the incongruity of the cosily liberal anti-racism in Susan Cooper's *Silver on the Tree* (1977) and the middle-class Stanton family compared with the mythic archetypes Cooper evokes is much more interesting in terms of "insights into human nature and the human condition" than is suggested by Margery Hourihan, *Deconstructing the Hero*, pp. 37–38. Instead of a "failed" attempt to marry the realities of 1970s Britain with a conservative "National Myth", it may be more rewarding to consider this as simply highlighting the need to re-examine the Myth itself. Archetypes are not fixed or final: Albion is a dynamic rather than a simple reverberating pattern.

12 Felicity Hughes, "Children's Literature: Theory and Practice", originally published in *ELH: A Journal of English Literary History* 45 (1978), pp. 542–62; reprinted Hunt, *Children's Literature*, see p. 81.

13 Hunt, *Children's Literature*, p. 77.

14 Hunt, *Children's Literature*, p. 83.

15 Hunt, *Children's Literature*, p. 83.

16 Michael Moorcock, reviewing a reprint of Poul Anderson's *The Broken Sword* in the *Guardian* of 25th January 2003 reminds us that it was first published in the same year (1954) as the first volume of *The Lord of the Rings*: "Tolkien times two" *Guardian* Review section 25/1/02, p. 28.

17 Diana Wynne Jones, "The Profession of Science Fiction, 51: Answers to Some Questions", *Foundation* 70 (Summer, 1997), pp. 5–14, at p. 7.

18 Ruth Nadelman Lynn, *Fantasy Literature for Children and Young Adults: An Annotated Bibliography* (4th edition) (New Providence, NJ: Bowker, 1995) p. xxvii. For Lin Carter, see especially his *Imaginary Worlds* (New York: Ballantine, 1973).

19 Brian Attebery, *Strategies of Fantasy* (Bloomington: Indiana UP, 1992), p. 18.

20 TzvetanTodorov, *The Fantastic: a Structural Approach to a Literary Genre* (Ithaca, NY: Cornell UP, 1980), Rosemary Jackson, *Fantasy: the Literature of Subversion* (London: Methuen, 1981) Christine Brooke-Rose, *A Rhetoric of the Unreal* (Cambridge: Cambridge UP, 1981), Kathryn Hume, *Fantasy and Mimesis: Responses to Reality in Western Literature* (New York and London: Methuen, 1984), and Brian Attebery, *Strategies of Fantasy*.

21 Stephens, *Language and Ideology*, p. 241.

22 Attebery, *Strategies of Fantasy*, p. 3.

23 Tom Shippey, ed., *The Oxford Book of Science Fiction Stories* (Oxford: Oxford UP, 1993), p. ix.

24 Peter Hunt, *Criticism, Theory and Children's Literature* (Oxford: Blackwell, 1991), p. 60.

25 Rose, *The Case of Peter Pan*, p. 10.

26 Lesnik-Oberstein, *Children's Literature*, p. 163. See also her "Childhood and Textuality" in Lesnik-Oberstein ed., *Children in Culture: Approaches to Childhood* (London: Macmillan, 1998), pp. 1–28.

27 Deborah Cogan Thacker and Jean Webb. *Introducing Children's Literature: from Romanticism to Postmodernism* (London: Routledge, 2002), p. 143.

28 Nicholas Tucker, *The Child and the Book: a Psychological and Literary Exploration* (Cambridge: Cambridge UP, 1981), p. 2.

29 Tucker, *The Child and the Book*, pp. 56–57, 97, 100 and 99 respectively.
30 Tucker, *The Child and the Book*, pp. 218–32.
31 Hunt, *Criticism, Theory and Children's Literature*, p. 45.
32 Hunt, *Criticism, Theory and Children's Literature*, p. 46.
33 Hunt, *Criticism, Theory and Children's Literature*, p. 47.
34 Hunt, *Criticism, Theory and Children's Literature*, p. 47.
35 Hunt, *Criticism, Theory and Children's Literature*, p. 48.
36 Hunt, *Criticism, Theory and Children's Literature*, p. 18.
37 Diana Wynne Jones's *Fire and Hemlock* (1985) retells the "Tam Lin" border ballad, and is published as a book for "young adults", but Ellen Kushner's *Thomas the Rhymer* is an "unbranded" adult book. Emil Petaja's *Saga of Lost Earths* (1966) and its sequels make up a sequence retelling in science-fiction terms the Finnish epic the *Kalevala*. The Sanskrit epic *The Mahabharata* is the root of a fantasy series forthcoming from the Indian writer Ashok Banker.
38 Peter Hunt and Millicent Lenz, *Alternative Worlds in Fantasy Fiction* (London: Continuum, 2001) pp. 28–32.
39 Brian Attebery, *The Fantasy Tradition in American Literature* (Bloomington: Indiana UP, 1980), pp. 134, 135.
40 *Children's Literature Quarterly* (*CLQ*), Spring 1987, p. 6.
41 *CLQ*, Spring 1987, p. 7.
42 *CLQ*, Spring 1987, p. 10.
43 *CLQ*, Spring 1987, p. 11.
44 *CLQ*, Spring 1987, p. 23.
45 *CLQ*, Spring 1987, p. 24.
46 *CLQ*, Spring 1987, p. 28.
47 In December 2002 parents at a carol service in Maidenhead, Berkshire were "shocked" to hear the vicar suggest that Father Christmas was a myth. "It is not his job to tell them things like this," said one mother of a nine-year old son. ("Vicar Tells Children Santa is Dead", http://news.bbc.co.uk/1/hi/england/2562109.stm)
48 Hunt and Lenz, *Alternative Worlds*, p. 4.
49 Hunt and Lenz, *Alternative Worlds*, pp. 28–32.
50 Hunt and Lenz, *Alternative Worlds*, p. 91.
51 Hunt and Lenz, *Alternative Worlds*, pp. 163,165.
52 Hunt, *Criticism, Theory and Children's Literature*, p. 97.
53 See Diana Wynne Jones "The Profession of Science Fiction, 51: Answers to Some Questions" in *Foundation* 70 (Summer, 1997), 7–8
54 In "Swallows and Eddisons", in *Strange Attractors: Kicking the Reality Fix* (Plymouth: AFFN, 1994, pp 15–28)
55 Hourihan, *Deconstructing the Hero*, pp. 11–12.

14

THE CHANGING STATUS OF CHILDREN AND CHILDREN'S LITERATURE

Eva-Maria Metcalf

Source: Sandra Beckett (ed.), *Reflections of Change: Children's Literature Since 1945*, Westport, CN: Greenwood Press, 1997, pp. 49–56.

Certainly, in no century before the twentieth have children been studied so intensely, gained so much recognition, and been valued so highly, and the same can be said for children's literature. The German scholar Gundel Mattenklott argues in her book *Zauberkreide* that the opportunity for children's literature to leave the literary periphery and become part of the literary avant-garde had never before been as great as it was during the late 1960s.[1] I fully agree with her argument and would like to take it a step further. In what follows, I will examine some of the preconditions and point to a few manifestations of this new status in German children's literature from the 1960s through the 1990s. Children's literature, as I approach it, is situated in the field of tension delineated by social and institutional structures, technological advances, market forces, pedagogical and political claims, literary norms, and discursive practices, and is defined by the currently dominant concept of childhood. Subtle or more substantial changes in any or all of these factors will affect the role and the makeup of children's literature. Here, I will highlight a few threads in this complex web of interrelationships, focusing on those that are linked to questions of power and prestige.

Before I embark on an analysis of the status of children's literature since the late 1960s, however, let me set the scene with some anecdotal and statistical evidence about its status and shape before the 1950s. In 1944, the Swedish publisher Hans Rabén launched a competition for the best Swedish manuscript for a girl's book, in an effort to boost the sales of children's books. When it came to opening the envelope containing the name of the winner, his worst fear came true: the winner of the prize was an unknown housewife. Fortunately both for the publisher and for children all over the world, it was an unusually gifted housewife who won the prize that year. The winner was Astrid Lindgren, who set a new tone in children's literature with the publication of *Pippi Longstocking* the following year.

The publisher's fear that the prize might go to a housewife was not unfounded. In fact, the likelihood was great, as evidenced by statistical data cited by the German author Erich Kästner, in an article in the Stockholm newspaper *Dagens Nyheter* in 1957.[2] According to this source, 30 percent of all Swedish children's books that year were written by housewives. Another 30 percent were written by teachers and 30 percent by other professionals, such as doctors and engineers. The remaining 10 percent were written by self-proclaimed authors, fully 70 percent of whom were no longer alive. In other words, only 3 percent of Swedish children's books on the market were written by currently active, professional authors.[3] If we believe the children's author James Krüss, who cited Kästner, the situation was very similar in Germany at that time, and we can assume it was the same all over Europe as well. Even if we grant that these statistics are somewhat inaccurate, they clearly reflect the low status of children's literature in the 1950s, when it was a field in which teachers and housewives with time on their hands could, and did, dabble. Children's literature, designed as the sugar coating around the bitter pill of education two centuries earlier, continued to be primarily a vehicle for educators with some talent for storytelling. Despite calls for better-quality children's literature like Heinrich Wolgast's at the turn of the century, literary quality was at best a secondary issue, and at worst, inconsequential. At the beginning of the twentieth century, children's literature was a totally separate and marginalized entity in the polysystem of literature, confined within its own system and guided by its own laws. It was effectively barred from the literary world of modernity by its association with the premodern world of folklore and fairy tale, discovered during the age of Romanticism and further cemented during the latter part of the nineteenth century. The belief that the child's naive, unadulterated, and uncritical view of the world should remain intact informed the idea of a separate world of childhood and children's literature, which, combined with a heritage of didacticism and an aura of dilettantism, barred children's literature from mainstream literature and even more so from the privileged status of high literature, which had raised its barriers by celebrating art for art's sake. Almost by definition, then, modernist stylistic experimentation and creative potential were anathema to children's literature, which, as a result, became stigmatized as imitative, backward, and unworthy of attention by any serious, self-respecting author.

Were we to conduct a survey about who writes children's books in Sweden, Germany, or the United States today, the results would be quite different. Lately, children's literature has experienced an unparalleled professionalization and literarization, as well as a concomitant and unprecedented growth in status. In *Criticism, Theory, and Children's Literature*, Peter Hunt argues that in order to accede to the privileged status of literature, from which children's literature has historically been excluded, either it must become part of the power structure, or the power structure must change.[4] I contend that the power structure has indeed changed, and that this has affected status, form, and content of children's literature. Two parallel developments have helped children's literature gain a more prominent voice: the demythification and democratization of childhood—on both conceptual and experiential levels—and the demythification and democratization of the literary establishment through attacks on the canon and the razing of hierarchical structures.

Postmodernism's attacks on logocentrism and its proclivity to erase barriers and flatten hierarchies have had a liberating and empowering effect on children's literature. It has become less provincial and, as a consequence, has gained greater access to and presence in the marketplace of ideas. As Alison Lurie remarks: "Once upon a time children's books were the black sheep of fiction . . . quarantined from the rest of literature. . . . Recently, though, children's literature is beginning to be discovered by mainstream theorists and scholars. Learned volumes on its significance crowd the library shelves, and the professional journals are full of articles that consider every classic from *Alice* to *Charlotte's Web* as a 'text.'"[5] Lurie might be overstating the case slightly, but it is certainly a fact that articles about and reviews of children's books have gained greater substance and prominence during the past decades.

The forerunners

The children's literature of the 1990s owes an enormous debt to the cultural revolution of the late 1960s and early 1970s, and to the philosophers and social scientists who prepared the ground for that revolution. In 1962, Philippe Ariès published his groundbreaking history of childhood. Its revelation of the bourgeois concept of childhood as myth and cultural construct still reverberates in theoretical discussions about childhood today. At the time, it renewed the debate about the status of children and adults, gave rise to a fundamental rethinking of intergenerational relationships, and cleared the way for a new social and cultural construct of the child that has affected much of the literature created for children since then. Children's literature also was affected by the cultural-revolutionary euphoria. In the wake of the civil rights movement, voices were raised for children's rights as well. The debunking of canons, of authority figures, and of authoritarian structures that took place in the streets and at universities in the late 1960s entered children's books surprisingly quickly, resulting in a creative push. Carnivalesque techniques of subversion, which were among the favored discourse strategies used in this social and cultural revolt, had had a long tradition in folklore and children's literature, and could easily be filled with new content to become part of the social and cultural protest movement. Publishers cooperatives—many of them with leftist and Marxist leanings—published children's books for the new child, and scholars and critics formed alternative working teams (*Arbeitsgruppen*). The most notable of these grassroots anti-establishment movements was Red Elephant (*Roter Elefant*), founded in 1975 by Jörg Becker, Malte Dahrendorf, and Wolfgang Frommlet. It later included other leading German children's literature scholars, among them Klaus Doderer.[6] Its mission and goal was to promote books that adopted the new model of childhood. To this end, the group presented alternative prizes for a number of years, in open opposition to Deutscher Jugendbuchpreis, the prize awarded each year by the German government.

Let me give you an example of the experimental character of a book published by Basis Verlag—a leftist publishing cooperative of children's books in Berlin, that is specifically interesting in light of my argument. *Die Geschichte von der Verjagung und Ausstopfung des Königs* (The Story About How the King Was Chased out and Stuffed) violates cultural taboos not only in subject matter and message but in narrative structure as well. It is a thinly disguised story about storytelling. Two not very imaginative and innovative poets, who are part of the plot, invent a traditional tale about a king in order to amuse the child protagonists. But the fictional children—and by extension the implied readers—reject these old-fashioned tales and throw them out along with the king, thus making room for new and more socially responsible, participatory ways of living and thinking. The new, politically correct, and quite utopian happy ending depicts everyone living together in peace and harmony in a country that now belongs to everyone. This story remains in the strong grip of socialist ideology and didacticism and seems outdated in the post-Cold War period, but its respect for—and overestimation of—the child's ability to read critically and its innovative use of narrative strategies have survived or, better, have been revived in postmodern writing. This tale about storytelling that uses the Brechtian alienation effect to get its point across has no single author. It is the product of a joint creative effort of children and adults, and in its introduction the authors reveal the production process much as John Scieszka does in *The Stinky Cheese Man and Other Fairly Stupid Tales*.

The rather slim production of leftist book cooperatives was admittedly the radical fringe. But skepticism of the established order, critical reading, and demythologizing soon became the order of the day in mainstream children's literature of the 1970s. Stories abounded in which children were taught to distrust adults and to question a dehumanized consumer culture. *The Cucumber King* (*Wir pfeifen auf den Gurkenkönig*, 1972), by Austrian author and Andersen Medal winner Christine Nöstlinger, is another throw-out-the-king story, exposing the father-knows-best, happy middle-class nuclear family as a myth. It, too, addresses class and gender conflicts head-on, drawing parallels between political dictatorship and power relationships in the patriarchal family. The novel ends predictably enough for its kind: the father and his alter ego, the Cucumber King, are deposed, preparing the way for a democratic family structure within a democratic society. The social and political awareness that entered children's fiction broke open the traditional "small world" of childhood, and liberated and challenged authors to use a variety of approaches and narrative techniques to coax readers into active and critical participation.

A new self-definition

How does children's literature in the 1990s differ from that of the 1970s? What has survived, and what has changed? In the 1970s, children's literature constituted an arena for assertiveness training of both author and reader. Authors assumed the role of children's advocates and spoke largely *for* children as they let children speak up in their fiction. Children's literature simply modeled behavior to be emulated. Contrary to that approach, cutting-edge children's books today do not want to patronize or colonize readers by speaking up for them or even by guiding them. Along with the teleological certainty of the socialist cause, agency and activism have mostly disappeared. Authors, like teachers, have resigned their authority as preachers and educators, choosing to function instead as "facilitators." Behind the open problematization of the authorial position lies the deeply democratic idea of empowerment and power sharing. Modeling several modes of action, authors let readers find their own temporary and unstable solutions in multivalent texts. The double-voiced discourse of anti-authoritarian literature that pitched the voice of the oppressor against that of the oppressed, refuting and ridiculing the dominant voice by means of carnivalesque subversive strategies, has grown into multi-voicedness or, rather, voicelessness.

We should not forget that the empowerment of children and a revaluation of children's literature would be unthinkable if the emancipatory drives of the countercultures had not conformed with information society's demands for a more sophisticated and flexible workforce and "capitalist society's hunger for incessant innovation".[7] Mainstream culture —including children's literature—has responded to the deprivileging of dominant groups and their discursive practices by annexing and appropriating parts of fringe discourses and counter-discourses, as well as aspects of avant-garde experimentation, while blunting and undermining their revolutionary potential in the process. As a result of these impulses, mainstream culture has become more diversified, more colorful, and more noncommittal in recent decades. Much of children's fiction today presents readers with choices, but without the hope and the vision of the 1970s or the stable and uniform ethical guidelines of a bygone era. Child readers are asked to embrace the kind of critical, even cynical, stance—previously reserved for adults only—that is replayed in the eclecticism and cynical indifference of mainstream culture and youth culture today.

The empowerment of the child has its price, and one may ask whether children are not overtaxed, confronted as they are with skepticism, contradictions, and ambiguities, and left awash in choices between sometimes equally valid ethical and behavioral codes. Nevertheless, the ability to make more or less informed choices even in the absence of grand narratives is a vital lesson for a child growing up in a democratic, consumer-oriented, information society. In a world in which competing authoritative discourses vie with each other for ever shorter durations of time, children are forced to grow up sooner, learn the language games, and participate in them. With the shift in the perception of childhood and in childhood experiences, authors are addressing more precocious children who share more experiences with adults than children did a generation or two ago. In content as well as in form, authors have severed themselves from traditional restraints. Issues raised in today's books no longer center on everyday concerns of school, friendship, and family only. Often, the family and school settings remain, but political, social, and economic issues, from AIDS to xenophobia, from ecology to homophobia are addressed. Increasingly, philosophical and epistemological questions enter children's fiction as well, and all this occurs very much in synchrony with issues that capture the public debate.

Highlighting the function of narrative and questioning author and reader positions within the work of fiction are becoming common in postmodern children's books. These books give readers an active part in the unfolding of the plot by admitting them into the writer's workshop. The demythification and decentering of the author and of the creative process of fiction writing erase borderlines between readers and writers, and make them accomplices by lowering the author and elevating readers, regardless of age or gender. Child readers are given a voice of their own, not by model or decree, as was the case in the early phase of empowerment, but by being expected to perform and consciously participate in the creative process. A growing number of books are on a par with books written for adults in terms of their poetics. Increasingly, "readerly texts," to use Roland Barthes's term, have been replaced by more interactive "writerly" texts whose messages to readers are more diffuse and subtle. These frequently elliptical texts require profound attention and cooperation on the part of the reader.

Still, it would be silly to argue that children's books are *intellectually* at the same level as books for adults. Maria Lypp's concept of asymmetric communication as it concerns children's literature still applies. The gap in life experience and cognitive development between children and adults has shrunk but not disappeared. It will continue to place special demands on authors writing for children and on critics reviewing children's books. The range of topics, as well as the complexity and ambiguity of the narrative, may seduce critics into treating these books as adult books or looking at them as "texts" only—as Alison Lurie suggested—and applying methods of literary analysis without taking into consideration the audience and the context in which they were written. *Functionally*, however, children's literature mirrors that of adults. There are high-brow and low-brow books for children, and both are part of the public debate.

Let me add one final consideration to my observations about the changing status of children's literature. The "mainstreaming" of children's literature has much to do with the specific qualities of postmodern discursive practice. It is imitative by nature, thus doing away with the stigma of children's literature not being original and on the cutting edge. In the postmodern replay of Dada and surrealism in children's literature, I find reflected the same questioning of social and symbolic hierarchies and power structures, the same fragmentation and absence of closure, the same self-reflection, and the same metaphorical language that characterized modernist adult literature, but it is presented with a levity, playfulness, and superficiality that characterizes postmodern sensibilities. "Post-Modernism," Charles Newman argues, "carries out the aesthetics of anti-realism in an external fashion, while rejecting the varieties of Modernism in both its extreme Transcendent and Nihilistic modes."[8] Postmodernism's levity and playfulness, its superficiality and ahistoricity, and its secondary orality (a term taken from Walter Ong's work *Orality and Literacy*) are all elements of postmodern culture that correspond closely to the developmental stage and language of childhood.

The ludic, fantastic, and kaleidoscopic elements characteristic of postmodern writing and culture have a long tradition in children's literature's wordplay, nonsense, and fantasy tales going back to nursery rhymes, *Alice in Wonderland*, and Lear's nonsense verse. German author Jörn Peter Dirx consciously picks up on that tradition in *Alles Rainer Zufall* (All Pure Coincidence, 1987). (The title is a play on words that remains pervasive in the book. Rainer is a German first name, but its homonym means "pure.") It is a pastiche of *Alice in Wonderland* in which serendipity and ambiguity reign and no causal logic ties the various episodes together. The "wonderland" into which Rainer Zufall falls is nothing but the fictional rendition of an already absurd yet commonplace world. In a fashion similar to the book about the king who was chased out and stuffed (from the early 1970s), Dirx makes the author an integral part of the plot, with the added twist that here Roman Dichter (literally "novel poet," again an untranslatable play on words), the author, is both inside and outside of the plot at the same time. As he types words and sentences on his keyboard, they instantly become real, and thus the protagonists are at his mercy. On the other hand, the plot moves forward through the actions of the child protagonists and seemingly independently of the author.

The creative process thus merges the imaginative powers of author and reader, and appears as a blend of serendipity and intentionality. In Dirx's work, nonsense no longer affirms sense, as it does in Carroll's *Alice*, yet through the intrusion of the absurd and the fantastic into fictional reality, the world assumes a Kafkaesque quality of illogic and absurdity. It is probably no "coincidence" that in one of the illustrations that exquisitely catches the play of illusion and allusions that makes up this book, Kafka appears next to Alice, Mary Poppins, Struwwelpeter, Babar, Tarzan, Superman, Mickey Mouse, Don Quixote, and other cultural icons from within and without the children's literature canon. This collage also illustrates the playful blending of high and low, adult and child cultures that has contributed to the integration of children's literature into the mainstream.

By questioning and erasing borders between the real, the fictional, and the fantastic, postmodern authors broach epistemological questions in a format that is understandable but challenging for children. Equally challenging are narratives told on various levels and from various perspectives (Peter Pohl, Tormod Haugen, for example). Books like these carry a fair amount of intellectual prestige—an important point for the status of children's literature today. Its new position has offered authors the full range of issues and topics addressed in adult fiction and a greater freedom to experiment, and it has offered readers and critics of children's literature a means to participate in the public debate.

Notes

1 Gundel Mattenklott, *Zauberkreide: Kinderliteratur seit 1945* (Stuttgart: J. B. Metzler, 1989), pp. 14, 165.
2 Cited in James Krüss, *Naivität und Kunstverstand. Gedanken zur Kinderliteratur* (Weinheim and Basel: Beltz, 1992), p. 76.
3 Ibid., p. 88.
4 Peter Hunt, *Criticism, Theory, and Children's Literature* (Cambridge: Basil Blackwell, 1991), p. 54.
5 Alison Lurie, "William Mayne," in *Children and Their Books: A Collection of Essays to Celebrate the Work of Iona and Peter Opie*, ed. Gillian Avery and Julia Briggs (Oxford: Clarendon Press, 1989), p. 369.
6 Otto Gmelin, *Böses aus Kinderbüchern und ein roter Elefant* (Frankfurt: Haag und Herchen, 1977), pp. 186, 212.
7 Charles Newman, *The Post-Modern Aura. The Act of Fiction in an Age of Inflation* (Evanston, Ill.: Northwestern University Press, 1985), p. 51.
8 Ibid., p. 178.

References

Dirx, Jörn-Peter. *Alles Rainer Zufall.* Ravensburg: Otto Maier, 1987.
Ende, Michael. *The Neverending Story.* Trans. Ralph Manheim. New York: Doubleday, 1983.

Ewers, Hans-Heino. "Zwischen Literaturanspruch und Leserbezug. Zum Normen- und Stilwandel der Kinder- und Jugendliteraturkritik seit don 70er Jahren." *Tausend und ein Buch* 4 (August 1993): 4–14.

Ewers, Hans-Heino, Maria Lypp, and Ulrich Nassen, eds. *Kinderliteratur und Moderne. Ästhetische Herausforderungen der Kinderliteratur im 20. Jahrhundert.* Weinheim and Munich: Juventa, 1990.

Gmelin, Otto. *Böses aus Kinderbüchern und ein roter Elefant.* Frankfurt: Haag und Herchen, 1977.

Haugen, Tormod. *Romanen om Merkel Hanssen og Donna Winter og Den store flukten.* Oslo: Gyldendal, 1986.

Hunt, Peter. *Criticism, Theory, and Children's Literature.* Cambridge: Basil Blackwell, 1991.

Krüss, James. *Naivität und Kunstverstand. Gedanken zur Kinderliteratur.* Weinheim and Basel: Beltz, 1992.

Lurie, Alison. "William Mayne." In *Children and Their Books: A Collection of Essays to Celebrate the Work of Iona and Peter Opie.* Ed. Gillian Avery and Julia Briggs. Oxford: Clarendon Press, 1989.

Mattenklott, Gundel. *Zauberkreide: Kinderliteratur seit 1945.* Stuttgart: J. B. Metzler, 1989.

Newman, Charles. *The Post-Modern Aura. The Act of Fiction in an Age of Inflation.* Evanston, Ill.: Northwestern University Press, 1985.

Scieszka, John. *The Stinky Cheese Man and Other Fairly Stupid Tales.* New York: Viking, 1992.

Zipes, Jack. "Down with Heidi, Down with Struwwelpeter, Three Cheers for the Revolution. Towards a New Socialist Children's Literature in West Germany." In *Children's Literature* 6 (1977): 162–179.

15

PLAYING IN THE PHASE SPACE

Contemporary forms of fictional pleasure

Margaret Mackey

Source: *Signal* 88 (1999): 16–33.

Storytelling has always been an important part of any society, and the forms and techniques of story adapt to the possibilities and pressures of different social arrangements. In our contemporary era of major techno-logical change, we can see stories shifting and altering their borders even as the world of make-believe expands beyond anything our ancestors might have imagined. Television provides instant access to fiction day and night in an unceasing flow; video games offer extended hours of highly concen-trated immersion; collaborative online fictional sites open the doors to co-operatively mandated and organized forms of storytelling where no one narrator is completely in charge. The commercial world supplies numerous prosthetics to fictional engagement in the form of toys and games and various 'lifestyle' accoutrements. An entire magazine industry feeds on back-up information about television and film stars, special effects and computer graphics, and the whole elaborate decision-making process involved in the creation of screened fiction.

Contemporary citizens of most societies, not just the Western or most prosperous ones, will recognize all or part of this picture, yet the vocabulary for describing new hybrid forms of story that cross media boundaries and variously impinge on our daily lives is surprisingly limited. A fiction de-scribes a possible world, but the boundaries of that world may seem nebulous when it can exist, more or less recognizably, in print, film, CD-ROM, audio, and website form, to name just the most obvious. The death of the author may or may not be finally established, but the issue of what is 'authorized' is one that affects stories in many ways, commercial as well as intellectual. How far can a story be attenuated through sequels and spin-offs before its original power is diffused through dilution and/or over-exposure? It is commonplace to see many transmutations of a single story: a picture book is made into an animation and turned back into a newly reworked picture book that then becomes a board book, to take a single and highly representative example. How many generations does it take before the sense of what made the story matter in the first place is rendered indecipherable, replaced by a generic impression that plurality and reproduction are the key elements of storytelling?

It is relatively easy for those invested in the culture of literariness to ignore such manifestations, to dismiss them as the epiphenomena of a corrupt commercial enterprise that ensnares too many of our children but need not affect those in the elite who still care for and look after the interests of print literature. Yet the impact of technology is not confined to the slick and heavily funded world of popular culture, although some of its most radical effects may be felt there. Questions about the powers and limits of a fictional universe arise in more strictly literary worlds as well.

One great storyteller of the 1980s and 1990s is Philip Pullman. He is the author of the *Dark Materials* fantasy trilogy that is captivating already avid readers and creating many new ones; he is also the creator of a number of other stories including a handful of graphic novels. Pullman both gives us an example of textual play that challenges our thinking about literary practice at the end of the twentieth century and offers useful critical vocabulary for discussing these matters.

The first novel of *His Dark Materials* is published in North America as *The Golden Compass*, although its original British title is *Northern Lights*. The second novel appears as *The Subtle Knife* in both jurisdictions, and the third is still being written. The underlying themes of the trilogy arise from Milton's *Paradise Lost*, which is the source of the titles and which informs many of the major structures of the story. There is no doubt that these books represent a serious literary enterprise in the best sense of the words.

At present, both books are available in hardback and paperback, and there is an abridged audio version of *The Golden Compass*. There is some talk of a film contract, but so far the world of *His Dark Materials* exists only verbally, apart from some appealing cover art. Both books have garnered rave reviews and *Northern Lights* won most of the awards going in 1995; sales figures to both children and adults are astonishing, and the impatience with which the third volume is awaited is a minor literary phenomenon in itself.

So far this description might just represent a consoling indication that the world of print fiction is still alive and well. The phenomenon of *His Dark Materials* is not floated on the back of tie-ins and commodities and television animations and advertisements. It represents the triumph of an intriguing and important words-only story, well told and compelling.

Yet even in this entirely verbal fictional world, there are some words that both do and do not belong to the published book. They appear on the lavish and fascinating website sponsored by Random House, the American

221

publishers of the trilogy.[1] Each book has its own site, and each site offers background information about the story world that does not appear in the novels but manifestly applies to them. The *Golden Compass* site offers a detailed history and symbol glossary of the alethiometer, the truth-telling compass of the American title. On the *Subtle Knife* site, there is information about the *Liber Angelorum*, the book of the angels, which now, we are told, survives only in the form of evocative 'scraps' saved after a fire in the Torre degli Angeli.

Here is an example of the kind of information offered from the *Liber Angelorum*:

> **Envy** The angels envy us our solidity. Death, they think, would be a price worth paying for the power and brilliance of our senses. If an angel were to see with our eyes, or hear with our ears, he would be dazzled and stunned by the force with which we perceive the physical world. With gifts like this, he would think, why do these creatures not spend their lives in exploration of the physical universe that they are so well equipped to understand? Why are they not consumed with intellectual bliss? This is a mystery to angels.[2]

This passage recognizably comes from the narrative voice of *The Subtle Knife*, dealing with substantive issues in a vigorous and lively manner. Yet it does not appear in the novel and the information does not really affect the story in any immediate way. What it does affect is the thematic underpinning that links *His Dark Materials* to its Miltonian predecessor; both poets and scholars can appreciate the extra layering and complexity such material adds to the story—and so, without a doubt, can many less credentialled readers who happen to find the website.

So we have an example of a kind of fictional add-on, an appendage that does and does not belong to the world of the novel. In the advertising world the name for this kind of material would be the back-story, the infilling fictional detail that sets up the parameters of play with advertised toys. For example, Stephen Kline describes a back-story (in this case, Barbie's) as 'a narrative that established her personality profile within an imaginary but familiar universe' (170).

The 'scraps' from the *Liber Angelorum* manifestly belong to the 'imaginary but familiar universe' of *His Dark Materials*, but it is inappropriate and unsatisfactory to think of this vivid and poetic fragment as akin to the manipulative world of what Kline calls the 'passive dictation' of the advertising back-story that is designed to place narrative constraints on children's imaginative engagement with toys like Barbie. Fortunately Pullman himself has supplied a more generous critical terminology that offers an opportunity to clarify some elements of contemporary story-making.

The phase space

In November 1997 Pullman delivered the Patrick Hardy Lecture to the Children's Book Circle in London. In this talk, he discussed some 'rules' of storytelling, and introduced the concept of phase space, a scientific term that he explored as a metaphor for discussing the artistic potential of story-making. With a certain generosity of interpretive licence, it also serves as a useful metaphor for exploring many different aspects of contemporary culture.

> As I understand it, phase space is a term from dynamics, and it refers to the untrackable complexity of changing systems. It's the notional space which contains not just the actual consequences of the present moment, but all the possible consequences. The phase space of a game of noughts and crosses, for instance, would contain every possible outcome of every possible initial move, and the actual course of a game could be represented by a path starting from the one move that was actually made first—a path winding past numbers of choices not made. Robert Frost:
>
> > Two roads diverged in a wood, and I—
> > I took the one less travelled by,
> > And that has made all the difference.
>
> Of course, it does make all the difference. And we do have to choose: we can't go both ways. I am surely not the only writer who has the distinct sense that every sentence I write is surrounded by the ghosts of the sentences I could have written at that point, but didn't . . .
> So the opening of your story brings with it a phase space. (47)

Pullman goes on to make a number of interesting points about this phase space, but perhaps the most pertinent at this point is the metaphor of the path through the phase space:

> It has to do with phase space again, with the path through the wood. And a path is a path *to*: it has a destination.
> For every story has to have an ending. Sometimes you know what the ending is before you begin. Well and good. Sometimes you don't, and then you have to wander about through the events until you manage to see the natural destination. But once you know where it is, you must make for it, and then go back and clear the path and make sure that every twist and turn is there because you want it to be: because this one shows a better view of the landscape to come, or that one illustrates the fate of someone analogous to our protagonist, or another because it reveals a deep romantic chasm

just at the moment when you need to introduce a note of sublimity . . . And all of them because they lead to the end. In other words you must design the path so that it leads to the destination most surely, and with the maximum effect.

(50–1; ellipsis in original)

Pullman here is undoubtedly describing the steady hand of the confident storyteller, working a crafted line through all the potential elements that might be realized in a particular story world. And yet in that background territory of the phase space, it seems to me we see something that is also relevant to many forms of contemporary storytelling. What is the information on the *Subtle Knife* website but data from the phase space—information that might have been in the book but is not because it does not lead to the end of the story? Pullman is very definite that the direction of a story must always be towards its ending: 'If a scene does not advance the story, it will get in the way,' he says on one occasion[3] and on another, 'Whatever doesn't add, subtracts' (1998, 50).

This clear-cut and even ruthless approach to storytelling has its own substantial satisfactions, but it seems evident that there is much productive potential left in the phase space of a story: things that might have happened in the plot but did not, aspects of characters or incidents that are known to the author or that can be imagined by readers but that are not laid down in the novel itself. The website of *The Golden Compass* and *The Subtle Knife* seem to have offered Pullman one venue for a different kind of play in the phase space he created for the world of the trilogy—imaginative, engaged, but not strictly narrative in the sense of driving to the ending. The author is a privileged player in this specialized game, of course, but in fact many school assignments invite students to explore the phase space. They are exhorted to write a 'missing' chapter including a scene that occurs offstage from the main action of the novel, or to supply school report cards or news bulletins relating to characters or incidents of a book. The imaginative and imaginary hinterland of a story, it would seem, is often perceived as fair game to its readers as well as to its original creator.

One important point to remember about a phase space is how necessarily it relates to its originating story. A set of all possible noughts-and-crosses moves might be very large but each member of the set would recognizably be a playable nought or cross. Some news bulletins or report cards are simply not admissible to the phase space of a particular story. The phase space may be large and bristling with possibilities but it is also consistent and identifiable, coherent as part of the world of a particular story.

A second point to keep in mind is how many contemporary texts for both children and adults make specific and often parodic use of the phase space. Pullman, with his one crafted path through the phase space towards the ending of the story, is describing a particular kind of story-telling technique.

Many stories play with that very decision-making process he describes, along the lines of, 'Yes, but what if a different choice were made at this point?' Hence we have books like *The Three Little Wolves and the Big Bad Pig* by Eugene Trivizas and Helen Oxenbury and many different titles by the Ahlbergs. We have books like *The Stinky Cheese Man and other Fairly Stupid Tales* where the play in the phase space becomes part of the story. This example of 'Cinderella', or 'Cinderumpelstiltskin' as it is called in the version by Scieska and Smith, is a recognizable phase-space game:

> One day the local prince announced that he was holding a fabulous ball at his castle. Everyone was invited.
>
> The stepmother and stepsisters got all dressed up to go. But, as usual, they made Cinderella clean the house, so she didn't have time to get ready. After the stepmother and stepsisters left for the ball, Cinderella sat down and began to cry.
>
> Just then a little man appeared.
>
> 'Please don't cry,' he said. 'I can help you spin straw into gold.'
>
> 'I don't think that will do me much good,' said Cinderella. 'I need a fancy dress, glass slippers, and a coach.'
>
> 'Would you like to try to guess my name?' said the clever little man.
>
> Cinderella looked at him. 'No. Not really.'
>
> 'Come on. Do you think it's "Chester"?'
>
> 'If you don't have a dress, it doesn't really matter.'

Clearly, in this as in many other such stories, part of the joke is knowing that the story is switching phase spaces as different characters speak. Very young children are expected to get the joke, and all the evidence suggests that they have little problem with what might seem a sophisticated task.

Meanwhile in another part of the culture, we have comic books reworking some of the basic decisions affecting Superman's career, killing him off and bringing him back to life. When Sherlock Holmes went through such a process at the turn of the century, the fans went wild; the nonchalance with which such a trick is greeted today may well reflect the degree to which contemporary readers are at home with the whole idea of fictional life in the phase space. Some of this familiarity is a feature of constant, even relentless, exposure to 'quick and dirty' storytelling on television soaps and sitcoms (American television is particularly specialized in this regard): the evil twin has amnesia; no, she was just pretending in order to get the handsome and stupid hero to the altar; no, really it was all a plot by the mother-in-law who was hoping to find a route to make contact with her third-last ex-husband. Some of the contemporary nonchalance about living with alternative possibilities is an effect of living with multiple personalities attached to single proper nouns: Winnie-the-Pooh is the saccharine-with-an-edge creation of A. A. Milne as well as being the saccharine-with-extra-sugar creation of Walt Disney.

The enormous success of the *Dark Materials* trilogy testifies to our pleasure in the kind of storytelling Pullman describes, but there are many other kinds of fiction in contemporary culture that substitute a meander round the world of potentials for a decisive path-clearing operation that strikes out for the ending. And even in many stories where plot more or less drives the engine of the story, there is often back-up material that returns us to the phase space; the handbooks and maps and websites that accompany the elaborate fantasy of Terry Pratchett's *Discworld* books provide one good example of this phenomenon.

Adaptations and misreadings

To a degree, any adaptation or retelling makes use of the world created by a story, not just the actual elements laid out in order on the page. Phyllis Bixler, discussing a musical made from *The Secret Garden*, suggests that 'narratives contain many secrets for a reader to discover—or buried seeds of many other stories which a reader's imagination can coax into bloom' (114). Bixler talks about the creative forces of 'misreading' an original text to produce an adaptation that has 'an energy of its own' (102). To some extent, what we judge when we view a movie developed from a familiar book is the degree to which we find the adaptation drawing successfully on the same phase space. We may not know what all the options in that phase space might be, but we certainly know what does not belong, and it makes us uncomfortable or angry when the film plays false. On the other hand, one of the true pleasures of a successful adaptation—and after all these years the television example of *The Jewel in the Crown* is still one of the best—is that it sheds light on the whole phase space of the original story, rendering it deeper and fuller and more intriguing. No matter how simplistic aspects of this particular story may appear to post-colonial eyes, the fictional phase space of both book and television series is undoubtedly rich and coherent in its own terms and the two different versions of the story are mutually illuminating. (Whether a story and its adaptation always share a common or identical phase space is an intriguing point. One image could be of overlapping phase spaces, another of separate spotlights into a single phase space. Whatever the image, there must be a sense that both versions are drawing on the same set of contingencies.)

What makes a fictional universe recognizable has implications for many forms of contemporary culture. In a survey of texts revolving round a single narrative starting point, the movie *Men in Black*, I turned up well over sixty examples in print alone, not counting television programmes and Internet sites that deal with various aspects of the phase space of that story. Some of these texts played with the boundaries of the phase space, another familiar contemporary game. At what point does actor Will Smith step out of his persona as Jay, the rookie alien hunter of *Men in Black*, and become his own self? Can he ever be completely dissociated from his specific embodiment of this fictional character? Such questions take on additional force when re-makes of films substitute new actors in the roles of familiar characters. It may even be that certain actors bring their own phase space to a part: the background shadings of Will Smith's persona probably affect his reception as Jay. Viewers of the film *Titanic* may well go one step further and associate the character of Jack with the Valentino-esque potential of Leonardo di Caprio rather than the other way around.

The various forms of retelling that are associated with most commercial productions of films these days also play in the phase space. Some, such as the printed screenplay of the movie, stick strictly to reproducing the original path, though it is remarkable how often such a reproductive text also includes an essay about the making of the movie, unpicking all the decisions that were eventually made to show how they might have been made otherwise.[4] Other approaches take the world of the movie and play around with it—literally in the cases of the many action movies that are turned into computer games, or in the case of children's films that act as source material for the production of toys. In a culture that values many forms of postmodern play with options and alternatives it might be argued that it is Pullman's steadfast pursuit of the single (though complex) path to the ending that is distinctive. Yet many (though not all) stories in contemporary popular culture feature a similar narrative drive, and it is often the surrounding galaxy of spin-off texts and toys that opens up the phase space.

Online narrative

The concept of phase space makes room for a productive consideration of hypertext narrative and the kinds of 'stories' developed in MUDs and MOOs, fictional online sites where each participant creates part of the scenario, typing in settings and characters that affect the larger picture.

Hypertext involves a computer text where readers follow different links from one paragraph, or lexia, to another. Sometimes it is possible for them to establish their own links but in most forms of hypertext fiction the links are developed by the author, and the reader simply makes choices between a varying number of pre-established options. At one level, readers read from the same text but in tracing different paths through the story their reading experiences are exceedingly diverse. In a very literal fashion, hypertext makes it possible for the writer to include all those sentences Pullman describes as ghosts, 'the sentences I could have written at that point but didn't'. This may not be the best or most constructive way to create a hypertext narrative either, but it now becomes possible to contemplate such an option in a realistic and material manner; indeed, it may well be that the format inveigles writers who would be terse and direct in standard print to opt for the recursive and meandering route when composing in this medium.

Jorge Luis Borges' story 'The Garden of Forking Paths' describes the fabulous Chinese novel of the same title as 'a shapeless mass of contradictory rough drafts' (96). Stuart Moulthrop, who converted the story into a hypertext version, quotes this line and comments, 'As it happens, this is precisely what a hypertext fiction looks like when reduced to the printed page' (274). Moulthrop describes the universe created by Borges in print and himself in hypertext as 'a cosmology of multiple universes containing all the plenary possibilities of selection', a phrase that could stand as an alternative definition of a phase space.

It is certainly clear that readers of hypertext narrative must assume they are taking only one of many possible paths through the phase space; pleasure in the phase space itself must form a major part of their engagement with the story. As Jane Yellowlees Douglas succinctly expresses it, hypertext 'propels us from the straitened "either/or" world that print has come to represent and into a universe where the "and/and/and" is always possible' (155).

Janet H. Murray describes some of the appeal of nonlinear stories in congruent terms:

> In discussing labyrinths we distinguish between those that are coherent and those that are purposely more tangled. The coherent labyrinths are like the one Theseus discovered or the ones in English gardens: they have a single solution, a path in and a path out. They can be solved . . . Other labyrinths, like the ones created by users of the Storyspace authoring system like Michael Joyce and Stuart Moulthrop are weblike in structure, multi-threaded, and have no single path. The pleasure here is not in solving but in dwelling in a seemingly inexhaustible resonant environment, luxuriating in a prolonged state of enticement and disorientation. (137)

Pleasure in the indwelling, in the phase space itself, is part of the appeal for participants in stories created online by groups of anonymous contributors to MUDs and MOOs (the rather obscure acronyms stand for Multi-User Domain and for Multi-User Domain, Object-Oriented). Sherry Turkle explains these complex fictions as follows:

> MUDs put you in virtual spaces in which you are able to navigate, converse, and build. You join a MUD through a command that links your computer to the computer on which the MUD program resides. Making the connection is not difficult; it requires no particular technical sophistication. The basic commands may seem

awkward at first but soon become familiar. For example, if I am playing a character named ST on Lambda MOO, any words I type after the command "say" will appear on all players' screens as "ST says." Any actions I type after the command "emote" will appear after my name just as I type them, as in "ST waves hi" or "ST laughs uncontrollably." I can "whisper" to a designated character and only that character will be able to see my words.

MUDs are a new kind of virtual parlour game and a new form of community. In addition, text-based MUDs are a new form of collaboratively written literature. MUD players are MUD authors, the creators as well as consumers of media content. In this, participating in a MUD has much in common with script writing, performance art, street theatre, improvisational theatre—or even commedia dell'arte. (11–12)

MUD makers often create elaborate settings, describing their virtual worlds with detailed enthusiasm. The very act of creating this alternative universe constitutes much of the appeal of the process.

Like Murray talking about hypertext fiction, Turkle describes two kinds of storytelling in the online communal narrative domains of MUDs and MOOs.

Two basic types of MUDs can now be accessed on the Internet. The adventure type, most reminiscent of the games' Dungeons and Dragons heritage, is built around a medieval fantasy landscape. In these, affectionately known by their participants as "hack and slay," the object of the game is to gain experience points by killing monsters and dragons and finding gold coins, amulets, and other treasure. Experience points translate into increased power. A second type consists of relatively open spaces in which you can play at whatever captures your imagination. In these MUDs, usually called social MUDs, the point is to interact with other players and, on some MUDs, to help build the virtual world by creating one's own objects and architecture. "Building" on MUDs is something of a hybrid between computer programming and writing fiction. One describes a hot tub and deck in a MUD with words, but some formal coded description is required for the deck to exist in the MUD as an extension of the adjacent living room and for characters to be able to "turn the hot tub on" by pushing a specially marked button. In some MUDs, all players are allowed to build; sometimes the privilege is reserved to master players, or wizards. Building is made particularly easy on a class of MUDs known as "MOOs" (MUDs of the Object Oriented variety). (182)

The phase space *is* the pleasure for many of the players in these fictional universes. In the social MUDs, the option of finding the single best path to the end is simply not available and indeed might be seen as arbitrarily short-circuiting the appeal of the whole process. We are in territory where very different rules of story-making apply.

Many commercially marketed computer games operate in a similar kind of fictional zone. The setting, the world of various options and alternatives, is the chief character in such games. Some, such as *Myst* and its sequel *Riven*, emphasize the lavish visual world on the screen but still offer a challenge to find the 'right' path through the story. Others, along the lines of *SimCity* and its successors, civic simulation games, appeal to their many players by virtue of the world-building powers they offer; what actually occurs in these worlds is open-ended, and in many ways unimportant. Still others, such as *Virtual Springfield*, a CD-ROM tour of the home town of television's Simpson family, offer what might be described as one version of the phase space of the more narratively organized animated stories. Playing the game amounts to little more than moving in and out of different Springfield buildings, opening cupboards and drawers, and developing an intimacy (carefully fabricated) with all the hidden corners of the town.

In a slightly different form, Mindscape's computer game *Creatures* sets up a phase space in which the human player hatches and then rears digital babies ('Warning: Digital DNA enclosed,' says the box). The renowned evolutionary biologist Richard Dawkins is quoted on the box as saying, 'This is the most impressive example of artificial life I have seen.' What is also impressive is the elaborate, even baroque play-space set up for the relatively uncomplicated 'plot' developments in which the little creatures grow, succeed or fail in learning to talk, mate, reproduce, age, and die, with their actions developed through their digital make-up and also through the care and education offered to them by the game's players. The sense that much of what happens is utterly arbitrary, that it could at any given stage happen otherwise if the digits lined up in a slightly different formation, is part of the appeal of this eerie game. That this primal (though digital) crap-shoot occurs in the kind of cute kitschy environment so familiar to young people from numerous cartoons and plastic toy universes may help to make this particular phase space recognizable and even cosy to young people reared with television. That children seem rather less uneasy about the 'life' created for and by these creatures than the adults watching over their shoulders may also partly reflect their life-long exposure to a culture full of many different kinds of phase space. A comparison of this game with more stilted adaptations of print stories in CD-ROM format[5] demonstrates that *Creatures* is predicated on a new kind of narrative development that can only be described as digitally organic. The strength of its long-term appeal is yet to be established but the sense of new fictional territory opening up is very powerful.

There are many ways in which our culture encourages engagement in the world of the story rather than the story itself. A few examples may give some idea of the range: a lavish book of *Little Women* offers many background pictures and notes supplying information about the social, cultural and historical matrix from which the book was developed (Alcott; Mackey); a CD-ROM of the Pulitzer-Prize-winning comic novel *Maus: A Survivor's Story* offers access to the background tapes that were used to develop the story and provides clips of the book's creator discussing why he made one decision rather than another (Spiegelman); the composite artform of the pop-up music video provides commentary in boxes on the screen describing scenes that were originally meant for the video but ultimately dropped.[6]

Many forms of literary tourism explicitly welcome you to the universe in which a story was set. The Prince Edward Island home of L. M. Montgomery, now turned into a living museum celebrating *Anne of Green Gables*, is highly seductive, for example. As a teenager I found myself straining to look through 'Anne's' window to see if I could spot her friend Diana's bedroom light. I felt remarkably foolish when I realized what I had done, yet of course I was merely answering the invitation of the setting. Theme parks celebrating, for example, the doings of Asterix provide another similar invitation: step into the phase space; participate in the matrix from which aesthetic decisions arise. The symbiosis between Beatrix Potter and the National Trust encourages a temptation to look on all the Lake District as a Potter park, full of living incarnations of the tiny stories she chose to tell.

Why does it matter?

In many ways, what I am describing here is familiar stuff. Children have probably always known about the phase space in its loosest definition, playing numerous pretend games in the virtual hinterland of their favourite stories. As a child of the 1950s I took many of my games from television and books, playing cowboys with my brothers on some occasions, and on others marking out territory in the field behind my house to be my own stately home and ruined abbey, in an imagined recreation of the desirable universe of the Abbey Girls books by Elsie J. Oxenham. In each case, the domain of the story was far more important to me than particular details of the plot.

The concept may not be entirely new but there has been a vast increase in the quantity and variety of contemporary texts that are undeniably fiction but not quite narrative, at least not in the straightforward sense we have understood it in the past and that Pullman's description still enticingly represents in the present. It seems fairly clear that the idea of following the narrative thread from beginning to end of the story is now perceived very broadly as just one option for engaging with a fiction. Young people will sit through a film in the decreed linear fashion but once that movie is out on video their viewing becomes far more recursive, dwelling longer in the good bits, skipping other parts, circling and repeating, adding information about story, actors, and special effects from other sources (for example, Wood, 189–91). Much of their leisure-time engagement with texts in one medium or another is spent in fictional settings where a leisurely exploration of the details of the what-if is the most important part of the encounter.

If such experience is an important part of young people's out-of-school encounters with fiction, it is very likely to show up in their own writing, and may also affect how they respond to the writing of other people. The impact of nonlinear story world-building may be even more striking when they are given the opportunity to work in multimedia. Geri Gay explored the responses of young people to an interactive second-language program that allows students of Spanish to create stories about travellers on an aeroplane. Her account of their creations has a familiar ring, in the light of some of the ideas discussed above; the connections are not conclusive but they seem suggestive:

> The analysis of the records revealed qualitative differences in the way students explored the program's content. Some students seemed to move from one segment to another in one direction only. Employing a weaving metaphor, Mazur . . . called this group Spinners, because although they were constructing meaning, the result was but a literal interpretation or description of events in the order in which they were viewed. Others' use was characterized by a back and forth movement among scenes accomplished by use of the video controllers and the program's navigation features. This group was labelled the Weavers.
>
> The "weaving" style of use also correlated to the kind of final stories the students wrote. The students who moved through the program in a linear way wrote stories primarily conveying actions, while students who displayed the nonlinear weaving pattern of program use wrote final stories which focused on the motivations or psychology of the characters. The Weavers' stories were more inventive, embellishing content by drawing connections between visual content viewed in particular scenes. (181)

There is not enough information about what really happens in English classes to develop any true sense of the degree to which the teachers of today's young people acknowledge and make room for the possible impact of new kinds of fictional experience and grounding. It seems likely that many, possibly still most of the texts used in English classrooms continue to represent the linear narrative drive. A survey of texts used in Grade 10 classes in Edmonton, in western Canada, established that the vast majority of authors being taught to fifteen-year-olds were born between

1900 and 1940, well before the advent of the new kinds of story-making I have been describing (Altmann *et al.*, 214–15). It would be reckless to suggest that this survey speaks for a wider world, but it would also be foolish to ignore the fact that English syllabuses around the English-speaking world tend to reproduce the same favourite titles and authors. (In Edmonton, for example, the most taught novel in Grade 10 is *To Kill a Mockingbird*; the most popular play is *Romeo and Juliet*. Both titles will obviously resonate with teachers of fifteen-year-olds elsewhere.)

Students who enter their secondary classrooms knowledgeable about the back-stories of many movies, familiar with the leisurely, nonlinear appeal of *The Simpsons'* universe courtesy of handbooks and CD-ROMs, at ease with the circular and repetitive attraction of many different online forms of fiction, will often find that their expertise is little valued in the academic forum. If they are truly unlucky, they will be taught about 'the' plot diagram and trained to think that there is only one way to write a valid story. Even in more enlightened classrooms, they may regularly wonder why their 'fit' with linear school stories is often so uneasy.

Similarly, teachers, reading the writing of students who operate from many experiences of what we might loosely describe as the phase-set school of story construction, may well perceive the kinds of works submitted to them as undisciplined and prolix, rather than recognizing amateur representatives of a different kind of discipline. Pullman himself, in a fascinating article written for *Signal* a decade ago, highlighted the kinds of writing done by young people who grew up in a world where the picture was an important part of the storytelling process, and provided a useful new lens through which teachers could look at their students' written productions (1989, 181–6). Ten years of technological change have broadened the potential for divergent storytelling repertoires, and contemporary students writing out of a background of extensive experience with different forms of popular culture may well be more sophisticated than their teachers recognize.

There are some signs of a new pedagogy being developed to address new kinds of narrative challenge. Nancy Welch, writing recently in *College English*, contrasts the linear implications of foreshadowing with a more open and plural approach to texts that she calls 'sideshadowing'. Her description of the contrast between the two seems to describe a form of phase space:

> Thus while foreshadowing doubles our sense of time—what is, what will be—sideshadowing works to triple, to quadruple. What is and what will be are joined by what else this present moment may suggest, what else the future could hold. Events no longer exist as points on a straight timeline but instead within fields of other potential actions that vie for our attention too.

> By shifting our attention back to the present moment and the field of potential actions that moment exists within, sideshadowing doesn't supplant the practice of foreshadowing. Instead it opens up that view to other realities, along with a glimpse of the consequences for each. Too often . . . we commit ourselves to a particular course of action without realizing that in the present moment there are other courses to be taken. Sideshadowing seeks out those might-have-beens and still-might-bes—other actions and outcomes, other interpretations and their implications . . . [I]t can teach us that understanding any given moment—including any moment in a student's draft—means understanding the field of possibility that moment exists within. (383)

As Welch describes the process of sideshadowing, drawing substantially on the insights of Bakhtin and his intellectual descendants, the concept seems almost to offer the relevant verb to accompany the noun phrase 'phase space'. Her article suggests fruitful avenues for exploring the implications of the issue for teaching both writing and reading in many different media.

Conclusions

Philip Pullman may well not recognize the free-and-easy use I have made of his concept of the phase space (never mind what a mathematician would make of such a cavalier takeover!). Obviously not one of my examples deals with a complete phase space for any given fiction; there is still no way to create or describe the complete world of *all* fictional possibilities relating to a single story, even a simple one. The texts I have described, the CD-ROM cities and islands, the online MUDs and MOOs, the reworkings and adaptations of given stories—all these complex representations still provide only samplings from any given phase space. My point is that contemporary culture leads us to be at home with plural possibilities. The old question, 'How many children had Lady Macbeth?' is askable again because our culture is now much happier to settle for an answer of *x*; Lady Macbeth might have had one child, or two children, or many, and all of these potential answers can co-exist in the phase space of *Macbeth*. The fact that no one single answer is possible does not mean that the question should not be asked nor that the answer is somehow outside of any kind of literary purview. Plural and speculative answers are now part of the imaginative landscape.

Today, even very young children manifest a new ease with *not knowing*, a comfort with juxtaposed alternatives all of which are equally plausible. Such a response is part of the culture that nurtures them. Adults, particularly those who engage with young people's reading and writing, can also benefit from exploring, extending, sometimes resisting and sometimes celebrating the enticements of the phase space. New forms of fiction resonate within the recreational lives of many young people today; the adults in their lives also need to start paying attention to these new narrative playgrounds.

Notes

1 http://www.randomhouse.com/features/goldencompass/
2 http://www.randomhouse.com/features/goldencompass/subtleknife/angelorum.html
3 http://www.randomhouse.com/features/goldencompass/subtleknife/pullman.html
4 The screenplay of *Men in Black* follows this format, and so does Kenneth Branagh's book about the making of the movie of *Hamlet*. Numerous other examples demonstrate that this approach is not confined to high or popular culture exclusively.
5 See, for example, the CD-ROM game of *My Teacher is an Alien* where plot developments are relatively laborious involving much trial and error.
6 The pop-up video format involves the insertion of printed captions over the top of previously made music videos; these captions offer all kinds of relevant and irrelevant information, often including references to decisions made, alternative scenes dropped, and other background insights into the original creation of the video.

References

Allan Ahlberg & André Amstutz, *Ten in a Bed*, Granada, 1983
Janet & Allan Ahlberg, *The Jolly Postman or Other People's Letters*, Heinemann, 1986
Janet & Allan Ahlberg, *It Was a Dark and Stormy Night*, Viking, 1993
Louisa May Alcott, *Little Women*, illustrated by Jame's Prunier,Viking, 1997
Anna Altmann, Ingrid Johnston & Margaret Mackey, 'Curriculum Decisions About Literature in Contemporary Classrooms: A Preliminary Analysis of a Survey of Materials Used in Edmonton Grade 10 English Courses', *Alberta Journal of Educational Research XLIV*(2), Summer 1998, 208–20
Phyllis Bixler, '*The Secret Garden* "Misread": The Broadway Musical as Creative Interpretation', *Children's Literature 22*, 1994, 101–23
Jorge Luis Borges, 'The Garden of Forking Paths', in *Ficciones*, edited by Anthony Kerrigan, Grove Press, 1962, 89–101
Creatures, CyberLife Technology, CD-ROM, Mindscape Entertainment, 1996–97
Jane Yellowlees Douglas, 'Will the Most Reflexive Relativist Please Stand Up: Hypertext, Argument and Relativism', in *Page to Screen: Taking Literacy into the Electronic Era*, edited by Ilana Snyder, Routledge, 1998,144–62
Geri Gay, 'Issues in Accessing and Constructing Multimedia Documents', in *Contextual Media: Multimedia and Interpretation*, edited by Edward Barrett & Marie Redmond, MIT Press, 1997, 175–88
Stephen Kline, *Out of the Garden: Toys and Children's Culture in the Age of TV Marketing*, Garamond Press, 1993
Margaret Mackey, '*Little Women* Go to Market: Shifting Texts and Changing Readers', *Children's Literature in Education*, December 1998, 153–73
Stuart Moulthrop, 'No War Machine', in *Reading Matters: Narratives in the New Media Ecology*, edited by Joseph Tabbi & Michael Wutz, Cornell University Press, 1997, 269–92

Janet H. Murray, 'The Pedagogy of Cyberfiction: Teaching a Course on Reading and Writing Interactive Narrative', in *Contextual Media: Multimedia and Interpretation*, edited by Edward Barrett & Marie Redmond, MIT Press, 1997, 129–62

My Teacher is an Alien, based on the series by Bruce Colville, CD-ROM, Byron Preiss Multimedia, 1997

Myst, Cyan, CD-ROM, Broderbund Software, 1993–94

Philip Pullman, *The Golden Compass*, Alfred A. Knopf, 1995

Philip Pullman, 'Invisible Pictures', *Signal* 60, September 1989, 160–86

Philip Pullman, 'Let's Write It in Red: The Patrick Hardy Lecture', *Signal* 85, January 1998, 44–62

Philip Pullman, *Northern Lights*, Scholastic, 1995

Philip Pullman, *The Subtle Knife*, Scholastic, 1997

Riven, Cyan, CD-ROM, Broderbund Software, 1997

Jon Scieska & Lane Smith, *The Stinky Cheese Man and other Fairly Stupid Tales*, Viking, 1992

SimCity Classic, CD-ROM, Maxis, 1989

Art Spiegelman, *The Complete Maus*, Voyager CD-ROM, CityROM, n.d.

Eugene Trivizas & Helen Oxenbury, *The Three Little Wolves and the Big Bad Pig*, Heinemann, 1993

Sherry Turkle, *Life on the Screen: Identity in the Age of the Internet*, Simon & Schuster, 1995

Nancy Welch, 'Sideshadowing Teacher Response', *College English* 60(4), April 1998, 374–95

Julian Wood, 'Repeatable Pleasures: Notes on Young People's Use of Video', in *Reading Audiences: Young People and the Media*, edited by David Buckingham, Manchester University Press, 1993, 184–201

16

FUTURES FOR CHILDREN'S LITERATURE

Evolution or radical break?

Peter Hunt

Source: *Cambridge Journal of Education* 30(1) (2000): 111–119.

[E]lectronic technology has brought us into the age of 'secondary orality'. This new orality has striking resemblances to the old in its participatory mystique, its fostering of a communal sense, its concentration on the present moment. . . . Unlike members of a primary oral culture, who are turned outward because they have little occasion to turn inward, we are turned outward because we have turned inward.

(Ong, 1982, p. 136)

Teacher surrounded by small children: 'There is no such thing as a wrong answer. However, if there WERE such a thing, Malcolm, that certainly would have been it'.

(Boynton, 1986, p. 62)

Electronic media are not simply changing the way we tell stories: they are changing the very nature of story, of what we understand (or do not understand) to be narratives.

How great the change is going to be in language/literature terms might be demonstrated by a simple analogy. Printing, in the West, dates from the mid 15th century; the first examples of what we now regard as one of the most *natural* forms of printed fiction, the novel, date from the mid 18th century. The Internet, which was first developed in 1973, and which is estimated to have 100,000,000 computers connected to it by the year 2000, has not yet found its equivalent of the novel. Whatever that equivalent form turns out to be, people brought up on the novel will have as much difficulty in conceptualising it as people brought up in an oral culture had in conceptualising the novel.

And this is precisely what the curriculum of the next century will have to face: this generation of teachers will have to deal not merely with the old questions of where children's books fit into education or how far texts validated by the culture of school are *therefore* endangered by popular cultural forms outside school. The new question is how to mediate the interaction between new media and established text forms, and the profound intellectual shift that this implies.

Fiction narratives for children, in whatever form—from print to video—have had a contentious position in the curriculum (and in school library budgets) for a century. Pragmatically, there is little reason to suppose that this will change: the skirmishes between reason and imagination, between system and freedom and between various definitions of 'literacy' (and the best ways of achieving it) will doubtless continue. They will influence, and be influenced by, more scarcely-thought-out political gestures (such as the sudden injection of ~ £115,000,000 for 23,000,000 books for schools in 1998–1999 (BBC, 1999) or the possibility that the dismembering of the school library services of the last 20 years may be remedied, at least in part).

What happens in the 21st century depends to some extent on the symbiotic relationship between children's books and schools. How books are treated in education is directly linked to the books that are produced and marketed. It may seem that the real power in publishing lies with the accountants (Chambers, 1993, pp. 13–14), and this has sustained the generally conservative form and content of the children's book and the dominance of a very few writers. The recent major survey, *Children's Reading Choices* confirms common observation in bookshops, that Dahl, Blyton and 'series' books outweigh all others (Hall & Coles, 1999, pp. 17–55): this puts the apparently encouraging fact that over 8,000 children's titles were published in the UK in 1997 in context (Astbury, 1998, p. 57).

However, behind the accountants are the teachers, who have a powerful influence, but who generally find themselves caught in two related and complex situations.

Firstly, they are faced with overwhelming numbers of books in theory, but, partly because of the (comparative) lack of library support, very few in fact. (This has been compounded by the concentration of 'school book fairs' in the hands of a small number of publishers.) Consequently, there is a tendency for teachers to reinforce conservative trends. (It is possible that the (un)steady growth of courses in children's literature will gradually raise awareness and critical acumen.) Indeed, it can be argued that over the last 20 years, after reaching a plateau of worthy (if perhaps rather dull) 'literary quality', children's novels are returning to their historical roots as extensions of the educational system: prizeworthy novels commonly address issues and ideas rather than 'merely' telling stories (Hunt, 1999). Books are published to fit 'key' educational stages or to support the 'literacy hour'. Consequently, although the evidence is that children are reading *more* than they were 30 years ago (Hall and Coles report that the 'average number of books read prior to (their) survey, across all age groups, was 2.52', whereas, in 1971, for a similar survey the average was 2.39 (Hall & Coles, 1999, p. 15)) *what* they are reading is (especially within schools) unrepresentative of the potentials of fiction.

Taken together with a general political emphasis on 'classic' or 'established' texts in schools, through the National Curriculum and Key Stage recommendations, all of this seems to imply, in simplistic terms, the valuing of certain 'established' types of narrative. Outside school, other kinds of narrative—indeed, texts that are not usually regarded as being narratives—are being read. A common reaction to this situation has been to see the division in oppositional value terms, as does Derek Meakin, Chairman of the publisher Europress:

> The sad fact is that for many years children have not been encouraged to lose themselves in books, as children of my generation were in the 1930s . . . and what stories they were . . . [a] far cry from the often tedious, politically correct schoolbooks that are around today—books that help dissuade young people from reading anything at all, and make them turn instead to the black hole of a TV set with its messages of violence, lust and greed.
>
> (Meakin, 1997, p. 8)

This does not recognise that the narratives encountered in reading done (primarily) outside school (magazines, non-fiction, video games) demand a *different* kind of perception and concentration: the book (and its associated narrative patterns and mindsets) is doing something rather different from video versions of the same texts and something *quite different* from 'inter-active' and net-based media. These are different *kinds* of narrative, reflecting different concepts of story. Nor does it acknowledge the obvious fact, evident in various forms since the 19th century, that if a certain kind of text/culture is supported in school but not elsewhere, then its study will probably be counter-productive. If the hand-held book is identified with school (especially if is identified with some vague 'literary' value), then other media will continue to dominate. Whether this is politically, sociologically or culturally a good thing is probably less important than the (often unacknowledged) change in what 'story' is understood to be.

The situation is, of course, complicated by the fact that boys and girls are 'differently literate' (Millard, 1997) and that classrooms (especially in primary schools) are largely a female province. For although, as Hall and Coles point out, 'overwhelmingly both boys' and girls' book reading at all ages is narrative fiction', there is a lot of *non-book* reading, which is (narrative or not) *non-fiction*, and 'when non-fiction is read the readers are mainly boys' (Hall & Coles, 1999, p. 85).

Margaret Mackey has summed up the situation:

> Students who enter their secondary classrooms knowledgeable about the back-stories of many movies, familiar with the leisurely, non-linear appeal of *The Simpsons'* universe courtesy of handbooks and CD-ROMs, at ease with the circular and repetitive attraction of many different on-line forms of fiction, will often find their expertise is little valued in the academic forum. If they are truly unlucky, they will be taught about 'the' plot diagram and trained to think that there is only one way to write a valid story. Even in more enlightened classrooms, they may regularly wonder why their 'fit' with linear school stories is often so uneasy.
>
> (Mackey, 1999, p. 30)

As a result, how children's literature develops in the future may depend on how well we understand and apply our understanding of intellectual changes, which may, at the basic level, involve a revision of what it means to be 'literate' and to be a 'good reader'.

Traditionally, to state what might seem to be the blindingly obvious, we have understood 'narrative' to be the act of communicating an abstraction —a story: it is *an act of communication to others*. We recognise the difference between the abstract *story* and the telling of it, *narrative*, because the *telling* has, ultimately, influenced the *story*. Equally obviously, something must happen in a *narrative*; stories can be seen to progress through 'narrative units', marked by change of some kind; these units are given coherence by links such as character, scene, atmosphere, theme or motif, and overwhelmingly aim towards a resolution. All of these elements and resolutions are guided by *generic* traditions.

The new hypermedia stories that we are now encountering/creating do not live by these rules. To appreciate the mental leap that will be required, we need to acknowledge the differences between what might broadly be called the three different narrative types, oral, written, and 'hypermedia'.

It is tempting to see in the structures and devices of the oral tale a 'natural' 'mental template for narrative structure' (Fox, 1993, p. 69), although the 'beginning–middle–end' structure is demonstrably 'culture-specific':

> ...many cultures have stories...that are expressed chiefly in circular or spiral terms. There might be a 'beginning', but there is no real 'middle' or 'end'. Cumulative stories in some cultures do not have a climactic event that then triggers actions moving the story to a final conclusion. ...
>
> (Pellowski, 1996, p. 670)

(For an exploration of the theoretical issues see Fox, 1993, pp. 68–83; Ong, 1982, pp. 31–77)

Certainly all the evidence is that modern audiences, whatever their background in media, respond enthusiastically to oral storytelling, when they are given the opportunity (Geoff Fox, personal communication; Colwell, 1991, pp. 85–91; Medlicott, 1996, pp. 541–543) and have the necessary skills of concentration and response.

However, it is not the sequence that is the essence, or meaning, of an oral tale. The *narrating*, the interactive building of mutual as well as personal meaning seems to be *more* important. Thus, as Carol Fox suggests (*pace* Propp *et al.*), the narrative units (the actions) are actually relatively uninteresting (Fox, 1993, p. 70), as is constantly demonstrated in 'mature' genres.

It is striking that in elements such as these, and especially in the fact that the experience of the oral narrative is not stable, thus making 'static' criticism (and the assignation of literary 'quality') difficult, oral storytelling resembles hypertext. Just as oral tellings may be passed on from narrator to narrator *within one telling*, so, Nigel Woodward predicted in 1983:

> [e]ven the literary work may be set to become less an isolated act by a single author, and more and more the product of a process in which the author is one of a group of several authors—a group that eventually includes the 'reader'.
>
> (Woodward, 1983, p. 8: see also Barratt, 1989)

With writing and printing, there were many quite fundamental changes to narrative, and hence to story—as Walter J. Ong put it, 'writing restructures consciousness' (Ong, 1982, pp. 78–115). The most obvious changes involve less dependence on memory, more subtle modes of imposing coherence, allusion, character development, more and different points of view and focalisation, and, perhaps above all, 'print encourages a sense of closure, a sense that what is found in a text has been finalised, has reached a state of completion' (Ong, 1982, p. 132).

Narrative changes fundamentally, and the kinds of story it tells changes. It removes itself from the spontaneous, the ephemeral and the 'disorganised', all characteristics of what child readers read for much of the time and all characteristics of hypertext. What has come to be valued in print-narrative, and especially in 20th century western culture, is anything *but* the narrative: as E. M. Forster intoned, 'Yes—oh dear yes—the novel tells a story. That is the highest factor common to all novels, and I wish that it were not so . . .' (Forster, 1976, p. 40) This is the culture that leads to the warnings to students '*not to tell the story*' in essays and exams (as if that were too simple a matter), to the relegation of narrative-driven children's literature almost to the bottom of the literary pile (Hunt, 1991, pp. 17–41) and to the relegation of texts which seem to be nothing but narrative, such as the 'Choose Your Own Adventure' books, to the lowest level of all.

But whether or not the central action becomes only part of the complex picture, printed narratives (with very rare exceptions, such as the work of William Burroughs, which are generally seen as experimental) remain linear and resolution-based. Some texts, in the name of post-modernism, have attempted, generally metafictionally, to repackage these linear narratives, but they almost always have to maintain some coherence by simple linearity or appeals to genre understanding (such as Gillian Cross's *Wolf*). Even multiple narratives, such as David Macaulay's *Black and White* are simply chopped up linear narratives. Books such as David McKee's *I Hate My Teddy Bear* or Janet and Allan Ahlberg's *The Babies' Catalogue* are exceptions that prove the rule, although even they retain traces of linear coherence.

Traditional linear narratives, then, offer fixed outcomes but imaginative opportunities. Thus, however many times we read *Charlie and the Chocolate Factory*, Charlie will always be given the factory at the end. What that factory looks like, however, is largely up to the images in our own heads. In contrast, a good many computer 'games' (which lean towards the conditions of hypertext) offer us landscapes, visualised characters and images of all kinds, but allow the player to choose different outcomes.

Some of the earliest attempts to break out of the straightjacket of resolution were the 'Choose Your Own Adventure' type series, from the 1970s. Although driven by crude decisions, pre-programmed links and consequences at narrative unit level, these (hugely successful) series shifted 'power' in the text towards the reader as an empowered partner.

It might have been expected that the new electronic media would have exploited these 'games', simply because more choices could be handled electronically. The fact that this has not happened points to the essentially different nature of the electronic media: they *can* handle old-fashioned devices (just as television could and did handle theatre before finding its own style), but they can do other things better.

What is important is that it is not the *increase* in narrative alternatives, but the *decrease* in what we anticipate—the decrease in the importance of narrative (or the very nature of narrative itself). There are many computer *games* which provide settings and then allow their 'players' to exist within them; 'what actually occurs in these worlds is open ended, and in many ways unimportant' (Mackey, 1999, p. 24). Some sophisticated games, instead of transferring print-originated stories to CD or the Internet, reflect children's 'life-long exposure to a culture full of many different kinds of (alternative narratives)' (p. 27). The fact that they are called 'games' indicates, of course, the attitude felt towards them by an older, embattled mindset.

The obvious consequence of these trends is that the concept of 'narrative' is stretched. We are in a transitional phase towards widespread hypermedia thinking and we have to accept that the MUDs (multi-user domains) which allow for multiple authorship, the annotated texts, the web sites and magazines that elaborate on narratives old or new, are all now part of narrative. What were previously thought of as external or extraneous items (back stories, actors' biographies, cut-out toys, adaptations) become part of the 'narrative'. A recent report on multiplayer 'online role-playing games' cited Ultima Online, which has 125,000 'players', or Everquest, which fills its virtual cities with 30,000 people every night, each adding to the complex narrative (Krantz, 1999, p. 96).

And so to 'hypermedia', the electronic linking of words, sounds and images. (For definitions (which are, perhaps inevitably, themselves shifting constantly) see Woodward, 1983, pp. 2–4).) If we regard written narrative as a fixed thread upon which we 'hang' our own private universe of interpretations and elaborations, then hypertext is the same thing without the thread. This 'narrative' can be constructed through a 'package' which allows the reader/writer to proceed associatively or at random on the Internet.

> It is conceivable that the linking power of hypertext packages will encourage some authors thereby to link everything to everything else, or keep adding further nodes of information according to some vague philosophy which espouses associations as 'natural' and hence desirable, leaving the reader to decide what they want to access.
> (McKnight *et al.*, 1991, quoted in Horton, 1994, p. 174)

If we use true hypertext (if such a thing exists or could exist), we can build up matrixes which don't *go anywhere*. (It is interesting that early versions of hypertext mark-up languages included 'browse sequences', ghosts, as it were, of linear narratives.) We end up (although, of course, we never *end up*) with narratives which, in 'linear' terms, are merely chaos or nonsense. Such texts are fairly difficult to describe from a linear point of view: most literary researchers/theorists (for example Culler, Gennette, Barthes, Applebee and Sutton-Smith (Fox, 1993, pp. 78–81)) seem unable to go beyond shapes, relationships and structures, which, however elaborate, relate to linear 'ground logics'.

More commonly, such a narrative is constructed by 'surfing' the Internet. By 'surfing' (interacting with the world of stored data) we build up a matrix or constellation of 'items': they are the story, but that story is complex and intensely personal. It is continually changing and cannot be transmitted to anyone else: the reader is making and claiming his/her own meaning. This leads to the paradox that these new narratives are both personal and involve 'shared authorship' and they are all unstable works in progress. Criticism, if it has a place at all, has to be to be an intervention, an interruption, and an extension of the story itself.

This makes whatever is generated (i) virtually unrecognisable as a narrative and (ii) singularly useless for and inaccessible to evaluation. Of course, this is exactly what happens when any reader interacts with any narrative in any form, although it would not be in the interests of the critical/educational establishment at any level to admit it. Or, to put it another way, for years we have discussed and advocated the necessity of our students' involvement and interaction with texts/story/drama. Now we are going to be taken at our word: 'Our young readers expect to learn actively; they do not expect always to think in a straight line' (Dresang, 1999, p. 265).

Or, perhaps, we have come full circle. If oral narratives and written narratives share the characteristic of linearity, then oral and hypertexts share the quality of the matrix.

Put at its least threatening, we might say that those untrained in certain ways of thinking (conveniently children) do not see narrative in the same way as older readers. Less comfortingly, we might say that the future narratives for the 'computer reader' seem to be no more or less than individual, unassessable chaos. But these readers still need to subsist in a linear educational system. What, then, are the more pragmatic implications?

The most likely scenario, given the massive inertia built into social and educational systems, is that linear and hypertext models of narrative will exist in parallel. Compromise seems to be inevitable, and possibly highly creative: Benjamin Wolley in *Virtual Worlds* quotes Michael Joyce, inventor of a hypertext authoring tool, 'Storyspace . . . which might be used to create a novel as supple and multiple as oral narratives' (Wolley, 1993, p. 163). Another consequence would be to cease to privilege any one narrative mode. As Carol Fox noted:

> Logical resolutions to stories are a late development in the history of literacy. For children there is plenty of scope in the rest of the telling to explore the huge variety of ways of narrating fictional events. To encourage children to experiment with these ways would be to give them metanarrative knowledge.
>
> (Fox, 1993, p. 198)

Fundamentally, for the foreseeable future, two quite different mindsets will be operating at the same time in our educational system, and what we now think of as children's literature—narrative for children—will be at the centre of it. It need hardly be said that the political implications are quite revolutionary. Just as the Internet has the potential to destroy cultures, so the acceptance of the validity of individual internal narratives (or cooperative narratives without any authoritarian centre) totally undermines politically and culturally established 'standards'. Negotiating that situation is what the curriculum of the future will be about.

References

ASTBURY, R. (1998) Editorial, *School Librarian*, 46(2), p. 57.

BARRATT, E. (Ed.) (1989) *The Society of the Text* (Cambridge, MA, MIT Press).

BBC (1999) Year of Reading puts 23 million books in schools, *BBC News*, 31 March 1999, http://news.bbc.co.uk/hi/english/education/.

BOYNTON, S. (1986) *Don't Let the Turkeys Get You Down* (New York, NY, Wildman).

CHAMBERS, A. (1993) The difference of literature: writing now for the future of young readers, *Children's Literature in Education*, 24(1), pp. 1–18.

COLWELL, E. (1991) *Storytelling* (South Woodchester, Thimble Press).

DRESANG, E. T. (1999) *Radical Change. Books for youth in a digital age* (New York, NY, H. W. Wilson).

FORSTER, E. M. (1976) *Aspects of the Novel* (Harmondsworth, Penguin).

FOX, C. (1993) *At the Very Edge of the Forest: the influence of literature on storytelling by children* (London, Cassell).

HALL, C. & COLES, M. (1999) *Children's Reading Choices* (London, Routledge).

HORTON, W. (1994) *Designing and Writing Online Documentation*, 2nd edn (New York, NY, John Wiley).

HUNT, P. (1991) *Criticism, Theory and Children's Literature* (Oxford, Blackwell).

HUNT, P. (1999) The Devil and Madame Doubtfire: Anne Fine and the revolution in contemporary British children's fiction, *The Lion and the Unicorn*, 23(1), pp. 12–21.

MCKNIGHT, C., DILLON, A. & RICHARDSON, J. (Eds) (1991) *Hypertext in Context* (Cambridge, Cambridge University Press).

KRANTZ, M. (1999) Grab your breastplate! *Time*, 153(24), p. 96.

MACKEY, M. (1999) Playing in the phase space, *Signal*, 88, pp. 16–33.

MEAKIN, D. (1997) Breathing electronic life into children's classics: the 1997 Woodfield Lecture, *New Review of Children's Literature and Librarianship*, 3, pp. 1–9.

MEDLICOTT, M. (1996) Story-telling, in: P. HUNT (Ed.) *International Companion Encyclopedia of Children's Literature*, pp. 539–545 (London, Routledge).

MILLARD, E. (1997) *Differently Literate: boys, girls, and the schooling of literacy* (London, Falmer Press).

ONG, W. J. (1982) *Orality and Literacy* (London, Methuen).

PELLOWSKI, A. (1996) Culture and developing countries, in: P. HUNT (Ed.) *International Companion Encyclopedia of Children's Literature*, pp. 662–675 (London, Routledge).

WOLLEY, B. (1993) *Virtual Worlds* (London, Penguin).

WOODWARD, N. (1983) *Hypertext and Hypermedia* (Wilmslow, Sigma Press).

Part 4

PICTURE BOOKS

17

INTRODUCTION TO PICTUREBOOK CODES

William Moebius

Source: *Word & Image* 2(2) (April–June 1986): 141–151, 158.

It is easy to be captivated by the lovable and endearing creatures that inhabit the modern picturebook. Whether our taste for picturebooks was formed by the work of Beatrix Potter[1] or by that of her distinguished successors, we know, even if we often disavow it, this infatuation with the image of her Mrs Tiggy-Winkle (a hedgehog), Mary Chalmers' Harry (a cat) or Cyndy Szekeres' Pippa Mouse, Ernest Shepard's or William Pene du Bois' bears, Clement Hurd's rabbits, or Bernard Waber's Lyle (a crocodile) and Arthur (an anteater). Disarmed, entangled in a net of affection, we are almost ready to eat, as it were, out of the handling of the illustrator.

The story 'behind' the image, a story often supplied by the illustrator, may lead us to form our attachment to such images; is it possible that the sweetness of Raphael's Madonna is made sweeter by the story of Jesus, or the poignancy of Rembrandt's self-portraits by the story of Rembrandt's own life? The story in the child's picturebook may have no such scriptural or historical pre-existence; it unfolds for us just now, a variety-show of images and texts. We anticipate the next while looking at the one before, we laugh now that we see what we had not noticed or expected before, we let our eyes wander off a familiar character's face to a puzzling word on the page and back again.[2] Unlike the framed settings of a Biblical text of a Raphael or Rembrandt, the pictures in a picturebook cannot hang by themselves; picturebook texts do not fare well when they are extracted and anthologized in various bibles of children's literature.[3] Each works with the other in a bound sequence of images/text, inseparable in our reading experience one from the other. In a contemporary artbook, we would be encouraged to read a succession of figures by Picasso, or of portrait-landscapes by the Douanier Rousseau as a record of each artist's creative development.[4] In the picturebook, we read images and text together as the mutually complementary story of a consciousness, of a Lyle the Crocodile's ways of being, his growing and suffering in the world.

Each page affords what Barbara Bader, the pioneer historian of the genre in its American development, has called an 'opening';[5] implied, of course, is a closing, a deliberate shutting out of what came before, and a constant withholding of what is to come.[6] Unlike a published reproduction of a mural or a frieze, upon which the eye can wander, scanning a wide field for pattern, for signs of unity, the picturebook opening allows only limited exposures. Each page, if read at the speed of a slow reader, has only a minute or less to impress itself on our attention, to earn a place in our memory, as the story compels us forward, in what Bader, borrowing from Rémy Charlip, calls 'the drama of the turning of the page'.[7] Even as H. A. Rey or Bernard Waber make introductions ('This is George. He lived in Africa . . .'; 'This is the house. / The house on / East 88th Street'), what they introduce remains elusive, images lost, tracked down, and lost again and again.

We can pour emotion and affection into these pages, if we choose, under the license of our second childhood; or, as I wish to do here, we can watch more closely, looking past the lovable expression on the monkey's or anteater's face, and attend to elements of design and expression that comprise what we might call 'codes'.[8] To do this is not to deny anyone the emotional truth of the image, a sensitive issue to many adults who admire children's books as the last frontier of innocence. Dorfman and Mattelart, in introducing their icon-smashing *How to Read Donald Duck*, state rather unequivocally: 'For the adult, in protecting his dream-image of youth, hides the fear that to penetrate it would destroy his dreams and reveal the reality it conceals'.[9] I make no claims to revealing realities hidden behind a screen of text and illustration, not do I seek to destroy any dreamimages. Close study of the picturebook may generate more dreamimages, more for the waking imagination to contemplate, not all of it pleasant or 'delightful'.[10]

Some historical considerations first. Readers of either of two recent, lavishly illustrated histories of the picturebook or its parent, the illustrated book for children, will recall the attention given by both Susan Meyer and Barbara Bader to developments in media and printing techniques; out of each technical advancement, certain picturebook artists found a personal style. But more to our point, both historians also give rather detailed accounts of how, from Edmund Evans on, the making of the picturebook was seen more and more to require an integral relationship between picture and word, a 'total design'. Rather than being an album of pictures, or a text with some 'tipped-in' illustrations, the picturebook was, after Edmund Evans, conceived of as a whole 'product'. Text was 'script' or libretto (sometimes, as we shall see, better seen as footnote, or even as decorative flourish). Cover, endpapers, title-page design, all were carefully chosen elements of a whole, an experience wrapped, not without conscious intention, as a gift.[11] Yet, as Bader's treatment of the subject reveals, distinctions were still to be made, almost 100 years after Evans' first publishing efforts, between 'illustration-as-communication' and 'illustration-as-art'.[12] In Bader's aesthetics, it appears that an emphasis on design is linked to the communicability of messages. Tomi Ungerer, a contemporary, is 'more the designer'.[13] Of Marcia Brown's work, she writes, 'and the design itself tells much of the story'.[14] While Bader's work investigates the development of the 'design' factors, allowing the work of former Disney artists Bill Peet and Hardie Gramatky a place in the development of the picturebook alongside the work of Wanda Gág, Margaret Wise Brown and Feodor Rojankovsky, it does not elaborate a poetics of the picturebook, except in passing reference to what a certain illustration 'does' for the text.

Meyer's work largely pays tribute to what Bader would call 'illustration-as-art', the tradition of Caldecott and Pyle, of Kay Nielsen and N. C. Wyeth. But Meyer singles out Walter Crane and W. W. Denslow, for whom 'the words themselves were part of the total picture, exquisitely designed letterforms integrated within the format of the unit of a decorated book'.[15] Devoting her final chapter to W. W. Denslow, 'a very different kind of American' from N. C. Wyeth,[16] Meyer tries to give her reader the sense of a different tradition, one which would demand that the picturebook be 'an object of beauty, designed carefully from cover to cover, with attention to every detail, including endpapers, frontis and title page, typography and illustrations'.[17]

No approach to the picturebook can overlook the importance of medium and design as a part of the reader's experience. Nor can we pretend to be unaffected by pictures we encounter in picturebooks that could be cut out, framed and placed over the fireplace, such as N. C. Wyeth's or Kay Nielsen's. Yet I believe that in the picturebook what matters is something more than the artist's mastery of materials and technique, or the felicity of the book's design. These may prove attractive features to some readers, and may even foster an appreciation of 'good' books, of 'objects of beauty' in younger readers. By focusing attention on codes in the picturebook, we are no less concerned with dignifying the artist's creation. We are, as it were, making soundings in the harbour of 'design-as-communication', marking the deeper channels of a modern art-form.

Such soundings must begin simply enough with the *world* as it is depicted in the picturebook, of what has been called the 'presented world'.[18] By using the word 'depict' I mean to include verbal as well as pictorial elements. What is presented in the text usually obeys certain conventions of recognizability and continuity. We depend on a number of stable visual cues, so that we can say 'There goes Curious George again', or ask 'Isn't he there behind that bush'? Whenever we ask 'Who's that'? of a picturebook character, we expect the answer to hold for that image during the entire story, unless we are alerted to a metamorphosis. We expect George to keep looking like George, and not like any monkey or anthropomorph, unless we are led to believe that George will now simulate such another. To remain recognizable, a character need only reveal a few signal traits such as curly hair (Ira), a proboscis (Arthur) a striped tail (Frances) or a blue jacket (Peter Rabbit). These metonyms of personality, species, gender, character type constitute elements of a semic code, but may also play a role in action, as the main character undergoes an identity crisis related to the presence or absence of a primary feature.

Characters remain recognizable despite the omission of particular features, lips, eyebrows, etc., we know they would possess if they were to step out of the book. And the world they inhabit remains imaginable even though it is sometimes not depicted at all at a given opening. What we refer to as the 'blank face' of the picturebook character might as well also apply to the carefully managed *'blanchissage'* of the world in certain illustrations.

Between text and picture, or among pictures themselves, we may experience a sort of semic slippage, where word and image seem to send conflicting, perhaps contradictory messages about the 'who' or the 'what' of the story. Here is a kind of 'plate tectonics' of the picturebook, where word and image constitute separate plates sliding and scraping along against each other. Let's look, for an example, at the cover and title page of *Where the Wild Things Are*.[19] The front cover features the title of the book like a headline across the top; reading down the page into the picture, our eye falls on a seated animal-like creature who is dozing off in the foreground at one corner of the page. Behind this creature runs a stream and a fringe of palm-like trees. The expression 'Wild Things' in the headline is generic, almost too abstract. What is a wild thing? In no bestiary will we encounter quite the specimen of 'wildness' shown here, bull's head and human feet, sporting a one-piece blue fur suit, sitting like a Manet gentleman in *Le Déjeuner sur l'herbe*. Perhaps we will be reminded of a Seurat or a Douanier Rousseau. Stillness and quiet prevail. We turn to the title-spread. Here, not quite so high, is the same expression 'Wild Things'. But now, in addition to two others of the original furry breed, pictured on the left, comes a new figure dancing onto the page from the right. Is this too a wild thing? It looks like a boy in some sort of wolf suit . . . Suddenly the title has acquired the status of a banner above a rogue's gallery. The images on both the cover and title page each angle for our respect under the firm, immutable authority of the inscription *Where the Wild Things Are*. But between these images lies a buffer zone, an undefined 'wilderness'. What Roland Barthes has called the 'reference code' is probably also active here, as we attempt to cross this buffer zone. Only later may we discover that Max has earned the appellation 'wild thing' from his mother, thanks to his 'mischief of one kind / or another'; the benign creature with the horns is 'wild' only in appearance, and is easily tamed by Max, 'the wildest thing of all'. In order to make this distinction of kind, we must first have had some acquaintance with the different connotations of the word 'wild' outside the text. The cover and title-page have hardly told us everything necessary to sort out the meaning of the 'wild thing'. The unresolved question of 'What is a wild thing?' coupled with the hint that not all 'wild things' think or act alike, prompts us to read on, to turn up or over new evidence, to become the loyal subjects of the hermeneutic code.

The convention of recognizability operates also in cases in which the name of the character is made to apply to an object that bears no physical resemblance to that character. The verbal text maintains the continunity of character's name and feeling, keeps the inner secret; the pictorial version presents two or more manifestations. Sylvester, in *Sylvester and the Magic Pebble*, must be distinguished from the large rock he becomes, even during the period in which he is indistinguishable from that rock.

In playing with the convention of recognizability, some picturebooks enable the reader to build a network of associations between two vastly different referents, as say between Sylvester and the rock, or between Max the devouring monster who says to his mother 'I'll eat you up' and the wild things that cry out at Max's departure, 'We'll eat you up, we love you so.' These associations arise in the active imagination only, and are not usually outright in the text. If we declare that 'Sylvester is now a rock',[20] we may mean superficially that on the page at this moment Sylvester, a donkey, has been turned into a rock. But the rock is originally Sylvester's *idea* of a defence against a lion. And as the seasons change around him, the rock reinforces *our idea* of the durable, patient, somewhat stolid personality of the donkey. And as it stands by itself in the field, the rock also conveys a sense of its own isolation, and gives tangible form to the idea of loneliness. When angry Max tells his mother 'I'll eat you up', we cannot help but take him at his word. After all, he is wearing a wolf-suit and a picture of a toothy monster bears his scrawled signature; even the Scottish terrier beats a retreat before this little devil. Maybe he would take a bite out if his mother. Only later, when at his parting from them, the beasts make 'We'll eat you up' the terms of an endearment, do we catch up with the metaphorical possibility of the phrase or the action it describes.

Nevertheless, the plain, the literal sense is the first we connect with in most picturebooks. As such, we usually attribute a plain, literal point of view to the main characters, who as problem-solvers seek plain, practical solutions to their problems, a supply of food, for example.[21] Yet the best picturebooks can and do portray the intangible and invisible, ideas and concepts such as love, responsibility, a truth beyond the individual, ideas that escape easy definition in pictures or words. With her lens as historian, Bader sees 'a new non-imitative way of working generally, a way of expressing intangibles, communicating emotion, sensation – one which invited the viewer, too, to see things in a new way'.[22] After Max has enjoyed his fling with the wild things, and exercised his enormous power over them, he falls into a reverie of a world that neither he nor the reader can see, a world 'where someone loved him best of all'. Max's mother never does appear in *Where the Wild Things Are*, except as represented by her tokens, shown in the final illustration, a three-layer cake, a glass of milk, a bowl of something steaming. On the final page, without a picture, the text tells us 'And it was still hot.' Here the 'it' emerges as unspeakable and unseeable motherlove. Likewise, 'rock' temporarily replaces Sylvester. Literally petrified, made to suffer through the seasons without companionship, movement, or speech, Sylvester, once restored to donkey shape, retains certain qualities of rockhood not readily apparent on the face of a jubilant donkey. He can no longer be quite as easily shaken or frightened, nor ever so quick to use magical formulas to protect himself.

That so many picturebook characters come, in the end, to recognize or to experience the value of the intangible over the tangible, of what is 'loved best of all' over what is closest at hand, the unseen over the seen, deserves an essay of its own. Here I would offer just two observations in passing. The first is that such a pattern of story (and pattern of reader response, from dependence on the plain and literal to the development of a sense of independence in the face of individually discovered yet intangible meanings) accords with a pattern of cognitive development described by Piaget in terms of the passage from preoperational and concrete operational thought to formal operations, from the various 'realisms' to the recognition of symbol.[23] Second, I would point out that the frequent depiction in picturebooks of gates, doors, windows and stairs, of roads and waterways, and the changing representation of light, artificial and natural, to accord with different degrees of character understanding, are not accidental or fortuitous phenomena, but downright basic to the symbolic force of the story. A character who looks out the window or stands in the door, as Max does in *Where the Wild Things Are*, is implicated in the unspoken meanings of thresholds. Whether stairs, steps or extended ramp, the incline may provide a measure of the character's stature or of progress towards a depth or height of understanding or confusion. There is nothing doctrinaire about such pronouncements. Nothing should tie interpretation of stairways or doorways and such in picturebooks to a single intention or effect. Such pieces of the symbolic code work differently in different stories, and will lend themselves to different interpretations. But they should not be overlooked.

'The presented word' may also bear the marks of 'presented worlds' in other texts. For example, Sendak plays with the familiar image of 'The Thinker',[24] or, more subtly, alludes to Rodin's Adam in the final illustration of *Where the Wild Things Are*, which shows Max, hand on forehead, striding into his room, still wearing his wolf-suit, but clearly emerging as a young man. The phenomenon of intertextuality is more common in the picturebook than might appear. Series books such as Waber's about Lyle, Rey's about Curious George, or Duvoisin's about Petunia, would seem to depend on it; yet they do each stand alone. In Waber, at a point somewhere after the middle, we sometimes encounter a plethora of signs borrowed from other places, rubber stamps (in Ira *Sleeps Over*) or political signs (in *Lyle Finds his Mother*). And it is not unlikely for a character to be found reading a book, the title of which is readable within the illustration.[25] We might treat such examples of intertextuality as tests of the reader's knowledge of the world of texts.

Each of the foregoing aspects of 'the presented world' requires our prior knowledge of the world outside the text for adequate recognition. The picturebook poses the challenge 'How much of the world to you know'? at the outset, and asks us, like Chukovsky's child before the nonsense-verse, to prove our knowledge of reality by affirming the resemblance of what we see on the page to some figure already stored in consciousness.

But the picturebook also asks us 'How much do you see'? To help us in this respect, it is likely to contain figures who represent points of view other than those of the main character. It may do this by editorializing in the text, or by depicting tacit witnesses on the fringes or in the foreground or background of the picture. Sometimes, the text will somewhat heavy-handedly ask the reader to look. In Rey's *Curious George*, a butterfly and a cat offer the disengaged viewpoint, not passing judgment as the narrator, in league with the 'man in the yellow hat', but smiling out at the reader, provoking our sympathy for George, for all living things, regardless of their moral aptitudes. Clement Hurd moves mice about the bedroom in *Goodnight Moon*. Even as early as Wilhelm Busch, we see animals in complicity with readers as the geese, backs to reader, gobble up the milled remains of Max and Moritz. From the grand final reception in Tibor Gergely's classic *Scuffy the Tugboat*, to that in Arnold Lobel's 'A Swim' or 'The Dream', the eye of the beholder in the text affords a vantage point for the wandering eye of the reader.[26]

As specific onlookers in the text tease us with their inside view, with what they see, we may ask ourselves, again, what indeed do we see? As Gombrich once pointed out, 'we are all inclined to judge pictures by what we *know* rather than by what we *see*.'[27] It is here that we may sketch out for further study the operation of certain graphic codes. These serve not so much to indicate the artist's command of the medium, or to demonstrate the artist's grasp of an ineffable beauty, as to enhance the reader's feeling comprehension of events and emotions. Graphic codes do not depend on the relation of objects to each other in a world outside the text; these we would call 'iconographic'.[28] The images of a child looking out of a window or of a boat winding its way down a watercourse belong to such inconographic codes. To be able to read a graphic code we must consider the disposition of objects on the page, the handling of line and colour, we must examine the 'presentational process'.[29] It would be misleading and destructive of the possibility of an 'open text' to say that within the graphic codes this particular gesture means one thing or another, regardless of the specific text. We must speak of 'dominances' and 'probabilities', to borrow from the language of de Beaugrande.[30] My intention in the following discussion is to toss out some leads, and to let each reader conduct research according to the demands of specific texts.

The codes of position, size and diminishing returns

The position of the subject on the page, what some might call the 'ham' factor, constitutes a code. It often matters whether the main character is depicted high or low on the page, in the centre or on the fringe, on the lefthand side or the right. Height on the page may be an indication of an ecstatic condition (as in *Curious George*) or dream-vision (as in Daugherty's *Andy and the Lion*) or a mark of social status or power, or of a positive self-image. Being low on the page is often by contrast a signal of low spirits, 'the pits', or of unfavourable social status. These figures may be strengthened or weakened depending on whether the character is centred or in the margin, large ('close-up') or small ('distanced') (we here introduce the code of size), or presented in one or in more than one scene on the same page (the code of 'diminishing returns'). The more frequently the same character is depicted on the same page, the less likely that character is to be in control of a situation, even if in the centre. Whenever Curious George is shown in a succession of vignettes on the same page or facing pages, he is probably having fun and about to lose his freedom. In such a succession of vignettes, those at the top of the page may signal a more competent character than those at the bottom. A character that is on the margin, 'distanced' or reduced in size on the page, and near the bottom will generally be understood to possess fewer advantages than the one that is large and centred. Large size alone is not a sufficient criterion for the reading of advantage; it may be a figure of an overblown ego.

As with the stage, it matters whether the actors are shown on the left or the right. A character shown on the left page is *likely* to be in a more secure, albeit potentially confined space than one shown on the right, who is likely to be moving into a situation of risk or adventure. The left-hand page will complete a thought, let us know that we can go on, that the thinking of the previous page is complete. In the *Story about Ping*, the duck family moves across the page to the right as they leave the safety of the boat in the morning, and boards the boat from right to left in the evening. When Ping finally returns from his wanderings, he moves up the plank to the right, not the left, as the boat has now become an adventure unto itself, a wise-eyed boat worth inhabiting, and no longer quite to be taken for granted.

Codes of perspective

Supplementing the codes of position, size and diminishing returns are those of perspective, in which we follow the presence or absence of horizon or horizontals, vanishing points, and contrasts between façades and depths. Where it has been present earlier, the sudden absence of a horizon, of a clear demarcation between 'above' and 'below' is likely to spell danger or trouble, as in Donald Carrick's illustration of Berniece Freschet's *Bear Mouse*, in which the stratified lines of the mouse's underground burrows and the snowline give way to an utterly white background as a hawk attacks the mouse. See also *The Story About Ping*: when the horizon disappears, Ping is about to get into trouble, to lose perspective. The play of the horizon can be complicated if there is a vanishing point, or if above the horizon there is sheer open space. Either complication may place the reader along with the character in a state of suspense. What lies 'beyond'? When Ping falls asleep in the bulrushes after losing track of his boat-home, or when he stands in shallow water, his boat-home in sight and a spanking in the offing, sheer open space covers the horizon.

A character located within a two-dimensional façade is likely to be less 'open-minded', less able to give imaginative scope to desire than one pictured within a three-dimensional 'depth'. In *Where the Wild Things Are*, the frustrated feelings of Max begin to find an outlet with the appearance of a window at the back; there is even a crescent moon, for more depth.

The codes of the frame and of the right and round

The code of the frame enables the reader to identify with a world inside and outside the story. Framed, the illustration provides a limited glimpse 'into' a world. Unframed, the illustration constitutes a total experience, the view from 'within'. *Where the Wild Things Are* demonstrates this point with considerable force, as Max's universe expands from the small, framed picture of himself in a room to the unframed doublespread of himself in the place where the wild things live. As the frame usually marks a limit beyond which text cannot go, or from which image cannot escape, we may associate a sense of violation or of the forbidden or of the miraculous with the breaking of the frame, as when the ocean-side tree spreads over the text as Max 'sailed off through night and day', or with the frame that blocks or screens out a part of the subject, as it does Petunia's head in her moment of extreme hubris, or at moments in which text suddenly intrudes itself into the picture, as in *Andy and the Lion*, when after 23 successive openings with text on the lefthand page and picture on the right, the text 'CAME' under the left side of a doublepage spread and 'OUT' under the righthand *underline* Andy's successful removal of the thorn.

I find it useful to relate the code of the frame to the code of round vs. rectilinear shapes. A character framed in a series of circular enclosures is more likely to be secure and content than one framed in a series of utterly rectangular objects. Often, an emphasis on rectangular shapes is coupled with a problem, or with an encounter with the disadvantages of discipline or civilized life. In the *Story About Ping*, Ping is held captive in an inverted basket, which appears on the page in broad bands at right-angles to one another.

One other aspect of the frame must be mentioned. The picturebook provides a temporal as well as a spatial frame. It has an opening and a closing page, a cover with two sides. What the front and back pages say is often mutually complementary, symmetrical even, as in *Curious George*, who begins and ends his story in a tree. And given the presence of the outer frame or covering, the 'heart' or 'core' of the book lies somewhere in its middle, in the wild things' wordless dance, or in the proliferation of verbal signs (Waber).

The codes of line and capillarity

The intensity of a character's experience may be represented by the thickness of thinness of lines, by their smoothness or jaggedness, by their sheer number or profusion or by their spareness, and by whether they run parallel to each other or at sharp angles. Thin, spare lines may suggest mobility and speed, thick, blurred or puffy lines, paralysis or a comfortable stasis. Jagged lines and those that run at sharp or odd angles to each other usually accompany troubled emotions or an endangered life, as when Ping fights for freedom from his captor in the water, or Bear Mouse eludes the diving hawk. Smooth and parallel lines, such as those of the junk Ping calls home, or of Bear Mouse's burrow suggest a settled, orderly world. What I call the code of capillarity refers to the presence or absence of capillary-like squiggles or bundles; an abundance of such marks often signals vitality or even a surfeit of energy, rendering the scene crowded, nervous, busy, as if each line were a living organism, part of a giant audience. Swabs of plain colour provide relief from such jungles of line.[31] It is interesting to watch the gradual progress towards a simple, painted backdrop in *Where the Wild Things Are*. Max begins his story in a room, the back wall of which is represented by myriad fine cross-hatchings. Draped over a line of tied handkerchiefs, a segmented or interrupted line, is a bedspread with a pattern of pink flowers. The cross-hatchings of the wall-covering, the knotted handkerchiefs, the pattern on the bedspread contribute to a high degree of capillarity, of nervous energy, as, of course, does the anger on Max's face. Once Max is shut up in his room three pages later, the cross-hatchings seem less complicated, and the top of the pink bedspread and the blue sky visible through the window show few traces of such capillarity. At the point a few pages on where Max has begun his moondance, the cross-hatched backdrop has disappeared, to be replaced by a smooth, yet white, speckled sky. Max has moved into a calm state from an anxious one, into a position of command from one of frustration.

The code of colour

While we may attribute colour-coding to factors outside the text, we should not overlook what colour can say inside the text. Apart from the traditional associations of certain colours with certain moods or feelings, and apart from the association of bright colours with exhilaration and discovery, and of dark colours with disappointment and confusion,[32] we need to be sensitive to colour as a linkage among different objects. In the *Story About Ping*, for example, the Yangtze and the uniforms of the Chinese fishermen are blue, the duck and the sunlight, yellow. Plunging into the depths of blue leads Ping into the clutches of the men in blue. Disobedience is associated with a blue captivity, freedom with yellow and white.

The graphic codes as we have outlined them above are interactive, simultaneous, though not always congruous with the codes of the verbal text, or of the presented world. As we have noted elsewhere,[33] at a glorious moment in *Curious George* in which George is depicted as central on the page, of medium size, associated with a round shape (the balloon) and contained within one, all indications of positive feelings fraught with uncertainty (it is the righthand page), the text tells us that George was 'afraid' and indeed George does hover high above the ground in that 'presented world'. But George is smiling broadly, confirming the message of the graphic code, unperturbed by the narrator's alarmism . . .

[Moebius then examines in detail Bernard Waber's *Ira Sleeps Over*]

Such a reading as this is never complete. Our hope is always that we will never read the same book twice in quite the same way. And that any reader will be willing to read picturebooks like *Ira Sleeps Over* over and over again. Soft and endearing as many picturebook characters may be, they exist in tougher environments than we might imagine, blank spaces of fear. It is up to us to discover their ways to meaning and form, to being-in-the world. Let us take them with us, not merely as the small fry charitable adults chuckle at, but as figures of our own dynamic confusion and search for order.

Notes

1 Do I speak only for myself? I wonder how many who enjoy picturebooks today discovered them not in the arcadia of childhood, but in the straits of early parenthood. The formation of our taste then would depend on a joint enterprise between parent and child, and not on our own preferences alone. We could speak

of 'households of taste'. For mine, then, the works of Beatrix Potter marked the beginning.

2 For some of the philosophical implications of such a process, Irving Massey's 'Words and Images: Harmony and Dissonance', *Georgia Review*, 34 (1980), pp. 375–95, provides a fine introduction. 'Thinking consists of a constant alternation between image-making and word-making' (p. 388).

3 In an interview, 'The Artist as Author: the Strength of the Double Vision', in Margaret Meek, Aidan Warlow and Griselda Barton (eds), *The Cool Web: The Patterns of Children's Reading* (New York: Atheneum, 1978), Maurice Sendak has remarked that 'in the United States we work to bring pictures and words together to achieve a wholeness in the book, which I was very surprised to find is not at all important in many European countries' (p. 252). Whether or not this view is representative, it is not reflected in the editorial practice of American anthologizers of children's books. In Judith Saltman (ed.), *Riverside Anthology of Children's Literature*, 6th edn (Boston: Houghton Mifflin, 1985), Steig's *Sylvester and the Magic Pebble* is reprinted with but a single illustration. In Francelia Butler (ed.), *Sharing Literature with Children: A Thematic Anthology* (New York: David McKay, 1977) Potter's 'The Tale of Two Bad Mice' appears as text alone.

4 See William Rubin (ed.), *Pablo Picasso: A Retrospective* (New York: Museum of Modern Art, 1980) and Yann le Pichon, *The World of Henri Rousseau*, tr. by Joachim Neugroschel (New York: Viking, 1982). In the Picasso volume, the editor notes (p. 13) that 'the photographs accompanying the chronology are intended to document events in Picasso's life'. In the Rousseau, le Pichon offers the following preliminary explanation (p. 19): 'Although slightly arbitrary, the thematic classification of Rousseau's works allows a better analysis of his biographical and iconographical inspiration. The illustrations are not always – indeed, may be anything but – the direct sources of his paintings. They are sometimes offered as indirect influences, as documents on Rousseau's ambience, sometimes ulterior, but as close as possible to the painter, his life, his mentality, the people surrounding him.'

5 Barbara Bader, *American Picturebooks; From Noah's Ark to the Beast Within* (New York: Macmillan, 1976), pp. 155, 316.

6 Cf. Massey, 'Words and Images', p. 376: 'Each act of vision is detached from other acts of vision; we do not see continuously. We see one thing, and then another. There is a closure in each experience of sight.' See also Roland Barthes, *S/Z*, tr. by Richard Miller (New York: Hill & Wang, 1974), p. 11: 'To read is to find meanings, and to find meanings is to name them; but these named meanings are swept toward other names; names call to each other, reassemble, and their grouping calls for further naming: I name, I unname, I rename: so the text passes: it is a nomination in the course of becoming, a tireless approximation, a metonymic labor.'

7 Bader, *American Picturebooks*, p. 359.

8 I wish to adopt Barthes' notion of the code as both a perspective of quotations and a force or voice, as he proposes in *S/Z*, pp. 20–1. In the ensuing discussion of 'presented world', I cheerfully and gratefully lift from the reading of *S/Z* notions that I find valuable in the reading of the picturebook.

9 Ariel Dorfman and Armand Mattelart, *How to Read Donald Duck*, tr. by David Kunzle (New York: International General, 1975), p. 31. This brilliantly argued book deserves a wider circulation.

10 In Lucy Robin, 'The Astonished Witness Disclosed: An Interview with Arnold Lobel', *Children's Literature in Education*, 15, 4 (1984), pp. 191–7, Lobel declares (p. 194), 'And yet children's books, the best of them, are not delightful.

My favourites, anyway, strike deep. The artists that do the best ones are able to make them delightful on one level, but that's just the whipped cream on top. Underneath there is something much more.'

11 For a more detailed summary, see Susan E. Meyer, *A Treasury of the Great Children's Book Illustrators* (New York: Abrams, 1983), pp. 37–8.

12 Bader, *American Picturebooks*, p. 289.

13 Ibid., p. 547.

14 Ibid., p. 322.

15 Meyer, *Treasury*, p. 43.

16 Ibid., p. 249.

17 Ibid., p. 256.

18 I follow Horst Ruthrof's distinction between 'presented world' and 'presentational process' as argued in *The Reader's Construction of Narrative* (London: Routledge & Kegan Paul, 1981).

19 For related insights into the workings of *Where the Wild Things Are* and other picturebooks, see Sonia Landes, 'Picturebooks as Literature', *Children's Literature Association Quarterly*, 10, 2 (1985), pp. 51–4. The issue reached me only after this essay had been completed. I am delighted to see confirmation, some of it uncanny, of ideas put forth here.

20 Whether or not young children can grasp the metaphorical significance of such a substitution is a matter of debate. See, for example, Ellen Winner, Anne K. Rosenteil and Howard Gardner, 'The Development of Metaphoric Understanding', *Developmental Psychology*, 12, 4 (1976), pp. 289–97; and Janice H. Dressel, 'Abstraction in Illustration: Is It Appropriate for Children?', *Children's Literature in Education*, 15, 2 (1984), pp. 103–12.

21 It is not my intention to read every picturebook narrative as a study in problem-solving. But in the many instances in which a picturebook character or community does have a problem, I find that the usual first remedy involves the manipulation of objects, to make the world a better place for the ego, etc. The book itself usually points to remedies beyond the concrete and factual.

22 Bader, *American Picturebooks*, p. 225; see also pp. 397–9.

23 See n. 18 above, and Charles Sarland's excellent 'Piaget, Blyton, and Story: Children's Play and the Reading Process', *Children's Literature in Education*, 16, 2 (1985), pp. 102–9.

24 Note the cover and the 17th opening of *Where the Wild Things Are*. Sendak's eclecticism is well known.

25 Observed by Barbara Kiefer in 'The Responses of Children in a Combination First/Second Grade to Picture Books in a Variety of Artistic Styles', *Journal of Research and Development in Education*, 16, 3 (1983), pp. 14–20, one young reader (p. 17) 'pointed out a tiny book lying on the floor in one double-page spread of Schulevitz's *Oh What a Noise* (1971). The book is less than one inch wide, yet Peter noticed that the title written on its spine was the same as the title of the book.'

26 Philippe Hamon, 'Pour un statut sémiologique du personnage', *Littérature*, 6 (1972), pp. 86–110, distinguishes for us (p. 95) 'une catégorie de *personnages-embrayeurs*', of characters who 'link us up' with what is happening in the text: 'Ils sont les marques de la présence en text de l'auteur, du lecteur, ou de leurs délégués . . .' See also Bader, *American Picturebooks*, p. 456.

27 E. H. Gombrich, *The Story of Art* (Oxford: Phaidon, 1966), p. 387.

28 To read inconographical codes, we need to know much more, often, than the text can tell us about symbolic usages. We acquire our knowledge of these figures from sources outside the text, from economic and political data, as Dorfman and

Mattelart do in their analysis of the inconography of Donald Duck, from the symbolism of ritual or dream, from mythical and literary sources, etc.

29 Elsewhere (Olga Richard, 'The Visual Language of the Picturebook', *Wilson Library Bulletin* 44, December, 1969, pp. 434–47) we are taught, after Gyorgy Kepes, to attend to 'the Elements of Art', namely 'color, shape, line, texture and the arrangement of these within a unified picture plane' (p. 436). But as in the 'Picturebooks: Stories for the Eye' chapter (pp. 167–8) of Saltman's *Riverside Anthology*, the purpose of such attention is, by providing a descriptive vocabulary, to help us appreciate the individual styles of different illustrators. The most elaborate of such approaches that I have seen is that of Ottilie Dinges, who offers an extensive 'grid' (*'Raster'*) for the linguistic and graphic analysis of picturebooks in 'Fragen über Fragen um das Bilderbuch – und eine Spielregel dazu/oder/ Hermeneutische Fragestellungen zu einer umfassenden Ästhetik and Didaktik des Bilderbuches', in Helmut Fischer and Reinhard Stach (eds), *Aspekte der Vermittlung von Jugend-literatur* (Essen: Arbeitskreis Das gute Jugendbuch e.V., 1980), pp. 63–9.

30 See Robert de Beaugrande and Wolfgang Dressler, *Introduction to Text Linguistics* (London: Longman, 1981), pp. xivff. *'Probabilistic* models are more adequate and realistic than *deterministic* ones . . . *Dominances* can offer more realistic classifications than can *strict categories.'*

31 Compare Meyer, *Treasury*, p. 30, for whom cross-hatching, a technical advance on the path towards a 'more truly realistic' method, is seen to render 'a semblance of modeling', with Landes, 'Picturebooks', p. 53, who can say of a section of *Where the Wild Things Are*, 'No borders, no limitations, and, within the pictures, the cross-hatching of reality has disappeared and all the straight lines have been transformed into nature's curves.'

32 In terms of the contrast of the colourful and the colourless, the picturebook has evolved an entire genre, one in which an opening of colour alternates with an opening without colour. For prime examples, see Rémy Charlip, *Fortunately, Unfortunately* (New York: Parent's Magazine, 1964); and Roger Duvoisin, *A for an Ark* (New York: Lothrop, 1952).

33 *'L'Enfant terrible Comes of Age'*, in Norman F. Kantor and Nathalia King (eds), *Notebooks in Cultural Analysis* (Durham, NC: Duke University Press, 1985), pp. 32–50.

Primary sources

Betty Boegehold/illustrations by Cyndy Szekeres, *Here's Pippa Again*, New York, Dell, 1975.

Margaret Wise Brown/illustrations by Clement Hurd, *Good Night Moon*, New York, Harper & Row, 1947.

Mary Chalmers, *Throw a Kiss, Harry*, New York, Harper & Row, 1958.

Gertrude Crampton/illustrations by Tibor Gergely, *Scuffy The Tugboat*, New York, Golden Press, 1946, 1955.

James Daugherty, *Andy and the Lion*, New York, Viking, 1938.

Roger Duvoisin, *Petunia*, New York, Knopf, 1950.

Marjorie Flack/illustrations by Kurt Wiese, *The Story About Ping*, New York, Viking, 1933.

Berniece Freschet/illustrations by Donald Carrick, *Bear Mouse*, New York, Scribner's, 1973.

Russell Hoban/illustrations by Garth Williams, *Bedtime for Frances*, New York, Harper & Row, 1960.

Arnold Lobel, 'A Swim', in *Frog and Toad Are Friends*, New York, Harper & Row, 1970, pp. 40–52.

Arnold Lobel, 'The Dream', in *Frog and Toad Together*, New York: Harper & Row, 1971–2, pp. 42–64.

A. A. Milne/illustrations by Ernest H. Shepard, *Winnie-the-Pooh*, New York, E. P. Dutton, 1926.

William Pene du Bois, *Bear Circus*, New York, Viking, 1971.

Beatrix Potter, *Mrs Tiggy-Winkle*, London, Frederick Warne, 1905.

H. A. Rey, *Curious George*, Boston, Houghton Mifflin, 1941.

Maurice Sendak, *Where the Wild Things Are*, New York, Harper & Row, 1963.

William Steig, *Sylvester and the Magic Pebble*, New York, Windmill/Simon & Schuster, 1969.

Bernard Waber, *The House on East 88th Street*, Boston, Houghton Mifflin, 1962.

Bernard Waber, *Lyle and the Birthday Party*, Boston, Houghton Mifflin, 1966.

Bernard Waber, *An Anteater Named Arthur*, Boston, Houghton Mifflin, 1967.

Bernard Waber, *Ira Sleeps Over*, Boston, Houghton Mifflin, 1972.

Bernard Waber, *Lyle Finds His Mother*, Boston, Houghton Mifflin, 1974.

18

THE IMPLIED VIEWER

Some speculations about what children's picture books invite readers to do and to be

Perry Nodelman

Source: *CREArTA* 1(1) (June 2000): 23–43.

Usually, when we talk about how picture books affect the children who read them, we talk about the form and content of specific books. We enthuse over how a particular set of pictures will delight them, or we think about whether they will be able to understand the visual style of an illustrator or the diction used in a particular text. We wonder if depictions of certain characters will encourage young readers to think in terms of gender stereotypes, or we worry about the morals they might derive from special tales. And of course, all of this is important. My own work as a scholar of picture books explores a range of ways in which individual writers can use semiotic and narrative codes in order to communicate specific meanings in individual books. I know, not only that these books do convey meanings, but that the meanings they convey are subtle and wide-ranging. Furthermore, I'm convinced that children can access these meanings in all their complexity, and both take pleasure and gain knowledge from doing so. We need only be willing to teach them the appropriate interpretive strategies.

But in focussing on these matters, I've ignored a number of ways in which picture books might affect child readers simply by virtue of the fact that they *are* picture books. The mere act of looking at the pictures in this particular kind of book requires a range of assumptions about it and attitudes towards it before one can even begin to make any sense out of it or gain any pleasure from it.

These attitudes and assumptions have profound implications. They help to shape our ideas about why we look at things (both pictures and the real objects they represent), and what in fact, the visible world is: what it is for, what it does, what it owes to us and what we owe to it. And in all these ways, the basic skills required for us to be able to respond as expected to any picture book contribute to our sense of who we are and why we are that way. In what follows, I consider what it means to be a viewer of children's picture books. What do these books invite one to be, or to do, or to think?

The assumptions upon which I base my exploration emerge from semiotic theory, which describes systems of *signs*: symbolic ways of communicating information.[1] According to Marshall Blonsky, "The semiotic 'head,' or eye, see the world as an immense message, replete with signs that can and do deceive us and lie about the world's condition" (1985, p.vii). While words and pictures are different media and communicate different things in different ways, both are sign systems and share the basic qualities of sign systems.

Signs tend to be arbitrary. They are representations of other things which they don't necessarily resemble. There's no reason, for instance, that a red light should signify the need to stop your car. It might just have well been a purple light, or a loud siren. Consequently, signs and the systems they form can communicate successfully only to those already in possession of the knowledge required to make the not-necessarily-obvious connections between the sign and what it signifies. In an important sense, and merely in existing and being used, the signs themselves imply someone capable of making the expected sense out of them. A red traffic light conveys, not only the idea of danger, but also the conviction that someone exists outside itself capable of responding to it as intended – someone who will be able to decipher it successfully enough to be thinking about stopping.

Reader response critics speak of the "implied reader" of a text – a person in possession of the knowledge and the methodology of thinking about signs that allow an understanding of the text more or less as its speaker or writer intended it.[2] Pictures, equally, can be spoken of in terms of their implied *viewer* – someone in possession of the knowledge and methodology of thinking about them that allows an understanding of the picture more or less as its creator intended it.

Pictures tend to be less arbitrary than written signs. A photograph of a cat resembles an actual cat far more obviously than do the letters *C A T*, so that it may seem a little less obvious that the implied viewer of a picture requires special knowledge in order to understand it. It is, nevertheless, true. Anthropological literature describing early contact with groups unfamiliar with contemporary Euro-American civilisation frequently contain reports of people without previous knowledge of photographs or representational drawings who could make little sense of the examples they were shown.[3] Meanwhile, my own college-level students, unfamiliar with the conventions of expressionist art as used in, for instance, Diaz' illustrations for Eve Bunting's children's story *Smoky Night*, often ask me why the characters' faces are blue or purple. Not knowing the sign system – not being the viewer these pictures imply – they interpret the information the sign system offers about emotional states of mind incorrectly, as literal information about the actually visible world.

The knowledge and the assumptions about the world and about people expected of both implied readers and implied viewers move well beyond just technical questions about knowing how to decipher a particular kind of sign or convention or image. They also include a range of assumptions about the reality the signs represent. Viewers won't be able to think about what a picture of a cat represents if they don't know what an actual cat is. They won't be able to figure out that the cat is a friendly one if they don't know how to interpret the shape of its mouth as drawn by the artist and identify it with a human smile, or that it is a poor cat if they don't understand the convention that clothing with patches sewn on in various places signifies the wearer's poverty, or that it is a French cat because of the beret it is shown to be wearing.

Furthermore, the conventions of visual representation add further information for a viewer about how to understand or make sense of the real objects depicted. Imagine, for a moment, a picture of a cat being thrown from a second-story window. Someone knowledgeable about the significations of certain styles of visual depiction will understand that laughter is the appropriate response if the picture is in a cartoon style, alarm if the picture is in a traditionally representational style, wonder if the picture is in a dream-like surrealistic style. The conventional means by which an artist or illustrator represents objects for us convey, not just the idea or the appearance of the objects, but also, how we should think about and respond to those objects.

Consequently, one of the effects for children of looking at pictures and picture books – particularly in the company of someone, a parent or a teacher or another child, who already understands the conventions of viewing them – is to make a real viewer resemble an implied one. Once a knowledgeable viewer gives us some ideas about questions to ask about and things to look for in pictures, the pictures themselves contain the information that will allow us to make sense of them in the terms the illustrator intended. Pictures thus encourage us to become the viewers they imply. They partake of what theorists of ideology call the construction of subjectivity – the ways in which the culture we exist in encourages us to think about who we are and the significance of what we think and feel and do.[4] If we come to understand that the cartoon of a cat is supposed to be funny, and we find ourselves actually looking at the picture and laughing at it, we have become constructed by the picture as subjects with a particular understanding of when laughter is appropriate – an understanding we share with others who have accepted the convention that this particular style of visual depiction implies comedy and requests laughter. In other words, and paradoxically, we have accepted as an understanding of who we are in our most essential and individual separate selves something that identifies us with the values and understanding of our larger group.

All of this suggests the potential danger of pictures and texts. The readers and viewers they imply might not be people we approve of. The subjectivity they work to construct might not be a subjectivity we would wish for our children or ourselves.

And indeed, that is exactly the case in terms of a wide range of adult responses to specific children's books. As I suggested earlier, we worry about the messages being given or the gender assumptions texts are making, and so on – and that we do so simply asserts the degree to which we worry about what the readers and viewers texts and pictures imply and the subjectivity they construct. Fortunately, there are a number of defences we can take against these specific acts of construction. We can simply (and, I think, dangerously) keep our children away from the books that we worry about – not buy them for our libraries, not allow children access to them at all. We can, just as simply, (and, I think, just as dangerously), assume that children naturally respond to texts in a wide variety of different ways, that they are what John Fiske, speaking of texts of popular culture, identifies as "active" reader/viewers and that they participate in the meaning – making process in ways that free them from the repressive intentions of texts, so that we simply needn't worry about what the texts imply their readers should be and do.[5] Or we can, with more effort (and, I personally think, more productively), provide children with the ability to think critically about what they read and view – to become more active readers than they might already be, to be aware of how texts work to influence them and thus resist the negative influences.

But as I said earlier, my focus here is not on the specific content of particular books, but on the viewer implied by *any* picture in *every* picture book. Unless we want to deprive children of books altogether, this we cannot avoid. That makes it all the more important to become aware of the nature of this generalised viewer. I will return to these matters after a look at what that nature is.

Let me begin by exploring my conviction that it exists at all. Do all picture books, just by virtue of being picture books, imply specific qualities or forms of knowledge or attitudes or assumptions in their viewers? Why might they?

One reason they might is suggested by Marshall McLuhan's decidedly unfashionable but still stimulating ideas about the ways in which media of communication shape the meanings of their content and the ways in which audiences respond to that content, famously formulated as "the medium is the message." According to McLuhan, ". . . any medium has the power of imposing its own assumptions on the unwary. Prediction and control consist in avoiding this subliminal state of Narcissus trance. But the greatest aid to this end is simply in knowing that the spell can occur immediately upon contact, as in the first bars of melody" (1965, p.15). We make assumptions along these lines when we talk about TV turning its viewers into couch potatoes, without reference to the actual content of the programming. While McLuhan's survey of the implications of various media in *Understanding*

Media doesn't cover children's picture books, it does allow the possibility that these books do work to impose "assumptions on the unwary" just by virtue of what they are.

So what might those assumptions be, and what do they suggest about the inherent basic nature of an implied reader/viewer? Let me outline some.

I begin with some qualities picture books share with other forms of children's literature. The implied reader/viewer is a child – a brutally obvious fact, perhaps, but the obviousness masks a whole realm of fascinating assumptions about what children are or should be. While different children's picture books make different assumptions about their readers, all children's picture books make the common assumption that their readers *are* children. They take it for granted that the mere fact of their implied readers' age means those readers have qualities unlike older human beings and like each other, qualities that require the existence of a certain kind of book to suit their needs *as* children. For much of human history in most cultures, no such thing as a children's picture book existed – in part, presumably, because no such thing as a child in need of that specific sort of book existed. So the existence of children's picture books implies the existence of children as a specific, definable, and necessarily defined sub-category of being human.

Furthermore, the child who is the implied reader/viewer of any children's picture book must *know* that – or at least be in the process of learning it, becoming conscious of the ways in which he or she is childlike, understanding what it means to be a child and understanding it to be important knowledge. Before you can choose to read a picture book or ask to have it read to you, you have to assume that you might in fact be a potential member of its intended audience. Parents and others often work to foster exactly that assumption in children: "Here's a book just for you!" Children who accept that such a book *is* for someone just like them then understand that they *are* children.

Nor is being a child simply a matter of being young. It is a matter of having certain abilities or tastes or interests – the abilities, tastes and interests implied by the style, subject, and level of difficulty of the book which now invites readers to imagine themselves as the specific audience it seeks. They are being encouraged to think of themselves as having these needs or tastes or interests not because they were born with them or because their parents have them, but simply by virtue of the fact that they *are* children, and therefore, childlike in the way the book implies children are.

In addition to helping children to think of themselves as being children, the books also encourage them to understand that the category "children" is an exceedingly important one, a key issue always operative and never to be forgotten in their relationships with other people, both adults and other children. We are a culture in which children as well as adults know that being a child means knowing that one is a child and therefore entitled to or expected to behave in certain ways defined as childlike.

Those ways are subtle and complicated – the books we offer children offer a range of different ways of being childlike. Picture books, for instance, imply an audience of *younger* children, and help children to understand that early childhood is a time when stories must be told in short and simple texts and when pictures are necessary to make sense of the words. They imply that early childhood is different in quality from later childhood, when longer books with fewer pictures become possible and appropriate. They imply, in other words, an idea of childhood as a time of development through a series of discrete stages: the idea that people get increasingly complicated as they mature.

In order to become more complicated one must start out being less complicated. Obviously, then, many of the qualities we define as childlike involve ways in which younger children are more limited than older children, and all children are more limited than adults – less wise, less capable, more prone to self-indulgence and more in need of certain kinds of adult control and regulation. Children who accept their resemblance to the implied child reader/ viewers of children's picture books have been given the freedom to be less wise and more self-indulgent that adults are often allowed to be.

At the same time, though, they have been invited to understand how much their limitations force adults to control and regulate and supervise them. The implied reader/viewer of picture books knows, not just that the books are intended for specifically childlike readers, but also, that they are provided for those childlike readers, not by other children, but by adults, adults with the best interests of children in mind. The mere existence of picture books then implies a world organized so that children need and can depend on benevolent adult intervention in, and supervision of, all aspects of their lives – including their imaginative lives as influenced by the content of children's books. The books suggest in merely being there the entire social structure that creates and shapes the nature of childhood as a position of dependency for children in our culture.

The child reader/viewers I have just been describing are complex and ambivalent, caught in a complex field of forces, pulled powerfully in opposite directions. On the one hand, they are childishly free of adult standards of behaviour, allowably amoral or anarchic since these are "childlike" qualities. On the other hand, though, because they are childlike they must accept adult supervision and control. On the one hand, they are childishly innocent; on the other, they *know* they are childishly innocent, have been taught to think of themselves as such, and know what childish innocence allows them – a form of knowledge that surely qualifies and undermines the innocence, since now the intuitiveness and spontaneity that define innocence are not actually intuitive and spontaneous but instead, it seems, performed, enacted by an actor who has learned to play it in order to satisfy adult expectations. This implied child reader/viewer is not so simple or straightforward or unlearned as our clichés about the childlike might suggest.

The learning the implied reader/viewer possesses has yet other dimensions. More generally, the implied reader/viewer of children's picture books, like the readers of all books, understands some basic conventions about books. Books have a front and a back, a top and a bottom. The words and pictures on the cover are separate from but related to the actual story itself, which is found inside. The story, at least in books in the English language, emerges when a reader begins at what we call the front (i.e., with the bound margin on our left) and moves consecutively through the pages, and from left to right and then top to bottom on each double-paged spread.

A reader/viewer who knows all this and acts on it appreciates some basic principles of convention and order, and has a willingness to adhere to them. The mere fact that a child can leaf through a book in the right order in order to perceive a narrative within it then means that the child has come to understand something about the rules and patterns that allow for social intercourse and communication. We like to talk about children being free and spontaneous and creative. The spontaneity and creativity of any child who knows and makes use of these basic facts about books has been qualified by and governed by adults. Reading a book is inherently an act that moves a reader/viewer beyond individual isolation and the freedom of anarchy. A child who knows which way is up and reads books with that way up is on the way to becoming a good citizen in a shared social reality.

It is ironic, then, that many children's books seem to be what Alison Lurie calls "subversive" – apparently celebratory of spontaneity and imagination and the defiance of adult values and assumptions. According to Lurie, "the great subversive works of children's literature mock current assumptions and express the imaginative, unconventional, noncommercial view of the world in its simplest and purest form" (1990, p.xi). But they can be so only for readers who have become conventional enough to respond to and make sense of the works more or less as intended. The supposed subversiveness emerges only once a safely conventional context has been established – and that, surely, dissipates any real danger to conventional values.

I spoke earlier of a child exploring books in a certain sequence in order to discover the narratives within them. The implied reader-viewer of these books knows about narrative – knows what a story is. Most picture books tend to be stories, and imply a reader who knows and takes pleasure in what a story is, in what it does and how it operates. Once more, this reader both knows and likes the satisfactions of order – in this case, the ways in which narratives organize events into a sequential cause-and-effect pattern and bring about a unified sense of completeness and closure that gives meaning to actions and events. The ability to take pleasure in these organizations of experience imply a more general commitment to meaning and order, and a flight from the spontaneity and freedom of random anarchy that confirms the ways in which picture books bind readers to their communities. As I suggested before, only once this binding has occurred can an indulgence in a safely contained and now merely fictional spontaneity and anarchy be allowed. Once more, the "childlike" becomes possible (and allowable for children) only within the context of an acceptance of an adult construction of reality which dissipates the actual subversiveness of anti-social behaviour.

An acceptance of the patterns of narrative also binds children to history, and perhaps to their very sense of what they are as individual beings. The master pattern of narrative – the sequence in which a moment defined as a beginning leads to a middle and eventually to an end – itself implies the idea that events can be usefully and satisfactorily explained in terms of what caused them and how they then lead to others. That concept not only organizes time's passage, but tends to become the shape by which we understand who we are. The idea that one can understand events in terms of their place in a chronological sequence of events is the basis of all developmental views of things in general. The idea that one can understand oneself by figuring out how previous events helped to shape one is central to our current sense of what our individual personalities and very beings are. Psychoanalysis, for instance, finds the sources and meanings of adult behaviour in the hidden events of childhood; and I have already spoken of how age-related theories of development encourage both adults and children to think of children as being too old for certain books they might once have enjoyed, or too young for books they will one day get to. Knowing how to decode narrative structures places us in history and makes us historians, of the world and of ourselves.

Furthermore, and equally important: a child who has that knowledge and takes pleasure in it – examines books in the order intended, seeks out stories and is satisfied by their sequencing and closure – has become a consumer. The audience picture books imply, merely in offering certain forms of experience, are people who expect the reward of a certain kind of experience in return for a special kind of effort. Merely in being and in purporting to be attractive, picture books hold out the promise of pleasure and profit to those willing to consume them.

That books exist to offer readers pleasure tells readers that they deserve to, even need to, be pleased. In other words: that the book exists to fulfil a need implies that the need exists that then must be fulfilled and can rightfully be fulfilled. In different times and places, children were not encouraged to seek enjoyment in stories and pictures or even, in more general terms, to think of themselves as people with a need or a right to indulge these forms of pleasure. That so many picture books exist, that they are often so opulently illustrated and designed, and that we encourage children to take pleasure in the delights they offer and to seek out yet more books and get more pleasure from them without any need to feel guilty about it – all these are evidence of the extent to which picture books imply an entire economy of consumption driven by satisfying one's urge to please oneself in certain ways understood to be satisfying.

Furthermore, the mere fact that picture books exist is flattering for their intended audiences. The books are often sumptuous, complex, expensive – and they tend to be found in sizeable collections, in stores and libraries and even moderately well-off homes, for clearly, having just one is not enough, and the more the better. Indeed, current pedagogical theory often highlights the importance of providing children with a spectrum of possibilities from which to make choices and thus develop their individual tastes and values. The message is clear: All of this is being done for you, child reader, to teach *you*, to please *you*, to make *you* happy, to help *you* be the best you can be. That means you and your right to take pleasure are important, that pleasing you has been an aspiration of a whole range of people, writers and illustrators and publishers and librarians and parents. To become the implied reader/viewer of these elaborate productions is, inevitably, to develop a strong sense of one's worth and one's desert – to understand that one does indeed deserve such elaborate attention and that wanting and getting what one wants are good things.

Meanwhile, however, the implied reader/viewer also understands that picture books don't just please: they also teach. One reads them to learn from them, to become a different and better version of oneself. In yet one more sense, then, these books allow pleasure only in order to co-opt it and undermine it: you are being pleased, and you are allowed to be pleased; but you are allowed only within the context of goals of self-improvement, and so just to be pleased is not enough. You may take pleasure only if you also understand how shallow it is to want pleasure in and for itself, and are prepared to move beyond it.

Often, in fact, children's books contain stories which replicate this allowing and undermining of pleasure, and work to make their readers feel guilty about the very pleasures they offer. These stories ask children to identify with characters who are creative or spontaneous or adventurous (and, perhaps, subversive), first, in order to enjoy the delights of adventurousness and spontaneity, and second, in order to learn how dangerous adventurousness and spontaneity are. The implied viewer of such books develops two intriguingly contradictory ideas about pleasure: it's good and bad, healthful and dangerous, harmless and harmful.

The two ideas tend to occur sequentially in texts – first the delightful indulgence in pleasure, then the dangerous consequences. But since so many books follow this pattern, a child reader of a series of children's books is taken back to the first stage and then moves on to the second again and again. The reader/viewer implied by a number of children's picture books taken together is, then, like the comically deficient characters on many American TV situation comedies, who delightfully indulge their vice or folly and then become aware of how badly they have behaved and learn to move beyond it in each episode, and then, at the start of the next episode, are always right back where they started, being vicious or foolish in the same delightful old way. These implied reader-viewers move back and forth between childlike folly and adult wisdom, between delightful subversiveness and sane conventionality, but never seem to completely give up one for the other. These reader/viewers are, once more, complex and ambivalent.

Part of the complexity is a consciousness of incompleteness – of not being *finished* yet. That there is a lesson to learn means that you have not yet learned it – that you are not yet all you can be or ought to be. The incompleteness is confirmed by the master narratives of development I discussed earlier. The ways in which our thinking about how people become what they are make childhood the crucible in which adult person-alities are shaped – and thus, a mere stage along the way to a more complete being. A child is, then, malleable, a subject-in-progress, a person in the making but not yet quite made. Such beings exist in time, and might change with it – indeed, must change, must always enter the next stage, must keep on moving forward. Their sense of self must be qualified by the knowledge that they are not yet the selves they should be and ideally ought to hope they will be.

Note, once more, the ambivalence. On the one hand, this magnificent book exists for *me* to enjoy: damn, I'm good. On the other hand, the book is about how someone like me turns out to be wrong. Or maybe it's just about things I don't know yet and obviously need to know before I can be a whole person. Damn, I'm not quite good enough yet.

But before becoming too depressed by the confusion of all this, I have to acknowledge that it is my own character as a reader – and also, I egocen-trically suspect, the character of the readers implied by most literary texts. These readers hope to be gratified by the text's ability to please the people they already are, *and* they want to move past pleasure, to be unsettled by knowledge that there are new things to know, to learn to be different and better from it. I might go even further, and say that this is, perhaps, the ambivalent and eternally divided character demanded of all members in good standing of democratic societies, which gives us the freedom to be ourselves and please ourselves only in return for learning and acting on the knowledge that our freedom must always take place within the context of, and be constrained by, the needs of other individuals and of the whole communities to which we belong. The basic assumptions of children's picture books about their readers help to accommodate the readers to the opposing pulls of thoughtless (and possibly subversive) self-satisfaction and communal understanding and the constraint of individual desire it inevitably results in that will define their lives as adults.

It appears to be no accident, then, that children's literature in general and children's picture books in particular have come to exist specifically and mainly in the context of middle-class-dominated western democracies, and help to create subjects comfortable with the nature of middle-class-dominated western democracies as they have developed within the last few centuries. It is hard to imagine a society of pure egotists or one that was totally repressive of individual desire developing a form so determined both to gratify and to constrain, so unwilling to give up either pole of this bilateral ambivalence in the subjects it constructs. (And note how these two impossible extremes, the totally repressible subject and the totally irrepressible one, are mirrored in the two ideas about child reader/viewers I rejected earlier – the totally impressionable subject implied by censors, the safely active meaning-makers postulated by theorists like Fiske. Each view equally fails to account for the inevitable pull towards the other in the culture that we occupy and that occupies us.)

So far, the reader/viewer I've been describing is the one implied by children's books in general. Now I'd like to look at some qualities more specifically related to picture books.

Picture books contain pictures, and pictures imply a specific sort of viewer merely in being pictures, a viewer unlike the reader implied by the words of a text. Compared to printed words, for instance, they offer a relatively dense sensuous experience. Pictures contain textures, colours, shapes, lines – a variety of things for the eye to respond to and he pleased by, for these aspects of pictures are and are meant to be pleasing in and for themselves, without reference to the meanings or objects they have been made to represent. To look at, say, a patch of intense red is sensuously arousing without any reference to the apple or fire truck the patch of red might be representing in a particular picture.

Of course, the colours and lines and shapes in pictures book do represent other things – the red patch is indeed an apple or a fire truck, not just a patch of red. As I said earlier, pictures operate as a system of signs, and as I try to show in my book *Words About Pictures*, every aspect of them helps to convey specific meanings to knowledgeable viewers. Their implied viewer knows these signs, has a conscious or unconscious awareness of how they allow lines and colours on a flat page to convey ideas of people and place and things. Such an implied viewer is caught up in and constrained by the cultural understandings that make the visible world meaningful. And as Fredric Jameson suggests, "as sight becomes a separate activity in its own right, it acquires new objects that are themselves the product of a process of abstraction and rationalisation which strips the experience of the concrete of such attributes as colour, spatial depth, texture and the like . . ." (1981, p.63). To interpret sensuous information as a sign is to deflect attention from it as a purely sensuous experience.

Nevertheless, the sensuous information which contains and conveys abstracted and rationalised cultural knowledge has no choice but to remain, and to convey itself all the while it is conveying the cultural knowledge. The patch of red is still, whatever it represents, a patch of red. In order to understand what it represents, the implied viewer has no choice but to see it and to respond to it in and for itself as well as in terms of what it has come to represent. According to the psychoanalytical theorist Julia Kristeva, that represents a path to liberation from the constraint of being constructed as a specific kind of subject placed within specific cultural values: "it is through colour – colours – that the subject escapes its alienation within a code (representational, ideological, symbolic and so forth) that it, as a conscious subject, accepts . . . The chromatic apparatus, like rhythm in language, thus involves a shattering of meaning and its subject into a scale of difference" (1980, p.221). So, too, it seems, do lines and shapes and textures shatter meanings merely by insisting on being themselves. The very act of observing that which contains and conveys meanings therefore undermines the meanings, just as the meanings undermine the pure sensations of the containers in and for themselves. The implied viewer, who can and must both respond to the containers and perceive the meaning they contain, is, once more, pulled in two ways, towards the meaningful and communal and constraining on the one hand and towards the purely sensuous and pleasurable and unconstrainedly anti-meaningful on the other. The implied viewer of picture books is a divided subject.

The division is confirmed by the fact that picture books contain both words and pictures. The viewer they imply knows not only what kind of information to expect from each of these two different media, each one requiring from those who would make sense of them a different set of assumptions, but also, how to put the information together into a whole. This includes some fairly basic strategies of meaning-making, such as, for instance, assuming that the house we see in a picture accompanying a text about a house is indeed the house the text mentions – that despite the fact we have two different signs for it in two different sign systems, there is just one house. It also includes somewhat more sophisticated strategies, such as guessing from the appearance of the house in the illustration information about its age, its possible location in time or space as implied by its architectural style, the relative degree of wealth of those who live in it, the possibility of someone being content to live in such a dwelling. The implied reader/viewer also knows how to apply all this visual information to the situation outlined by a text – interpret the words and their implications in the light of information provided by a perusal of the pictures. Such a reader/viewer then knows how to be analytical, how to compare and combine information from different sources, how to make the implied sort of sense of a complex field of possibilities, how to solve a puzzle (and to enjoy solving it). Children encouraged to become such reader/viewers are becoming meaning-makers, actively engaged in solving the puzzles.

But there is, once more, a paradox, and a division: the mastery they develop as puzzle solvers masters them, as they increasingly become able to realise solutions to the puzzles that were the ones intended by the author and illustrator, become increasingly aligned with the subject the text intends to construct.

Meanwhile, the mere act of looking at both the words and the pictures in picture books in order to make meaning out of them adds yet a further dimension to the implied reader/viewer. In order to understand both the words and the pictures, we need to position ourselves at some distance away from them: we can't make anything like the sense an author might have intended out of the words and/or illustrator out of the picture with our noses pressed firmly against the books they appear in. Marshall McLuhan suggests that "Psychically the printed book, an extension of the visual faculty, intensified perspective and the fixed point of view" (1965, p.172). If that is true – and literally speaking, it is – pictures, even more intimately connected with the visual faculty, must do something similar. Both, then, require reader/viewers to distance themselves from what they observe in order to observe it in what they will then consider to be a meaningful and accurate manner. Such reader/viewers will tend to trust the value and validity of the detached, isolated point of view – and tend to mistrust the value and validity of what they perceive by other means – by touch, for instance. They have become gazers; I will say more shortly about the economy of the gaze and the character of he or she who gazes.

Younger children who have not yet developed that trust in the gaze often tend to scan picture books, giving equal attention to all parts of the picture plane – and they often find interesting or unexpected details that more experienced viewers miss completely. Experienced viewers, who know how to stand back and read the information in a picture that suggests perspective, and consequently, a focus on certain objects within it under-stood to be central – what the picture is "really" about – tend to interpret the discoveries of inexperienced, unfixed scanners as errors: they themselves know the one right way to view.

And the right way, merely in existing and in being right, establishes hierarchies, priorities, centres and margins. The act of looking at a picture and establishing which of the group of visual objects it depicts is actually its subject – the person, or the cat on the person's lap, or the lamp on the table beside the person, or the flower in the drapery in the background – con-structs the reader/viewer as conscious of and operating within the context of such hierarchies. Such a subject views the world politically: children who can read and enjoy picture books have become politic beings, conscious of and seeking out the inevitably varying dispositions of power and interest and attention in the world around them.

Yet they are, also, individuals with a consciousness of their individuality, their separateness from and difference from the world around them. According to Walter J. Ong, oral storytelling, which takes place in the context of a shared experience as many listeners become an audience, tends to create communities. Cultures in which oral storytelling predominates imply and therefore, presumably, tend to consist of people who think of them-selves primarily in terms of their place in the community as a whole, and who take little interest in the subtle distinctions that make them unique or just different from others. In order to read a printed book, on the other hand, one must separate oneself from the community, have a private experience in isolation from others. Consequently, cultures with print imply and therefore, presumably, tend to develop individuals conscious of and interested in their separation from and differences from each other.

Picture books can and do offer that isolated and individuality-building sort of experience to solitary reader/viewers. But the books are often read by adults to children singly or in groups, and thus can also support more communal forms of experience and self-perception. Furthermore, the pictures can be viewed by more than one person at a time, although, of course, all the viewers must be positioned in front of the pictures and at an appropriate distance from them in order to make something like the implied sense out of them. So picture books support the relatively un-self-conscious community of oral cultures as well as the self-absorbed isolation of books consisting of nothing but print and read privately. They suggest, once more, a compromise between the self and the communal, possibly even an ambivalent pull in both directions. Is the story just for you alone, or for you as a member of a group? Are you most significantly yourself, or a part of a community? Once more, a picture book viewer must feel both pulls at once – possess a divided subjectivity.

Finally, the division is confirmed yet again by the human figures who appear in the picture in picture books, and the relationships those figures imply between themselves and those who view them. Like the actors in a play or a movie, they are there to be looked at. In many books they even smile out at us, apparently conscious of and happy about the presence of viewers. Whether they acknowledge their position or not, these figures share in a somewhat less aggressive form the invitation to voyeurism that John Berger discovers in both contemporary pin-up photographs and traditional European paintings of nudes. Their implied viewer of all these pictures is a peeping Tom with the right to peep, to linger over details, to enjoy and interpret and make judgements about it. He or she is a person of great power in relation to that which he or she views.

In the depictions of nude adults Berger talks about, the implied viewer is someone quite different from the person being viewed: a male rather than a female, probably a clothed male rather than a naked one (such clothed males sometimes even appear in famous painting of naked women, looking at the women who look out of the painting at us as we view it), and specifically a male with the right to view. As Berger suggests, then, the person in the picture is defined in a power relationship with the viewer: men have the right to look, the power to hold what they see in their gaze; women are primarily that which men have the right to look at, a possession, something whose primary duty is to look good and to be seen. The nude and its implied viewer then sum up a power dynamic that defines what was the traditional relationship of men and women in the European civilisation that produced such paintings. Indeed, a sizeable feminist discourse based in the psychoanalytical theories of Jacques Lacan talks about women and others becoming "subject to the gaze" – at the mercy of a more powerful being whose power is defined by the right and ability to stand at some distance from them and view them. In learning to become the implied viewer of picture books, children simultaneously learn to identify with the powerful gazer, and to subject others to their gaze. They learn to be in charge.

In picture books, however, the viewer and the viewee, the gazer and the gazed at, are, in some important sense, the same person. A child views a child who represents him or herself, for we encourage children to see themselves in terms of the characters represented in picture book stories – to identify with them in order to learn from their stories. If children are meant to see themselves in these pictures, then they must imagine themselves as having the power to gaze at themselves, and to see themselves as depicted. On the one hand, they have the power of the gaze. On the other hand, they are subjected to a gaze – which is, strangely, their own gaze.

In fact, picture books offer a repetition of the moment Lacan defines as the mirror stage; that moment in infancy in which a child identifies itself with its image in a mirror. At this point, the child, who previously lived in a seamless universe and made no distinction between itself and other things, develops an ego, a sense of self, and does so by realising that there are things outside it, such as the space around its image in the mirror. The child perceives it exists as a separate self only inside a context which is larger than itself, and which makes it feel small in relation to it. Once we identify ourselves with the smaller versions of ourselves we see in the mirror, therefore, we are always conscious of ourselves as diminished, lacking a wholeness we once had, eternally striving for it and never achieving it. The image constrains and constricts us – as smaller-than-life representations of children in picture books construct child viewers who identify with them, as the safely contained representations of subversive anarchy in children's books contain children within adults ideas of the childlike.

Inevitably, furthermore, to be conscious of oneself in terms of the imagery of mirrors is to be divided. Lacan speaks of "the very bipolar nature of all subjectivity" (1977, p.10). A self is both that which thinks or views, the separate detached consciousness, and that which is being viewed or thought about. I am that which sees myself as this: in demanding and therefore confirming this relationship in the number of ways I have been describing, picture books play their part in establishing what Lacan calls "an alienating identity" (p.4) built on what is only an "illusion of autonomy" (p.6). We are only what the pictures have encouraged us to believe ourselves to be – and inevitably sense how incomplete and illusory that is. We are free and not free, autonomous and constrained, isolated and enmeshed.

But of course, that can happen only for those whose subjectivity has been constructed as the books invite. A child inexperienced in the language of pictures might, for instance, look at a serious representational picture of the falling cat and laugh, or at a cartoon picture and cry – or even look at a picture of a child and not identify with it. Indeed, inexperienced viewers often have exactly this sort of unintended response – one that an illustrator who worked hard to convey specific information would probably view as inaccurate. Meanwhile, children with the knowledge and experience to view as implied might consciously or unconsciously refuse to do so, might actively participate in making a different meaning that implies a different sense of their own subjectivity. These possibilities raise an important question about the argument I have made here. How *do* young, inexperienced viewers look at pictures? Are they in fact the viewers the pictures in picture books imply?

I believe either that they are, or that they are in the process of learning to become so. Theorists like Claude Levi-Strauss teach us that all artifacts of a culture manifest and replicate their basic structures – that each of the artifacts contain a little or has some contrapuntal but still supportive relationship to the central meanings and values of the culture.[6] As artifacts of our own culture, picture books require and help to construct readers and viewers who will take their place in that culture. That place may appear to be oppositional to its central concerns, but if it's possible to take it publicly, and recommended as a desirable position to take by those ensconced centrally or marginally within the culture, then the apparent opposition is bound to turn out to be just another way of supporting those central concerns. No other subjectivity is possible for the sane members of such a culture but some version of the form of subjectivity picture books help to construct.

If that's true – and I find it hard to understand how it could not be true – then the sort of active participator in meaning-making postulated by Fiske would have to turn out to be less free from the constraints of our culture than might first appear. According to Fiske, his approach,

Instead of concentrating on the omnipresent, insidious practices of the dominant ideology . . . , attempts to understand the everyday resistances and evasions that make ideology work so hard and so insistently to maintain itself and its values. This approach . . . is essentially optimistic, for it finds in the vigour and vitality of the people evidence of the possibility of social change and of the motivation to drive it.

(1989, p.20–21)

I accept the possibility of resistance, deny the likelihood that the change it allows actually threatens the dominant ideology in any serious way. A community that conceives of itself as a site of freedom for its members has to allow resistance to its dominant values – and obviously, has to do so in ways that prevent any real shift in those values or the power structure they support. The kinds of alternative meaning-making Fiske describes are best understood, I think, as allowable divergences from dominant values, allowable because they don't actually in any serious way threaten the dominance of those values. The most central and most paradoxical of those values is the idea that each of us is and must always be an individual, an ambivalent being essentially at odds with the community we essentially belong to, a community that then survives exactly by requiring and celebrating our sense that we are resistant to it in ways that co-opt and absorb true resistance.

We should not be surprised, then, that the reader/viewer implied by picture books is conflicted, divided, ambivalent. As I suggested earlier, our culture of equally free subjects sharing a single space is inevitably and necessarily conflicted about insoluble issues of separation and community, freedom and constraint. In learning how to look at picture books, then, in becoming the conflicted, divided, ambivalent subjects they imply, children are merely in the process of entering into the conflicts, divisions, ambivalences and complexities of life as it is in our time. Their – and our – one chance of changing that situation in any truly fundamental way comes with the development of an awareness of it, and particularly of the ways in which our culture allows and at the same time polices and defangs the making of meanings that appear to threaten its dominance.

Notes

1 For more about semiotic theory, see my discussion in *Words About Pictures*, (1988, p.9–10).
2 The basic ideas of reader-response criticism, including the concept of "implied reader" are discussed more fully by Wolfgang Iser.
3 See, for instance, my discussion of these matters in *Words about Pictures*, (1988, p.10–16).
4 For more about construction of subjectivity, see my *Pleasures of Children's Literature*, (1996 p.136–139).
5 While Fiske's ideas relate to texts of popular culture such as television and advertising, they represent a view of the freedom of reader/viewers frequently found in discussions of children's literature, and frequently used to downplay the significance of implied refers and viewers. It's for this reason that I refer to it here.
6 Lévi-Strauss speaks, for instance, of "the unconscious structures underlying each institution and each custom" of a culture (1967, p.21).

References

Berger, J. 1972, *Ways of Seeing*, British Broadcasting Corporation, London; Penguin, Harmondsworth.
Blonsky, M. (ed.) 1985, *On Signs*, Johns Hopkins UP, Baltimore.
Bunting, E. 1994, *Smoky Night*, Illus. David Diaz, Harcourt Brace, San Diego, New York, and London.

Fiske, J. 1989, *Understanding Popular Culture*, Unwin Hyman, Boston, London, Sydney, Wellington.

Iser, W. 1974, *The Implied Reader*, Johns Hopkins UP, Baltimore.

Jameson, F. 1981, *The Political Unconscious: Narrative as a Socially Symbolic Act*, Cornell UP, Ithaca, New York.

Kristeva, J. 1980, *Desire in Language: A Semiotic Approach to Literature and Art*, ed. Leon S. Roudiez, Columbia UP, New York.

Lacan, J. 1977, "The Mirror Stage as Formative of the Function of the I as Revealed in Psychoanalytic Experience." in *Ecrits: A Selection*, trans. Alan Sheridan Norton, New York and London, pp. 1–7.

Lévi Strauss, C. 1967, *Structural Anthropology*, Doubleday Anchor, Garden City, New York.

Lurie, A. 1990, *Don't Tell the Grownups: The Subversive Power of Children's Literature*, Back Bay/Little Brown, Boston, New York Toronto, London.

McLuhan, M. 1965, *Understanding Media: The Extensions of Man*, McGraw Hill, New York.

Nodelman, P. 1988, *Words about Pictures: The Narrative Art of Children's Picture Books*, University of Georgia Press, Athens, GA.

Nodelman, P. 1996, *The Pleasures of Children's Literature*, 2nd edn, Longman, White Plains, New York.

Ong, W. J. 1982, *Orality and Literacy: The Technologizing of the Word*, Methuen, London.

19

THE DYNAMICS OF PICTUREBOOK COMMUNICATION

Maria Nikolajeva and Carole Scott

Source: *Children's Literature in Education* 31(4) (2000): 225–239.

Recently, a number of critical studies have focused on the various aspects of word/image interaction in picturebooks (Schwarcz, Joseph, H., *Ways of the Illustrator: Visual Communication in Children's Literature*, 1982; Schwarcz, Joseph, Schwarcz, Chava, *The Picture Book Comes of Age*, 1991; Moebius, William, "Introduction to picturebook codes", 1986; Nodelman, Perry, *Words About Pictures. The Narrative Art of Children's Picture Books*, 1988; Rhedin, Ulla, *Bilderboken: På päg mot en teori* (*The picture Book—Towards a Theory*), 1991; Doonan, Jane, *Looking at Pictures in Picture Books*, 1993; Bradford, Clare, "The picture book: Some postmodern tensions", 1993; Sipe, Lawrence R., "How picture books work: A semiotically framed theory of text-picture relationships", 1998). These and other works have included thoughtful terminology, such as iconotext (Hallberg, Kristin, "Litteraturvetenskapen och bilderboksforskningen", 1983), imagetext (Mitchell, W. J. T., *Picture Theory. Essays on Verbal and Visual Representation*, 1994), or synergy (Sipe), that helps to convey the essence of this interaction. While these terms all indicate the complex relationship between text and image, they do not recognize or explore in any systematic way the wide array and diversity of the dynamics that picturebooks embody.

In our new book *How Picturebooks Work* (Garland Press), we examine a broad spectrum of word/image interaction and identify a number of characteristic dynamics. For example, in *symmetrical* interaction, words and pictures tell the same story, essentially repeating information in different forms of communication. In *enhancing* interaction, pictures amplify more fully the meaning of the words, or the words expand the picture so that different information in the two modes of communication produces a more complex dynamic. When enhancing interaction becomes very significant, the dynamic becomes truly *complementary*. Dependent on the degree of different information presented, a *counterpointing* dynamic may develop where words and images collaborate to communicate meanings beyond the scope of either one alone. An extreme form of counterpointing is *contradictory* inter-action, where words and pictures seem to be in opposition to one another. This ambiguity challenges the reader to mediate between the words and pictures to establish a true understanding of what is being depicted.

While these terms are not absolute (the relationship between words and pictures in a picturebook will be never be completely symmetrical or completely contradictory), we have found them very useful in analyzing the ways in which picturebooks present such features as setting, characteriza-tion, point of view, and temporality, focusing on the specific way word/image interaction works—or sometimes fails to work—to express each of these aspects of narrative. Just as the terms are not absolute, so the com-plex works we discuss rarely fall neatly into any one category. While some simple word/picture relationships are easy to characterize, more complex works involve a variety of aspects. For example, although characterization might be predominantly complementary or enhancing, plot line or modal-ity might be counterpointing or even contradictory.

Several picturebook studies (Gregersen, Torben, "Småbørnsbogen", 1974; Hallberg, 1982; Golden, Joanne M., *The narrative Symbol in Childhood Literature. Exploration in the Construction of Text*, 1990; Rhedin, 1993) have made some preliminary attempts at picturebook classification, but have not gone far beyond the basic distinction between illustrated books (where the words carry the primary narrative while pictures are supportive or decorative) and books in which both the visual and the verbal aspects are both essential for full communication. We identify this second category by the single word "picturebooks" and have focused on these in our study. Kristin Hallberg's term "iconotext" and her definition of a picturebook as a book with at least one picture on each spread serve as useful tools to assist in this identification.

While we agree that the distinction between the two categories of illus-trated books and picturebooks is indeed crucial, we do not find it nearly adequate enough to describe the broad spectrum of the word/picture dynamic, which stretches from verbal narratives illustrated by one or two pictures to picturebooks with one or two words. To make the variety even more challenging, it is clear that each of these extremes can be either narrative or non-narrative in form. This discussion will focus on the narrative ones.

The spectrum of word/picture dominance: illustrated books and picture narratives

In a predominantly verbal narrative, pictures are usually subordinated to the words. A number of very significant children's stories have been illustrated by various artists who may impart different and even, on occasion, inappropriate interpretations to the text. But the story will remain basically the same and can still be read without looking at the pictures. The many illustrated editions of Bible stories, folktales, Perrault's, Grimms' or Andersen's tales fall into this category. Even if we have preferences for certain illustrations, perhaps because we have grown up with them, the text is not dependent on illustrations to convey its essential message.

At the other end of the word/picture spectrum is the predominantly picture narrative. Jan Ormerod's *Sunshine* and *Moonlight* are very simple stories in which all of the individual frames—between two and ten on each spread—depict consecutive moments with almost no temporal ellipses between them. They are easy to follow, with no substantial gaps in the story that readers must fill from their own imaginations. Quentin Blake's *Clown* is perhaps more demanding visually, but there is also, as in Ormerod's books, a clear sequence of events and few gaps which cannot very readily be bridged by the reader.

Tord Nygren's *The Red Thread* (*Den röda tråden*) is a picturebook almost completely devoid of words, and the very few that appear are part of the illustration, not a linear text. Despite its juxtaposition of pictures with no apparent relationship one to another (although there are some recurring figures and scenes), the book, in clear contrast to Ormerod's and Blake's works, involves a highly sophisticated self-conscious focus on the nature of the narrative. The red thread that gives the book its title is featured running across the cover, both back and front, and across each and every doublespread, traversing the page turn so that its position as it exits the right-hand edge of the page is identical to its position as it enters the left-hand margin of the next doublespread. Its journey across each page is meandering, with a varying succession of twists and turns and different levels of involvement in the pictures: It may simply run across the page, or it may play a part in the scene, such as forming the rope across which the tightrope walker makes his perilous way.

The concept of the thread itself, so often used metaphorically to represent narrative progression, challenges the reader to create a narrative that successfully bridges the gaps between the wide variety of picture presented. In addition, the recurring elements within the pictures themselves suggest that there must be a narrative, if the reader could just unravel the code and understand what it is. Furthermore, the path the thread takes directs the movement of the eye, which would otherwise explore the elements of the picture in a different manner, ranging from point to point according to visual cues of form, color and design. This tension between the eye's path as directed by the thread and the visual pull of the picture itself, together with the constant search for meaning, alert the reader to the interplay inherent in picturebooks between the linear narrative usually presented in the text and the apparent static aspect of the pictures. These impulses stimulate the reader to an ongoing evaluation of their interaction.

The teasing presence of the thread provokes the reader to an awareness of the different kinds of narrative order that exist. One doublespread provides a very specific narrative presented through a series of 15 miniature pictures. This series tells the clear story of a man who dreams of a woman and goes on a journey to find her, the pictures portraying the events of his journey and ending with the happy couple standing with their arms around each other.

But most of Nygren's doublespreads are far less revealing, presenting more questions than answers. What is the meaning that lies behind the doublespread of the magician, the masks, and the mirrors, with their reflections and refractions? What is the story of the skywatchers' doublespread where a tightrope walker crosses the sky balanced on the red thread anchored to a crescent moon? What is the connection between the diverse spreads, a connection posited not only by the thread itself, but by other devices? Certain characters appear in a number of illustrations. Are we to believe that they are part of a progressive narrative, or are they just recurrent favorites of the author-illustrator? And, does the inclusion in the final scene of some of these characters, as well as some of the scenes pictured earlier, suggest that we are to infer some sense of an ending, or finale of action? The perceptive reader notes that the red thread does not end here, but runs from its final point in the last picture onto the back cover, thence onto the front cover, and onto the first page, in an eternal circle. One cannot help but wonder whether Nygren is not laughing at our earnest attempts to penetrate the puzzle.

The series of Sam books created by Barbro Lindgren and Eva Eriksson are good examples of the picture narrative in a dominant relationship with words. Although there are some very short, simple sentences to accompany the pictures, the plots can easily be understood from the pictures alone. Unlike Ormerod's wordless picture narrative, Sam books have only one picture on each spread, so the "drama of page turning" is fully realized here. Each of the Sam books focuses on one problem, or rather one object, featured in the title: *Sam's Ball, Sam's Wagon, Sam's Teddy Bear*, and so on. They portray everyday situations that most children (in the Western world at least) can easily recognize. There are few details that have no correspondence in the verbal text, but all details are essential. The books are addressed to a very young child whose experience of the world is quite limited, and the settings are sparsely depicted. The universe consists only of the immediate surroundings and does not reach beyond the material things the child is able to see here and now. The temporal span is extremely tight, and there are few gaps to fill.

Enhancing and complementary word/picture relationships

Most picturebooks are characterized by what we have termed symmetrical relationships and those we call enhancing or complementary. When they are enhancing or complementary, with words and pictures supporting one another by providing additional information that the other lacks, the additional material may be minor, or quite dramatically different. Exemplifying these kinds of interaction are many classics and award-winners such as *The Little House* by Virginia Lee Burton, the *Babar* books by Jean de Brunhoff, *Curious George* by H. A. Rey, *Sylvester and the Magic Pebble* by William Steig, *Frog and Toad Are Friends* by Arnold Lobel, and *Bread and Jam for Frances* by Russell and Lillian Hoban.

Minimal enhancement

Let us take a brief look at William Steig's Caldecott Medal winner *Sylvester and the Magic Pebble*. To begin with, we might observe that the verbal text does not initially mention that Sylvester is a donkey. The text merely states that Sylvester Duncan lived with his mother and father and collected pebbles as a hobby. But for the pictures, we would assume that Sylvester was a boy. An interesting feature of this book, which makes it in some ways different from many picturebooks involving humanized animals, is that the characters are only partly anthropomorphic. For instance, some of the animals in the story wear clothes and walk on their hind legs, while others behave more like animals, such as the dogs who sniff the neighborhood in search of Sylvester. Sylvester himself does not wear clothes, but otherwise seems to behave like a human child.

Apart from these elements of visual characterization, there is little in the verbal text that allows expansion by means of the pictures. We may find the pictures charming, and we may note the richness of the characters' postures and facial expressions, corresponding to words describing their emotions. But we must admit, however, that the pictures do not add much that is different to the narrative. Moreover, the text is richer than the pictures: there are several episodes in the verbal text that are not illustrated. There are other textual gaps that another artist might have decided to fill: pictures detailing wishes, for example, or pictures expanding imaginary situations. The artist has chosen to let the verbal text carry the narrative, while the visual text enhances it.

Significant enhancement: complementary relationship

In Beatrix Potter's case we see a very effective balance between pictures and prose that complement and enhance one another. They rarely overlap, but rather work together to strengthen the ultimate effect. *The Tale of Peter Rabbit* offers a good example. The opening doublespread presents some apparent contradictions, some devices to keep the reader alert and involved. The verbal text tells us that there are four little rabbits but the picture shows only three. Closer attention reveals that the hind legs and tail on the left belong to a rabbit whose head is underneath the tree root, rather than to the rabbit whose head appears the other side of the root. This little puzzle immediately sets up a tension between picture and text, because we want to figure out how to resolve the discrepancy. More familiarity with the book will lead us to the interpretation that this is probably Peter, checking out his surroundings underground instead of taking his cue from his mother.

The verbal text presents the names of the rabbits listed in a slanted line, leaning, like a backslash, from right to left rather than the usual left to right reading movement, and bringing the eye toward the picture and the puzzle of the four names and three rabbits. The text and picture are thus interrelated in several ways: in the apparent discrepancy between the information that is imagistically and verbally presented; in the impact on eye movement that plots a back-and-forth pattern between text and picture pages, reinforced by the line of names which points to the picture; and in the questions of interpretation provoked by the behavior of the rabbit whose head is hidden from the reader —questions that introduce the subversive message of the book (motives for behavior may be hidden, anti-authoritarian, exciting, and adventurous).

An excellent example of complementarity may be found in the second spread where the rabbits have metamorphosed from ordinary wild creatures crouched on all fours to characters with human attributes; they are standing up and wearing clothes, and distinctive clothes at that. This instant human-ization is reinforced by the text on the opposing page where Mrs. Rabbit is talking to her children, addressing them with an endearment, giving them advice, and a little family history. Them is another interesting dynamic. Although the text refers, backwards in time to Mr. Rabbit's "accident" (he was put in a pie by Mrs. McGregor), the picture is alerting us to the future. The girls are clustering round and paying attention to their mother, but Peter stands apart with his back to her, either not listening, or else rejecting what she says. The combination of text and image communicates to the reader a sense of imminent peril, the meeting of a dangerous situation (words) with the refusal to be guided by experience (picture), a combination of backshadowing and foreshadowing.

Complex dynamics: counterpoint and contradiction

The closer words and images come to filling each other's gaps, the more passive is the reader's role since there is little left to the imagination. This is also true when there are few gaps, or if the gaps in words and images are very similar, However, as soon as words and images provide alternative information or contradict each other in some way, we have a variety of readings and interpretations. Since the range of counterpointing examples is so varied and so rich, we will examine several books that illustrate some of the different features of counterpoint and range from the easily understood to the highly challenging.

Ironic counterpoint

Babette Cole's *Princess Smartypants* provides a fascinating word/picture relationship that offers much stimulation to the reader's imagination through its ironically humorous counterpoint. The verbal text begins: "Princess Smartypants did not want to get married. She enjoyed being a Ms." The accompanying picture shows the princess lying on her stomach on the floor in front of a television set, surrounded by her pets (including two little dragons). She is eating chocolates from a box, while around her is a mess of dirty clothes and dishes, banana skins and apple cores, a crushed Coke can, and a Mars bar wrapper. Her horse is spread comfortably on the sofa. This humorous and somewhat surprising visualization of the joys of "being a Ms." sets the stage for an intensification of the techniques introduced where the sometimes bland verbal text is expanded.

The tasks that the princess gives her many admirers sound quite straightforward when described in words: "stop the slugs from eating her garden," "feed her pets," "challenged [. . .] to a roller-disco marathon," "invited [. . .] for a cross-country ride on her motorbike," "rescue her from her tower," "chop some firewood in the royal forest," "put her pony through its paces," "take her Mother, the Queen, shopping," and "retrieve her magic ring from the goldfish pond." But pictures reveal the truly daunting nature of the tasks and the reasons why the princes fail: the slug is as large as a dinosaur, the pets are ferocious dragons, the tower is made of glass, the forest is enchanted, the goldfish pond is inhabited by an enormous shark, and so on. In each case, the reader encounters the words before seeing the picture, which thus functions as an ironic counterpoint. When the last suitor arrives, the words state only that he accomplishes all the tasks, while the pictures show with detailed humor and inventiveness exactly how he manages it.

The verbal narrative ends with the princess, rid of her victorious, but ultimately unsuccessful suitor, "liv[ing] happily ever after." Once again the pictures expand on the words by showing the princess, leaning back in a beach chair, wearing a bikini, and once again surrounded by her hairy and scaly pets. Thus, while the story that the pictures tell is not radically different from the one told by words, much of the humor and irony of the narrative would be lost without the pictures. The feminist content of the book may perhaps be conveyed by the verbal narrative alone, but its aesthetic whole would be destroyed. The complete narrative is definitely dependent on the pictures to produce the desired effect.

Perspectival counterpoint

Pat Hutchins's *Rosie's Walk* is often used to exemplify words and pictures telling a story from two very different perspectives—to the point where one might suggest that there are two stories (e.g., Nodelman, 1988, p. 224f). John Burningham's *Come Away from the Water, Shirley* and *Time to Get Out of the Bath, Shirley* are two more favorites (e.g., Schwarcz, 1982, p. 17f). However, the nature of interaction is radically different in these books. In *Rosie's Walk* the visual narrative is more complicated and exciting than the verbal one, which contains one sentence of 25 words. In the Shirley books, words are fully in accord with one set of pictures, but totally contradictory to the parallel story told by the pictures on the right-hand pages, which thus constitute a wordless narrative. The two narratives in the Shirley books are, among other things, conflicting in their genres: one is "realistic," the other a fantasy.

The same duality is the narrative principle of Satoshi Kitamura's *Lily Takes A Walk*, but the counterpoint between perspectives is much more highly developed, involving contradiction and ambiguity. A girl takes a walk with her dog, going first through a green suburban landscape and then down some streets, stopping to shop, to point out the stars for the dog (appropriately enough, the Dog Star), waving to a neighbor, watching the ducks in a canal, and coming safely home. The text specifies that Lily "is never scared, because Nicky is there with her." Looking at the pictures, however, we see that the dog is extremely frightened, and following his gaze—that is, sharing his perspective rather than the girl's or the omniscient narrator's—we discover the sources of his fear: a huge snake winding around a tree stem, a tree formed into a monstrous grin, a mailbox gaping with sharp teeth and dropping letters from a ghastly red tongue, an arch and two street lamps metamorphosing into a dragon, the moon and the tower clock together forming a pair of huge eyes, a giant emerging from a shop window, a dinosaur stretching its long neck from a canal on the other side of the bridge, and finally a garbage bin full of dreadful creatures.

One of the final spreads shows the happily smiling Lily and her parents around the dinner table, with the words, "Lily's mother and father always like to hear what she has seen on her walks." Apparently, her account is as unexciting as the preceding verbal story itself. The thought-balloons coming from the dog reiterate, in images, what he has seen, and this serves to alert the readers in case they have missed any of the details. On the last spread, but covered by a half-page, we see the dog's basket being invaded by an army of mice, accentuating that at least some of his fears are true. Lily, sound asleep, is oblivious to what is taking place. If we turn the half page over, we see the dog asleep and the mice retreating into their hole. This alternative perspective suggests that this episode might be interpreted as the dog's imagination or nightmare. It also raises questions about the reliability of the dog's point of view.

The fact that the focalizing character of the visual narrative is a dog in an otherwise realistic story—that is, the dog is not a humanized, talking animal—creates an interesting situation for the reader. Like a very young child, the dog cannot verbalize his fears, which obviously stimulates the reader's empathy. The images emphatically imply that the character does have emotions, even though he cannot articulate them. As readers, we are allowed to feel superior to both the girl and the dog. We see clearly that the girl is unobservant and perhaps lacks imagination (she has the role in the story often given to unaware or insensitive parents), but we also suspect that the dog's view of things is also probably exaggerated. The counterpoint between the two perspectives and the ambiguity of the actual events shape the book's impact and the reader's involvement in decoding it.

Counterpoint in characterization

It is clear that the picturebooks that employ counterpoint are particularly stimulating because they elicit many possible interpretations and involve the reader's imagination. Characterization is one aspect where the counterpoint has especially strong potential to create irony and ambiguity, and to call for resolution of apparent contradiction. Inger Edelfeldt's *Nattbarn* (*Nightchild*) illustrates such potential, posing a number of puzzles for the reader, and resolving some of them, but only if the reader pays thoughtful and perceptive attention. The work presents a young girl, a princess, who discovers a poor girl living in the nearby forest and develops a continuing relationship with her. The two figures are explicit opposites. The princess, with fair skin and curly blonde hair, wears light, bright colors and is pictured surrounded by sunshine. Nightchild is pictured with drab clothes, lank, dark hair, and a pale, sullen expression. Their dolls mirror their owners: the princess's chubby dolls project her golden image, as do their names— Goldenhair, Rosycheek, Sunny-soul, and Little Sweetie—while Nightchild's have names such as Moss, Chunk, Stoneheart, and Squealing Liza. The girls' relationship is the focus of the tale.

Because the princess's mother is unable to see Nightchild, and neither parent notices when the princess stays away over night with her, the reader is faced with a dilemma involving the genre of the piece. Is this a tale of magic or is Nightchild simply a fantasy of the princess? Certainly the setting in the turreted castle surrounded by forest, and the visit to Nightchild's miniature, rustic castle in the trees could come from a Grimm-like tale. But when, at last, Nightchild comes to the castle at the end of the book, she disappears into a mirror and talks to the princess from this looking-glass world. This clearer manifestation of genre suggests that this is a psychological study rather than a fairy tale, and the sense of the forest girl as the shadowy side of the princess, her mirrored alter-ego, becomes more apparent.

The pictures are not explicit about this point, but the similarity between the two girls does reinforce this interpretation, particularly in the illustration where the two girls share a bed and begin to take on the other's characteristics: Nightchild lies peacefully asleep, almost smiling, clutching her doll, while the wakeful princess, her hair bedraggled, looks solemnly on while her doll sits on the pillow. The light and shade are evenly distributed between them. This picture follows a very significant conversation between the two girls in which Nightchild claims that the princess is her sister: "Your mother is my mother too. But you were born in the daytime, and she liked you at once. I was born at night, and as soon as she saw me, she turned away [. . .] She has never seen me." The princess's reply, "I see you," connotes recognition and acceptance of Nightchild.

Thus, pictures and verbal text reinforce this interpretation, particularly when the princess embraces the notion of both dark and light in her life: "it will be both wild and quiet and funny and serious, and the castle will be called Castle of Day and Night in the land of Sun and Moon." The text goes further to say that the girl in the mirror "turned on the light inside the mirror so that I could see her. She even smiled." The very last page shows the castle with a sun and moon at the top right and left corners and a smiling girl in a framed, crowned circle in the center at the bottom.

The readers are comfortably proud of their decoding, until they are alerted to yet another problematic contradiction, this time posed in just some of the illustrations. Is it because this is a Swedish picturebook that the Royal Family is not regal? While the external view of the castle in which the princess lives is old and traditionally turreted with high narrow windows, the views of the inside are very different. The windows are double paned and modern in appearance, and the rooms are intimate, cozy, and furnished with a traditional stove and rather ordinary furniture. Furthermore, the breakfast table offers just bread, rolls and jam, and boiled eggs, and mother and father appear in their housecoats looking rumpled, and, in mother's case, in her curlers. It is also clear, in the evening scene when mother, in her slippers, brings hot chocolate and warm scones, that this "castle" has no servants, and no pomp and circumstance. Rather, it seems just like an ordinary home with ordinary parents. In fact the only regal touch is the breakfast mugs, which bear fun pictures of people wearing crowns.

Although the verbal text includes nothing to verify what the pictures show, the reader is led to the ultimate conclusion that the division of the self into a daytime and a shadow persona carries by implication not only the rejection of the dark side, but also the distortion of the acknowledged aspect of the self. Thus, the distinction between the real world of the castle and the fantasy world of the forest (where the breakfast table in Nightchild's house-holds mugs and bowls shaped into sad, grotesque faces) is subtly altered to suggest the spawning of two fantasies—the world of the castle and the world of the forest—with the real world serving as the springboard to both. The characterization of the girl is thereby made even more complex and true to the psychological dimension: an ordinary girl who likes to dream that she is special, a princess, and who makes herself the focus of an elaborate fairy tale where the division in the self is articulated and resolved through fantasy. While this feels like an accurate and penetrating interpretation, it is still obviously somewhat ambiguous because the verbal narrative does not acknowledge it.

Conclusion: directions for further work

In this article we have presented a few illustrations of our approach to the word/picture dynamic, which we find so rich and so promising in its ability to penetrate and unlock the intricacies of picturebook communication. Our book's analysis of the different kind of dynamics—such as symmetrical, complementary or enhancing, and counterpointing—permits us to explore many aspects of picturebooks, but this focus on word/picture interaction also opens up many new opportunities for further work. For example, we have not examined pedagogical or cognitive aspects of picturebooks in our study of dynamics, and have not pursued questions concerning the ways in which young readers understand different textual or pictorial codes, or whether certain books can be used for educational purposes.

Another natural question arising from our focus on dynamics concerns the ways in which counterpoint and contradiction are decoded by various categories of readers. Great children's literature speaks to both adults and children, and the two audiences may approach textual and visual gaps differently and fill them in different ways, a process that the picturebook creator may deliberately manipulate or bring about unintentionally. We believe that our approach does open new perspectives for examining the ways in which picturebook creators handle dual address in reaching both adult and child audiences, and in the possible differences of interpretation that sophisticated and unsophisticated readers might make.

References

Bradford, Clare, "The picture book: Some postmodern tensions," *Papers: Explorations in Children's Literature*, 1993, 4(3), 10–14.

Doonan, Jane, *Looking at Pictures in Picture Books*. Stroud: Thimble Press, 1993.

Golden, Joanne M., *The Narrative Symbol in Childhood Literature. Explorations in the Construction of Text*. Berlin: Mouton, 1990.

Gregersen, Torben, "Småbørnsbogen," in *Børnel-og ungdomsbøger: Problemer og analyser*, Sven Møller Kristensen and Preben Ramløv, eds., pp. 243–271. Copenhagen: Gyldendal, 1974.

Hallberg, Kristin, "Litteraturvetenskapen och bilderboksforskningen," *Tidskrift för litteraturvetenskap*, 1982, 3–4, 163–168.

Mitchell, W. J. T., *Picture Theory. Essays on Verbal and Visual Representation*. Chicago: University of Chicago Press, 1994.

Moebius, William, "Introduction to picturebook codes," *Word and Image*, 1986, 2(2), 141–158. Also in *Children's Literature. The Development of Criticism*, Peter Hunt, ed., pp. 131–147. London: Routledge, 1990.

Nodelman, Perry, *Words About Pictures. The Narrative Art of Children's Picture Books.* Athens: The University of Georgia Press, 1988.

Rhedin, Ulla, *Bilderboken: På väg mot en teori.* Stockholm: Alfabeta, 1993. (Studies published by the Swedish Institute for Children's Books no. 45—with a summary in English: *The Picture Book—Towards a Theory.*)

Schwarcz, Joseph H., *Ways of the Illustrator: Visual Communication in Children's Literature.* Chicago: American Library Association, 1982.

Schwarcz, Joseph, and Schwarcz, Chava, *The Picture Book Comes of Age.* Chicago: American Library Association, 1991.

Sipe, Lawrence R., "How picture books work: A semiotically framed theory of text-picture relationships," *Children's Literature in Education,* 1998, 29(2), 97–108.

Picturebooks discussed

Blake, Quentin, *Clown.* London: Jonathan Cape, 1995.

Burningham, John, *Come Away from the Water, Shirley.* New York: Crowell, 1977.

Burningham, John, *Time to Get Out of the Bath, Shirley.* New York: Crowell, 1978.

Cole, Babette, *Princess Smartypants.* London: Hamish Hamilton, 1986.

Edelfeldt, Inger, *Nattbarn.* Stockholm: Alfabeta, 1994 (*Nightchild*).

Hutchins, Pat, *Rosie's Walk.* New York: Macmillan, 1968.

Kitamura, Satoshi, *Lily Takes a Walk.* New York: Dutton, 1987.

Lindgren, Barbro, and Eriksson, Eva, *Sam's Ball.* New York: Morrow, 1983 (*Max boll* 1982). The first of many "Sam" books.

Nygren, Tord, *The Red Thread.* Stockholm: R & S Books, 1988 (*Den röda tråden,* 1987).

Ormerod, Jan, *Moonlight.* London: Lothrop, 1982.

Ormerod, Jan, *Sunshine.* London: Lothrop, 1981.

Potter, Beatrix, *The Tale of Peter Rabbit.* New York: Warne, 1902.

Steig, William, *Sylvester and the Magic Pebble.* New York: Windmill Books, 1969.

20

THE INTERACTION OF WORD AND IMAGE IN PICTUREBOOKS

A critical survey

David Lewis

Source: *Reading Contemporary Picture Books: Picturing Text*, London: RoutledgeFalmer, 2000, pp. 31–45.

> The big truth about picture books ... is that they are an inter-weaving of word and pictures. You don't have to tell the story in the words. You can come out of the words and into the pictures and you get this nice kind of antiphonal fugue effect.
>
> (Allan Ahlberg cited in Moss 1990:21)

Introduction

The picturebook began to be taken seriously as an object of academic study during the latter years of the twentieth century. The first major works in English to address the form and its nature, for example, *Ways of the Illustrator* by Joseph Schwarcz and *Words About Pictures* by Perry Nodelman were published in the 1980s (Schwarcz 1982; Nodelman 1988) and since then there has been a steady increase in the flow of articles, conference papers and book chapters dedicated to the study, criticism and analysis of the picturebook. There has been a gathering sophistication in the attempts to understand its properties but I believe we are still some way off under-standing many of the picturebook's most significant features. Even though we are experienced readers of verbal text we are still learning how to read the picturebook, both in the sense of reading individual books, and in the sense of understanding how they work. In this chapter I examine some recent attempts to characterize the special ways in which pictures and words are used in picturebooks to tell stories and create imaginative fictions. Some of what follows is critical but my intention is not simply to find fault. My main aim is to establish the imperfect and provisional nature of what we know so far. I certainly have no straightforward answers to the questions that I raise but at the end of the chapter I suggest a way in which we might conceive of word–picture interactions in picturebooks that opens up possibilities for study rather than closing them down. But to begin with, let us go back to the basic facts of reading a picturebook – what we do with our eyes and minds – and then consider some of the ways that expert readers have attempted to characterize the process.

Describing the interaction of word and image

When we read picturebooks we look at the pictures and we read the words and our eyes go back and forth between the two as we piece together the meaning of the text. In *Have You Seen Who's Just Moved in Next Door to Us?* (see page 11) the rhyme at the top of each page directs our attention to characters and events, one or two at a time, represented in the street scene below. The scene itself, however, always overflows whatever the words say about it and our eyes are tempted to wander around, roving up and down the street, inspecting the houses and their occupants, reading the captions and speech balloons, grasping (or missing) the jokes and the puns. In *So Much*, the pictures show us a family at play. The words give us the sounds and rhythms and intonations of their speech so we watch what the aunties, cousins and grans do with the baby and 'hear' their exclamations of delight and declarations of affection. In *Drop Dead*, much of the verbal text is in the form of captions to preposterous pictures so that when we read of Gran and Grandad that '[They] forget things!' we look to the picture to see what has been forgotten and smile at the old man's missing trousers and polka-dot boxer shorts.

Children reading picturebooks must also find routes through the text that connect words and images. Here six-year-old Jane reads to me from *Time to Get Out of the Bath, Shirley* by John Burningham. As she reads, she moves from the words to the pictures below the words and across the gutter to the scene on the right-hand page (words in capital letters represent book text read aloud).

> J: HAVE YOU BEEN USING THIS TOWEL SHIRLEY OR WAS IT YOUR FATHER? . . . (*looking at picture below*) probably her father 'cos it's got big hands
>
> DL: Hmm
>
> J: (*examining the picture to the right of the gutter*) She's gone on the back of the horse . . . is that an owl or a bat? . . . bat!
>
> DL: Don't know . . . could be
>
> J: Oh look, there's a witch.

Time to Get Out of the Bath, Shirley, and its sister text, *Come Away From the Water, Shirley* are justly famous for their teasing quality, the way words and pictures do not seem to fully match. In the former story, Shirley is taking a bath while her mother potters around the bathroom uttering banal remarks like the one in the extract above. At each page-opening the pictures beneath the words show mother at the moment of speaking while those to the right of the gutter show Shirley to be involved in an adventure involving storybook knights and kings and queens which we may suppose is taking place in her imagination. The words act as a prompt for further investigation of the page, for on their own they simply do not tell us enough about what is going on. Jane actively scans and interrogates both pictures, searching for semantic links that will help her piece together the story.

Picturebook text is thus usually composite, an 'interweaving of words and pictures' as Allan Ahlberg puts it (see quotation at the head of the chapter). The metaphor of weaving is useful for not only does it pick out for us the sensation we have when reading a picturebook of shuttling between one medium and another, but it is also related, through sense and meaning to the term *text* which is itself etymologically and semantically close to *textile*. A text in this sense is something woven together, a cohesive patterning of inter-related strands that adds up to more than a mere accumulation of individual parts. For this interweaving to proceed, however, we need to have the images and the words displayed before us in fairly close proximity to each other. It is not much use if the two strands – the weft and the warp, so to speak – are on different pages or are so far apart that they cannot be brought together in the act of reading. If the words are on one set of pages and the pictures elsewhere in the book, as is frequently the case in longer texts and illustrated novels, then it becomes difficult for the two forms of representation to enter into the construction of the story together. We now take sophisticated combinations of word and image in books, magazines and advertising for granted but it is only relatively recently that printing technology has permitted this creative freedom. The emergence of the picturebook from earlier forms of illustrated text has been slow and hesitant.

Musical metaphors

Despite the suggestive power of metaphors such as 'interweaving', the task of describing and analysing the interaction of text and picture in picturebooks is far from straightforward. All metaphors and analogies have their limitations and it is always a mistake to push them too far or to interpret them too literally. They may also distort what they are intended to illuminate. Take, for example, the analogy that follows the interweaving metaphor in the quotation from Allan Ahlberg's interview with Elaine Moss, 'You don't have to tell the story in the words. You can come out of the words and into the pictures and you get this nice kind of antiphonal fugue effect.' Once again we are offered an image of movement between two or more parts, this time the separate voices or lines in a piece of music. Once again the metaphor is suggestive but it will not withstand much pressure once we test it out against some real examples. There is indeed a sense in which pictures and words 'echo' or 'answer' each other in a vaguely antiphonal way and we can perhaps see it and feel it in books like *The Park in the Dark* or *The Little Boat*. But a book like *Rosie's Walk*, by Pat Hutchins, or even *Gorilla*, is not well served by the analogy. The pictures are richer in information than the words and might be said to introduce and develop new themes rather than echo the one introduced by the words.

Perhaps it is a little unfair to push such an analogy as far as this as its purpose would seem to be to hint at a very general kind of relationship rather than account for the diversity of kinds of relationship in detail. After all, Allan Ahlberg was responding to questions in an interview rather than committing a considered view to print. Nonetheless he does suggest that there is a 'big truth' about picturebooks that his images from weaving and music can capture. In fact musical metaphors are commonplace in discussions of the picturebook and they are worth examining for what they reveal about how the picture–word relationship is sometimes conceptualized. Maurice Sendak, for example, has remarked that the true illustrator has '. . . an odd affinity with words . . . almost like a composer thinking music when reading poetry' (Lorraine 1977:329). Philip Pullman, a writer with experience both of writing graphic novels for children and of studying the effects of pictures on words (see Pullman 1989, 1993), sees the interaction of word and image in the best picturebooks as being essentially a matter of *counterpoint*. The same term is used by Schwarcz in *Ways of the Illustrator* (Schwarcz 1982) and, more recently, by Maria Nikolajeva and Carole Scott in *The Dynamics of Picturebook Communication* (Nikolajeva and Scott, 2000) and *How Picturebooks Work* (Nikolajeva and Scott, 2001).

One of the problems with counterpoint is that different writers use the term in different ways. For Pullman, counterpoint as it has been developed in the picturebook, the comic and the graphic novel is a matter of simultaneity, the potential possessed by words and pictures in combination to 'show different things happening at the same time' (Pullman 1989:171). Nikolajeva and Scott use the term in a somewhat similar fashion, arguing that only certain books exhibit features of counterpointing and those are the ones where the words and the images provide different kinds of information that the reader must make some effort to reconcile and integrate. As an example they suggest the work of Babette Cole who often captions outrageous pictures with banal phrases, as in *Drop Dead*. The authors explain that at the outer extremity of this category lies a smaller group of books where the words and the pictures seem to be saying such different things that they appear to be contradicting each other. *Time to Get Out of the Bath, Shirley* seems to possess some elements of this kind of relationship. For Schwarcz, however, the situation is reversed: the relationship that Nikolajeva and Scott call counterpoint, Schwarcz calls *deviation* and he reserves the term counter-point for the more specific and extreme subset where words and pictures seem opposed or contradictory (Schwarcz 1982). One outcome of this confusion is that we remain unsure whether counterpoint is an appropriate metaphor for the workings of words and pictures in all picturebooks or only in some picturebooks. And if it is the case that only some picturebooks are truly contrapuntal, then exactly which sub-category of picturebooks does the term most accurately describe?

The most important weakness of musical analogies, however, is that they risk keeping the words and the pictures apart: they might reflect each other, echo each other, weave around each other in a play of voices and images, but hardly ever do they seem to influence each other. Allan Ahlberg, for example, in the sentences that connect his two metaphors, says explicitly that 'You don't have to tell the story in the words. You can *come out of the words and into the pictures . . .*' (Moss 1990, my emphasis). The following 'antiphonal effect' then suggests a kind of bouncing back and forth between the two. Ahlberg would no doubt acknowledge the mutual influence that words and pictures exert upon one another but in this interview he seems to be speaking as a creator of picturebooks rather than a reader of them. Or rather he seems to be collapsing the two roles into one, superimposing the experience of the writer ('You don't have to *tell* the story in the words') onto that of the reader ('you get this nice kind of antiphonal fugue effect').

Interanimation

The experience of reading picturebooks would suggest that as our eyes move from words to pictures and back again, far from leaving behind the meaning or effects of one medium as we enter the other, we carry with us something like semantic traces that colour or inflect what we read and what we see. Margaret Meek, in a discussion of how writers and illustrators support young readers, writes of the words of one particular book being 'pulled through the pictures' and of how 'pictures and words on a page *interanimate* each other' (Meek 1992:176, 177). The liveliness of these images is appeal-ing and suggests vividly how the two media act upon each other. Perry Nodelman's gloss on this process is as follows: '. . . the pictures themselves can imply narrative information only in relationship to a verbal context; if none is actually provided, we tend to find one in our memories' (Nodelman 1988:195). And again, 'Words can make pictures into rich narrative resources – but only because they communicate so differently from pictures that they change the meaning of pictures. For the same reason, also, pictures can change the narrative thrust of words' (Nodelman 1988:196). This is a most important observation for it alerts us to the fact that although pictures and words in close proximity in the picturebook influence each other, the relationship is never entirely symmetrical. What the words do to the pictures is not the same as what the pictures do to the words. Roughly speaking, the words in a picturebook tend to draw attention to the parts of the pictures that we should attend to, whereas the pictures provide the words with a specificity – colour, shape and form – that they would otherwise lack.[1]

In Anthony Browne's *Voices in the Park* for example, when we look at the picture which dominates the first page we see a rather handsome white house set in a neat lawned garden with autumn trees in the background and a white fence in the foreground. Also in the foreground, but set off to one side, a smartly dressed lady gorilla walks with her son and her dog along the pavement. The picture thus has a life of its own in that we recognize what it depicts and read some of its general significance: the clean, white neatness and smartness of the house and the purposeful air of the lady gorilla, for example. But the picture only gains the life it needs in and for Browne's story when we read the words that accompany it: 'First Voice. It was time to take Victoria, our pedigree Labrador, and Charles, our son, for a walk.' The picture is thus not primarily about the house, as we may have thought, despite its prominence, but about the characters in front of it. Moreover the words take us inside the head of one of the characters and tell us something about her personality – careful, slightly pedantic – as well as her intentions. Thus do the words breathe life into the image. They frame the image for the reader by directing attention, and offering interpretation. The central point, however, is that the image can only live and have meaning *as part of the picturebook* when informed – or 'limited', as Nodelman would say (Nodelman 1988:221) – by the words.

The reverse is also true, at least inasmuch as the words are 'animated' and given a specificity and locality that on their own they simply do not possess. Reading the words alone will tell us that here is a voice speaking, or possibly silently ruminating, on a commonplace domestic event. But the words on their own cannot tell us exactly where the event takes place, cannot convey the clear light and clean lines of the setting and nor is there any indication of gender: this could be mother or father speaking. The words clearly mean something we can understand, but on their own the words are attenuated, partial, and they only come fully to life and gain their complete meaning within the story when read alongside the accompanying picture.

There is, however, a further point to be made about what results from this interanimation. Nodelman continues, 'good picture books as a whole are a richer experience than just the simple sum of their parts' (Nodelman 1988:199). A picturebook's 'story' is never to be found in the words alone, nor in the pictures, but emerges out of their mutual interanimation. The words change the pictures and the pictures change the words and the product is something altogether different. Roland Barthes, one of Nodelman's sources here, makes a somewhat similar point when discussing what he calls *relaying* in comics and cartoons. He argues that in these mixed media forms 'language . . . and image are in a complementary relation; the words are then fragments of a more general syntagm, as are the images, and the message's unity occurs on a higher level: that of the story, the anecdote, the diegesis' (Barthes 1986:30). There is thus a synergy about picturebooks that ensures that if a reader wants the whole experience, then pictures and words have to be taken together.[2] And this is true even of those picturebooks where the language makes perfectly good sense on its own. Errol Le Cain's *Aladdin* works very well when the verbal text alone is read aloud, but when we see the pictures as we hear or read the words, Aladdin's world is no longer the one we envisage in our heads but Le Cain's very particular world with its highly patterned surfaces and elongated figures. When we see the pictures, Le Cain's characters enter into our apprehension of the tale most determinedly.

One of the greatest advantages of looking at the word–picture relation in picturebooks in this way is that it offers a perspective on them that is more realistic than some of the looser, musical metaphors. If we are prepared to see language and image working productively upon each other then we have the beginnings of a model upon which to build an account of the picturebook that fits our experience of reading. What is lacking at the moment is a way of acknowledging and examining differences. All picturebooks may exhibit the interanimation of word and picture, but not all picturebooks do it in the same way.

Taxonomies and types

During the 1970s, 1980s and 1990s writers and illustrators of picturebooks pushed outwards at the limits of what could be said in words and pictures and how it could be said. Formal experimentation went hand in hand with attempts to address wider and more diverse audiences and more and more sophisticated kinds of subject matter. Critics and commentators have responded by looking, amongst other things, for emerging patterns and themes within the work of those who are judged to be the major practitioners. One approach has been to categorize picturebooks according to the different ways in which words and pictures are perceived to interact. I do not intend here to review every attempt that has been made at this project but I shall look briefly at three relatively recent examples to try and illustrate their strengths and weaknesses.

One of the most recent attempts to create a sophisticated taxonomy of picturebook interactions is that of Maria Nikolajeva and Carole Scott. Nikolajeva and Scott (2000, and forthcoming)[3] identify a 'broad spectrum of word–image interaction' (2000:225) reaching from *symmetry* at one end to *contradiction* at the other, symmetry being, roughly speaking, an equivalence of word and image, contradiction, a maximal dissonance. At various points along the continuum between these two poles they locate what they consider to be significant forms of interaction and these become the categories within which different kinds of picturebook are sited. The main categories are *symmetry, enhancement, counterpoint* and *contradiction*. These are explained as follows.

Words and images are considered to be in a symmetrical relationship when they come as close as possible to conveying the same information or telling the same story – roughly the equivalent of Sendak's narrative illustration. Thus if the words tell us of a boy standing in the rain in a garden, the pictures show us precisely that – a boy in a garden with the rain falling. The relationship between words and pictures becomes enhancing when the pictures expand upon the words or vice versa, the possibilities within this category ranging from minimal enhancement to significant enhancement or complementarity. In the former case (minimal enhancement) there is little difference between what the words say and what the pictures show, but in the latter case, one strand within the text will be seen to enlarge upon the other in ways which clearly affect the overall meaning. William Steig's *Sylvester and the Magic Pebble* is cited as an example of minimal enhancement, the argument being that the pictures do only a little more than echo the words and thus barely shift the text beyond the condition of word–image symmetry. On the other hand, when words and pictures enhance each other significantly something quite distinctive is held to be added to one strand of the text by the other. Beatrix Potter's *The Tale of Peter Rabbit* is, for Nikolajeva and Scott, a good example of a book where words and pictures are in such a complementary relationship. Potter's verbal text gives us the bare tale but her pictures tell us things about Peter's relationship with his family not mentioned in the words. As we have already seen, for Nikolajeva and Scott, when words and pictures counterpoint one another they offer the reader 'alternative information' so that an effort must be made to forge a connection. Contradiction, the extreme form of counterpoint, pushes the words and pictures even further apart so that they seem to be saying entirely different things.

There is enormous variety within the picturebook form, and categorizing the dynamic relationships between words and pictures seems to offer a means of gaining some purchase on the differences between picturebooks. A particular strength of Nikolajeva and Scott's approach lies in the fact that they not only discriminate between types of interaction but also explore the way they intersect with narrative features such as character, setting and point of view. In relation to these features some combinations of word and picture do seem to be relatively static and uncomplicated, the pictures appearing to do little more than shadow, or echo, the story told in the words. Others seem to demand more of the reader in terms of active synthesis and there are, indeed, those that challenge the reader with discontinuous or bizarre combinations. Nikolajeva and Scott are also careful to remind readers that the categories they describe cannot be considered to be wholly watertight, but even allowing for their sensitivity in this area their account gives rise to a number of conceptual and terminological difficulties.

Consider for example the authors' use of the term 'symmetrical'. In their view, a relationship is symmetrical when 'words and pictures tell the same story, essentially repeating information in different forms of communication' (Nikolajeva and Scott, 2000:225). The difficulty here is that a picture can only offer 'the same information' in the loosest possible sense and, as Nodelman demonstrates very clearly, it can only do this insofar as the words tell the reader what he or she should attend to.[4] The symmetry that many picturebooks appear to exhibit is thus illusory, an artefact of word–picture interanimation. Such relationships are often better understood in terms of the practical process of illustration, that is, the way illustrators sometimes try to match in pictures what they read in a prior written text. A further problem arises out of the fact that, although Nikolajeva and Scott purport to be exploring the dynamic interaction of word and image, to claim a symmetrical relationship for many picturebooks is to side-step the question of interaction altogether. If the two parts of the text appear to be saying the same thing then there would appear to be no interaction to examine. The pictures and words would simply be running on parallel tracks. What would be far more useful would be an investigation into how the effect of symmetry is achieved. To what parts of a verbal text are pictures responding when the resultant impression is one of congruence or symmetry? As we saw in the case of *Gorilla*, the words and sentences that make up a narrative are not all of the same kind and some are clearly easier to set 'symmetrical' pictures alongside than others.

Similar problems arise when we consider the category of contradiction. If this is taken to mean something like 'stating the opposite' then we have the same problem as with symmetry. Nodelman's warning that '. . . pictures . . . can imply narrative information only in relationship to a verbal context' (Nodelman 1988:195) alerts us to the fact that we simply cannot identify what it is that a picture 'states' in relation to the narrative outside of its animation by the words. Pictures certainly do possess an ideational function – that is, they are perfectly capable of representing facts, events and states of affairs – but words, whether in the form of captions or fragments of narrative, will always affect how we take up and interpret those facts. In other words, the impression of contradiction is once again an artefact, a product, of the pictures and words coming together and acting upon one another rather than simply a matter of two modes offering transparently contrary meanings.

What Nikolajeva and Scott are really interested in, like most researchers in this field, are the effects of difference and incongruity, the ways in which pictures and words rub up alongside each other in ways that make us stop and think. In this respect, Denise Agosto, in her article, 'One and inseparable:

interdependent storytelling in picture storybooks' follows a similar route (Agosto 1999). At the outset she distinguishes between what she terms twice-told tales – those where '. . . the texts and the illustrations . . . tell the same stories simultaneously' – and interdependent tales, where '. . . the reader must consider both forms of media concurrently in order to comprehend the books' stories' (Agosto 1999:267). Twice-told tales are said to employ parallel storytelling rather than interdependent storytelling, but parallelism is simply symmetry by another name and as such must be seen as the result of interdependence rather than as a separate category altogether. However, Agosto's purpose is not to investigate the whole range, but to propose and elaborate upon a model of interdependent storytelling in those cases where there are clear differences between words and images. She begins with a diagrammatic representation of her model, dividing up the terrain into super-ordinate, interordinate and subordinate categories (see Figure 1).

Agosto's two major sub-categories are therefore storytelling by augmentation and storytelling by contradiction. In the case of books that work by augmentation, '. . . the texts and the illustrations each amplify, extend and complete the story that the other tells'; in the case of contradiction, '. . . the texts and illustrations present conflicting information, such as the words describing a sunny day where the corresponding pictures show a rainstorm' (Agosto 1999:269, 275). Agosto provides some fairly clear examples of contradiction and manages to find some books where at least some features of the verbal text are illustrated in a manner that indicates something like opposition or negation. For example, in Steven Kellogg's *Pinkerton, Behave!*, a puppy in the process of being house-trained refuses to comply with its master's commands. The words tell of commands such as 'Come!' and 'Fetch!' while the pictures show Pinkerton responding by respectively

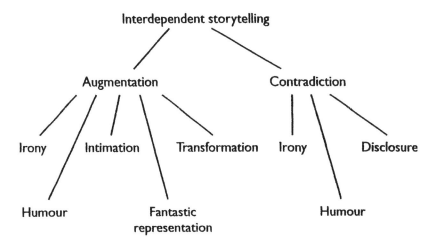

Figure 1 A theoretical model of interdependent storytelling, from Agosto 1999.

jumping out of the window and shredding the newspaper. But the same objections could be raised here as in the paragraphs above. The putative opposition of 'Come' and the image of a dog leaping through a window is the result of an interpretative act and not the outcome of the simple co-presence of two logically incompatible statements.

A further difficulty arises out of the attempt to subdivide these two main types. Agosto provides two titles as examples of each subdivision and although she nowhere makes it explicit, it seems clear that the categories of augmentation through irony, humour, intimation etc., are intended to be categories or types of book. *Tidy Titch*, by Pat Hutchins, is thus an example of ironical augmentation and Ellen Raskin's *Nothing Ever Happens on My Block* turns out to be an example of disclosing contradiction. The problem is that, as Agosto admits, an individual book may exhibit more than one effect. Irony and humour, for example, come together more often than not: indeed, it would be very strange if they did not. In fact it would not be difficult to imagine a book exemplifying several traits at once. One of Agosto's own examples of fantastic representation – John Burningham's *Come Away from the Water, Shirley*, the sister text to the one mentioned at the beginning of the chapter – is a particularly indeterminate picturebook possessing ironical, humorous, fantastic and even contradictory features. What this suggests is that the categories as they are described are not particularly useful for characterizing individual books but are far more useful as an indication of the kinds of effects that pictures and picture sequences can have when placed alongside different kinds of verbal texts. The ironical augmentation of words by pictures, if it is anything at all, is the result of a particular kind of word–image interanimation, not a kind of book. It may well be the case that certain books exhibit very clearly a particular form of interanimation throughout, but the very fact that many books exhibit several forms, either simultaneously or sequentially, suggests that in looking at types of book, we are looking at too large a unit of analysis.

Joanne Golden alerts her readers to this fact in her chapter on the picturebook in *The Narrative Symbol in Childhood Literature*. In her own words, 'It is important to note, however, that while particular relationships between picture and text may be predominant in certain picture books, a given book may also reflect more than one type of relationship' (Golden 1990:104). Golden attempts to '. . . examine the nature of the picture storybook' by describing and exemplifying five different types of text–picture relationship. These are:

(i)   text and picture are symmetrical;
(ii)   text depends on picture for clarification;
(iii)   illustration enhances, elaborates text;
(iv)   text carries primary narrative, illustration is selective; and
(v)   illustration carries primary narrative, text is selective.

Symmetry is again considered to be the simplest, most basic word–image relationship. Golden, like Nikolajeva and Scott, and Agosto, finds nothing to say about the interaction or interanimation of the two strands other than that the words echo, or shadow, the pictures and vice versa: 'In this type of text–picture relationship, the picture provides redundant information to the text. It serves literally to convey what the text conveys.' Once again, this is both an inaccurate description of the case and a sidestepping of the issue of interaction (although, to be fair, Golden does not claim to be examining how words and pictures interact, only how they are 'related'). Her examples are taken from *The Tale of Peter Rabbit* (remember that Nikolajeva and Scott considered this to be a good example of significant enhancement, or complementarity, not symmetry) and *Titch* by Pat Hutchins. Of *Titch* she says:

> On one page, the text reads 'Pete had a big drum' and under the text is a picture of Pete holding two drumsticks with a large drum hanging from a string around his neck. In a comparable picture on the opposite page, the text reads 'Mary had a trumpet' and a picture of Mary blowing a trumpet is depicted below the text.
>
> (Golden 1990:106)

It should be fairly clear that the pictures can only be said to convey 'literally' what the text conveys by virtue of the fact that the words are telling us what to notice and what to think of what we see. Taken away from the words in the book, the pictures might better be thought of as being symmetrical with something like 'Peter holds a drum and drumsticks', and 'Mary plays a trumpet' – that is, words from a book about 'doing things'. The pictures will not 'literally convey' anything in particular until they are brought to life by the words around them.

Golden is more helpful about clarification (type ii) and enhancement/ elaboration (type iii). Pictures clarify the written text when the words alone are insufficient to carry the narrative. In Ezra Jack Keats' *The Snowy Day*, the words 'He walked with his toes pointing in, like that:' make a clear gesture towards the picture where we see exactly what kind of a walk it is. '[A]nd he made angels,' is unclear for a slightly different reason. Without the picture it is assumed we would not know that what is being referred to are 'snow angels' made by moving the arms up and down and the legs from side to side while lying in the snow. When the relationship between word and picture is one of elaboration, '. . . the essential narrative is conveyed in the text but the illustrations extend and elaborate the text by delineating further details' (Golden 1990:110). It is here that we begin to see that Golden's is essentially a word-centred view of the picturebook. Although she quotes with approval the picture theorist W. J. T. Mitchell on the complex word–image relationship of 'mutual translation, interpretation, illustration and embellishment' (Mitchell 1987:44) she tends to look at the words first and then the pictures to see what relationship the latter seem to have towards the former. This position becomes even clearer when we move on to the fourth kind of relationship. This is where the written text carries the primary narrative and illustration is selective, the illustrator singling out just one or two of the many scenes and events conveyed to the reader through the words.

In describing the picture–word relationship in her final category 'Illustration carries primary narrative, text is selective' she betrays a misunderstanding of how words and pictures interanimate one another and in her choice of example inadvertently reveals the limitations of her scheme. *Hey Diddle Diddle* by Randolph Caldecott does indeed appear to be a narrative told in pictures but if we were to take away the words of the traditional rhyme and (this is necessary also) forget that we ever knew them, I am not at all sure that we could make consistent narrative sense out of Caldecott's sequence of pictures. It is therefore simply untrue to say that the pictures 'carry the primary narrative'. Once again, if they appear to do so, it is only because we are guided by the words alongside or in our heads. Furthermore, to say that the text is 'selective' is to suggest that the words chronologically came after the images: the 'author' choosing which of the many features of the illustrations to mention. But this is plainly not the case for we know that Caldecott, as was his usual practice, chose a popular short text and embellished it with sequences of pictures. Golden acknowledges that this was so. If that is what happened, then would not *Hey Diddle Diddle*, along with other similar picturebooks, be better considered as an example of enhancement and elaboration, that is, of her type iii?

Once again, confusion and misunderstanding seem to take over when attempts are made to label picturebooks according to how the words and pictures seem to be related to one another, or how they interact. There is a singular lack of agreement over how categories – that is, types – of book might be described, and a pervasive lack of understanding of the nature of word–picture interanimation, particularly in relation to narrative. Individual texts are described differently by different authors (e.g. Beatrix Potter's *The Tale of Peter Rabbit*) and there is a general unwillingness to recognize that the appropriate unit of analysis is the form of word–picture interaction and not the whole book. Why should this be so?

Part of the problem, I believe, stems from the fact that picturebooks do not take kindly to being corralled into six, eight or even ten determinate categories. Part of the argument of this book is that the picturebook is a particularly flexible form of text and that picturebooks in general are extraordinarily diverse. I tried in Chapter 1 to hint at the heterogeneity of the form and suggested that one way of linking different kinds of picturebooks together is through the concept of family resemblances. Picturebook A may be like picturebook B, and B may be quite like C, but that does not mean that A and C will be much alike except in the most general terms. Furthermore, taxonomies, once established, exert a considerable magnetic attraction. If it seems that picturebooks are divisible into the complementary, the contrapuntal and the contradictory, then there is a strong temptation to make individual examples fit the available categories. If there seem to be contradictory elements to a particular book then into the bag it goes, foreclosing more detailed examination. There clearly are differences in the ways that illustrators manipulate word–picture relationships, and there clearly are books that are consistent in their treatment of those relationships, but there are also many, many books that are subtle, indeterminate and resistant to easy categorization.

Where does this discussion leave us? If neither musical analogies nor simple taxonomies will do, where might we go from here? What we need is a way of looking at picturebooks that in the broad view recognizes the interanimation that always occurs when words and pictures are intertwined as they are in picturebooks, but that also posits the flexibility of the relationship, the way it can twist and turn within the supple telling of a tale. At the risk of burdening the reader with yet another metaphor, I want to suggest that we might develop the notion of an interanimation of word and image by considering the two strands to be held together in an *ecological* relationship.

Notes

1 It should already be clear that this is a great oversimplification. Words in picturebooks can do far more than simply point to what should be attended to in the pictures, and the pictures almost always do more than dress up the words in colour and form. Nonetheless it cannot be emphasized too much that 'what the words do to the pictures is not the same as what the pictures do to the words'. For further clarification and discussion readers are advised to turn to Nodelman's Chapter 7, 'The relationships of pictures and words', in particular, pp. 193–201.
2 Lawrence Sipe adopts the term 'synergy' in his article 'How picture books work' (Sipe 1998:98) and follows *The Shorter Oxford Dictionary* definition: 'the production of two or more agents, substances, etc., of a combined effect greater then the sum of their separate effects.' This formulation, along with Nodelman's, seems to me to be more inclusive than Barthes' and thus more appropriate to the varied form of the picturebook.
3 At the time of writing neither Nikolajeva and Scott's book, *How Picturebooks Work*, nor the article based upon the book was published. The article has now been published in the winter 2000 issue of *Children's Literature in Education*. I was fortunate enough to be able to read the finished draft and the comments in this chapter are based solely upon that draft.
4 See the arguments earlier in this chapter. Also, consider Nodelman again:

> pictures can communicate much to us, and particularly much of visual significance – but only if words focus them, tell us what it is about them that might be worth paying attention to. In a sense, trying to understand the situation a picture depicts is always an act of imposing language

upon it – interpreting visual information in verbal terms; it is not accidental that we speak of 'visual literacy', of the 'grammar' of pictures, of 'reading' pictures. Reading pictures for narrative meaning is a matter of applying our understanding of words.

(Nodelman 1988:211)

References

Agosto, D. E. (1999) 'One and inseparable: interdependent storytelling in picturebooks', *Children's Literature in Education* 30(4): 267–280.

Barthes, R. (1986) 'Rhetoric of the image', in R. Barthes, *The Responsibility of Forms, Critical Essays on Music, Art, and Representation*, trans. R. Howard, Oxford: Basil Blackwell.

Golden, J. M. (1990) *The Narrative Symbol in Childhood Literature: Explorations in the Construction of Text*, Berlin: Mouton.

Lorraine, W. (1977) 'An interview with Maurice Sendak', in S. Egoff, G. T. Stubbs and L. Ashley (eds) (1980) *Only Connect: Readings on Children's Literature*, 2nd edn, Toronto: Oxford University Press.

Meek, M. (1992) 'Children reading – now', in M. Styles, E. Bearne and V. Watson (eds), *AfterAlice*, London: Cassell.

Mitchell, W. J. T. (1987) *Iconology: Image, Text, Ideology*, Chicago: Chicago University Press.

Moss, E. (1990) 'A certain particularity: an interview with Janet and Allan Ahlberg', *Signal* 61: 20–26.

Nikolajeva, M. and Scott, C. (2000) 'The dynamics of picturebook communication', *Children's Literature in Education* 31(4): 225–239.

—— (2001) *How Picturebooks Work*, New York: Garland.

Nodelman, P. (1988) *Words about Pictures: The Narrative Art of Children's Picture Books*, Athens, Georgia: University of Georgia Press.

Pullman, P. (1988) 'Invisible pictures', *Signal* 60: 160–186.

—— (1993) 'Words and pictures: an examination of comic strip technique', in K. Barker (ed.), *Graphic Account*, Newcastle-under-Lyme: The Library Association Youth Libraries Group.

Schwarcz, J. H. (1982) *Ways of the Illustrator: Visual Communication in Children's Literature*, Chicago: American Library Association.

Sipe, L. R. (1998) 'How picture books work: a semiotically framed theory of text–picture relationships', *Children's Literature in Education* 29(2): 97–108.

Picturebook references

Gorilla by Anthony Browne, Walker Books, 1983.

Voices in the Park by Anthony Browne, Doubleday, 1998.

Come Away From the Water, Shirley by John Burningham, Jonathan Cape, 1977.

Time to Get Out of the Bath, Shirley by John Burningham, Jonathan Cape, 1978.

Aladdin by Errol Le Cain, Faber & Faber, 1981.

Hey Diddle Diddle and Baby Bunting by Randolph Caldecott, first published George Routledge & Son, 118821; New Orchard Editions, 1988.

Princess Smartypants by Babette Cole, Hamish Hamilton, 1986.

Drop Dead by Babette Cole, Jonathan Cape, 1996.

So Much by Trish Cooke, illustrated by Helen Oxenbury, Walker Books, 1994.

The Little Boat by Kathy Henderson, illustrated by Patrick Benson, Walker Books, 1995.

Rosie's Walk by Pat Hutchins, The Bodley Head, 1970.

Tidy Titch by Pat Hutchins, Julia MacRae, 1991.

The Snowy Day by Ezra Jack Keats, The Bodley Head, 1967.

Pinkerton, Behave! by Steven Kellogg, Dial Press, 1979.

Have You Seen Who's Just Moved in Next Door to Us? by Cohn McNaughton, Walker Books, 1991.

The Tale of Peter Rabbit by Beatrix Potter, Frederick Warne, 1902.

Nothing Ever Happens on My Block by Ellen Raskin, Athenium, 1966.

Sylvester and the Magic Pebble by William Steig, Simon & Schuster, 1969.

The Park in the Dark by Martin Waddell, illustrated by Barbara Firth, Walker Books, 1989.

21

THE NATURE OF PICTUREBOOKS

Theories about visual texts and readers

Evelyn Arizpe and Morag Styles

Source: *Children Reading Pictures*, London: RoutledgeFalmer, 2003, pp. 19–38.

> Picturebooks successfully combining the imaginary and the symbolic, the iconic and the conventional, have achieved something that no other literary form has mastered.
>
> (Nikolajeva and Scott 2000: 262)

> Pictures form a point of peculiar friction and discomfort across a broad range of intellectual inquiry.
>
> (Mitchell 1994: 13)

Defining picturebooks

In the opening to *American Picture Books*, Bader (1976) offers a succinct definition:[1]

> A picture book is text, illustrations, total design; an item of manufacture and a commercial product; a social, cultural, historical document; and foremost an experience for a child. As an art form it hinges on the interdependence of pictures and words, on the simultaneous display of two facing pages, and on the drama of the turning page.

In this book we will be concerned with most of the notions mentioned by Bader: sophisticated picturebooks which require sophisticated readings; picturebooks which are simultaneously art objects and the primary literature of childhood; the importance of design and the interconnections between word and image; picturebooks as compelling narrative texts which, indeed, work on the basis of 'the drama of the turning page' (1976: 1). The fact that texts carry cultural, social and historical messages and that they are constructed as items of merchandise will not feature prominently in our discussion, but will be part of the implicit theoretical background to our study.

Nodelman takes the definition a little further when he argues that 'picture books are a significant means by which we integrate young children into the ideology of our culture. Like most narratives, picture book stories most forcefully guide readers into culturally acceptable ideas about who they are through the privileging of the point of view from which they report on the events they describe ... (in other words) to see and understand events and people as the narrator invites us to see them' (Nodelman in Hunt 1996: 116–18). Similarly, in *Language and Ideology in Children's Fiction* (1992), Stephens discusses the socialising and educative intentions of picturebooks and considers how the reader is positioned according to style, perspective and word–picture interaction, stressing that picturebooks can never be said to exist 'without a specific orientation towards the reality constructed by the society that produces them' (Stephens 1992: 158).

Although this book is about what children say about picturebooks and not about the picturebook itself, scholarly work on the subject has obviously informed our research. We shall therefore give a brief account of the theories that have furthered the study of the picturebook as an aesthetic object and, in some cases, of children's understanding of this object.

How picturebooks work

Our understanding of the reading process owes a great debt to Iser[2] and Rosenblatt. At the heart of the reading experience is the gap in the text which has to be filled by the reader, particularly pronounced, of course, in picturebooks. Iser draws on Laing's belief, forcefully argued in *The Politics of Experience*, about human beings 'continually filling in a central gap in our experience ...' and goes on to say, 'it is the gaps, the fundamental asymmetry between text and reader, that give rise to communication in the reading process' (1980: 165–7). Rosenblatt took up a similar theme when she argued that: 'The literary work exists in a live circuit set up between reader and text; the reader infuses intellectual and emotional meanings into the pattern of verbal symbols and these symbols channel his thoughts and feelings. Out of this process emerges a more or less organised imaginative experience' (1978: 25).

Whereas Iser and Rosenblatt focus on literary texts, Nikolajeva and Scott examine picturebooks which, they argue, lend themselves to hermeneutic analysis; the reader starts with the whole, looks at details, then goes back to the whole picture, as the process begins anew.

Whichever we start with, the verbal or the visual, it creates
expectations for the other, which in turn provides new experiences
and new expectations. The reader turns from verbal to visual and
back again, in an ever-expanding concentration of understanding. . . . Presumably, children know this by intuition when they
demand that the same book he read aloud to them over and
over again. Actually, they do not read the same book; they go
more and more deeply into its meaning. Too often adults have
lost the ability to read picturebooks in this way, because they
ignore the whole and regard the illustrations as merely decorative. This most probably has to do with the dominant position of
verbal, especially written, communication in our society, although
this is on the wane in generations raised on television and now
computers.

(2000: 2)

This description of the hermeneutic circle may seem self-evident, but
our study showed how complex such a process could be with regard to
sophisticated picturebooks.

If anyone still doubts that picturebooks are anything more than vehicles
of childish entertainment, a glance at a number of recent critical texts
devoted to understanding the nature of this apparently simple genre
should suffice to convince them. Such critics draw on the latest literary
theories – from poststructuralism to postcolonialism, from psychoanalysis
to gender theory – to analyse these books and still they cannot encompass
the multi-modal dynamic between image and text (which has no equivalent in adult literature as it goes well beyond that of even the graphic
novel).

To the parent or teacher who may chiefly come across picturebooks at
children's bedtime or during the Literacy Hour, at the very least picturebooks can provide some escape from routine and reality. But to adults
who approach them with some awareness of how they work, the reading
of a picturebook can be much more significant as intellectual excitement
converges with aesthetic pleasure, sometimes with emotional resonance
and often with some humour thrown in. As Nikolajeva points out, most
adults may need even more help than children in appreciating a picturebook
beyond the plot level. In fact, conventional criteria about what constitutes
culture, art, literature (including children's 'classics' and memories of
childhood reading) can get in the way, as can certain kinds of 'fixed' moral
and religious beliefs. Fortunately children, especially very young children,
do not approach picturebooks with these preconceptions and prejudices
and their openness and curiosity can teach many of us adults lessons
about looking.

The relationship between words and pictures

It must be emphasised that we are talking here about picturebooks – not books with illustrations, but books in which the story depends on the inter-action between written text and image and where both have been created with a conscious aesthetic intention (not just for pedagogic and commercial purposes). We are talking about picturebooks composed of pictures and words whose intimate interaction creates layers of meaning, open to differ-ent interpretations and which have the potential to arouse their readers to reflect on the act of reading itself. With some notable exceptions, we are referring to picturebooks published within the last twenty years or so where a quiet revolution has been taking place within children's literature. These picturebooks (along with other branches of children's literature) diverge from any concept of children's books as 'simple', if by simple we are refer-ring to such aspects as clear-cut narrative structures, a chronological order of events, an unambiguous narrative voice and, not least, clearly delineated and fixed borders between fantasy and reality. We can observe a shift in artistic representation from the mimetic toward the symbolic. This shift in approach may be correlated with the postmodern interrogation of the arts' ability to reflect reality by means of language, or indeed by visual means. (See, for example, Nikolajeva and Scott 2000: 260–1.)

The relationship between word and image in a picturebook is particularly interesting. Mitchell (1994) talks about a complex relationship of mutual translation and interpretation, while Kress and van Leeuwen focus on the visual component of a text as an 'independently organised and structured message connected with the verbal text. . . . The two sets of meanings are therefore neither fully conflated, nor entirely opposed' (1996: 16–17). Kümmerling-Meibauer suggests that the relationship between word and image is always dialogical and that, in learning from text and pictures, the cognitive functions they perform are the most significant: 'the tension between the text and the pictures is the central subject of these picture books. Visual discovery, isolation of things, and disruption of traditional context lead to transformation and demand higher cognitive awareness on behalf of the viewer . . . the pictures change the meaning of the words' (1999: 163–76). In an article exploring the possibility of a semiotically framed theory of text–picture relationships, Sipe shows us how sophisticated picturebooks demand recursive reading: 'There is thus a tension between our impulse to gaze at the pictures . . . and not to interrupt the temporal narrative flow. The verbal text drives us to read in a linear way, where the illustrations seduce us into stopping to look' (1998: 101).

Sipe (1998) and Lewis (2001)[3] both review recent attempts to theorise the relationships between written text and pictures and to find appropriate metaphorical language to describe this complex and varied interaction.

Between them they cite Moebius's attempts at a geological comparison with 'plate tectonics' and 'polysystemy'; Schwarcz's use of 'congruency' for harmonious relationships between word and image; Nodelman's use of irony to describe the dynamic way 'the words change the pictures' and vice versa; Meek's 'interanimation', Mitchell's 'mutual translation', Sipe's 'transmediation' and Lewis's own ecological analogy, which he develops at length in *Reading Contemporary Picturebooks*; and various musical metaphors such as author, Ahlberg's, 'antiphonal fugue effect' and illustrator, Sendak's, conceptualisation of his craft as 'almost like a composer thinking music when reading poetry' or 'counterpoint' used differently by Pullman (1989), Schwarcz (1982) and Nikolajeva and Scott (2001).

Art, educational and literary criticism

Since the 1960s there has been a growing body of writing about illustration in children's literature in general, including picturebooks. The work of Hurlimann (1968), Alderson (1973), MacCann and Richard (1973) and Bader (1976) among others has pioneered the study of illustration. According to Nikolajeva and Scott, the first book to consider the picturebook as a whole, as a sequence of 'symbolic communication' rather than individual pictures, was Schwarcz (1982). He not only tried to understand how pictures carry meaning but also how they relate to the verbal text and he explored specific elements such as motifs, metaphors, patterns and contexts in order to raise awareness of how the illustrator worked. Others, such as Roxburgh (1983), Moebius (1986), Bradford (1993) and Sipe (1998) have tackled the issue of text–picture dynamics from different theoretical angles.

One of the most influential studies which raised the tone of the discussion around picturebooks and gave it greater academic status, is that of Nodelman. In *Words About Pictures* he examines visual features in depth (as well as style, symbols and movement) to show how communication is achieved. He was one of the first critics to consider the relationship between words and pictures for the text's meaning as a whole, believing that: 'placing them into relationship with each other inevitably changes the meaning of both, so that good picture books as a whole are a richer experience than just the simple sum of their parts'. He goes on to say that the most successful picturebooks seem to be those in which 'unity on a higher level' emerges from pictures and written texts which are noticeably fragmentary and whose differences from each other are a significant part of the effect and meaning of the whole (1988: 199–200).

It is the differences between words and pictures that make us reinterpret each in the light of the other; this led Nodelman to theorise that their relationship is mainly ironical. However, as Kümmerling-Meibauer points out in her detailed exploration of irony in picturebooks, the picture–text relationship is not always ironical, it only applies to some instances of the genre. Whether or not a picturebook is ironical, she concludes:

> what should be abundantly clear is that most of the key elements of sophisticated narratives are present in a simpler form in picture books. These statements suggest that the modern picture book as an art form is now ready to claim its own territory, both artistically and as a field of research.
>
> (1999: 177)

Another fruitful approach was taken by Graham (1990) in *Pictures on the Page*, as she discussed how artists convey emotions through themes, character, settings and story. Graham also shows how this teaches the reader about narrative conventions and develops their literary competence, arguing that children react to these emotions and have the ability to interpret complex 'post-modern' books such as those by Browne, Sendak or Burningham which take the implied reader seriously.

Doonan is a most perceptive and original critic; in *Looking at Pictures in Picture Books* (and various articles in international journals), she uses her extensive knowledge of art and individual artists to show us how to become 'beholders'.[4] Doonan (1986) examines picturebooks as aesthetic objects and increases readers' understanding of how visual features work, pointing out that abstract elements of picture making – colour, line, shape, composition – together with chosen materials and style, 'allude to complex psychological states through images which function as the visual equivalent of simile, metaphor and intertextuality'. Doonan explains that readers must 'tolerate ambiguity' and 'remain genuinely open-minded and prepared to give the whole process plenty of time' (1986: 9–11). She is outstanding in her analysis of Browne and Kitamura's work; her influence on the present authors is evident as her wise commentaries are studded throughout this book.

In *How Picturebooks Work*, Nikolajeva and Scott argue that, although the work of Schwarcz, Moebius, Nodelman and Doonan provide help in decoding pictures, it does not go far enough in 'decoding the specific text of picturebooks, the text created by the interaction of verbal and visual information' (2000: 4). By building on the work of other international scholars,[5] Nikolajeva and Scott attempt to arrive at a system of categories which describe this interaction. A thorough examination of picturebooks where the words and the pictures provide 'mutually dependent narratives' (a category of picturebook they label 'counterpointing') allows them to arrive at a terminology which, as their title says, helpfully describes how these books work.

Although Nikolajeva and Scott are interested in how the reader's imagination is involved in the reading, they do not discuss children's responses. While admitting that they avoid the problem of audience, they believe picturebooks provide a special occasion for a collaborative relationship between children and adults, for picturebooks empower children and adults much more equally. 'Those less bound to the accepted conventions of decoding text are freer to respond to the less traditional work, so children's very naïveté serves them well in this arena, making them truer partners in the reading experience. Children's ability, therefore, to perceive and sift visual detail often outdistances that of the adult' (2000: 261). We would argue that it is not only children's 'ability to perceive and sift' that empowers them, but that, although they may be 'naïve' with respect to literary conventions, they are equally if not more sophisticated than adults in other respects.

Unlike the scholars above, Lewis does actually report children's responses to some of the picturebooks he discusses. In his article on Burningham's *Where's Julius?* (1992), Lewis compares his own reading of this picturebook with that of his two children. He describes the book in detail and the way in which his understanding of it changed through hearing the children's difficulties with retelling this story. He then discusses the way in which the conventional relationship between image and text is subverted and how a game is played by the readers in order to make sense of a metafictive and open-ended picturebook such as this one. He argues that this type of book forces the child (and adult) reader to involve critical skills that teach us about the actual nature of reading pictures.[6]

In a later article Lewis says:

> I can see at least two routes to finding ways forward in the study and criticism of the picture book, neither of them new, and both involving a focus upon individual texts in an attempt to accommodate diversity and difference. One route involves careful and patient listening to what children say as they read, the other an equally patient, careful description of individual books.
>
> (1996: 113)

In Lewis's recent study he decided to take the latter route because, although he does occasionally draw on his conversations with primary school children about some of the books, and in various places emphasises the importance of taking into account both children's and adults' responses, *Reading Contemporary Picturebooks* (2001) is more about understanding the nature of the picturebook than about children's understanding of them. Lewis begins by discussing formal features of picturebooks and reviewing taxonomies (including those of Nikolajeva and Scott) of the interaction between words and pictures. He goes on to explore the multiform and constantly developing nature of this genre through the concepts of ecology, play, postmodernism[7] and Wittgenstein's later philosophical work on language games etc. He also experiments with applying Kress and Van Leeuwen's grammar of visual design to the images in picturebooks. Lewis alerts us to the many forms that picturebooks take and will continue to take in the future. It is because of this constant change that he claims 'the picturebook is thus ideally suited to the task of absorbing, reinterpreting and re-presenting the world to an audience for whom negotiating newness is a daily task' (2001: 137). Once again he reminds us of the importance of looking closely at the reading event itself.

Discordant voices

Unfortunately, we live increasingly in an official educational culture which 'underestimates the power of the picturebook to give rise to a variety of intellectual and emotional responses' as Kiefer tells us in *The Potential of Picture Books*. She goes on to document how educational systems have:

> neglected the potential of picture books to develop visual literacy, just as reading and writing researchers have overlooked the opportunities for language and literacy learning provided by picture books. Children live in a highly complex visual world and are bombarded with visual stimuli more intensely than most preceding generations. Yet few teachers spend time helping children sort out, recognise, and understand the many forms of visual information they encounter, certainly not in the same way teachers deal with print literacy.
>
> (1993: 10)

Goldsmith, author of *Research into Illustration*, admits as much: 'although a number of researchers had investigated the place of illustration in the teaching of reading, not only were the findings apparently contradictory, but few ... paid proper attention to the nature of the illustration itself' (1984: 2).

We believe that these attributes should be valued in schools, but in Britain and America, and probably most educational systems across the world, the skills of visual literacy are under-rated or, in extreme cases, despised. Take the work of Protheroe; in a book whose title says it all – *Vexed Texts: How Children's Picture Books Promote Illiteracy* – she asserts that at school

> [children] are being exposed to what is called 'contextualised' or 'context-embedded' language ... (they) do not have to imagine anything. ... How can they [create meaning for themselves] if 'meaning' is always provided in the form of objects or pictures? They can't. ... My contention [is] that illustrated books are harmful to developing reading skills ... and may permanently stunt their intellectual growth. ... Right from the beginning [children] need stories without pictures.
>
> (1992: 8–10,158)

Not only do we think that Protheroe is misguided, but the whole of *Children Reading Pictures* provides evidence in support of the opposite argument. Our research shows that picturebooks encourage intellectual growth in children and we believe that they should be used more widely with older pupils as well as with younger children who are learning the rudiments of reading.

There is, however, some evidence to suggest that pictures are not always beneficial to young readers. Although Goldsmith asserts that 'in communicating in print with people who cannot read, pictures are essential', she goes on to quote Hale and Piper (1973) who found that under research conditions 'children younger than thirteen have difficulty in ignoring irrelevant material. This means that a picture, if not a positive help, could become a hindrance.' She also notes that Donlan (1977) found that children were more imaginative in their drawing and use of colours in response to a story if they had not previously seen the illustrations (1986: 111). Goldsmith also suggests that, 'once the ability to produce internal structures exists (around 8/9 years) for tasks of a given level of difficulty, pictures hinder rather than help learning . . . [and] can have a leveling effect, helping slower learners and retarding the others'. But Goldsmith's understanding of the possibilities made available by complex picturebooks seems rather limited, as she also suggests that text and picture 'should convey as nearly as possible the same message to the viewer' (1984: 78–9, 354–95). From *Rosie's Walk* to *The Stinky Cheese Man*, and most pointedly in *Zoo* and *Lily*, picturebook artists have successfully demonstrated how the opposite can be true; indeed, most ironic picturebooks work precisely on the principle that the words and pictures tell contrasting stories which challenge readers to make their own interpretations.

Readers and teachers

All of the scholars discussed above have furthered our understanding of the picturebook, particularly in its most recent and complex forms, and all of them are aware of the importance of audience. However, there is another body of recent work which has attempted to bring children's voices into the picture and suggested how pedagogy may help extend children's knowledge and enjoyment of picturebooks.

One of the main influences has been Meek's seminal *How Texts Teach What Readers Learn* (1988) which describes how children's books can initiate readers into understanding how different kinds of narratives work. These reading 'games' can only be properly learned by immersion in a wide range of texts which gradually reveal their secrets. These ideas probably influenced Hollindale (1997), who argues for a 'childist criticism' of children's literature, a critical approach which values the child's opinions and preferences and also reflects on the context in which the act of reading takes place. It is an approach often linked to reader-response theory which focuses on the active role of the reader in the reading process, a process Rosenblatt calls 'transactional' because reader and text 'shape' each other. According to Watson, the result of this interaction is not only that the text is multi-layered but that so is the act of reading: readers bring their 'potential for engaged responsiveness' to the texts which at the same time invite the reader to increase their engagement and realise the potential of those texts. A good teacher will recognise this and build on both of these potentials (Watson in Styles and Drummond 1993).

Michaels and Walsh (1990) discuss different types of picturebooks and reader response to the visual text, and how they can be used in primary and secondary classrooms to teach aspects such as narrative, gender and register. Baddeley and Eddershaw (1994) follow a similar line in *Not So Simple Picture Books*, where they analyse children's responses to show how picturebooks demand sophisticated visual and intellectual skills from the reader and how children are able to rise to the challenge. Consequently, they criticise the National Curriculum in Britain for not taking advantage of the teaching picturebooks can offer to both younger and older readers. They show, in a variety of ways, how this can be achieved with teacher guidance. Anstey and Bull's *Reading the Visual* (2000) provides a comprehensive introduction to the genre and discusses the place of the picturebook in the curriculum within the Australian context. *Talking Pictures* (Watson and Styles 1996), particularly the chapters by Bromley, Rosen, Styles and Watson, puts children in the spotlight, often analysing shared readings which demonstrate how very young readers can engage intellectually with picturebooks. The importance of young readers' response is also emphasised in another collection of articles, *What's in the Picture?* (Evans 1998).

At the heart of the work by both art specialists and educationalists is the desire to understand how picturebooks work and to use this understanding to further both adults' and children's knowledge and appreciation of this art form. Nodelman's study, for example, intended to:

> bring such invisible knowledge to the surface so that we may better appreciate the amazing learning capabilities of children and so that we can allow children themselves to appreciate it also. My own experience with children confirms that many of them can learn to develop a rich and subtle consciousness of the special characteristics of picturebook narrative and can immensely enjoy doing so. But such knowledge cannot be learned if it is not taught.
>
> (1988: 37)

In what follows, we explore some of the ways in which this learning develops in children and how it can be more fruitfully taught.

Cognitive psychology and visual literacy

Much of the literature on how children read pictures comes from developmental psychology. The main focus of research in this field examines, usually under test conditions, how children respond to particular, often isolated images, or pictures in text books. Because of its close focus on the cognitive, such research mostly fails to take account of the outstanding art work in many picturebooks which provokes affective as well as cognitive reactions in young readers, and also ignores the dynamic relationship between viewer and text which is so evident to those of us studying children's overall reactions to picturebooks.

Although neither Piaget nor Vygotsky refer specifically to the ways in which children look at artistic images of the kind we are concerned with, their theories (and later, Bruner's) on cognitive development underlie our understanding of how children learn to think. In observing how children from 4 to 11 make sense of pictures, it was inevitable that we returned to their seminal ideas, though we do not pretend to be conversant with all the debates surrounding their work or the huge scholarship in this field.

One of Piaget's major theories linked thinking with experience; children act upon the world through their senses and develop hypotheses based on the consequences of their actions. Vygotsky takes a different tack: while he goes along with Piaget's view that action is crucial to learning, for Vygotsky it is language that plays an indispensable role in mediating internal thought processes such as the ability to reason and to reflect. Like Dewey, Vygotsky goes on to argue that language is a way of sorting out thoughts, a primary vehicle for cognition and socialisation, emphasising the social, collaborative and cultural aspects of learning. Vygotsky did attempt to link psychology with art, literature, emotion and other aspects of culture; had he lived longer he might well have extended his thinking to children learning specifically through image.

Piaget showed how babies discovered predictable patterns and learned to anticipate. He believed that perception was subordinated to action so that children could only make sense of the world within their developmental stage. Piaget's influence on educators has been enormous, including those interested in visual texts such as Sipe discussing what he calls the 'transmediation' of word and image in picturebooks:

> Each new page opening presents us with a new set of words and new illustrations to factor into our construction of meaning. Reviewing and rereading will produce ever-new insights as we construct new connections and make modifications of our previous interpretations, in a Piagetian process of assimilation and accommodation. In other words, we assimilate new information and in

the process we change our cognitive structures, accommodating them to the new information.

(1998: 106)

It follows from Piaget's theory that young children are not capable of seeing the world as older children or as adults do because they lack the mental operations to make sense of what they see. Wood,[8] however, argues that perhaps it 'is not young children's inability to perform logical operations but their general lack of expertise which leads them to perceive situations in different ways from the adult' (1998: 36). This is in tune with Vygotsky's notion that children's development interacts with their cultural experience, and that perception, action and speech are inseparable and necessary for the acquisition of knowledge.

As Bruner has pointed out (1983), in Piaget's theory the child is very much alone in sorting out actions and thoughts, receiving little help from others. Bruner also stresses the importance of problem-solving in learning but he is more interested in the social processes it implies. According to Bruner,[9] building on Vygotsky's insights, the development of knowledge and the formation of concepts can be accelerated by 'scaffolding', particularly through the use of mediated language as the more experienced inducts the less experienced learner into understanding. Like Vygotsky, he believes that language has a crucial role to play in developing knowledge and thinking, so these processes are developed in the child through social interaction rather than tackled by the child on her own. This is where Vygotsky's influential concept of the 'zone of proximal development' also comes into play. He defined this as 'the distance between the actual developmental level as determined by independent problem solving and the level of potential development as determined through problem-solving under adult guidance or in collaboration with more capable peers' (1978: 86).

In our research, the results of co-operatively achieved learning were evident particularly in the group discussions and follow-up interviews. Questions were not only working as tools for inquiry, but also as the 'planks' and 'poles' of scaffolding which allowed children to move further into their zones of proximal development. Researchers became facilitators, especially in terms of providing a language through which the children could talk about pictures, modelling concepts and using prompts and leading questions. More experienced peers (those who had had greater access to the culture which produced the picturebook) unconsciously helped their schoolmates in their understanding as they talked about what they saw and how they made sense of it. This leads us to concur with the idea that communal expertise played a more crucial role than individual logical mental operations in determining how far children could make sense of visual texts. We also noted the central role of language in developing thought, but found that, with the younger children what could not be communicated verbally, could sometimes be shown in their drawings.

Perhaps the following example (an observation of Flora aged 17 months as she read *Peepo!* taken from Evelyn Arizpe's informal literacy journal of her children) can show how cognitive theories can be applied to reading pictures.

> I have always had misgivings about reading the Ahlbergs' *Peepo!* with a toddler. Although Flora enjoyed the story with its rollicking verse and repetitions and, of course, the peep-hole, I felt there was too much detail in the pictures for her to distinguish any of it clearly, except for the baby which constantly appears on the left-hand page. But my older daughter loved the book, so Flora must have seen it about a dozen times before the particular reading I will now describe. For some reason, it struck me that this time Flora was enjoying the book more fully and this was because she had made the connection between the baby on the left, the peep-hole, and the picture on the other side. Although it is hard to explain this intuition in words (especially as Flora could not talk at this stage), the evidence for thinking she had made a leap in understanding was her keen and prolonged scrutiny of the pictures after the reading. On the page where the baby is in a high chair, Flora pointed to the foot without a shoe. 'Where's the shoe?' I asked her, then turned the page with the peep-hole and showed her the missing shoe under the table. Flora's finger then went from the shoe under the table, back to the shoe-less foot and on to her own feet. She began pointing to the things she was familiar with on other pages, such as the bowl of porridge, cake and toy duck. I thought it was interesting that this awareness had occurred after Flora had spent two weeks in another house which was chaotic and full of objects and extended family, not unlike those in the book. It was as if this experience had helped Flora to distinguish individual objects amongst all the rest and connect them to the baby and herself.

This shows how Piaget's 'pre-operational child' is dealing with the environment at a perceptual level and acting upon it, using both eyes and hands (literally grasping, turning pages, putting fingers through the holes and pointing). Flora has learnt to predict and anticipate there will be a baby, a peep-hole and a larger picture on every page. Flora's behaviour also gives an illustration of Nikolajeva and Scott's hermeneutic circle in action, and relates to Clark's first phase of understanding a visual work of art in which the viewer engages with a text by getting a general impression of the whole and then goes on to the second stage, which is careful looking –

something that needs to take time. Through my asking questions (about things which I know she has experience of) and providing cues and prompts, we have now reached Flora's zone of proximal development and she is moving towards a new level of understanding.

In Clark's third phase, the viewer connects to her own experience (sitting on a high chair watching lots of family members going in and out of a cluttered room) and knowledge (shoes often get lost). This leads to a re-examination of the images, where Flora registers what she knows and is on the alert for other objects that she might recognise; in this case, in the next reading she suddenly saw the little objects at the corner of the frame around the baby. It is difficult to say in what way Flora's everyday world has been altered by looking at the pictures (Clark's final stage), but it is certain that the accumulation of knowledge from looking at this and many other picturebooks will have an impact on how she views the world.

The intelligent eye

> To read the artist's picture is to mobilise our memories and our experience of the visible world and to test his image through tentative projections. . . . It is not the 'innocent eye', however, that can achieve this match but only the inquiring mind that knows how to probe the ambiguities of vision.
>
> (Gombrich 1982: 264)

As Barthes and others have shown us, far from coming to texts with an innocent eye, the reader is 'a socialised being', a collection of 'subjectivities' responding to the visual world with a body and mind shaped by the realities in which he or she grew up' (Raney 1997: 39).

In his book, *Visual Thinking*, Arnheim is concerned with visual perception as a cognitive activity. He argues that artistic activity is a form of reasoning, in which perceiving and thinking are indivisibly intertwined: 'My contention is that the cognitive operations called thinking are not the privilege of mental processes above and beyond perception but the essential ingredients of perception itself.' Arnheim takes us back to Plato's belief in 'the wisdom of direct vision' and his equation of Socrates' blindness with 'losing the eye of the mind'. Arguing that the Greek philosophers first conceived the dichotomy of perceiving and reasoning, Arnheim reminds us that they never forgot that 'direct vision is the first and final source of wisdom' (1970: 7–13).

In a later work, Arnheim describes the process by which children gain their first 'intellectual concepts' through intelligent observation:

> Perceptual intuition is the mind's primary way of exploring and understanding the world. Before the young mind defines its notion

of what is, say, a house, it grasps intuitively something of a large object that keeps presenting itself in daily experience. All those buildings look different from one another, but they have something in common, and this common character is what is apprehended intuitively by the observant mind. I call it a 'perceptual concept'.... The young mind now acquires its first 'intellectual concepts'.

(1989: 28)

Langer had already discussed the power of the image and how it works on the human psyche back in the 1940s in her important work, *Philosophy in a New Key*. In a later book she elaborates: 'The exhilaration of a direct aesthetic experience indicates the depth of human mentality to which that experience goes. What it does to us is to formulate our conceptions of feeling and our conceptions of visual, factual and audible reality together. It gives us forms of imagination and forms of intuition itself. That is why it has the force of a revelation, and inspires a feeling of deep intellectual satisfaction' (1953: 397).

Few educationalists, other than those concerned in arts education and some psychologists, seem aware of what hard discipline is required in looking attentively at pictures. In *Iconology: Image, Text, Ideology*, Mitchell asserts: 'More clearly than any other use of the eyes, the wrestling with a work of visual art reveals how active a task of shape-building is involved in what goes by the simple names of 'seeing' or 'looking' (1986: 36). In a similar vein, writing in the foreword to Arnheim's *Thoughts on Art Education*, Eisner points out:

The eye, as Arnheim tells us, is a part of the mind. For the mind to flourish, it needs context to reflect upon. The senses, as part of an inseparable cognitive whole, provide that context ... The optimal development of mind requires attention not only to intellectual processes but to intuitive ones as well. Children and adolescents should be encouraged to see the whole, not only the parts. Art can teach this ... The gist of Arnheim's message is that vision itself is a function of intelligence, that perception is a cognitive event, that interpretation and meaning are an indivisible aspect of seeing, and that educational processes can thwart or foster such human abilities.

(Eisner in Arnheim, 1989: 4–7)

Visual literacy and the arts

The work of Gardner and his Project Zero Team based at Harvard University has produced much evidence and ground-breaking theories on arts education, including work on multiple intelligences and visual analysis. In his attempt to link human development and the artistic process, Gardner studies the moment in which children begin to understand and use symbolic systems. He describes this moment as a 'revolution' because the child is no longer limited to making, perceiving and feeling in relation to material objects and events, but can now invent imaginary objects and events and use them to mediate feelings, experiences, ideas and desires. He also thinks it probable that, by the ages of 3 or 4, children can experience 'discrete emotions', including those in response to a work of art, though they will not be able to articulate those emotions. In opposition to cognitive theorists, Gardner believes this transition – from operating with direct actions on the world to operating on a plane of symbols – happens in the early period between the ages of 2 and 7 even though the child might lack the words to express this new knowledg.[10] Both means of operating are present when making or responding to art:

> I contend that, as the child develops, he may continue to make, feel and respond to objects and experiences, both in the direct way characteristic of the sensorimotor period, and on a superimposed plane of symbolic experience. Making a painting involves acting upon objects and performing motor skills, as well as dealing with a symbolic system of great delicacy; similarly viewing a painting involves consideration of its status as a 'thing' in the world, as an attractive object, and as a comment on aspects of the world couched in a symbolic medium. The power and fascination of the arts rests precisely on the fact that individuals become involved with them on both the sensorimotor and the symbolic planes.
>
> (1973: 132)

However, Gardner also quotes Piaget to warn us depressingly that this artistic aptitude can regress 'without an appropriate arts education which will succeed in cultivating these means of expression and in encouraging these first manifestations of aesthetic creation. The actions of adults and the restraints of school and family life have the effect in most cases of checking or thwarting such tendencies instead of enriching them' (1973: 19).

Perkins was also part of the Project Zero research team; his illuminating observations about how looking at art engenders thinking set us off on a fruitful line of inquiry. In *The Intelligent Eye: Learning to Think by Looking at Art*, Perkins shows how this works:

> looking at art has an instrumental value. It provides an excellent setting for the development of better thinking, for the cultivation of what might be called the art of intelligence . . . [and] a context especially well suited for cultivating thinking dispositions . . . as [works of art] demand thoughtful attention to discover what they

have to show and say. Also, works of art connect to social, personal and other dimensions of life with strong affective overtures.

(1994: 3–4)

Perkins goes on to identify six categories which help foster a thinking disposition:

- *sensory anchoring* – it is helpful to have a physical object to focus on;
- *instant access* – art is open to everyone who can see and by its nature encourages looking closer or offers a fresh angle on the familiar;
- *personal engagement* – art is made to hold the attention and helps to sustain prolonged reflection;
- *dispositional atmosphere* – art cultivates thinking dispositions and brings an atmosphere of heightened affect;
- *multi-connectedness* – art encourages connection-making through social and moral issues, philosophical allusions, historical themes, formal structures, relevance to personal experience . . .
- *wide-spectrum cognition* – looking at art recruits different kinds of cognition such as visual processing, analytical thinking, posing questions, testing hypotheses, verbal reasoning.

(1994: 4–5)

Perkins goes on to develop the idea of what he calls 'experiential and reflective intelligence' which he describes as 'the deployment of one's intellectual resources to intelligent behaviour . . . By cultivating awareness of our own thinking, asking ourselves good questions, guiding ourselves with strategies, we steer our experiential intelligence in fruitful directions' (1994: 11). His conclusions perfectly mirror our findings, which is why we have quoted them at length in this chapter.

Kress and van Leeuwen point out that, although the image is now at least as powerful as the word, this recognition has not been understood by decision-makers, particularly those involved in education: 'the dominant visual language is now controlled by the global cultural technological empires of the mass media [and we now see] the incursion of the visual into many domains of public communication where formerly language was the sole and dominant mode'. Kress and van Leeuwen go on to bemoan 'the staggering inability on all our parts to talk and think in any way seriously about what is actually communicated by means of images and visual design' (1996: 4, 13–16).

Notes

1 Like Lewis (2001) and Nikolajeva and Scott (2000), and unlike Bader (1976), we spell 'picturebooks' as a compound word, indicating that its nature is dependent

on both words and pictures. (Some of our quotations spell picture books as two separate words.)

2 Iser gave us concepts like the 'implied reader' and taught us about the co-construction of meaning between the reader and the writer: 'the text represents a potential effect that is realised in the reading process . . . the poles of text and reader, together with the interaction that occurs between them, form the ground-plan on which a theory of literary communication may be built . . . [aesthetic response in reading is] a dialectic relationship between text, reader, and their interaction' (1980: ix–x).

3 For a fuller discussion see Lewis's *Reading Contemporary Picturebooks* (2001), chapters 2 and 3.

4 Doonan uses this term to describe someone with formal understanding of visual images that are not free-standing works of art, or one-off decorations, but sequences of scenes, comic-book frames or illustrations in books.

5 We have not included them here as their work has not been translated into English.

6 Although Lewis refers to the image of parent and child sharing a book, it is important to remember that this may not be the case for many children whose 'reading events' are more likely to take place in school.

7 Anstey and Bull point to the postmodern picturebook as aiding readers to become more active in their interaction with the text precisely because of the multiple narratives, ambiguity and contradictions the text offers.

8 Wood (1998) provides one of the most influential of many critiques of Piaget's work.

9 Bruner coined the term 'scaffolding' with Wood and other colleagues but, as this tends to mean one-to-one tutoring, the more inclusive term, 'guided participation' (Rogoff 1990) is also useful.

10 We certainly saw evidence of this among the youngest children in our study.

References

Alderson, B. (1973) *Looking at Picture Books*, London: The National Book League and Bocardo Press.

Anstey, M., and Bull, G. (2000) *Reading the Visual*, Sydney: Harcourt.

Arnheim, R. (1970) *Visual Thinking*, London: Faber.

—— (1989) *Thoughts on Art Education*, Santa Monica, CA: Getty Center for Education in the Arts.

Baddeley, P., and Eddershaw, C. (1994) *Not So Simple Picture Books: Developing Responses to Literature with 4–12 Year Olds*, Stoke-on-Trent: Trentham Books.

Bader, B. (1976) *American Picture Books: From Noah's Ark to the Beast Within*, New York: Macmillan.

Bradford, C. (1993) 'The picture book: some postmodern tensions', *Papers: Explorations in Children's Literature* 4: 10–14.

Bruner, J. S. (1983) *Child's Talk: Learning to Use Language*, Oxford: Oxford University Press.

Doonan, J. (1986) 'The object lesson: picturebooks of Anthony Browne', *Word and Image* 2: 159–172.

Evans, J. (ed.) (1998) *What's in the Picture? Responding to Illustrations in Picture Books*, London: Paul Chapman.

Gardner, H. (1973) *The Arts and Human Development*, New York: John Wiley & Sons.

Goldsmith, E. (1984) *Research into Illustration: An Approach and a Review*, Cambridge: Cambridge University Press.

Gombrich, E. H. (1982) *The Image and the Eye*, Oxford: Phaidon Press.

Graham, J. (1990) *Pictures on the Page*, Sheffield: NATE.

Hollindale, P. (1997) *Signs of Childness in Children's Books*, Stroud: Thimble Press.

Hunt, P. (ed.) (1996) *International Companion Encyclopedia of Children's Literature*, London: Routledge.

Hurlimann, B. (1968) *Picture-Book World*, Oxford: Oxford University Press.

Iser, W. (1980) *The Act of Reading*, London: Johns Hopkins University Press.

Kiefer, B. (1993) *The Potential of Picture Book: From Visual Literacy to Aesthetic Understanding*, Englewood Cliffs, NJ: Merrill.

Kress, G., and van Leeuwen, T. (1996) *Reading Images: The Grammar of Visual Design*, London: Routledge.

Kummerling-Meibauer, B. (1999) 'Metalinguistic awareness and the child's developing concept of irony', *The Lion and the Unicorn* 23: 168–176.

Langer, S. (1953) *Feeling and Form: A Theory of Art Developed from Philosophy in a New Key*, London: Routledge and Kegan Paul.

Lewis, D. (2001) *Reading Contemporary Picturebooks*, London: RoutledgeFalmer.

—— (1992) 'Looking for Julius: two children and a picture book', in K. Kimberley *et al.* (eds), *New Readings*, London: A & C Black.

—— (1996) 'Going along with Mr Gumpy: polysystemy and play in the modern picture book', *Signal* 80: 105–119.

MacCann, D., and Richard, O. (1973) *The Child's First Books: A Critical Study of Pictures and Texts*, New York: H. W. Wilson.

Meek, M. (1988) *How Texts Teach What Readers Learn*, South Woodchester: Thimble Press.

Michaels, W., and Walsh, M. (1990) *Up and Away: Using Picture Books*, Melbourne: Oxford University Press.

Mitchell, W. J. T. (1994) *Picture Theory: Essays on Verbal and Visual Representation*, Chicago, IL: University of Chicago Press.

—— (1986) *Iconology: Image, Text and Ideology*, Chicago, IL: University of Chicago Press.

Moebius, W. (1986) 'Introduction to picturebook codes', *Word and Image* 2: 141–158.

Nikolajeva, M., and Scott, C. (2000) 'The dynamics of picturebook communication', *Children's Literature in Education* 31: 225–239.

—— (2001) *How Picturebooks Work*, London: Garland.

Nodelman, P. (1988) *Words about Pictures: The Narrative Art of Children's Picture Books*, London: University of Georgia Press.

Perkins, D. (1994) *The Intelligent Eye: Learning to Think by Looking at Art*, Cambridge, MA: Harvard Graduate School of Education.

Protheroe, P. (1992) *Vexed Texts: How Children's Picture Books Promote Illiteracy*, Sussex: The Book Guild Ltd.

Pullman, P. (1989) 'Invisible pictures', *Signal* 60: 160–186.

Raney, K. (1997) *Visual Literacy: Issues and Debates*, London: Middlesex University, School of Education.

Rosenblatt, L. M. (1978) *The Reader, the Text and the Poem: The Transactional Theory of the Literary Work*, Carbondale, IL: Southern University Press.

328

Roxburgh, S. (1983) 'A picture equals how many words? Narrative theory and picture books for children', *The Lion and the Unicorn*: 7–8, 20–33.

Schwarcz, J. H. (1982) *Ways of the Illustrator: Visual Communication in Children's Literature*, Chicago, IL: American Library Association.

Sipe, L. R. (1998) 'How picture books work: a semiotically framed theory of text – picture relationships', *Children's Literature in Education* 29: 97–108.

Stephens, J. (1992) *Language and Ideology in Children's Fiction*, Harlow: Longman.

Styles, M., and Drummond, M. J. (eds) (1993) *The Politics of Reading*, Cambridge: Cambridge Institute of Education and Homerton College.

Watson, V., and Styles, M. (eds) (1996) *Talking Pictures*, London: Hodder & Stoughton.

Wood, D. (1998) *How Children Think and Learn*, London: Blackwell.

Part 5

CRITICISM AND TEXTS

22

BEGINNINGS

Roderick McGillis

Source: *The Nimble Reader, Literary Theory and Children's Literature*, New York: Twayne, 1996, pp. 1–26.

> Jack be nimble,
> Jack be quick,
> Jack jump over
> The candle stick.

Here is a simple, well-known nursery rhyme. I offer it as an example of writing we think of as children's literature, an example of literature for the very young child. But how do we know this is literature for the very young child? Our calling it a "nursery rhyme" indicates that we think it is suitable for children, and indeed this rhyme appears in countless collections of such rhymes lavishly illustrated and marketed for a child audience. Its brevity, its bounce, and its bumptious fun mark it suitable for children. Nothing complicated lurks between the lines; nothing polysemous calls out to us from the nine different words. No author's name comes tagged to this rhyme, and consequently we need not worry ourselves about unconscious expressions of an author's anxieties or wishes. Further, we do not have a date of composition, something that is usually available when a work of literature comes to us from a named author. The rhyme appears to exist in a timeless zone; it actualizes a freedom that confirms our hope that once upon a time purity and innocence were ours. We want our children's literature—we want our children—to signify the truth of an absolute beginning when nothing needed to be explained, analyzed, scrutinized, or interpreted. We accept this truth to be self-evident: to dissect is to murder. And that, dear reader, is that.

But of course that, dear reader, is not that. We all know that rhymes, for children or for adults, are not found beneath trees; nor do they emerge fully formed, pristine and transparent, from mysterious vaults presided over by powerful publishers. We know that someone someplace and at some time made up this rhyme, just as we know Lewis Carroll made up *Alice's*

Adventures in Wonderland while living in Oxford in the 1860s or William Wordsworth made up *The Prelude* in stages between 1798 and 1805 and then tinkered with it until he died forty-five years later, and knowing this prompts us to speculate on or investigate the rhyme's origins.

Now, I confess to meeting readers each year in my university classes who are content to say this rhyme jauntily, without manifesting a desire to know where it came from or what it is about. The best of such readers do genuinely appreciate the experience of reading; they read for innocent pleasure. Others, however, are more canny; they sense that this apparently innocent rhyme might have once had a design upon its readers. The most cynical of such readers wish to recast many of the well-known nursery rhymes to bring them up to date, to smooth away rough edges, to remove all vestiges of violence, sexuality, and disorder that might lurk between the lines. The best of such readers, however, wish to re-create the experience of the rhyme, not to destroy it, and such re-creation may take the form of critical commentary, commentary based on knowledge of literature, its forms and conventions. These canny readers wish to become competent, that is, informed, readers.

The canny reader wants to know something about this apparent piece of trivia not only because anything perpetuated in and by our culture tweaks our curiosity, but more importantly because our children are implicated in this rhyme. We offer it to them as something valuable when they are very young, and we rightly ask ourselves, why do we do this? What does this rhyme have to offer children? What effect will it have on them? What meanings does it hold? What meanings will be apparent to children? What meanings will be accessible, even unconsciously, to them? Such questions beg others: What is the meaning of meaning? Is meaning important at all, and if so, then how do we arrive at the meaning of this or any text? What do we want children to get from this rhyme and why?

In short, anyone who offers this rhyme or any other work of literature to a child must do so for a reason, and that reason must have some connection to a sense of what the rhyme or work of literature is and does. For example, a mother or father might offer "Jack be nimble" to a child in order to initiate a period of quietude in the home, and in so doing she or he tacitly accepts a critical sense that the words of this rhyme work in opposition to their obvious meaning. Whereas the words describe a rambunctious activity—leaping over a presumably lighted candlestick—their effect on the child will be to calm the rambunctious spirit. These words work to internalize gusto, and in internalizing gusto they might happily lead to nap time. On another occasion the father or mother might wish to promote verbal exercise by encouraging the child to play with language by learning to say the rhyme. Something about the rhyme and its rhythm makes it fun to repeat. To make this judgment, the father or mother implicitly accepts the form of the rhyme as valuable. On yet another occasion a parent might repeat the rhyme simply to elicit laughter from a child. Laughter is life affirming, and to speak the rhyme in this context is to sense something life affirming either in the very fact of the rhyme or in its meaning, its theme. Whatever the occasion for the repetition of this or any other rhyme, implicit or explicit reasons must accompany the decision to repeat it, and these decisions have something to do with the literary merit or coherence of the rhyme. In other words, we all bring some literary analysis, however incipient, to our experience of what we read, even if what we read is nothing more intricate than "Jack be nimble."

Partly because I hope that mothers and fathers, as well as professional academics and researchers, want to know more about the rhymes and other literature children receive either directly or through the mediation of adult readers, I embark on this examination of the ways we have of reading. My intent, however, is not to provide information regarding specific works of literature nor to offer authoritative interpretations of specific works. Instead, I hope to describe the possibilities for each reader finding out about works of literature herself, in a manner most suited to the individual reader. My assumption is that no one interpretation of a work of the imagination is perfect, and that interpretations are the work of individual readers at particular times and in particular places. What any reader in his or her particular time and place needs to know in order to experience a work of literature as fully as he or she might varies. Take the two-year-old child who listens to "Jack be nimble," for example. What she needs to know will have more to do with the occasion in which the rhyme comes to life and with the voice that brings it to life than with the rhyme's internal consistencies of diction and rhythm. She quickly learns that the tone of voice and the accompanying bounce on the seat of her diapers that form her experience of this rhyme are its meaning. What this two-year-old needs to know has more to do with what Wellek and Warren, in *Theory of Literature* (1942), call the "extrinsic" approach to literature. The adult who reads or recites the rhyme to the child will need to know different things: the rhythmic pattern of the rhyme, its theme or themes, its type. These are matters Wellek and Warren term "intrinsic" to literature, and they are necessary to the adult for two reasons: so that he or she can read the rhyme aloud effectively, and so that he or she can decide whether the rhyme is suitable to read to a particular child. Now we might add to this brief summary of readers the adult reader who is either a professional researcher or someone who is simply curious about our culture and its creative products. This reader might wish to know where the rhyme comes from or what it tells us about the person or people who invented it. This reader might want to know something about the symbolic import of the rhyme's image: the candlestick. To satisfy such curiosity, this reader will employ methods of inquiry that might be "extrinsic" or "intrinsic." It is these methods, either "extrinsic" or "intrinsic," which are my subject.

Extrinsic approaches might take us in four directions. We might study the historical circumstances of the origin of the rhyme as the Opies have done in *The Oxford Dictionary of Nursery Rhymes,* and consider the centuries-old custom of candle leaping "both as a sport and as a form of fortune-telling" (Opie, 227). Such an approach might shift into a consideration of various appearances of this rhyme in collections over a period of years, and we might wish to note how, if at all, the audience for the rhyme changes both in its profile and in its reception of the rhyme. For example, an obvious change in the audience is the narrowing down to children what was at one time a community experience. Another possibility, since we are speaking of audience, is to examine individual responses to the rhyme, raw data, as it were. One child might express joy at the image of a young person leaping over a candlestick, accomplishing successfully a feat that in most houses would probably be frowned on. I know that my own response involves the appreciation of subversive or transgressive activity in this rhyme. This shift to personal response might move again toward the psychological impact or implication of a rhyme such as "Jack be nimble." Does my interest in the rhyme actually have to do with a castration anxiety? Or is it more positively a phallic joy, the release of libidinal energies in a suitably subliminal way?

These four ways of reading the rhyme take us away from the rhyme itself as we try to place it in a historical, emotional, or psychological perspective. The four approaches might look something like this: History–Reception–Response–Psychology. The movement is from context to audience to intertext (I mean here by "intertext" the connection between the text in words, the rhyme, and the text in motion, the mind). Each of these— context, audience, intertext—has balancing subjects in an intrinsic approach to the text. (See Figure 1.)

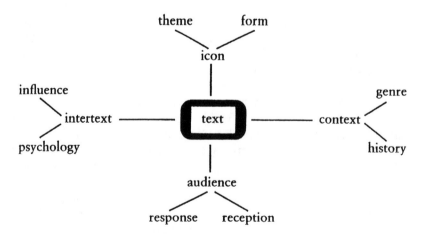

Figure 1

Whereas an extrinsic approach to literature looks to historical circumstances related to the origin and reception of the works of literature or to their psychological implications for a specific reader or for the general reader, an intrinsic approach looks at literary history, conventionally thought of as the study of genres or literary types, or at the influences on, or the form and message in, specific works. In short, the intrinsic approach is what we think of as "close reading" and *explication du texte*. In the case of "Jack be nimble," we might concern ourselves with the type of literature called "nursery rhyme," and trace its development from early collections of rhymes in the eighteenth century or from appearances of the rhymes in Renaissance works to argue for the radical nature of this type of poetry, its connections to a countertradition to court poetry or later to what came to be known as high art. The rhyme joins a tradition of accentual poetry in English that for centuries finds itself associated with folk art, primitive art, nonsense, nonserious verse. It is, from an ideological perspective, an expression of antibourgeois feeling.

If we concentrate on the form of the rhyme, we might conclude that the form *is* the content or the theme and that this content is self-referential; that is, the rhyme draws our attention to its language because this—the musical sound of the rhyme—is the meaning. Like music and dance, rhyme celebrates life. In fact, the words communicate this celebratory sense: to jump or cross over an object is to exhibit speed, agility, and energy. "Nimble" means "take quickly," "agile," "quick." But "quick," as well as meaning "fast," also means "alive." The potential pleonasm—nimble, quick—accentuates Jack's lively behavior, his seizing the day. Whatever that candlestick signifies, Jack's agility in jumping it testifies to his engagement in life. Having said this, however, we still have not explained the rhyme. Who is Jack, and why does he jump the candlestick? What does it mean that he jumps a candlestick and not some other object? For answers to these questions, we will have to set the rhyme in another context.

The context for the rhyme is forever renewed each time someone reads it. Although we might think that the act of jumping over a candlestick, just like the act of reading the four-line rhyme itself, has a beginning and an ending, we are mistaken. Jack is, like the figures on Keats's Grecian urn, suspended forever above the candlestick. Or perhaps the image of the repeated jump cut in film serves us better here; Jack forever jumps that stick, and he does so precisely because we have no original context for his action. Readers will provide the context they think most appropriate for an understanding of the rhyme. And the context they provide will depend upon their experience of the rhyme. Do they *see* the text, that is, read it silently? Do they *hear* it, that is, hear themselves or another person read it aloud? Do they read it for themselves or for others such as their children; do they read it as part of a community of readers, as part of a class assignment, for example? Do they read it because they want to or because they have to? Do they read to confirm their sense of things, to lose themselves, to have experiences only available in language, to learn something?

What I want to indicate is that an understanding of something as simple as "Jack be nimble" may take us in several directions. No single meaning, beyond the obvious meaning (what E. D. Hirsch in *Validity in Interpretation* terms intentional meaning) that someone observes a fellow named Jack jump over a candlestick, is available ready-made to the reader of this rhyme. Even my assumption of an "obvious meaning" is rather a presumption since it does not take into account that this might be an exhortation and not simply a description, and that Jack is a person and not an animal. The punctuation would suggest description ("Jack be nimble" rather than "Jack, be nimble"), but the syntax and grammar suggest exhortation ("Jack jump over" rather than "Jack jumps over"). Despite the possibility of general agreement to my assertions, the possibility remains for another reading. And another.

But this talk of multiple readings, familiar enough to readers of literary criticism and theory, presumes we know *what* we are reading. In this case, what we are reading is a rhyme conventionally placed in that body of work we in literary studies call children's literature. If I practiced a different discipline, anthropology say, then I might well consider this rhyme as part of a different body of material called folklore. My purpose here is not to debate the naming of academic territory, but rather to point out that what I call children's literature is itself problematic. What is children's literature? The easy answer is that it is literature written for or by children. The difficulty here is that in many cases we must accept what publishers publish in their children's lists as "children's literature," thereby accepting as fact that specific authors wrote with children in mind. But we know that the authors of some books (e.g., *A Sound of Chariots* by Mollie Hunter, *Red Shift* by Alan Garner, and *The Tin-Pot Foreign General and the Old Iron Woman* by Raymond Briggs, to name only three) did not write with children specifically in mind and were surprised when their books ended up in the children's lists. And publishers have recently complicated matters by publishing fiction for adolescent readers under the tag YA (Young Adult) Fiction. The best of this fiction—by such authors as Robert Cormier, Virginia Hamilton, Alice Childress, Margaret Mahy, William Mayne, and Kevin Major—may be read with pleasure and thoughtfulness by adults as well as by young adults.

As for literature written by children, this is almost never considered by professional literary critics or theorists, presumably because they either do not have access to a body of this work or because they do not consider it worthy of the nomenclature "literature" (my guess is the latter). Whatever definition we subscribe to, we tacitly indicate that we know what "literature" is when we offer our definition of "children's literature." I suspect, however, that Northrop Frye was right when he noted that we "have no real standards to distinguish a verbal structure that is literary from one that is not" (*Anatomy of Criticism*, 13), and Terry Eagleton, more recently, voices a similar truism. "There is no 'essence' of literature whatsoever" (9). Clearly, we all behave as if we do know what literature is because we all have a sense of what we perceive as literature. The attempt of the Children's Literature Association to create a canon of children's literature in the 1980s indicates what we should have known all along: canons of literature for adult and child readers have existed for centuries because people who think about these things and who are in positions of influence and power have ideas about what literature is and does. Whatever it is and can do, we can say several things about it without defining it in any more rigorous way than I have done in the preface to this volume.

Literature, according to Wellek and Warren, must include "oral literature" (10), and this is worth stressing when we consider the use of oral forms with young children. It might not be too much to say that all children's literature is the ghost of an oral form. The visual, in the sense of graphic art—book illustration—is also an important aspect in children's literature. Wellek and Warren further argue that literature distinguishes itself through a particular use of language; "it stresses the awareness of the sign itself" (12). This seems adequately appropriate to children's literature, especially to literature for the very young that stresses sound above sense. The very young child needs to like language before he or she needs to understand it. Yet from the eighteenth century to the present, those who assume responsibility for children have also stressed the sense that literature should contain. "Good" literature is good for children. The nineteenth century was rich in platitudes on the importance of reading literature, platitudes that we still echo: reading literature strengthens the imagination, toughens the moral fiber, sharpens our sense of beauty consequently improving our sense of taste, and deepens our spiritual awareness. In short, the reading of literature is a civilizing activity; it makes us better human beings. It makes us more discriminating than we are if we do not read. Knowing good from bad in literature helps us know good from bad in life. And make no mistake, we can know good from bad; we can find truth in literature and in life. This line of thought would see a rhyme such as "Jack be nimble" as preparatory; it is a piece of ephemera, useful, if at all, only as material to help children begin to read and become comfortable with the language of poetry.

The nineteenth century generally accepted Matthew Arnold's championing of poetry; to read poetry was to receive fine impressions as well as cogent criticisms of life. Fine impressions, although they seem as important to many now as they did a hundred years ago, began to lose their luster as investigations into the psychology of reading indicated that readers need not respond to a poem or a novel in similar ways. Impressions also proved inadequate to account for the complexities of form and language we could perceive in the literary text. Comparing a poem to music or to the true voice of feeling, even describing a novel as a comic epic in prose, proved inadequate to account for the vagaries of form in fiction or the nuances of ambiguity in poetry. The early decades of the twentieth century saw forms of close critical reading become popular—either the practical criticism of I. A. Richards, the morally rigorous reading of F. R. Leavis and the *Scrutiny* group, or the writers influenced by the Formalist trends in Russia. In the United States, as Gerald Graff points out, "much of the program of the latter-day New Criticism had already been formulated by the mid-nineties" (*Professing Literature*, 123). By mid-century the work of literature came to be revered as an icon; this was especially true of poetry. What we still refer to as the New Criticism—a form of careful close reading practiced by American and British critics in the 1930s, 1940s, and 1950s—articulated a new vocabulary for literary discussion: ambiguity, irony, paradox, coherence. For the New Critics, the study of literature as a coherent discipline was, in itself, valuable: "our starting point must be the development of literature as literature" (Wellek and Warren, 255).

The New Critics saw no use for psychology as a method for literary study: "In the sense of a conscious and systematic theory of the mind and its workings, psychology is unnecessary to art and not in itself of artistic value" (Wellek and Warren, 81). The study of psychology had, however, affected some readers' interpretations of literature for years; Freud himself had written about literature and drawn many of his ideas from it, ideas that go beyond the famous Oedipal complex into areas such as the family romance, narcissistic neuroses, the uncanny, and the creative process. Freudian concepts proved useful to many practicing critics during the years of New Criticism's ascendancy; for example, see the work of Lionel Trilling. Somewhat more recently, we can find in Norman Holland's Freudian analysis of literary response, *The Dynamics of Literary Response* (1975 edition), the following: "In this day and age, few of us have not heard of phallic and feminine symbols—they have even penetrated the nursery rhymes:

> Jack be quick, Jack be nimble,
> Jack jump over the phallic symbol." (56)

The impact of psychology, though, did not derive from Freud alone. Jung, Rank, and others began to influence not only the interpretation of literature, but also the way we think about the totality of literature. New Criticism accepted the work of literature as discrete, but Jungian oriented critics, as well as anthropologists such as Jesse Weston and James Frazer, who furthered the investigations of such nineteenth-century scholars as Andrew Lang and Max Müller, drew attention to recurring symbols, motifs, and characters within literature. The connection with myth also became clearly apparent and available to critical thinking. The result was myth criticism, or the study of archetypes and archetypal patterns in literary works, often associated with the influential studies of Northrop Frye.

Whereas the New Critics viewed literature as a number of discrete texts that formed a canon of great works, Frye was willing to include any and all works of the imagination in the literary universe. New Criticism is unlikely to take serious scrutiny of something as apparently frivolous as "Jack be nimble," but Frye would include it in the structure of words that forms the literary universe. As the fragment of a myth, "Jack be nimble" tells the story of someone named Jack—a name with connections to folk traditions of the peasantry (Fr. *jacque*, ME *jacke*) with its various associations: jack-of-all-trades, jack-in-the-box, jack-in-the-pulpit, jackanapes, jack-o'-lantern, and of course, the coarser connotations concerning toilets and phalluses. The jack-o'-lantern shows a connection between Jack and light also apparent in the jacklight, a light used for hunting or fishing at night. The connection here between Jack, light, and fishing might lead the mythically inclined reader to think of biblical types, and the name "Jack" has connections both to James and John. Jack is, we might remember from our reading of traditional fairy tales, a giant killer and a rescuer. His jumping the candle testifies to his luck, and perhaps to his heroic association with the light of the world. To jump the candle successfully is to preserve life. This connection between Jack and the life force might remind us that Jack is that most paradoxical of creatures: the trickster.

Frye, however, had another end in view than the study of mythic patterns in literature; he was deeply committed to the view that literature presented the reader with a total world, one that stands over against our world with its own conventions and its own structures. Unlike the New Critics, Frye wanted to see how individual works cohere in a body of work, the totality of what the human imagination has created. How does a particular story relate to the traditions of story? His aim was to articulate the conventions and structures of literature so that the readers, any readers, could better grasp the imaginative possibilities in whatever work of literature they read. The study of literature, then, was based on a growing body of knowledge, the knowledge of how literature works. What the student of literature studied was criticism and critical thinking, rather than literature per se. Knowledge of literature is dependent upon knowledge of "the criticism of literature," which is "all that can be directly taught" (*Anatomy of Criticism*, 11). And this knowledge has a liberating power; the critic becomes a Blakean creator "able to construct and dwell in a conceptual universe of his own" (12). Frye implicitly attacked the canon-making activity of New Criticism; his was a democratizing activity. Despite his fierce championing of the work of art's independence from ideology, he argued that we must consider "the participation of the work of art in the vision of the goal of social effort, the idea of complete and classless civilization" (348).

Frye's "liberal humanism" came under attack from both the right and the left, from conservative critics such as E. D. Hirsch who maintain the authority of the author's intention, and from those who viewed literature from a political and sociological perspective. Hirsch's criticism, perhaps more implicit than explicit, lies in his attempt to reinstate the author as final arbiter of meaning. Finally, however, both Hirsch and Frye share an Arnoldian faith in the power of literature to civilize and humanize. A more radical attack on Frye comes from Marxist and feminist critics who argue that literature is not above ideology, that it does not liberate us from social codes but rather enforces those codes. Literature has a powerful and direct effect on the reader; it has a socializing power because readers assume a one-to-one relationship with the characters and actions depicted in a work of literature. To put it plainly, if a sympathetic character in a novel accepts as a good the authority of state, church, gender, or institution, then the reader is apt to accept these as a good in life. The best that can be said for the New Critics and Frye as exemplars of liberal humanism is that they are "impotent" to alter social reality (Eagleton, 199). The liberal humanist cannot make the social implications of a rhyme such as "Jack be nimble" apparent. The Marxist critic, however, will point to the connection between candle jumping and the working class. Historically, the practice of jumping over a lighted candle is associated with guilds such as the lace makers of Wendover, Buckinghamshire, who did their jumping on November 25, Saint Catherine's Day. The rhyme, then, becomes an expression of working class solidarity, and perhaps a reminder of the working man's jump into the light of a new day, as much as an expression of superstition. Might we even go so far as to say that this rhyme contains a call to action?

If it does, then the call to action is oblique. And I daresay Frye's liberal humanism divorced from action ought not to be glibly dismissed. Clearly, Frye has a social vision, a radical one. But what he also generated within literary studies was an interest in the structure of a literary work. Frye's interest is in the structures or building blocks of literature, whether these be traditional symbols, recurring character types, or shapes of plot. According to John Carlos Rowe, Frye's *Anatomy of Criticism* "may be the only 'native' version of structuralism that we have had" (34). This interest in structures Frye holds in common with critics whose work derives from structuralism, a term deriving from both linguistics and anthropology and dating from the early years of this century and the work of Ferdinand de Saussure (1857–1913) and, later, Claude Lévi-Strauss (b. 1908).

Structuralists from linguistics, anthropology, and psychology had for some time previous to the work of Frye investigated humanity's instinct for creating structures. Unlike Frye, who focuses his attention on literature, structuralists turn their attention to all aspects of the human sciences. They study anything seriously, from the color of traffic lights to wrestling matches. In literature, they will take any work seriously, not worrying over its "greatness"; for the structuralist there is no great tradition. Each object of study is a structure of images, effects, characters, actions, whatever, that reflects on itself in a series of binary opposites. By organizing the binary oppositions of

342

a work, we can come to understand the significance of that work, the tensions that hold it together, and the gaps that might weaken it. For example, a structuralist might draw our attention to the opposition between animate and inanimate objects in "Jack be nimble": Jack and the candlestick. This drawing into tension of a moving and an immobile object is accentuated in the rhyme "quick" and "candlestick." Examination of the two objects might bring us to an awareness that life and death are not as opposed as we might at first assume; Jack may leap, but the candle also burns. Both objects function through energy. Nothing is static. The candlestick, too, is quick. But whereas structuralism tends to privilege one aspect of the binary opposite—life as opposed to death, Jack as opposed to the candle—and to see the poem or whatever it looks at as a closed system, the so-called poststructuralists focus on the energy that refuses to allow Jack to land or to envisage the candle as burning out.

Poststructuralism finds fragments everywhere. Nothing is neatly packaged except nothing. In literary criticism, deconstruction is the most pertinent form of poststructuralism. To deconstruct a work of literature is to show how it does not cohere. As Alvin Kernan puts it: "The razor-close readings of deconstruction always eventuate in discovering that all texts, because of the indeterminate nature of language, contradict themselves in ways that cancel out even the possibility of any meaning, however ironic or ambiguous, and this is about as far away as it is possible to get from the position of the new criticism that works of literature are sacred texts so intensely meaningful that any paraphrase is heresy" (*The Death of Literature*, 81). The deconstructive critical activity gives free play to the interpreting mind and focuses on the point in the text in which gaps appear, gaps that indicate language's tendency to contradict itself. The written work leaves traces of different meanings, and it is these traces that prevent interpretation from ever closing a text. Unlike the New Critics, who ground interpretation in a belief in the unified work of art, the deconstructionist ungrounds interpretation. The power of the text to create meaning weakens, and deconstruction, in Jonathan Culler's words, "puts in question the claim that anything in particular is definitively in the text" (*On Deconstruction: Theory and Criticism after Structuralism*, 83).

The reason for this refusal to delimit meaning lies in an attitude to language. In traditional formulations, language is, in effect, imitative. That is, human beings choose a word (sign) to signify some object or concept that exists in the phenomenal world. For example, "dog" signifies a creature all of us blessed with the power of sight can perceive with our eyes; it has four legs and a tail that wags when it is happy or content, and it appears to enjoy fetching. In a similar fashion, "blue" signifies that an object has a certain color. Users of the language take it for granted that such words put us in touch with reality, the world as it really is. For purposes of literary criticism, this means that readers can assume that a text has definite meaning that derives from the transparency of its language. The linguist Ferdinand de Saussure, however, unsettled this commonsense view of language when he pointed out that words such as "dog" and "blue" are arbitrary. Clearly, for a French-speaking person the three letters "d-o-g" do not signify a four-legged animal who enjoys fetching. In English, the word "dog" is a purely conventional sign; it only means what we allow it to mean. It means something different from "dig" or "dot" or "dip," and so on, because we agree that it does. But "dog" has other meanings: a lazy fellow, an andiron, affected stylishness (to put on the dog), an inferior thing, and so on. Then we have many expressions that use the word "dog": hot dog, dogtrot, dog days, dog-ear, and so on. Any and all of these variant meanings and implications are potentially effective when we hear the word "dog" in a context, and it is not completely possible for a speaker (and even less so for a writer) to control what sense(s) of the word are active in a listener. Language is, as Belsey notes, "in an important sense arbitrary" (41). For purposes of literary criticism, the arbitrary aspect of language means that texts do not have absolute meaning. Instead, they mean whatever a community of readers agrees that they mean.

Since the rhyme before us uses the word "candle stick" and not "candle," we might ask whether Jack jumps over something that contains a candle, or whether the candlestick is empty. Or we could approach the candlestick from another perspective: is it silver or brass, shining or dull? Is the absence of such details accidental or intentional? The fact that we cannot know the answer to these questions, or the many others we might ask, leaves the implications of the rhyme forever open to the free play of the reader. Deconstruction is interested in that free play, but we might note again the authority that has passed from text to interpreter or to the interpretive community.

The interest in the interpreter is, of course, an interest in the reader. How does the reader receive a work of literature? Does the text create its reader or does the reader create the text? Such questions lead to what we know as reception theory and reader response theory. Reception involves, among other things, the implied reader of a text or the kind of person a text supplies as its ideal recipient (Iser, 27–38), or what Chatman refers to as "the audience presupposed by the narrative itself" (150). Response, on the other hand, involves what happens in the mind when we read a text. The response critic is interested in the web of connections the reader inevitably makes to his or her literary or extraliterary experiences. Our response, the feelings and thoughts we have when we read, directs our interpretation and our evaluation of texts. To a large extent, we read the book we wish to read; we make the text as we read it. All reading occurs within a context, perhaps most often the context of a community: a classroom, or a book discussion group, or a community of fans (fandom). The result is that readers, in Stanley Fish's nifty expression, "mis*pre*read" texts (311); that is, they inevitably shape the words they read to fit prior assumptions about both the world and the literature they are reading. Our interpretation, then, may have little or nothing to do with what the author intended when he or she wrote the book. In the most extreme reader response criticism, exemplified by the work of David Bleich and Michael Steig for example, interpretation recedes in importance. What really matters is both our awareness of ourselves as we read and the understanding of our own psychic lives that reading can help us attain. Books that attract us do so because they speak to something deep within our psychological makeup. To talk about these books is to open a path into our emotional lives. The term "bibliotherapy" is appropriate here.

All these theoretical approaches may be, and have been, used by critics of children's literature. Recent criticism has forthrightly applied the work of structuralists, deconstruction, feminism, Marxism, Freud, Jung, and so on to children's books. Unease, however, accompanies such treatment of children's books simply because books for the young are hardly thought of as "difficult," and even if they are, young readers are unlikely to turn to critical readings of *Charlotte's Web* to understand the myth of eternal return and the nature of the hero, or to learn of their own psychological dependence on the mother and of their emergence from that dependence. The audience for critical readings of and approaches to children's books is, generally, other critical readers: in other words, professional "book people." The hope is, I guess, that sophisticated readings of children's books will affect how and what children read by reaching those (teachers, librarians, parents) who influence children's reading habits. Does this, in fact, actually happen? Or does the hermeneutic activity in this instance produce a particularly vicious circle? Critics speak to critics and not to the people directly involved with children's books: teachers, librarians, parents, and most important, children themselves. But because the texts upon which critics of children's literature write are for children, and because the audience for these texts is relatively unlettered, children's literature critics find themselves looked upon with some suspicion by academic critics who work on mainstream literature. From the other end, the teachers, librarians, parents, and children who read children's literature look with some suspicion on those who spend their lives intellectualizing these ostensibly simple books. This double estranging of the children's literature critic puts him or her in an awkward position: wanting to speak to those both within and without the academy and finding, if not hostility, then at least disrespect from both groups. In the middle, the children's literature critics speak among themselves, more often than not forgetting the children who are the impetus for the enterprise in the first place.

In part, this is the burden of Jacqueline Rose's *The Case of Peter Pan, or the Impossibility of Children's Fiction* (1984). Rose argues that adults write children's fiction and evaluate it, and in doing this they take into account not children, but their conception of what children ought to be and ought to learn. Children themselves are powerless to create their own literature or to control what they receive. They do not, generally, have the economic power to purchase books for themselves; they do not control what books their school or local library places on its shelves. Some adult authority figure mediates most, if not all, of a child's reading, and that mediation is not disinterested. Adults want children to read certain books for social reasons. Consequently, children's books and the criticism of children's books are a form of social power.

Many commentators on children's books readily accept this function of literature to form its readers; for example, Fred Inglis in *The Promise of Happiness* (1981) sets out to show that the "best prose is itself evidence of human goodness and a way of learning how to be virtuous." "Only a monster," he writes, would not want to give a child books "which will teach her to be good." Literature helps the reader to "live well" (4). Speaking specifically about fairy tales and from quite a different ideological position from Inglis, Jack Zipes insistently points out that fairy tales inscribe cultural values in order to perpetuate the power of the male bourgeoisie in this our capitalist system (see such works as *Breaking the Magic Spell, Fairy Tales and the Art of Subversion*, and *Don't Bet on the Prince*). Zohar Shavit, in *Poetics of Children's Literature* (1986), explains the formative aspect of children's literature as a feature of its connection to "the educational apparatus." In Shavit's view of the "literary polysystem" (33), children's literature is "a vehicle for education, a major means of teaching and indoctrinating" (35). A similar view is implicit in E. D. Hirsch's *A First Dictionary of Cultural Literacy* (1989), which sets out to provide the "specific knowledge that is the true foundation of our children's academic skills" (xii). And for a writer such as Robert Leeson (*Reading and Righting*, 1985), both the child and the oral tradition are pure sources of communal value that we have left behind and are in danger of losing (13 and passim).

By setting up the child as a "pure point of origin in relation to language, sexuality and the state" (Rose, 8), children's fiction and the criticism of children's fiction cover the traces of their own weakness. For these writers and critics, the child serves as the touchstone for all that is instinctively and purely human; the child is truly father of the man. Yet Wordsworth's famous words hold an ambiguity: the child might teach us what we are, inscribe us, author us, serve as the authoritative version of what we should be, but at the same time the child is that from which we come and from which we tear ourselves away. In other words, the child and the father represent an impossibility: that which we have been, that which we continuously seek, and that which we can never find. Both child and father are unknowable in any absolute sense. What we know is what we create, and we create both fathers and children through language: we create an identity in language. As Rose argues, creating an identity in language is not the same as reflecting an identity. Language does not simply state truths; it creates them. We forget this when we blithely assume that we know what is best for our children, that we know what literature they should and should not read. Yet much criticism of children's books insists on an evaluative stance: "The shocking ugliness and cruelty of image and action in the latest horror comics and movies can only be horrible and harmful, and any sane teacher will want to keep his children out of such harm's way" (Inglis, 6).

This assertion by Inglis is an extreme example of evaluative criticism. Evaluation implies moral worth, and just as children's books themselves have traditionally had a strong didactic element, so has the criticism of children's books. Good books make us better people than we would have been had we not read these good books. Even the formulaic approach to literature traditionally used in the schools rests on the notion that the competent reader is a humane reader. Evaluation suggests a standard of value that transcends historical fashion. It rests on the belief in the "concrete universal," which the "objective critic" can explain to the uninitiated reader:

> The function of the objective critic is by approximate descriptions of poems, or multiple restatements of their meaning, to aid other readers to come to an intuitive and full realization of poems themselves and hence to know good poems and distinguish them from bad ones.
>
> (Wimsatt, 83)

This passage, a fundamental statement of New Criticism's credo, assumes objectivity is unproblematic; it implies in its use of the singular "meaning" that a work of literature has a unified and single meaning; and it is confident that standards of value, which all readers can and should accept, exist. Yet contradiction lurks in these lines. If meaning is single, then why do we need "multiple restatements" of this meaning? Would not one statement suffice for all readers? Further, what does Wimsatt imply by the words "approximate descriptions"? The answer to this question is available in the title of another New Critical essay, Brooks's "The Heresy of Paraphrase" (*The Well Wrought Urn*, 192–214). Language can never reproduce a work of literature without simply repeating the words of that work of literature. And even then, as Borges's "Pierre Menard, Author of the 'Quixote'" shows, a literal transcription of *Don Quixote* in the 1990s must render the meaning and significance of the work different from its meaning and significance in the seventeenth century. Questions as to why someone would transcribe it arise, as do questions of historicity. For Wimsatt and the New Critics, this irreducibility and unrepeatability of the work of literature argues the sanctity of the verbal icon, the power of logos to invest a work of literature with inviolable power.

Recent literary and cultural theory, however, takes up Saussure's argument in *Course in General Linguistics* (1916) that language is a system of signs which is purely conventional. The relationship between words (signifiers) and the objects to which they refer (signifieds) is arbitrary and unstable. The meaning of words is something that social groups agree on, and this agreement is an important aspect of social coherence. Clearly the best interests of a social group are in maintaining existing connections between signifieds and signifiers. Whatever disrupts or extends such connections must present a threat to social cohesion. This is one explanation for the powerful conservative force of most canonical children's literature, and for the attempt over the years to denigrate what Shavit refers to as noncanonical works (comic books, pulp or chapbook material, the fairy tale in the late eighteenth and early nineteenth centuries). Inevitably, however, the meaning and significance of words, and by extension works of literature, change as accommodation and adaptation and downright subversive tendencies affect what authors write. A critical activity that concentrates on the polysemous nature of language has the potential to liberate readers from reified codes of meaning.

If interpretation of literary works is ongoing, without closure as they say, then how are we to understand what we read? And how are we to teach children to become competent—even insightful—readers? As practicing critics, we answer these questions through example; our interpretations of literary works implicitly or explicitly imply a theoretical position, and because of the nature of language as a social institution, our theoretical position must reflect an ideology. Most intrinsic approaches to works of literature accept the notion that language expresses reality; the text expresses a vision of social reality, a vision of the way things really are, or it articulates coherently and fully an author's intention. Most extrinsic approaches accept the idea that texts participate in the nonliterary as well as the literary world; the text expresses cultural beliefs and emotional content beyond the control of the author. Of course, some intrinsic approaches exhibit a belief in language's inherent instability, and some extrinsic approaches exhibit a belief in its stability. The important thing is that we, as practicing critics and teachers, raise to consciousness our own presuppositions when we interpret literature. What is our theoretical position? Why do we read texts the way we do? At the very least, we should be aware of the possibilities for reading texts and of the implications of choosing a particular methodology.

The possibilities for reading texts form the substance of this book. But before I can begin to examine specific methods of reading and interpreting, I must acknowledge some of the difficulties that have silently moved through this first chapter. I have spoken of "works of literature," "children's literature," "children's books," "oral literature," and "texts." These are not simple formulations, nor are they synonymous. "Works of literature" refers to printed books of an imaginative nature (although this definition in itself is problematic), whereas "oral literature" is oxymoronic in that oral forms of discourse are not written and therefore are preliterate. Should we include oral forms such as story and rhyme in a discussion of literature? Are "children's books" the same as "children's literature"? Not necessarily. And what is children's literature? This question returns us to the beginning of this chapter. Children's literature, like all literature, lives two lives: an institutional one and a wandering one. More and more, as Alvin Kernan has argued in *The Death of Literature*, literature survives not by wandering but by its tenuous existence within an institution. But what we need to point out here is that whatever children's literature is, it is not only lettered. In other words, children's literature includes words accompanied by pictures as well as words spoken without the aid of a printed book. In fact, children's literature includes pictures without words. And when words and pictures occur together, their relationship varies as Perry Nodelman has brilliantly shown in *Words About Pictures* (1989).

The most accurate word to use when speaking of stories and poems for children, as it is the most accurate word to use for any narrative or other form of poetic discourse, is "text." "Text" is not only fashionable, it is also precise. It signifies a change in attitude to the "work" of literature. Whereas "work" suits the New Critical notion of the literary object—closed and coherent—"text," coming as it does from the Latin *textus* (that which is woven), suggests the bringing together of disparate things in an inchoate process that is literature, whether for children or adults. As Barbara Johnson says: "'Work' and 'text' are thus not two different kinds of object but two different ways of viewing the written word" (40). My own position has always moved in the direction of what Georges Bataille terms the hetero-logical theory of knowledge; that is, a theory of knowledge that respects scientific rigor and also opposes "any homogeneous representation of the world" (Bataille, 97). Heterology does not reject closed systems; rather, it delights in that which closed systems leave behind. The notion of "text" suits such a theory of knowledge. The text can never be closed, for to close it is to shelve it, fit it into a neat and repeatable system. To accept hetero-geneity is to subvert our desire for certainty, for the comforting swaddle of single meaning.

Children, like adults, exhibit both conservative and subversive tendencies. Whatever meaning we may ascribe to "Jack be nimble," children are quick to offer another, as naughty versions indicate. Mary and Herbert Knapp cite this version:

> Jack be nimble, Jack be quick,
> Jack jump over the candlestick.
> But Jack wasn't nimble, Jack wasn't quick,
> Now Jack's in the hospital with a French-fried dick. (180)

The creator of this version is not as literal-minded as we might first suspect. No, the allusion to French fries turns Jack into something akin to Mr. Potato. From my own childhood, I recall: "Jack be nimble, Jack be quick/Jack jumped over the candlestick/Great balls of fire!" The intertextual allusion here takes us, I have no doubt, to a famous song by Jerry Lee Lewis. The Knapps suggest that rhymes such as these are means by which sixth-grade boys "get used to their own sexuality" (180), and, who knows, this may be the case. What interests me, however, is the impetus to keep the rhyme going, to let its meaning escape reification, especially when reification means, in Bataille's terms, "the establishment of the homogeneity of the world" (96). How exciting for me, then, to discover just this last March (1993) on a visit to a local elementary school, a collection of poems by the students themselves. The third poem in the collection is:

> Cat be nimble
> Cat be quick
> Cat see doggie
> Cat give kick
> Cat show quickness
> Cat show skill
> Cat find dog paw
> Quicker still

Here the transgressive and libidinous energy of the schoolyard versions finds expression in understated but very present violence. The rhyme shows considerable sophistication in its linguistic transgressions too.

My concern as a practicing critic of literature is, then, to stain the pellucid consciousness of my reader clear again, and I can accomplish this only by the force of my readings. In other words, theory and practice must connect. To read with understanding we must have some means of entering the system of discourse that we confront, and to read with some chance of situating ourselves outside dominant beliefs we must have several means (strategies of reading) at our disposal. We must, as Eagleton has argued, be pluralists: "Any method or theory which will contribute to the strategic goal of human emancipation" will do (211). The reader who knows the passage from Eagleton's *Literary Theory: An Introduction* that I cite here will note that I do not include the rest of his sentence, which speaks of method and theory contributing to "the production of 'better people' through the socialist transformation of society." "Human emancipation," it seems to me, does not necessarily produce "better people," if "better" means morally superior to others. What Eagleton must refer to is people better than those who subscribe to a capitalist system. I have no design to offer a series of methodologies that we can use to "better" our child readers in this way. It seems to me naive to assume that either literature or theory can make people "better," either morally or politically. The position that it can and does is one that links, surely, the radical theorist Eagleton with the conservative program of someone like F. R. Leavis.

Literary theory is for the adult reader a means of self-consciousness. Why do we read what we read? Why do we interpret one way and not another? What do we wish to do when we read and interpret? Without some answers to questions like these, we remain innocent readers, happy in our ignorance that we are imposed upon by what we read, that we are powerless to escape the enforced quiescence reading can put upon us. But if we read with the confidence of knowing why we read and how we interpret, then we have some chance of passing on such knowledge to our children, thereby encouraging them to become active readers too. Making children active, self-aware readers like the ones who originated the subversive rhymes quoted above offers them the opportunity of understanding the codes and conventions they meet with at every turn in their daily lives from their television viewing to their experience of urban sprawl. In this sense, then, they have the opportunity of standing aside from the whirligig of the market system to understand how it impinges upon them.

The difficulty arises when we ask how we might teach critical theory to children. How do we bring an end to their innocence? This is a pedagogic question, and questions of pedagogy are often divorced from questions of critical practice. Such a divorce is fatal to the study of children's literature.

[* * *]

[One] last point regarding older and more recent books for the young, raises an issue dealt with in Peter Hunt's *Criticism, Theory, and Children's Literature* (1991). Hunt argues that the study of children's literature must take into account what children actually read. No canon exists in children's literature; rather, what we have are canons. The only literature that we can truly call "children's literature" is that which is "alive" (Hunt, 14). What literature remains alive, of course, depends on what literature we as a social and educational group keep alive. Recently, at a conference on children's literature, I heard one educationalist remark that in the inner city schools of New York children did not, in fact, read anything; rather, they received their stories and narratives from television and other visual media. Be this as it may, my passionate belief is that the competent and informed reading of literature prepares us to understand and stand apart from the narratives we receive in whatever form. Further, because narrative feeds on narrative, because all forms of imaginative thinking partake of previous constructions of the human imagination, knowledge of the past and its cultural products is formative. To deprive children access to—indeed, to fail to encourage knowledge of—the so-called classics of children's literature is to deprive them access to their history as well as to ours. Purely practical concerns keep us from knowing everything, but tolerance and perpetuation of texts from past and present are surely as important in children's literature as they

351

are in adult literature. [. . .] Reading is, after all, an activity. And to act is to affirm life. Jack acts when he jumps the candlestick.

Children's books cited

Briggs, Raymond. *Fungus the Bogeyman*. London: Hamish Hamilton, 1977.
Garner, Alan. *Red Shift*. New York: Macmillan, 1973.
Hunter, Mollie. *A Sound of Chariots*. New York: Harper Trophy, 1988 (1972).
Opie, Iona and Peter. *The Oxford Dictionary of Nursery Rhymes*. Oxford: Oxford University Press, 1984 (1951).

Works of literary theory and criticism cited

Bataille, Georges. *Visions of Excess: Selected Writings, 1927–1939*. Tr. Allan Stoekl. Minneapolis: University of Minnesota Press, 1985.
Belsey, Catherine. *Critical Practice*. London: Methuen, 1980.
Bleich, David. *Subjective Criticism*. Baltimore: The Johns Hopkins University Press, 1978.
Brooks, Cleanth. *The Well Wrought Urn*. New York: Harcourt, Brace, 1947.
Chatman, Seymour. *Story and Discourse: Narrative Structure in Fiction and Film*. Ithaca, NY: Cornell University Press, 1978.
Culler, Jonathan. *On Deconstruction: Theory and Criticism After Structuralism*. Ithaca, NY: Cornell University Press, 1982.
Eagleton, Terry. *Literary Theory: An Introduction*. Oxford: Basil Blackwell, 1983.
Fish, Stanley. *Is There a Text in This Class? The Authority of Interpretive Communities*. Cambridge, Mass.: Harvard University Press, 1980.
Frye, Northrop. *Anatomy of Criticism*. New York: Atheneum, 1966 (1957).
Graff, Gerald. *Professing Literature: An Institutional History*. Chicago: University of Chicago Press, 1987.
Hirsch, E. D. *Validity in Interpretation*. New Haven, Conn.: Yale University Press, 1967.
Holland, Norman N. *Dynamics of Literary Response*. New York: Norton, 1975 (1968).
Hunt, Peter. *Criticism, Theory, and Children's Literature*. Oxford: Basil Blackwell, 1991.
Inglis, Fred. *The Promise of Happiness: Value and Meaning in Children's Fiction*. Cambridge, England: Cambridge University Press, 1981.
Iser, Wolfgang. *The Act of Reading: A Theory of Aesthetic Response*. Baltimore: The Johns Hopkins University Press, 1978.
Johnson, Barbara. "Writing", *Critical Terms for Literary Study*, Frank Lentricchia and Thomas McLaughlin (eds). Chicago: University of Chicago Press, 1990, pp. 39–49.
Kernan, Alvin. *The Death of Literature*. New Haven, Conn.: Yale University Press, 1990.
Knapp, Mary and Herbert. *One Potato, Two Potato: The Folklore of American Children*. New York: Norton, 1976.

Leeson, Robert. *Reading and Righting: The Past, Present and Future of Fiction for the Young*. London: Collins, 1985.

Nodelman, Perry. *Words About Pictures: The Narrative Art of Children's Picture Books*. Athens: University of Georgia Press, 1988.

Rose, Jacqueline. *The Case of Peter Pan, or the Impossibility of Children's Fiction*. London: Macmillan, 1984.

Rowe, John Carlos. "Structure", *Critical Terms for Literary Study*, Frank Lentricchia and Thomas McLaughlin (eds). Chicago: University of Chicago Press, 1990, pp. 22–38.

Saussure, Ferdinand de. *Course in General Linguistics*. Tr. Wade Baskin. New York: The Philosophical Library, 1959.

Shavit, Zohar. *Poetics of Children's Literature*. Athens: University of Georgia Press, 1986.

Steig, Michael. *Stories of Reading: Subjectivity and Literary Understanding*. Baltimore: The Johns Hopkins University Press, 1989.

Wellek, Rene, and Austin Warren. *Theory of Literature*. New York: Harcourt, Brace, 1956 (1942).

Zipes, Jack. *Breaking the Magic Spell: Radical Theories of Folk and Fairy Tales*. London: Heinemann, 1979.

—— *Don't Bet on the Prince: Contemporary Feminist Fairy Tales in North America and England*. New York: Methuen, 1986.

—— *Fairy Tales and the Art of Subversion: The Classical Genre for Children and the Process of Civilization*. New York: Wildman, 1983.

353

23

THE READER
IN THE BOOK

Aidan Chambers

Source: *Booktalk: Occasional Writing on Literature and Children*, London: Bodley Head, 1985, pp. 34–58.

I

1. Two to say a thing...

There is constant squabble about whether particular books are children's books or not. Indeed, some people argue that there is no such thing as books for children but only books which children happen to read. And unless one wants to be partisan and dogmatic—which I do not, having had my fill of both—one has to agree that there is some truth on both sides and the whole truth in neither.

The fact is that some books are clearly *for* children in a specific sense —they were written by their authors deliberately for children—and some books, never specifically intended for children, have qualities which attract children to them.

But we must go further than that truism, which helps us very little to deal critically with books or to mediate them intelligently and effectively. We need a critical method which will take account of the child-as-reader; which will include him rather than exclude him; which will help us to understand a book better and to discover the reader it seeks. We need a critical method which will tell us about the reader in the book.

For it seems to me that all literature is a form of communication, a way of saying something. Samuel Butler once observed that it takes two to say a thing, a sayee as well as a sayer—a hearer as well as a speaker. Thus, if literature is a way of saying something, it requires a reader to complete the work. And if this is so, as I am convinced it is, it must also be true that an author addresses someone as he writes. That someone has come to be called 'the implied reader'.

2. *The implied reader*

Let me defend myself against an obvious objection. I am not suggesting that, as an author writes, he necessarily has in the front of his mind a particular reader. F. H. Langman in a useful article, 'The Idea of the Reader in Literary Criticism', puts it this way:

> I do not say we need to know what readers the author had in mind. An author may write for a single person or a large public, for himself or for nobody. But the work itself implies the kind of reader to whom it is addressed and this may or may not coincide with the author's private view of his audience. What matters for the literary critic is to recognize the idea of the reader implied by the work. Not only correct understanding but also evaluation often depends principally upon correct recognition of the implied reader.
>
> [p. 84]

I would go further. I would say that, until we discover how to take account of the implied reader, we shall can fruitlessly for serious attention to be paid to books for children, and to children as readers by others than that small number of us who have come to recognize their importance. What has bedevilled criticism of children's books in the past is the rejection of any concept of the child-reader-in-the-book by those who have sought most earnestly for critical respectability. And they have done this, have set aside the reader-in-the-book, in the belief that mainstream criticism requires them to do so, when in fact literary criticism has for years now been moving more and more towards a method that examines this very aspect of literature. If children's book critics look for parity with their colleagues outside the study of children's books, they must—if for no other more valuable reason—show how the concept of the implied reader relates to children as readers and to the books they read.

The idea of the implied reader derives from the understanding that it takes two to say a thing. In effect it suggests that in his book an author creates a relationship with a reader in order to discover the meaning of the text. Wolfgang Iser, in *The Implied Reader*, puts it this way: he says that such a critical method 'is concerned primarily with the form of a work, insofar as one defines form basically as a means of communication or as a negotiation of insight' [p. 57].

To achieve this, an author, sometimes consciously sometimes not, creates, in Wayne C. Booth's words: 'an image of himself and another image of his reader; he makes his reader, as he makes his second self, and the most successful reading is one in which the created selves, author and reader, can find complete agreement.' [*The Rhetoric of Fiction*, p. 138]

The author's second self[1] is created by his use of various techniques: by the way, for example, he puts himself into the narrator—whether that be a third-person godlike all-seer or a first-person child character; by the way he comments on the events in the story; and by the attitude he adopts towards his characters and their actions, which he communicates in various ways, both subtle and obvious.

In the same way (and let me stress again, deliberately or otherwise) the reader's second self—the reader-in-the-book—is given certain attributes, a certain persona, created by techniques and devices which help form the narrative. And this persona is guided by the author towards the book's potential meanings.

Booth points out that a distinction must be made 'between myself as reader and the very often different self who goes about paying bills, repairing leaky faucets, and failing in generosity and wisdom. It is only as I read that I become the self whose beliefs must coincide with the author's. Regardless of my real beliefs and practices, I must subordinate my mind and heart to the book if I am to enjoy it to the full.' [p. 137]

3. *The unyielding child reader*

Booth expresses something mature literary readers have always understood: that a requirement of fulfilled readership is a willingness to give oneself up to the book. They have learned how to do this: how to lay aside their own prejudices and take on the prejudices of the text, how to enter into the book, becoming part of it while at the same time never abandoning their own being. In C. S. Lewis's words literature allowed him 'to become a thousand [people] and yet remain myself'.

Children, of course, have not completely learned how to do this; they have not discovered how to shift the gears of their personality according to the invitations offered by the book. In this respect they are unyielding readers. They want the book to suit them, tending to expect an author to take them as he finds them rather than they taking the book as they find it. One of the valuable possibilities offered by the critical method I look for is that it would make more intelligently understandable those books which take a child as he is but then draw him into the text; the books which help the child reader to negotiate meaning, help him develop the ability to receive a text as a literary reader does rather than making use of it for nonliterary purposes.

The concept of the implied reader and the critical method that follows from it help us to do just that. They help us establish the author's relationship with the (child) reader implied in the story, to see how he creates that relationship and to discover the meaning(s) he seeks to negotiate. Clearly, such understanding will lead us beyond a critical appreciation of the text towards that other essential activity of people concerned with children's books: how to mediate the books to their readers so that not only are individual books better appreciated by children but children are also helped to become literary readers.

II

We must examine one book closely in an attempt to reveal its implied reader. But before we come to that, it might be useful to consider some of the principal techniques by which an author can establish his tone—his relationship with his desired reader—and, of particular importance in children's books, by which he can draw the reader into the text in such a way that the reader accepts the role offered and enters into the demands of the book.

4. Style

Style is the term we use for the way a writer employs language to make his second self and his implied reader and to communicate his meaning. It is far too simplistic to suppose that this is just a matter of sentence structure and choice of vocabulary. It encompasses an author's use of image, his deliberate and unaware references, the assumptions he makes about what a reader will understand without explication or description, his attitude to beliefs, customs, characters in his narrative—all as revealed by the way he writes about them.

A simple example which allows a comparison between the style a writer employed when writing for adults and the alterations he made to it when rewriting the story for children, is provided by Roald Dahl. 'The Champion of the World' is a short story first published in *The New Yorker* and now included in *Kiss Kiss*. Some years afterwards Dahl rewrote the story for children under the title *Danny: The Champion of the World*. The original version could hardly be called difficult in subject or language. A ten-year-old of average reading ability could manage it without too much bother, should any child want to. Both versions are told in the first person; the adult narrator of the original is in some respects naïvely ingenuous, a device Dahl employs (following *New Yorker*-Thurber tradition) as a foil for the narrator's friend Claud, a worldly wise, unfazable character, and as a device to exaggerate into comic extravagance the otherwise only mildly amusing events of a fairly plain tale.

Because the original is written in this first-person, easily read narrative, which is naïve even in its emotional pitch, Dahl could transfer parts with minimal alterations straight from the original into the children's version. Yet even so, he made some interesting and significant changes. Here, for example, is the original description of the entry into the story of its arch-villain, Victor Hazel (differently spelt in the two tellings), whose unforgivable snobbery and unscrupulous selfishness are justification enough in the narrator's eyes to warrant poaching his pheasants:

I wasn't sure about this, but I had a suspicion that it was none other than the famous Mr Victor Hazel himself, the owner of the land and the pheasants. Mr Hazel was a local brewer with an unbelievably arrogant manner. He was rich beyond words, and his property stretched for miles along either side of the valley. He was a self-made man with no charm at all and precious few virtues. He loathed all persons of humble station, having once been one of them himself, and he strove desperately to mingle with what he believed were the right kind of folk. He rode to hounds and gave shooting-parties and wore fancy waistcoats, and every weekday he drove an enormous black Rolls-Royce past the filling-station on his way to the brewery. As he flashed by, we would sometimes catch a glimpse of the great glistening brewer's face above the wheel, pink as a ham, all soft and inflamed from drinking too much beer.

[p. 209]

Here is the version recast for the children's telling:

I must pause here to tell you something about Mr Victor Hazell. He was a brewer of beer and he owned a huge brewery. He was rich beyond words, and his property stretched for miles along either side of the valley. All the land around us belonged to him, everything on both sides of the road, everything except the small patch of ground on which our filling-station stood. That patch belonged to my father. It was a little island in the middle of the vast ocean of Mr Hazell's estate.

Mr Victor Hazell was a roaring snob and he tried desperately to get in with what he believed were the right kind of people. He hunted with the hounds and gave shooting parties and wore fancy waistcoats. Every week-day he drove his enormous silver Rolls-Royce past our filling-station on his way to the brewery. As he flashed by we would sometimes catch a glimpse of the great glistening beery face above the wheel, pink as a ham, all soft and inflamed from drinking too much beer.

[pp. 49–50]

Dahl has simplified some of his sentences by chopping up the longer ones with full stops where commas are used in the adult version. And he does some cutting: he takes out the abstractions such as the comment about Hazel loathing people of humble station because he had once been one of them himself. Presumably Dahl felt children would not be able (or want) to cope either with the stylistic complexities of his first version or with the motivation ascribed to Hazel's behaviour. Whatever we may think about this, it certainly reveals Dahl's assumptions about his implied reader.

What he aims to achieve—and does—is a tone of voice which is clear, uncluttered, unobtrusive, not very demanding linguistically, and which sets up a sense of intimate, yet adult-controlled, relationship between his second self and his implied child reader. It is a voice often heard in children's books of the kind deliberately written for them: it is the voice of speech rather than of interior monologue or no-holds-barred private confession. It is, in fact, the tone of a friendly adult storyteller who knows how to entertain children while at the same time keeping them in their place. Even when speaking outrageously about child-adult taboo subjects (theft by poaching in *Danny* and, in this extract, harsh words about a grown-up), the tone has a kind of drawing-room politeness. At its most typical it is a style that speaks of 'the children' in the tale. Arthur Ransome marks a high point in that traditional manner:

So the letters had been written and posted, and day after day the children had been camping on the Peak of Darien by day, and sleeping in the farmhouse by night. They had been out in the rowing-boat with their mother, but they had always rowed the other way so as not to spoil the voyage of discovery by going to the island first. But with each day after the sending of the letters it had somehow seemed less and less likely that there would ever be an answer. The island had come to seem one of those places seen from the train that belong to a life in which we shall never take part. And now, suddenly, it was real. It was to be their island after all. They were to be allowed to use the sailing-boat by themselves. They were to be allowed to sail out from the little sheltered bay, and round the point, and down the lake to the island. They were to be allowed to land on the island, and to live there until it was time to pack up again and go home to town and school and lessons. The news was so good that it made them solemn. They ate their bread and marmalade in silence. The prospect before them was too vast for chatter. John was thinking of the sailing, wondering whether he really remembered all that he had learnt last year. Susan was thinking of the stores and the cooking. Titty was thinking of the island itself, of coral, treasure, and footprints in the sand. Roger was thinking of the fact that he was not to be left behind. He saw for the first time that it was a good thing to be no longer the baby of the family. Vicky was youngest now. Vicky would stay at home, and Roger, one of the crew of a ship, was to sail away into the unknown world.

[pp. 16–17]

Ransome achieves precisely the same relationship with his reader as Dahl, and by pretty much the same stylistic qualities. Ransome's style is more fluid than Dahl's, gentler on the ear, better balanced and more tuneful. But it is essentially writing for children; no one, surely, can believe that, had Ransome been writing for adults—in the sense of an implied adult reader— he would have adopted the tone of voice so evident and so well created in *Swallows and Amazons*, from which the extract is taken.

Style can, as I say, work in a much more complex and subtly effective way than these two extracts suggest—or rather than my use of them here suggests. And we will look further into this aspect of the writer-reader relationship when we come to examine a major text.

5. Intermission: What the writers say . . .

Mention of Ransome calls to mind his famous much-quoted words about writing for children: 'You write not *for* children but for yourself, and if, by good fortune, children enjoy what you enjoy, why then you are a writer of children's books.'

All very well and, obviously, what Ransome believed about himself. But it is difficult to believe on the evidence of Ransome's books that, had he really thought he was speaking to an adult audience primarily, he would have adopted the same tone of voice or would have treated his stories in the ways he does. Even a traditional critical examination of his books, eschewing all thought of the reader, implied or otherwise (excepting of course the critic who never considers himself anything but an objective, and there-fore somehow never a specific, reader—a matter Langman in the article already mentioned deals with very effectively), must surely reveal that Ransome's books are for children in quite specific ways, whatever Ransome himself said. Which is not to suggest that he, or any other writer who adopts this idea about himself as a writer, is dissembling. Rather, I want simply to reinforce Langman's observation: 'An author may write for a single person or a large public, for himself or for nobody. But the work itself implies the kind of reader to whom it is addressed and this may not coincide with the author's private view of his audience.'

Which proves one thing, if anything at all: we must be wary of using as evidence in criticism what an author says about himself, publicly or privately: a caution we have not sufficiently taken to heart in commentating on children's books. Over recent years there has been a fashion for calling the authors on stage to explicate themselves and their work in public and to defend it against the worst ravages of pedagogy and off-the-cuff criticism. That has been beneficial neither for the authors nor for their audiences.

6. Point of view

Tone of voice, style as a whole, very quickly establishes a relationship between author and reader; very quickly creates the image of the implied reader. In books where the implied reader is a child, authors tend to reinforce the relationship by adopting in their second self—giving the book, if you prefer—a very sharply focused point of view. They tend to achieve that focus by putting at the centre of the story a child through whose being everything is seen and felt.

This is more than simply a device. If literature for children is to have any meaning at all, it must primarily be concerned with the nature of childhood, not just the nature commonly shared by most children but the diversity of childhood nature too. For, like all literature, children's literature at its best attempts 'to explore, recreate and seek for meanings in human experience' (the phrase is Richard Hoggart's); this attempt is made with specific reference to children and their lives through the unique relationship between language and form.

But, at the level of creating the implied reader and of an author's need to draw a child reader into his book, this narrowing of focus by the adoption of a child point of view helps keep the author's second self—himself in the book—within the perceptual scope of his child reader. And the child, finding within the book an implied author whom he can befriend because he is of the tribe of childhood as well, is thus wooed into the book. He adopts the image of the implied child reader and is then willing, may even desire, to give himself up to the author and the book and be led through whatever experience is offered.

Thus the book's point of view not only acts as a means of creating the author-reader relationship but works powerfully as a solvent, melting away a child's non-literary approach to reading and reforming him into the kind of reader the book demands.

Some authors, feeling constricted by a too narrowly child-focusing viewpoint, try to find ways of presenting a fuller picture of adulthood without losing the child-attracting quality of the narrower focus. A few have tried to do this directly, using adult characters and a point of view that shifts between a child-focus and an adult-focus, but very few of the few who have tried have succeeded. It remains one of the major problems for children's writers now. *Carrie's War* by Nina Bawden is well worth critical consideration as a very fine example of how an author creates an implied reader and of how adult characters can be revealed in much of their complexity without loss of definition for young readers.

Most writers approach the problem of adult-portrayal less directly. They tend to cast their tales in the form of fantasy, usually with animal-human characters. Robert C. O'Brien's *Mrs Frisby and the Rats of NIMH* provides a much enjoyed modern example; Kenneth Grahame's *The Wind in the Willows* probably the best known and most affectionately regarded; and Russell Hoban's *The Mouse and His Child* one of the most complexly layered and handled (for which reasons, no doubt, it is finding its most responsive audience not among children but among adolescents).

But if I wanted to select, in the context of my theme, two superlative examples that encompass a possible readership of about seven years old right on to adulthood, I would choose Alan Garner's *The Stone Book* to demonstrate the direct approach and Ted Hughes's *The Iron Man* as an example of the solution through fantasy.

7. *Taking sides*

It does not follow, of course, that a writer who places a child at the narrative centre of his tale necessarily or even intentionally forges an alliance with children. *Lord of the Flies* is entirely peopled by children, but no one would call it a book for children in any sense. (Adolescents enjoy it—or at least their teachers have decided they shall study it; but adolescents are not children, an understanding I have so far taken for granted.) Even the point of view of William Golding's book, though the narrative restricts itself to the child characters' points of view, is in fact profoundly adult in range and perceptions. And this is to say nothing about the style and the implied reader it helps create.

William Mayne, always published as a children's author but notoriously little read by children and much read by adults, may, for all I know, intend to be a writer for children. But what the tone of his books actually achieves, as Charles Sarland brilliantly uncovered in his article, 'Chorister Quartet', is an implied author who is an observer of children and the narrative: a watcher rather than an ally. Even his dramatic technique seems deliberately designed to alienate the reader from the events and from the people described. This attitude to story is so little to be found in children's books that even children who have grown up as frequent and thoughtful readers find Mayne at his densest very difficult to negotiate. He wants his reader to stand back and examine what he, Mayne, offers in the same way that, as nearly as I can understand it, Brecht wanted his audiences to stand back from and contemplate the events enacted on stage.

As Sarland says, Mayne 'requires a degree of sophistication in the reader that would not normally be found in children of the same age as his characters. It is clear from the way he uses pace, dialogue, causal relationships, puns and wordplay that the last thing he wants is that the reader should be carried along on the tide of the narrative'. [p. 113]

There is, in other words, an ambivalence about Mayne's work that disturbs his relationship with his child reader. And this is made more unnerving by a fracture between a narrative point of view that seems to want to ally the book with children and narrative techniques that require the reader to disassociate from the story—to retreat and examine it dispassionately.

What Mayne may be trying to do—I say 'may be' because I am not sure that he *is* trying for it—is not impossible to achieve, though it is very difficult indeed to achieve for children. I have no space to delve into the matter here,

362

fascinating though I find it, except to say as a pointer to those who want to follow this direction for themselves: Alan Garner's *The Stone Book*, besides the other extraordinary qualities it possesses, manages to balance these paradoxical demands, involving the reader with the narrative while at the same time helping him to stand back and contemplate it. And Garner makes it possible for children to participate like this at even quite an early time in their growth as readers, though the younger ones may require the mediation of an adult alongside them in order to enter into such a profound experience.

Taking sides can be crudely worked for, simply as a way of 'getting the child reader on your side'. Enid Blyton provides the obvious example. She quite literally places her second self on the side of the children in her stories and the readers she deliberately looks for. Her allegiance becomes collusion in a game of 'us kids against them adults'. Nothing reveals this more completely than her treatment of adult characters like the policeman Mr Goon in *The Mystery of the Strange Bundle*. The unfortunate constable's name itself—chosen by the author, remember—indicates Blyton's attitude to the man, to his office, and her stance as one of the gang, one of the children in the story. Let's play this game together, she says openly and without embarrassment; let's have fun at the expense of the grown-ups; let's show them who's best; let's solve a mystery and have an adventure.

The very titles of her books reinforce this taking of sides. They act as an attraction to the book, raising in the reader expectations about the nature of the story to come that she never fails to satisfy. There are ten books in the *Mystery of . . .* series, eight in the Adventure series, and twelve 'about the Five Finder-Outers and Dog'.

Incident by incident Blyton sustains the collusion with her implied reader, sometimes letting him have the edge on the characters by telling him what they don't yet know, sometimes letting the characters have the edge on the reader by withholding details it later turns out the characters knew all the time. And adults get the edge only so that they can be done down later by the narrator, her characters and her readers.

There is about her stories a sense of secrets being told in whispers just out of earshot of the grown-ups, a subversive charm made all the more potent for being couched in a narrative style that sounds no more disturbing than the voice of a polite maiden aunt telling a bedtime story over cocoa and biscuits. Ultimately Blyton so allies herself with her desired readers that she fails them because she never takes them further than they are. She is a female Peter Pan, the kind of suffocating adult who prefers children never to grow up, because then she can enjoy their pretty foibles and dominate them by her adult superiority. This betrayal of childhood seeps through her stories: we see it as the underlying characteristic of her children who all really want to dominate each other as well as the adults.

Richmal Crompton is quite as canny; she too allies herself strongly with her child reader.[2] But her work has a redeeming quality—one among others:

her ironic treatment of William, the Outlaws and their adventures. A skilled short-story writer, she structures her tales with an elegance outstanding in its craftsmanship and finish. But above all she brings to children's reading that essential element they must discover if they are to grow beyond the kind of writing Blyton's epitomizes. For without an understanding of irony, literature—beyond the merely plotful level—will never provide much pleasure and certainly cannot yield up its deepest meanings.

Once an author has forged an alliance and a point of view that engages a child, he can then manipulate that alliance as a device to guide the reader towards the meanings he wishes to negotiate. Wolfgang Iser provides a useful example, not from a specifically children's book, where such a manoeuvre is too rarely used, but from *Oliver Twist*. Iser cites the scene in which the hungry Oliver

> has the effrontery (as the narrator sees it) to ask for another plate of soup. In the presentation of this daring exploit, Oliver's inner feelings are deliberately excluded in order to give greater emphasis to the indignation of the authorities at such an unreasonable request. The narrator comes down heavily on the side of authority, and can thus be quite sure that his hard-hearted attitude will arouse a flood of sympathy in his readers for the poor starving child.
>
> [p. 116]

What such manipulation of the reader's expectations, allegiances, and author-guided desires leads to is the further development of the implied reader into an implicated reader: one so intellectually and emotionally given to the book, not just its plot and characters but its negotiation between author and reader of potential meanings, that the reader is totally involved. The last thing he wants is to stop reading; and what he wants above all is to milk the book dry of all it has to offer, and to do so in the kind of way the author wishes. He finally becomes a participant in the making of the book. He has become aware of the 'tell-tale gaps'.

8. Tell-tale gaps

As a tale unfolds, the reader discovers its meaning. Authors can strive, as some do, to make their meaning plain, leaving little room for the reader to negotiate with them. Other authors leave gaps which the reader must fill before the meaning can be complete. A skilful author wishing to do this is somewhat like a play-leader: he structures his narrative so as to direct it in a dramatic pattern that leads the reader towards possible meaning(s); and he stage-manages the reader's involvement by bringing into play various techniques which he knows influence the reader's responses and expectations, in the way that Iser, for example, described Dickens doing in *Oliver Twist* (7).

364

Literature can be studied so as to uncover the gaps an author leaves for the reader to fill, these gaps taking two general forms.

The first is the more superficial. These gaps have to do with an author's assumptions, whether knowingly made or not, about his readers. Just as we saw in the Dahl extracts (4) how a writer's style revealed his assumptions about his implied reader's ability to cope with language and syntax, so we can also detect from a writer's references to a variety of things just what he assumes about his implied reader's beliefs, politics, social customs, and the like. Richmal Crompton in common with Enid Blyton, A. A. Milne, Edith Nesbit and many more children's authors assumed a reader who would not only be aware of housemaids and cooks, nannies and gardeners but would also be used to living in homes attended by such household servants. That assumption was as unconsciously made as the adoption of a tone of voice current among people who employed servants at the time the authors were writing.

These referential gaps, these assumptions of commonality, are relatively unimportant until they become so dominant in the text that people who do not—or do not wish to—make the same assumptions feel alienated by them as they read. This alienation, this feeling of repugnance, affects the child just as much as the adult, once the referential gaps become significant.

Far more important, however, is another form of tell-tale gap: these are the ones that challenge the reader to participate in making meaning. Making meaning is a vital concept in literary reading. Laurence Sterne refers to it directly in *Tristram Shandy*:

> No author, who understands the just boundaries of decorum and good breeding, would presume to think all: The truest respect which you can pay to the reader's understanding, is to halve this matter amicably, and leave him something to imagine, in his turn, as well as yourself.
>
> For my own part, I am eternally paying him compliments of this kind, and do all that lies in my power to keep his imagination as busy as my own.
>
> [p. 127]

Of course, it doesn't all depend on the author; he can deploy his narrative skills brilliantly, 'halving the matter amicably' with his reader. But unless a reader accepts the challenge, no relationship that seeks to discover meaning is possible. It is one of the responsibilities of children's writers, and a privileged one, so to write that children are led to understand how to read: how to accept the challenge.

Let me offer the crucial gap in Sendak's *Where the Wild Things Are* as example. In its pictorial as well as its textual art this masterpiece is compactly authored. One might be forgiven for supposing at first sight that there are no gaps of any kind for the reader to enter. But not so; there is one so vital that, unless the reader fills it, the profound meaning of the book cannot be discovered. It is the gap which demands that the reader supply the understanding that Max has dreamt his journey to the Wild Things, that in fact the Wild Things are Max's own creation. Once understood, that meaning having been made, the book opens itself to all sorts of other pleasurable discoveries which actually were clues to the meaning all along and which, once realized, present themselves as clues to yet further meaning. There is, for instance, in the first picture in the book, the Wild-Thingish doll hanging from a coathanger; and then, in the very next picture, there is the portrait of a Wild Thing framed and hung on the wall and signed 'by Max'.

Such guides to the reader may seem obvious to an adult, but children of four and five and six, who are the book's implied readers, make such a significant contribution and discover such details only if they give the book a willing attention of the same order as adults must give to filling the gaps in, say, Joyce's *Ulysses*.

Alan Garner's *The Stone Book* is built around three main images, each placed in precise relationship to each other so that they create two vital gaps which the reader must enter and fill before the potential meanings of the book become plain. Reiner Zimnik's *The Crane* is as halved as Sterne could wish; Zimnik's tone of voice is so sensible, so matter of fact, so gentle and everyday, you can suppose the meaning(s) of his story must be so too. But in fact the book is heavy with possibilities and is not at all easy to plumb intellectually, though emotionally—as an increasing number of teachers are finding after introducing it to their nine- to twelve-year-olds—it is powerfully attractive.

9. In sum . . .

. . . and before we begin an exploration of one text.

I am suggesting that the concept of the implied reader, far from unattended to by literary critics in Europe and America, offers us a critical approach which concerns itself less with the subjects portrayed in a book than with the means of communication by which the reader is brought into contact with the reality presented by an author. It is a method which could help us determine whether a book is for children or not, what kind of book it is, and what kind of reader (or, to put it another way, what kind of reading) it demands. Knowing this will help us to understand better how to teach not just a particular book but particular books to particular children.

I have been trying to sketch in some of the more significant ways in which specific responses are provoked in a reader, the techniques that make up what Kenneth Burke in *The Philosophy of Literary Form* has called 'the strategy of communication'. This is achieved by major techniques such as I have described and by a variety of other devices such as what an author discloses to his reader and what he conceals, the way he signals his intentions, his evocation of suspense, the introduction of the unexpected, and the way he can play about with the reader's expected responses to the narrative.

All these create a relationship between author and reader, which I have used the word 'tone' to denote; and an author, consciously or otherwise, reveals in his narrative, through the way he uses all these techniques and by other signals too, what he wants from his reader, what kind of relationship he looks for.

Now I want to examine some of these matters at work in one book, Lucy Boston's *The Children of Green Knowe*.

III

10. Why The Children of Green Knowe?

For three reasons.

Mrs Boston is a much admired and respected writer; her first children's book lends itself to my critical needs here.

Not only is she much respected, but she is historically important. *The Children of Green Knowe* appeared in 1954 and was one of the first of the new wave of children's books that marks the outcropping since the Second World War. I think it intelligently arguable that this book directly influenced a number of the writers who began work in the 50s and 60s. (Philippa Pearce's *Tom's Midnight Garden*, Alan Garner's *The Weirdstone of Brisingamen* and the work of William Mayne owe a considerable debt to Lucy Boston. Discuss.)

Mrs Boston has said publicly some interesting things about her work, which provide an example of the kind of authorial self-comment I warned against earlier. During a talk given in November 1968 to the Children's Book Circle (a gathering of children's book editors in London who meet to discuss their professional concerns) Mrs Boston said:

> Is there a conscious difference in the way I write for grown-ups and children? No, there is no difference of approach, style, vocabulary or standard. I could pick out passages from any of the books and you would not be able to tell what age it was aimed at.
>
> [p. 36]

Let's see. The opening of *Yew Hall*, Lucy Boston's first book, and written for adults (or, to use her word, grown-ups):

> Possibly it was their voices that made me decide that I could share my house with them, so that after having once refused, I repented and told them that they could come. He was a huge man, handsome

like a statue in St Paul's. His martial features and great neck suggested at once to the imagination the folds of a marble cloak drawn
back across a superlative torso and looped over an arm to free
the incredible giant legs in their marble tights. He was so near to the
type classified as admirable at the turn of the eighteenth century
that his own personality might have escaped my notice if it had not
been that his voice was as soft and warm in quality as a man's voice
could possibly be. There was nothing feminine about it. It was like
a breeze in the tops of a forest, and he gave the impression, that
afterwards was amply confirmed, of having so much space to live in
that he need never knock elbows with or trip over anyone else. Well
might he be self-satisfied—like America he had no need of imports.
A general comfort radiated from his bigness—a big heart, a big fire,
a big meal, a big bed, a big pair of shoes; and, I suppose, we must
also think of a big stick, a big clap of thunder.

[pp. 9–10]

Compare the opening passage of her first children's book, published
the same year (see extract below): there are unmistakable differences in
approach, style and vocabulary. The urbanity of *Yew Hall* establishes very
quickly a tone that implies a literate, adult reader. The handsome statues
of St Paul's, the martial features and superlative torso, the type classified
as admirable at the turn of the eighteenth century, America having no need
of imports: this one paragraph is littered with references that expect a
reader who can match the author's cultural and social background: the
educated English middle class. The writing is confident, witty, slightly
superior ('Possibly it was their voices that made me decide that I could
share my house with them . . .'), the kind of writing one would not be
ashamed to be caught reading by one's butler.

What of *The Children of Green Knowe*? Who is its implied reader? Let's
look at it under the headings suggested in II.

11. Style

Here are the opening paragraphs of *The Children of Green Knowe*:

A little boy was sitting in the corner of a railway carriage looking
out at the rain, which was splashing against the windows and blotching downward in an ugly, dirty way. He was not the only person in
the carriage, but the others were strangers to him. He was alone
as usual. There were two women opposite him, a fat one and a thin
one, and they talked without stopping, smacking their lips in
between sentences and seeming to enjoy what they said as much as
if it were something to eat. They were knitting all the time, and

whenever the train stopped the click-clack of their needles was loud and clear like two clocks. It was a stopping train—more stop than go—and it had been crawling along through flat flooded country for a long time. Everywhere there was water—not sea or rivers or lakes, but just senseless flood water with the rain splashing into it. Sometimes the railway lines were covered by it, and then the train-noise was quite different, softer than a boat.

'I wish it was *the* Flood', thought the boy, 'and that I was going to the Ark. That would be fun! Like the circus. Perhaps Noah had a whip and made all the animals go round and round for exercise. What a noise there would be, with the lions roaring, elephants trumpeting, pigs squealing, donkeys braying, horses whinnying, bulls bellowing, and cocks and hens always thinking they were going to be trodden on but unable to fly up to the roof where all the other birds were singing, screaming, twittering, squawking and cooing. What must it have sounded like, coming along on the tide? And did Mrs Noah just knit, knit and take no notice?'

The two women opposite him were getting ready for the next station. They packed up their knitting and collected their parcels and then sat staring at the little boy. He had a thin face and very large eyes; he looked patient and rather sad. They seemed to notice him for the first time.

[pp. 9–10]

The language in *Yew Hall* tends towards the Latinate. *Green Knowe* is much more firmly Anglo-Saxon. Rain is splashing and blotching, lips are smacking, knitting needles click-clack, not to mention Tolly's own list of participial verbs describing Noah's animals. This makes for a style not only simpler to read but far more active than a Latinate one, far more concrete in an everyday and child-appealing sense.

There is, however, as Mrs Boston claims, no lowering of standard between the two books. *Green Knowe* is just as densely and richly textured—perhaps is even more richly textured—than *Yew Hall*. But the images and the words used to communicate them are quite different in the experiential demands made on the reader. At the crudest level *Yew Hall* requires familiarity with St Paul's Cathedral, the late eighteenth century and the economy of the United States if one is to enjoy all Mrs Boston has to offer. *Green Knowe* requires no such sophistication. You need only to have seen some rain, have been on a train, know something about the story of Noah and the Flood, and to have observed women knitting for the text to be completely open to you. After that you need only put at Mrs Boston's disposal a sympathetic imagination and she leads you off in a very clearly signposted direction. Even from these three opening paragraphs we can see she is busy with sensual experience: the sight, sound, feel, and sense of things. It is a direction in which her story will take young readers a very long way.

For sure, then, the style of *The Children of Green Knowe* is much more accessible to a child reader, and comparison with the style of *Yew Hall*, which seems so much more confidently natural to Mrs Boston—one feels it is closer to her own thinking voice—leads one to suppose its implied reader is a child. At the very least the style appeals to the child-in-the-adult, possessing that very tone of voice I earlier suggested is traditionally the English tone used in telling stories to children: direct, clear, polite, firm, uncluttered. And Mrs Boston achieves it admirably.

We must discover whether or not the other aspects of her book reinforce the impression given by her style.

12. Point of view

Tolly is seven; remarkable for his age, a child of a very particular class. His father and stepmother are in Burma; the boy has been put into boarding school, left for the holidays with the headmistress and her old father, and then sent alone on a train journey to visit his great-grandmother, Mrs Oldknow, who lives in a large old house. Throughout, the story is told from Tolly's point of view. Only occasionally is there a brief shift for some narrative purpose, as when the two women in the train 'sat staring at the little boy. He had a thin face and very large eyes; he looked patient and rather sad. They seemed to notice him for the first time.' Otherwise, the perceptions are all the boy's.

Even Mrs Oldknow, so central a character in the story, is seen only from the outside. Her private thoughts and perceptions remain enigmatic, and influentially so: she occupies a somewhat mysteriously attractive place in the book. One wonders about her, and feels too a little daunted by her, a little afraid of her secret knowingness. The reader gets that impression from a subtly handled feature of the book. All along one cannot help feeling that it is Mrs Oldknow who is telling the story. And probably the feeling would not be so strong were it not for the stories Mrs Oldknow tells Tolly at night. They are about the children who lived in the house and died in the Plague of 1665. But then, the rest of the book is also about a boy in the house. Isn't the whole book therefore a story by Mrs Oldknow? Has she, in fact, invented Tolly? Or isn't she, at the very least, telling his story, and doing it so well because she *knows*—can see into children's minds, as children so often believe some adults can, and tell what is going on in them?

So, though the story is told from Tolly's point of view—apart, of course, from Mrs Oldknow's stories about the other, long-ago children—Mrs Oldknow herself seems in control of it. These two things together stimulate a strong sense of alliance among Mrs Oldknow, Tolly and the reader, thus placing the author unmistakably on the reader's side.

13. Taking sides

Before the story has gone far enough to establish the strong relationship I've just described, Mrs Boston is signalling her allegiance. The opening paragraphs of the book reveal her sympathetic understanding of a small boy's response to the world about him, and in particular the world as it surrounds Tolly at that moment on the train. Every slight detail serves this end, from the clacking needles and the train being more stop than go, to the child-accurate observation of the rain and the flood and the train noise.

Then the two women take notice, and their conversation with Tolly sets him thinking about his circumstances. Now Mrs Boston reveals unequivocally whose side she is on: Tolly being miserably shy of his headmistress, the kind Miss Spudd, who yet always calls him 'dear'.

When Tolly at last meets his great-grandmother, wondering if she is a witch and whether he will be afraid of her (the terrible business of meeting strange relatives), Mrs Boston-Oldknow (for Mrs Boston's second self must surely be Mrs Oldknow) declares her allegiance openly: 'What does one generation more or less matter? I'm glad you have come. It will seem lovely to me. How many years of you have I wasted?' A declaration of friendship, if not of love, which is reinforced by a further shift from adult-child allegiance to collusion no more than a page later:

> At that moment the fire went *pop!* and shot a piece of wood out into the room. *Pop!* again.
> 'Buttons! Who said buttons? Poor Mrs Noah.' Tolly chased the sparks and trod on them to put them out.
> 'Why do you live in a castle?' he said, looking round.
> 'Why not? Castles were meant to live in.'
> 'I thought that was only in fairy tales. Is it a real castle?'
> 'Of course.'
> 'I mean, do things happen in it, like the castles in books?'
> 'Oh yes, things happen in it.'
> 'What sort of things?'
> 'Wait and see! I'm waiting too, to see what happens now that you are here. Something will, I'm sure.'
>
> [p. 20]

Something is being proposed here: at the least a game, at the most something more mysteriously magical, and it is to be an adventure enacted between Tolly and Mrs Oldknow.

Next morning, the adventure begins: it involves Tolly's long-ago child relatives—whether as ghosts or not we hope to discover—household toys, garden animals, and Mrs Oldknow. Being cut off by the flood simply asserts actually and symbolically the private collusive world inhabited by the boy and the old woman.

371

But the collusion is not just a means of disposing the reader to the book: its profoundest meaning depends upon the nature of the relationship.

14. Tell-tale gaps

Game or ghost story? More than a game and not just a ghost story. Each time we think that at last Tolly is indisputably seeing apparitions of Toby, Alexander and Linnet, Mrs Boston withdraws confirmation.

A crucial scene comes after the snowfall. A tree's branches form a cave, which Tolly enters and there seems to meet and hear speaking the three ghosts; Alexander even plays his flute. But the scene ends: 'Had he been dreaming?' And when Tolly creeps out of his snowcave, 'Somewhere in the garden a thrush was trying to whistle Alexander's tune.' We are left wondering still.

Later Mrs Oldknow leaves Tolly alone in the house, and Boggis too is gone. Surely now the ghosts will emerge and they, Tolly and the reader can meet undeniably. But no. Despite the house being empty of others and dark coming on, so that the stage is set for a final exciting ghost-drama, our expectations raised for a climax (how many other writers have prepared us so before), Mrs Boston will not satisfy us: 'For some reason [Tolly] felt convinced that until his great-grandmother returned, not so much as a marble would move in the house.' She has employed a device similar to Dickens's in *Oliver Twist*: reader's expectations raised, and deliberately dashed. We are forced to wonder why.

Here is the amicable halving of this book; here is a tell-tale gap which the reader must enter if the book's true meaning is to be negotiated. Whatever is going on in the story can only be enacted between Mrs Oldknow and Tolly. Nothing happens when they are apart. Together, their lives have followed a pattern. During the day, Tolly explores and plays, sometimes on his own, sometimes with Mrs Oldknow, sometimes with Boggis, but always, however gently and subtly suggested, at the instigation of his great-grandmother. She, like a superlatively wise play-leader, offers opportunities for Tolly to enjoy himself through experiences that enliven the world to him. He is led to look closely, hear clearly, touch sensitively, think imaginatively. The book is laden with instances in which Tolly encounters objects and, by sensing them and playing with them, imaginatively perceives the life in them.

These moments extend from the purely sensational—

> In the fire the snow drifting down the chimney was making the only noise it ever can—a sound like the striking of fairy matches; though sometimes when the wind blows you can hear the snow like a gloved hand laid against the window.
>
> [p. 64]

—to lengthy passages in which Tolly's exploration of a room or a part of the garden or of a toybox is described in close and carefully imaged detail. The walk through the snow that leads to the snow-cave scene is one such.

Punctuating these descriptions of the day-to-day activities are four stories told by Mrs Oldknow to Tolly at bedtime. This device suits the apparently naturalistic plot: Tolly is on holiday with his great-grandmother; the house and gardens provide his daily adventures; before bed he is given his fictional adventure. But these four stories are not just any stories: they are about the three long-ago children and their horse Feste, one story for each. Some critics—John Rowe Townsend in *A Sense of Story*, for instance—have felt this an awkward construction. To my mind it is not only a pattern that creates a satisfying rhythm in the book—entirely suited, as I say, to the plot's boy-on-holiday structure—but it actually makes the book's true meaning possible.

We are led to see things this way: Tolly and Mrs Oldknow fantasize about Toby and Alexander and Linnet. Tolly may or may not actually see their ghosts, and enjoys the game. But the three long-ago children have undeniable reality only in the stories Mrs Oldknow tells about them. There they live in their own right, not as spectres raised by Tolly and his great-grandmother, just as Tolly and Mrs Oldknow have a reality in their own right only as characters in Mrs Boston's story about them. Stories, Mrs Boston is telling us, are the means by which we give life to ourselves and the objects around us. Stories, in fact, create meaning.

Strangely enough, in the very talk to the Children's Book Circle in which she claimed no difference between her writing for adults and her writing for children, Mrs Boston also said:

> My approach has always been to explore reality as it appears, and from within to see how far imagination can properly expand it. Reality, after all, has no outside edge. I never start with a fantasy and look for a peg to hang it on. As far as I deliberately try to do anything other than to write a book that pleases me, I would like to remind adults of joy, now considered obsolete—and would like to encourage children to use and trust their senses for themselves at first hand—their ears, eyes and noses, their fingers and the soles of their feet, their skins and their breathing, their muscular joy and rhythms and heartbeats, their instinctive loves and pity and their awe of the unknown. This, not the telly, is the primary material of thought. It is from direct sense stimulus that imagination is born . . .
> [p. 36]

Nowhere has an author so exactly stated her aims, and in few books has an author achieved her highest aims so certainly as Mrs Boston does in *The Children of Green Knowe*. Through Tolly, guided by Mrs Boston's second self, her implied reader is brought to grips with the direct sense stimulus that gives birth to life-expanding imagination. By any standard this is a fine achievement, all the more remarkable for its simplicity.

15. Lucy Boston's implied reader

Mrs Boston makes no impossible demands on her child reader's ability to construct meaning from words. Her style is approachable, uncomplicated, specific rather than abstract. The first Green Knowe book is not long; its episodic and day-by-day rhythm punctuated by the stories-within-the-story makes it easy to read in unexhausting parts. Her alliance with her young reader is persuasive. The now almost old-fashioned middle-classness of Tolly's and Mrs Oldknow's life (and Mrs Boston's preference for it) is strong but not so dominantly obtrusive as to be a disadvantage. (The polite formality of the collusion between Mrs Oldknow and Tolly is nowadays amusing. Even though they are playing a game, Tolly must always behave impeccably; he commits only one naughty act throughout the whole book: he writes on the newly whitewashed wall in Boggis's room, a wickedness allowed to pass without censure, of course, because it is done in a servant's room, not in the main house. Even Boggis, old retainer, wants to preserve the benevolent hierarchical social tradition, to the point of tolerating his daughter's indiscretion because it provides him with a male heir to his post. The book is deeply conservative and traditionalist; a political attitude which disposes children all the more readily to the story, for most children prefer things to remain as they always have been.)

All Mrs Boston requires of her reader is a willingness to enter into the spirit of sensuous discovery. Given this, she deploys her craft very subtly indeed towards her stated aims. And that she is speaking primarily to children I have no doubt.

Notes

1 The term was revived by Kathleen Tillotson in her inaugural lecture at the University of London, published under the title 'The Tale and the Teller' (1959): 'Writing on George Eliot in 1877 Dowden said that the form that most persists in the mind after reading her novels is not any of the characters, but "one who, if not the real George Eliot, is that second self who writes her books, and lives and speaks through them." The "second self", he goes on, is "more substantial than any mere human personality" and has "fewer reserves"; while "behind it, lurks well pleased the veritable historical self secure from impertinent observation and criticism".' [p. 15]
2 Of course, the William stories were first written for adults. But children soon adopted them, after which Richmal Crompton was never in doubt about her true audience.

24

PROBLEMS OF AUDIENCE

Barbara Wall

Source: *The Narrator's Voice: The Dilemma of Children's Fiction*, London: Macmillan, 1991, pp. 20–36.

All writers take cognisance of audience, though it is true that they may look for audience no further than themselves. Writers who set out to write for children, however, must look further than themselves, for they are separated from children, even from the children they once were, by a substantial barrier of age and experience, a barrier which, though it may in some ways be surmounted or traversed, cannot be removed. Whatever some of them have said to the contrary, writers for children must serve two masters, themselves and their chosen audience.

While this fact may seem self-evident, the difficulties writers have experienced in the last one hundred and fifty years in coming to terms with it, are barely beginning to be analysed or understood. As early as 1855, two years before the publication of *Tom Brown's Schooldays*, William Calder Roscoe, in an essay 'Fictions for Children', pointed to one major and limiting difficulty for writers for children.

> Many books ostensibly written for children, are spoiled because the author always has a side-glance at a wider audience. The possible verdict of an adult reader exercises a disturbing influence on his work, his subject no longer possesses his mind in its integrity, and he deserves to fail, as he almost inevitably does, not because a work must be written expressly for children in order to suit their wants, but because a man cannot without confusion undertake a work of art from two different points of view.
>
> (p. 40)

Roscoe's comment serves to remind us that criticism has rarely accorded stories for children the status of works of art – they are seldom mentioned in histories of literature – and suggests one reason why this should be so. Even without the 'side-glance at a wider audience' the single-mindedness needed to produce a work of art is likely to be compromised by the need to take into account the existence of a double audience. And for some writers the fact that there is unavoidably a double audience to be considered results in the highly self-conscious cultivation of two distinct and separate audiences. Michael Egan, in an essay on James Barrie, 'The Neverland of Id: Barrie, *Peter Pan* and Freud', implies that this type of 'Double Address' as he calls it, is widespread and widely accepted.

> Barrie appears to be making use of one of the important but un-recognized conventions of writing for children: the Double Address. On the one hand the author speaks directly to his principal audience, his voice and manner serious and gentle, even conspiratorial. From time to time, however, he glances sidelong at the adults listening in and winks. Naturally, his jokes and references on these occasions are not meant to be understood by the children.
>
> (p. 46)

There is no doubt that what Egan describes is to be found in fiction for children, though less frequently in the last fifty years than before. Generally, however, Egan's comments show insensitivity to this still under-discussed aspect of narrative technique. 'Double Address' as he defines it, with the author 'winking' at the adult audience, a term which, unlike Roscoe's 'side-glance', implies that children are deliberately excluded from the joke, can hardly be called a 'convention', recognised or not, of writing for children (though it certainly occurs) since most writers avoid it. It occurs, as I have said, only in the work of the most self-conscious writers – and Barrie is an almost painfully self-conscious writer – and inevitably detracts from the integrity of the work. Far from being a solution to the problem of how to write simultaneously for child and adult, Egan's 'Double Address' is commonly rejected by critics, who accuse authors who use it of writing down.

The problem is this: who is to be addressed by the narrator of a story when the author can no longer unselfconsciously write for himself or herself, or for a reader like himself or herself? If children are addressed then the book is likely to be perceived as being 'only' a children's book. If children are not addressed it is likely not to be a children's book at all. Children, who are usually familiar with the voice of the oral teller and may therefore expect to be addressed, have little choice in the matter. They may or may not like the voice which an author uses to address them, or even to avoid addressing them. Children can do little except express preferences – some authors become popular with children and others do not. Adults too may or may not like the voice which an author uses to address children. Critics and reviewers may accuse writers of pandering to childish predilection or of writing down, and even condemn outright the use of the 'children's book register'. The challenge is to find a way not merely to be acceptable to, but to address both children and adults simultaneously, to find, in fact, not a double, but a dual audience.

My examination of the ways in which the narrators of nineteenth-century children's fiction address their narratees will show with what effort and how gradually authors learnt to free themselves from self-conscious awareness of a potential adult audience so that they could concentrate on writing for children, and in so doing, in some cases at least, achieve a dual audience. At the same time it will be seen that most stories for children which have achieved the status of classics are stories whose narrators satisfactorily address adults, either as part of a dual audience, or by oscillating between child and adult narratee, as does Thomas Hughes's narrator in *Tom Brown's Schooldays* or Barrie's in *Peter and Wendy*. That it is possible to demonstrate that narrators are always addressing someone, and possible to decide whether that someone is a child, or an adult, or neither one nor the other specifically, or neither one nor the other consistently, enables those who wish to do so to determine empirically which books are for children and which are not, and whether it is possible for books to be for both children and adults at the same time. Consciousness of audience is at the heart of the narrative process as it is undertaken by writers of stories genuinely for children.

An examination of the work of three notable writers of fiction for children will help to anatomise the difficulties writers experience in finding a voice in which to speak to children without compromising their adult integrity: one, Arthur Ransome, whose books have been outstandingly successful with children, emphatically denied that he wrote for children at all; a second, James Barrie, in spite of the fact that his Peter Pan has become a genuine legendary figure, can be seen as a writer who failed to come to terms with his child audience; and a third, T. H. White, also recognised as a 'classic' children's writer, though his work is uneven and less well known, has brilliantly, if only fleetingly, demonstrated that it is possible, not just to attract, but to address, a dual audience. The narrators of these three writers are put forward as examples of the three modes of address to children in fiction: Ransome uses *single address*, Barrie *double address* and White *dual address*, at least at times.

Of the three, Barrie (1860–1937) is the earliest and his case the most complex. As a children's writer he has recently begun to attract a good deal of critical attention, and there can be no doubt that the creation of Peter Pan is his most lasting contribution to literature. But, strangely, unlike Alice, Peter Pan is not firmly fixed in a text. It is an idea, rather than a character, that has captured the twentieth-century imagination.

Although Peter Pan had appeared first in 1902 in Barrie's whimsical adult novel *The Little White Bird*, it was the play, *Peter Pan*, written when Barrie had already established a reputation as a playwright and first produced in

1904, which, by its immediate and continuing success, released the character into the mythology of childhood. Michael Egan has argued most persuasively that the reason for this lies in the fact that *Peter Pan* is 'a psychodrama of the unconscious': 'Barrie unconsciously created a vast, symbolic metaphor – the Neverland – of the child's id; and . . . he populated it with figures of an almost archetypal resonance' (p. 37). Egan's demonstration that *Peter Pan* is an oedipal fantasy, with Peter both husband and son to Wendy, and father of her 'children', as well as killer and supplanter of the father-figure Captain Hook (always doubled in productions with Mr. Darling), makes it clear why *Peter Pan* has proved so astonishingly enduring.

As a prose fiction however *Peter Pan* has never quite succeeded. Barrie's own *Peter and Wendy*, written after a number of other writers had tried to capture the story of the play in fictional form, is still the richest and most satisfying version. But there have been many retellings of the story. Jacqueline Rose in *The Case of Peter Pan* lists eleven different writers as having been involved in such retellings. One can only conclude that the story exerts a strong fascination but that no one, not even Barrie himself, has been able to tell it definitively. A study of his and other attempts high-lights the importance of narrative stance, and narrative personality, and the relationship of narrator to narratee, in establishing whether or not a fiction is for children. Barrie's inability to define his audience is at the heart of his problem.

R. L. Green, in *Tellers of Tales*, expresses outrage at the fact that modern writers still attempt to retell the story:

> A recent attempt to rewrite Barrie's book at full length for the age-group to which he himself addressed *Peter Pan and Wendy* is one of the most astonishing and unnecessary pieces of impertinence in the history of children's literature.
>
> (p. 221)

He has inadvertently put his finger on the problem. For *Peter and Wendy* is not addressed to children of any age-group, at least not consistently. It has in fact no consistent narrative manner; it fits no formula, is shot through with ironies, sets up norms of storytelling which it then subverts; the narrator's attitude to his narratee is as hard to grasp as the character of the elusive Peter himself. It is impossible to guess whether this is the result of Barrie's incompetence in writing for children or whether he aimed deliber-ately – or even perhaps unconsciously – at pleasing too diverse an audience. The children of Arthur and Sylvia Llewelyn Davies, to whom Barrie had told the original Peter Pan and desert island stories, were all adolescents by 1911, when *Peter and Wendy* was published. George, the original of David of *The Little White Bird*, was now eighteen. All five boys were by then orphaned and under Barrie's legal guardianship; but the youngest, Nicholas, was only seven. Barrie had, besides the boys whom it is clear he was always anxious to please, a wide and appreciative adult public both for plays and novels. Another difficulty was that the story he was about to tell was a confusing and elusive mixture of fantasy and reality; fantastic events which had worked well on the stage would now require explanations.

The absence of a clearly defined and stable narratee or implied reader is obvious from the start. The description of Mrs Darling's mind and of her husband's impercipience are jokes which are illsuited to a children's book – there seems some unexplained sexual animosity on the author's part here – although the images and language have the flavour of a children's book.

> Of course they lived at 14, and until Wendy came her mother was the chief one. She was a lovely lady, with a romantic mind and such a sweet mocking mouth. Her romantic mind was like the tiny boxes, one within the other, that come from the puzzling East, however many you discover there is always one more; and her sweet mocking mouth had one kiss on it that Wendy could never get, though there it was, perfectly conspicuous in the right-hand corner.
>
> The way Mr. Darling won her was this: the many gentlemen who had been boys when she was a girl discovered simultaneously that they loved her, and they all ran to her house to propose except Mr. Darling, who took a cab and nipped in first, and so he got her. He got all of her, except the innermost box and the kiss. He never knew about the box, and in time he gave up trying for the kiss.
>
> (p. 1)

The attitude of this narrator to his narratee is very hard to determine. Barrie was too confused in his attitudes to be able to concentrate consistently on any one audience, although two at least are clearly defined. At times his narrator addresses in avuncular fashion a child narratee: 'I don't know whether you have ever seen a map of a person's mind' (p. 7). At other times he straightforwardly addresses an adult narratee: 'On these magic shores children at play are for ever beaching their coracles. We too have been there; we can still hear the sound of the surf, though we shall land no more' (p. 9).

Although in real life Barrie, it seems, easily made friends with young children, the narrator of *Peter and Wendy* is always uncomfortable in his stance as he addresses children. His most consistent tone is one of teasing. People who tease do so because they cannot establish a more equable relationship and in so far as they are teasing are not to be trusted. Barrie's is an untrustworthy narrator, one who constantly and without warning breaks the illusion he pretends to be creating, and cannot resist the opportunity to make fun of the convention he is exploiting, thereby putting his narratee suddenly in an unanticipated position.

Tootles, [the narrator here apostrophises Tootles] the fairy Tink who is bent on mischief this night is looking for a tool, and she thinks you the most easily tricked of the boys. 'Ware Tinker Bell.

Would that he could hear us, but we are not really on the island, and he passes by, biting his knuckles.

(p. 65)

Which of these adventures shall we choose? The best way will be to toss for it.

I have tossed, and the lagoon has won. This almost makes one wish that the gulch or the cake or Tink's leaf had won. Of course I could do it again, and make it best of three; however, perhaps fairest to stick to the lagoon.

(p. 102)

The story of the play *Peter Pan* grew out of Barrie's games with the Davies boys. The framework of the play, and of the novel too, the Darling household, is sentimental and whimsical, though touched with astringency in Barrie's treatment of that male competitor, Mr. Darling, but the adventures on the island are of a different kind, and still carry signs of the games which were their inspiration. At one level they are games for the participants (narrator and narratee) to be absorbed in: at another, they are seen by the author as literary rituals, and at this level Barrie cannot resist caricaturing the kind of story which at another level he is practising; and at this point he severs the bond between narrator and narratee. While some of the most brilliant patches of writing in *Peter and Wendy* come from the tension produced by this double intention, the feeling of intimacy which he has created for a young reader must dissipate when with irony and cynicism he attacks the convention.

In that supreme moment Hook did not blanch, even at the gills, but Smee and Starkey clung to each other in terror.

(p. 113)

The pirate attack had been a complete surprise: a sure proof that the unscrupulous Hook had conducted it improperly, for to surprise redskins fairly is beyond the wit of the white man.

By all unwritten laws of savage warfare it is always the redskin who attacks, and with the wiliness of his race he does it just before dawn, at which time he knows the courage of the whites to be at its lowest ebb. The white men have in the meantime made a rude stockade on the summit of yonder undulating ground, at the foot of which a stream runs; for it is destruction to be too far from water. There they await the onslaught, the inexperienced ones clutching their revolvers and treading on twigs, but the old hands sleeping

380

tranquilly until just before the dawn. Through the long black night the savage scouts wriggle, snakelike, among the grass without stirring a blade. The brushwood closes behind them as silently as sand into which a mole has dived. Not a sound is to be heard, save when they give vent to a wonderful imitation of the lonely call of the coyote. The cry is answered by other braves; and some of them do it even better than the coyotes, who are not very good at it. . . .

That this was the usual procedure was so well known to Hook that in disregarding it he cannot be excused on the plea of ignorance.

(p. 149)

It is the difficulties which such sophistication and detachment in the narrator present to children of an age to be entertained by the events of the story that have caused the numerous rewritings. Such retellers attack the book's strength by removing the idiosyncratic narrator and all signs of his connivance with an adult audience, but they can find nothing to put in his place. Barrie's practice may be wayward and unpredictable, but his idiosyncratic use of double address is the hallmark of this work. Sometimes his narrator addresses children both covertly and overtly, and sometimes adults; sometimes his narrator addresses adults while pretending to address children. Modern readers, especially adults, often find his narrator so arch and knowing as to be repulsive and offensive. But he is con-spicuously *there*: a personality to be encountered and reckoned with, a purveyor of ironies, and a stimulator of thought. When this personality has gone, only a wishy-washy sentimentality remains. The passage just quoted, for instance, loses, in Eleanor Graham's retelling, its irony, its sense of a joke shared with the reader, and most of its meaning.

> Hook had broken the two unwritten laws of savage warfare: first, that it is always the Indians who attack first, and second, that they always fall upon the white man at dawn, knowing with the cunning of their tribe, that at that hour the white man's courage is at its lowest ebb.

(p. 119)

Even more striking is the transformation of the famous 'Do you believe in fairies?' passage. At the first performance of the play, before a mainly adult audience, a claque had been arranged. It proved unnecessary as the audience broke spontaneously into applause. The *Peter and Wendy* version shows clearly that Barrie recognised the dangers inherent in such a question.

> 'If you believe,' he shouted to them, [all children 'who might be dreaming of the Neverland'] 'clap your hands; don't let Tink die.'

Many clapped.

Some didn't.

A few little beasts hissed.

The clapping stopped suddenly; as if countless mothers had rushed to their nurseries to see what on earth was happening; but already Tink was saved. First her voice grew strong; then she popped out of bed; then she was flashing through the room more merry and impudent than ever. She never thought of thanking those who believed, but she would have liked to get at the ones who had hissed.

(p. 167)

This is no serious, gentle, conspiratorial voice. Instead a self-conscious tartness acknowledges that not all children will be entertained by this fantasy, and although child and adult readers might react differently to this passage, there is no suggestion of a 'wink'. The narrator exhibits, if momentarily, feelings of dislike towards a narratee he suddenly evisages as threatening. In contrast is the bland sentimentality of a version which removes this astringency and substitutes a comfortable world where disagreement is impossible.

Peter leaped to his feet. It was night, and there were no children anywhere near, but he yelled for all he was worth.

'All of you out there, if you believe in fairies, clap your hands. Clap them hard, and go on clapping. If you don't, Tinker Bell will die.'

There was hardly a moment before, suddenly and miraculously, the silence was broken by a tremendous clapping of hands.

'More,' he cried, delighted.

The clapping grew louder, voices cheered – and Tink's light shone out again. It became very bright, and she popped off the bed with a gay chime of her bells, herself again.

(Graham, 1962, p. 132)

Although in *Peter and Wendy* the personality of Barrie's narrator is consistently forceful and obvious, it is clear that Barrie experienced difficulty in finding a voice and stance when he transformed his story from stage to novel: the mixture of satire and sentimentality in which he cloaked his fantasy caused confusion in his mind about whom he was really writing for. In *Peter and Wendy* his preoccupation with the nature of children, his deepseated resentment at their self-sufficiency, his recognition of their selfishness, their heartlessness, and their ability to wipe out the past and to lose themselves entirely in the activities of the moment, prevented him from addressing the child reader within his book with continuing friendliness and respect. His narratee – child or adult – is always at the mercy of the narrator's dissatisfaction with child nature and his ambivalent feelings about family relationships.

J. M. Barrie's adult novels and plays reveal him as a man who had great difficulty in growing up and putting fantasy behind him; *Peter and Wendy* shows his subconscious resistance to becoming a writer for children. He could not readily submit himself to the child as audience but needed constantly to retain his idea of himself as an adult writing for adults. This adult self-consciousness resulting in the use of a very obvious form of double address as a narrative manner is at the heart of the unsatisfactory nature of *Peter and Wendy*.

Arthur Ransome (1884–1967), on the other hand, and some other writers of the thirties whose best work is still in print and still read, notably John Masefield and Noel Streatfeild, had no such difficulty. Reconciled to, even delighted by, the idea of writing for children, they were comfortable with what they were doing. Yet Ransome paradoxically insisted that he wrote only for himself. Unfortunately, by denying that he wrote for children he gave tacit support to the idea that there is something demeaning in deliberately writing for children, a view that has led to the harmful assertion that there is no real difference between fiction for children and fiction for adults. That his much-quoted statements on the subject are contradicted by his practice has made his influence double-edged: writers adopted his manner of addressing children, while critics insisted that good writers did not write for children.

In 'A Letter to the Editor' written for *The Junior Bookshelf* in 1937, shortly after he had been awarded the Carnegie Medal for *Pigeon Post* (1936), Ransome forthrightly denied that he wrote for children. Quoting Stevenson, 'It's awful fun, boys' stories; you just indulge the pleasure of your heart', he expressed his concurrence. 'You write not *for* children, but for yourself, and if, by good fortune, children enjoy what you enjoy, why then you are a writer of children's books' (p. 4). From this it is clear that Ransome did not object to being a writer of children's books; indeed he went on to say 'Every writer wants to have readers, and than children there are no better readers in the world' (p. 4). Nevertheless, his words are disingenuous, and depend on a special interpretation of what writing 'for children' means. Earlier in the article he had been even more anxious to dissociate himself from 'writing for children'.

> I do not know how to write books for children and have the gravest doubts as to whether anybody should try to do any such thing. To write a book *for* children seems to me a sure way of writing what is called a 'juvenile', a horrid, artificial thing, a patronising thing, a thing that betrays in every line that author and intended victims are millions of miles apart, and that the author is enjoying not the stuff of his book, but a looking-glass picture of himself or

herself 'being so good with children' . . . a most unpleasant spectacle for anyone who happens to look over his shoulder.

(p. 3)

Ransome objected in fact to being in the company of those writers whom he saw as addressing children without true seriousness, of those writers who, to adapt Helen Garner's words, were presenting the little play called 'Writing for Children'.

The reiterated denial that he wrote for children, which is in such strong contrast to the stance which he adopted as narrator in his twelve highly successful children's novels, suggests that he was fearful of the problems created by a double audience and needed to protect his integrity by finding in himself a single audience. Perhaps unconsciously – though it is difficult to believe that he was not aware of what he was doing – he made a distinction between writing *for* children and writing *to* children. He developed a type of narrator – a friendly adult talking seriously and without condescension to children –and a narrative style which overcame most of the problems with which earlier writers had struggled, problems which I shall consider in more detail in later chapters. The style which he developed, a manner of single address, imperceptibly pervaded writing for children from then on. He was not uncomfortable, nor self-conscious, in addressing children, because he so loved what he was doing – that is, recreating his childhood, exercising on paper his practical skills and his knowledge relating to sailing and the outdoor life, and sharing the company of 'a family of imaginary children', with whom he tells us in his autobiography he 'had for some time been growing intimate'. He simply put himself in the place of the children he was writing about and described what they saw and did, felt and thought. He has no viewpoint apart from theirs. Although the voice and knowledge are those of an adult, the narrator is consistently – extraordinarily so – a contemporary of the characters.

They carried their mugs and the kettle and the tin plate piled with thick slabs of brown bread and marmalade to the edge of the cliff. The island lay about a mile away towards the lower, southern end of the lake, its trees reflected in the glassy water. They had been looking at it for ten days, but the telegram had made it much more real than ever it had been before. Looking down from Titty's Peak in the evening of the day on which they had come to the farmhouse where their mother had taken lodgings, they had seen the lake like an inland sea. And on the lake they had seen the island. All four of them had been filled at once with the same idea. It was not just an island. It was *the* island, waiting for them. It was their island. With an island like that within sight, who could be content to live on the mainland and sleep in a bed at night?

(*Swallows and Amazons*, 1930, p. 17)

384

When adults, the children's mother, or the Blacketts' Uncle Jim, enter the story, they are presented as the children see them. We are told only what they do and what they say, not what they feel and think. The voice of the narrator is unobtrusive, undogmatic, uncondescending, but distinctively adult too, in its unwavering intention to make absolutely clear what is described.

> Susan had got the sail ready. On the yard there was a strop (which is really a loop) that hooked on a hook on one side of an iron ring called the traveller, because it moved up and down the mast. The halyard ran from the traveller up to the top of the mast, through a sheave (which is a hole with a little wheel in it), and then down again. John hooked the strop on the traveller and hauled away on the halyard. Up went to the brown sail until the traveller was nearly at the top of the mast. Then John made the halyard fast on the cleats, which were simply pegs, underneath the thwart which served to hold the mast up.
>
> (p. 27)

All readers, young and old, know when reading these words that this passage with its carefully and simply explained detail is addressed to children. The absence of an overt narratee cannot hide the fact. Ransome, whatever he said, was writing both to and for children; he knew it, and took pleasure in it.

> With so many look-out men Captain John might have been content, but just once he looked round for himself and saw the two lights one above the other like the stop called a colon, which I am just going to make here: there, like that.
>
> (p. 130)

Ransome's claim to fame as a children's writer has been that he pioneered a formula for holiday adventure stories which is still not exhausted. But an achievement as important, though less understood and less acknowledged, was his development of a narrative manner, a way of writing *to* children without showing consciousness of the existence of adults who might look over his shoulder, a mode of address which I have called single address, which set the pattern for the next fifty years. Because he was writing about activities he intensely enjoyed, he readily found a voice in which to talk about them. His genuine eagerness to share his knowledge and experience with others, especially with children who had so much to learn, made communication – comparatively – simple. Although he did not invent single address, he helped to extend its range and influence.

Ransome is a straightfoward case of a writer who accepted that he was writing for an audience of children and addressed them accordingly.

He satisfied children. Clearly he satisfied himself. He maintained his integrity. He is a limited writer, however, and appeals, now his innovative force is spent and his middle-class values suspect, only to those adults who lose no status in their own eyes by becoming child narratees. In addressing his stories so directly to children he excluded the possibility of a dual audience. It is not surprising that Humphrey Carpenter, whose *Secret Gardens: A Study of the Golden Age of Children's Literature* reveals an unacknowledged preference for children's classics which have at least in part an adult narratee, should refer to a 'certain plodding predictability' (p. 210) in the work of Ransome and Lofting, both writers who write *to* children.

T. H. White (1906–64) is a writer more to Humphrey Carpenter's taste than Ransome. According to Carpenter and Prichard's *The Oxford Companion to Children's Literature, The Sword in the Stone* (1938) and *Mistress Masham's Repose* (1947; New York, 1946) are 'classic children's novels'. Yet each was selected on publication by the Book of the Month Club, which suggests that initially at least the books were not felt to be for children: adult readers were able comfortably to adopt the implied reader role assigned to them. T. H. White, unlike Ransome, was a writer who genuinely wrote so much 'for himself' that he was unable to define clearly, either in his own mind or in his practice, the audience he was writing for. In a letter to his friend L. J. Potts at the beginning of 1938 he commented on the nature of *The Sword in the Stone.*

> It is not a satire. Indeed, I am afraid it is rather warm-hearted – mainly about birds and beasts. It seems impossible to determine whether it is for grown-ups or children. It is more or less a kind of wish-fulfilment of the things I should like to have happened to me when I was a boy.
>
> (Quoted in Warner, 1967, p. 98)

An examination today of its narrative stance still does not reveal whether it was addressed to children or adults. Certainly the narrator's satirical eye is directed toward the adult characters, and the jokes tend to be for the initiated.

> Sir Ector said, 'Had a good quest today?'
> Sir Grummore said, 'Oh, not so bad. Rattlin' good day, in fact. Found a chap called Sir Bruce Saunce Pité choppin' off a maiden's head in Weedon Bushes, ran him to Mixbury Plantation in the Bicester, where he doubled back, and lost him in Wicken Wood. Must have been a good twenty-five miles as he ran.'
> 'A straight-necked 'un,' said Sir Ector.
>
> (p. 8)

On the other hand, the child, the Wart, soon appears as the main character, it is to him that things happen, and most of the story is seen through his eyes. The narration is in language tempered to the child presence, even if, for adults, much of the humour comes from the contrast between the language usually used in the retelling of the Arthurian story, and that used by the Wart and his narrator. He certainly did not patronise children; but many of his jokes are jokes primarily because his young protagonists and his young readers will not understand them.

His technique in *Mistress Masham's Repose* is, if anything, more extravagant, more crammed with learning and humour way above children's heads than was the case in *The Sword in the Stone*. White was aware that his book might be spoilt for children because of arcane language and of jokes put there at the child's expense. After reading the manuscript, David Garnett rebuked him for using words and jokes 'which the child does not understand & which it rightly feels are in bad taste as you would not put them in if you were telling the child the story' (White, 1968, p. 193). Although White made some attempt to eradicate this element of wildness and extravagance he did not have the energy or the patience to reconstruct his story with due regard for child readers. *Mistress Masham's Repose* does however demonstrate what a brilliant 'dual' novel White might have achieved if he had been able to maintain the kind of narrative stance which in fact he exhibits only spasmodically, a stance in which the narrator addresses child and adult narratees genuinely in the same voice. There are many short passages in the novel in which this is achieved. In the following extract Maria has just picked up the walnut shell in which is encradled the Lilliput baby.

> Now in spite of the homicides or other torts which she might have committed as a pirate, who was partial to the Plank, Maria was not the kind of person who bore malice for injuries, and she was certainly not the kind of kidnapper who habitually stole babies from their heartbroken mothers, for the mere cynical pleasure of hearing them scream. She guessed immediately that this was the mother of the baby, and, instead of feeling angry about the harpoon, she began to feel guilty about the baby. She began to have an awful suspicion that she would have to give it back.
>
> Yet the temptation to keep it was severe. She would never drop on another find like this, she knew, not if she lived to be a thousand.
>
> Think to yourself, truly, whether you would have returned a live one-inch baby to its relatives, if caught fairly in the open field?
>
> (p. 18)

The 'you' addressed here is both child and adult. To a child the question is a serious one, an invitation to stand in Maria's shoes and become a part of the fantasy world, sharing Maria's dilemma. To an adult the question is an ironical acknowledgement of the complexity of motives that prompt human action. It is not surprising that many adults have read the book without suspecting that it was intended for children. Yet White initially aimed at a child audience; and knew that he had chanced on a brilliant subject.

> It has taken me getting on for forty years to realise that I can never be a Shakespeare. I must try, at best, to be a Lewis Carrol [*sic*] i.e. I must be content to write for children. I have therefore begun, and written 40,000 words of a book for Amaryllis Virginia.
>
> (1968, p. 140)

His attitude, however, was always ambivalent. His comment on Arthur Ransome whose *The Picts and the Martyrs* he bought 'to see what I ought to write like' shows that in spite of his desire to emulate Carroll, his first interest was not to write for children, though on occasion he does so brilliantly. Of Ransome he said, 'He does not write with one eye on the grown-up, as I do' (1968, p. 174). White wrote in fact with rather more than one eye on the grown-up. An examination of his work to provide an answer to the question 'Is it for children?' must produce the response 'Sometimes'. Yet few writers have shown so convincingly that writing simultaneously for children and adults is possible. Genuine dual address of this kind is, however, very rare.

I have suggested that there are three distinct ways in which writers known as writers for children address children in their stories. First, they may write as Ransome does for a single audience, using single address; their narrators will address child narratees, overt or covert, straightforwardly, showing no consciousness that adults too might read the work. Concern for children's interests dominates their stories. Secondly, they may write for a double audience, using double address, as Barrie does; their narrators will address child narratees overtly and self-consciously, and will also address adults, either overtly, as the implied author's attention shifts away from the implied child reader to a different older audience, or covertly, as the narrator deliberately exploits the ignorance of the implied child reader and attempts to entertain an implied adult reader by making jokes which are funny primarily because children will not understand them. Barrie uses both these forms of double address. Thirdly, they may write for a dual audience, using dual address, as White has shown is possible, although he more often uses double address. More usually, however, writers who command a dual audience do so because of the nature and the strength of their performance. Their narrators address child narratees, usually covertly, but often openly as White does, either using the same 'tone of seriousness' which would be used to address adult narratees, or confidentially sharing the story in a way that allows adult narrator and child narratee a conjunction of interests. Concern for something other than purely children's interests dominates their stories: pride in the artist's craft, perhaps, or commitment to an idea; in the case of the greatest of all writers for children, the Charles Dodgson of the *Alice* books, a delight in language and logical problems.

Although double address, in both its forms, flourished as a mode in the nineteenth century and persisted into the twentieth century in the work of writers like C. S. Lewis, it is rare today. Single address is a phenomenon of the twentieth century, and is the result of a change in the attitudes of adults writing for children which took place about the turn of the century. Dual address, which might be found at any time, is rare and difficult, pre-supposing as it does that a child narratee is addressed and an adult reader simultaneously satisfied. Works which draw a dual audience in spite of being addressed to children, however, are not so rare. But the fact that some writers have been able to address children directly and yet at the same time command an adult readership by putting the adult reader comfortably in the position either of observer-listener or of teller-surrogate, has helped to obscure the fact that writers who address children and leave adult readers no other role than child-addressee may also be both fine writers, and writers who serve children's needs.

Primary sources

Barrie, J. M., *Peter and Wendy* (1911; London: Hodder, 1913).
Ransome, Arthur, *Swallows and Amazons* (1930; London: Cape, 1964).
White, T. H., *The Sword in the Stone* (1938; London: Collins, 1968).

Secondary sources

Carpenter, Humphrey, and Mari Prichard (eds), *The Oxford Companion to Children's Literature* (Oxford: Oxford University Press, 1984).
Carpenter, Humphrey, *Secret Gardens: A Study of the Golden Age of Children's Literature* (Boston: Houghton, 1985).
Egan, Michael, 'The Neverland of Id: Barrie, Peter Pan and Freud', *Children's Literature*, 10 (1982): 37–55.
Ransome, Arthur, 'A Letter to the Editor', *The Junior Bookshelf*, 1(4) (1937): 3–5.
Roscoe, William Caldwell, 'Fictions for Children', in Lance Salway (ed.), *A Peculiar Gift: Nineteenth-Century Writings on Books for Children* (Harmondsworth: Kestrel, 1976), pp. 23–45.
Warner, Sylvia Townsend, *T. H. White* (London: Cape, 1967).
White, T. H., *The White–Garnett Letters*, ed. David Garnett (New York: Viking, 1968).

25

NECESSARY MISREADINGS

Directions in narrative theory for children's literature

Peter Hunt

Source: *Studies in the Literary Imagination* 18(2) (1985): 107–121.

"I would also maintain that traditional categories like 'plot', 'character', [and] 'theme' are often less than useful in discussing the literary experience of young children: the categories that matter, as far as I can discern, are 'chunks' like 'two opposed characters dialoguing' or 'protagonist-acting' . . . And finally, 'text-as-mediated' is the crucial variable more often than 'text' in itself."—Hugh and Maureen Crago

"In assessing their value [the *Alice* books], there are two questions one can ask: first, what insight do they provide as to how the world appears to a child?; and, second, to what extent is the world really like that?"—W. H. Auden[1]

I

Narrative theory cannot escape the problem of audience. Perception/reception controls what the text is seen to be, and, consequently, how it is described. As Rimmon-Kenan puts it, "the reader . . . is both an image of a certain competence brought to the text and a structuring of such a competence within the text."[2] Most narrative theory automatically assumes peer-reader discriminations—"literary competence"—and perceptive skills that are nuclear rather than linear, synchronic rather than diachronic.

If we take narrative theory to be primarily concerned with higher level units than stylistics (which considers grammar, lexis, phonology, etc.), then we are immediately confronted with problems of validating any analysis: "an individual's perceptions and judgements are a function of the assumptions shared by the groups he belongs to."[3] We are not dealing with that

390

which "can be described and referred to as unarguably given" by the texts.[4] Robert Protherough, following D. W. Harding, has suggested a progression from "matters of fact which are demonstrable from the text," through "clear implications", "manifest literary effects", "shared associations", "significance based on a particular stance", to "private associations" in our reading of texts. Only the first of these categories is really "unarguable".[5]

In discussing narrative units, structure, character, background, and so on, narrative theory deals with distinctions generated by the analytic methods used (rather than residing in the texts), and by the ideology of the discriminators. Normally, within peer-group "interpretive communities" this does not matter; but with children's books we can make no simple assumptions about text or audience. Unlike any other type of writing, we cannot "locate actual readers by looking at writings about literature that have been published and are thus available to us."[6] Just as there has been an inevitable move towards feminist poetics and black poetics[7] so we need to reconsider our adult analytic strategies with regard to a poetics of children's literature. There is, as Stanley Fish points out, "always a formal pattern, but it is not always the same one."[8] Our perceptions of narrative patterns are based on an appeal to a common culture, and the culture of the primary readers of children's literature is not necessarily common with ours; it may be in opposition to it, or a sub-culture of it, or in a power relationship with it.[9] In any case, we have to be aware that "ordinary" theory, methods, and terminology may not be relevant. The anthropologist and linguist Shirley Brice Heath has pointed out, for example, that in the two different US cultures that she studied, "they structure their stories differently; they hold different scales of features on which stories are recognized as *stories* and judged as good or bad."[10]

I would suggest that the critic of children's literature has only two choices. The first is to read the texts as if they were decontextualised (ignoring intended or implied or actual readers) and to apply whatever ready-made narrative theory seems appropriate. The second is to acknowledge that the very category of "children's literature" implies a set of texts distinguished not by textual characteristics[11] but rather by the interactive construct to which they contribute by virtue of a distinctive relationship with their audience, and the distinctive nature of that audience. If we do this, we must then ask: can we adopt our current methodology, or do we need a new one?

Jonathan Culler has also made this point:

> Once we see as our task the analysing of literary competence as manifested in the interpretive strategies of readers, then the activities of readers . . . present us with a host of facts to explain. . . . It is . . . this notion of what readers can and will do, that enables an author to write, for to intend meanings is to assume a system of conventions and to create signs within the perspective of that system.[12]

Reader affects text affects analysis. As Suleiman notes (with reference to Jauss), "we must take into account *different* horizons of expectation coexisting among different publics in any one society."[13]

This paper explores the implications of this position. I suggest that "conventional" narrative theory must recognise that its analyses of children's literature can also be more than usually provisional. In terms of the child culture (that is, not merely child competence) encountering texts, we may have to accept counter-readings or "misreadings" in terms of narrative analysis, as an inevitable part of the complex process of reading the children's book.[14]

To examine whether this is so, I would like to apply "conventional" narrative analysis (using "narrative units") to a classic novel, *The Wind in the Willows*, and then to examine this and other texts in terms of "narrative shape"—a method which, because it has links with developmental psychology, may be more appropriate, revealing, and valid.

II

If there is a "cultural dislocation" between the child's reading of a text, and the adult's, what does it consist of, and how does this affect narrative and narrative theory?

Experience (or "creation") of text is the convergence (or clash) of two code-sets; those of "life" (knowledge of the world/probability/causality, etc), and of "text" (knowledge of conventions, generic expectations, intertextual reference, etc). Both are important for narrative theory, and for the production of texts for children, but here I will be primarily concerned with "text"-codes. The implied audience for "children's literature" is a *developing* one: integrating the codes of text and of genre will be an important part of the reading process, while, diachronically, a developing reader may change more radically between re-readings than a "skilled" or "mature" reader. "Customary" reading allows us, on our first reading, to "reach a preliminary hypothesis about genre, bear it in mind as we glance back over earlier passages, and reread the whole work in the light of our assumptions about its literary form."[15] But we have to have knowledge of the divisions and discriminations implicit in genre in order to form hypotheses or make assumptions. Margaret Meek has written that "successful early readers discover that a story happens like play. They . . . feel quite safe . . . because they know that a story is a game with rules,"[16]—yet, as E. D. Hirsch notes, "a genre is less like a game than like a code of social behavior."[17]

Hence the developing encounter with text entails reacting against, as well as conforming to, and manipulating, narrative conventions. To the developing reader, the ritualised forms of text may seem alien because they do not have any referential "truth"; even the simplest structure of "beginning-middle-end" is patently artificial. (Some sub-cultures, of course, never appreciate the validity of story. As the mystically-inclined Buddy remarks in Salinger's "Seymour: an Introduction": "Whatever became of that stalwart bore Fortinbras? Who eventually fixed *his* wagon?"[18]) Perceptions of how texts are "ordered" (clozure, open endings, etc) appeal to concepts of psychological satisfaction which, as Piaget and many others have pointed out, are neither universal nor static.[19] Readers may select completely different conceptual sets from the same text (despite—or perhaps because of—authors' attempts to tailor texts to specific audiences).

It is possible to argue that children belong (however briefly) to a primary oral culture, although one that is in close contact with a written culture. Walter Ong notes in his *Orality and Literacy*:

> Little has thus far been done, however, to understand reader response in terms of what is now know of the evolution of noetic processes from primary orality through residual orality to high literacy. Readers whose norms and expectations for formal discourse are governed by a residually oral mindset relate to a text quite different[ly] from readers whose sense of style is radically textual. . . . Even today . . . readers in certain subcultures [of high-literacy cultures] are still operating in a basically oral framework, performance oriented rather than information oriented.[20]

Ong points out that the literate necessarily have difficulty in conceiving of an oral universe. The written word is not simply a transcription of the spoken word: contained in the transition between the two is the paradox that orality unites people in finite, interactive groups (especially where narrative is concerned), whereas reading/writing is a solitary activity which gives access to a much wider, if absent, group. It is in this transition that the dislocation of children's literature occurs.

The oral mindset has a "spectacular" influence on narrative and plot "which in an oral culture is not quite what we take plot typically to be."[21] It is not simply that formulae are used because they are essential for the preservation of thought in the oral culture (and, of course, for the development of learning and understanding for the child), or that "heavy" characters are mnemonic and aid noetic economy.[22] Rather, "you do not find climactic linear plots in people's lives [except by] ruthless elimination of all but a few . . . incidents."[23] In "performed" narratives, the use of "strings" rather than patterned groups, disregard for temporal sequence, apparently random analepsis and prolepsis,[24] limited cataphoric reference, the opening *in media res*, and so on, are not simply devices to aid memory: they are not "proto-written" strategies.[25] Rather, they relate to a distinctive world view. It is interesting that the one example of narrative that Suzanne Romaine gives in her recent study, *The Language of Children and Adolescents* is discontinuous. "There may be," she concludes, "crucial differences between adults and children . . . in the social significance of performed narratives. . . . [T]he notion of complexity as far as narrative structure is concerned must take into account both linguistic and social factors."[26]

If we place these characteristics of performed narrative beside the child's natural tendency towards performance, "easy access to metaphor", and an ability to handle complex narrative acts, described by Gardner[27] it is clear that we are not dealing with *lesser* ability, but with a different kind of ability: one that seems likely to view narrative (and consequently perceive its structures) in a way not accounted for in conventional theory. Further, the text may actually seem to symbolise an alien culture, and as such may be perceived perversely or subversively. In turn, because the reader is assumed not to have code-skills equivalent to those of the writer, texts intended for children tend to be "overcoded", either by unusually strong narrational control, or by frequent summary.[28] The paradox is that such modifications are beside the point, and merely re-inforce the illusion that the structures of children's literature are easily accessible.

III

To clarify the possible range of alternative readings, or "misreadings", and to demonstrate what modifications to conventional theory might be appropriate, let us take an example from a "classic", Kenneth Grahame's *The Wind in the Willows*. Although originating in oral stories for Grahame's son[29] the book has few oral mannerisms surviving in the text, and its secure status tends to be challenged only in terms of large narrative elements such as its divided structure, "adult" characterisations, and its social and sexual implications.

To perceive and codify such elements—indeed, to perceive narrative at all, we have to discriminate discrete *events* which make up the text, and theory has spent much time in considering how these might be distinguished.[30] Such elements (or narrative units, or "plotemes") can be seen, in Culler's words, as

> culturally marked significant actions. . . . What the reader is look-
> ing for in a plot is a passage from one state to another—a passage
> to which he can assign thematic value. . . . The analyst's task is not
> simply to develop a metalanguage for the description of plots, but
> to bring to the surface and make explicit the metalanguage within
> the reader himself.[31]

The problem is, of course, *whose* culture?—and will the metalanguages be mutually comprehensible?

Consider the opening of Chapter 12, "The Return of Ulysses", in terms of how its "events" or narrative units might be described.

When it began to grow dark, the Rat, with an air of excitement and mystery, summoned them back into the parlour, stood each of them up alongside of his little heap, and proceeded to dress them up for the coming expedition. He was very earnest and thoroughgoing about it, and the affair took quite a long time. First, there was a belt to go round each animal, and then a sword to be stuck into each belt, and then a cutlass on the other side to balance it. Then a pair of pistols, a policeman's truncheon, several sets of handcuffs, some bandages and sticking-plaster, and a flask and a sandwich-case. The Badger laughed good-humouredly and said, "All right, Ratty! It amuses you and it doesn't hurt me. I'm going to do all I've got to do with this here stick." But the Rat only said, "*Please*, Badger! You know I shouldn't like you to blame me afterwards and say I had forgotten *anything*!"

When all was quite ready, the Badger took a dark lantern in one paw, grasped his great stick with the other, and said, "Now then, follow me! Mole first, 'cos I'm very pleased with him; Rat next; Toad last. And look here, Toady! Don't you chatter so much as usual, or you'll be sent back, as sure as fate!"

The Toad was so anxious not to be left out that he took up the inferior position assigned to him without a murmur, and the animals set off. The Badger led them along by the river for a little way, and then suddenly swung himself over the edge into a hole in the river bank, a little above the water. The Mole and the Rat followed silently, swinging themselves successfully into the hole as they had seen the Badger do; but when it came to Toad's turn, of course he managed to slip and fall into the water with a loud splash and a squeal of alarm. He was hauled out by his friends, rubbed down and wrung out hastily, comforted, and set on his legs; but the Badger was seriously angry, and told him that the very next time he made a fool of himself he would most certainly be left behind.

So at last they were in the secret passage, and the cutting-out expedition had really begun![32]

The simplest view is that units are marked grammatically: "When it began to grow dark . . .", "When all was quite ready . . .", ". . . when it came to Toad's turn . . .", or indicated by summary: "Rat . . . proceeded to dress them up . . .", ". . . the animals set off . . .", "So at last they were in the secret passage. . . ." But as Michael Stubbs has demonstrated in his "Stir until the plot thickens", paraphrase (which is evidence of the mode of comprehension, as well as of comprehension itself) is essentially a matter of semantic concepts.[33] It is not simply a question of grammar, and although grammar may indicate authorial judgements, what is perceived as significant could be categorised in various other ways.

For example, units could be discriminated by scenes (in Rat's parlour/on the river bank (and the tunnel entrance)/in the tunnel); by actions (dressing up/walking/swinging/Toad falling/drying/talking); or by the successive focii on characters (Rat/all characters/Badger/Toad/Badger/Mole and Rat/Toad/ all characters/Badger). At one extreme there might be a close paraphrase (summoning/dressing/Badger-Rat conversation, etc ...); at the other, the whole extract might be seen as a macro-unit of the complete novel ("The cutting-out expedition began.") In terms of narrative facilitation we might classify the elements as preparation/advance of action/delay/sum-mary; thematically, they might be, aggression/assertion/travel/success/failure/ re-unification; in terms of character, they might be, successively, Rat's reliability/Badger's bluffness/Mole's quiet efficiency/Toad's incompetence.

Any of these, and many others, are possible descriptions; but, I would argue, not all are equally *likely*. If this section of the text is taken as (or presented as) part of an unreflective "action" plot, then the broadest divisions, centering upon nodes of particularly "striking" action might be made. Thus Toad's slip might be seen as the central significant event because (a) it is the most violent action, (b) it re-inforces an apparently dominant character, (c) it fulfils a prediction about Toad's character, and (d) it is deviant—and thus threatening—in the story context. As we shall see, psychological evidence suggests that this may be an appropriate form of narrative unit; certainly it should not be assumed that the child's reading will be, *ipso facto*, the crudest. If *The Wind in the Willows* is read as a series of moves to and from the security of home, then the shape and nature of the units would shift. Equally, the stratification of relationships might be important, however the characters are seen (for example, Badger as father figure, Rat, brother figure, Toad, child as rebel, Mole, child as con-formist); in that case the organisational nodes might be as small as segments of speech acts.

If narrative theory is to concern itself with matters of discrimination, or to subscribe to the basic concepts of histoire-récit-narration or Culler's "autonomous level of plot structure", we must be aware of the multiple ways of describing the story's realisation: not merely the level of abstraction, but the type of abstraction involved.[34] To do this may mean escaping from the systems which are adult readings of children's behaviour, and which speak so confidently of "appropriate" story shapes.[35]

IV

The Wind in the Willows has been seen by many critics to be divided, if not fractured, between action, and reflection; between Toad's adolescent (or manic, or socially irresponsible) adventures, and the more lyrical and static experiences of "Dulce Domum", "The Piper at the Gates of Dawn", and "Wayfarers All". (The division has, perhaps, been confirmed by A. A. Milne's skillful stage adaptation, which brings Toad to the centre, and which virtually eliminates Grahame's *fin-de-siècle* mysticism on the grounds that it is untheatrical).[36]

Certainly, the "reflective" chapters can be read as having considerable structural similarity; few characters, few scenes, few "incidents" (although the last is, of course, more arguable), and firm "clozures"—they all end in sleep or stasis. These chapters punctuate the much more varied and densely packed chapters devoted to Toad's adventures ("Mr Toad", "Toad's Adventures", and "The Further Adventures of Toad") not at points of clozure, but at nadirs—Toad in the dungeon; Toad lost and asleep in a hollow tree. Such a reading seems to support the view that two distinct audiences are specified by the book.[37]

However, the remaining chapters that feature Toad, "The Open Road", and the two final chapters, "'Like Summer Tempests Came His Tears'" and "The Return of Ulysses" are hybrids: they have few scenes, but many "incidents", and such unity as there is, is provided by the characters of Mole and Rat. Toad is, after all, only at first an incidental character, seen through the eyes of Mole; in the first chapter he appears only in passing, and by the end of the book Mole has a central role, and Badger has the last word.

In a sense, then, at least part of the book may be seen as Mole's *bildungsroman*, as he moves from his suburban villa to acceptance as a hardened campaigner: it is a multiple development from outsider to insider, of child to adult, of lower class to middle class. (Badger, clearly of the old squirearchy, is drawn to Mole, as is the way of English society, by their mutual work-ethic). These potent elements, which form a very fluid book-wide series of interrelationships, are crystallised in the inversions of Chapter 5 ("Dulce Domum") when Rat is benevolently in control of Mole, and Chapter 9 ("Wayfarers All") when Mole takes charge of Rat; of Chapter 2 ("The Open Road") in which Toad dominates Mole, and Chapter 12 ("The Return of Ulysses") when Mole quietly patronises Toad.

Structurally or operatively, then, the first five chapters of *The Wind in the Willows* might be read as a unit, pivoting, classically, at Mole's lonely nadir in The Wild Wood in the middle of chapter 3, and beginning and ending at Mole's home. Mole has, of course, grown, but home remains for him a reference point. Indeed, his final speculations in "Dulce Domum" could almost be taken from a textbook on the psychology of children's literature:

> ... the upper world was all too strong, it called to him still, even down there, and he knew he must return to the larger stage. But it was good to think he had this to come back to, this place which was all his own, these things which were so glad to see him again, and which could always be counted upon for the same simple welcome."[38]

If there are two texts in *The Wind in the Willows*, then they are sequential, rather than interleaved: Mole's serious story once resolved, we can move on to Toad's more farcical one.

In appealing to psychological patterns for validation of significance, we might note the progression in Mole's story from chapters which have a strong, secure ending (1, Mole in bed at Rat's house; 2, Mole among the society on the river bank) to those which are less resolved: in chapter 3, although they reach safety at Badger's house, Mole and Rat are still away from home, while in chapter 4, Mole is on his way home from the Wild Wood: "As he hurried along, eagerly anticipating the moment when he would be at home again. . . ."[39] These endings may symbolise Mole's growing maturity; the circles, within the larger circle of the five-chapter unit, do not need to be completed.

The assumption that circularity is an appropriate narrative pattern, for a given audience, and that texts can usefully be described in these terms suggests that a book like *The Wind in the Willows*, for all that it apparently requires a skilled readership, might appeal and satisfy in ways not necessarily accounted for in conventional readings.

The obvious difficulty is that I have based all these descriptions on my own "adult" perception of story-grammar, assuming that an "event" (for example, Mole and Rat go to Mole End) is an unarguable fact, with boundaries that can be more or less agreed—something that the text gives *us*, and therefore a unit that can be conjectured about. If we have any respect for the language system, it might be said, how can we escape this solipsism? Perhaps we could usefully consider associative semantic fields as the cohesive feature in children's literature, each field activated or given direction by significant single stimuli (in Applebee's terms, a form of primitive narrative). For, as the Cragos noted, the concept of narration itself may be formed and motivated by the intensity, vividness, and relevance of the text.[40]

V

The ideal proving ground for these ideas is the one area of children's literature which has developed away from the "classic realist" text towards the genuinely discontinuous and interactive.[41] This is the picture book—that is, a text in which verbal and visual components both carry the narrative rather than merely illustrating or clarifying each other. Far from being merely the province of the beginner reader, it has become so complex as really to require a new metalanguage to describe it.[42] Despite the problem of visual conventions, the encounter with the picture book seems to be akin, for the child, to an oral encounter, and the combined text is likely to be read far more fluidly and flexibly than the purely verbal text. And so, as satisfying and seductive as the perception of circularity may be (the "need" for it has become a commonplace of psychologically-oriented criticism of children's literature), the picture book may undermine its validity.

Take, for example, the notorious case of David McKee's *Not Now, Bernard*.[43] One paraphrase of this apparently innocuous text might be: Bernard, a small boy, tries to tell his parents that there is a monster in the garden; he is ignored, and duly eaten ("every bit") by the monster in the garden. The monster takes over Bernard's place in the household, eats Bernard's supper, and is sent to bed ("'But I'm a monster,' said the Monster"). The bedroom light is switched off—and the book ends. One set of readers may see this as a variation on the classic *The Shrinking of Treehorn*[44] —superior child versus insensitive adults; another may see it as a simple equation from an adult point of view—Bernard = Monster. I have heard it said that some children are worried about the lack of resolution (although not about Bernard being eaten), but it seems to me equally likely that the segments which are really important could be visual elements which extend between successive "openings" (or "spreads") of the physical text. These may well provide "units" quite at odds with grammatically or "significantly" marked units. Indeed, my paraphrase of the text (which only communicates with you, my reader, because, as Stanley Fish has it, "a way of thinking, a form of life, shares us"[45]) is almost certainly, for the primary audience, a "misreading", making the "wrong" units, and tracing less than central significances.

Another classic, Russell Hoban and Quentin Blake's *How Tom Beat Captain Najork and his Hired Sportsmen*,[46] may seem to appeal simply because of Tom's triumph over his iron-hatted Aunt Fidget Wonkham-Strong and the fairly fearsome Captain Najork. Yet the shape of the narrative reinforces this triumph from a different perspective. Instead of resolving the plot within the context of home, Tom escapes:

> Tom took his boat and pedalled to the next town down the river. There he advertised in the newspaper for a new aunt. When he found one that he liked, he told her, "No greasy bloaters, no mutton and no cabbage-and-potato sog. . . . Those are my conditions."
>
> The new aunt's name was Bundlejoy Cosysweet. She had a floppy hat with flowers on it. She had long, long hair.
>
> "That sounds fine to me," she said. "We'll have a go."

The contrast in aunts, and Hoban's neat parallels (the flowers drooped where Aunt Fidget walked) and Tom's complete triumph implies an ending—but there is a coda. On the last page, we look back at the happily married Aunt and Captain, and the unfortunate hired sportsmen (who have taken over Tom's tasks). Tom has not simply escaped, he has, in a sense, left the central scene, left the book. And the triumph is as much a visual one: throughout, the pictures stress the innate superiority of the child's world, and, importantly, they circumvent the adult, literate mechanism, the verbal text.

This covert anarchy can be followed most rewardingly through the work of John Burningham. In his *Come Away From The Water, Shirley*[47] the adult-oriented and the child-oriented versions of the same time-span are presented on facing pages. On the left-hand pages, in muted colours, Shirley's parents settle in their chairs on the beach, and conduct a one-sided conversation (full of adult evasions and peremptory commands) with Shirley, who remains offstage. Although there is considerable fragmentation of the "conversation", there is no discontinuity in the time-sequence. Shirley's adventures, with pirates and buried treasure, wordless and (literally) highly coloured, take place on the facing pages. The point may be obvious, but the contrast of codes is interesting. The "adult" pages rely for their comprehensibility on reference to extra-textual experience, whereas Shirley's (imagined?) adventures are based on inter-textual reference (the reverse, of course, of what might normally be expected). This structure, of parallel "focussed chains"[48] reflects the performative patterns of the counter-culture of childhood and perhaps allows some interchange between child and adult culture.

Burningham moves closer (in structural terms) towards a true "children's book" in *Granpa* (1984).[49] The broad pattern of this book is of a full-colour picture on the right of each opening, usually featuring various encounters between a small girl and what we may assume to be her grandfather (no particular sequence is suggested). On each facing page are fragments of dialogue, and below these, in sepia, outline drawings which variously decorate or elaborate or comment upon the pictures opposite, by showing details, or flashbacks, or fantasies. Thus the first opening has the dialogue:

"There would not be room for all the little seeds to grow." "*Do worms go to heaven?*"

facing a picture of girl and Granpa in a greenhouse. The sketch adds details of the greenhouse. The third opening shows Granpa nursing a female doll, and a teddy bear; facing is the line "'I didn't know Teddy was another little girl'" above a sketch of a female teddy bear making up in a mirror. Another has Granpa skipping (rope); "'*Were you once a baby as well, Granpa?*'" inquires the girl, and the sketch gives us a box of old sports equipment. Even the ending is ambiguous and unpredictable. In successive openings, girl and Granpa walk in the snow; Granpa is unwell ("'Granpa can't come out to play today'"); they watch TV together ("'*Tomorrow shall we go to Africa, and you can be Captain?*'"); and, penultimately, the girl sits looking at Granpa's empty chair. The final page, in very bold colours, shows a little girl pushing a baby energetically in a very old-fashioned pram. Does life go on? Or is this Granpa's childhood?

This fragmentation, the possibility of reading in several different planes, with, if anything, under-coding of conventional elements (like dialogue), may seem to be over-sophisticated for its audience. But I would argue that its very complexity, together with the relinquishing of any authorial control in the verbal text, makes *Granpa* closer to the comprehension patterns of an orally based reader than the vast majority of texts that purpose to be "for children". As such, it contains a serious challenge for critics.

VI

The adult critic tends to seek firm connections between elements, to build coherent wholes from what must be (most obviously in the picture book) a repetitive and continually variable experience. Not only do we not read sequentially, but our concept of text is perpetually being revised. Similarly, the adaptations made by adult authors for children (producing books that are shorter, more schematic, less philosophical, with fewer sub-plots, and so on, than their adult equivalents)[50] are far too simplistic.

It is clear, then, that our description of children's literature texts above stylistic levels needs to be re-thought. We cannot make assumptions about textual relationships, even where they are grammatically marked (as even grammatical analyses are not absolute: distinctions depend on the distinguishing system). Thus the concept of "misreadings" is variable, and must be rooted in theory, even though it may be demonstrated pragmatically, for the "authority of the interpretive community" is, in this case (and perhaps all cases), extremely local and impossible to measure.[51] To some degree, lateral thinking is essential to our task.

If this paper has seemed needlessly evangelical, it is because, as Helen Huus puts it, there are four stages necessary to the development of any new discipline: "the creation of a unique body of knowledge ... the establishment of standards ... recognition by peers ... and acceptance by the academic world."[52] One has to doubt whether any of these can be achieved for children's literature until the distinctiveness of the critical act is recognized. Some critics have noted differences, but do not follow them through. For example, Purves and Monson observe that the child's perspective on the world is one "that differs from others but which is highly valid in its own right", and at the same time maintain that "children's literature ... is ... a meaningful art form differing very little from other art forms", without apparently finding any incongruity in the two statements.[53] Likewise, to say with Margaret Meek, that children's writers "keep pace" with the growing reader, linking "his growing understanding of the succession of events, of duration and simultanaety, with the presentation of time ..."[54] is both to take an over-generous view of writers, and to avoid the underlying problem of the socialisation inherent in most writing for children. What writing for children *is*, is taken to be what it *must be*.

Of all texts, children's literature is the most "self-deconstructing", because its adult structures and assumptions declare themselves as part of the purposed education of their audience into adult (that is, *text*) ways of thinking (quite apart from any overt or covert "didactic" intent). Consequently it seems inevitable that it will be read in ways which, if not actually inaccessible to us, require a good deal of thought to discern.

Auden's epigraph to this paper may fail to take into account the fact that Carroll was not a child—but the remark is still salutary. We need, in children's book narrative theory to be aware that we are dealing with legitimate "misreadings", and that therefore we must cultivate a double viewpoint, and learn to look for fluid meanings rather than fixed relationships.

Notes

1 Hugh and Maureen Crago, "The Roots of Response". Paper delivered at the session on Literary Experience in Early Childhood, MLA, Washington, December 1984. p. 10; W. H. Auden, "Today's 'Wonder-World' Needs Alice", *Aspects of Alice*, ed. Robert Philips (Harmondsworth: Penguin, 1974), p. 37.

2 Shlomith Rimmon-Kenan, *Narrative Fiction: contemporary poetics* (London: Methuen, 1983), p. 118.

3 Jane P. Tompkins, "An Introduction to Reader Response Criticism", *Reader Response Criticism: from formalism to post-structuralism*, ed. Jane P. Tompkins (Baltimore: The Johns Hopkins University Press, 1980), p. xxi.

4 Winfred Nowottny, *The Language Poets Use* (London: The Athlone Press, 1965), p. 1.

5 Robert Protherough, *Developing Response to Fiction* (Milton Keynes: Open University Press, 1983), p. 30.

6 A. B. England, "The Perils of Discontinuous Form", *Studies in the Literary Imagination* 17:1 (1984), 3. The difficulty is that children can only rarely usefully articulate their reactions, and, as most empirical researchers have found, children tend to mediate their ideas to suit the researcher.

7 See, for example, Wendy Mulford, "Socialist-feminist criticism: a case study, woman's suffrage and literature", *Re-Reading English*, ed. Peter Widdowson (London Methuen, 1982), pp. 180–181.

8 Stanley Fish, *Is There A Text In This Class? The Authority of Interpretive Communities* (Cambridge: Harvard Univ. Press, 1980), p. 267.

9 See Peter Hunt, "Childist Criticism: the sub-culture of the child, the book, and the critic", *Signal*, 43 (1984), 45–59; Jacqueline Rose, *The Case of Peter Pan, or, the impossibility of children's fiction* (London: The Macmillan Press, 1984), pp. 1–11.

10 Shirley Brice Heath, *Ways with Words: language, life, and work in communities and classrooms* (Cambridge: Cambridge University Press, 1983), p. 184.

11 Compare Myles McDowell, "Fiction for Children and Adults: some essential differences," *Writers, Critics, and Children*, ed. Geoff Fox *et al.* (New York: Agathon Press, 1976), pp. 141–142; Dennis Butts, *Good Writers for Young Readers* (St. Albans: Hart-Davis Educational, 1977), p. 10.

12 Jonathan Culler, "Prologomena to a theory of reading" *The Reader in The Text*, ed. Susan R. Suleiman and Inge Crosman (Princeton: Princeton Univ. Press, 1980), p. 50.

402

13 Susan R. Suleiman, "Introduction: Varieties of Audience-Oriented Criticism", *The Reader in the Text*, p. 37.

14 Peter Hunt, "Questions of Method and Methods of Questioning: childist criticism in action" *Signal*, 45 (1984), 185–7.

15 Heather Dubrow, *Genre* (London: Methuen, 1982), p. 107.

16 Margaret Meek, *Learning to Read* (London: The Bodley Head, 1982), p. 37.

17 E. D. Hirsch, *Validity in Interpretation* (New Haven: Yale Univ. Press, 1967), p. 93.

18 J. D. Salinger, "Seymour, an Introduction" *Raise High the Roofbeam, Carpenters and Seymour: an Introduction* (Harmondsworth: Penguin, 1964), p. 156.

19 See, for example, Nicholas Tucker, *The Child and the Book* (Cambridge: Cambridge University Press, 1981).

20 Walter Ong, *Orality and Literacy* (London: Methuen, 1982), p. 171.

21 *Orality and Literacy*, p. 142; compare W. Labov, *Language in the Inner City* (Philadelphia: University of Pennsylvania Press, 1974), p. 363; A. K. Pugh, "Construction and reconstruction of text" *The Reader And The Text*, ed. L. John Chapman (London: Heinemann Educational, 1981), pp. 70–80. Pugh cites J. M. Mandler and N. S. Johnson, "Remembrance of things parsed: story structure and recall" *Cognitive Psychology* 96 (1977), 111–151. See also, Nancy Stein "The comprehension and appreciation of stories: a developmental analysis" *The Arts, Cognition And Basic Skills*, ed. S. S. Madeja (St. Louis: Cemrel, 1978), pp. 231–249.

22 The child's view of character, as has often been observed, may be essentially different to that of an adult, and where it is reproduced in text, is recognised as deviant. See, for example, Walter Allen on Charles Dickens' characterisation in *The English Novel* (Harmondsworth: Penguin, 1958), pp. 163–5.

23 Ong, p. 142.

24 Rimmon-Kenan, *Narrative Fiction*: p. 46.

25 See Jeffrey Wilkinson, "Children's Writing: Composing or Decomposing?" *Nottingham Linguistic Circular*, 10:1 (June 1981), 85–99; M. A. K. Halliday and R. Hasan, *Cohesion in English* (London: Longman, 1976), pp. 32–33; Arthur N. Applebee, *The Child's Concept of Story: ages two to seventeen* (Chicago: Chicago Univ. Press, 1978), pp. 56–70.

26 Suzanne Romaine, *The Language of Children and Adolescents: the acquisition of communicative competence* (Oxford: Blackwell, 1984), pp. 149–150.

27 Howard E. Gardner *et al.*, "Children's Literary Development: the realms of metaphors and stories," *Children's Humour*, ed. Paul E. McGhee and Antony J. Chapman (Chichester: John Wiley, 1980), pp. 98, 111.

28 See Christine Brooke-Rose, *A Rhetoric of the Unreal: studies in narrative and structure* (Cambridge: Cambridge Univ. Press, 1981), who notes (p. 247), that, as an example, *The Lord of the Rings* is frequently "overcoded" because it concerns a world which, because it is "wholly invented and unfamiliar, has to be constantly explained."

29 Roger Lancelyn Green, *Writers and Places* (London: Batsford, 1963), p. 46; Humphrey Carpenter and Mari Prichard, *The Oxford Companion to Children's Literature* (Oxford: Oxford Univ. Press, 1984), p. 573; Brian Doyle, *The Who's Who of Children's Literature* (London: Hugh Evelyn, 1968), p. 120.

30 For example, Rimmon-Kenan, pp. 13–19; Seymour Chatman, *Story and Discourse: narrative structure in fiction and film* (Ithaca: Cornell Univ. Press, 1978), pp. 31–33.

31 Jonathan Culler, "Defining Narrative Units" *Style and Structure in Literature*, ed. Roger Fowler (Oxford: Blackwell, 1975), pp. 138, 139, 141.

32 Kenneth Grahame, *The Wind in the Willows* (1908; rptd. London: Methuen, 1978), pp. 236–237.
33 Michael Stubbs, "Stir Until the Plot Thickens" *Literary Text and Language Study* ed. Ronald Carter and Deirdre Burton (London: Edward Arnold, 1982), p. 62.
34 See Rimmon-Kenan, p. 3; Culler, "Defining Narrative Units", p. 123.
35 Discussed in *The Child and the Book*, pp. 14–16, 97.
36 A. A. Milne, *Toad of Toad Hall* (London: Methuen, 1940), pp. v–vii.
37 *The Oxford Companion to Children's Literature*, pp. 274–5.
38 *The Wind in the Willows*, p. 106.
39 *The Wind in the Willows*, p. 83.
40 Maureen and Hugh Crago, *Prelude to Literacy* (Urbana: University of Southern Illinois Press, 1983), p. 40; Applebee, *Child's Concept of Story*, pp. 62–63.
41 I exclude here the "game" book, which provides the reader with binary choices at predetermined nodes. Although apparently "interactive" these books are in fact dominated by adult prescription to a far higher degree than any "conventional" text.
42 See Elaine Moss, *Picture Books for Young People, 9–13*, 2nd ed. (South Woodchester: Thimble Press, 1985), p. 4.
43 David McKee, *Not Now, Bernard* (London: Andersen Press, 1980). Unpaginated.
44 Florence Parry Heide, *The Shrinking of Treehorn* (New York: Holiday House, 1971).
45 *Is There A Text in this Class?* pp. 303–304.
46 (London: Cape, 1974). Unpaginated.
47 (London: Cape, 1977). Unpaginated.
48 *The Child's Concept of Story*, pp. 58, 63–4.
49 (London: Cape, 1984). Unpaginated.
50 "Fiction for Children and Adults: some essential differences," pp. 140–142.
51 Hugh Crago with Molly Travers, "The Opening Door: readers text and child listeners as a novel begins," *Developments in English Teaching*, 3:1 (August, 1984), 1–18.
52 Helen Huus, "Literature for Children—an Emerging Discipline Internationally." Paper presented at the Children and Books Session of the World Congress of the International Reading Association, Hamburg, August 1978, p. 1.
53 Alan C. Purves and Dianne L. Monson, *Experiencing Children's Literature* (Glenview: Scott, Foresman, 1984), p. 5.
54 Margaret Meek, "Speaking of Shifters" *Signal*, 45 (1984), 157 (reprinted from *Changing English: essays for Harold Rosen* (London: Heinemann Educational, 1984).

26

FROM THE EDITORS

"Cross-writing" and the reconceptualizing of children's literary studies

Mitzi Myers and U. C. Knoepflmacher

Source: *Children's Literature* 25 (1997): vii–xvii.

The Victorian satirist and evolutionist Samuel Butler once tried to depict ancestral genes at cross-purposes with each other. These "former selves," wrangling for "possession" of a single psyche, create a din of jarring voices: "Faint are the far ones, . . . loud and clear are the near ones. . . . 'Withhold,' cry some. 'Go on boldly,' cry others. 'Me, me, me, revert hitherward. . . . Nay, but me, me, me'" (Butler 43).

The notion of "cross-writing" we advance in this special issue of *Children's Literature* resembles Butler's dramatized crossover in one important respect: we believe that a dialogic mix of older and younger voices occurs in texts too often read as univocal. Authors who write for children inevitably create a colloquy between past and present selves. Yet such conversations are neither unconscious nor necessarily riven by strife. Instead of the competing ancestral voices that Butler posits, we stress creative cooperation. Most of the writers, artists, and editors we consider in this volume manage to integrate the conflicting voices they heed. Their constructs involve interplay and cross-fertilization rather than a hostile internal cross fire.

Cross-writing is not limited to texts written for children. In an "adult" novel such as *The Mill on the Floss*, George Eliot's Mr. Tulliver is puzzled by the genetic "crossing o' breeds" that makes the dark daughter to whom he gave his own mother's name so unlike his blonde wife. Yet the man who sees everything in terms of contraries cannot help his precocious child cross into a new order of reality. The adult is at odds with the child in an inimical world that has no room for Maggie Tulliver. In contrast, George Eliot's next child-man, Silas Marner, who also gives his mother's name to the orphan who has crossed his threshold, benefits from the reactivation of hitherto dormant childhood memories. Like that other solitary, Robinson

Crusoe, whose family name was *Kreuzner* (crosser), Silas mends a wounded psyche by reverting to a more elementary and childlike world. Given its pastoralism, George Eliot's fable was at one time deemed as suitable for child readers as Defoe's romance. Yet, as two generations of American schoolchildren discovered to their chagrin, the book remains preeminently "adult." Despite its primitive setting and fairy-tale elements, the novel relies on the authoritative voice of an ultra-sophisticated expositor. This linguistically adroit narrator brings out existential complexities that the tongue-tied Silas can bypass, but which her readers cannot read as merely a "simple twist of fate."[1]

Indeed, it might be argued that any text that activates a traffic between phases of life we persist in regarding as opposites demands, yet seldom receives, readings that should reflect a similar critical elasticity. Whether addressing adult or child audiences, or both, such fluid texts often rely on settings that dissolve the binaries and contraries that our culture has rigidified and fixed. Crusoe's island hut and Marner's valley cottage offer blendings not possible in the civilizations each man has fled; and although the raft that acts as a temporary haven for Huck and Jim cannot remain immune to the divisive communities that dot the river, the boy who plans to cross into still open territories at the end of Twain's novel refuses to succumb to the new form of enslavement that Jim accepts.

In transcending the binaries imposed by culture, Huckleberry Finn thus anticipates that other strange pilgrim-navigator, E. B. White's Stuart Little. Himself a cross between different species, the mouse-boy resists the allurements of a human mate his own size, the pretty dwarf child of Ames's Crossing. Instead, he prefers to pursue an elusive bride of still another order, Margalo the Shelleyan (or Mater-linked?) bird who never was on land or sea. Were he to find her, his new family would be as cross-grained as that formed by the hunter, the mermaid, and the furry and non-furry foundlings in Randall Jarrell's *The Animal Family*, an enigmatic fairy tale enhanced by Sendak's equally enigmatic crosshatched drawings.

As a writer-artist whose ability to maintain contact with "the psychic reality of my own childhood" shapes an original classic such as *Where the Wild Things Are* (Lanes 247), Maurice Sendak's wonderful understanding of the interplay between adult and child has also made him a key interpreter of such diverse figures as the Grimms, George MacDonald, Lewis Carroll, Melville, and many others. His shrewd grasp of the "cross-writing" at work in Wilhelm Hauff's sly and delightful *Dwarf Long Nose* even exceeds, as Maureen Thum points out in the first essay in our collection, that of the story's translator. Like Sendak's own Max, whose mother sends him away for being too wild, Hauff's boy-protagonist Jacob is repudiated by his biological mother when he returns to her in an alien shape. And yet, like the boy in a wolf suit, the deformed Jacob can adopt a maternal identity. As one who has learned to feed others, he follows the career of the misshapen herb-fairy he now physically resembles. For his part, Max also tries out the adult identity of one more powerful than he. As undaunted by the monsters he unleashes as his mother had been by her own wild thing of a boy, he fashions a self by blending child and adult—the rebel rumpus dancer and the authoritarian grown-up who can keep wildness in check. When this Mowgli-like wolfboy and king of the jungle returns to maternal domestication and restraint, his recrossing ratifies the blending he has achieved.

One of the delights of teaching children's literature is to ask college students, those recent "adults" still in contact with earlier selves, how their present, more analytical reencounters with texts such as *Where the Wild Things Are* or *Charlotte's Web* ratify, alter, or complement their childhood responses. Their accounts vividly confirm the duality of such texts. One reader notes that the terrible claws and gnashing teeth of the Wild Things had never disturbed her as a child, when she trustfully regarded the creatures as "incredibly kind and unthreatening." Pondering about this discrepancy, she adds a long postscript:

> Perhaps this was because I focused more on Sendak's illustrations than on his verbal description of the Wild Things. I always thought they were heading towards Max to welcome him when his boat arrived. The most remarkable thing in comparing my responses, then and now, is the realization of the willing suspension of disbelief that I extended to the book when I was young. There is a different gratification in reading children's books as an adult. One marvels at the wit of an author who can delight the child's parents as much as the child. While the development of analytic faculties has afforded me the opportunity to enjoy children's books from fresh perspectives, I also like to believe that I could sit in my room and have a wild rumpus with some terrible looking beasts.[2]

Using *Charlotte's Web* for their comparison of childhood and adult readings, two other students recall near-opposite responses. Whereas Andrea M., a psychology major, remembers that she and all the other students in Mrs. Murray's first-grade class had joyfully identified with Wilbur, Douglas M., an English major who was first exposed to the book in "Mrs. Hutching's third grade classroom," privileges Wilbur's two caretakers, Charlotte and Fern. In rereading the book at age twenty, Andrea realizes that her investment in Wilbur's survival had totally obscured the importance of Charlotte's role; she even recalled "being slightly angry at Charlotte for leaving Wilbur all alone." Now, however, Wilbur seems less important to her than the spider's "so enviable and admirable ability to accept the natural course of life."

Douglas M.'s impressions also underwent a radical revision. Although as a third-grader he had regarded Fern "as a heroine, not only in the beginning, but throughout the story," as a grown-up he faults her for failing to "fling herself at her father" a second time, when Mr. Arable assures Homer Zuckerman that this "wonderful" pig would yield "some extra good ham and bacon" (126). Yet the self-pitying Wilbur himself now seems diminished: "he is not 'Some Pig,' 'Terrific,' or 'Radiant,' and thus did not really qualify to be saved while all other pigs are slaughtered. As an adult reader, you start to wonder why Charlotte went through all the work to save a pig who never considered the fragility of her own life until death became readily apparent." If the six-year-old Andrea and the eight-year-old Douglas once regarded Wilbur as a threatened fellow-child, both now preeminently identify themselves with the nurturance and wisdom of the adult Charlotte.

Charlotte's ability to metamorphose a "humble" pig into a radiant, special child through the criss-crossings of her intricate web is, of course, inseparable from White's own craft as a cross-writer. Although adult and child readers of his text express discrepant priorities, it is the web that allows both constituencies to believe in talking animals and in a spiderly interest in pigs. Whether read as an assault on the credulity of adults for whom advertising has replaced religion or as a Thoreauvian document that celebrates continuity and renewal, *Charlotte's Web* will continue to appeal to the child in us all.

White is a humorist, as are Hauff, Kipling, and Nesbit, the writers taken up in the first third of this collection. Like the *New Yorker* ironist who so strongly identifies with children and animals, Hauff uses indirection to question the norms imposed on the young by their elders. Yet if the deceptively conventional and benign surface of his children's stories allows Hauff, as Maureen Thum shows, to evade adult censorship, Kipling's invention of a genre of his own in the *Just So Stories* opens up a meeting place for father and daughter, an adult survivor and a dead—but ever living and infinitely renewable—child. Moreover, as U. C. Knoepflmacher demonstrates in his analysis of Kipling's composite drawings, the writer's graphic wit, like Sendak's, amplifies his verbal text and frees a space for endless interplay. Kipling and his children revered the work of E. Nesbit, his fellow cross-writer. Although her own attitude toward the "Mowgli-man" was more ambiguous, the Bastable children are uncritical of *The Jungle Books* they act out. Nesbit transports the Bastables into an adult novel, *The Red House*, and the significance of that transportation is assessed here not by one, but by three different interpreters—Mavis Reimer, Erika Rothwell, and Nesbit's most recent biographer, Julia Briggs. We felt that a volume devoted to polyphonic texts should include at least one colloquy by different voices. And, as an author whose wonderfully individualized children are typically treated as dynamic members of a larger group, E. Nesbit seems the ideal candidate.

"Salutations" is the first word uttered by the spider who immediately apologizes for her Latinism: "it's just my fancy way of saying hello or good morning" (White 35). Yet Charlotte's contravention of Strunk and White is deliberately implanted. The spider who knows that "humble" is related to "humus" and hence to one who lives close to the ground surely also knows that "salvus" is embedded in her choice of greeting. After salving a boy pig's wounded self-esteem and soothing his night fears, she will use her steadying voice to bring about his salvation. White's mentoria thus follows the path of those wise and impeccable dames who supervised the growth of English and American children in the eighteenth and nineteenth centuries. Four of these influential figures are taken up in the second third of our collection of essays. That the first, Charlotte Smith, should share the name of the hairy-legged Charlotte A. Cavatica may merely be a felicitous coincidence. But the fact that the other three, Maria Edgeworth, Margaret Gatty, and Mary Mapes Dodge, were also involved in revisionary cultural work does make them the foremothers of White's weaver of words. Charlotte the wordsmith is, after all, based on the brilliant Katharine White, "a true friend and a good writer," whose discriminating yet nurturing stewardship at the *New Yorker* helped bring distinction to those she supervised.

As Donelle Ruwe's analysis of the Lambs and Smith demonstrates, the cross-writing of genders and generations can reinforce or challenge existing cultural ideologies. If our historical positioning makes us notice textual fissures papered over by the Lambs, recent feminist theory enables us to appreciate Smith's artistry and cultural ambitions. But Ruwe notices what contemporary resuscitations of Smith's literary achievement have undervalued: how much of her poetic virtuosity is grounded in her work for young persons. Smith (who gave birth to twelve children) could use juvenile relatives for both inspiration and critical reception. Similarly, as Mitzi Myers reminds us, the twenty-two children produced by her father's four marriages provided Maria Edgeworth with an ongoing supply of juvenile readers, critics, and potential story subjects and allowed her to reexperience childhood and continually reactivate her own child self. Moreover, as Myers maintains, Edgeworth's Anglo-Irish identity, her hybrid literary careers, her cross-disciplinary curiosity, her conflicting political allegiances, and her allusive intertextuality also coalesced to designate her as a paradigmatic border-crosser.

Like Smith, Edgeworth, and many other women writers, Margaret Gatty melds scientific and literary interests. Her multidisciplinary parables not only conspire against later "adultist" notions of aesthetic purity, but also address dual audiences and fulfill surprisingly ambitious dual aims. As Alan Rauch notes, this wife of a provincial clergyman has designs on a British national consciousness and can debate "big" issues like evolution: not all Victorian sages are named Carlyle or Ruskin, nor do they all inveigh in strident polemics. Engagingly oblique and scientifically informative, Gatty remains indubitably political. Her work confirms the profound impact exerted by works all too often ignored in current cultural reconstructions.

As Graham Greene and so many others have testified, "It is only in child-hood that books have any deep influence on our lives. What do we ever get nowadays from reading to equal the excitement and the revelation of those first fourteen years?" (13).

Rauch, Ruwe, and Myers, as well as Susan R. Gannon in her subsequent study of the dual readership of *St. Nicholas Magazine*, remind us that child readers produce adult thinkers and writers. Given the critical attention paid to texts read by adult writers in their later years, it seems odd that what they imbibed as children has gone unremarked. The memoirs, autobiographies, and letters of a host of eighteenth- and nineteenth-century figures defy our modernist clichés about the deadening effect of all those boring, adult-chosen works shoved down the throats of unwilling tots. Despite invectives against one's youthful reading, like Nesbit's own *Wet Magic* (1913), what impresses about these reminiscences is how beloved many writers we now dismiss were and how influentially they shaped future audiences—and future writers.

Perhaps no periodical production succeeded so well in amalgamating the aims and needs of a dual audience as did *St. Nicholas*. Gannon's rich analysis of the magazine as a bi-text urges us to explore what happens to the *adult* audience for all ambiguous writings directed at multiple readers. As she shows, Dodge converted *St. Nicholas* into a meeting ground: genera-tions of future adults could interact in its pages with their young peers as well as with their elders. This harmonious coalition, befitting a nation begin-ning to insist on its identity as a "melting pot," thus offers one more example of the transformative spaces created by the cross-writing contributors to Dodge's journal. Frances Hodgson Burnett and Kipling, for example, not only transport boy heroes into England and India, the remembered lands of their respective childhoods, but also open up new terrains for girls: the fantasyland in Burnett's "Behind the White Brick" anticipates the secret garden Mary Lennox will revitalize (see Auerbach 133), and the Whale, Camel, and Rhinoceros tales are preludes to the story in which Taffy can create a sign-system of her own. Here, adult and child, as well as girls and boys, can become reconciled, mutually strengthened.

Young and mature audiences, however, could also meet in other kinds of ventures—undertakings that perfected the "art of teaching in sport" long before our own multimedia artifacts and even before the educational inno-vations rightly celebrated by Carolyn Steedman and Juliet Dusinberre.[3] The virtually complete teaching tool assembled by Lady Ellenor Fenn, dis-cussed in our "Varia" section by Andrea Immel, is just one example of the extraordinary teaching devices that delighted our ancestors of all ages. Fenn's charming box miniaturizes the extravagant devices and exhibits examined by scholars such as Richard D. Altick and Barbara Maria Stafford. Her visual and verbal cornucopia opens out an entire Lilliputian world that parent and child can reassemble and deconstruct as their whimsy takes

410

them. As innovative in its day as post-modern hypertextuality is today, and certainly requiring a more active and imaginative participation, this specimen of child-adult interplay challenges the constructions of our own media culture by the sophistication of its high literary and intellectual standards.

The last two essays in the collection, however, stress fissures as much as coalitions. Can *Goblin Market* and *The Lord of the Flies* be read as child-texts, or are they irrevocably shaped by an adult understanding? Like so many of her fellow Victorians, Christina Rossetti aligns herself with the traditions of folklore in order to recover a female space. Even more important, she razes the distinction between child and adult when she has a cured Laura wake up from her trance: laughing and tossing "gleaming" locks that show "not one thread of gray," Laura is a sexualized woman who has fully recovered her "innocent old way" (Rossetti, ll. 540, 538). But even though Rossetti conflates girlhood and maturity, she also tries to cleanse Lizzie's and Laura's world of all male contamination, of the unsavory fraternity of goblin men who are both sexually threatening and childish. As Lorraine Janzen Kooistra shows, the transpositions at work in this masterpiece thus affect its readership. As she notes, the poem's blending of near-pornographic descriptions with materials highly attractive to child readers resulted in a dual marketing that persists to this day.

If merchant men are barred from Lizzie's and Laura's agrarian world, women are absent in an island world where British boys degenerate into goblin-like sadists. Maternal memories fade as the blinking Piggy—a Wilbur without a Charlotte—is immolated by his peers. Golding's irony is exacerbated by his cross-references to an antecedent text, a boys' book, Ballantyne's *Coral Island*. As Minnie Singh notes, this earlier robinsonade exulted in the Crusoe-like resourcefulness of civilized Victorian boys. Yet Golding, who has a uniformed officer wonder whether such feral creatures could once actually have been British boys, has shifted genres. *The Lord of the Flies* not only harks back to Defoe via Ballantyne; it also takes its readers into the fourth book of *Gulliver's Travels*, the one omitted from all those children's editions that feature the voyages to Lilliput and Brobdingnag. Mowgli the boy who feasts with wolves and Max the boy who dances with wild things have, in Golding's own alchemy, turned into Yahoos. And yet this so emphatically "adult" text owes its power to its own distinct mode of cross-writing.

Cross-writing, we believe, has a dual value for those eager to gain for children's literature the recognition now given to formerly marginalized fields such as women's literature or ethnic literatures. It helps us conceptualize this emerging scholarly discipline more clearly and more globally. And it will help us to relocate children's literature at the center of the curricula at our schools and universities. The pioneering interdepartmental program in Children's Studies instituted at Brooklyn College by Gertrud Lenzer, professor of sociology at the City University of New York

Graduate School and University Center, features courses in children's literature at its core. If a greater attention to cross-writing in such courses can benefit fields that are themselves in need of cross-fertilization, mainstream courses in literature might be equally enriched. We received essays on writers whose "adult" works are much taught and reprinted, but whose work for the young has persistently been segregated: Hawthorne and Kate Chopin, Stein and Ionesco. As Sandra Lee Beckett noted in a special Modern Language Association (MLA) session on cross-writing we sponsored in 1993, a writer like Michel Tournier (who, like Golding, returns to the Robinson-story from a modern perspective) persistently rewrites his children's books for adults and his adult books for children.[4]

Only when current revisionists of all stripes—feminists, Americanists, modernists—count children in will we be able to see the full cultural space that we continue to subdivide into separate little parcels. Even though formerly neglected adult female poets of the period between the late eighteenth-century Revolutions and the reformist 1830s are currently undergoing serious revaluation, the Romantic depictions of childhood—masculinist and anti-masculinist—still go unquestioned. When Charlotte Smith or Letitia Barbauld write grown-up poems, they are hot; yet as authors of work for the young, they are passed over. Despite the success of adult fictions such as *Turtle Diary* (1975) and *Riddley Walker* (1980), Russell Hoban seems to have been denied a place in American literature courses. His many children's books, including the one that, according to him, could just as well have been marketed as an adult fiction, have unquestionably contributed to that neglect: a pair of mechanical mice who resemble Huck and Jim and a living rat as obsessed as Captain Ahab seem to lack the "high seriousness" demanded by Arnoldian academics.

Without too much overstatement, we hope to claim cross-writing as an unlocker of doors that have shut off and devalued our field. More than a simple key, however, cross-writing offers the versatility of a critical Swiss Army knife. That versatility, we feel, is well exemplified by the essays we have collected. As delineated in this special issue, cross-writing is not just one topic among others. Currently proliferating articles on gender and postcolonialism anticipate what might be the eventual place of children's cultural studies. Cultural studies itself, as most centrally the study of *relationships* within and between cultures, has to go back to how cultures produce and construct citizens and consumers. Thus cross-writing involves more than one topic. To study the relationships within and between cultures, we need to go back and consider how cultures that transform children into citizens and consumers produce and reproduce themselves through literacy and the literary.

Our coinage brings together many disciplines and lines of inquiry, [and] cross-writing may even help us revise, once and for all, the notions of a "Romantic" natural childhood which still tend to dominate most readings of children's literature and the child. But such airy projections are premature. We prefer to stay "humble," which, in Charlotte's helpful gloss, means "near the ground" as well as unproud (White 140).

Notes

1 Steve Martin's recent film by that name is a laudable attempt to "update" *Silas Marner*, and yet his "translation" cannot capture the existential dimensions of George Eliot's text.
2 C. D., an English major at Princeton University, 12 May 1995.
3 Despite their sophisticated critical attention to juvenile writing and representation in nineteenth- and twentieth-century culture, Dusinberre and Steedman start too late: the history of cross-writing begins long before the Victorian period. Although Steedman's 1995 book, *Strange Dislocations*, ostensibly begins in the 1780s, she looks at Goethe's Mignon rather than actual maternal educators.
4 As Marilyn Fain Apseloff notes in *They Wrote for Children Too*, most readers seem astonished by the sheer number of major authors who also wrote for children.

Works cited

Altick, Richard D. *The Shows of London*. Cambridge, Mass.: Harvard University Press, Belknap, 1978.

Apseloff, Marilyn Fain. *They Wrote for Children Too: An Annotated Bibliography of Children's Literature by Famous Writers for Adults*. Westport, Conn.: Greenwood, 1989.

Auerbach, Nina, and U. C. Knoepflmacher, eds. *Forbidden Journeys: Fairy Tales and Fantasies by Victorian Women Writers*. Chicago: University of Chicago Press, 1992.

Butler, Samuel. *Life and Habit*. Vol. 4. The Shrewsbury Edition of the Works of Samuel Butler, Ed. Henry Festing Jones and A. T. Bartholomew. 20 vols. London: Jonathan Cape, 1923–26.

Dusinberre, Juliet. *Alice to the Lighthouse: Children's Books and Radical Experiments in Art*. New York: St. Martin's, 1987.

[Fenn, Lady Ellenor.] *The Art of Teaching in Sport: Designed as a Prelude to a Set of Toys, for Enabling Ladies to Instill the Rudiments of Spelling, Reading, Grammar, and Arithmetic, under the Idea of Amusement*. London: J. Marshall [not before 1785].

Greene, Graham. *The Lost Childhood and Other Essays*. London: Eyre and Spottiswoode, 1951.

Lanes, Selma G. *The Art of Maurice Sendak*. New York: Harry N. Abrams, 1980.

Rossetti, Christina. *Goblin Market*, in *The Complete Poems of Christina Rossetti: A Variorum Edition*, ed. R. W. Crump, vol. 1. Baton Rouge: Louisiana State University Press, 1987.

Stafford, Barbara Maria. *Artful Science: Enlightenment Entertainment and the Eclipse of Visual Education*. Cambridge, Mass.: MIT Press, 1994.

Steedman, Carolyn. *Strange Dislocations: Childhood and the Idea of Human Interiority, 1780–1930*. Cambridge, Mass.: Harvard University Press, 1995.

White, E. B. *Charlotte's Web*. New York: HarperCollins, 1980.